THE HANDBOOK FOR
SPIRITUAL
WARFARE

REVISED AND UPDATED

DR. ED MURPHY

THOMAS NELSON
Since 1798

NASHVILLE DALLAS MEXICO CITY RIO DE JANEIRO BEIJING

Published in Nashville, Tennessee, by Thomas Nelson, Inc.

Thomas Nelson, Inc., titles may be purchased in bulk for educational, business, fundraising, or sales promotional use. For information, please email SpecialMarkets@ ThomasNelson.com.

Unless otherwise noted, all Scripture quotations in the Introduction through chapter 7 are from the New King James Version. Copyright © 1982 by Thomas Nelson, Inc. In the remainder of the book, Scripture quotations are from the NEW AMERICAN STANDARD BIBLE®. Copyright © 1960, 1962, 1963, 1968, 1971, 1972, 1973, 1975, 1977, 1995 by The Lockman Foundation. Used by permission.

Other Scripture quotations are noted by abbreviation:

AMPLIFIED for the Amplified® Bible. Copyright © 1954, 1958, 1962, 1964, 1965, 1987 by The Lockman Foundation. Used by permission.

KJV for KING JAMES VERSION

PHILLIPS for J. B. PHILLIPS: THE NEW TESTAMENT IN MODERN ENGLISH, Revised Edition. Copyright © 1958, 1960, 1972 by J. B. Phillips. Used by permission of Macmillan Publishing Co.

NEB for the NEW ENGLISH BIBLE. Copyright © 1961, 1970 by the Delegates of the Oxford University Press and the Syndics of the Cambridge University Press. Used by permission.

NIV for HOLY BIBLE, NEW INTERNATIONAL VERSION®. Copyright © 1973, 1978, 1984 International Bible Society. Used by permission of Zondervan. All rights reserved.

Permission has been secured from the publishers of works from which more than five hundred words have been quoted. Each of these works is documented fully in the endnotes. The author and publisher hereby gratefully acknowledge the permissions granted for use in this book by these publishers.

Chapter 64, "Dangers and Pitfalls of Spiritual Warfare," is an adaptation and expansion of material by Edward F. Murphy, first published in *Behind Enemy Lines,* Charles H. Kraft, ed. (Ann Arbor, Mich.: Vine Books, 1994) and used by permission.

Library of Congress Cataloging-in-Publication Data

Murphy, Edward F., 1929–
    Handbook for spiritual warfare / Ed Murphy—Rev. ed.
        p. cm.
    Includes bibliographical references and indexes.
    ISBN-10: 0-7852-5026-3
    ISBN-13: 9-780-7852-5026-5
    1. Spiritual warfare. I. Title.
BV4509.5.M89   1996
   235'.4—dc20
                                    96–8955
                                        CIP

Printed in the United States of America
11 12 - 16 15 14

Contents

Dedication

The original still stands. "To some who have influenced my life towards living as a good soldier of Christ Jesus" (2 Tim. 2:3) I wrote, "They are Warner Hutchinson, Dr. N. Paul Gupta, now with Lord, Dr. Dick Hillis, gravely ill as I write, Dr. Donald McCurren, now with the Lord, Rev. Ernest Rockford, now with the Lord, to my four children, Carolyn, Dr. Ed Murphy Jr., Barbara, and Paul. I ended saying, "To Loretta, who became my bride when we were but young people, who has lived with me and warred with me against evil since 1950: my wife, my beloved, my companion, my fellow-missionary warrior and intercessor, the greatest treasure God has given to me after Himself."

Loretta was quite suddenly ushered into the presence of the Lord at 12:50 A.M. on Sunday, August 4, 2002, with her family gathered around her singing one of her favorite hymns, "There is a land that is fairer than day, And by faith we can see it afar, For the Father waits over the way, to prepare us a dwelling place there. In the sweet by and by, we shall meet on that beautiful shore, In the sweet by and by, we shall meet on that beautiful shore."

I was holding her in my arms as she breathed her last. I saw with my own eyes the radiance of her life slip out of her body from her feet to her head. It was awesome to see the life substance depart from her suddenly, leaving only a shell behind.

One morning a few days before our Heavenly Father promoted her to higher service she greeted me with a radiant, peaceful, angelic face. "Honey," she said quietly, as was her manner, "my mother, father and all my believing relatives now with the Lord, came together to me this morning. My mother said, 'Loretta, we are waiting for you to *join* us in heaven.'" I rejoiced for her, but wept for me. That was the turning point in her two-year battle with metastasized stage-two breast cancer.

What a privilege has been mine to passionately love this woman since she was only 14 and I 16 years of age. She was my first and only true love. Not only was she one of the greatest women to have ever lived, but one of the most beautiful, loving, kind, gentle, compassionate, and guileless human beings I have ever met. She had such integrity, she could not and would not lie. While never judgmental, she could not comprehend the willful sin of high visibility Christian leaders. She would ask me again and again, "How can that leader face God and His people, and yet he lies and deceives? I cannot reconcile such conduct with a God-like life."

The morning after Loretta's death, my younger son, Paul, told me in the presence of our family, "Dad, to me, after Jesus Himself and the Virgin Mary, Mom was the most perfect human being I have ever known." I had to agree. Thus to you, my beloved wife, I dedicate this revision of the *Handbook*. Thank you for being, as I always called you, "The wife of my life. How I love and miss you!"

Preface to the Second Revised Edition

As I wrote in the revised edition of 1996, the widespread acceptance of *The Handbook for Spiritual Warfare* has been very gratifying to me as its author. While dozens of other books on spiritual warfare have been written since its appearance in 1992, the book still stands, to my knowledge, as the only beginning definitive study, still in print, written in the history of the church. It was with that purpose in mind that I wrote the book in the first place. Clinton E. Arnold, whom I will mention later, calls the *Handbook*, "the most detailed book about spiritual warfare currently available." The events of September 11, 2001, have awakened the entire world to the fact that we are at war. The shock for many is to discover that spirits of radical evil, like hate, rage, homicide, death, and destruction have joined hands with the religious spirits of Radical Islam to do indescribable evil in the name of God.

I did my undergraduate studies in Philosophy. One philosopher whose name I have long forgotten wrote, "Religion represents one of the most dangerous areas of human life. In the name of one's God and/or the gods, every conceivable barbaric act has been committed—all in supposed obedience to the wishes of that god." This is spiritual warfare at its most devastating dimension.

When the original manuscript of the handbook was turned over to my editors in 1991, it was 1,200 pages long. It took one year to condense it to its present 660 some pages. That was more difficult to me than writing the full-length book in the first place. I am still satisfied with the book with the few changes I have added to this new revision.

I have learned a great deal more about the deceptions of evil supernaturalism and how to free bruised believers from their influence—enough to write a new book—but not now. My African ministry is too vast, too satisfying, and too time-consuming. God has His perfect timing for each stage of my multidimensional ministry. Oh how I love serving my awesome Lord and redeemer! How I love His church! How I love human beings reflecting in my servant life God's amazing love for mankind. (John 3:16) This love extends to every unreached people group, which has yet to hear the truth of God's amazing saving grace. (Matt. 24:14; 28:1820; Acts 1:6–8)

I am grateful scholars have written books covering areas I was unable to write on in detail in the original *Handbook for Spiritual Warfare*. Most notable are the two on spiritual warfare by Jeffery Boyd. His first book, *God At War*, is more general, while his second one deals with one of the most crucial philosophical and theological issues of our day, thiodicy. The book is entitled, *Satan and the Problem of Evil*.

My close friend and former student, Clinton E. Arnold[1], Professor of New Testament at Talbot School of Theology, has written three superb books on spiritual warfare. His first, *Ephesian, Power and Magic* I used extensively in my studies in the Handbook on Ephesians. His second book, *Powers of Darkness, Principalities and Powers in Paul's Letters* and *Three Crucial Questions About Spiritual Warfare* were not yet in print. His treatment of territorial spirits in the latter book adds some provocative insights into this complex, but controversial issue.

I trust that this second revision will make the *Handbook* an even more effective tool in the hands of God's spiritual warriors. I am dissatisfied with some of my comments in the revision done in 1996. This is especially true with the section entitled, "Equating Church Culture with Renewal Itself." Everything I write there is true, but not in the context of what occurs during all revivals in which the Holy Spirit directly takes control during public meetings. All such divine interventions will inevitably produce an atmosphere very similar to what we are witnessing today. The meetings take on a format often found in Pentecostal-Charismatic revivals. The same was true in the revivals led by amazing renewal leaders like John Wesley, George Whitefield, and even Jonathan Edwards in the 18th century. I will return to this issue more in depth in my revisions in chapter 64. Even in the midst of these blessings, the greatest hope of all committed believers is perfectly reflected in the last prayer of the Bible, "Even so, come quickly Lord Jesus." (Rev. 22:20)

Preface

As you read Carolyn's story in the Introduction, you will recognize that I, like most involved in direct spiritual warfare ministry, did not choose this dimension of kingdom activity. It was chosen for us by Another, whose servants we are. As you continue to read, you will discover how the post-Enlightenment Western world view has filtered out much that the Bible reveals about the evil spirit world from our understanding.

The church is revealed in Scripture not only as the people of God and the body of Christ, but also as a part of God's warrior kingdom in ongoing conflict with internal evil (the flesh), social evil (the world), and supernatural evil (the spirit world). I call this a multidimensional sin war.

Today God seems to be awakening His church anew to the vivid reality that we are at war: we are at war with evil; that evil is personal, not impersonal; it is supernatural evil, the kingdom of Satan. Jesus, the Lamb (the gentle, sacrificial Savior) and the Lion (the mighty warrior) calls us out of our complacency to be soldiers of the Cross. Girded with the full armor of God, we are to overcome the Evil One, to challenge the principalities and powers who hold individuals and peoples in bondage with the authority we have in Christ through declaration and intercession (see Acts 26:18).

This book has arisen

- *out of pain:* my own encounters with personal evil and labors to help set the captives free.
- *out of confusion:* Why are the church's leaders so reluctant to lead God's people to engage the powers? Why haven't they grasped the dominant place spiritual warfare has in God's biblical revelation?
- *out of conviction:* The entire biblical revelation of God's redemptive activity (salvation history) is set in the context of warfare between the two kingdoms.
- *out of concern* that we recover the biblical, radical warrior lifestyle that won cities and communities for Christ in the early centuries; that God revive His worldly church; that we not compromise with evil nor live for ourselves but for God, for the lost, and for the healing of the bruised among us; that our teaching and practice of spiritual warfare be rooted in reverent reflection upon Scripture, church history, and valid experience—not in dogmatic theology, on one hand, or in sensationalism, on the other.
- *out of appreciation* for the faithful spiritual warriors in all nations who engage the enemy in the authority that is ours in Christ and through intercession (often called "warfare praying").
- *out of prayer* that our reigning Lord, to whom all the principalities and powers are in subjection, will again, through His church,

preach the gospel to the poor, proclaim release to the captives, recovery of sight to the blind, set free those who are downtrodden, proclaim the favorable year of the Lord. (Luke 4:18 NASB)

As a *missionary* I have been involved in encounter with the powers for years, since 1958. Unfortunately, most of those years I was untrained as a spiritual warrior. As a *missiologist*, my graduate studies all focused on how to take *panta ta ethne* (all the peoples) from Satan to God, and in practice I have experienced both success and failure. As a *pastor-counselor*, I have ministered to hundreds of demonically afflicted people both one-on-one and in groups. Some of their stories are in this book. As a *teacher*, I want to share what I have learned from God, from my colleagues who minister continually to the bruised among us, and from the suffering people who have ministered to me even as I have ministered to them.

This is a *work in progress*. It is a beginning attempt to go deeper into the warfare dimension of the Christian life, and to some degree, into evangelism. The main focus is pastoral, with a secondary focus evangelistic.

I have tried to both broaden and deepen the studies already done in this arena of warfare, especially with the spirit world, to produce a comprehensive work on the subject. Since spiritual warfare touches every dimension of human life, I have been forced to move into areas of study and experiences outside my areas of expertise, and I ask my readers who are specialists in these areas to keep this in mind as they discover any shortcomings in this work.

I write this preface after finishing the book. I am comfortable with most of what I have written, yet uncomfortable with some of what I have written. I only wish time had permitted a rewrite of some of the exegetical sections with more input from biblical scholars, but deadlines made this impossible. So I release the book, hoping it will open the flood gates, inspiring others more knowledgeable and gifted than I to write and help God's army fight the good fight in these closing years of this century, and, if the Lord tarries His Coming, in the opening years of the twenty-first century.

By its very nature, this is a controversial book. Some dimensions of spiritual warfare are controversial both theologically and in practice. My mission organization, O.C. International (formerly Overseas Crusades), is committed to power encounter as a valid dimension of evangelism and Christian living and spiritual warfare as the context of the church's life and mission. Yet the views expressed in this book are my own. They do not necessarily represent the views of O.C., its leadership, and its missionaries. I am grateful to O.C. for allowing me time to do this writing.

I am grateful to the dozens of publishers, writers, and people who have allowed me to quote their material. Because of the comprehensive nature of this book, I have felt it right and necessary to quote many of the experts and not to rely upon my own limited knowledge and experience.

I am grateful also to my former administrative assistant, Mrs. Betty Sparks, who typed the first draft of this book, which was three times the size of what you see here. Her beloved husband, Charles, was diagnosed with incurable cancer about the time we began the work. Betty hung in there with me until the emotional and physical strain was no longer bearable. Charles went to be with the Lord before the book was completed. Betty's daughter, Mrs. Melissa Parle, stepped into the gap along with one of O.C.'s faithful staff workers, Mrs. Lois Vogen, who with others, finished the manuscript. I could not have done this work without Betty, Charles, Melissa, Lois, and Loretta, my faithful wife, who again put up with months of my absence until the work was complete. Thank you in Jesus' dear name.

Deep heartfelt thanks go to Mrs. Dolly McElhaney and my editor, Mr. Mark E. Roberts, for condensing the volume of material I first submitted to the present, more manageable size. I had enough for three volumes. I owe them an immeasurable debt for their gracious labors and critical help. I also thank them in Jesus' dear name.

Introduction

"Ed, you must come home right away." My wife's voice trembled across the long distance line. "Carolyn has been acting strangely since you've been away. As I dealt with her last night, I saw a demon glaring at me through her eyes."

"A demon!" I exclaimed. "That's impossible. Carolyn is a Christian. Christians can't have demons."

"I know she is a Christian," Loretta replied. "I also know Christians aren't supposed to have demons. But it was a demon that stared at me through her eyes. That was not Carolyn."

I was shocked, incredulous, angry, and confused. How could demons abide in the same body with the Holy Spirit?

As the oldest of our four children, Carolyn had always assumed leadership for the other three, being an example to them of stability, discipline, and strong commitment to Christ.

True, we had been having our first behavioral problems with her on this missionary furlough from Colombia, South America. I was not overly concerned, however. Any fourteen-year-old girl dropped suddenly into the turbulent environment of the 1960s in the United States would experience readjustment difficulties. Besides, Loretta and I were so busy in ministry that I felt Carolyn was reacting to our neglect of her.

Demons were the furthest thing from my mind. I knew nothing about them except that, according to Scripture, they existed, were especially active in Bible times, and in modern times were to be found "on the mission field." To my knowledge, however, I had never met one during my then ten years as a missionary.

"Loretta," I declared, "you must be mistaken. Carolyn can't have demons. Besides, I can't come home yet. The conference won't be over for several days."

"You have to come home," she insisted. "I can't handle this by myself. Ask Dick Hillis for permission to come home today.

"Last night I went into Carolyn's room to talk with her. I found her lying on the floor with her feet up on the bed listening to some weird music. When I called to her she did not answer. She was in a trance.

"As I spoke to her about her recent rebelliousness towards us and the Lord, she suddenly changed before my eyes. She became hostile and began yelling at me to get away and leave her alone. I noticed a mysterious 'darkness' in her eyes. It was not Carolyn who glared at me through those eyes but another personality, an evil personality, totally unlike the Carolyn we know and love. I am sure it was a demon.

"The words that came out of her mouth were not Carolyn's. They were evil, cynical, haughty, and God-defying. I spoke to the evil thing and commanded it in the name of the Lord Jesus to release Carolyn so I could speak directly to her alone. Suddenly her eyes changed and Carolyn was back in control of herself."

Deeply disturbed by the conversation with my wife, I told Dick Hillis what Loretta had said. To my amazement, he affirmed that under certain circumstances Christians can be partially controlled by demons. I had never heard of such a thing before. In all my years of theological and missionary training, no one had ever taught me that true Christians could experience demonic bondage.[1]

"If Loretta says Carolyn has demons, you had better get home and help her," Dick said. "Someone else can cover your responsibilities here in the conference."

On the journey home to Los Angeles from San Jose, California, I was both angry and fearful: angry over the possibility that evil spirits could disturb the life of my lovely daughter and fearful that, if true, I wouldn't know how to free her from their influence. *What do I do?* I thought. *Where do I begin?*

I arrived late and Carolyn was already in bed. Awakening her, I told her what Loretta had said about her rebellious attitude and the demons glaring through her eyes.

Within moments her usually sweet personality changed into something evil. With a strange glare in her eyes she screamed at me. "Leave me alone!" she yelled.

I forbade the demons to speak directly through Carolyn. When she calmed down, I spoke to her very quietly about her walk with the Lord. Suddenly she became her usual sweet, responsive, and obedient self.

"Dad," she said, "I don't know what's the matter with me. There seems to be something inside of me that takes over and I do weird things. Dad, help me. I'm scared. I love Jesus and I want to do what is right. What's wrong with me?"

Carolyn and I got down on our knees in prayer. She confessed her rebellion and disobedience, crying to the Lord to break the power of evil oppressing her life. She was having unusual difficulty in praying, however, especially in declaring the lordship of Christ over her life.

In the past I had noticed she had a small object hanging on a chain around her neck, but hadn't thought anything of it. As I was praying with her, trying to resist the Devil on her behalf, my attention was drawn to that object. It looked like a Star of David.

"Where did you get that star?" I asked. She told me the name of the boy who had given it to her. I knew him. He was a professing Christian but definitely not a committed believer.

"What is it supposed to symbolize?" I inquired.

"I don't know what it symbolizes," she replied. "It's just a kind of good-luck charm. It's found on the dust covers of some musical albums. All the kids wear them."

The "star" turned out to be a pentagram, a symbol of the occult world. At that time I was almost totally ignorant of occultism, its symbols and practices. Yet somehow I knew that thing was an evil symbol. Its presence on her body served as an amulet, drawing evil spirits to her life.

"Carolyn, you will not find full freedom from the demon spirits afflicting you until you remove that object and renounce the spirit forces associated with it," I told her.

She took it off her neck and threw it on the floor. She confessed and renounced her occult involvement, her recent interest in heavy metal rock music, and her rebellious attitude and selfishness. Soon we were in a face-to-face confrontation with evil spirits.

"Dad, they're after me. I'm afraid," she cried. "They have a hold on my life. I want them to go. Dad, please help me get rid of them."

"Get away from my daughter's life," I commanded. "She has broken all allegiance with you. Get out! Leave her alone! In the name and authority of my Master, the Lord Jesus Christ, who defeated your master on the Cross, I command you to go away from Carolyn and do not return. Get out of her life! Let her alone. Carolyn does not belong to you. She has given her life to the Lord Jesus Christ."

Within a few minutes the struggle ceased. Carolyn became calm. She joyfully began praising the Lord for setting her free. The evil spirits had left. We both cried and rejoiced before the Lord for His grace in releasing her from the demonic spirits.

We went to bed happily thinking that the battle was over. About two A.M., however, Carolyn banged on our bedroom door.

"Dad, the demons are back," she cried. "Help me! They seem to be coming at me from under my bed. They want to get back inside of me."

I went to her room with her. "What do you have under your bed?" I asked.

"I have a small box filled with more of those stars and other paraphernalia. I forgot about them when we were praying last night. Dad, please get them out from under my bed."

"No, Carolyn," I replied. "I won't do it for you. You have to do it yourself. By your choice you got involved with them and by your choice you'll get rid of them."

"I'm afraid," she said, "but I'll do it if you will help me." She reached under the bed, pulled out the little box, and handed it to me. "Dad, will you destroy them for me? I don't want anything further to do with them."

"No," I replied. "You must destroy them. This will declare to the spirit world that you are making a complete break with them. I'll walk out in the back yard with you, but you must do it yourself."[2]

She did. We returned to her room for another talk and time of prayer. It was then that I began to discover the extent of the demonic evil influence that had come against her life through her involvement in demonic rock music and through the influence of her boyfriend.

Carolyn had never been fond of extreme rock music. She liked some of the more mild, almost folk, rock groups but showed no interest in heavy rock groups with their grotesque dress, vulgar gestures, and immoral, rebellious, often occultic lyrics. We had never allowed them in our home.

While on furlough things were different, however. Both Loretta and I were continually involved in ministry and were neglecting our children. Most of the time I was away from home on mission business or in missionary conferences. Loretta had her own missionary meetings to attend, plus heavy correspondence and personal contact with our supporters.

Unknown to us, Carolyn's friend had introduced her to the fringes of the hippie-occult protest movement of the sixties. He had also exposed her to heavier rock music and transcendental meditation. She found that she could go into a trance while listening to the music of certain rock groups.

Carolyn confessed her sins to the Lord, renouncing transcendental meditation and all evil music. She destroyed her offensive rock music and everything in her possession which she knew dishonored the Lord.[3]

This was the beginning of what later became the most important world view shift[4] in my Christian life. Little did I know that over a period of several years I would not only come to understand that true believers, under unusual circumstances of sin, can come under direct partial demonic control, but I would also find myself involved in a ministry of helping to rid believers of these evil personalities.

We are all aware that Satan and his demons are our enemies. We know that they war against true believers, churches, and other Christian institutions. Most of us can quote verbatim parts of Ephesians 6:10–20, James 4:7–8, 1 Peter 5:8–11, and other spiritual warfare passages.[5] The question is, do we really comprehend the power hurled against us by Satan and his demons? Do we really know what Satan can do in the lives of believers who violate God's Word, even through ignorance?

THE REALITY OF DEMONIZATION:
RELATING SCRIPTURE AND EXPERIENCE

Perhaps the most controversial question to be raised is, "Can a true believer be demonized?" Note that I am speaking not of demon possession, but of *demonization.*[6] *Possession* implies ownership and total control. Christians, even disobedient ones, belong to God, not to Satan. Thus, Satan cannot control them totally. *Demonization* is a different matter, however. By demonization I mean that Satan, through his demons, exercises direct, partial control over an area or areas of the life of a Christian or non-Christian.

Can that really happen to Christians?

According to Scripture and Christian experience it can. Scriptures warn believers not to "fall into the same condemnation as the devil" or "fall into reproach and the snare of the devil" (1 Tim. 3:6–7).[7] They also tell us of believers who have "turned aside after Satan" (1 Tim. 5:15).

The apostle Peter wrote to warn believers of the terrible danger they faced as a result of Satan's attacks. He said that if they did not learn how to "resist him firm in [their] faith," they could be "devoured by the devil" (1 Pet. 5:8–9). Those are strong words. No wonder the apostle Paul writes about the danger of believers being ignorant of Satan's schemes (2 Cor. 2:11).

Much is being written about demons today, also. We are witnessing what one scholar called "a demonic deluge." Some of it is excellent; some of it is very bad. Studies on Satan lean toward sensationalism on one hand and rigid dogmatism on the other. The very act of studying demons causes one to focus so intently on them that extreme views often result, understandably but unfortunately.

For many, any theology of demons they have is built primarily on subjective experience. They uncritically believe what demons tell them and write books accordingly. This, combined with their emotional subjectivism and their tendency to see all evil, and all personal, and all social malfunctions as primarily and directly demonic (they are always indirectly demonic), further divides the church on this crucial area of reality and turns the unbelieving critic away from Christ and the Bible.

On the other hand, there are others whose theology of demons is built on their own limited interpretations of Scripture with little or no experience in direct, ongoing confrontation with evil spirits. Declaring what demons can and cannot do, they produce their books from this monocultural, dogmatic perspective.

The result is the church divided again. Just as tragic, millions of terribly hurt people, believers as well as unbelievers, go without help or go to counselors who may be atheists or Christians inexperienced in the demonic realm.

The Scripture-versus-experience issue is unfortunate, unbiblical, and illogical. Never in Scripture are the two held to be mutually exclusive. They are always seen to be two sides of the same coin. God's written revelation is the Bible. That written revelation is not given in an abstract theological form, however. It is given in historical form as God makes Himself known to His people and to the world in the context of human experience. A knowledge of God divorced from the experience of God led to the Crusades, the Inquisition, and other chapters in the colonization of the heathen world by organized Christianity too shameful for words.

We all recognize this in our evangelism. We commonly say we want to help people find Christ as "their personal Savior." We know informing them about God and Jesus is not enough—they must experience Him personally. God must first be experienced before He is understood.

We all recognize this to some degree in our development of theology. We realize that God's truth is not discovered primarily by the human brain but by the human heart as revealed by the Holy Spirit (1 Cor. 2:10). Thus if we had to make the choice of being taught about God by a brilliant, highly trained, but "unsaved" theologian, or a semi-literate but Spirit-filled believer, we would probably choose the believer. While he may not be able to define God theologically, he can lead us to God experientially.

Why do we evangelicals so distrust experience with the spirit world? Why do we develop theologies about this dimension of reality about which we are personally ignorant except through biblical exegesis? Can a theology of Satan and demons that is both true and useful for ministry really be developed by theologians studying their Hebrew and Greek Bibles while sitting in their air-conditioned offices apart from at least some personal experience?

If the theologians in question did not bring limiting preconceptions about what demons can and cannot do to their study, they could possibly, exclusively through the Scriptures, develop guidelines to practical demonology that could then be tested by experience. Based on the results of that experience, they would then need to readjust their demonology to fit the contemporary assault of evil supernaturalism the church is facing today.

This is exactly what has happened to me and many other theology professors, Bible teachers, counselors, missionaries, and pastors in the past few years. We were all taught theology in college and seminary. We accepted what we were taught because we trusted our teachers. As we read Scriptures through their eyes, we found what they told us we would find. Occasionally we found things they told us we would not find, but, with a few exceptions, we remained quiet.

Then we were launched into ministry and our theology put to the test of experience. The basic tenets of our historic Christian theology probably did not change. In fact, they only became firmer. What did happen, however, is that we were forced to return to Scripture for help, again and again. We began to examine anew certain dimensions of our unreflective theology when it did not prove congruent with our own valid experience with God, with people, and, in many cases, with Satan and demons.

Therefore, correct biblical interpretation is that interpretation which is most consistent with experience. Theology which is contradicted by experience, or at the least brought into question, is theology that needs to be reexamined. To declare that theology must be maintained even if it is challenged by on-going experience is legalism, pharisaism, dogmatism, and evidence of subtle arrogance. To continue with theology that hurts already hurting people is sin. We cannot sacrifice people on the altar of theological presuppositions.

In the wake of the eighteenth-century rise of rationalism known as the Enlightenment, Western theology lost an intuitive, historic understanding of the spirit world. As in all other areas where the church has ignored or resisted dimensions of biblical reality, the process of rediscovery usually comes through experience. This experience calls theology into question at that point. The theological status quo will always resist the reformers, however.

The status-quo theologians and Bible teachers, if they hold a high view of Scripture, will go back to Scripture, not to openly challenge their own presuppositions in light of the experience of their brethren, but to defend their presuppositions against their misguided brothers.

The reformers, if they also hold to a high view of Scripture, will also return to

Scripture. If they are honest, they will return not to prove themselves right and their status-quo brethren wrong, but to better understand what their experience is telling them. When they do, they will either call into question their experience, their understanding of Scripture, or both.

Usually the latter will occur. If their experiences are valid they will find that they are supported by Scripture much more than they had first imagined. They will also find that Scripture will cause them to restate their experience and not go to extremes. They will recognize that they too, as all men, are susceptible to both deception and error. The result should be a newly formulated theology more consistent with both Scripture and experience.

This is what is occurring today with the church's "new" experience with demons. The demons have always been with us. But, as conservative evangelical theologians and Bible teachers have been telling us for years, as we see the day of the final conflict between the kingdom of God and the kingdom of evil approaching, an outpouring of demonic evil such as the church and the world has not known since the early centuries of the Christian era will occur.

If we are entering that period, and most biblical scholars suspect we are, then we should expect Satan to come into the open and through lying, deceitful spirits assault mankind in general and the church in particular.

Is that what we are witnessing today? Only time will tell. One thing is absolutely certain, however: *Our theology of the spirit world must fit the reality of contemporary human anguish.* Particularly for us in the West, where materialism is the religion of many, and where occultism, Satanism, and the New Age movement flourish, a status-quo practical demonology will not do. With sexual abuse and even Satanic Ritual Abuse (SRA) of children no longer a secret, but almost a national epidemic, status-quo counseling will do no longer.

Demons flow where abuse flows. Demons flow where Satanism, Satanic occult practices, and the New Age movement flourish. Demons enter the bodies and lives of abused children, especially those who have experienced SRA, and of practicing New Agers. The church in the West will find it difficult to bring salvation and healing to the survivors of such evil if it maintains its present status-quo, unworkable theology of experiential demonology. This is true for both salvation and sanctification.

Worldwide, evil supernaturalism manifests itself in two major religions. Hinduism is shedding its traditional pacifism and becoming militant and missionary. Elements of it thrive in the West in the form of the New Age movement. Islam too is on the rise, militant and missionary, increasingly intolerant of other religions, especially Christianity. It is still the most powerful religious competitor of Christianity. Demonic activity is rampant in both Hinduism and Islam.

While much is being written in our day about spiritual warfare, the church is still basically ignorant of the spirit world. That ignorance is most pronounced in the Western world, but it exists in the non-Western world also.

Africans, Asians, Latin Americans, and the inhabitants of Oceania know intuitively the reality of the spirit world. They know invisible spiritual beings both good and evil continually interact with human beings. They strive to maintain the right balance of relationships with the spirits to avoid harm by evil spirits and to gain help from the good spirits.

What happens to their world view when they become Christians? It becomes confused. That confusion has at least a dual source: First, Western missionaries, though looked upon as experts about things spiritual, are primarily ignorant of the activity of the spirits. Second, their national church leaders were trained in their ministry by missionaries ignorant of the spirit world. I was one such missionary.

The unfortunate result worldwide is that, in general, our churches are filled with believers who are hurting through the activity of evil spirits. Many are Spirit-filled believers by anyone's definition of that term. Yet a war rages inside of them and around them. Often areas of their lives are in bondage to feelings, thoughts, and practices not compatible with their Christian faith. They know something is wrong, but few suspect the possibility of a direct demonic dimension to their problem. That was true with my daughter, Carolyn. But it was also true of me, her father. She was not the only victim of spiritual warfare in our family. I was, also, because I was ignorant of the operations of the evil spirit world.

Beyond our churches, effective worldwide evangelism is impeded by our having missed the biblical teaching regarding *territorial spirits*. These high-level principalities and powers hold whole people groups in their grip. How is their power broken (2 Cor. 4:3–4) so that people become free to choose for or against Christ?

Without doubt, Carolyn's story and my comments have raised many questions in the minds of my readers. While the Bible contains a vast amount of material about Satan, his evil angels, demons, and evil spirits, we will often be left still questioning because of what the Scriptures do *not* reveal. For example, the Scriptures do not directly explain the origin of Satan and his demons. They do not explain the relationship between malfunctions natural to human personality and personality malfunctions caused supernaturally. We are left mostly on our own in these and many other areas. The Bible does not develop a doctrine of satanology or demonology as clear and complete as other teachings such as hamartology and soteriology.[8]

I am not interested in simplistic answers to profound questions. Probably the reader shares my attitude at this point. I want to know all God wants me to know within the natural limitations we possess as earthly human beings (1 Cor. 13:9–13). I only wish He wanted us to know more.

I will attempt to explore the spirit world from four perspectives in this book. In Part One we will see how our world view—understanding of the ultimate nature of reality—affects our view of spiritual warfare.[9] Part Two looks at spiritual warfare from a theological perspective by examining the progressive development of the spiritual warfare motif in both Old and New Testaments. Parts Three and Four approach the subject from an exegetical perspective, studying key passages of Scripture. While the Scriptures leave us without all the information we often feel we need, they say more about spiritual warfare than most of us realize. Finally, Part Five examines spiritual warfare from a practical perspective, seeking to discover the implications of our study for human life in general and the Christian life in particular. This section will perhaps be the most important of the book, but it should not be examined without studying the scriptural foundation that supports it.

PART One

World Views

1

World View Clash

The World Vision organization planned to dig a well for a needy African village called Walamo.[1] They were warned not to go to the village because the most powerful *marabout*, or witch doctor, of the region had cursed it. They were told something bad would happen to them or their machinery if they tried to dig a well in the village under so strong a curse that people from other villages would not go there.

The team went anyway. In time they dug a well which filled with sweet, pure water. The people of Walamo were ecstatic. Nearby villages heard of it and, convinced the curse had been broken, resumed trade with Walamo. When asked why nothing evil befell the workers or their equipment, they responded, "Francois's god is more powerful than the *marabout's* god."

Francois, who led the drilling crew, was tempted to dismiss their views as pure superstition. The well had come in by understanding and working with the relevant scientific laws. The people, however, saw it as evidence of the superior power of Francois's god. Two world views had clashed.[2]

I am a missionary. A missionary leaves behind his own familiar culture and seeks to contextualize himself within a foreign culture.[3] He does this for the sake of the gospel and out of love for God and for the people to whom he is sent. As fully as possible, he seeks to understand their world view. He faces a serious problem, however: He carries with him his own world view. James W. Sire in *The Universe Next Door* defines world view as "a set of presuppositions (or assumptions) which we hold (consciously or unconsciously) about the basic make up of our world."[4] The working definition of world view I will use is even more basic: *World view* refers to "one's basic assumptions about reality."

Everyone holds world view assumptions whether or not they are reflective persons. All persons believe their own assumptions about reality are the correct ones, or at least the best ones, for the present. All persons' beliefs and behavior, in that order, are based upon their world view, whether or not they are conscious of that fact.

While world view is closely related to religion, the two are not identical. Paul Hiebert affirms that "a world view provides people with their basic assumptions about reality. Religion provides them with the specific content of this reality."[5] If one holds to an atheistic world view, atheism functions as a religion.

Aside from the agnostic position, only two conceivable world views exist. The *spiritualistic world view* affirms that ultimate reality is spiritual: immaterial, not physical or material. According to this view, whether ultimate reality is looked upon as personal or impersonal, it is spiritual. The vast majority of the world's more than five billion inhabitants hold to some form of a spiritualistic world view. Intellectually convinced atheists are very rare even in Western and in Marxist societies. Ours is not a world of philosophical materialists, but of convinced spiritualists.

This common spiritualistic world view gives the church a beginning point with most of humanity. Even the present occult explosion within the Western world is advantageous at this point. We can say to the occultist, "You are basically correct in your view of reality at one major point. Humans exist as spiritual beings, and not merely as material ones."

Second, the *materialistic* or *naturalistic world view* affirms that ultimate reality is material or physical, not spiritual. This view assumes that all life generated spontaneously from non-life and that by this process primitive single-celled life forms evolved over vast periods of time into the vast range of life as we know it today.[6]

Five important conclusions result from this view of reality:[7]

1. The universe is a cosmic accident that has no ultimate purpose.
2. Human life is a biological accident that has no ultimate significance.
3. Life ends forever at death for each individual life form.
4. Mind has no separate existence or survival apart from brain.
5. Humanity's intuitive, historic belief in an ultimate mind, spirit, or God behind, within, and outside of the physical universe is a form of self-deception. Thus, humanity's corresponding belief in human uniqueness, dignity, purpose, and survival beyond death is a non-real view of reality.

No wonder life is so empty to intellectually convinced but honest atheists. The word *honest* is important because most atheists do not want to honestly face the nihilistic implications of their world view. When they do, death would be better than life because it leads to eternal non-existence.

Western theology has been influenced by the Western world view more than most of us are aware of. By *Western theology* I mean the broad, generally accepted interpretations of Scripture embodied in mainstream works of systematic theology, covering the broad range of theological viewpoints and ecclesiastical groupings one finds among all believers who hold to a high view of Scripture and propagate a common historic Christian faith.

By *Western world view*[8] I mean the view of reality that arose out of the historical movement of the eighteenth century called the Enlightenment. It is often summed up in one word, *naturalism*. Sire traces the historical swing from theism to naturalism, and by way of deism, to nihilism.[9] One scholar defines methodological naturalism as "the name for that characteristic of scientific method which constructs its pattern of thought on the basis of natural causation as distinguished from a supernatural or occult explanation."[10]

This Western world view arches over almost all of the many diverse world view variations within the Western world, and is closely allied to the scientific method. Such a method, when adopted as one's *model* for reality, views the universe as a uniform system based strictly on the cause-and-effect relationships between its constituent parts, each in a determinate relationship one to the other, utterly closed to any dimensions of reality that transcend the natural. Sire observes that history thus becomes a "linear system of events linked by cause and effect but without an overarching purpose."[11] Thus, naturalism explains everything on the basis of impersonal natural and therefore predictable causes that account for all of reality.

How does all of this affect our study of spiritual warfare? Although we Christians have rightly rejected naturalism as an acceptable view of ultimate reality and hold faithfully to historic theism, naturalism nonetheless deeply influences our view of the daily events of our lives. This influence helps shape our view of the world of spirit beings, both benevolent and evil. Anthropologist Paul G. Hiebert of

Trinity Evangelical Divinity School writes of his own struggles in this area as a missionary to India in an article entitled "The Flaw of the Excluded Middle."[12]

John's disciples asked, "Are You the Coming One, or do we look for another?" (Luke 7:20). Jesus answered not with logical proofs, but by a demonstration of power in the curing of the sick and casting out of evil spirits. So much is clear. Yet when I read the passage as a missionary in India, and sought to apply it to missions in our day, I had a sense of uneasiness.

As a Westerner, I was used to presenting Christ on a basis of rational arguments, not by evidences of His power in the lives of people who were sick, possessed and destitute. In particular, the confrontation with spirits that appeared so natural a part of Christ's ministry belonged in my mind to a separate world of the miraculous—far from ordinary everyday experience.

Hiebert then presents the following diagram which reflects the Western Christian view of reality, a by-product of our Western theology:

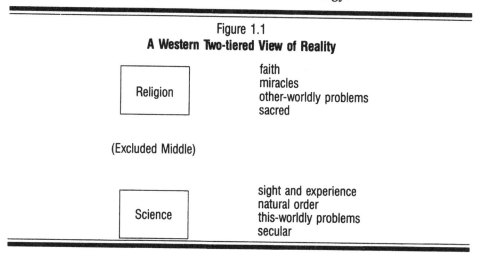

Figure 1.1
A Western Two-tiered View of Reality

Religion

faith
miracles
other-worldly problems
sacred

(Excluded Middle)

Science

sight and experience
natural order
this-worldly problems
secular

He comments:[13]

The reasons for my uneasiness with the biblical and Indian world views should now be clear. I had excluded the middle level of supernatural but this-worldly beings and forces from my own world view. As a scientist I had been trained to deal with the empirical world in naturalistic terms. As a theologian, I was taught to answer ultimate questions in theistic terms. For me the middle zone did not really exist. Unlike Indian villagers, I had given little thought to spirits of this world, to local ancestors and ghosts, or to the souls of animals. For me these belonged to the realm of fairies, trolls and other mythical beings. Consequently, I had no answers to the questions they raised.

In "The Excluded Middle," an article published in the *MARC Newsletter,* Bryant Myers expands Hiebert's concept of a two-tiered world. He points out that "the most important feature of this Enlightenment world view is that the spiritual and real worlds do not touch . . . . This is the major difference when we compare the western world view to how traditional folk understand their world."

Myers further explains that most traditional religions

believe the world is a continuum between those elements of the world which are mostly spiritual in nature and those which are mostly material . . . . There is no gap between the two worlds. The spiritual and physical co-exist together, inseparable parts of each other.[14]

According to Myers, there is a "middle part" of the traditional word view, a level of reality comprising witch doctors, shamans, curses, idols, household gods, and the evil eye. This spiritual part of reality operates in the material world and is rejected, or excluded, by the Western world view.

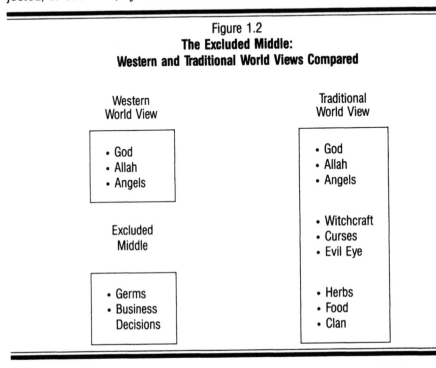

Figure 1.2
The Excluded Middle:
Western and Traditional World Views Compared

To traditional peoples there is no natural-versus-supernatural dichotomy. The supernatural directly involves the natural. Traditional peoples live in the middle zone. That is why much of our preaching and teaching seem to have little relevance to their daily life. We explain sickness on the basis of germs, nutrition, and related factors. They explain sickness on the basis of curses, the evil eye, witchcraft, or karma, all set against them.

Myers then applies this difference in world views to evangelism and missions:[15]

Christians in the west believe that God and Jesus Christ are part of the world of high religion, and that others are wrong to believe in Allah or some other high god. This means we believe that the critical question for evangelism is "Whose god is the true god?" . . . .

For people who still hold a largely traditional view of the world, the critical question is not "What is true?" as much as it is "Who is the most powerful?" After all, it is the stuff in the excluded middle that affects their lives for good or ill. This means that news about a God whose Spirit is more powerful than curses, witch doctors and demons is very attractive. This is one of the reasons the Charismatic and Pentecostal movements are growing as fast as they are today.

Francois, whom we met at the opening of this chapter, found himself in the excluded middle in the well-drilling incident. He could have reverted to the two-tiered view of reality in explaining the well of pure water to the people of Walamo. He could have told them that God was not involved because the well was part of the natural world of science, natural laws, and technology. He could have dismissed their view as pure superstition. He could have tried to impose his secular Western world view upon the traditional world view held by the villagers.

He could have, but he didn't.

Francois understood about the excluded middle. He realized that the people probably now saw him as a shaman more powerful than the sorcerer. He had to bridge the two world views and help the people understand, in Myers' words, the "difference between the idea of 'Francois's god' and 'the God of Francois.'" Their world view needed to be challenged by a biblical or kingdom framework, not a secularizing Enlightenment one." Francois explained that he did not own a god or have any power of his own. He was not a shaman; he had no magic. He was only a servant of the one true God "who was more powerful than the shamans and western science. This God created a world that was rational and understandable, and created human minds with the ability to figure out where the water was likely to be."[16]

In his explanation, Francois challenged both the Western world view and the traditional world view of the Walamos. Neither is completely harmonious with the biblical world view. The traditional world view, while closer to the biblical view, is like the Western world view, also filled with error.[17] It is polytheistic, pantheistic, magical, and animistic, and in these ways completely contrary to biblical revelation. In spite of these errors, the traditional view stands closer to the biblical world view because it fully acknowledges the reality of the spirit world.

As we will see in detail in future chapters, in the Bible the spirit world is real, alive, and everywhere invading daily life. It is portrayed in both the Old and New Testaments but more vividly in the New, where Christ and his followers engage evil supernaturalism intensely and triumph decisively. Nor did awareness of such dimensions of the spirit world and of conflict with evil spirits die with the apostolic church. The post-apostolic fathers took the realm of the demonic so seriously that they automatically took new converts from paganism through rites of deliverance from evil supernaturalism, a practice we have lost to our own detriment.[18]

Effective ministry in our day demands that we must recover the knowledge and experience of the spirit world that the early church possessed. We must relearn the forgotten art of spiritual warfare. Probably not since the days of the apostolic and patristic churches has there occurred the present revival of evil supernaturalism that we are experiencing today. The Western world is being shaken by what Michael Green has called an "occult explosion."[19]

Overseas the story is the same. Western missionaries gave birth to most of the mother churches of Asia, Africa, Latin America, and Oceania. These missionaries believed that demons were automatically kept in check by Christ's defeat of Satan on the Cross and by His resurrection. Evil supernaturalism, while recognized, was seldom openly challenged and defeated through power encounter.[20] In missionary work among animists or spirit worshippers, the first generation of converts was and is often won through power demonstrations on the part of God through His servants. Following conversion, however, no biblically nor culturally relevant theology of the demonic world or power encounter is usually developed for the new converts. Most of the intuitive recognition of and fear of the world of evil spirits, ghosts, and the spirits of the ancestors or of animals held by the host cultures is regarded as "superstition." It is thus relegated to the unreal and becomes something to be ignored in Christian living and evangelism. National Christians often feel timid in speaking of "the old ways." They usually do not receive from their spiritual fathers, the missionaries, an adequate biblical and functional theology of the spirit world, power encounter, and spiritual warfare. They are left unprepared for the spiritual warfare into which they are being thrust as Christians.

But today national Christians everywhere are asking questions for which adequate answers are not forthcoming: "Can true believers be demonized? If so, what can be done to set them free?

"What can Satan through his demons (Eph. 6:10–20) do against true believers? Can believers be hurt by demons? Can Satan severely injure believers physically, emotionally, and even spiritually? Can he kill believers?

"What about our churches?" they ask. "Can evil spirits work their way into positions of power and quench the flow of the Spirit and His gifts? Can they counterfeit the gifts of the Holy Spirit? How can such demonic strongholds be recognized and broken?

"What about the place of evil supernaturalism in evangelism? Do high level spirit princes of evil rule territorially? Can they so oppress and control individuals, communities, peoples, and even nations that the Word of God does not take root, but rather is rejected or expelled?"[21]

These questions spring out of the concrete experiences of our Christian brothers and sisters in other cultures. The answers, however, can not only help non-Western Christians but also awaken us in the West to the cross-cultural reality of evil supernaturalism, whose manifestation in the current occult explosion has surprised many of us. Our surprise reveals our world view blindness.

To see people who are immersed in demonized cultures be set free by the gospel; to truly and completely deliver men, women, and children from the kingdom of Satan and bring them into the kingdom of God; and to minister to believers who are still subject to abuse by the spirits, *we Christian leaders must relearn the spirit world*. We must remove our Western-world view eyeglasses, which blind us to the biblical view of the spirit world, and be willing to become incarnate into the same world into which our Lord entered—a world of deadly spiritual warfare.

2

The Spiritual Warfare Dimension of a Biblical World View

All the writers of Scripture, regardless of their divergent cultural contexts, held to a common theistic world view. Furthermore, all the Scripture writers held to a common view of God. The God revealed in the earliest chapters of Genesis is the same God revealed throughout the entire Old and New Testament. He is both transcendent (Gen. 1:1) and immanent (Gen. 3:8). He is never seen as a localized tribal deity but as the creator "of the heavens and the earth" (Gen. 1:1f). While Abraham and the nation of Israel are called to restore His name on earth, He is, from the beginning, revealed as the God of all the peoples of the earth (Gen. 12:3; 14:19–20).

H. B. Kuhn, Professor of Philosophy of Religion at Asbury Theological Seminary, traces the progressive unfolding of dimensions of God's personality and His relationship both to creation and to His people which are found in the different names by which God reveals Himself in the Old Testament in an excellent encyclopedia article.[1] According to Kuhn, God's self-revelation to His people revolves around four central names: El, Elohim, Adonai, and Yahweh. Most of His other names are compound names built upon these four.

The name *El* is one of the oldest designations for deity in the Bible and the entire ancient world. It became the general name for God in Babylonia, Arabia, and the land of Canaan, as well as the Israelitish peoples.[2] Kuhn comments that El connotes not only the idea of might but also the idea of transcendence. Kuhn calls *Elohim*, the plural name for God, the plural of intensity. It is used over 2,000 times in the Old Testament to refer to Israel's God. It is frequently used with the article *(ha-elohim)*, meaning "the one true God." The third primary name by which God reveals Himself, *Adonai*, does not seem to have been in common use among Semitic peoples generally. It was used mainly by the Hebrews.

Kuhn then writes about God's fourth and final primary name of self-revelation, *Yahweh*, a name unique with the Israelites:[3]

> The other Semitic peoples do not seem to have known it or at least did not use it in reference to the Deity except as contacts with the Hebrew people brought it to their attention. It was the special property of the covenant people.

It was in the Exodus story that God gave this name as His covenant name between Himself and His people (Exod. 3:13–15). Thus from this time onward the events of the Exodus formed the core of the Hebrew proclamation: "I am Yahweh your God (Elohim) who brought you out of the land of Egypt, out of the house of bondage" (Exod. 20:2).[4] Kuhn observes that

God has taken the initiative in restoring the knowledge-bond which existed between God and fallen man, a bond which was fractured by the Fall. And it was through His revelation to Israel of Himself under the name of *Yahweh* or Jehovah that the unfolding of saving history became visible. The unveiling of God's nature by the giving of His name to Israel was of supreme significance to the entire Biblical system.

All through the Old Testament, Israel's God is declared to be the only true God. He is the God of creation. He is the Lord of all, even of the nations, though the latter are seen as in rebellion against Him, having degenerated from monotheism into polytheism, idolatry, and immorality. (This process was devolution, not evolution.) The three almost always go together. The Scriptures reveal that the gods of the nations are *no-gods*. They are not realities in themselves. They are powerless to save their followers. In essence they are demons who manipulate the pagan god systems and actually receive the homage paid to the no-gods (Lev. 17:7; Deut. 32:17; Ps. 106:37, cf. 1 Cor. 10:20–21).

Thus it is possible to speak of a biblical world view when it comes to the person of God Himself. While admitting the progressive nature of God's disclosure of Himself to humanity after the Fall, He is the same God who had established personal relationships with man before the Fall. In that sense, His self-disclosure has never varied. He was then what He is now. He Himself affirms, "I am the LORD, I do not change" (Mal. 3:6).

It could be objected that the biblical world view is far more extensive than my presentation. I am aware of that. However, my world view study is limited to its relationship to spiritual warfare and to six key dimensions of a biblical world view that impinge on our study of spiritual warfare.

A SPIRITUAL WORLD VIEW

The fundamentally spiritual character of ultimate reality represents the broadest possible dimension of a biblical world view. As already mentioned, the Bible and Christians share this perspective with the vast majority of the world's over five billion inhabitants.

A THEISTIC WORLD VIEW

James Sire's world view study first points out the historic swing within Western culture from theism to deism to naturalism.[5] The rest of his book records the continuing movement within Western culture from naturalism to nihilism, to existentialism, to Eastern pantheistic monism, to what he calls the "new consciousness." I would label it by its better known name, the New Age movement.[6]

Edward T. Ramsdwell, writing in Ferm's *Encyclopedia of Religion,* states that the term *theism* means more than monotheism. Theism connotes something more than mere contrast with polytheism. The essential ideas behind theism are that of a God who is both one and personal. He is also both transcendent (apart from the universe as its creator and sustainer) yet immanent as everywhere present and accessible to humanity.[7] Biblical theism declares that God is a true person and the only truly perfect person. As such He possesses perfect mind. He knows all. He has perfect emotions. He loves with a perfect love and hates with a perfect hatred: His perfect love makes heaven possible; His perfect hatred makes hell a reality. He possesses perfect will. He chooses what He wills and what He chooses will eventually come to pass.

This high view of God contrasts directly with both pantheism and polytheism.

Pantheism is "the doctrine that the universe, the all of reality is God . . . the cosmic whole is equated with God . . . all is God."[8] Pantheism has made a resurgence in the so-called secular society of the West in the New Age movement. The declarations of actress Shirley MacLaine and other exponents of the movement reflect a pantheistic world view. "If you don't see me as God," says MacLaine, "it is because you don't see yourself as God."[9] "You are God. You are each and every one, part of the second coming," says the extraterrestrial being named Soli, speaking through his channel, Neville Rowe.[10]

Polytheism is the belief in and worship of a plurality of gods. Polytheism and its by-product, idolatry, became the prevalent religious view of the ancient biblical world after the fall. It was out of the polytheism and idolatry of Ur of the Chaldeans that God called Abraham. Israel's most persistent spiritual battle was the fight to maintain itself pure from the polytheism and idolatry of its neighbors. It was a battle that Israel often failed to win. In judgment God immersed His fickle people in the very heartland of polytheism and idol worship during the Exile. After the return to the land of Israel, the nation never again was tantalized by the immoral luxuries of polytheism and idolatry.

It is important to note that Christians share this theistic, spiritual world view in common with both Jews and Moslems. This common point becomes the beginning of Christian witness to members of these two great theistic religions.

A REVELATIONAL WORLD VIEW

Christian theism is based on divine revelation, not on human intuition. Christians do not believe in the one true God as a product of human intuition or common sense. We know what we know about God only because He has chosen to reveal Himself to humanity. The writer to the Hebrews declares that God "at various times and in various ways spoke in time past to the fathers by the prophets" (Heb. 1:1).

The apostle Paul writes to young Timothy:

Continue in the things which you have learned and been assured of, knowing from whom you have learned them, and that from childhood you have known the Holy Scriptures, which are able to make you wise for salvation through faith which is in Christ Jesus. All Scripture is given by inspiration of God, and is profitable for doctrine, for reproof, for correction, for instruction in righteousness, that the man of God may be complete, thoroughly equipped for every good work. (2 Tim. 3:14–17)

We Christians share some dimensions of this world view in common with both Jews and Moslems, since they too hold that the Old Testament is the Word of God. They do not, however, believe this is true of the New Testament.

A TRINITARIAN WORLD VIEW

The one true personal God exists as Father, Son, and Holy Spirit (Matt. 28:19; Rom. 5:1,5; 15:30; 2 Cor. 13:14). While the Trinity is nowhere specifically stated in the New Testament, it is everywhere implied. We know this because of the second and final phase of God's self-revelation. As we have already seen, the writer of Hebrews declares that God "at various times and in various ways spoke in time past to the fathers by the prophets" (Heb. 1:1). Hebrews 1:2 continues saying, "[God] has in these last days spoken to us by His Son."

The verses which follow declare that His Son is "[the one] through whom also He made the worlds." They declare further that the Son is "the brightness of His glory and the express image of His person, and upholds all things by the word of His power."

Next, after declaring Jesus to be His Son, God declares:

> "Let all the angels of God worship Him."
>
> But to the Son He says:
> "Your throne, O God, is forever and ever . . .
>
> You, LORD, in the beginning laid the foundation of the
>   earth,
> And the heavens are the work of Your hands.
> They will perish, but You remain;
> And they will all grow old like a garment;
> Like a cloak You will fold them up,
> And they will be changed.
> But You are the same,
> And Your years will not fail."
> (Heb. 1:2–3,6,8,10–12)

The Trinity becomes a further limiting dimension of a biblical world view. It is at this point that we Christians separate from Jews or Moslems. Most Jews consider Jesus as an impostor, or at best, as a misguided Jewish reformer. Moslems have a higher view of Jesus. They declare Him to be one of the greatest of the prophets, second only to the last and greatest of the prophets, Mohammed.

The Koran calls Jesus "the Spirit of God" and even "the Word of God." Moslems, however, strongly reject his title as "the Son of God." He was not divine, or God, they affirm, but only a man like the other great prophets of God: Noah, Abraham, Moses, David and, finally Mohammed, the last and greatest.[11]

A REDEMPTIVE WORLD VIEW

God's revelation is primarily centered on redemption. It focuses on God's activity to bring men and women back to Himself after the Fall. The moment people sin, God comes to them. He not only comes to humanity in judgment for their rebellion against the lordship of God (Gen. 3:16–19), but He also comes to them in redemption. He provides the original sinful pair with clothes to cover one of the results of their sin, a sense of shame of their nakedness (Gen. 3:21). Most important of all, He promises a redeemer to free them from bondage to their new master, the serpent, whom we later know as the Devil or Satan (Gen. 3:15). The rest of the Bible from Genesis 4 through Revelation 22 is the story of God's providing redemption for sinful men and women.

A biblical world view must thus be a redemptive world view. Indeed, the closing chapters of God's revelation focus on the joys of the redeemed people of God forever in the presence of God in all His glory and the Lamb in all His majesty (Rev. 21—22).

The Christian reader who holds to a high view of the Old and New Testament Scriptures probably will not have found himself in major disagreement with anything found in these world view considerations, at least up to this point. What I have stated thus far represents the historic view of biblical Christianity. There is, however, one more major biblical world view dimension which must be presented. For the purpose of our study this is the most vivid, dynamic, and all-pervading biblical world view dimension. At the same time it is probably the most neglected, least understood, and least applied to our Christian life and ministry.

A SPIRITUAL WARFARE WORLD VIEW

This biblical world view dimension can be expressed in one statement: present reality exists in a state of cosmic-earthly conflict or spiritual warfare. In philosophical terms, modified dualism exists in the universe. The kingdom of God and the kingdom of evil supernaturalism are engaged in fierce conflict one against the other. *Absolute dualism* affirms that ultimate reality is eternally dualistic, that evil and good have always existed, and always will exist.[12] Biblical dualism declares a *modified dualism:* present reality exists in a state of dualism, but such was not so in the beginning nor will it be so in the future. "In the beginning God . . ." is the view of Scripture. There was no evil, no opposing force, only God, and God is good. Then God created moral beings, the angels, and placed them within His kingdom. Still there was no dualism. They obeyed His will. At some point in the hidden past, rebellion occurred within the angelic kingdom. Dualism was born. Evil entered God's kingdom, dividing it into two kingdoms, the kingdom of God and the kingdom of Satan. This is the biblical view of the distant past.

As the focus of Scripture moves through time from the "eternal" past to the "eternal" future, dualism vanishes. The ultimate state is that of eternal monism. Only God and His perfect kingdom will exist in the eternal future. (The very concept of eternity past and eternity future presents an apparent contradiction to our minds. Can that which is eternal truly have a past and a future? Such words are helpful, however, to talk of the past and the future.)

Dualism, however, is a present reality. The universe exists in a state of cosmic-earthly conflict or spiritual warfare. Cosmic dualism is a reality: spiritual warfare exists in heaven. Earthly dualism is a reality: spiritual warfare rages on earth.[13]

Some dimensions of this warfare world view are recognized and described in different ways by different people. Some speak of the struggle between good and evil. Others talk of the battle between right and wrong, or between light and darkness. Still others refer to the conflict between the positive forces which seek to preserve life and order in the universe and the negative forces which tend to disturb and even destroy life and order. From a biblical perspective, however, this dualism is revealed to be an on-going conflict waged on two fronts: God and His angelic kingdom confront Satan and his demonic kingdom, while the children of God contend with the children of Satan. To understand and further equip ourselves for this cosmic-earthly struggle, we must explore the realms of theology, biblical exegesis, and the experience of the people of God.

PART TWO

Theological Considerations

The Origin and Scope of Spiritual Warfare

3

Cosmic Rebellion
The Problem of Evil

Spiritual warfare is an evil issue. Warfare in itself is evil. If evil did not exist there would be no warfare of any kind. Evil is the most perplexing problem ever faced by humanity. Thinking men have been facing it for millennia. The Greek philosopher, Epicurus (341–270 B.C.), quoted by the philosopher Lactantius (260–340 A.D.), is supposed to have written that

> God either wishes to take away evils, and is unable; or he is able and unwilling; or he is neither willing nor able, or he is both willing and able. If he is willing and is unable, he is feeble, which is not in accordance with the character of God; if he is able and unwilling, he is envious, which is equally at variance with God; if he is neither willing nor able he is both envious and feeble, and therefore not God; if he is both willing and able, which alone is suitable to God, from what source then are evils? or why does he not remove them?[1]

This was the problem that kept the great C. S. Lewis bound to the shackles of atheism for most of his life. He writes about it in his provocative book, *The Problem of Pain*.[2] As Lewis recounts his former defense of atheism, he graphically describes the evil and misfortune which faces all human beings. He concludes:

> If you ask me to believe that this is the work of a benevolent and omnipotent spirit, I reply that all the evidence points in the opposite direction. Either there is no spirit behind the universe, or else a spirit indifferent to good and evil, or else an evil spirit.

Lewis' response to his former line of reasoning is interesting.

> I never noticed that the very strength and facility of the pessimist's case at once poses us a problem. If the universe is so bad, or even half so bad, how on earth did human beings ever come to attribute it to the activity of a wise and good Creator? Men are fools, perhaps; but hardly so foolish as that. . . . At all times, then, an inference from the course of events in this world to the goodness and wisdom of the

Creator would have been equally preposterous; and it was never made.[3] Religion has a different origin.

Lewis' footnote mentions the word *theodicy*. It comes from the Greek *theos*, God, and *dike*, justice. Webster defines theodicy as the "defense of God's goodness and omnipotence in view of the existence of evil."

Edgar S. Brightman, Professor of Philosophy of the Graduate School of Boston University, defines theodicy as "the attempt to justify the way of God to man, that is, to solve the problem of evil in the light of faith in the love and justice of God."[4]

> The problem of evil is obviously more acute for theism than for any other type of philosophy or theology; if it cannot be solved, theism must be abandoned, retained by faith in hope of a future, as yet unattainable, solution, or held as a truth above reason.

C. S. Lewis would probably agree that the solution is presently unattainable. He would declare that the truths behind theism are truths above and beyond present human reason. As Pascal is attributed to have affirmed, "the heart has reasons that the mind knows not of." Lewis is correct that theodicy is not something new, adequately wrestled with only in the modern scientific age. Indeed, Gnosticism, the greatest division to arise within the early patristic church, was centered on this issue of evil in God's universe.

In *Satan: the Early Christian Tradition,* Jeffrey Burton Russell explains that Gnosticism probably had its roots as far back at least to the Qumran community with its theology of cosmic conflict between good and evil.[5] Yet Gnosticism was essentially a Christian attempt at theodicy which went astray. It threatened to split the post-apostolic church by the middle of the second century. Most of the apologetic writings of the early fathers were directed against this devastating heresy. Gnosticism thus performed a long-range service to the church by provoking thought on the problem of evil, especially by the great apologetists—Justin Martyr, Tatian, Athenagoras, Theophilus, Irenaeus, and Tertullian.[6]

> By bringing the question of theodicy front and center, the Gnostics forced the fathers to devise a coherent diabology, which had been lacking in New Testament and apostolic thought. Gnostic emphasis upon the power of the Devil caused the fathers to react by defining his power carefully; Gnostic stress upon the evil of the material world elicited their defense of the essential goodness of the world created by God.

Perhaps the most complex and profound dimension of the spiritual warfare view of present reality has to do with the origin of that conflict. It did not originate on earth with the fall of man. The Bible is clear on that point. Did it originate somewhere or sometime in the heavenly realm, evidently before the creation of man? This seems to be the case.[7] The Old Testament clearly hints at cosmic rebellion against the rule of God by frequent reference to evil, supernatural beings which seek to injure men and lead them away from a life of obedience to God.[8]

We cannot begin with Genesis 3 because the serpent who tempts Eve is nowhere called a supernatural being in the Old Testament. The New Testament, however, clearly identifies him as the Devil and Satan (2 Cor. 11:3; Rev. 12:9). One point is certain: at least by the intertestamental period, when Genesis 3 was read and explained to Jewish listeners by Jewish teachers, the serpent was identified with Satan. The New Testament interpretation of the fall of man and that of the Jews is identical at this point.[9] While references to Satan are not as common in the Old Testament as they are in the New, Satan is mentioned several times: once in

1 Chronicles, fourteen times in Job 1 and 2, once in Psalm 109:6, and three times in Zechariah 3:1–2.

Satan's Pattern of Operation

Satan's first recorded appearance by name is found in 1 Chronicles 21:1. This passage reveals his attempt to draw David, a man of God, into disobedience to God. It suggests a *pattern* of operation against humanity found all through Scripture, discovered throughout history, and experienced by believers and unbelievers everywhere in our day. In it we find Satan's main strategy, his primary target, and his essential purpose.

Deception, the Strategy

First, we unveil Satan's main *strategy* of temptation, *deception*. The writer recounts that Satan "moved David to number Israel" (v. 1). (See 2 Samuel 24:1 for a typically Old Testament view of the divine side of this Satanic temptation.) David, like Eve before him, had no idea of the origin of the thoughts which suddenly appeared in his mind. As he reflected upon them they seemed to be correct, logical, the thing to do. While his conscience evidently disturbed him (v. 8), he went ahead with his plan. What David proposed to do was wrong. It was so wrong that even Joab, his military commander, who was no saint by anyone's standards, saw the wrongness of David's decision and voiced his opposition to it (vv. 2–4).

It was so wrong that when God's judgment fell upon Israel, David knew he was at fault and immediately repented of his wrongdoing (v. 8). "I have sinned greatly," he confessed. "Take away the iniquity of Your servant, for I have done very foolishly."

Here we discover what we will find all through the Bible. Human sin always has a *dual* source. It has a human source, one's wrong choices. But it also has a supernatural source, Satan's temptations. He plants the seeds of evil thoughts and imaginations into human minds and hearts, intensifying the evil already there (Acts 5:1–3; 1 Cor. 7:5; 2 Cor. 11:3; 1 Thess. 3:5; cf. 2 Cor. 10:3–5; Phil 4:8).

The Scriptures speak much of deception. It takes *Strong's Concordance* two full columns to record the number of times the words and its derivatives are found in the English Bible! The words occur over 150 times, spread equally throughout both Testaments. Vine says that *deception* essentially means giving "a false impression."[10] That's how Satan approaches people, and that is evidently how he first approached his angelic peers to lead them in rebellion against God.

Satan almost always begins with deception—thus Paul's warning in 2 Corinthians 11:3 and his mention of Satan's schemes in 2 Corinthians 2:11. However, once Satan has established a strong foothold in a person's life (Eph. 4:27), deception may no longer be so important. He will often unmask himself to torment and enslave his victims further.

Leaders, the Target

Second, we discover his main *target* for deception, *leaders*. In the case of those who do not love our God, he moves in deception against persons in all levels of leadership. Political, military, economic, religious, educational, media, family, and other kinds of leaders become the target of his deception. Why? Because they control the destiny of humanity.

Someone has stated that if a solitary man sins, he alone may be affected. If a family man sins, his entire family is affected. If a community leader sins, the community is affected. If a leader over a given structure of a given society sins, the entire society is affected. If a national leader sins, the entire nation is affected. If a world leader sins, the whole world is affected. Who can forget Adolf Hitler!

If a Christian leader sins, a church, a Christian institution, or a Christian home is damaged or possibly paralyzed. Who can argue with this? We are all to some degree the victims of the sinful acts of Christian leaders exploited by the media to the discredit of God's church.

Dishonor, the Purpose

Third, we discover the main *purpose* for his deception. It is to *dishonor* God by bringing shame and even judgment upon His children. Through deceiving God's leader, David, Satan brought shame upon God's people. He also indirectly caused God's righteous judgment to fall upon His own children (v. 7).

Thus in this first recorded appearance of Satan by name in Scripture we discover the major features of his evil schemes against God and His people. He is a deceiver who seeks to seduce the leaders of God's people into actions of disobedience to God. He exists to dishonor God and injure His people. The diabology of the rest of Scripture is but an expansion of these major features of evil supernaturalism.

Belief About Evil Spirits Universal in Antiquity

As a study of ancient history reveals, belief in some form of evil supernaturalism was universal in the Old Testament world. The late Dr. Merrill F. Unger writes that

> the history of various religions from the earliest times shows belief in Satan and demons to be universal. According to the Bible, degeneration from monotheism resulted in the blinding of men by Satan and the most degrading forms of idolatry (Rom. 1:21–32; 2 Cor. 4:4). By the time of Abraham (c. 2000 B.C.), men had sunk into a crass polytheism that swarmed with evil spirits. Spells, incantations, magical texts, exorcisms,[11] and various forms of demonological phenomena abound in archeological discoveries from Sumeria and Babylon. Egyptian, Assyrian, Chaldean, Greek, and Roman antiquity are rich in demonic phenomena. The deities worshiped were invisible demons represented by material idols and images.[12]

Unger continues, quoting Dr. George W. Gilmore in the *Schaff-Herzog Encyclopedia of Religious Knowledge,* who says that "the entire religions provenience out of which Hebrew religion sprang is full of demonism." Unger then states that "early Christianity rescued its converts from the shackles of Satan and demons" (Eph. 2:2; Col. 1:13). To an amazing degree the history of religion is an account of demon-controlled religion, particularly in its clash with the Hebrew faith and later with Christianity.

Other hints of the belief in evil supernaturalism and cosmic rebellion held by the Jewish people can be found throughout the Old Testament. The *serpent* as symbolic of an evil spiritual being or beings is mentioned many times (Gen. 3:1–24; Job 3:8; 41:1; Ps. 74:14; 104:26; Isa. 27:1).[13] *Evil spirits* are spoken of some eight times, all involved in the demonization of Saul (1 Sam. 16:14–23; 18:10; 19:9). Lying spirits are mentioned six times (1 Kings 22:21–23). These verses must be studied in light of the full context, beginning with the first verse. *Familiar spirits* are also mentioned six times (Lev. 20:27; 1 Sam. 28, KJV). The NAS translates the underlying Hebrew words "one who has a familiar spirit," the KJV as "one who is a medium."

Unclean perverse spirits are referred to at least once (Isa. 19:13–14, KJV). John D. W. Watts in his excellent commentary on Isaiah interprets the expression as "a spirit of distorting."[14] Whether or not this refers to personal evil or simply an atmosphere of confusion is an open question. The false counsels and plans of Egypt, however, did come through divination. Thus, both meanings could be true.

Spirits of religious and physical harlotry are mentioned several times. The most frequent references are in Hosea in conjunction with idol worship, divination, and Baalism. *Demons* as identical with the gods and idols of the pagan nations are referred to at least four times (Lev. 17:7; Deut. 32:17; 2 Chron. 11:15; Ps. 106:19–39; cf. 1 Cor. 10:20–21). *Evil spirits who rule over territories* and nations and fight against both God's angels and His people are mentioned in the historical books, the Psalms, and Daniel. Daniel 10:10–21 is the best known passage.[15]

Key Questions

At least four important questions arise as we read these passages.

1. *Where did these evil, supernatural, created cosmic beings come from?*
   The Old Testament is emphatic that they are not true gods (Gen. 1:1f; Isa. 45:5–6; 21–23). The Old Testament is equally emphatic that God did not create evil creatures. All He made was declared "good" (Gen. 1—2). Somehow, good creatures became bad in a cosmic rebellion that continues to have devastating effect on all of creation.
2. *Why are they always revealed to be God's enemies,* the enemies of mankind in general, and of God's people in particular?
3. *Why do they incessantly seek to resist God's purposes,* corrupt His creation, defile and ensnare His people, and torment, afflict, and destroy mankind? What is their purpose in authoring such evil?
4. *How is it that, while being God's enemies, at the same time they are ultimately subject to God's will?* In other words, how is it that God uses them to defeat themselves and enhance mysterious, profound dimensions of God's sovereign purposes (Gen. 3:1f; 1 Sam. 16:14; 18:10; 19:9; 1 Kings 22:20–22; Isa. 19:13–14)?

The Old Testament hints that these invisible, evil, supernatural, created cosmic beings are fallen angelic creatures. Somewhere, sometime, evidently before the creation of mankind, they were led by a mighty angelic creature, perhaps called Lucifer, into rebellion against the lordship of God. Job 4:18 and Isaiah 24:21 seem to indicate this. Isaiah 14:12–17 and Ezekiel 28:11–19 are often used to refer to this cosmic rebellion. While there is reason to doubt the validity of this traditional secondary interpretation (all agree the primary interpretation has to do with the king of Babylon and the leader of Tyre), it is consistent with the biblical picture of Satan and his fallen angels.

When we come to the New Testament, however, the picture is much clearer. We are not left with mere hints of cosmic rebellion. Instead the New Testament declares that such a rebellion did occur. From the Gospels to Revelation we confront spiritual warfare both in heaven and on earth. The New Testament opens with the world of evil supernaturalism in open confrontation with the Son of God. In the first chapter of Mark, Jesus confronts Satan in His forty-day wilderness temptation (vv. 12–13). Having won that initial and, in many ways, decisive battle with the enemy, Jesus launches Himself into His public ministry.

His synagogue ministry is interrupted by demonic resistance. Jesus quickly silences and dispatches the angry, fearful evil spirits (1:21–26). In the same chapter, before the sun had risen the next day, Jesus confronts and casts out demons late into the night (1:29–34). The next day after His intense nighttime deliverance activity, Jesus begins His itinerant ministry. He visits the synagogues in city after city. Mark records that in these synagogues Jesus carried out a twofold activity. He was "preaching and casting out the demons" (1:39). Incredible! What a world of spiritual conflict!

As John's gospel story unfolds, for the *first time* in Scripture we are clearly told of the origin of evil. In John 8:44, Jesus says it originated with Satan. He informs us that He has come to bind Satan, break his power, and release those he holds captive (Luke 4:11–19; Matt. 12:22–29). Jesus reveals that Satan directs a mighty kingdom of evil. He has his own evil angels, just as God has His holy angels (Matt. 25:41). Next we discover that these angels are the same as the demon spirits who bind and oppress men (Matt. 12:22–29; Luke 13:10–16; Rev. 12:4–17; 13:1f).

Levels of Authority in Satan's Kingdom

As the story of evil supernaturalism unfolds in the New Testament, we discover that there are different ranks of authority in Satan's kingdom (Eph. 6:12 with Matt. 12:24–45; Mark 5:2–9). Furthermore, demons, evil spirits, and fallen angels (all synonymous terms in this book) *seem* to fall into at least four different classifications, not three as is often affirmed.

First, there are those who are free to carry out Satan's evil purposes. They inhabit the heavenlies (Eph. 3:10; 6:12) but also are free to operate on earth. These demon spirits afflict and even indwell the bodies of men (Matt. 12:43–45).

Second, there are rebellious angels who seem now to be bound in the abyss or pit.[16] They will evidently be released at a future date and will wreck havoc on the earth (Rev. 9:2–12). Satan and all free demons will be bound in this same pit during the thousand-year reign of Christ on earth (Rev. 20:1f).

Third, there *seems* to be another group of fallen angels which evidently became so wicked or were guilty of evil so horrendous they were not permitted to exist in the heavenlies or on earth. They are bound forever, not in the abyss, but in hell. The Greek word is *tartarus*, incorrectly translated "hell." Vine says that

> Tartarus . . . is neither Sheol nor Hades nor Hell, but the place where those angels whose special sin is referred to in that passage (2 Peter 2:4) are confined "to be reserved unto judgment." The region is described as "pits of darkness."[17]

These spirits evidently will never be released. They seem to be held in darkness until the day of their judgment (2 Pet. 2:4; Jude 6).[18]

Finally, there is a fourth group of evil angels who seem somehow to be bound within the earth, if we are to take the words literally. Four of them are mentioned as being "bound at the river Euphrates." When they are released they will lead a demonic army of destruction against mankind (Rev. 9:13–21).[19]

Paul tells the church at Corinth that believers will someday judge angels (1 Cor. 6:3). These must be fallen angels because God's angels are called "the holy angels" (Mark 8:38). Thus the evidence that evil spirits and demons are rebellious angels mounts (see Job 4:18; Isa. 24:21–22).

Cosmic Conflict: Facts From the Future (Revelation 12)

Revelation 12 speaks of a future day when there will be a final cosmic conflict between the angels of God under Michael and the angels of Satan (Rev. 12:3f). Even if one does not hold to a futuristic view of Revelation, this passage still reveals several undeniable facts.

1. Satan rules over a kingdom of evil angels (vv. 3–7).
2. This kingdom of evil supernaturalism opposes God and His kingdom (vv. 3–7).
3. The kingdom of evil is defeated by the archangel Michael, who evidently serves as the commander of God's holy angels and His angelic army (vv. 7–8).
4. Satan and his angels will be (or already have been) dethroned from their place of prominence in heaven (v. 9a).
5. Satan and his angels will be (or already have been) cast down to earth to bring woe to mankind (vv. 9b,12b).
6. The kingdom of evil supernaturalism is a kingdom of intense hatred against the people of God. They make war against those who "keep the commandments of God and have the testimony of Jesus" (vv. 13–17).
7. Because the activity of these wicked angels is identical with that of the evil spirits and demons found in Scripture, they must represent the same evil creatures.

Even with this brief overview, one thing is certain. The New Testament clearly declares that sometime, somewhere, cosmic rebellion occurred. A vast army of angels evidently exercised their free will and chose to resist their God and Creator. That army of fallen angels has one master over them. He is called "the great dragon . . . that serpent of old, called the Devil and Satan." Their purpose is to deceive "the whole world" (Rev. 12:9) and war against the children of God (Rev. 12:13–17).

Sin, therefore, first originated with Satan, the Evil One (John 8:44). He next evidently deceived some of the angels into following him in rebellion against God. Together they form the cosmic kingdom of evil. One group of these fallen angels seems to constitute the demons, those evil, unclean spirits who afflict mankind and oppose the church of the living God. It is primarily against them that the church's warfare is directed.

Thus, evil was "born" in the heavenlies. Now it is time to examine the entrance of evil into the experience of humanity.

4

Rebellion in the Heavenlies and on Earth

How was it possible for sin to arise in a kingdom of complete sinlessness, that is, the kingdom of God? How could sinless angels sin? The Scriptures nowhere attempt to explain how or why Satan and the angels were created with the capability for sin. Nor do they explain how or why human beings were created with the same capability. These represent but two in a series of givens which are recorded in Scripture.

By *given* I mean a fact or event which is recorded in the Bible without any explanation. The first and greatest given in all of Scripture is found in Genesis 1:1, "In the beginning God . . . ." No attempt is made to explain the existence of God. His existence is simply declared. The second greatest given is found in the same verse, "God created the heavens and the earth" (v. 1b). No explanation either of the time or the manner of the original creation is revealed. The third great given is found in the very next verse, "The earth was without form, and void; and darkness was on the face of the deep" (v. 2a).

In verse one the heavens and the earth are mentioned. Beginning with verse two the focus is exclusively upon the earth. No explanation about the earth's state of formlessness, void, and darkness is revealed. The six days of creation (or recreation) which follow are, themselves, givens.[1] The same is true with the sin of both angels and men. They, also, are givens.

The following explanation provides a partial answer. I share it in common with many biblical commentators.[2] God is the only non-creature in the universe. As eternal God, He is without beginning and without end. He exists but He was not created. He is here, but He never began. He always was, is, and shall be. Thus He and *He alone is absolutely perfect.* He has perfect *mind.* He knows everything about everything. He has perfect *emotions.* What He feels is always what should be felt. He has perfect *will.* He always chooses what is right. Indeed, by very definition as perfect God, He cannot choose evil. He cannot sin.

All creatures are imperfect, however. By very definition God cannot create God. He can create only beings which are less than God, and therefore, imperfect. The creation can never be equal to the Creator. By the very act of creating creatures in His own image and likeness, God is creating creatures with mind, emotions, and a will similar to His own.[3] By definition He cannot create creatures in His own image and likeness which are not free to think, feel, and choose for themselves.

Furthermore, creatures cannot be created in God's image and likeness and, at the same time, be preprogrammed only to do God's will. Paul Schilling in his excellent book, *God and Human Anguish,* says if this had occurred

> even though all participants might think they were free, *they would not actually be free,* and though superficially happy, they would be unable to make their own de-

cisions or to grow in genuinely responsive relations to other persons. . . . They would *lack all intrinsic value,* since all would be *robots* unconsciously living out their predetermined destiny in one vast and tightly organized system. . . . This arrangement would conceive *God as the Great Hypnotist,* whose subjects would unknowingly and irresistibly carry out the commands given them during hypnosis . . . *the notion of human beings* [and angels] *created so that they would always choose the good is self contradictory.* If they were *really free,* there could be *no guarantee* that they would always choose rightly, while if they were so constituted as to exclude choices, they would not be free. (italics mine)[4]

Furthermore, freedom of choice *untested* is only theory, not reality. Therefore, both angels and mankind had to face the choice between obedience to God and disobedience.

The American psychiatrist, Dr. Scott Peck, in his book *People of the Lie,* tells of his conversion to Christ. He too wrestles with the problem of evil.[5]

To create us in His image, God gave us free will. To have done otherwise would have been to make us puppets or hollow mannequins. Yet to give us free will God had to forswear the use of force against us. We do not have free will when there is a gun at our back . . . *In agony He must stand by and let us be.* (italics mine)

Freedom of choice was given to Lucifer (if that was his name) and the angels, also. In the heavenly realm all of God's angels were evidently put to the test of obedience. Although the story of that test is nowhere recorded, it is everywhere implied. Those who withstood the deception of the fallen angel, possibly Lucifer (Isa. 14:12),[6] were confirmed in holiness. They are described as "the holy angels" (Mark 8:38) and the "elect angels" (1 Tim. 5:21, KJV). Those who were deceived and followed the rebellious Lucifer are now, like their master, confirmed in their iniquity. According to Scripture, no provision is made for their redemption.[7]

Experience with demons confirms this fact. They hate God and will never repent or seek His forgiveness, even though they recognize with horrible fear that they are doomed to the lake of fire. They are truly confirmed in evil.[8] That the rebellion in heaven had its origin in the initial rebellion of one angelic being, Satan or the Devil, seems certain. All through Scripture He is revealed as the sole originator of evil and temptation (John 8:44; Luke 4:1–13). Furthermore, the Devil is always seen as the master over an angelic army of evil supernaturalism (Matt. 25:41; Rev. 12:3–17). It is his tail which swept away "a third of the stars of heaven and threw them to the earth" (Rev. 12:4). (These stars probably represent angels.[9]) He is revealed to be in command of "principalities, . . . powers, . . . the rulers of the darkness of this age, . . . spiritual hosts of wickedness in the heavenly places" (Eph. 6:12).

Two Kinds of Evil on Earth

This cosmic rebellion reached earth soon after man's creation. The evil it brought affected the universe on two levels: the natural and the moral.

Edward J. Carnell defines *natural evil* as "all of those frustrations of *human values* which are perpetrated, *not* by the free agency of man, but by the *natural elements* in the universe, such as the fury of the hurricane and the devastation of the parasite."[10]

Carnell next quotes the poet John Mills:[11]

Killing, the most criminal act recognized by human laws, Nature does once to every being that lives; and in a large proportion of cases, after protracted tortures such as only the greatest monsters whom we read of ever purposely inflicted on their living fellow-creatures. . . . Nature impales men, breaks them as if on the wheel, casts them to be devoured by wild beasts, burns them to death, crushes them with stones like the first Christian martyr, starves them with hunger, freezes them with cold. . . . All this, Nature does with the most supercilious disregard both of mercy and of justice, emptying her shafts upon the best and noblest indifferently with the meanest and the worst.

Carnell follows with a word about one of the greatest of all evils, death. He speaks of the heartlessness of death which strikes down the good, along with the bad, in blind indiscrimination. He observes that

the overt reason why natural evil is peculiarly a Christian problem is that Christianity teaches not only that all of nature was originally created by the Almighty and pronounced by Him to be *good,* but also that the present movement of all things is *guided* and *guarded* by the very watchful eye of Him "who accomplishes all things according to the counsel of his will" (Eph. 1:11).

Can the Christian walk through the crowded corridors of a children's hospital or stumble through the rubble left by the devastating force of a hurricane, without feeling the force of Job's words? "Surely I would speak to the Almighty, and I desire to reason with God" (Job 13:3).[12]

The Bible is in no way silent about natural evil. Beginning with Genesis and moving through the entire biblical record ending in Revelation 22, natural evil has a place of prominence in Scripture second only to its more devastating twin, moral evil. However, Scripture does not attempt to explain natural evil outside of the context of human *moral* evil. It says nothing about the existence of natural evil in the universe before the birth of moral evil in the experience of mankind.

Carnell defines *moral evil:* "[It] includes all of those frustrations of human values which are perpetrated not by the natural elements in the universe, but by the free agency of man." In his definitions of both natural and moral evil, Carnell limits his discussion exclusively to the relationship of evil to humanity.[13]

I differ from Carnell in that I see evil as originally pre-human, existing before the fall of man. Out of the context of pre-human, cosmic evil, human evil is introduced in Scripture. The anthrocentric focus of Scripture ignores direct references to the existence of natural evil in the heavens or on earth before the fall of man. Was there a pre-Adamic earthly moral creation which suffered a similar fall as that recorded in Genesis 3 with mankind? Is the gap theory, which affirms that a pre-Adamic fall occurred on earth between verses 1 and 2 of Genesis 1, accurate?[14] Was there physical death in the universe or on earth prior to man's fall? Did the present disorder within the order of the stellar heavens exist prior to man's creation and fall?

About these and similar issues of natural evil *the Scriptures are silent.* Furthermore, we do not go to God's Word for answers to some of the fundamental questions raised by the natural sciences other than the declaration of Scripture, "In the beginning God created the heavens and the earth" (Gen. 1:1). The Scriptures clearly indicate, however, that the *Fall of humanity and the present groanings of nature are intimately related.* In one of the greatest cosmological passages in Scripture Paul affirms that

the creation was subjected to futility, not willingly, but because of Him who subjected it in hope; because the creation itself also will be delivered from the bondage of corruption into the glorious liberty of the children of God. For we know that the whole creation groans and labors with birth pangs together until now. Not only that, but we also who have the firstfruits of the Spirit, even we ourselves groan within ourselves, eagerly waiting for the adoption, the redemption of our body. (Rom. 8:20–23)

With this in mind the apostle introduces his cosmological reasonings with the words, "For the earnest expectation of the creation eagerly waits for the revealing of the sons of God" (v. 19).

Why? Because humanity's full redemption, which will occur only at the redemption of our bodies (v. 23), will transform the entire physical creation. At that point and only at that point will natural evil be annihilated forever.

The apostle Peter declares that at some point, probably concurrent with or soon after the redemption of our bodies referred to by Paul, "the heavens will pass away with a great noise, and the elements will melt with fervent heat; . . . Nevertheless we, according to His promise, look for new heavens and a new earth in which righteousness dwells" (2 Pet. 3:10,13).

All of this is harmonious with John the Revelator's words:

Now I saw a new heaven and a new earth, for the first heaven and the first earth had passed away. Also there was no more sea. Then I, John, saw the holy city, New Jerusalem, coming down out of heaven from God, prepared as a bride adorned for her husband. (Rev. 21:1–2)

The result will be the eternal and *nearly* total annihilation of natural and moral evil, from God's creation and mankind's experience. I say "nearly" because the mysterious exception is called hell or the lake of fire.[15] Whatever one's views of hell or the lake of fire may be, such a "place" does exist. Jesus says hell was made "for the devil and his angels" (Matt. 25:41). He warns men that they too will go there if they continue living in disobedience to God (Matt. 5:21–22,27–30).[16]

Paul describes that place of eternal evil as a place where men shall "be punished with everlasting destruction from the presence of the Lord and from the glory of His power" (2 Thess. 1:9), a penalty reserved for all who "do not know God, and on those who do not obey the gospel of our Lord Jesus Christ" (v. 8). John pictures hell as a "lake of fire and brimstone" into which the Devil and his servants will be thrown to be "tormented day and night forever and ever" (Rev. 20:10). He further adds that "Death and Hades were cast into the lake of fire. This is the second death. And anyone not found written in the Book of Life was cast into the lake of fire" (vv. 14–15).

A horrid, vivid, terrifying picture of eternal evil, the lake of fire evidently parallels the new heavens and the new earth of eternal bliss, of eternal non-evil. Mystery of mysteries!

COSMIC REBELLION BECOMES EARTHLY

With the introduction of humanity into the conflict between the two kingdoms, the formerly exclusive cosmic rebellion now becomes a cosmic-earthly rebellion.

The historical-pictorial account is given in Genesis 3:1–24.[17] The *historicity* of the Fall is confirmed in Scriptures such as 2 Corinthians 11:3 and Revelation 12:7–9. The historic fact of the Fall is also used by Paul in Romans 5 and 1 Corinthians 15 in connection with the historic, redemptive action of Jesus as the last Adam and the second man. I call Genesis 3 a *pictorial* account because of the vivid symbolism used to describe the historical events. The main truths of the story are just as real and historic if one admits to symbolism as they are if one follows a strict literalism.[18]

Three Lessons From Genesis 3

I consider Genesis 3 to be the most important passage on spiritual warfare in the entire Old Testament. We will deal with it in detail later. Three of the many lessons to be learned from this story contribute to the discussion at this point.

1. *Humanity was led into rebellion against the rule of God by an already existing evil, supernatural being.* In the symbolism of the story, that evil supernatural being is revealed as a serpent, an animal, part of God's good creation.[19] Whether or not the physical animal we know today as the serpent is the creature revealed here is entirely beside the point. The main point of the story is that mankind was deceived into an act of disobedience to God by an already existing wise, but evil, being.

   He reveals his evil wisdom by disguising himself so that the woman is unaware of his evil. She believes she is in conversation with a familiar creature, part of God's good creation. Then he leads Eve into a discussion about God and the limitations He has placed on her and Adam in the Garden. Until now she has only seen the positive side of her Edenic state. Satan awakens within her mind the realization of the negative side, what she and Adam *cannot* do in the garden. The deception was directed against her mind which, by definition, also includes her emotions and will.

2. *He outwits the sinless but inexperienced woman.* Carefully he chooses his words to cause her to think his thoughts after him. This subtle transition confuses her mind and distorts her view of reality. She fails to reject the lies now being planted within her mind. She accepts the lies and half-truths she is hearing as the real truth.

3. *Being a former sinless creature himself, the serpent (Satan) is aware when her thinking has become distorted.* He knows when she is ready to receive in her mind a direct denial of God's Word and a total misrepresentation of God's purposes: "You will not surely die. For God knows that in the day you eat of it your eyes will be opened, and you will be like God, knowing good and evil" (vv. 4–5). That was all that was needed. *The deception is complete.* Eve's *mind* embraces Satan's thoughts. She now sees the forbidden tree from an entirely new and wrong perspective. Satan has awakened within her *emotions* she had never known before. She sees, she delights, she desires, and she takes the fruit of her deception.

   Sin is born. As is sin's nature, it never remains by itself. It always seeks company. Eve immediately shares her new-found pleasures with her husband, Adam. Evidently there is not as yet any visible, negative evidence of sin's consequences in her appearance. Adam exercises his free will and eats the forbidden fruit, disobeying the Word of God. The goal of Satan's deception is now realized. The head over God's new creation falls.

Consequences of the First Earthly Deception

One major consequence is the defilement of all of God's new creation. Satan's delight is at its zenith. He has not only deceived God's angelic creation, but he has also succeeded in defiling God's earthly creation.

Second, *the cosmic rebellion has now become a cosmic-earthly rebellion.* Mankind has joined the fallen angels in rejecting the revealed will of God. History, both cosmic and earthly, will never be the same.

Third, *humanity not only participates in the conflict between the two kingdoms but also becomes the central person around whom the conflict revolves.* Thus humanity both by nature and by choice belong to Satan's kingdom (Luke 4:5–6; John 12:31; 14:30; 16:11; Acts 26:18; Eph. 2:1–3; Col. 1:13). God, however, out of sovereign love, mercy, compassion, and grace (Eph. 2:4–9; cf. 1:13–14), has acted to provide full redemption for all humanity (John 3:16; 2 Cor. 5:18–21; 1 John 2:1–2).

God's enemy, having deceived the human race into following his deception into independence from the will of God, now becomes man's mortal enemy. Through his demonic hosts he resists God's program of redemption for humanity. Satan does not want people to hear or obey the gospel of God's love. He does all within his evil power to resist the spread of the gospel to the nations (Matt. 13:19,25–30; Acts 5, 8, 13, 19; 2 Cor. 4:3–4; 11:3–4,13–15; 1 Thess. 2:18; 3:5; Rev. 2—3; 12:17—13:7).

The battle centers on humanity. Satan deceived and enslaved the whole race; God potentially has redeemed it (2 Cor. 5:18–19; 1 John 2:1–2). All that is lacking is people's response to God's redeeming love. To stop them from responding is Satan's goal, which he seeks to accomplish through continued deception.

In this context of sin and deception the gospel is preached. The Spirit of God convicts people of sin, righteousness, and judgment (John 16:18). The enemy fights back to hold them in continual bondage (Matt. 13:19; 2 Cor. 4:3–4). Thus, again, in this sense humanity not only participates in the conflict between the two kingdoms, but it is the central being around which the conflict revolves. Building on humanity's sinful flesh energized by this evil world, Satan assaults the human mind with continual lies. People, thus being deceived, in turn become deceivers (2 Tim. 3:13). They spread Satan's lies on a worldwide scale as they unwittingly assume the nature of their deadly enemy.

5

The Source of All Rebellion

When Liars Tell the Truth

Although all demons, like their master, Satan, are liars, they can be forced to tell the truth. First, they never lie to Jesus. Second, they can be made to confess to their deception by Satan and subsequent rebellion against God, as the following incident illustrates.[1]

With the permission of the demonized victim, I was using a deliverance as a teaching session for some sincere, but somewhat incredulous observers. A few days earlier my wife Loretta, my younger daughter Barbara, and I, with a few prayer helpers, had begun the deliverance process. We knew that there were yet more demons to be expelled from the victim's life.

I purposely entered into a controlled dialogue with one of the demons beyond what is normal and usually appropriate. I allowed the demons to use the victim's vocal cords and speak out loud.[2] I was dealing with a demon called Fear.[3]

"How long have you been around?" I asked Fear.

"For ages," it replied.

"You rebelled against God, didn't you?" I prodded.

"Yes."

"Why did you do that?"

"We were fooled."

"Who were you fooled by, Satan?"

"Yes."

"Yet you say you love him."

"We must."

"He is the Prince of Darkness. Do you know where he is going?"

"We were betrayed."

"Then you betray him. Would you like to betray him?"

"No."

In the only story in the Acts of a one-on-one demonic encounter and deliverance story which records demonic speech, the demons declare the truth. "These men are the servants of the Most High God, who proclaim to us the way of salvation," they exclaim (Acts 16:17).

Evidently, demons are often compelled to tell the truth in the presence of greater spiritual authority (Luke 10:17–19; Eph. 2:6; 3:10). They will often voluntarily proclaim the truth about God, the Lord Jesus Christ, and the defeat of Satan their master by the Lord Jesus Christ. They will also confess their own defeat and our authority over them during the fear and pain they experience during deliverance sessions. In spite of their defiant and arrogant bluffing, demons go through progressive torment during prayerfully and carefully planned deliverance sessions.

With increasing experience in challenging and evicting evil spirits through the authority in Jesus' name, the believer learns to detect when the unclean spirits are lying, when they are fearfully confessing the truth, and how to compel them to speak the truth. I do not usually enter into involved dialogue with demons during deliverance ministry. If I am led by the Holy Spirit to seek information from a demon, it is only for a specific purpose and under certain conditions. Also, as the Lord's servant, I am always in charge. The demons are never allowed to take over the proceedings.

The purpose of deliverance is always to help free the victim from demonization and lead him into a life of obedience to God. The conditions, however, will vary depending upon the circumstances. Sometimes time is a crucial factor. The demons must be expelled from the victim's life in a short period of time. I will set up post-deliverance counseling sessions with the counselee, which will often involve further deliverance.

At times I am compelled to force the demons to reveal the "places" (Eph. 4:27) they are holding in the victim's life to expel them more easily. This is not always necessary, for if effective pre-deliverance counseling is followed, the victims themselves will usually reveal that information. Sometimes, however, those places may be hidden deep within the victim's damaged personality. The demons know the places and can be made to reveal them. This process often takes time; deliverance counseling is not a ministry for impatient or preoccupied people.

In some serious cases of demonization involving extreme child abuse and often Ritual Sexual Abuse (RSA), personality splitting or dissociation may occur. Amnesia is almost always involved. Demons may attach themselves to the alter personalities also (see chapter 59). This type of deliverance and healing is in a class by itself. The "rules" are now in the process of being formulated, because this is new territory in both counseling and deliverance ministries. Most major books on deliverance procedures totally or almost totally ignore such Multiple Personality Disorders (MPD).* The normal procedures suggested often do not work well with this type of personality bruising.

Again, we do not build our theology on the fearful cries of demons. Yet when faced with the presence of the reigning Lord in the person of His servants, they will confirm the biblical account concerning their relationship to Satan, their deception, their fall, and all other dimensions of biblical truth. They are forced to tell the truth.

The Origin of Evil in Satan

We still face a difficult question, however. While the fallen angels and humanity were deceived by Lucifer (we will use this name for Satan before his fall, but it is not certain that this was his name), who deceived Lucifer? We have just removed the troublesome question of theodicy one step backwards, to the birth of evil within Lucifer himself. The biblical answer is clear, even though how it could occur is nowhere explained. Satan is the father of lies because he is himself a liar, Jesus affirms. He lied both to the angels and to humanity because he was already a liar. Furthermore, Jesus declares that "He was a murderer from the beginning" (John 8:44; cf. 1 John 3:8.) What does this mean?

According to Leon Morris, "the term rendered 'beginning' can also denote 'origin' in the sense of basic cause . . . first cause."[4] Applying this truth to John 8:44

---

*I use "alter personality" and "Multiple Personality Disorder (MPD)" through most of this book because these are the words used most frequently by counselors, both Christian and secular, to refer to extreme personality dissociation. For my preferred terms see chapter 59, note 1.

gives us important insight. Jesus is affirming that murder has its origin in Satan. He is its first cause. Jesus next connects that origin with Satan's nature as "a liar and the father of lies." Morris connects this murder with the human race. "It was through Satan that Adam became mortal (Rom. 5:12; cf. Wisdom 2:24). Satan thus became the murderer of the whole human race. . . . a 'man killer.' "[5]

We can take this truth one step farther back to the true origin of murder through lying. It occurred not on earth, but in the angelic realm probably before the creation of humanity. Remember the demon Fear and its mournful lament, "We were fooled (by Satan). We were betrayed!" Thus murder through lying had its origin in the Devil. Jesus is saying that Satan originated murder and deception. He evidently did so when he deceived a host of God's angels into rebellion against God, thus bringing about their death; that is, their eternal separation from God.

The Remaining Mystery

As to how Satan himself was transformed from a good creature into the liar who then became the murderer of some of the angels and the entire human race, the Bible is totally silent. Where the Bible is obviously and consistently silent about such matters we do well also to remain silent.

Our earlier discussion of the price that God had to pay to create creatures with true freedom of choice throws some light on the question of how Lucifer could become the Devil, liar and murderer. Yet we are ultimately left with a mystery which our mortal minds cannot fully fathom. In matters like this I continually refer to verses in Scripture like these:

> The secret things belong to the LORD our God, but those things which are revealed belong to us and to our children forever, that we may do all the words of this law. (Deut. 29:29)

> Such knowledge is too wonderful for me; It is high, I cannot attain it. (Ps. 139:6)

> Oh, the depth of the riches both of the wisdom and knowledge of God! How unsearchable are His judgments and His ways past finding out! For who has known the mind of the LORD? Or who has become His counselor? Or who has first given to Him And it shall be repaid to him? For of Him and through Him and to Him are all things, to whom be glory forever. Amen. (Rom. 11:33–36)

We have seen again and again that the lie that penetrated the innocent, free minds of Adam and Eve and which led to their murder (John 8:44; 1 John 3:8) originated outside themselves. They possessed no inner inclination toward evil, no independence from God. They did not live in "the world," that is, human society organized toward life independent of the will of God. Their "society" was the Garden of God. Yet they sinned.

So we see that sin and rebellion against the lordship of God are not normal to the human race *as God created us*. The *normal* human life was meant to be one of total obedience to God and unbroken, peaceful, indescribable fellowship both with God and our fellow man. In their innocence, both in their intimate relationship with God and in their naked relationship with each other, Adam and Eve felt no shame (Gen. 2:25; cf. 3:7–11). All God made was good. They lived in the warm, pure light of primeval goodness and innocence.

Sin and rebellion against God, resulting in both natural and moral evil, are thus an abnormality which has now become normal for humanity. Edith Schaeffer comments on this transition.[6]

Adam and Eve had experienced the transition from living in a perfect world to living in a spoiled world. Adam and Eve had known what it was to be "normal human beings" living in the "normal world" but they were the only ones who were to compare by personal experience what "normal" and "abnormal" were like. Their choice to act upon the lie of Satan, as if it were truth, brought about the result that God had predicted. The world became abnormal. We have lived in—and do live in—an abnormal world. Things have been spoiled, vandalized by Satan, by a whole period of cause-and-effect history.

A detailed study of Genesis 3 will serve us well. Satan's tactics and his strategy have not changed since the Garden of Eden. Becoming aware of what he did to our first parents and how he did it will serve to forewarn and arm us for the spiritual battle we all face here and now.

6

Cosmic-Earthly
Warfare Begins
Genesis 3

The major focus on spiritual warfare as experienced by humanity begins with Genesis 3. I will make no attempt to deal in any depth with the critical issues often raised about this story. As mentioned previously, Genesis 3 is both an historical and a pictorial account of the fall of humanity. It actually happened the way it is recorded. There really was an historical Adam and Eve. Not only were they the first human beings created in the image of God, but they stand as the representatives of the entire human race. Their transgression, particularly that of Adam as the head of the human race, is seen in Scripture as the fall of the human race (Rom. 5; 1 Cor. 15).[1]

Mysteries in the Genesis 3 account have disturbed the minds of biblical scholars, both Jewish and Christian, for centuries.[2] The prince of Bible commentators, John Calvin, writes that the story raises "many and arduous questions."[3]

Moses, the writer of Genesis,[4] begins his account with another given, the talking, seducing serpent:

> Now the serpent was more cunning than any beast of the field which the LORD God had made. And he said to the woman, "Has God indeed said, 'You shall not eat of every tree of the garden'?" (Gen. 3:1)

Three Views of Genesis 3

There seem to be only three major ways of viewing the serpent's role in the temptation story. First is to see it *literally*. The serpent spoke to Eve and, indirectly, to Adam through Eve bringing about humanity's fall. Second is to view it *allegorically*. Webster defines allegory as "the expression by means of symbolic fictional figures and actions of truths or generalizations about human conduct or experience." For those who hold to a high view of Scripture, as I do, we can pass over most of Webster's first definition of allegory when it comes to Genesis 3. His second definition fits the case better, however. The story is historical, but is described through "symbolic representation."[5]

The third manner of viewing the story is both *literal and symbolic*. I lean towards this historical-pictorial (symbolic) view of Genesis 3. The events involving Adam and Eve actually happened the way Moses records them. He does, however, use symbolism to tell his story. If strict literalism is correct, or if the allegorical view is best, or if we have here literalism mixed with "symbolic representation," the story is still the same. R. Payne Smith notes that

> The leading point of the narrative is that the temptation came upon man from without, and through the woman. Such questions, therefore, as whether it was a real serpent or Satan under a serpent-like form, whether it spake with a real voice, and

whether the narrative describes a literal occurrence or is allegorical, are better left unanswered.

God has given us the account of man's temptation and fall, and the entry of sin into the world, in this actual form; and the more reverent course is to draw from the narrative the lessons it was evidently intended to teach us, and not enter upon too curious speculations.[6]

The historical account of the Fall is obviously given in story form and with vivid imagery and symbolism. In this manner the truth the story was meant to convey could best be communicated to the common people of that day.[7] One thing is absolutely certain in light of the testimony of the rest of Scripture, however. Satan was the source of the voice that spoke to Eve's mind through the serpent.

Calvin raises the possibility that the ability of the serpent to talk on this occasion could be considered as the first direct intervention by God into the normal course of His creation, the first miracle.[8]

The serpent was not eloquent by nature, but when Satan, by divine permission, procured it as a fit instrument for his use, he uttered words also by its tongue, which God Himself permitted. Nor do I doubt that Eve perceived it to be extraordinary and on that account received with the greater aridity what she admired . . . if it seems incredible that beasts should speak at the command of God, how has man the power of speech, but because God has formed his tongue.

There is certainly biblical support for some aspects of Calvin's position. What about Balaam's donkey? The biblical record states, "Then the Lord opened the mouth of the donkey, and she said to Balaam, 'What have I done to you, that you have struck me these three times?'" (Num. 22:28). It is interesting to note that Balaam conversed with the donkey and was apparently neither surprised nor fearful, and the same appears to have been true for Eve.[9]

Did not Jesus himself affirm that God will make stones to speak His glory if people refuse to do so? His exact words were, "I tell you that if these should keep silent, the stones would immediately cry out" (Luke 19:40). Cannot the God who can make stones and donkeys to speak also allow a serpent to provide the channel of communication for Satan when such fits His sovereign plan? Indeed He can, and did. Whether it was audible, verbal communication or the implanting of thoughts into Eve's mind is also a question for which there is no easy answer. Either way, the story remains exactly the same.

Finally, there is the question as to why Moses does not mention the presence of Satan in the account of the Fall. My first answer is the obvious one: No one really can be certain since the answer is not given. Again, I appeal to Deuteronomy 29:29.

Lessons on Spiritual Warfare From Genesis 3

Now the main teachings of the story about warfare with evil supernaturalism begin to unfold. We start with the danger of a two-way conversation, either verbally or within the mind, with the Devil on his terms. Satan began with the question, "Has God indeed said . . . ?" Instead of silencing him, Eve answered his question. He then subtly responded to her answer and the trap was set (Gen. 3:1–6).

It is always dangerous to engage in a two-way dialogue with the Devil *on his terms*. To all of his doubts, lies, and boasts our response must be that of Jesus, "Away with you, Satan! For it is written" (Matt. 4:10). "It is written" is equivalent to "the sword of the Spirit, which is the word *(rhema)* of God" of Ephesians 6:17. That is exactly how I handle demons in deliverance ministries. Often, once they have been exposed, demons tend to switch from total silence to rambling verbosity. They must be shut down by a word of command in Jesus' name:

> You are not allowed to speak unless you are asked to speak. You will answer what you're asked and no more. Then I will determine if you speak out loud or only in the mind of _____ (the victim). I will decide that, not you. This is a one-way conversation and I am in charge, not you. Be silent until I give you permission to speak.

To those who feel that we should not use the personal pronoun "I" but instead ask the Lord to silence evil spirits, my answer is simple and biblical: Nowhere in Scripture is that procedure taught nor practiced. It sounds very pious but it is erroneous.

Jesus gives us authority over the demonic realm. We do not need to ask for what is already given. That such authority is given to all God's servants is clear in that it was not only given to the twelve apostles (Luke 9:4) but also to the seventy other disciples (Luke 10:1f). Since they were disciples of Jesus but not part of the apostolic band, they can be seen as representatives of Christians in general.[10]

When the seventy returned from their witnessing ministry, they were not bashful in referring to *their* authority over demons as it was evidenced in their ministry. They exclaimed, "Lord, even the demons are subject to us in Your name" (Luke 10:17).

Jesus, far from rebuking them for "arrogance," affirmed their words. After declaring the fall of Satan that He beheld in the spirit realm, which was evidently directly connected to their ministry (v. 18), He joyfully declared, "Behold, I give you the authority to trample on serpents [interesting in light of Genesis 3!] and scorpions [Rev. 9:1–11], and over all the power of the enemy, and nothing shall by any means hurt you" (v. 19). Their authority, *exousia*, delegated to them by Jesus Himself, was greater than the power, *dunamis*, of the enemy. They had nothing to fear (v. 19).

The only caution Jesus laid upon them was to maintain balance in their life, ministry, and priorities. While it was a cause of rejoicing to know that the enemy was subject to them (vv. 17–18), it was more important to rejoice in their relationship to God and His kingdom (v. 20).

In the only case outside of the Gospels where the Scriptures describe a one-on-one deliverance "session" from demonization (Acts 16), the apostle Paul followed the exact pattern of deliverance ministry practiced by the seventy. To the demons afflicting the slave girl of Philippi he declared, "I command you in the name of Jesus Christ to come out of her." Luke writes, "And he came out that very hour."

Doubting God's Goodness

Returning to Genesis 3, we note that once Satan deceived Eve into conversing with him on his terms, he subtly attacked God's goodness: "Has God indeed said?" Lange comments:[11]

> The deluding ambiguity of his utterance is admirably expressed by the particles. . . . The word in question denotes a questioning surprise, which may have in view now a yes, and now a no, according to the connection. This is the first striking feature in the beginning of the temptation. In the most cautious manner there is shown the tendency to excite doubt. Then the expression aims, at the same time, to awaken mistrust, and to weaken the force of the prohibition.

What is Satan saying to Eve? "God is not really good to you since He is denying you all the delicacies of the garden, is He? How can He be a good God and treat you this way?"

We have all heard that voice in our minds! "How can God be good and allow you to suffer as you do? How can He be good and deny you what you really want, deep within you? How can God be good and allow your child, wife, husband, loved one to die of cancer? How can God be good and . . . ?" The reader can add his own often-heard words of doubt about God's goodness.

Eve made a serious error in allowing that line of thinking to continue. She could not stop it from beginning, but she could and should have stopped it from progressing. It is the same error we often make under similar demonic attacks.

Satan, through his demons, assaults our minds with doubts. He attacks our faith. He undermines our confidence in God's goodness by pointing out perceived inconsistencies in God's treatment of us and others. We must learn "to shut him down" by rejecting his accusations against God within our minds. This is where we use the sword of the Spirit, the Word (*rhema*, a particular verse or truth of Scripture, not the entire Bible) of God.

Next Eve tries to defend God. I paraphrase her words, "No, you have it all wrong," she replies. "We can eat of the trees of the garden, from all of them except the fruit of the tree in the middle of the garden." In her reply to Satan it is possible the thought has begun to cross her mind, *Why did God put that forbidden tree there, anyway? Why did he have to plant it right in the middle of the garden where we have to see it every day? That doesn't seem fair.*

Eve walked right into Satan's trap. While she did not know it was Satan with whom she was conversing, her actions were still inexcusable. She knew God personally. Also she knew what God expected of her: obedience. She should have exclaimed, "I don't know *who* you are or *what* you have in mind, but I will not listen to your doubts. Be silent! How dare you affront the goodness of my God! He is God! He is Lord! He is sovereign! He is the maker and owner of all! He is good to us! Look at all He has done for us! Look at the hundreds of trees from which we can eat. Why do you single out the one from which we are commanded not to eat?

"I love God and I choose to obey Him even in the areas where I do not understand. Whatever His purposes may be for denying us the fruit of that one tree, I will believe! I will obey! I reject all doubts about His goodness!"

Denying God's Word

Unfortunately Eve followed the wrong course of thinking. When the Evil One saw that her confidence in God's goodness had been weakened, he took the next step. He overtly denied God's Word: "You will not surely die!" (v. 4). Calvin comments that

> Satan now springs more boldly forward; and because he sees a breach open before him, he breaks through in a direct assault, for he is never wont to engage in open war until we voluntarily expose ourselves to him, naked and unarmed. . . .
>
> He now, therefore, . . . openly accuses God of falsehood, for he asserts that the word by which death was pronounced is false and delusive. Fatal temptation! When, while God is threatening us with death, we not only securely sleep, but hold God himself in derision![12]

The same occurs in our Christian life. Once we have been deceived by the Evil One into doubting God's goodness, we will automatically begin to doubt His Word. The latter naturally follows the former.

I was counseling a young woman who, among other things, was plagued by an extremely poor self-image. Her mind was continually bombarded with doubts about God. She wanted to love Him but found, at the same time, she emotionally almost hated Him.

"Why did God make me so ugly?" she asked. (She was a reasonably attractive blue-eyed blonde.) "Why does God make my life so difficult? If He is really my loving Father, why does He not treat me with the gentle love, compassion, and kindness of a good father? Why does He allow me to be so unhappy?

"I once had the assurance of my salvation. Now I am not so sure. I know the Bible promises assurance of salvation to all who repent and believe, but because I have lost my confidence in His goodness how can I trust His Word?

"I want to love God, but secretly I almost hate Him. I'm angry at Him. He's unfair and unkind. He doesn't hear me when I pray. So how can I trust anything He tells me in His Word?"

This is spiritual warfare. The young lady was a committed Christian. She was also an honest one. She only spoke *openly* what many believers feel *secretly* when their world begins to crumble around them, when their minds are under severe demonic assault.

Winning the Battle in Our Minds

How do we resist these attacks against our mind? The apostle Paul gives us the sure answer in 2 Corinthians 10:3–5:

> For though we walk in the flesh, we do not war according to the flesh. For the weapons of our warfare are not carnal but mighty in God for pulling down strongholds, casting down arguments and every high thing that exalts itself against the knowledge of God, bringing every thought into captivity to the obedience of Christ.

"Though we walk in the flesh" (here "flesh" probably refers to our humanity), we are at war, Paul is affirming (v. 3). In every war weapons must be used. Spiritual warfare is no different. God has given us weapons with which we engage in effective battle.

"Our weapons do not arise out of our humanity," Paul is declaring. "Even the most brilliant, resourceful, and strongest among us cannot overcome the enemy with whom we war. But our weapons are divine. Since they come from God, they are more powerful than anything the enemy brings against us. They are sufficient to destroy every fortress of evil we encounter," Paul promises (v. 4).

What is our responsibility in this matter? Paul tells us in verse 5. In one word, we are, by God's power, to take control of our minds, our thought life. As was true of Eve in Genesis 3 so it is true of us. Our mind, which includes our heart, emotions, and will, represents the real battleground between the two kingdoms within our lives as believers. That is the testimony of the entire New Testament confirmed by daily experience. If we win the battle in our minds, we have won the war.

That is the battle that Eve, and later Adam, lost. We all suffer the consequences of that defeat to this day, but the battle is reenacted almost daily in the mind and heart of every child of God. Thus the importance given in Scripture to the mind and to its almost equivalent term, the heart.

What does the Bible mean by "the mind of man"? What does it mean when it refers to "a man's heart"? These questions carry us into the next chapter, the area of biblical psychology.

7

Warfare in the Garden

Biblical psychology makes no attempt at precise definitions and distinctions about human nature as does modern psychology. The Bible is not a textbook on psychology just as it is not a textbook on geology, astronomy, or any of the sciences. Where it touches on any of the areas covered by these disciplines, however, the Bible is without error.[1] But since its purposes lie in another direction, the Scriptures should not be used to attempt to create a full-orbed science. In the words of D. M. Lake,[2]

> Biblical concepts of psychology lack analytical and technical precision. Both the Old Testament and the New Testament focus attention on man's concrete and total relationship to God and where psychological terms do appear their intention seems to be emphasis rather than a concern to divide or compartmentalize man's activity. For this reason, no consistent pattern or terminology can be determined in either Testament.

Meanings of *Heart*

Also for this reason it is difficult to come up with precise definitions of words like *heart, mind,* and similar words used in the Scriptures to refer to man's immaterial nature. J. M. Lower notes that "heart [refers] to the inner man; the function of mind; where man remembers, thinks; the heart, the seat and center of all physical and spiritual life; the soul or mind as the fountain and seat of thoughts, passions, desires, affections, appetites, purposes, endeavors."[3] Thus the heart refers to "the inner man," the hidden person of the heart. It can also denote "that central agency and facility within man whereby he images, intends, purposes, thinks, and understands." The heart is also "that center, essence, and inner substance of man which needs to be reconciled to God, redeemed, that being righted with God may be reconciled to others." Finally, the heart is "the core and seat of emotions; the center of emotional reaction, feeling, and sensitivity."

Meanings of *Mind*

When one considers the wide variety of Hebrew and Greek words translated "mind" in the English Bible, one encounters confusion and overlapping, with the biblical use of heart and similar words. After surveying this variety, Lake concludes:[4]

> . . . no one term occupies an exclusive meaning, nor is one term alone used to indicate the faculty of reflection or cognition. It is equally clear because of this constellation of terms that man's being defies precise definition. All these terms call attention to man's inner being . . . that controls the self.

According to Lake, the "Hebrew mentality was strikingly different from the Greek." Although the Bible regards man as a thinking being, he is presented as a united whole whose reflexive or cognitive faculties are an indivisible element of his total being.

There are two Greek words used primarily by the apostle Paul for mind. The first word is *nous*. William Vine says *nous*, or mind, "Generally speaking, [refers to] the seat of reflective consciousness, comprising the faculties of perception and understanding and those of feeling, judging and determining."[5] The second word is *noema*. Vine says it means "thought, design, [and] is rendered 'minds' in 2 Corinthians 3:14; 4:4; 11:3; Philippians 4:7."

Nous, translated mind, is found all through the New Testament. Luke puts the word in the mouth of Jesus in Luke 24:45: "And He opened their understanding *(nous)* that they might comprehend the Scriptures."

Paul uses *nous* to write of the reprobate mind, a mind controlled by sin and under the judgment of God (Rom. 1:28–32, Eph. 4:17; Col. 2:18; 1 Tim. 6:5; 2 Tim. 3:8; Titus 1:15). He uses *nous* to stress the renewed mind in Romans 12:2 and to refer to the believer as possessing the mind of Christ in 1 Corinthians 2:16. He uses the plural of *nous* to speak of "the peace of God, which surpasses all understanding, will guard your hearts and minds through Christ Jesus" in Philippians 4:7. *Nous* thus becomes primarily a Pauline word, even as warfare within the human mind of both believers and unbelievers is primarily a Pauline emphasis.

Noema also is a Pauline word. It is used exclusively by the apostle in the New Testament. In 2 Corinthians 3:14 Paul speaks of men whose minds "were blinded." In 2 Corinthians 4:4 he declares that Satan is the primary source of the spiritual blindness of the unbelieving mind: "whose minds [*noemata*] the god of this age has blinded, who do not believe, lest the light of the gospel of the glory of Christ, who is the image of God, should shine on them."

The apostle next turns his attention to believers. Referring to Eve's deception by the serpent, he declares, "But I fear, lest somehow, as the serpent deceived Eve by his craftiness, so your minds [*noemata*] may be corrupted from the simplicity that is in Christ" (2 Cor. 11:3).

Mind and Motive

With this we return to Genesis 3 and Satan's attacks against the mind of Eve. With the door into Eve's mind now opened wide to his lies, the enemy next assaults God's motives. In doing so he actually is assaulting God's character: "For God knows that in the day you eat of it your eyes will be opened, and you will be like God, knowing good and evil" (v. 5).

What is the serpent insinuating?

"There is more to life than what you are presently enjoying," the Tempter whispers. "God is keeping a wonderful realm of reality and experience from you. I'll tell you how to have it. You don't have to deny your relationship with God. You only need to listen to me. I'll help you really enjoy life to its fullness."

Adam and Eve, deceived by this lie, have led the parade of humanity along this same course of deception. From materialism on one hand to modern Gnosticism (hidden esoteric wisdom) on the other, Satan's lies have detoured men from a life of simple obedience to God.

For those who seek pleasure, Satan offers the delights of forbidden fruit from all kinds of trees: illicit sex, material possessions, mind-mood altering drugs, unrestrained fun. "Live it up. Enjoy yourself. You only live once so get all the gusto out of life that you can." Through the media of the world, Satan appeals to the hidden evil of the flesh.

Contemporary Religious Deceit

For those who will not accept the "simplicity that is in Christ" (2 Cor. 11:3) as the way to spiritual fullness, the liar offers other sources of "spirituality." This is what I mean by a modern Gnosticism that suggests that there are other gospels, other Christs, other "holy" spirits, other hidden spiritual mysteries to understand and experience (2 Cor. 11:4; cf. Matt. 24:23–28; Gal. 1:6–9).

"You don't have to deny Christ" the seducer whispers to doubting, troubled minds. "I offer you the true 'Spirit of Christ,' a Christ not bound by traditional Christian bigotry. He is the cosmic, everywhere present Christ who has returned with great liberating truth. You can discover truth hidden from the closed minds of fundamentalists, bigots, and church leaders. Listen to his word revealed to you in this new age through . . ."

This deception unifies the syncretistic theology of the New Age movement. This is the message of spirit channeling, a branch of that movement.[6] One of the main teachings of the New Age movement is "You are God." What did the serpent promise Eve? "You will be (like) God . . ." The New Age movement is not so new after all.

Unfortunately, some teachings of New Age theology have been embraced by the "Christian" gurus who often appear on television, radio, and in the printed page with words of knowledge or prophecy which subtly dilute or contradict the message of the written Word of God, just as the serpent did in our story.

I am not speaking to the question concerning whether the gifts of prophecy and words of knowledge are in manifestation in the church today. Different points of view are held among Christians, all of whom have a high view of Scripture. Believers have the right to differ at this point.

Deception Through Signs and Wonders

I will take a stand, however, on the abuse of these gifts within Christendom. Deceiving, persuasive "Christian" leaders are leading sincere believers worldwide into doctrinal, spiritual, and even moral error. Their message subtly undermines the Old and New Testament Scriptures as the sole authority for eternal truth. They speak messages in tongues and write words of prophecy, knowledge, and revelation which are supposed to be followed as equal to the Word of God.[7] While in principle some may deny this, in practice they do it. "God has spoken . . ." is their trademark when God has not spoken. He never contradicts His written Word.

Believers sometime assume that the release of spiritual power through the lives of some of these dynamic leaders is proof that they are God's prophets. Signs, wonders, miracles, casting out demons—all performed in the name of Jesus—are taken as the absolute guarantee that their words are true. Such believers refer to Jesus' words:

> "Do not forbid him, for no one who works a miracle in My name can soon afterward speak evil of Me. . . . And these signs will follow those who believe: In My name they will cast out demons; they will speak with new tongues; they will take up serpents; and if they drink anything deadly, it will by no means hurt them; they will lay hands on the sick, and they will recover." (Mark 9:39; 16:17–18)

They argue, "Does not Mark conclude his gospel saying, 'And they went out and preached everywhere, the Lord working with them and confirming the word through the accompanying signs'" (Mark 16:20; cf. Heb. 2:4)? Jesus did utter these words. Mark and the other New Testament writers do refer to visible releases of

God's power as signs and confirmations of the truth declared along with the life-style modeled by the Lord's bond servants (Heb. 2:4). This is still true.

However, that is only one side of the coin. The other side is that of demonic counterfeit and Satanic deception. The world of evil supernaturalism is both allowed by God and able to counterfeit, even in the name of Jesus, the works of power performed by God's true messengers. Did not Jesus himself say that in the last times, deception will be so complete that through signs and wonders false prophets will mislead, if possible, even the elect (Matt. 24:24)? Did he not also declare that works of power in themselves, even those done in His name, are not evidence alone of spiritual truth and genuineness? Listen to His words in Matthew 7:15,20–23:

> "Beware of the false prophets, who come to you in sheep's clothing, but inwardly they are ravenous wolves. . . . Therefore by their fruits you will know them. Not everyone who says to Me, 'Lord, Lord,' shall enter the kingdom of heaven, but he who does the will of My Father in heaven. Many will say to Me in that day, 'Lord, Lord, have we not prophesied in Your name, cast out demons in Your name, and done many wonders in Your name?' And then I will declare to them, 'I never knew you; depart from Me, you who practice lawlessness!' "

In this passage Jesus presents holiness, a life of moral and spiritual purity and blameless character, as the evidence of a genuine relationship with Him rather than just works of power done in His name.[8]

Deception in the Garden

Satan had performed a great work of power in entering the body of the serpent. He even gave it the faculty of speech with which he communicated his words of deception into the mind of Eve. Under the impact of the doubts about God's person and His word, Eve is soon going to begin to move away from a godly lifestyle.

Satan's attack upon God's motives (Gen. 3:5) in withholding the forbidden tree is an attack upon His character. Satan is declaring, "God is not honest. He is taking advantage of your ignorance. He says your eyes will close in death, but I tell you, your eyes will be opened. Moreover, you will be like God."

Calvin asserts that Satan is censuring

> God as being moved by jealousy, and as having given the command concerning the tree, for the purposes of keeping man in an inferior rank.

> Because the desire of knowledge is naturally inherent in all, happiness is supposed to be placed in it; but Eve erred in not regulating the measure of her knowledge by the will of God.

> And we all daily suffer under the same disease, because we desire to know more than is right, and more than God allows; whereas the principal point of wisdom is a well-regulated sobriety in obedience to God.[9]

Eve begins to sin. The essence of sin is acting independently of the will of God. That is exactly what she is about to do. Sin had already begun this way in the cosmic realm when Lucifer chose to act independently of the will of God. In essence he himself wanted to be God. This is how the idea of sin is first planted within the heart and mind of Eve. "Act independently of God," Satan cajoles. "Be God yourself."

This is still humanity's problem. Men and women want to live the way they choose to live, not as God declares they should live. In other words, men and women outside of Christ want to be their own god. Unfortunately, Christians also face that struggle and often make the same selfish choices. We have to choose, not just once but daily, who will be God in our life.

Ray Stedman speaks of the flesh which controls the life of unbelievers and battles to influence the life of believers as "The urge to self-centeredness within us, that distortion of human nature which makes us want to be our own god—that proud ego, that uncrucified self which is the seat of willful defiance and rebellion against authority."[10]

How many of us as believers have accepted similar ego-centered thoughts as totally our own, not recognizing them as the voice of the serpent? Though they may first arise from within "that uncrucified self," as Stedman calls the flesh, they are always reinforced by Satan, who has assigned evil spirits against each of us (Acts 5:3–9; 1 Cor. 7:5; 1 Thess. 3:5).[11] This attack continues relentlessly against Eve's mind. "You will be like God. Your eyes will be opened . . . you will be like God, knowing good and evil." What does it mean to "be like God, knowing good and evil"? Lange writes:

> The knowledge . . . of good and evil, as the words are employed by Satan, must here denote not merely a condition of higher intelligence, but rather a state of perfect independence of God. They would then know of themselves what was good and what was evil, and would no longer need the divine direction.[12]

Eve has now almost reached the point of no return. I say "almost" because it is still not too late. She can still turn back. She can still resist the Devil even though she did not know there was a devil in God's good creation.[13]

She did know that God is love. He had made her beautiful and given her a perfect mate. They were, as no other human beings since, truly "made for each other." Most of their deepest human longings were fully satisfied in each other. Their home was Paradise, a garden which the Lord Himself had planted for them and their promised children. Except the fruit of the tree in the middle of the garden, all its pleasures were available for them to enjoy.

They were at peace with nature. The animals had all appeared before Adam to be named by him. Thus all were at peace with them and with each other. They had been given the blessing of work. They were daily occupied with each other, with the animals, and with the Garden of God. It was their privilege to cultivate and keep God's garden (Gen. 2:15). Finally, joy of all joys, God was constantly with them. They had the potential to know God as no other creature has known Him.[14]

Also, God had made obedience simple for Adam and Eve. They had no complicated laws or rituals to memorize. All they had to do was enjoy all God had given them while recognizing He had kept only one prerogative to Himself: He alone was God. They were always to honor Him as the Lord God (Gen. 3:8a).

That's why there *had to be* a forbidden tree. Being almost godlike in their lifestyle, they had to be reminded, daily, where all their blessing came from. And that only God was God. It was that simple.

Three Steps Backwards Make a Fall

But Eve was not satisfied. Her innocent but imperfect human nature has now responded to the subtle lies of the serpent. Instead of resisting him, realizing that whoever he was, he was anti-God, she succumbs to his deception. She soon loses her innocence. Eve then takes three fatal steps, steps which always are part of sin's curse.

1. She yields to her defiled imagination.

Her mind begins to fantasize about the fruit attached to the forbidden tree. Soon it becomes more important to her than everything else in life, even more important than God.

Martin Luther writes that "The Satanic promise drove the divine threatening out of her thought. Now she beholds the tree with other eyes (v. 6). Three times it is said how charming the tree appeared to her."[15]

Calvin sees Eve's capitulation as a fall from faith:

> The faith she had in the word of God was the best guardian of her heart, and of all her senses. But now, after the heart had declined from faith, and from obedience to the word, she corrupted both herself and all her senses, and depravity was diffused through all parts of her soul as well as her body. It is, therefore, a sign of impious defection, that the woman now judges the tree to be good for food, eagerly delights herself in beholding it, and persuades herself that it is desirable for the sake of acquiring wisdom; whereas before she had passed by it a hundred times with an unmoved and tranquil look. For now, having shaken off the bridle, her mind wanders dissolutely and intemperately, drawing the body with it to the same licentiousness.[16]

As Eve begins to fantasize, mental images of the forbidden fruit arouse her emotions. She can almost taste the pleasures that await her. Her stirred desires override the warnings of her reason. Her defiled imagination leads to wrong choices. Eve yields to physical desire. She sees "that the tree [is] good for food" (v. 6a). There is nothing wrong with food. But this is forbidden food—food eaten out of the will of God.

Eve succumbs to emotional delight: "and that it [is] pleasant to the eyes" (v. 6b), and to intellectual pride: "and a tree desirable to make one wise" (v. 6c).

Was she not already wise enough? Was she not, in company with Adam, beginning to learn the wonders of God and His creation? Though physically fully mature at creation, Adam and Eve, like Jesus after them, were certainly designed to increase "in wisdom and stature, and in favor with God and men" (Luke 2:52).

All of creation was before them to explore and understand, year upon year. As they did, their wisdom would expand until they knew everything God willed for them to know. Why this lust for the forbidden "wisdom" which only that single forbidden tree and its fruit would provide? Such is the way of sin!

2. She willfully disobeys God.

"She took of its fruit and ate" (v. 6d).

Now she will be delivered from all restraints. All her doubts will disappear. She will be a truly independent being. She will finally be free to choose for herself, not to have another choose for her. In other words, she will be her own god. Eve turns her back upon all that has governed her life up to now. She willfully chooses disobedience to God. She eats of the forbidden fruit, evidently with no noticeable negative effects.

Sin is that way, isn't it? At first it is delightful. The promises it holds out to us seem true. Sin *does* bring immediate pleasures, the writer of Hebrews admits (Heb. 11:25). If it were not so, men would not be so easily engulfed by its allurements.

3. She leads her loved one, Adam, to join her in the pleasures of sin.

"She also gave to her husband with her, and he ate" (v. 6e).

This is the social dimension of sin. Sin not only hurts the sinner, it hurts all who are closely related to the sinner. Sin craves company. It will breed more sin in the lives of others, especially our loved ones. Such is the way of sin!

Much has been written about Adam's participation in the sin of Eve. Some declare that he mutely stood by watching and listening to the entire temptation scene, doing nothing to come to the aid of his confused wife. Others affirm that he could not resist his wife's persuasion. Still others assert that he had to make a choice between the allurements of his wife and obedience to God.

First Timothy 2:14 is often quoted to support these views. Paul writes, "And Adam was not deceived, but the woman being deceived, fell into transgression." I agree with Newport J. D. White's comment in *The Expositor's Greek New Testament* that Paul is not attempting to absolve Adam for his sin nor place the entire blame on Eve. All Paul is doing in that passage is declaring that it was the woman who first transgressed and not Adam.[17]

In Romans 5:12–21 the same apostle puts the entire blame on Adam for having transgressed, thus bringing ruin upon the whole human race. Calvin feels that while Adam did wish to comply with Eve's wishes, there was another reason that he

> became partaker of the same defection with her. And Paul elsewhere states that sin came not by the woman, but by Adam himself (Rom. 5:12) then the reproof which soon afterwards follows, "Behold, Adam is as one of us," clearly proves that he also foolishly coveted more than was lawful, and gave greater credit to the flatteries of the devil than to the word of God.[18]

Perhaps Donald Guthrie sums it up best: "Whereas Eve was deceived or beguiled, Adam sinned with his eyes wide open."[19]

I would like to close this chapter with several comments from Calvin. He asks, "What was the sin of Adam and Eve?" He gives various answers, including that of Augustine, who asserts that "pride was the beginning of all evils, and that by pride the human race was ruined." Calvin then comments that

> if anyone prefers a shorter explanation, we may say unbelief has opened the door to ambition, but ambition has proved the parent of rebellion, to the end that men, having cast aside the fear of God, might shake off His yoke. . . . But after they had given place to Satan's blasphemy, they began, like persons fascinated, to lose reason and judgment; yea, since they were become the slaves of Satan; he held their very senses bound.

> At the same time, we must keep in memory by what pretext they were led into this delusion so fatal to themselves, and to all their posterity. Plausible was the adulation of Satan, "Ye shall know good and evil"; but that knowledge was therefore accursed, because it was sought in preference to the favour of God.

> Wherefore, unless we wish, of our own accord, to fasten the same snares upon ourselves, let us learn entirely to depend upon the sole will of God, whom we acknowledge as the Author of all good. And, since the Scripture everywhere admonishes us of our nakedness and poverty, and declares that we may recover in Christ what we have lost in Adam, let us, renouncing all self-confidence, offer ourselves empty to Christ, that He may fill us with His own riches.[20]

8

The Potential Demonization of the Unredeemed

The immediate result of humanity's fall was the spiritual death of the man and the woman: They were separated from the life of God. Their access to the tree of life was cut off. God "drove the man out from the Garden of Eden, to cultivate the ground from which he was taken" (Gen. 3:22–24).

John Murray mentions five long-range results of the Fall:[1]

The first was *subjective:* The Fall altered man's dispositional complex and changed his attitude toward God (Gen. 3:7–16). Man once found his supreme delight in the presence of God; now he flees from God's face.

The second was *objective:* The Fall changed God's relationship to man. The wrathful aspect of God's nature hinted at in Genesis 2:17 was revealed after Genesis 3:9.

The third was *cosmic:* All of creation was "injured." The ground was cursed because of the Fall (Gen. 3:17–19). Paul expands this by saying that "the creation was subjected to vanity." That vanity would not be removed until the day of "the revealing of the sons of God," the day of "the glory of the children of God," the day when the redeemed experience "our adoption as sons, the redemption of our body" (Rom. 8:18–23). Murray explains that "with [man's] fall came the bondage of corruption for all over which he was to exercise dominion. Only with the consummation of redemption will the cosmos be released from the curse incident to man's sin" (cf. Rom. 8:19–23; 2 Pet. 3:13).

The fourth result was *racial:* Adam's and Eve's fall affected the whole human race. Murray remarks:[2]

> Adam was not only the father of all mankind but he was also by divine institution the representative head. "Through one trespass the judgment came unto all men to condemnation . . . through the one man's disobedience the many were made sinners" (Rom. 5:18–19, ASV). As all died in Adam (1 Cor. 15:22), so all sinned in Adam; "for the judgment came of one unto condemnation" (Rom. 5:16, ASV; cf. 5:12, 15).
>
> All mankind is reckoned as participating with Adam in his sin and therefore in the depravity which his sin entailed. This is the Biblical explanation of universal sin, condemnation and death and no other validation of racial involvement in sin is necessary or justifiable.

The fifth result was *death*.

THE FALL OF THE HUMAN RACE IN ADAM

Without doubt, the effect of greatest consequences of Adam's fall was the fall of the entire human race. The New Testament emphasizes this devastating consequence more than all the others combined. In one sense, the other four mentioned by Murray are but part of this consequence (Ps. 51:5). In Ephesians 2:1–5, the apostle Paul succinctly describes the condition of all men before being made alive by grace in Christ. Men are dead in their "trespasses and sins." They walk "according to the course of this world." They walk "according to the prince of the power of the air, of the spirit that is now working in the sons of disobedience." Men live "in the lusts of the flesh." They live "indulging the desires of the flesh and of the mind." Men are "by nature the children of wrath." This is true of all mankind apart from Christ without exception, "even as the rest."

What an incredibly dark and graphic picture of fallen humanity! No one escapes this description. The apostle Paul includes himself, the Ephesian Christians, and all humanity.

THE BONDAGE OF HUMANITY TO THE DEVIL

As we review the apostle Paul's sevenfold description in Ephesians 2 of humanity's sinful condition apart from faith in Christ, I would like to stress the dimension that focuses on humanity's bondage to Satan.

The apostle states that all men and women outside of Christ live "according to the prince of the power of the air, of the spirit that is now working in the sons of disobedience" (2:2b). This portion of Scripture is not the only teaching that all those who live separated from Christ are bound by Satan. Jesus Himself said that there are only two families of humanity, "the sons of the kingdom" (of God) and "the sons of the evil one" (Matt. 13:38). He underscored this when He described even the devout, religious men and women of His day who did not believe in Him as the children of the Devil. He distinguished clearly between true believers who are of God and the merely religious who are not of God (John 8:38–47). The apostle John declared that the human race is composed of only two families, consisting of "the children of God and the children of the devil" (1 John 3:10; 5:18–20).

The Lord Jesus further amplified His teaching on the demonic state of all unbelievers when He declared three times that Satan is "the ruler" of this world (John 12:31; 14:30; 16:11). In His redemptive commission to Saul, who became the apostle Paul, the Lord Jesus again spoke of the satanic bondage of all men, both Jews and Gentiles, apart from faith in Him:

> I will deliver you from the Jewish people and from the Gentiles, to whom I am sending you, to open their eyes so that they may turn from darkness to light and from the dominion of Satan to God, in order that they may receive forgiveness of sins and an inheritance among those who have been sanctified by faith in Me. (Acts 26:17–18)

It is the apostle Paul, however, who develops this dark, demonic side of human nature perhaps more than all the other New Testament writers combined (1 Cor. 10:20–21; 2 Cor. 4:3–4; Eph. 2:1–3; Col. 1:13–14; 2:8,20; 2 Thess. 2; Heb. 2:14–15). Even if Paul had not said a single additional word about the demonic state of the redeemed beyond what he says in Ephesians 2, we would have sufficient basis for our concern for those outside of Christ. There the apostle emphatically states that "the prince of the power of the air" (no reputable biblical scholar questions that the apostle is referring to Satan) is "the spirit who now works in the sons of disobedience" (v. 2). Adam Clark comments that

> the operations of the prince of the aerial powers are not confined to *that region*, he has *another* sphere of action, viz. the wicked heart of man; and *in* this he *works* with *energy*. He seldom inspires *indifference* to religion; the subjects *in* whom he works are either *determinate* opposers of true religion, or they are *systematic* and *energetic transgressors of God's laws.*

Children of disobedience. Perhaps a Hebraism for *disobedient children;* but taken as it stands here, it is a strong expression in which *disobedience . . .* appears to be *personified;* and wicked men exhibited as her children, *the prince of the power of the air* being their *father,* while *disobedience* is their *mother.* Thus they are emphatically what our Lord calls them, Matthew 13:38, *children of the wicked one;* for they show themselves to be of their *father the devil* because they *will* do his *works* (John 8:44).[3]

Calvin adds his own characteristically pointed words:[4]

[Paul] explains the cause of our corruption to be the dominion which the devil exercises over us. A more severe condemnation of mankind could not have been pronounced. . . . There is no obscurity in the Apostle's language. . . . All men who live *according to the world,* that is, according to the inclinations of the flesh, are here declared to fight under the reign of Satan.

2 Corinthians 4:3—4

If we add to this Paul's description in 2 Corinthians 4:3–4 of the supernatural cause of the unbelief of the lost, we do not err in speaking of the potential demonization of the unredeemed.

And even if[5] our Gospel is veiled, it is veiled to those who are perishing. In whose case the god of this world has blinded the minds of the unbelieving, that they might not see the light of the Gospel of the glory of Christ, who is the image of God.

Calvin's discussion of this passage deals not only with the unbeliever of Paul's day but with the Manicheans who greatly disturbed the church by their doctrine of two first principles: a good first principle, God, and an evil one, Satan—much like the positive and negative sides of the first principle called "the Force" in the modern Star Wars cosmology. The Manicheans used Paul's description of Satan as *o theos,* "god," to support their heresy.[6]

Commenting on 2 Corinthians 4:4, Calvin writes, "The sum is this—that the blindness of unbelievers detracts nothing from the clearness of the Gospel; for the sun is not less resplendent, that the blind do not perceive his light."[7] He continues:[8]

The devil is called the god of the wicked, on the grounds of his having dominion over them, and being worshiped by them in the place of God . . . the power of *blinding* is ascribed to Satan, and dominion over unbelievers. . . . Paul's meaning . . . is that all are possessed by the devil, who do not acknowledge his doctrine to be the sure truth of God . . . [they are] slaves of the devil.

Lewis Sperry Chafer, commenting on the same verse, says, "Satan is said to be 'the god of this world' (2 Cor. 4:4) and in authority over this world to the extent that he gives its kingdoms to whomsoever he wills (Luke 4:6)."[9]

Michael Green includes the world and the flesh with the power of Satan when he says that the pull of the world is so powerful against both believer and unbeliever that only "the Spirit of the Lord within us is a force greater than the world and can preserve us from its downward pull. The devil, we are reminded, endeavors to get us to 'walk according to the course of this world' (Eph. 2:2). He is, after all, the 'god of this world' (2 Cor. 4:4)."[10]

Neil Anderson writes in *The Bondage Breaker* about

the condition of blindness which Satan has inflicted on unbelievers (2 Cor. 4:3–4). People cannot come to Christ unless their spiritual eyes are opened. Theodore Epp wrote, "If Satan has blinded and bound men and women, how can we ever see souls saved? This is where you and I enter the picture. Spoiling the goods of the strongman has to do with liberating those who Satan has blinded and is keeping bound. . . . This is where prayer comes in.[11]

Tom White speaks of three levels of spiritual warfare. He speaks of the cosmic level, the level of the redeemed, and the level of the unredeemed, the level we are considering in this chapter.

Disobedience to the Gospel is promoted by the devil, who holds unbelievers in spiritual darkness and death. Jesus' commission to Paul thus makes sense, "to open their eyes and turn them from darkness to light, and from the power of Satan to God, so that they may receive forgiveness of sins . . . ." (Acts 26:18).[12]

In his classic book, *What Demons Can Do to Saints,* the late Dr. Merrill F. Unger broke new ground in the area of biblical demonology and the controversial area of the demonization (which he unfortunately often termed "demon possession") of some believers.[13]

Demons attack the mind to gain a foothold in the lives of people. Satan blinds the minds of the unsaved taking them away from the light of the Gospel (2 Cor. 4:3–4). To resist demon influence [one] must guard against what he reads and what sort of television he permits himself to view. . . . If he is not wary, demon influence may merge into demon obsession. If not curbed, demon invasion may ultimately eventuate.

Few believers with a high view of Scripture raise any serious objections when they read these words because this state of bondage, slavery, even partial control by the Devil is biblical. But the moment an experienced evangelist-Bible teacher-counselor-"deliverance minister"[14] like myself or one of my colleagues raises the issue of the potentially demonized state of the unredeemed, people get nervous. One reason for this reaction is the equating of demonization with demon possession.

REVERSING AN UNFORTUNATE PRACTICE

It is difficult to say when the terms *demon possession* and *demon possessed* first began to appear in translations of the Bible. Evidently Bible translators chose these terms as they endeavored to describe the more advanced stages of demonization revealed in Scripture. The practice perhaps came from the Latin Vulgate, which uses both. The King James Version, done in the seventeenth century, uses both terms, as does the New American Standard and many other modern versions. Some, however, have wisely chosen more neutral terms like "demoniacs," "having evil spirits," or "one under the power of demons." These are much more accurate translations from the Greek than "demon possessed" and "demon possession."

Probably none of the Bible translators had any personal experience with the demonized. Also, most probably had little accurate information how demonization really occurs and what its true impact is upon the life of its victim. Besides, the translators were thrice removed from the biblical context.[15]

As has been true since biblical times, there have probably been many cases of demonization which were not as far advanced as the advanced cases mentioned in Scripture. What kind of ministry those people received is not clarified in the New Testament.

Theologians, Bible scholars, commentators, preachers, evangelists, and missionaries for centuries have unfortunately followed the practice of the KJV in its use of "demon possession," "demon possessed," even "devil possessed." These words have been almost universally used to refer to the more serious cases of the invasion of human beings by alien spirits.

Books and articles describing deliverance from severe demonization have also used the same terms. This is evident in *Demon Possession,* edited by J. Warwick Montgomery, which contains the major papers presented at the "Theological, Psychological, Medical Symposium on the Phenomena Labeled As Demonic" sponsored by the Christian Medical Society at the University of Notre Dame, January 8–11, 1975.[16]

"Demon possession" is certainly more sensational than "demonization," but sensationalism must be thrown out. Many of us who are involved in ministry to the demonically afflicted are saddened by all the sensationalism. There is no room for dramatics, grandstanding, and platform spectacles. Deliverance is often hard, even agonizing work, but necessary for the extension of God's compassion to hurting, demonically afflicted people.

I believe Satan is happy with the words "devil possessed," "demon possessed," and "demon possession." These words magnify Satan's power and degrade human beings. Satan loves this. I want to magnify God's power and degrade Satan. Why not join the cause, and once and for all reject the misnomer "demon possession"? I believe that will be a real "psychological" blow to Satan's kingdom and help demonically afflicted people as well.

Fortunately, the practice of using these terms is now in the process of correction because of renewed historical-contextual studies of Scripture and renewed experience with the demonized.

I would probably be safe in saying that this present generation of Christian leaders is perhaps the first in centuries, perhaps since the days of St. Augustine and the pioneer missionaries, to break into an aggressive ministry to the demonized, both believers and unbelievers.[17]

This renewed experience in counseling severe cases of demonization with diverse types of power encounters and deliverance experiences over a period of years has caused thousands of us who are theologically trained to look anew at our interpretation of biblical satanology and demonology. As a result, we have found that some dimensions of our traditional theology of evil supernaturalism are inaccurate both biblically and historically.

As Dr. Timothy Warner points out, the best word to refer to all forms of demonic invasion, attachment, or partial control of a human life is *demonization* not demon possession.[18]

> We obtained our English word demon by transliterating the Greek word *daimon.*
> We should have done the same thing with the Greek word *daimonizomai*—a verb
> form from the same Greek root. It would come into English as "demonize," and we
> could then speak of the degree to which a person could be demonized rather than
> being limited to the either-or options imposed by the "possessed"—"not possessed"
> view. . . . A Christian may be attacked by demons and may be affected mentally
> and sometimes physically at significant levels . . . , but spiritual possession clearly
> implies ownership and would seem to include the control of one's eternal destiny.
> In either case it would be impossible to be owned and controlled by Satan and have
> a saving relationship with Christ at the same time. So if the question is, Can a Christian be demon-possessed? The answer is clearly no.

Unger defines demonization as being "under the control of one or more demons."[19] I temper that definition by adding "being under the *partial* control of one or more demons."

Christians can be demonized, but not demon possessed. The issue must be taken further, however. Can unbelievers really be demon possessed? Can they be so totally controlled by Satan and his demons they have *no* control over themselves nor *any* responsibility for their actions? I don't think so.

A LOOK AT THE BIBLICAL WORDS

The main biblical words used in reference to demonization are, first, the nouns *daimon* and *daimonion* in Greek, both translated "demon." They are also used to refer to pagan gods which, as the Scriptures teach, are demons, not God (Deut. 32:17; 1 Cor. 10:20–21; Rev. 9:20).

Next is the noun *pneuma*, "spirit," in this case for a demon spirit. It is often accompanied with the adjective *akatharotos*, "unclean," or *poneros*, "evil." If *pneuma* is combined with *akatharotos* we have "unclean spirit." This title is common for demons in Mark, Luke, Acts, and Revelation (Mark 1:23,26–27; 3:11,30; 5:2f; 6:7; 7:25; Luke 4:33,36; 6:18; Acts 5:16; 8:7; Rev. 16:13; 18:2). If *pneuma* is combined with *poneros* we have "evil spirit" (1 Sam. 16:14–16,23; 18:10; 19:9; Luke 7:21; 8:2; Acts 19:12–13,15–16).

On one occasion we find the unique phrase "having a spirit of an unclean demon," *echon pneuma daimonion akatharton* (Luke 4:33). Unfortunately the KJV translates it "had a spirit of an unclean devil" and the NAS "possessed by the spirit of an unclean demon." The NIV translates it "possessed by an evil spirit," the AMPLIFIED by "possessed by the foul spirit of a demon." This is the type of unfortunate Bible translation one faces with most English versions of the New Testament when they deal with the spirit world.

Next is the adjective *daimonides*. It is used only once, in James 3:15. Vine says it "signifies proceeding from, or resembling a demon, 'demoniacal'."[20] The KJV unfortunately translates it "devilish." The NAS has it right; it uses "demonic."

One of the most important words used to describe the action of a demon within a human being is the verb *daimonizomai*. Dr. Merrill F. Unger in his earlier writings translated the word "demon possessed." In *What Demons Can Do to Saints,* Unger admitted this is not the best translation.[21] He says "*daimonizomai* (means) 'being demonized', i.e., under the control of one or more demons. . . . *All* demonic invasion is demonization of whatever degree of mildness or severity."

Then there is *echei daimonion*, "to have a demon" (Luke 7:33; John 7:20). This, along with *demonized* are probably the best words in English to refer to those who have been invaded by evil spirits.[22]

Finally, we have the participle *daimonizomenos*, used some 12 times in the Greek Testament. C. Fred Dickason says that

> it is used only in the present tense, indicating the continued state of one inhabited by a demon, or demonized. . . . The participle in its root form means "a demon-caused passivity." This indicates a control other than that of the person who is demonized. . . . He is regarded as the recipient of the demon's action.[23]

A final reason for rejecting the words *demon possession* is that the state of being completely, continually, and totally possessed or controlled by demons would be very, very rare, if it even exists at all.[24] Such persons would be totally unresponsible for any of their actions since the demons would possess and control them at all times. The Scriptures never place total responsibility for human evil upon Satan and his demons. Persons are always held accountable for their actions. However, persons severely demonized over a long period of time by extremely powerful demons find it difficult to maintain self-control when the demons are in manifestation, leading to what psychologists call "diminished capacity." Mark 5 is a case in point. Mark 9 with Luke 9 give added details of the story.

Thus the terms I am endorsing benefit our gospel ministry in these ways: they conform more closely to the biblical words and do not import extra-biblical ideas; they preserve the dignity of those suffering from demonization; and they help acknowledge and deal with a broader front of spiritual warfare, overcoming the all-or-nothing split communicated through the label of demonic possession.

A wild-looking, young wrestler was brought to me for counseling. As I tried to lead him to Christ I was quite certain that he was demonized but did not try to make contact with the demons. I tried only to lead him to Christ. Suddenly another personality took control of him, screaming, swearing, and threatening me and a friend sitting in on the counseling session. The wrestler was big and strong enough to kill us with his bare hands even if no demons were present. I took authority over them and forbid them to hurt me, my friend, or my office. The demons then turned on their victim, the wrestler. Using his own mammoth hands, they tried to choke him to death. With my hands, I was easily able to pull his hands from his throat with a word of command, while asking the Lord to send his angels to subdue him. They did so, and the demons were powerless to do any more harm.

The young man wanted to be free. He had great difficulty, however, in regaining self-control. He needed my help and that of God's angels to hold in subjection the destructive evil personalities raging in his body. Like the Gerasene demonic of Mark 5, he had little control over his own actions when the demons were in manifestation.

DEMONIZATION AND INDIVIDUAL RESPONSIBILITY

Psychologist Rodger K. Bufford speaks of a state of "diminished mental and volitional capacities" that exists not only in some cases of brain-mental malfunctions but also in severe cases of demonization.[25] In such a state not only may an individual lose control when the demons take it, but the individual may become so effectively disabled mentally that the person may be unable to seek help or even realize a need for it. Bufford compares the diminished capacity of the severely demonized with that of those who abuse alcohol, especially "those who are genetically predisposed to alcoholism [and] may be unable to stop [drinking], and may have greatly lessened abilities to think rationally or to act morally as well." Yet Bufford concludes that such demonized persons remain morally responsible because they

> have reached this state through a variety of conscious decisions involving choosing to come under demonic influence. The Christian, with the indwelling Holy Spirit, belongs to God's kingdom, thus is protected from possession, and has the resources through the Body of Christ and the power of the Holy Spirit to resist Satan's efforts. (Eph. 2:1–6; 6:12–18; Col. 1:13–14)

I give general support to Bufford's observations. I cannot concur with what Bufford states in this last paragraph, however. Most individuals do not chose "to come under demon influence." This is especially true if they have been demonized from infancy or childhood. It is true, however, that God still holds them responsible for all their choices. Humans, though fallen, still bear the image of God. As such, we possess the right and the capability to resist the entrance of demons into our lives *if we are aware of what is occurring.*

The Case of Thadius

While serving as Associate Professor of Intercultural Studies at Biola University and Talbot Theological Seminary, my wife Loretta and I were occasionally invited as guests of the senior graduation class for their annual graduation banquet. One year we were seated at a round table with about a dozen students. Most knew about my counseling-deliverance ministry, and one of them asked, "Dr. Murphy, have you had any unusual cases of demonic encounter in these days?"

"Why, yes," I replied. "I had one just a few hours ago. I had to hurry to get here in time for the banquet."

"Please tell us what happened," several asked.

I told them some of the events leading up to the power encounter which had occurred early that afternoon. This was my third session with the young woman. Several demons had been expelled in the past. That day I had kept one in manifestation[26] in the presence of God and the deliverance group. He was a weak, fearful demon who called itself Fear.[27]

I forced him to expose the entire demonic hierarchy working in the woman and in her entire family. I have learned how to keep demons from lying to me, so the demon's "finking" on the other demons was later checked out and proved to be truthful.

In the process of working with Fear, who was continually pleading with me to send him out because he was terrified of the other demons, another demon came into manifestation with such brazenness and arrogance that all of us were startled for a moment. He burst into manifestation and yelled at me,

"I am Thadius, and I am in charge here. What do you think you are doing? Trying to destroy us?"

"No, not yet," I replied. "Not until the Lord tells me to get rid of you. Then *He will destroy you, not me.* I command you to shut up. You will not say one more word but will only answer my questions truthfully."

I then went through the process of assuring as much as possible that his answers would be true. What demons voluntarily reveal may not be true. What they are forced to reveal will usually be true.[28] That is why I do not allow demons to lead any type of conversation. I always lead the conversation in the authority of the reigning Christ.

"Who are you?" I asked.

"I am Thadius, and I am in charge here," he replied.

"I thought Liar was in charge," I said.

"Yes, he was," he replied. "But you sent him out yesterday and now I am in charge."

"Aren't you sad that Liar the strong demon has gone out?" I asked.

"No, because now *I* am the one in charge," he boasted.

Thadius was one of the most arrogant demons I have ever dealt with. His sense of self-importance and command permeated the atmosphere, in contrast to Fear's whining. I had to immediately assert authority over him, or he would have taken authority over me and the entire session. When he saw that I was not intimidated by him, he soon obeyed every command I gave, but always with defiance and arrogance.

Awareness and Effective Resistance:
Why Deception Is Satan's Key Strategy

"Oh, I know Thadius," said a young woman seated across the banquet table.

The young man seated next to her was one of my students. He was from a Jewish home. He said, "Dr. Murphy, forgive me for not introducing you to my wife, Ruth. She is also from a Jewish home. She had some demonic problems before finding Christ."

"Ruth, you say you know Thadius! Please tell us your story," I asked.

"Several years ago before I came to believe in Jesus as the Messiah, I was engaged to a young man. He was into some kind of cult, some form of witchcraft or the like. He continually tried to persuade me to accept his spirits into my life. He said we had to believe the same things if we were to be married. He said his chief spirit guide was called Thadius.

"As a Jewess I had problems with what he was saying. I thought I loved him, however. I wanted to be one with him in marriage, but I was troubled by this thing of spirit guides.

"One night in bed I was wrestling with all this when I became aware of another presence in the room with me. I can't tell you how it happened, but a spirit appeared. He called himself Thadius. He said he wanted to come into my life and make me one with my fiance.

"I was terrified. Suddenly I realized what was happening. From my Old Testament background I remembered the evil spirits of paganism that troubled my people. I wanted it to go away from me. Suddenly I found myself crying out loud, 'In the name of the God of Abraham, Isaac, and Jacob, I tell you I want nothing to do with you, evil spirit. Get away from my life and do not return.'

"Immediately it left me and has never come back. I don't know who Thadius is, but I do know he is an evil religious spirit," she said.

This story illustrates my point that even persons like Ruth who was not a believer in Jesus as Christ and Lord at the time can resist the entrance of demons into their life *if they know what is occurring.*

Again, that is one reason why the Devil's main strategy is *deception.* Usually demons, who are "devils" in the sense of sharing the Devil's nature and being totally identified with his cause, do not make the bold approach followed by Thadius with Ruth. And this is further evidence that though Satan and his fallen angels possess wisdom man does not possess, they are far from being omniscient. They often blunder as Thadius did. In fact, sometimes they appear quite stupid.

Ruth, a woman created in the image of God, was able to forbid the entrance of Thadius into her life. This is probably true of all normal, rationally-minded adults, young people, and even children, if the latter are taught about the spirit world. Otherwise, children, because of their innocence and passivity, are more easily susceptible to demonic indwelling than adults.

Thus no one can truthfully say, "the Devil made me do it." Regardless of how demons are able to gain entrance into human lives either in infancy or in later adulthood, the Bible always holds the individuals accountable for their actions. Regardless of the amount of control demons presently exercise their victims at one point had enough authority to resist their evil desires. I have heard more than one demon say on the way out, "I might just as well go. He doesn't listen to me anymore."

That is why in pre-deliverance counseling[29] it is crucial to bring the counselee to at least two firm convictions. First, if in truth they do have demons, they must recognize it. Second, they must realize that *they* have authority over these demons. They must learn the difference between their thoughts and those of the demons residing within them. When they recognize which is which, the demons, who have hidden their presence until now, are exposed and their control over areas of the victim's life is weakened.

DEMONIZATION AND EVANGELISM

I do not simply cast demons out of the life of unbelievers. I first try to lead the unbelievers to faith in Christ. That is my mission. Jesus did not say, "Go into all the world and cast demons out of all creation," but "Go into all the world and preach the Gospel to all creation" (Mark 16:15).

If someone refuses to come to Christ, do I leave them with their demons? That depends on each individual case. In my experience to date in individual deliverance sessions, if the deliverance is preceded by careful pre-deliverance counseling, the unsaved person will always come to Christ. I can't remember any who have refused.

I suggest that if the person is having difficulty coming to Christ, demons possibly are blocking their mind, emotions, and will. The counselor must go after these demons and either expel them or bind them from interfering in the individual's faith act. They will usually be spirits of confusion, unbelief, antichrist, religious spirits, witchcraft, sexual spirits, death spirits, rebellion spirits, or the like. Once their activity is nullified, the victim can easily come to Christ if he wants to. This is true of Muslims, Hindus, cultists, Satanists, witches and warlocks, or whomever.

Very often the most difficult hand-to-hand warfare with demons that the counselor faces will be with these blocking demons. If possible, therefore, we should enlist the resistance of the victim and not quit until all the evil spirits are either expelled or shut down. In every case, we have always won this battle if the victims (who often suffer most during this kind of direct confrontation) and the deliverance team have been willing to hold the battle lines until the enemy is defeated. If this can be done without the demons coming into manifestation, and it usually can, so much the better.

Conclusions

Scripture describes the unredeemed as follows:

1. The unredeemed are all children of the Devil (Matt. 13:37–39; John 8:44; 1 John 3:3–10a).
2. They are in the kingdom of Satan (Col. 1:12–14).
3. They are all bound by Satan (Acts 26:18).
4. They are all blinded by Satan so that they cannot in themselves receive the gospel (2 Cor. 4:3–4; see 2 Cor. 3:14–15 for the human source of this blindness).
5. They are all in the power of the Evil One (1 John 5:19); "in his grip and under his dominion . . . asleep in the arms of Satan," John R. W. Stott affirms.[30]
6. They are all Satan's property (Matt. 12:22–29).
7. They are all enslaved to a world system controlled by Satan (John 12:31; 14:30; 16:11; 1 John 5:19).

8. They are surrendered to the prince of the power of the air. "Their life is energized by the power of evil supernaturalism," one commentator affirms (Eph. 2:2).[31]

Four Conclusions

In light of these scriptural declarations we draw the following fourfold conclusion about the status of the unredeemed and the warfare we will face in bringing them to faith in Christ.

1. *All non-Christians are spiritually "lost" without faith in the Lord Jesus Christ* (John 14:6; Acts 4:12; 26:18; Rom. 1:3).

2. *All non-Christians are potentially demonized, to one degree or another.* I am *not* affirming that demons have been able to invade the life of all unbelievers. I believe that in most cases they would like to do so if they could get in, but they cannot. Our discussion about humans bearing the image of God and thus being able to resist the entrance of demons fits here.

What I am asserting is that since the unredeemed are spiritually lost and belong to Satan, *potentially all could become demonized.* We must always be alert to the possible attachment of demons to the lives of all non-Christians, even when they do not manifest the personality malfunctions usually associated with demonization.

3. *Our ministry of world evangelism definitely includes the dimension of demonic warfare.*

4. *This spiritual warfare dimension of Christian witness arouses the resistance of the kingdom of darkness* against our every step to win men to Christ and bring them under the rule of God (Dan. 10:10–21; Acts 13:6–12; 16:16–24; 19:11–18).

Therefore, we must learn the spirit world as the Scriptures instruct us (2 Cor. 2:11). We must not be ignorant of Satan's schemes against both believers and unbelievers. Through prayer, the spoken Word, and persistent faith, we must learn to challenge the principalities and powers who rule over individual human lives, societies, and areas of the world (Eph. 3:10; 6:12–18; Rev. 12:11).

Effective evangelistic ministry to the demonically influenced demands that we truly believe that evil supernaturalism is already defeated! Satan and his demons have been dethroned from their position of authority in the heavenlies through the Lord's redemptive activity.

The Key Issue: Authority

The basic issue in spiritual warfare is that of *authority.* Perhaps for this reason our Lord declared His absolute authority in heaven and earth and His continual presence with His disciples before He sent them out into world evangelism (Matt. 28:18–20). A paraphrase of the Lord's words in verse 18 of Matthew 28 could be, "There exist powers, both in heaven and on earth, which will oppose you as you seek to carry out my redemptive mission. Be of good cheer! I have been given absolute, total authority both in heaven over the cosmic beings who will oppose you and on earth over their human agents who will resist you. No authority is greater than my authority; I am the Lord over heaven and earth. Therefore, you can go and you will be able to make disciples of all the people groups among the nations of the earth."

A paraphrase of our Lord's words in verse 20b could be, "I want to give you a further word of encouragement. As you seek to fulfill my redemptive mandate, you will be successful. Even though you will face evil cosmic and earthly power which will oppose you and harass you, be of good cheer! I your Lord, the Lord of this universe, will be with you, because, by my Spirit, I will be within you always (John 15—17; Acts 16:6–7; Rom. 8—9; Gal. 4:6), until the every end of this age of redemption."

Our Authority Is Delegated

Ours is a delegated authority. In Luke 10 Jesus gives total authority over all dimensions of evil supernaturalism to *all* of His disciples, not just the twelve apostles (Luke 10:1,17–19). The identity of the seventy disciples is unknown. This group of men was large enough for the Lord both to train and to oversee. Because this is the only reference to them, it is assumed they did not give up their jobs and homes to follow their Master as did the twelve apostles. Today we would call them laymen.

Calvin suggests that as the twelve symbolized the twelve tribes of Israel, the seventy symbolized the elders chosen by Moses to help him administer the affairs of the people, which later became the Jewish council of the seventy, the Sanhedrin.[32]

The Lord Jesus appointed the seventy along with the twelve: They are called "seventy others." He sent them "two and two," following the pattern He had established earlier with the twelve (Mark 6:7; 11:1; 14:13). This team ministry pattern had strong historical precedent in the Old Testament.

Biblical Precedent for Team Ministry

When God established His laws for His covenant people, the principle was "on the evidence of two witnesses." Punishment was never to be handed out on the evidence of one (Deut. 17:6; 19:15; 1 Tim. 5:19). The principle soon became, "Every fact is to be confirmed by the testimony of two or three witnesses" (2 Cor. 13:1; cf. Matt. 18:16). God said that by His power one shall "chase a thousand" but "two put ten thousand to flight." The writer of Ecclesiastes reinforced this principle: "Two are better than one because they have a good return for their labors. For if either of them falls, the one will lift up his companion. But woe to the one who falls where there is not another to lift him up . . . if one can overpower him who is alone, two can resist him" (Eccl. 4:9–12). Amos brought one necessary requirement to this team, however: "Do two men walk together unless they have made [are in] an agreement?" (Amos 3:3).

Jesus showed the spiritual authority behind two godly men who are in agreement when He said, "If two of you agree on earth about anything that they may ask, it shall be done for them by my Father who is in heaven. For where two or three have gathered together in My name, there am I in their midst" (Matt. 18:19–20). Christian prophets are instructed to speak two or three per church service and the others "pass judgment." Finally, when the last days of God's witness upon earth arrive, He will raise up two witnesses, not just one, who will speak His word and manifest His power before the nations (Rev. 11:1f). Evidently God does not usually call or send out Lone Rangers who are a law unto themselves. Certainly this has been proven to be true in a spiritual warfare ministry. He always calls men to function within a team, even if one, like the apostle Paul, is the outstanding leader of the team (Acts 13—28). It is interesting to observe the apostle Paul as a team leader. He definitely was the leader, yet in certain crises when his team had to take leadership, they did. Paul submitted to the team consensus (Acts 19:30–31).

Jesus sent His disciples out "two and two ahead of Him to every city and place where He Himself was going to come." They were to be His heralds to prepare the way for His coming. No wonder they immediately ran into spiritual warfare (vv. 17–20).

Although the seventy were not apostles, in Calvin's well chosen words they were "His secondary heralds."[33] It was to them, not to the twelve, that Christ spoke the all-inclusive, authoritative, spiritual warfare revelation.

> And He said to them, "I was watching Satan fall from heaven like lightning. Behold, I have given you authority to tread upon serpents and scorpions, and over all the power of the enemy, and nothing shall injure you." (Luke 10:18–19)[34]

Demonization, Responsibility, and Authority: Pat's Story

We all have the authority over "all the power of the enemy" promised by our Commander-in-Chief in verse 19. In His name, that is, in His authority, we too can exclaim "Lord, even the demons are subject to us in your name!" (v. 17).

My daughter Carolyn attended college while living at home. Being a swimmer, she spent each evening at the college pool. There she became acquainted with a young man who was on the college swim team. One day she told me about him.

"Dad, I met this handsome, neat guy named Pat at school. He's on the swim team. I have been trying to witness to him but he says he's an atheist. He's one of the most moral guys I have ever met. He never swears. His talk is always above reproach and he's a perfect gentleman around girls. I wish I could reach him for Christ. Could we all pray for his salvation?"

Of course we all agreed. Weeks went by, but Pat's spiritual resistance remained unchanged. He was quite willing to talk about God and Christ, but he had no personal interest in God for his own life. He was interested in Carolyn, however.

One day Carolyn asked if we could invite Pat to go to church with us the next Sunday morning and have lunch with us afterwards. Then I could have some time alone with him to talk to him about Christ. We agreed. I happened to be speaking in the college Sunday school class that Sunday, and Pat attended. He was polite and seemed right at home with the other college young people. After lunch that Sunday I asked if we could talk alone, and he readily agreed.

We talked for at least an hour, but got nowhere. Though Pat listened attentively and was very courteous, he maintained his unbelief in the existence of a personal God.

"I wish I could believe like you and Carolyn, Mr. Murphy," he said, "but I cannot. I don't know why, but I cannot. It's all very confusing to me. I don't usually have trouble thinking things through, but when it comes to God and Christ I draw a blank. It doesn't have any meaning to me."

Later I told Carolyn that Pat's mind was like the mind spoken about by the apostle Paul in 2 Corinthians 4:4. "The god of this world has blinded his mind until he cannot grasp even the elementary things about God, man, sin, Christ, and salvation," I told Carolyn. "I have never dealt with a person so totally blind to spiritual truth.

"I know you like him. I do too. We all do. He is a gentle, kind, and courteous young man. But unless his mind and heart are opened by God, there is no future for you with him. You would not want to spend the rest of your life with an atheist."

Carolyn agreed but determined to continue her witness. I could see she felt drawn to him but trusted her to make the right decision at the right time.

A couple of months later I was on a long overseas trip. In Greece I found a letter from Carolyn waiting for me. It was a "bombshell."

"Dear Dad," Carolyn wrote. "The most amazing thing happened with Pat. After you left I really began to press him about his need of Christ. I told him I was tired of his intellectual reasons for being an atheist. I was just as intellectual as he; yet Christ was the most real person in my life.

"I told him his problems were not intellectual but moral and spiritual. He was a sinner but too proud to admit it and humble himself before God, confess his sins, and choose to believe in the Lord Jesus Christ as his Lord and Savior. I told him he was blinded, confused, and bound by the Devil and that he was responsible to turn against the Devil and believe God.

"I had learned that Pat had come from a very dysfunctional home. His mother and dad separated when he was a teenager. He loved his dad very much, but he had no respect for his mother. He saw his home disintegrate before his eyes. Shortly after the separation, his dad suddenly died of a heart attack. His mother then lied about his age and put him in the military to get him out of the home when he was only 17.

"He asked me, 'Where was this so-called God of yours while my home was breaking up? What kind of God is He to allow such evil in the world?'

"I told him that I did not have all the answers for his anger with God and life," Carolyn wrote. "But I had the answer to his confusion, and that answer is in Christ. Finally I told him that unless he opened his mind and heart to give God a chance in his life, we would have to stop going out together. The boyfriend I wanted had to love Christ even as I did.

"Dad, we were sitting together on a park bench in Starboard Park near our home. It had rained heavily the night before, and the ground was covered with water and mud puddles. Suddenly the weirdest thing I have ever seen in my life happened before my eyes.

"Pat's body levitated off the bench and he was thrown backwards over the back of the bench. He hit a mud puddle with a splash. He rolled around until he was totally covered with mud. He suddenly sprang up and jumped around on his haunches, just like an ape. His eyes were glazed over and radiated hatred against me. He stuck his tongue out and hissed and spit at me. Then from his throat came a torrent of swear words and blasphemies that were totally demonic.

"Dad, I knew that was not Pat glaring at me, spitting at me, cursing me and Christ, and hopping around me in the mud. It was a demon.

"I tried to remember all you had taught us about dealing with demons in manifestation, but I was alone and I was scared. I began to quote God's word against them and that made them even more furious. I prayed, cried, and continued to quote God's promises of protection for me and salvation for Pat through the blood of Christ. That really agitated the demons. Finally, I began to sing the children's testimony chorus, 'Jesus Loves Me This I Know.' I changed the words and sang by faith Pat's salvation in his behalf since he could not do it himself,

Jesus loves Pat, this I know,
For the Bible tells me so.

"As I did so I began to march in circles around Pat, singing with all my heart. The demons never took their eyes off me but hopped around in the mud as I circled them.

"After an hour of this I was so tired I could hardly walk. I knew I needed help. I remembered that two of our mission leaders who had experience with demons lived near by, so I jumped in the car and went to their home. Thank God both were home and agreed to return with me to help set Pat free.

"When we reached the park Pat was not there. He lives in an apartment not too far away, so we went there. We found the door open and Pat sitting on the couch, half dazed but in his right mind. The men prayed with him. There were still some hang-on demons, but basically Pat was free.

" 'Carolyn,' Pat said, 'I do not remember one thing that happened from the time you began to speak firmly to me about my sin of pride and my need to repent, humble myself, and accept Christ as my Lord and Savior. Suddenly everything went blank. The next thing I knew, I was sitting in a mud puddle in the park covered with mud, and you were gone. I could not figure out what had happened to me or why you had left. I walked home in total confusion.

" 'I took off my filthy clothes and began to take a shower. As I looked up to adjust the shower head I saw a vision. The cross of Christ was superimposed across the shower head and suddenly I was free. All that raced through my mind was,

> Jesus loves me this I know,
> For the Bible tells me so.

" 'I cried my confession to God, and He heard me. I called upon Jesus, and He came into my life and washed all my sins away.

" 'I now know there is a God and He is my Father. I know that Jesus Christ is real, and He is now my Lord and Savior.' "

Though I have told this story dozens of times, it still brings tears to my eyes and joy to my heart. When I returned from overseas I spent hours with Pat in prayer and Bible study. He had already joined the college group of a local church and was witnessing for Christ.

Was he demonized? Yes, he was severely demonized. When did the demons go out? I don't know. Possibly they left when Carolyn was commanding their exit in the park and proclaiming Pat's salvation by faith in song. I have seen it happen that way.

Perhaps they went out when the Lord came to Pat in the shower and, for the first time in his life, he could believe and proclaim his own salvation.

Was that the last of Pat's problems with demons? No. He was attacked again and again. He had to learn ongoing self deliverance. He had to come to stronger Christians for prayer and even more deliverance. *Deliverance is more of a process than a once-and-for-all-crisis-event for almost all severely demonized persons.* It was so for Pat.

How is Pat today? He has walked faithfully with God for many years now. He is a wonderful husband and father. He is an outstanding church leader. He is one of my closest Christian friends.

The Normal Christian Life

9

Abundant and Conquering
John 10, Romans 6–7

To understand dimensions of spiritual warfare, we must first discover what Christ came to accomplish in our life. We have already referred to salvation and God's plan as salvation history. Also we have referred to justification for our sins and regeneration to newness of life.

When we talk of the Christian life we are in the area of sanctification. The word comes from the Greek word *hagiasmos,* very commonly used in the New Testament. Vine says it refers to a life of separation unto God and the holy life which results from that separation.

> [It is] that relationship with God into which men enter by faith in Christ, Acts 26:18; 1 Corinthians 6:11, and to which their sole title is the death of Christ, Ephesians 5:25,26; Colossians 1:22; Hebrews 10:10,29; 13:12.

> Sanctification is also used in the New Testament of the separation of the believer from evil things and ways. Sanctification is God's will for the believer, 1 Thessalonians 4:3, and His purpose in calling him by the Gospel, verse 7; it must be learned from God, verse 4, as He teaches it by His word, John 17:17,19; cf. Psalms 17:4; 119:9, and it must be pursued by the believer, earnestly and undeviatingly, 1 Timothy 2:15; Hebrews 12:14.

> . . . The holy character, *hagiosune,* 1 Thessalonians 3:13, is not vicarious, i.e., it cannot be transferred or imputed, it is an individual possession built up, little by little, as the result of obedience to the Word of God, and of following the example of Christ, Matthew 11:29; John 13:15; Ephesians 4:20; Philippians 2:5; in the power of the Holy Spirit, Romans 8:13; Ephesians 3:16.[1]

This sanctified life I call the Normal Christian Life. God wants us to live a holy life. The enemy resists our efforts to comply. Thus the normal Christian life is lived in the context of on-going spiritual warfare.

Among the many features describing the Christian life, I have chosen two, one given by Jesus and the other by the apostle Paul. These two cover probably all the other general dimensions of the normal Christian life. They are an *abundant life* and a *conquering life.*

Jesus portrays Himself as the Good Shepherd in John 10:1–18. In verse l0b He states succinctly the purpose of His incarnation: "I came that they may have life; and might have it abundantly."

THE ABUNDANT LIFE

One of the results of this abundant life in Christ Jesus is that we as His sheep now walk in the light. We often sing, "Once I was blind but now I can see. The light of the world is Jesus." We are testifying that before coming to Christ we looked for life but did not find it. We lived a make-believe life of striving for "self" fulfillment and so-called happiness. We actually lived and walked in darkness, though we called it light. This is what Jesus meant when He said, "If the light that is in you is darkness, how great is that darkness!" (Matt. 6:23).

There is a twofold source of that darkness in which we walked! The human source, the hardness of the human heart (1 Cor. 3:19; Eph. 4:17–19), and the supernatural source (2 Cor. 4:3–4).

Whether we felt miserable or happy, we preferred our misery or happiness to God. As one young man told me, "I know I am not living as God would have me live, but, frankly, it is fun. The world is very attractive to me." That is the natural, human source of that darkness.

Then there is the supernatural source, the mind-blinding work of "the god of this world," Satan (2 Cor. 4:3–4). Paul minces no words in his graphic description of the operations of the Devil within the mind and life of the unbelieving. Add to it Ephesians 2:1–3, and the picture grows even darker. Satan does not want men to "see the light of the gospel of the glory of Christ, who is the image of God."

I was once trying to lead a man to Christ whom I suspected might be demonized. Suddenly an angry demon came into manifestation, protesting my efforts at leading his victim to faith in Christ.

"Shut up!" it screamed at me. "Don't tell him that. He is mine. He belongs to me. I won't let him believe in your Jesus. I keep him from understanding your so-called gospel. I hate you."

I shut the demon down. I refused to let it interfere with the man's right to exercise his will to accept or reject Christ. While the man was not fully aware of what was occurring in his life, he knew an alien personality had taken partial control of his mind and vocal cords. That frightened him so much that he came to Christ with all of his heart. This demon and many others were expelled over a period of several months. The man had been into witchcraft and was severely demonized.

In contrast to his instantaneous salvation, his total deliverance was neither instantaneous nor automatic. Salvation is one thing. Sanctification, which *can include* deliverance from binding demonic powers, is something else. He was saved instantly. He was delivered progressively. Both can, and often do, occur at the same time, but not always.

Returning to our experience as unbelievers, one miraculous day the darkness was removed by God's sovereign saving mercy and "His great love with which He loved us ... He made us alive together with Christ (by grace you have been saved)" (Eph. 2:4–5).

The scales fell from our eyes (Acts 9:18). We saw what we never understood before, "the treasure" which is Jesus Himself (2 Cor. 4:5–11). We exclaimed with the blind man, "Once I was blind but now I can see" (John 9:25).

While we have all had our spiritual ups and downs since that day God first opened our eyes, we have never been the same. We no longer live in the darkness, but in the light of his presence. This is the universal testimony of all of us who love God in sincerity (And how we do love Him! Don't we?) With this as a background we will look at one of Jesus' most profound descriptions of the normal Christian life.

I Have Come That They Might Have Life

"Life" is one of the characteristic words used by the apostle John. John uses life in two ways in his gospel. He uses it to refer to all life as we know it in the universe (John 1:3–5). That life has its source in the Lord Jesus. John says "apart from Him [Jesus, the Logos of God] nothing came into being that has come into being" (1:3).

More importantly, life represents eternal life. Leon Morris says that "life in John characteristically refers to eternal life, the gift of God through His Son."[2] Also most characteristic of John is the use of the word "life" with or without the definite article to refer to "the life" or "the true life," the life of the Lord Jesus shared with believers as by His Spirit He comes to abide in them (John 14—17).

To John, therefore, true human life is eternal life, a life uniquely given by God only to believers in Christ (John 1:4; 3:15–16,36).[3] John will interchange "life" and "the life" for "eternal life" 15 times and "everlasting life" 8 times. Thus to John, true human life is meant to be eternal—everlasting life. This is particularly vivid in Revelation. There the word life is used almost exclusively for the "tree of life" (Rev. 2:7; 22:2,14); "the crown of life" (Rev. 2:10); "the Book of Life" (Rev. 3:5; 13:8; 17:8; 20:12,15; 21:27; 22:19); and the water of life (Rev. 21:6; 22:1,17). Man's association with these sources of life brings him into union with God's gift of eternal life (Rev. 1:17–18; 2:7,10,11; 11:11; 21:6; 22:1–12,17).

But "eternal life" refers not only to its everlasting *duration* but also to its *quality* as life possessed by the believer in the present. George Eldon Ladd in *A Theology of the New Testament* notes this distinctive emphasis of John.[4]

Eternal life is the central theme of Jesus' teaching according to John; but according to the synoptic Gospels [Matthew—Luke], it is the proclamation of the kingdom of God. Furthermore, the primary emphasis in John is upon eternal life as a present experience—an emphasis that is quite lacking both in the Synoptic Gospels and in Judaism.

Ladd does not deny the future-oriented character of eternal life. He points out that when Jesus said, "Whoever does not obey the Son shall not see life" (John 3:36), He was referring to humanity's ultimate destiny. This eschatological character of life is most vividly seen in John 12:25, "He who loves his life, loses it, and he who hates his life in the world will keep it for eternal life."[5]

Ladd affirms that in the above and other statements quoting Jesus, John "more clearly sets forth the antithetical structure of the two ages than the sayings in the synoptic Gospels where the similar thought occurs" (Mark 8:35; Matt. 10:39; 16:25; Luke 9:24; 17:33). C. H. Dodd says that John alone has given such statements "a form which obviously alludes to the Jewish antithesis of the two ages." John 4:14, 6:27, and 5:29 speak of "life," "eternal life" and "the resurrection of life" all with the age to come in view and relate closely to Daniel 12:2: "And many of those who sleep in the dust of the ground will awake, those to everlasting life, but the others to disgrace and everlasting contempt." As C. H. Dodd says, all of these sayings "represent life as an eschatological blessing," that is, a blessing given at the time of the fulfillment of all God's promises.[6] At the same time, it is eternal life as the *present possession* of the believer that is unique to John among the gospel writers.

Finally, Ladd says, this life is not only mediated through Jesus and His Word, but it is resident in His very person (5:26). He is the living bread (6:51ff) and the living water (4:10,14). God is the ultimate source of life; but the Father has granted the Son to have life in Himself (5:26). Therefore Jesus could say, "I am the life" (11:25; 14:6).

In John 10:10, Jesus is thus saying that believers may possess the life of the age to come in the present and in abundance. This is the Normal Christian Life.

. . . And Might Have It Abundantly

One of the advantages of this abundant life is that as troubled believers we can go back often to the Word, alone on our knees with God. There we can read His promises out loud back to God. We can also read them out loud to ourselves. We need to hear them spoken by our own lips into our own unbelieving ears. In time their living impact will set our soul on fire with the assurance of what we already are and have by simple faith in Christ. The Holy Spirit of God who abides within will then fill our hearts with all joy in believing.

We can also speak them aloud to the spirit world, to the demons of doubt, unbelief, hardness of heart, defeat, anger, self pity, depression, rejection and shame who have constantly lied to our mind.[7] They have been telling us that we are failures, that we are too sinful, too unbelieving, too hurt, too disappointed and rejected by others and even by God due to past failures. That we are too stubborn, too rebellious, and too hard-hearted to ever be able to live the normal Christian life.

As always, these demons are liars. They have been lying to us about who we are in Christ. All the promises of Jesus refer to each of us. They were spoken to us or for us (John 6:33–58) to help us live abundantly.

The abundant life assures us of who we are in Christ. It is a reality because Jesus, who is our life, abides within. When we understand who we are in Christ, and that He abides within us, we first affirm it to God in prayer. My close friend, Dr. Mark Bubeck, calls this Doctrinal Praying,[8] a companion of what is often called Warfare Praying.

Next we declare to ourselves who we are in Christ and the reality of the fullness of His indwelling presence. I have made my own affirmation of faith prayer which I carry in my daily calendar. I speak it both to God and to myself to keep my eyes off of my own sense of weakness, insufficiency, and worthlessness, on one hand, or foolish feelings of pride and self-sufficiency, on the other.

Then we speak this word of our testimony to all the powers of evil assigned us. As we declare who we are in Christ, what He has and is doing for us, that He now abides in His fullness in us and we are thus "made complete in Him" (Col. 2:6–10; see 2 Pet. 1:2–4), we begin to become strong in the Lord and the power of His might (Eph. 6:10). We are then able to affirm with authority, "Since God is for me, who is against me? I overwhelmingly conquer through Him who loved me."

One Key to the Abundant Life

How do we enter into this abundant life? How is the abundant life to be lived out in daily experience? While these are simple questions, the answers are evidently not simple, though one would think they should be. After all, if this is the life Jesus came to give us (and it is) and if He is that life (and He is), where is the difficulty?

The difficulty is at least twofold. One, the difficulty lies within each of us, even as it lay within the disciples. We, like they before us, still lug around with us this thing called the flesh, as we have just examined in past chapters. The flesh-life (the self-life) and the Christ-life are continually at war with each other. Thus any attempt to live the abundant life in this world means spiritual warfare.

Two, we all tend to latch onto one dimension of the abundant life revealed in Scripture, give it a "catch word" name, and declare that this is *the key* to living the abundant life. Years ago the late Dr. V. Raymond Edman, then President of Wheaton College, wrote a fascinating book called *They Found the Secret.*[9] It is a series of short biographies of some of the most godly men and women through the centuries who lived the abundant life in a vivid manner. He points out that all described that life in their own way. Some examples are the victorious life, the abundant life, the exchanged life, the Spirit-filled life, the surrendered life, the obedient life, the abiding life, the fruitful life, the peaceful life, the resting life, etc.

Edman points out these are all different descriptions of the same reality. That reality is this: the normal Christian life is the life of the Lord Jesus lived within the life of the believer. He is our abundant life.

Jesus implies this in John 10. He says that He is the door into the abundant life (vv. 7–9); His sheep belong to Him. He calls them "my own" (vv. 14,16). He says His sheep know Him just as He knows the Father (vv. 14–15,27–30). He is one with the Father. His sheep are one (but on a different level since they are created beings) with Him.

He gives His sheep "eternal life" (vv. 27–29). This is quality, not duration. It is God's life which Jesus has with the Father and shares with His sheep (John 5:26; 10:28–29). Finally Jesus says continually in John that this life results from His indwelling presence through His indwelling Holy Spirit (John 4:13–14; 6:41–58; 7:37–39; 11:25–26; 14:1–18,25–27; 15:1–11; 17:1–23).

We all would agree, I believe, with what has been said. The question is, How do we enter into that life?

This is probably one of the most difficult and controversial questions which has confronted believers for the entire 2,000 years of the Christian era. I certainly do not expect to answer it to the satisfaction of all my readers. There are hundreds of books available which attempt to answer this question. In my own personal library one entire section is devoted to this issue. It contains over 100 books. All are excellent. All contain part of the answer. None are *the* answer, however.

Some stress crisis. You enter into this abundant life by a crisis subsequent to salvation. Some stress process. You live that life progressively growing up into Christ. Others emphasis both crisis and process.

Let's see if I can bring us all together by finding the common grounds we all have in Christ. First, it is *crisis*. It begins with the crisis of salvation. We are born again. Christ, by His Spirit, comes to live within us. "It is because you really are His sons that God has sent the Spirit of His Son into our hearts to cry Father, dear Father" (Gal. 4:6, PHILLIPS).

Next is *process*. Paul describes it this way, giving his personal testimony to the secret of his abundant life: "And my present life is not that of the old 'I' but the living Christ within me" (Gal. 2:20a, PHILLIPS).

This leads to a *process of crisis*. The apostle puts it this way: "Oh, my dear children, I feel the pangs of child birth all over again until Christ be formed within you" (Gal. 4:19, PHILLIPS). It is Christ being born within us (Gal. 4:6). It is Christ living His life within us (Gal. 2:20). The goal is that Christ "be completely and permanently formed and molded within" us, as Bishop Lightfoot paraphrased Galatians 4:19 so long ago.[10]

This perspective is biblical enough and broad enough to fit all the particular emphases on the way to the abundant life given by all believers of all ages. The abundant life leads to the conquering life, the subject of the rest of this chapter and the next two.

THE CONQUERING LIFE

If I had only John 3 and Romans 8 of the Bible in my possession, I would have almost everything I need to begin and to live the Christian life. While this may over-simplify, it does reveal the importance of these two chapters. Romans 8 is one of the most majestic chapters in the entire Bible.

Romans 1—5

It is crucial to see the relationship between Romans 8 and the earlier chapters of the book.[11] Paul begins Romans with the proof of his apostleship in Romans 1:1–15. As he was not known by sight at the church of Rome and was not one of the twelve apostles, this was important. Next he introduces his subject, the gospel and the necessary faith response to its message in 1:16.

He follows with a vivid picture of the desperate need for this Gospel both among the Gentiles (1:18–32) and the Jews (2:1—3:8). He concludes that all—both Jew and Gentile—are totally lost in sin and separated from God (3:9–18). Even the Jews, who thought that by possessing the law they had escaped the sin and judgment resting upon the Gentiles, find themselves "without excuse" (3:19–20).

All of this lays the foundation for detailed teachings on the major theme of the first part of the book, justification by faith apart from the deeds of the law for the Jew and for all humanity (3:21—5:21). Thus the first five chapters focus almost exclusively on salvation through faith in Christ.

Romans 6

Chapter 6 opens a new theme in the epistle, that of sanctification; that is, the effects of salvation in the life of the believer while living in this hostile, sinful world. Most of us were probably raised on the concept of the believer's two natures. Thus, when we were regenerated, in one sense, we were not absolutely regenerated, not given a totally new life in Christ. We were taught that our sinful nature was left intact. A new nature was implanted in our body which co-existed with the old nature. Thus we were half regenerate and half degenerate. One moment the old nature, the old self, was in charge. The next it was the new nature, the new self in Christ.[12]

But the apostle Paul says differently in Romans 6. He writes, "We died to sin by our baptism into Jesus' death. We were buried with Him through baptism in death that as Christ was raised from the dead through the glory of the Father, so we too might walk in newness of life" (Rom. 6:2–4).

"Might" here does not imply doubt. It begins a purpose clause. "We died to sin with Christ," the apostle says. "We were raised with him with this purpose, to enable us to live a totally new life."

He then follows with another purpose clause: This occurred in order that our (Paul includes himself with the rest of us) body of sin will be done away with, in order that we no longer should be enslaved to sin, as in the past. We are dead to the old sinful nature. Thus we are freed from sin (vv. 7,18,22a) and enslaved to God (v. 22b).

"Now," Paul continues, to paraphrase his words, "since we have died with Christ, in that our sin nature died with Him, we believe that we are alive with Him. Look at what 'with Him' means," the apostle continues. "Death, which is the result of sin (v. 23) no longer has any more power over Him (Christ) because He died to sin, once for all. He was then raised from the dead (v. 9). The life He now lives is lived to God.

"By our identifying with Him through faith, we enter a union with Him in which His death to sin is our death also," to continue the paraphrase. "We too now live to God. It has already happened. Declare it to be so. Work it out in practice by presenting yourself and the members of your body to God as instruments of righteousness, just as you formerly presented yourself and the members of your body as instruments of unrighteousness."

Does this mean we enter into a state of sinless perfection? Are we totally incapable of sinning any longer? "No," the apostle says. "We know that is not true. Our experience reveals this to be false. We still live in this mortal body (vv. 12–13) which is made up of 'members of my body' which in turn are 'slaves to sin' (v. 13). In fact, I find sin warring within my mortal body."[13]

Romans 7

Again we face the spiritual warfare motif of Scripture, in this case warfare with the flesh. This is most vivid in Paul's words in Romans 7:14–25:

> For we know that the Law is spiritual; but I am of flesh, sold into bondage to sin. For that which I am doing, I do not understand; for I am not practicing what I would like to do, but I am doing the very thing I hate. But if I do the very thing I do not wish to do, I agree with the Law, confessing that it is good. So now, no longer am I the one doing it, but sin which indwells me. For I know that nothing good dwells in me, that is, in my flesh; for the wishing is present in me, but the doing of the good is not. For the good that I wish, I do not do; but I practice the very evil that I do not wish. But if I am doing the very thing I do not wish, I am no longer the one doing it, but sin which dwells in me. I find then the principle that evil is present in me, the one who wishes to do good. For I joyfully concur with the law of God in the inner man, but I see a different law in the members of my body, waging war against the law of my mind, and making me a prisoner of the law of sin which is in the members. Wretched man that I am! Who will set me free from the body of this death? Thanks be to God through Jesus Christ our Lord! So then, on the one hand I myself with my mind am serving the law of God, but on the other, with my flesh the law of sin. (Rom. 7:14–25)

What an incredible passage of Scripture! With what other passage can we compare it? Even the most godly of saints, in moments of deep internal warfare with sin, have wept in God's presence, knowing this autobiographical passage written by Paul was their autobiography also.

Dr. Mark Bubeck tells an interesting story that involved this passage.[14] It took place in a neighborhood Bible study. A highly educated professional man was asked to read out loud this passage from Romans 7:14–25. Dr. Bubeck writes: "At this point, his wife, who was in another part of the room, asked the lady next to her if her husband was making a confession. She recognized these words as so aptly describing her husband's struggles."

Bubeck continues:

The one doing this reading told me later that he just couldn't believe these words were in the Bible. He was sure that those leading the Bible study had deliberately chosen the passage for him to read. Being aggressive and vocal, he told them so, and they all had a good laugh over the incident.

Bubeck then remarks, "How relevant the Word of God is! How pointedly it speaks to us about the experiences we are having!"

Two Uses of "Flesh"

I believe it is important to note that Paul uses the word the flesh in two different ways in Romans 7.[15]

One, he says, "While we were in the flesh" (v. 5). Here the flesh refers to something which has already passed away. It would probably be equal to the old nature, "the old self," "the body of sin," which was crucified with Christ (cf. 6:6).

Two, he says once, "I am of the flesh" and twice "my flesh" (vv. 14,18,25). This is something which has not passed away but must be dealt with daily by the believer through the Spirit, the theme of 8:1–17 and of other passages of Scripture like Galatians 5:13–21.

In most of Romans 7 the apostle contrasts the law of the mind with the law of sin which was at work in his flesh. I have tried to show the contrasts on the following chart.

Figure 9.1
The Law of My Mind vs. The Law of Sin

1. "We know that the law is spiritual," v. 14a.	1. "I am of the flesh," v. 14b.
2. I would like to do different than what "I am doing," v. 15a.	2. I am "sold into bondage to sin," v. 14c.
3. "What I do, "I hate," v. 15d.	3. "I am doing (what) I do not understand," v. 15a.
4. "I do not wish to do" what I am doing, v. 16a.	4. "I am not practicing what I would like to do," v. 15b.
5. "I agree with the law, confessing that it is good," v. 16b.	5. "I am doing the very thing I hate," v. 15c; I am doing "the very thing I do not wish to do," v. 16a.
6. I am not doing what I am doing, v. 17a.	6. The "sin which indwells me" is doing these evil things, v. 17.
7. "The wishing (to do good) is present in me," v. 18b.	7. "The doing of the good is not" (in me), v. 18b.
8. "I wish" to do good, v. 19a.	8. "I do not do the good I wish," v. 19a; "I am doing the very thing I do not wish," v. 20a.
9. I am not doing what I am doing, v. 20b.	9. "Sin which dwells in me" is doing what "I do not wish," v. 20b.
10. I am one "who wishes to do good," v. 21.	10. "Evil is present in me," v. 21.
11. "I joyfully concur with the law of God in the inner man," v. 22.	11. There is a "law in the members of my body, waging war against the law of my mind," v. 23a.

12. "The law of my mind" (the opposite of the law of sin), v. 23.	12. That different law makes "me a prisoner of the law of sin which is in my members," v. 23b; I am a "wretched man," v. 24a; I am a prisoner of "the body of this death," v. 24b.
13. "With my mind (I) am serving the law of God," v. 25.	13. "With my flesh, (I serve) the law of sin," v. 25b.

Before the apostle finishes revealing his own inner struggles to find victory in Christ over the warfare with the flesh (the theme of chapter 8), he answers his own despairing cry for freedom from "the body of this death." He declares that there is sure victory "through Jesus Christ our Lord" (v. 25a).

Romans 6—8 Overview

Paul's thinking seems to progress through chapters 6—8. In chapter 6 he tells of our death to sin through our identification and union with Christ in His death to sin. He also tells of our present spiritual resurrection to newness of life which comes through our identification and union with Christ in His resurrection (6:1–13). Chapter 7 reveals the warfare which the true believer faces with the flesh while striving to live that resurrection life, a common theme in the epistles of Paul. The child of God rejoices that the sin nature is dead with Christ. He has a totally new resurrection life, not two opposing lives or natures. Therefore potentially he is able to consider himself "dead to sin, but alive to God in Christ Jesus" (v. 11).

As he begins to do so, however, he finds that sin still dwells within him. It is joined to his flesh. The flesh, unlike his old self or his sin nature, was not crucified with Christ once and for all. It is at war with the law of God written in his mind. He longs to discover the way to live in victory over the lusts of the flesh, the subject of at least the first 17 verses of chapter 8.

This is the meaning of Paul's "therefore" in 8:1. It takes us naturally into his discussion of the way of victory over "the law of sin and death" described in chapter 8. I call it the ecstacy of the normal Christian life.

10

Its Ecstasy
Romans 8

The victory described in Romans 8 is lived in the context of spiritual warfare. I submit a natural threefold outline of Paul's teachings in Romans 8: one, the ecstasy of the normal Christian life, verses 1–17a; two, the agony of the normal Christian life, verses 17b–27; three, the agony within the ecstasy of the normal Christian life, verses 28–39.[1]

THE ECSTASY

The apostle Paul begins his study on the ecstasy of the normal Christian life with three of the most foundational truths about Christian living found anywhere in the New Testament. The first is the believer's union with Christ Jesus. The second is the believer's life in the Holy Spirit. The third is the interrelationship between the two, verses 1–4.[2]

In Christ

The apostle first declares, "There is therefore now no condemnation for those who are in Christ Jesus." When I was a new believer, struggling to find victory in my Christian life, I heard the late Dr. J. Vernon McGee, then pastor of the Church of the Open Door in Los Angeles, preach on this text. The details of what he taught I have forgotten, but I have never forgotten the impact of that sermon on my life and one phrase he continually repeated.

"The most important word in the New Testament for the believer is the preposition *in,* in Christ and in the Spirit," McGee affirmed. This truth came to my parched heart like rain on arid ground. All I needed or would ever need to live the normal Christian life was already mine in the person of the indwelling Christ and His indwelling Spirit. I began a personal study of every passage in the New Testament which speaks of my union with Christ through His indwelling me in the person of the Holy Spirit (8:9).

As I prayed over the Scriptures dealing with the indwelling Christ and Holy Spirit, my life began to be transformed. While that transformation continues and will continue until I am finally with Him, the personal experience of that dual truth became a true "second blessing" or "a second work of grace" in my life.

Jesus is not only my Savior and Lord, He is my life. The Holy Spirit not only indwells me to seal me unto the day of redemption, but He also fills me with the person of God's Son. Through His gifts He empowers me for holy living and effective ministry. While many stress the one and ignore the other, the normal Christian life is both holy living and power in ministry. Both come from the indwelling Spirit of God's dear Son (Gal. 4:6).[3]

This is why Paul insists that everything we need to overcome the evil within (the flesh), the evil without (the world), and the evil from above (evil supernaturalism) is ours in union with our Lord (Eph. 1:3—2:10; 3:14–21; Col. 1:13—3:4) through the Holy Spirit (Rom. 8:1–17a). He also insists, however, that nothing is automatic or magical. If a believer does not know who he is in Christ and the Spirit and what Christ is to him as He indwells by His Spirit, that believer will be defeated most of his Christian life.[4]

Our acceptance before God has nothing to do with our performance as Christians. It has nothing to do with the stage of victory over the flesh we are now in. It has only to do with being "in Christ Jesus." All that needs to be done to bring us to God has already been done. No personal merit brings us to God. No personal demerit can keep us from God. If we are in Christ, we are "accepted in the beloved." For us there is no condemnation. John Murray writes:[5]

> To be reminded of union with Christ . . . is no less pertinent than to be assured of freedom from condemnation because the potency of sin and of the flesh evident in the conflict of 7:14–25 makes it all the more necessary to appreciate the victory which belongs to the believer in the bonds of Christ Jesus. It is a succinct way of alluding to all the grace implied in the argument of the earlier passage.

Verse 2 and verse 1 are closely related. Again, both refer to our union with Christ. Murray says, "not only bound together by the particle 'for,' but also by the repetition in verse two of 'in Christ Jesus.' Verse two unfolds the implication of the union with Christ emphasized at the close of verse one."[6]

Dunn, writing in the *Word Biblical Commentary* on Romans, says:[7]

> It is the "in Christ" which makes the difference. To have identified oneself with Christ while still belonging to this age was bound to precipitate or increase existential tension, but that being "in Christ" is what gives the assurance that the end result will be acquittal. The "in Christ" will triumph over the "in Adam," the tension of living between the two is temporary, the sobering realism of 7:14–25 is matched by the reaffirmed assurance of 8:1.

Two Laws

Paul next speaks of two laws in verse 2. First there is "the law of the Spirit of life in Christ Jesus." Second, there is "the law of sin and death." What laws are these?

"The Spirit of life" is clearly the Holy Spirit, not just an influence. The Holy Spirit is the dominant person of the Trinity mentioned in verses 4–16 and again in verses 23 and 26–27. He is called "the Spirit" who is life in verse 10. Murray says this is consistent with both "Pauline and New Testament usage. . . . The law of the spirit of life" would thus be the power of life operative in the Spirit. It is a commanding and authoritative power, because law has not only "a regulating and activating power" behind it but also a "legislative authority" behind it.[8]

In 7:22–23 Paul mentions two opposing laws, "the law of sin" and the "law of my mind." The law of sin operates in the flesh. The law of the mind, in the case of the believer, is also useless in itself to help the struggling Christian if it were not energized by "the law of the Spirit of life in Christ Jesus." Thus the power of sin is no match for the power of the Spirit. The believer who walks in the spirit (8:4f) is set free from "the law of sin and of death," the law of sin which leads to death operating in his flesh.

It is important to see, therefore, that the "no condemnation" of verse 1 is not deliverance from sin's guilt and penalty, but from sin's power. Paul has already dealt with the former in the early chapters of Romans. Since Romans 6 he has been dealing with the believer's deliverance from sin's power, that is, from "the law of sin and of death."

This view is further supported by verse 3, indeed, by all the rest of this first part of Romans 8. In verse 3 Paul speaks of the Old Testament law. It could never free us from sin's power because of the weakness of the flesh, the flesh here being human nature. God did this for us by sending His Son "in the likeness of sinful flesh—human nature which is weak and unable to do the will of God—and, as an offering for sin, He condemned sin in the flesh."

Murray repeats again that "the governing thought of this passage is concerned with deliverance from the law of sin and death, and therefore, from sin as a ruling and regulating power."[9] Murray's discussion of this act of God in Christ by which "He made sin forfeit its dominion" over the believers is a spiritual warfare interpretation to the passage.[10]

> Since then judicial language is applied to the destruction of the power of the world and of the prince of darkness and since the term "condemnation" is used here respecting the work of Christ, there is warrant for the conclusion that the condemning of sin in the flesh refers to the judicial judgment which was executed upon the power of sin in the cross of Christ. God executed this judgment and overthrew the power of sin; he not only declared sin to be what it was but pronounced and executed judgment upon it.

John Calvin takes a similar position. He says that "the burden of sin being laid on Christ, it was cast down from its power so that it does not hold us now subject to itself so the kingdom of sin in which it held us was demolished.[11]

Calvin's editor writes that because of the phraseology used we should "conclude that the *power* of sin and not its *guilt* is the subject treated of."[12]

> "Law" here is used of a ruling power, for that which exercised authority and secures obedience, "the law of sin," is the ruling power of sin; "the law of the Spirit of life," is the power of the Spirit the author of life: "the law of death" is the power which death exercises. Then "walking after the flesh" is to live in subjection to the flesh as "walking after the Spirit" is to live in subjection to Him. All these things have reference to the *power* and not to the *guilt* of sin. The same subject is continued from chapter 8:5 to the 15th verse.

The Battle: Sin Energized by Flesh vs. the Spirit

Thus we see that the battle in Romans 7—8:15 is warfare with the power of sin energized by the flesh of the believer. Paul's answer to the sin war we face with the flesh is the answer he also gives in Galatians, "But I say, walk by the Spirit, and you will not carry out the desire of the flesh" (Gal. 5:16).

In 8:4 the apostle says that the believer does not "walk according to the flesh, but according to the Spirit." He says in us "those who are according to the flesh [the unredeemed] set their minds on the things of the flesh, but those who are according to the Spirit [the redeemed], the things of the Spirit. For the mind set on the flesh is death, but the mind set on the Spirit is life and peace."

Next he describes the condition of the unregenerate. Since their mind is set on the flesh, they live in hostility to God. They do not nor cannot subject their fleshly minds to the law of God. Thus they are not nor cannot be pleasing to God (vv. 7–8).

Finally, he returns to believers who are "not in the flesh but in the Spirit." They are at war with the flesh and the flesh with them. They do not win every battle. If they did, they would never sin nor come short of any dimension of God's plan for their life. Still, they are not in the flesh, but in the Spirit. The proof? The Spirit of God dwells within them. If the Spirit of God does not dwell within them they are not regenerate (v. 9).[13]

In verse 10 Paul says, "And if Christ is in you . . . ." What he had declared to be true of the Spirit, he now declares of the Son. This is because the Spirit is "the Spirit of Christ" (v. 9). Thus Paul says, "If Christ is in you" (v. 10), and then "if the Spirit of Him who raised Jesus from the dead dwells in you" (v. 11). This is perfect unity between the Son of God and the Spirit in our life.

In verse 10, Paul, who has been affirming that the Spirit of Christ who indwells our being brings life and victory over the power of sin operating against us through the flesh, affirms that there is a part of our being where this life-giving power of the Spirit is not yet fully operative. That part of our being is our mortal body. Even though our body is God's temple and though Christ by His Spirit dwells within our body, Paul says "the body is dead because of sin." This is not meant to discourage us. He then states that "the spirit is alive because of righteousness." By saying this, Paul is not declaring a negative dualism of body and spirit. Both exist together in this world, and both will be joined together in the world to come at the Resurrection (1 Cor. 15:35–37; Phil. 3:20–21).

Thus the redemption provided for the whole person is experienced in two phases. By faith our spirit is born again and receives eternal life through the indwelling Spirit of Christ, but the body does not (Rom. 8:10). This is phase one. Phase two occurs only at "the revealing of the sons of God," at the moment of our full "adoption as sons" (vv. 19,23). Only then will the full redemptive benefits of the Cross be experienced by these sinful, mortal bodies; only then will we experience "the redemption of our body" (v. 23).[14]

The apostle continues promising hope for this sinful body in verse 11. Verses 12–17 are a summary and application of all he has been saying until now. We are again reminded to walk in the Spirit, which I take as synonymous as "being led by the Spirit of God" (v. 14).[15]

As to Paul's blunt warning in verse 13a, "for if you are living according to the flesh, you must die," Calvin rightly remarks, "Let then the faithful learn to embrace Him, not only for justification but also for sanctification, as He has been given to us for both these purposes lest they render Him asunder by their mutilated flesh."[16]

The Holy Spirit vs. Spirits of Slavery and Fear

Verse 15 is one of the great verses of Scripture setting the "Spirit of adoption," the Holy Spirit, over against the opposing spirit, "the spirit of slavery leading to fear." The Spirit of God, even when He is the Spirit of conviction of sin, is always the Spirit who lets us know we belong to God and His kingdom, Paul is implying. He builds up. He encourages. He blesses. He enlightens. He makes Jesus more and more precious to us. He empowers us to the defeat of the flesh, the world, and Satan and his demons. It is he and he alone who cries within us, "Abba! Father!"

It is the other spirit who tells us lies.[17] The writer of Hebrews says that the other spirit, Satan, is the one who binds us in fear (Heb. 2:15). We have been delivered from him, however, so we are not to fear him or his.

I am not declaring dogmatically that the apostle specifically has a demon in mind, though Dunn says he probably does. I am saying that Satan and his evil spirits are spirits of fear and bondage whether they build upon these pre-existing negative human emotions or initiate the attempted slavery themselves. Whatever binds us in fear or brings us into bondage or slavery is that other spirit.

The Holy Spirit is the Spirit of liberty, of adoption. He lets us know that we belong to God. He "bears witness with our spirit that we are children of God" (v. 16). The other spirits either whisper denials of our true sonship or say we are unacceptable to God, even though we may be His sons. Thus Jesus says the other spirit is "a liar, the father of lies, whenever he speaks a lie he speaks from his own nature" (John 8:44). When he speaks lies to us, we are to shut him up as Jesus did (Matt. 4:10; 16:23). We are to resist him with the words of truth (Eph. 6:17; James 4:7–8).

Crisis and Process in Full Deliverance: James' Story

I was counseling a troubled, out-of-town Christian by telephone. My schedule was so full a face-to-face counseling session was not possible. Yet he was hurting badly, and I felt compelled to try to minister to him by telephone.

James was a new believer who had been a practicing warlock in a local witch coven. His wife was a witch in the same group. They had one child, a young boy named Tommy, about six years old. James came from a troubled family. He was a victim of physical and sexual child abuse by his father. He grew up with a deep sense of shame, powerlessness, worthlessness, and anger. Witchcraft gave him a sense of power over others, over circumstances, and above all, over his own life.

He had had some exposure to Christianity as a youth, and he had friends who were Christians. He had gone to church with them occasionally but did not understand the Gospel. He was greatly impressed with the person of Christ but did not know how to appropriate Him for his own life.

Into Witchcraft

He met his wife while in high school. She introduced him to witchcraft. It seemed just right for him. After their marriage, he and his wife gave their lives to the spirit world. While there was "fun" in witchcraft, there were also things that disturbed his sensitive spirit. Everyone was on a power trip. Each sought to gain control over others. The spirits, while helpful to a bruised person like James, were also evil. They promoted free sex among the group. He did not like seeing his wife involved sexually with members of the group, both men and women. He felt degraded when he participated with the group in such activities.

Hate for others, particularly Christians, was a dominate feature of his coven. They were always putting curses on Christians and calling upon the spirits to harm them. Frankly, he liked a Christian co-worker who had begun to witness to him about the joy of the Christian life.

The controlling spirit of the group reminded him of the Devil he had read about and was hearing about from his Christian friend. He wondered if, unknown to him, his wife, and the other members of his coven, Satan was not manipulating them behind the scenes. As one of the coven leaders, he dared not voice his concerns, however.

A Christian Witness and a Desire to Change

One evening he, his wife, and child returned home from a particularly upsetting coven meeting characterized by expressions of deep hatred towards Christians. The spirits were upset with the group for not working harder to earn witchcraft a place of acceptance as a good "religion" which, in contrast to Christianity, stressed the values of earthly happiness, peace, and brotherhood. At the same time he recognized that they were filled with hatred against anyone who opposed them.

James voiced his concern to his wife. He also told her of his Christian co-worker and how kind, affirming, gentle, and moral he was. All his co-workers knew James' friend was a Christian, not because he constantly preached at them or argued with them, but by his lifestyle. While he ate his bag lunch with his fellow workers, he did not participate in their dirty talk or language. He occasionally reminded them when the swearing got too bad that they were misusing the name of his Lord, and he would firmly but gently ask them to stop. They would apologize, and their language and subjects of conversation would actually moderate when they were in his presence. James was deeply impressed with his Christian friend.

His wife was furious. "Christians are our worst enemies," she replied. "They say we worship Satan, which is a lie. They also say their God is the true God and Jesus the only Savior. This is also a lie. There are many gods. Our religion is the answer to the needs of humanity. We don't live for some future heaven. We enjoy life now. When we die, we become one with the spirits so we have the best of both worlds. How can you even think for a moment that your Christian friend may be right?"

The Break for Freedom

One Sunday while his wife was away, James went to church with his friend. He loved the singing, the prayers, and the sermon from the Bible. Most of all he was drawn to the person of Jesus. He cried when he began to understand that God loved him so much that He would send His own Son to die for his sins.

No matter what he had been taught and was teaching others, he knew sin was real. All the sex, hatred, pride, ambition, and disrespect for one's fellow man that his group was promoting was sin; he knew that. He wanted to get out. The pressure to continue promoting evil in the name of love was too much. He wanted to do good to all men. He wanted to be free.

Day after day at lunch break he talked with his Christian friend. One day he bowed his head, prayed, and received Jesus as his Savior. He could no longer continue calling evil good and the goodness of Christ and God, evil.

Ultimatum at Home

When he told his wife she was beside herself in rage. "You always have been a weak person," she said. "I don't know why I ever married you. Unless you return to the coven I'm leaving you and taking Tommy with me." They talked for hours. Rather, he tried to talk, but she railed at him, heaping insult upon insult. The next day when he returned from work she was gone. Just as she had threatened, she had taken Tommy with her.

She left no phone number where he could reach her. James called one of the leaders of the coven to see if he knew of her whereabouts. He did, but he would not tell James where she was. "You have become a Christian," the man said. "You are a traitor. You have joined our enemies. Unless you renounce Christianity and return to the coven you will never see your wife and child again." With that he hung up.

Continued Attack, Progressive Deliverance

It was then that James began to come under demonic attack. The spirits would bombard his mind with threats and insults. They would not let him sleep at night. They confused his mind so badly he had difficulty doing his work. He was desperate. His Christian friend took him to one of the leaders of his church who was gifted at expelling evil spirits. He supposedly had special gifts of discernment which would help him identify the spirits operating in James' life. Many demons were cast out. At first James was greatly relieved. In time, however, the demons either came back or others came to torment him. They were spirits of "slavery to fear" (Rom. 8:15). He was terrified. They threatened to kill him, and he feared they would.

At this point, James called me to help him get rid of his fears and bondage to the accusing spirits. Instead, I went through the Scriptures with him to help him understand who he was in Christ. I wanted him to recognize that Satan was already defeated by the Son of God in his behalf. I told him that though the Devil might not immediately and totally back off, he would eventually have to cease his accusations and fear tactics. He always does. He has no choice in the matter (James 4:7–8).

I call this pre-deliverance counseling. It would have been ineffective just to try to cast demons out of a life so severely demonized with powerful demons of witchcraft, fear, and bondage. Because he had been into witchcraft for years, including several years as a warlock, his deliverance was not instant, but progressive.

Full Deliverance

On more than one occasion the demons came into manifestation while we were talking by phone. I would bring them into subjection and continue with the scriptural counseling. James faithfully studied Dr. Mark Bubeck's book, *The Adversary.* He began to do Doctrinal and Warfare Praying.

He purchased and carefully followed my 16 audio-cassette tape series with accompanying study syllabus called *Spiritual Warfare.*[18] Eventually he began to sense the demons releasing their hold on his life and in his mind. While it took several months, the final self-deliverance occurred all at once one night while James was alone in bed. He suddenly became aware of the exodus of the last of the bondage spirits. They screamed their protest in his mind, "This is not fair. You belonged to us, but we have to go. Jesus is saying we must leave you right now. This is not fair. This is not fair."

With that they left.

As James drew near to the Lord in worship, prayer, and thanksgiving, the Lord drew near to him (James 4:7–8). Never had he experienced such a sense of the Lord's presence. *He was finally free.* He now understood Paul's words, "For you have not received a spirit of slavery leading to fear again, but you have received a spirit [the Holy Spirit] of adoption as sons by which we cry out, 'Abba! Father!' (Rom. 8:15; Gal. 4:6). James now knew for sure that he was both a child of God, an heir of God, and joint heir with Christ (v. 17). He knew that his sufferings were sufferings with Christ. All were meant for his good. He also knew that some day he would "be glorified with Him" (vv. 16–17).

This is an overview of Paul's teachings on the ecstasy of the normal Christian life. While some agony is involved, the focus is on ecstasy, the freedom from the law of sin and death through the indwelling Christ and His Holy Spirit. Our next chapter deals with Paul's overview of the agonies of the normal Christian life.

11

Its Agony
Romans 8

Paul's treatment in Romans 8 of the agony of the normal Christian life begins with the statement in verse 17 that the Christian life is a life of suffering with Christ and continues through verse 27. The contrast between this portion of Romans 8 and the prior portion (vv. 1–17a) is remarkable. That is why I call verses 1–17a the Ecstasy of the Normal Christian Life and this second portion the Agony of the Normal Christian Life.

If the apostle had halted his treatment of the normal Christian life with the "ecstasy" presentation, he would have been less than realistic, even in terms of his own Christian life. When he reaches the point of the greatest of all ecstasies of the Christian life, that of our real status as "heirs of God and joint heirs with Christ," he begins treating the agony of suffering (v. 17b).

Suffering With Glory

The apostle, always one to encourage, makes one of the most comforting statements in all of the Bible regarding our suffering with Christ. I like the NEB translation, "For I reckon that the sufferings we now endure bear no comparison with the splendor that is as yet unrevealed, which is in store for us."

John Murray notes that

> this verse is an appeal to the great disproportion between the sufferings endured in this life and the weight of glory reserved for the children of God—the present sufferings fade into insignificance when compared with the glory to be revealed in the future. The apostle appeals to this consideration an inducement to patient endurance of sufferings.[1]

In 8:18–27 Paul mentions three groanings: the groaning universe or the natural creation (vv. 18–22); the groaning church (vv. 23–25); and the groaning Holy Spirit (vv. 26–27).[2]

The apostle here personifies the physical creation, comparing it to a woman in the pangs of childbirth (v. 22). The universe is anxiously longing for "the revealing of the sons of God" (v. 19). As it was made to participate in the negative effects of humanity's fall, not by its own will but by the will of God (v. 20), it will also participate in the positive effects of redeemed humanity's entrance into "the freedom of the glory of the children of God" (v. 21). The church (that is, the children of God) and the creation groan together, waiting eagerly for the same things—"our adoption as sons" (vv. 22–23a).

This adoption is totally different than that already experienced by the children of God (Gal. 4:5; Eph. 1:4–5), though not unrelated. The adoption already entered into is spiritual: It does not include as yet the physical body (v. 15).[3] The adoption for which we still wait is "the redemption of our body" (v. 23b). This will only occur at "the last trumpet" for both those dead in Christ and for those who are alive at His coming (1 Cor. 15:50–57; 2 Thess. 4:13–18).

The Spirit Intercedes

While we and creation groan, waiting for the day when our bodies will be redeemed (v. 23), and we will be revealed for what we already are—"the sons of God" (v. 19), another groaning is occurring: the "Spirit himself intercedes for us with groanings too deep for words" (v. 26).

There is no end to suggested interpretations of this verse. Many have much to commend them. In my opinion, however, the one that is most objectionable is the one which declares that the Spirit's intercession "for us with groanings too deep for words" refers to praying in tongues. If this were so we would have to affirm that Jesus never prayed in the Holy Spirit, for He is never recorded as speaking or praying in tongues. This would also mean that when one prays with the mind (1 Cor. 14:14–19), that is, with the full use of his faculties, which is characteristic of all prayers recorded in Scripture, he is not praying in the Holy Spirit. If not, then he is praying in the flesh. Such a conclusion would be totally repugnant to most Christians.

Also, this would mean that Christians who do not have what is commonly called "a prayer language" do not have this benefit of the Spirit interceding for them "with groanings too deep for words." That means most of the Christians who have ever lived were deprived of what Paul here ascribes as a ministry of the Spirit in behalf of all believers, for most did not have a "prayer language."[4]

John Calvin says the correct interpretation has to fit the context:[5]

> [Paul] brings before them the aid of the Spirit, which is abundantly sufficient to overcome all difficulties. There is then no reason for anyone to complain, that the bearing of the cross is beyond their own strength, since we are sustained by a celestial power. And there is great force in the Greek word (used here) which means that the Spirit takes on Himself a part of the burden . . . so that He not only helps and succours us, but lifts us up as though He went under the burden with us.

Weaknesses and Sufferings

His editor remarks that the word for *weakness* "is taken metaphorically from assistance afforded to infants not able to support themselves, or to the sick, tottering and hardly able to walk." A beautiful picture indeed! "Weakness" (v. 26) is plural, indicating the great variety of burdens and sufferings (agonies) we feel. Calvin comments:[6]

> For as experience shows, that except we are supported by God's hands, we are soon overwhelmed by innumerable evils. Paul reminds us, that . . . there is yet sufficient protection in God's Spirit to preserve us from falling and to keep us from being overwhelmed by any mass of evils.

These weaknesses and suffering are not meant to break us down, but to cause us to look upwards. They make deep, heartfelt prayer as necessary as our daily bread. They tend to have a twofold possible effect upon the elect, however. Response to them can make some burdened hearts become harder, bitter, and complaining. In others, they bring us to God in heartfelt prayer.

We are often baffled about how or what we should pray. All we can do is come into His presence on our faces, weeping and confused. Words totally fail us. They seem completely limited in expressing our crushed spirit or troubled heart. No matter, the apostle says, the Spirit "intercedes for us with groanings too deep for [our] words."

His intercession, we must be assured, always reaches the Father's heart. God is always searching "the hearts" to understand our cries. At the same time, He knows the mind of the Spirit because what He intercedes for us is always according to the will of God (v. 27).

Later in this epistle Paul tells us that Jesus is at the right hand of God interceding for us (v. 34). Here Paul shows us the indwelling Spirit interceding for us from deep within us. How then can our prayer ever fail or our true needs ever go without being met? Before His throne and within our hearts God is interceding to God in our behalf. What an amazing life is this Christian life! In the midst of our agonies we must always contemplate the ecstasies.

THE AGONY WITHIN THE ECSTASY

The two words *agony* and *ecstasy* well describe the dramatic line of teaching found in these Romans 8:28–39. Almost every facet of God's redemption in Christ and the spiritual warfare we face in living out that redemption is found here.

Paul first begins with God's eternal sovereign purpose to glorify all his elect (vv. 28–30). What do we know? "We know that God causes all things to work together for good . . ." (v. 28a).

For whom is this true? "To those who love God, to those who are called according to His purpose" (v. 28b).

How do we know what we know?

1. *God has foreknown us.* The subject of God's foreknowledge is a subject of endless controversy. Does it simply mean God knows beforehand what will happen, that is, is it the same as God's omniscience; or does it mean God has ordained beforehand what will come to pass?[7]

I believe, in spite of the intellectual problems involved, the weight of evidence comes down strongly upon the latter view. As John Murray says, "to 'know beforehand' is to know with peculiar regard and love from before the foundation of the world (cf. Eph. 1:4) and 'foreknew' (Rom. 8:29) can have the persons as direct object with no further qualification."

2. *God has "predestined [us]* to be conformed to the image of His Son, that He might be the first-born among many brethren." It is to conformity "to the image of His Son" that He has predestined us, not just to escape hell and gain heaven. Jesus, while always in a different and higher category than his brethren, is to be the leader of many "Jesuses," men and women who bear His image.

3. *Those "He predestined, these He also called."* That is what it means to be the elect of God. God called us to His Son and to Himself, or we could not have come to Him at all (John 6:37–40,44,64–65).

4. *"Whom He called, these He also justified."* God has fully imputed His righteousness to His elect.

5. *These "whom He justified, these He also glorified"* (v. 30). Calvin comments that Paul speaks to us as believers, all of whom "are now pressed down by the cross" so that we may know that His Cross also leads to our glorification. We do not have that glorification yet. Only He does. Yet, Calvin says, "His glory brings to us such assurance respecting our own glory that our hope may be justly compared to a present possession."[8]

Calvin then comments that Paul uses the past tense for all of these blessings.

His editor comments, "Paul speaks of these things as past, because they are as already done in God's decree, and in order to show the certainty of their accomplishment."

Certainty of Our Calling

Next Paul emphasizes the certainty of our calling by God (from foreknowing us to our glorification) with a series of seven rhetorical questions, all of which begin with the words *what? who? how?* and *shall?* (vv. 31–39).

"What then shall we say to these things?" In other words, since we have been foreknown, predestined, called, justified, and glorified, what more can God do for us to assure us that He is directing all the good, and also the evil, which comes to our life for our good and His purpose (vv. 28–32a)?

"Who is against us" since *God is for us?* (v. 31b) Are there people who are against us? In such circumstances, how unimportant they are since God is for us! Is evil supernaturalism totally against us? Of course it is, but what can Satan and his evil spirits really do against us? They can hassle, afflict, threaten, scare, bruise, but they cannot really hurt us. God uses them eventually to help us.

We all become weary in the battle and often complain, "I am tired of the pressure Satan continually brings against me." When that happens, we can counter his attack by turning against Satan and his demons and declaring our acceptance by God (v. 31b) in the beloved (Eph. 1:3–8); their defeat by the King of Kings and the Lord of Lords (John 12:31–32); our authority in Christ's power over them (Luke 10:17–19); and their destiny in hell, the eternal lake of fire (Matt. 25:41; Rev. 20:10). I believe that is the meaning of resisting the Devil until he flees (James 4:7–8).

When we resist in such a manner we are fulfilling Ephesians 3:10 and Revelation 12:11. There Paul and John affirm:

That the manifold wisdom of God might now be made known through the church to the rulers and the authorities in the heavenly places. (Eph. 3:10)

And they overcame him because of the blood of the Lamb and because of the word of their testimony, and they did not love their life even to death. (Rev. 12:11)

How would He fail to "give us all things" that we need to live the normal Christian life? Look at what He has done for us! He did not spare His own Son on our behalf. He "delivered Him up for us all" (v. 32). How could He fail to give us all else that we need to live the life He commands us to live?

"Who will bring a charge against God's elect?" That charge can come from only three possible sources: from others, from ourselves, and from Satan. Satan is the main one to charge or accuse us (Zech. 3:1–3; Rev. 12:10). He not only does so before God but before our own damaged emotions and conscience, and he uses others to accuse us as well. Paul answers, "God is the one who justifies." He has already justified all of His own (vv. 29–30). So all other condemnation is pure rubbish. It holds no merit before God and should hold no merit before us.

Who is the one who condemns? Paul gives a fourfold answer which removes all ground for Satan's or anyone else's condemning God's own:

1. "Christ Jesus is He who died" for God's own. Calvin says, "As no one by accusing can prevail when the judge absolves, so there remains no condemnation when satisfaction is given . . . and the penalty is paid."
2. "Yes, rather who was raised." Paul's argument here is that Jesus' sacrifice

of His life to justify His elect was all that God's law demanded. He raised Him from the dead as "the conqueror of death, and triumphed over all its power."[9]

3. "Who is at the right hand of God." Christ at the place of glory, power, and dominion—that is, at the right hand of God—is one of Paul's joyful themes (Eph. 1:20; Col. 3:1–4; Heb. 1:3, 8–13; 8:1; 10:12; 12:2). He is Lord! He rules! He reigns! All authority is given Him in heaven and on earth! Read Hebrews 1:3,8–13 to see Him through the eyes of the Father and verse 6 through the eyes of the angels. Paul declares in Ephesians 2:6, We are seated "with Him in the heavenly places." Who dares condemn us?

4. "Who also intercedes for us." In other words, His very presence before the throne of God, at the right hand of God in our behalf, is itself an eternal intercession in our behalf.

Dunn calls all of this "the courtroom metaphor."[10]

The risen Christ pleads His sacrificial death before the Judge on behalf of those who have died with Him. . . . The verdict of acquittal or condemnation lies wholly with God alone. God's commitment to His own in Christ is how His acquittal comes to effect. . . . The Judge's own "Right Hand Man" is on our side, a more powerful, and more favored advocate than *any* who may plead against Him. . . . The success of His advocacy over that of any challenge is assured since His resurrection and exaltation to God's right hand was God's own doing. . . .

How blessed! How comforting! Who dares condemn us when He appears in God's presence for us? Satan, fool as he is, tries to do so but all in vain (Rev. 12:10). As for his demons, when the Father raised Jesus from the dead and seated him at His own right hand, it was "after angels and authorities and powers had been subjected to Him" (1 Pet. 3:22). This includes all of Satan's fallen angels of all classes as well as God's angels who joyfully submit to Him (Heb. 1:3–14).

"Who shall separate us from the love of Christ?" (v. 35). The expression "the love of Christ" is rare in Scripture. It is usually the love of God which is in focus (v. 39). Why is it used here?

While Paul does not say, one can venture a guess. In verses 33–34 the focus has been upon God's giving His Son to die for us, to be raised for us, to be glorified for us, and to intercede for us. Now Paul wants us to see Christ's love for us in all of this. In fact he will continue to feature not only God's love, but Jesus' love for us to the end of this chapter.

Jesus Himself had said that no one, not even the Father, took His life from Him. He laid it down of His own accord (John 10:18). Paul now tells us why He laid down His life for us: He loves us. If the believer allows that truth to penetrate his heart, mind, soul, emotions, indeed his very being, he will never be the same. The great theologian Karl Barth was once asked by a friend what was the greatest theological truth ever to enter his mind. He quickly answered,

> Jesus loves me,
> This I know,
> For the Bible
> Tells me so.

"Who shall separate us from the love of Christ?" Shall tribulation, or distress, or persecution, or famine, or nakedness, or peril or sword?

Calvin comments that Paul

preferred ascribing personality to things without life, and for this end—that he might send forth with us into the contest as many champions as there are of temptations to try our faith.[11]

As he had personified the creation which fell in man's fall and groans with the church's groaning, so Paul now personifies the things that try our faith so severely. Look at them. Think of what they have done, are doing, and will yet do to our faith and the faith of our loved ones. What an evil list!

Tribulations
Distress
Persecution
Famine
Nakedness
Peril
Sword

Shall any separately or all of these together separate us from the love of Christ? No, Paul says. In the midst of experiencing any or all of them, we "are more than conquerors through Him who loved us" (v. 37, NKJV). Yet, while going through them we usually feel that He has forsaken us.

Perpetua and Felicitas

Consider the story of the martyrdom of the 22-year-old Roman aristocrat, Perpetua, and her slave girl, Felicitas. It is told in a third-century writing called *The Passion of Perpetua and Felicitas*. Their faithfulness to Christ never ceases to stir my heart. The following paraphrase and quotations are taken from Ruth Tucker's exciting book *From Jerusalem to Irian Jaya*.[12]

Vibia Perpetua was the mother of an infant son. She and her personal slave, Felicitas, who was eight months pregnant, were imprisoned in the Roman city of Carthage, North Africa. Their imprisonment occurred under the rule of Emperor Septimus Severus, the vile emperor who launched the first empire-wide persecution of Christians in A.D. 202. Tucker says, "The emperor himself worshiped Serapis, an Egyptian god of the dead, and he feared Christianity was a threat to his own religion."

Christianity was growing rapidly in Carthage at the time, and the persecution there was the most intense in all the Roman Empire. Perpetua, Felicitas, three men, and their leader, a deacon named Saturus, were arrested. Perpetua's father, a respected nobleman, endured distress and humiliation when he "was informed that his only daughter had been arrested and imprisoned as a common criminal. He came and pleaded with her to renounce the new faith . . . [and] she refused." When he later heard that Perpetua was to be thrown into a public arena with wild beasts, he came to the prison and tried forcibly to rescue her. He failed and was beaten by the Roman officials. Perpetua wrote, "I was grieved by my father's plight as if I had been struck myself." Again he pled with her to consider the shame and suffering she was bringing upon her family and to renounce her Christian faith. She responded, "This will be done on the scaffold which God has willed, for I know that we have not been placed in our own power but in God's."

Perpetua's greatest sufferings while in prison awaiting her execution were due to her anxiety for her family and especially for her infant son. She said she was "racked with anxiety" almost to the breaking point. Permission was finally given for her baby to be with her in prison until the day of her death. She wrote, "At once I recovered my health, relieved as I was of my worry and anxiety over the child."

When the day of their execution drew near, the condemned believers met for prayer and to share an *agape* love feast, "more concerned about their worthiness, their loyalty to Christ than about the suffering ahead of them." Perpetua and Felicitas had already experienced five of the seven worst evils mentioned by Paul: tribulation, distress, persecution, famine (prison food was just enough to keep them alive), and peril. They were soon to experience the last two sources of trials, nakedness and the sword.

The men were first tortured for the entertainment of the crowd before their execution "by being mauled by 'a bear, a leopard and a wild boar.' Finally they were put to death. The two women were saved for last."

> Perpetua and Felicitas, who had given birth to her baby in prison, were stripped (nakedness) and sent into the arena to face a mad heifer. The gory torture soon became too much for the crowd and the people began shouting, "Enough."
>
> When this preliminary exhibition was ended, the young women were brought to the executioner, at which time Perpetua called out to some grieving Christian friends, "Give out the word to the brothers and sisters; stand fast in the faith, love one another, and don't let suffering become a stumbling block to you."
>
> She was taken to the gladiator to be beheaded. . . . His first blow was not sufficient. Perpetua cried out in pain, and took the gladiator's trembling hand and directed the sword to her throat and it was over.

Tucker says that this ended the wave of persecution in Carthage. The church continued to grow steadily, however. Many were attracted to the faith by the serenity and courage of Perpetua and her companions. Even Pudens, the prison governor, later turned to Christ and became a martyr for Christ.

Young Perpetua and Felicitas experienced all seven of these curses for Christ. Did they feel that God had abandoned them? That they had been separated from Christ? No. They knew with Paul that, "For thy sake we are being put to death all day long; We were considered as sheep to be slaughtered" (v. 36).

Paul's climactic note to all the agonies of our Christian life is the ecstatic cry, "But in all these things we overwhelmingly conquer through him who loved us" (v. 37). Bible translators and commentators struggle to grasp the full power of Paul's triumphant exclamation in this verse. Williams translates, "And yet in all these things we keep on gloriously conquering." PHILLIPS translates the phrase, "No, in all these things we win an overwhelming victory."

THE ECSTASY WITHIN THE AGONY

Finally come two of the most powerful verses of testimony to victory in spiritual warfare found anywhere in Scripture:

> For I am convinced that neither death, nor life, nor angels, nor principalities, nor things present, nor things to come, nor powers, nor height, nor depth, nor any other created thing, shall be able to separate us from the love of God, which is in Christ Jesus our Lord. (Rom. 8:38–39)

" 'For I am convinced,' " John Murray says, "is an express declaration of the confidence entertained respecting the impossibility of separation from the love of Christ."[13] William Barclay in his characteristic style says, "So Paul goes on with a poet's fervor and a lover's rapture to sing of how nothing can separate us from the love of God in our risen Lord."[14]

The nine expressions listed in Romans 8:38–39 are meant to universalize in the most emphatic way that nothing shall separate us from the love of Christ. They are also meant to reinforce the dogmatic declaration that we overwhelmingly conquer through Him who loved us.

Several of the expressions occur in pairs, the one expression being the opposite of the other: "death—life; things present—things to come; height—depth." Others are not so constituted but provide vivid imagery of powers greater than all human powers, such as "angels—principalities—powers." Finally, Paul exhausts all other possibilities by saying, "nor any other created thing."

The first pair, "neither death nor life."

Barclay says, "In life we live with Christ, in death we die with Him; and because we die with Him, we also rise with Him, and death so far from being a separation is only a step into His nearer presence. Death is not the end, it is only 'the gate of the skyline leading to the presence of Christ.' "[15]

The second pair, "nor angels nor principalities."

One interpretation of this pair is that they both refer to God's angels. Thus the two expressions do not reveal "a pair, the one expression the opposite of the other." Both refer to God's angels (including perhaps "powers").

A second interpretation is that they, like "death, nor life," are an opposing pair. "Angels" refers to God's elect angels of all classes while "principalities" refer to fallen angels of all classes.

A third view is more agnostic. It affirms that we do not know if Paul was actually trying to contrast good angelic powers and evil angelic powers in his use of "angels" and "principalities" and later "powers." All we do know is that none of these supernatural, created beings can separate us from the love of God in Christ.

James D. G. Dunn represents the more agnostic position. He says that we cannot say for sure what Paul had in mind when he speaks of angels and principalities (and later "powers"). We do not know the detail of Paul's views concerning the essential differences between angels which were good angels and those angels which were evil. All we do know is, whatever be the case, none of these created, disembodied, supernatural spirits can separate us from the love of God in Christ.[16]

> Paul uses terms which would embrace the complete range of spiritual forces, however conceived—good or evil, every possibility and eventuality is included (as with death and life). . . . His concern, here, however, is pastoral rather than speculative. Whatever names his readers give to the nameless forces which threaten the Creator's work and purpose, they are in the end impotent before Him who is God over all.

Since we are in an area of opinion, I will give mine. I believe Dunn is correct.[17] In this verse the apostle is dealing with the normal Christian life. Thus he declares that nothing in the universe can ever "separate us from the love of God which is in Christ Jesus our Lord" (v. 39b). If, hypothetically speaking, angels were to attempt that separation (Gal. 1:8)—and they don't—they would fail. If demonic powers were to attempt to do so—and they do—they too would fail. He is not here speaking hypothetically, however, because as Paul teaches elsewhere, such a goal would be consistent with demonic purposes.

The former Archdeacon of London and Canon of St. Paul's Cathedral, the Rev. E. H. Gifford, wrote a book on Romans first published in 1886. He says, "St. Paul's familiarity with Hebrew poetry" led him to outline ten possible sources that threaten to separate the believer from God. He puts them in poetic form, numbering each source as recorded below.[18]

<pre>
        1   2
Neither death, nor life
      3   4
Nor angels, nor principalities
         5   6
Nor things present, nor things to come
      7
Nor powers,
      8   9
Nor height, nor depth
             10
Nor any other creature.
</pre>

This is a beautiful arrangement. Gifford himself holds the more agnostic view.[19]

In our present passage *angels* and *principalities* must both have the widest possible application: the point in question is not the moral disposition, whether good or evil, but the power of the angelic order of created things.

He then states the distinction between angels and principalities is not a moral distinction but only a distinction in rank. "Principalities are angels of greater power and might" (Eph. 6:12; 2 Peter 2:11).[20] His entire discussion of these verses is worth studying.

The third pair, "nor things present nor things to come."

Here we have a linear dimension: time. Paul is as human as the rest of us. He knows that the past is past. Even though it does affect us in the present and the future, we cannot really change the past. What happens in the present and the future does cause us true apprehension, however.

Nothing that is presently occurring or will yet occur and nothing in the uncertain future can separate us from God's love in Christ Jesus our Lord. There is a further word worth considering here, however. William Barclay says, "*no age in time* can separate us from Christ." He reminds us of the Jewish view of time. The Jews divided all time into this present age and the age to come. Thus according to Barclay,[21] Paul is saying that "In this present world nothing can separate us from God in Christ; the day will come when this world will be shattered and the new age will dawn. It does not matter; even then, when this world has passed and the new world come, the bond is still the same."

The fourth element is "powers."

"Powers" seems isolated from the rest. It probably is to be connected to the second pair, unless the apostle has something else in mind which commentators have not been able to understand as yet. I do not see why it cannot be seen as he uses it consistently in Ephesians and Colossians for high-level cosmic powers of evil. While not being dogmatic, I believe that is what Paul has in mind.

The fifth pair is "nor height nor depth."

Dunn says Paul is "deliberately drawing on current astronomical terms to denote the full sweep of the heavens visible and invisible to the human eye." He also affirms that this would include "all astrological powers known and unknown which could be thought to determine and control the fate and destiny of human beings. Whatever force they might bring to bear on believers,[22] the love of God is greater still."[23]

The final words, "nor any other thing."

Romans 8 is like a sermon, a poem, or a piece of beautiful prose, as it reasons towards its climax in this final word of Paul's. Like a choir, the words build in ever-growing crescendo and beauty until they reach this final word, "nothing in all of creation shall ever be able to separate us from the love of God in Christ Jesus our Lord." All that needs to be added is, "Amen."

Murray's, Dunn's, and Barclay's comments are worth noting, however. Murray says, "this concluding negation is for the purpose of leaving no loophole—no being or thing in the whole realm of created reality is excluded."[24] Dunn says,

> Lest any thing or power within reality could be said to have been omitted from the above list, Paul rounds it off with an all-embracing addendum. Since God alone is creator and since God is one, any other creature means everything else! Nothing, but nothing, can separate from "God's love in Christ Jesus our Lord."[25]

Barclay writes that

> here is a vision to take away all loneliness and fear. Paul is saying, "You can think of every terrifying thing that this or any other world can produce. Not one of them is able to separate the Christian from the love of God which is in Jesus Christ, who is Lord of every terror and master of every world. Of what shall we be afraid?[26]

Dunn concludes his commentary on Romans 8:[27]

> In this mystery—God for us in Christ Jesus, the crucified as Lord—lies the heart of Paul's assurance. This towering confidence rests foursquare on Christ, on God's commitment to His own in Christ and on their commitment to this Christ as Lord, Master and determiner of all. With this much said, no more need be said, and both chorus and soloist fall silent.

E. H. Gifford writes that Romans 8:31–39 "is a noble hymn of victory (which) while growing out of its immediate context (vv. 28–30), and having a primary reference to the sure triumph of them that love God, forms at the same time a grand conclusion to the whole doctrinal portion of the Epistle." He quotes Godet.[28]

> It is the crown of that edifice of salvation in Christ, of which St. Paul had laid the foundation in his demonstration of the righteousness of faith (1—5) and raised the superstructure in his exposition of sanctification (6—8). After this it will only remain for us to see this salvation thus studied in its essence, unfold itself upon the stage of history.

That salvation can only unfold itself "on the stage of history" as the people of God demonstrate their abundant and conquering Christian life to an incredulous and doubting public.

A Passion for Purity and Power

While living in this world we are continually grieved at the spread of sin and lawlessness. We yearn that His kingdom "will come" and that His will shall be done "as in heaven also on earth" (Matt. 6:9, literal translation). We know this will never be fully realized until God makes new heavens and a new earth, where only righteousness dwells. Thus we long for His coming. In the meantime, we seek to be "blameless and innocent, children of God above reproach in the midst of a crooked and perverse generation among whom [we] appear as lights in the world" (Phil. 2:15). In essence, that is the abundant but normal Christian life (John 10:10b).

Rev. Keith Benson, missionary in Argentina since 1957, labors in the interior of that vast country where God is presently moving in such mighty power after years of awful resistance to the Spirit of God.[29] The area where Keith is laboring is the center of indigenous, demonic worship called Difunta Correa. "Superstition, lust, demonism, and spiritism is the daily experience," he writes. He recently wrote me a letter which expresses well the burden to see Christians truly live an abundant life of holiness and power.

> My burden—in a word—is evangelism with holiness. I long that people get converted because they see the holiness of God, and not merely because they have a need. May they feel their need of holiness, is my prayer, my burden.

I read that Ghandi once said,

> I like your Christ but I don't like your Christians.

May God work so deeply in our lives that people who know us will say,

> I like your Christ and I am inspired by your Christians.

12

The Reality of Below Normal Performance

BPWMGINTWMY.

This strange string of letters are displayed on a button given to those who attend one of Bill Gothard's seminars on "Basic Christian Conflicts." The arrangement translates to *Please Be Patient With Me. God Is Not Through With Me Yet.*

The apostle Paul was acutely conscious of this problem in his own life. Thus he wrote in Philippians 3:12–14:[1]

Yet, my brothers, I do not consider myself to have "arrived" spiritually, nor do I consider myself already perfect. But I keep going on, grasping ever more firmly that purpose for which Christ Jesus grasped me.

My brothers, I do not consider myself to have fully grasped it even now. But I do not concentrate on this. I leave the past behind, and with hands outstretched to whatever lies ahead, I go straight for the goal—my reward, the honor of my high calling by God in Christ Jesus.

The normal Christian life as described in the previous chapters and the entire New Testament is not the norm among the majority of the world's Christians. Why?

All of us as believers will always fall short of the biblical ideal until the day of our glorification in the kingdom of God. The ideal is always meant to be the ideal, the goal towards which we continually move without ever reaching it. In other words, there must always be progress. There must never be stagnancy in our Christian life. We need to know Him better, to be more like Him, to love Him more, to obey Him more completely, to walk more fully in the Spirit, putting to death all works of the flesh and obeying with deeper insight His Holy Word. This ideal is always, in one sense, unattainable in this life.

Jesus once expressed the ideal of the normal Christian life with these words: "You are to be perfect, as your heavenly Father is perfect."[2] This is our purpose or ideal. This side of glory can we ever say, "I have finally become perfect in my relationships both to God (Matt. 19:21a) and my fellow man (Matt. 5:48)? What's next?"

The ideal is the absolute goal or purpose towards which all of us progress. We are to be continually transformed to the image of Christ, Paul tells us in Romans 8:28–30. This side of "the glory that is to be revealed to us" (Rom. 8:18), that goal will not be fully realized in this earthly life. We will always come short of God's ideal for our lives. As God is patient with us, we must, therefore, be patient with ourselves as well as with each other (Eph. 4:31—5:23; 1 Cor. 11:1; 1 Pet. 2:21; 1 John 2:6 with John 8:29; James 1:2–4 with Heb. 12:10–14).

BARRIERS TO THE NORMAL CHRISTIAN LIFE

Many Christians, including Christian leaders, fall far short of the biblical ideal, however. Why? There may be as many different reasons as there are struggling Christians.

Viewing Salvation as an Escape From Sin's Judgment

Perhaps many believers fall far short of the biblical norm because they are not truly interested in reaching it. For those who fit this category, the focus of their encounter with Christ is often on personal salvation from the guilt and the penalty for their sins. While this emphasis is harmonious with Scripture as one begins his walk with God, it is not sufficient for a life that could be called "Christian" in the full sense of the word.

The experience of one of my high school classmates is a case in point. At the time I was a sincere Roman Catholic with a deep God consciousness. I had a hunger to know the Lord in a personal way but did not find him within my church. I lived a very moral life and was known as one of the "good religious boys" on campus.

The only Protestant churches I knew anything about we called "holy roller" churches. And they were! I remember one located a few blocks from my home. While walking near the church during evening services I could hear their "worship" half a block away from the church.

At first I was amused by it all. Later I became repelled by their emotional frenzy. It seemed eerie, almost fearful. I was glad I didn't belong to that kind of church. A group of us would occasionally stand outside one of the windows to watch the spectacle. The noise level was unbelievable. Men and women were shouting and falling on the floor. Everything seemed to be in total confusion.

One of my high school friends was a nice "unsaved" Protestant even as I was a Roman Catholic. He too lived a very moral life. We enjoyed our friendship, loved the outdoors, sports, and the good things kids did in high school without getting involved in "sinful" activities.

One day I heard that my friend had "gotten saved" at a "holy roller" meeting. "John, we heard you 'got saved' last Sunday. What does that mean?" a group of us asked him.

"Well, the pastor preached a sermon on hell. It scared me so much I was determined I didn't want to go there if I could avoid it," he replied. "He said if we would come to the altar and confess our sins we would 'get saved' from hell. So I did. I don't want to go to hell."

"What else did he tell you?" we asked.

"He said it is a sin to go to the movies and dances. I have to stay away from those things or I could still end up in hell," he replied.

This was too much for all of us, me included. While I understood sin and believed in hell, I had never heard that movies and dances were sinful and would send you to hell. We all told him to leave the holy roller church. After a short time he did.

By his own confession he went forward to "get saved" to "escape hell."[3] Evidently the love and beauty of God's plan of salvation was not presented or, at least, did not reach him.

Did he truly find the Lord? I don't know. Perhaps we were the voice of the Evil One through whom the Word sown was removed from his heart (Matt. 13:19). Perhaps he never was given the "word of the kingdom," so there was really no firm truth to remove from his heart.

Viewing Salvation as Receiving "God the Servant"

Others who fit the category of believers who do not truly desire to live a life totally pleasing to God have embraced a gospel of "God the servant," as I choose to call it. They have been told, directly or indirectly, that if they come to Christ, life will be pleasant from then on. All will go well. God will become their divine servant. He will provide all of their needs. "God wants to make you happy," they are told, "and is available to prosper you in life."

If they don't like their present job and want a better one, God will provide it. If they are sick, God will heal them. If they need a newer, more comfortable car, it is available for the asking. "God owns all the cattle on a thousand hills," they are told. "He is your Father and will share his material riches with you."

When I first made my decision to live totally for the Lord three years after my conversion, things did not go nicely for me. In fact, totally the opposite occurred. My mother disowned me as her son, somewhat of a sacred duty in those days for Roman Catholic parents whose children became Protestants. I went directly to Bible school but had so little money I barely had enough to eat one meal a day weekends when the school cafeteria was closed.

My fiancee broke off our engagement. I was convinced God had called me into missions, but she did not want to be married to a missionary. She said I had to choose between her and the will of God. I wanted her, but I also wanted to obey God. I finally chose God's will and the pain that accompanied it.

Soon I came under direct demonic attack. I thought I was losing my mind. The focus of the attack was on the words of a Roman Catholic priest who told me that if I left the Catholic church to become a Protestant missionary I was doomed to hell. One morning I awakened to a sense of evil in my dorm room. I was filled with fear. I thought I saw the Devil or a demon in my room. "You are going to hell," it said. "You have left the true church of Jesus Christ. You are lost."[4]

Fear swept over me. My stomach felt nauseous. I trembled from head to foot. Terror pulsated through me. My mind became confused. I tried to assure myself that it was a lie. I knew Jesus had said, "He that hears my Word and believes on Him who sent me has eternal life, and does not come into judgment, but has passed out of death into life" (John 5:24).

The Holy Spirit had used this verse three years earlier to bring me to the assurance of salvation as a gift of God solely through faith in the Lord Jesus Christ. It had meant everything to me before. It meant nothing to me now. It contained only words. They were words that to me were without the power they had before. I was lost! There was no hope for me! I was going to hell!

I prayed. My roommate, a strong believer, prayed for me. Nothing helped. I felt I was slipping deeper and deeper into a pit of darkness. It was a pit of fear, anxiety, and sheer terror.

While I knew it was from the Devil, that did not change matters. I could not resist him. I could not find the faith or strength to counterattack. I tried to use "the sword of the Spirit which is the Word of God," but it seemed that the sword was dull and that the Spirit had abandoned me.

I cried out to God, but He did not seem to hear me nor answer me. He hid Himself from me. My despair did not begin one early morning and end that night. It continued day and night for a week. I became so sick and afraid, I could neither get out of bed nor go to my classes. I was convinced I was going to hell. I was terrified. My godly roommate sent word to the various prayer groups which met on campus. They faithfully prayed for me, but nothing helped. In fact, I became worse.

In the providence of God, the semester day of prayer came at the end of that week. Although attendance was compulsory, I did not attend. I was too afraid. As I lay in bed, I suddenly felt compelled to get up and go to one of the rooms where the men students would be praying. I was convinced that if God was going to deliver me it would probably be there, with them in prayer.

As I entered the room I was still afraid. The men were standing up one by one, leading out in prayer. I had never prayed out loud in a public meeting before. However, before I knew it I was on my feet, praying with all my soul. I cried out unashamedly to the Lord. I reminded Him I was His child. I loved Him and wanted Him to fill my life with His love and peace and to take away all fears. I spoke back to Him His promises of eternal life in His Son.

On and on I prayed, afraid, yet determined to be free from my fears. The more I prayed back to God His promises of life and peace in His Son, the greater became my conviction that He was hearing me and was going to answer. Peace slowly began to flood my soul. The darkness slowly receded. Finally all became light. The darkness was totally gone. I knew God had heard and restored unto me the joy of my salvation (Ps. 51:12).

God the Sovereign Provider

Sometime after this terrible experience I was listening to an evangelist pleading with people to come to Christ. His message was what I now call a "God the servant" message. One of my friends who was with me called it "rose bed" theology: Come to Christ and life will become a bed of roses. I remember remarking, "The only problem with roses are the thorns."

This is not to say that God is not the provider. One of His names is *Jehovah Jireh*. It means "the Lord, our Provider" or "the Lord will provide." He is our helper, our deliverer, our healer; but He is God, and He is not our servant. In His wisdom and sovereignty, He does not always provide as we expect provision to be. He does not always help as we understand help to be. He does not always deliver as we suppose deliverance to be. He does not always heal as we believe healing to be.

We read Hebrews 11:4–35a, which gives the account of those who were provided for, helped, delivered, healed, even raised from the dead. This is "the good news" from a totally human perspective. The "bad news" from the same perspective occurs in verses 35b–40. This is the account of those who were not provided for, not helped, not delivered, not healed. The dividing words between the two groups are found in verse 35b, "and others were . . . ."

The Barriers of Ignorance, Wrong Choices, and Blindness

The third observation as to why so many believers do not live the normal Christian life is quite different. Many are truly interested but are facing problems in their life about which they themselves are baffled and confused. Millions of Christians want to follow Christ with all their heart. They truly love the Lord Jesus and want to obey Him. They seem to be stymied in their Christian life, however, and they do not know why. It has nothing to do with sincerity. They could not be more sincere.

Recently I had the privilege of participating in a Bible study for Christian leaders led by Dr. Bill Lawrence, Associate Professor of Pastoral Studies of Dallas Theological Seminary. Bill was speaking on "Adequacy and Inadequacy in the

Christian Life."[5] His message was partly autobiographical. Bill told of his own struggles in learning how to live the normal Christian life. He said,

"I tried to live the Christian life for years. I read God's Word where it said we are to be obedient, and I tried to be obedient. I saw we are to have faith, and I tried to have faith. I read that we are to submit to the lordship of Christ, and I tried to submit to His lordship. I was taught that all I had to do was learn His commands in His Word and choose to do them, and I would be able to do them. I tried it, but I was totally inadequate.

"The result? A big cover-up. I did not want people to really know me, so I built walls around my life to keep people away. I worked hard at appearing as a victorious Christian, especially as a pastor. I tried to prove to everyone my great value to God. I did not know that the Lord was setting me up so I could fail."

Using the story of the feeding of the 5,000 in Luke 9:12–17, Bill developed his theme showing how this entire incident was "set up" by Jesus to teach His disciples their inadequacy and His adequacy to make them what He wanted them to be.

"We are all like water polo players," Bill said. "We live all the time in the deep end of the pool with no time outs allowed. We are to learn that we are never adequate to feed the multitudes.

"We are given an impossible responsibility with totally inadequate resources facing overwhelming problems, all in the context of spiritual warfare. Therefore our ministry is always a supernatural ministry.

"Jesus follows the 'bless and break' principle in our lives as He did with the loaves and fishes (Luke 9:16). The disciples were first told to do what they could do with the resources they had, verses 13b–15. They obeyed. Next Jesus took what they had and blessed it, verse 16a.

"He will take the gifts and experiences we already have and bless them. We are to bless Him for what He has given us," Bill said. Then he admonished us, "Don't play the comparison game. Don't say 'I wish I were somebody else' or 'I had what others have.' This is an identity crisis. God has made each of us a new man in Christ. He will work through each of us.

"We all have three things. We have strengths, limitations, and flaws. He will bless and multiply the gifts and experiences He has given. These are our strengths. God also gave us our limitations. They are sovereignly defined limitations. To know my limitations is as important as knowing my strengths. My flaws are the weakness of the flesh. These are the areas in my life where I need to grow."

I was greatly interested in his reference to flaws, because I was working on this chapter at the time of the Bible study. When asked the source of the flaws, Bill replied that there are three: ignorance, wrong choices, and blindness.

Often believers are *ignorant of who they are in Christ*.[6] When we know who we are in Christ we begin to truly trust the Lord. Also, we are then free to take risks for God, even to fail and to learn through our failures.

Making wrong choices is wilful disobedience to the Word of God.

Finally, *blindness is failure to recognize our own weaknesses*. Much comes out of how we were raised both in our homes and in our churches. We fail to recognize the reality of the sin which is in our life, that is, how marred we really are. We build our life on flawed foundations.

In talking about the way out of our blindness, Bill shared three suggestions: "One, we are to walk in the Spirit of God. Two, we are to be open to the Word of God. Three, we are to be open to the help and admonition of others."

As Bill affirmed, in most teaching about the normal Christian life, the ideal is strongly presented. We are told what type of life we are to live. The believer is then told to submit to the lordship of Christ and strive to follow the biblical model.

The problem, however, is this: The normal Christian life is more than a question of human resolve. It is more than an issue of correct attitude. It is even more than an issue of submission to God and the lordship of Christ. The missing element in much teaching about the normal Christian life is the full biblical dimension of spiritual warfare. Part of that dimension includes our dealing realistically with the very real difficulties of everyday life.

BEARING THE BRUISES OF BATTLE

The Christian life is full of apparent contradictions. We are told that the way to rest in God is to be totally submitted to His will (Rom. 12:1–2). Yet the believer who does so immediately discovers that he is at war. From within, from without, and from above he is harassed, resisted, afflicted, tormented, tripped up, sabotaged, and too often, defeated.

When this happens over a long period of time, even though we are told not to grow "weary in well doing" (Gal. 6:9 NKJV), we do grow weary. We become discouraged. We begin to suffer battle fatigue. We become critical, bitter, even cynical, and too often deliberately sinful.

Dealing With Failure

Peter E. Gilquist's helpful article "Spiritual Warfare: Bearing the Bruises of the Battle" touches on this area.[7] He says, "The successful Christian life must have built into it a certain expectation of failure."

Our pride says, "No! Others fail, yes! But not me." But truth and reality say, "Yes, even me." We are too proud to admit to or accept any failure in our personal life, our families, or our ministry.

I was participating in a men's retreat several years ago, sharing the teaching sessions with another brother, a good friend of mine. In the course of his teaching on the family, he used the illustration of one of his teenaged children. He said, "If there ever was a perfect daughter, my Mary is that girl." His words went through me like a knife. I had been suffering for weeks trying to counsel one of my teenage children. While a good youngster, he was anything but perfect. I felt that his struggles reflected on me as a father and a Christian leader. Guilt for neglecting my son because of my erratic schedule made me squirm.[8]

I also was concerned for another close friend who was present for the conference. He and his wife were two of the most loving, kind, godly, and consistent Christian parents I had ever known. Their daughter graduated from college, married, and had an ideal Christian home. The boy, however, got into trouble in college, going from one tragedy to another. At the time he was living anything but a victorious Christian life. He was an alcoholic.

What was my brother feeling inside on hearing my fellow speaker continue on, talking about his "perfect" child? I could not bear to ask him.

Our churches are filled with hurting people. Many of them, like my friend referred to above, are heart-broken parents who have seen one or more of their children walk away from the Lord, the church, and even from a stable moral life in youth or later in adulthood. Every time someone else gives testimony of how their children all walk with God, quoting Proverbs 22:6, "Train up a child in the way he should go. Even when he is old he will not depart from it," they die a little more inside. Their sense of failure becomes almost unbearable.

"Where did we go wrong?" they ask themselves. "We must have failed as parents. There must be sin in our life. Why is that promise true of everybody else, but not of us?"

Such hurting people are often so ashamed they dare not talk to anyone about their problem. They often think they are the only ones suffering such guilt and sense of failure. If they only knew the truth, they would find they are not alone in their agony.

Seldom or never do the brethren who boast of their success as parents, claiming this verse, ask themselves who it was who wrote these words. It was Solomon. What happened when Solomon himself became "old"? The Bible tells us in no uncertain terms.

> Now King Solomon loved many foreign women along with the daughter of Pharaoh: Moabite, Ammonite, Edomite, Sidonian, and Hittite women . . . For it came about when Solomon was old, his wives turned his heart away after other gods; and his heart was not wholly devoted to the LORD his God, as the heart of David his father had been. (1 Kings 11:1,4)

Was his departure from God and a moral life the fault of David his father or Bathsheba his mother? While they had their own guilt before God, the Lord never pointed his finger at their failures as the cause of Solomon's failure. Solomon alone (with the Devil) was to blame, and only he was punished for his sins.

David is always held up by God as the ideal man of God and godly ruler. Remember 1 Kings 15:5 declares, "David did what was right in the sight of the LORD, and had not turned aside from anything that He commanded him all the days of his life, except in the case of Uriah the Hittite."

Yet the sin of Solomon, David's most outstanding son, the man chosen by God himself to sit on David's throne, the one to whom "the Lord, the God of Israel, had appeared twice" (1 Kings 11:9), had consequences so devastating for Israel it would be difficult to exaggerate its affects.

Perspective on Parental Responsibility

Furthermore, if the godliness and consistency of parents is to be measured primarily by the lifestyle of their children, God Himself is the greatest failure as a father. Adam was His son (Luke 3:38). Yet that son rebelled against Him, dragging the entire human race to the brink of hell with him.

God later called Israel to be His son (Hosea 11:1). Read the laments of the Father God over the waywardness of His rebellious sons (vv. 2–12). They remind me of God's later lament for Israel in Isaiah 1:2–4:

> Listen, O heavens, and hear, O earth; For the LORD speaks, "Sons I have reared and brought up, But they have revolted against Me. An ox knows its owner, And a donkey its master's manger, But Israel does not know, My people do not understand." Alas, sinful nation, People weighed down with iniquity, Offspring of evildoers, Sons who act corruptly! They have abandoned the LORD, They have despised the Holy One of Israel, They have turned away from Him.

I believe Proverbs 22:6 is the expression of a general principle. As we teach our children the way to walk, they may have their ups and downs, but they will *usually* return to God's ways. This is what has occurred with my four children, including the son already mentioned. But it does not always happen that way.

When children raised in a godly, happy Christian home rebel and turn away from the Lord, Proverbs 22:6 is *not* the verse those heartbroken parents need. They need verses of encouragement, promises they can claim, examples they can follow. I myself have followed Job's practice (Job 1:4–5). I claim promises for my children and grandchildren like Isaiah 43:25; 44:3–5,21–23; 55:2–3; 59:21 and others. Each can make his own promise list as God speaks by His Spirit to his heart.

For those whose children or other loved ones have already died apparently in rebellion against the Lord, we can rest in Genesis 18:25b, "Shall not the Judge of all the earth deal justly?"

Another dimension of bruising in battle must be mentioned. An increasing number of once-model Christian homes are being shaken, some destroyed by infidelity, divorce, incest, and other forms of child abuse. To whom do the innocent turn for help? To whom do the guilty come when they repent and return to the Lord? Will they be able to find a home among all the "successful Christians" who hide their own sinfulness and failures?

Gilquist writes, "May the Lord give us victory over the belief that we always have to be victorious." *We will eventually win the war, but we will not win every battle.* If this were not so then the war would not be a true war. But it is. Though the ferocity of the war waxes and wanes, it never ends while we live in "this body of sin." Believers must be taught the ways of spiritual warfare as soon as they enter God's family.

SPIRITUAL WARFARE IN THE BELIEVER'S SANCTIFICATION

The last major point I want to address in this chapter can hardly be overemphasized. For the unbeliever, spiritual warfare is a salvation issue. The god of this world blinds the minds of all unbelievers "that they might not see the light of the gospel of the glory of Christ, who is the image of God" (2 Cor. 4:4).

This is not true of the believer, however. For the child of God spiritual warfare is not a salvation issue, but a sanctification issue.

The Believer's Salvation Is Secure

Our salvation is already secured by the grace of God and the blood of the cross. The believer's salvation has its origin exclusively in the sovereign operation of divine grace entered into solely by faith (Eph. 1:3–14; 2:1–22). When it comes to that salvation the stress in Scripture falls upon:

1. The sovereign election of God (Eph. 1:3–12; 2:10).[9] Regardless of how we define election, we are the elect of God, period.

2. The grace of God (Eph. 1:6–7; 2:5–9).

3. The love of God (Eph. 1:4–5; 2:4).

4. The mercy of God (Eph. 1:5,9; 2:4).

5. The substitutionary, propitiatory, redemptive death of the Lord Jesus Christ for our sins, that is, His precious blood shed on the cross for our sins (Acts 20:28; Rom. 3:23–25a; 5:9).[10]

6. The regenerating ministry of His Holy Spirit, that is, the new birth produced by the indwelling Spirit of God (John 3:3–8; Rom. 8:1–4,9,15).[11]

7. The intercessory ministry of the Spirit of God within us and that of the glorified Son of God at the right hand of God on our behalf (Rom. 8:26–27; 8:34; Heb. 7:25; 9:24).

Thus the strong note of assurance of salvation, eternal redemption, eternal life, "the life of the age to come" in the New Testament. This life is provided for every believer regardless of his maturity or immaturity in Christ (Eph. 1:4–8a,13–14; Phil. 1:6).

The Bitter Fruit of Insecurity Regarding One's Salvation

The failure to enter into the rest of the assurance of salvation leads to havoc in the Christian's life. The writer of Hebrews felt so strongly about this that he wrote, "Therefore leaving the elementary teaching about the Christ, let us press on to maturity, not laying again a foundation of repentance from dead works and of faith toward God, of instruction about washings, and laying on of hands, and the resurrection of the dead, and eternal judgment. And this we shall do, if God permits" (Heb. 6:1–3).

I was once teaching a series on spiritual warfare in a large church in a major U.S. city. The Sunday morning church services were televised, and a telephone counseling service operated during and after the televised service. Among the phone calls was one from the wife of a former pastor. The lady and her husband were desperate for help and asked if I could counsel them. While it had been announced that I was not available for counseling, because this case pertained to needy Christian leaders and I was remaining in the area for a few days, I agreed to see them.

Accompanied by mature lay leaders from the church so the couple could have further counseling when needed, I met with them. The wife came from a dysfunctional family. She grew up with a bad self-image. She became a perfectionist, always trying to excel, but never reaching her expectations. She had severe sexual problems. She loved her husband and was faithful to him, yet she was never satisfied with their intimate relationship. She took the initiative in leading her husband into unwholesome sexual practices, and her husband, who loved her very much, went along with anything she suggested. Nothing worked, however. Her sense of unworthiness and guilt only increased.

Nor could she find rest in her relationship with God. Nothing she did pleased Him. She felt He was always angry with her and never accepted her, even though she continually sought ways to please Him. As a result, she and her husband became "church hoppers," looking for some type of spiritual experience which would satisfy her spiritual longing.

Finally, they found a church which seemed to meet her needs. She did have a dramatic experience with the Holy Spirit, which she had been told would transform her life and give her personal peace and power to live for God. To some degree it did—for a while.

Unfortunately, this church was strong on a "guilt," "unworthiness," "I am a worm" (Ps. 22:6) concept of the Christian life. Exposure of sin was central in its message. Believers were made continually aware of their sinfulness and unworthiness. When they confessed their sins they were to receive Christ all over again as sin separated them from God. The last part of each Sunday evening service was dedicated to encouraging believers to repent of their sins and come back to the Lord. Those who did were asked to give public testimony to what God was doing in their lives. The testimonies always seemed to focus on loss of salvation through sin and spiritual rebirth when sin was confessed and forsaken and Christ was newly received.

The troubled woman had always struggled with the assurance of salvation. Witnessing these testimonies only increased her sense of guilt and unworthiness. She lost what assurance of salvation she already had. She sought counseling, but her counselors could not help her. She became desperate. Her husband also became desperate. He did not know how to help her.

Spiritual Warfare and Achieving Spiritual Wholeness

As they listened to the television message that Sunday morning, a whole new dimension of the Christian life was opened to them. While they always believed in Satan and demons, they had little practical insight into spiritual warfare. They wondered if evil supernaturalism was involved in her problems and requested a counseling session with me.

The difficulties this woman was facing were not necessarily demonic. Probably in most such cases demons, even if they are present, are not the principle problem. And even if demons are involved, their expulsion does not necessarily cure the problem.[12] This case, however, involved direct demonic activity in at least three areas of her life: her poor self-image which began when she was an only child, brought up in a dysfunctional home; her inability to rest in God's promise of salvation; and her sexual malfunctions.

The counseling she had received was not effective for several reasons. The counselor was not trained well enough to help complex cases like hers. The counseling had not been going on long enough. After a few sessions the woman became discouraged and did not return. Finally, the demonic dimension had not even been considered. No one suspected that demons were involved in her problem, directly or indirectly.

The point at which her problems became so intensified she could no longer function satisfactorily as a person and a Christian focused around her complete loss of the assurance of her salvation. While she had battled for years over this issue, she had been able to muster up enough faith and continue functioning as a believer. The church culture into which she had recently moved had only served to make her situation critical.[13]

As we counseled her, many dimensions of her early bruising came to light, and her damaged sexual life began to come into focus. At this point the first group of demons surfaced. They left her one by one or in groups without much difficulty. In spite of her up-and-down Christian life, she truly loved the Lord and had a strong desire to walk in holiness and healing.

It was not long before the story of her loss of all assurance of salvation came to the forefront. Most of our counseling then focused on helping her know who she was in Christ. After helping to free her from demonic oppression and after many hours of counseling, she and her husband went away with a sense of assurance and guidelines for further counseling.

To enter into victory in spiritual warfare, the believer must rest in the fact that his salvation is totally of God. The believer's part is repentance for sin and faith in the Lord Jesus Christ as Savior and Lord (Acts 20:21). The one who exercises such faith is secure in Christ, be he a strong Christian or a weak Christian.

Spiritual Warfare Ministry to Believers
Builds on the Assurance of Salvation

Spiritual warfare for the believer belongs exclusively to the arena of sanctification, not at all to the arena of salvation.[14] Before we come to Christ, it is a salvation issue. After we come to him, it becomes a sanctification issue. *Satan knows he cannot take us to hell with him once we come to Christ. He does seek to disturb our Christian life so we do not live as true children of God.*

On one occasion I was ministering to a demonically afflicted Christian. The demons had been telling their victim in his mind that he was not a true believer, that God had abandoned him, and that he was going to hell. While I was trying to help him accept himself in Christ as a redeemed child of God, a demonic voice yelled through his lips, "He is not a Christian. He belongs to us. He is not going to heaven. He is going to hell with us. Let him alone. He is ours."

I shut off his lies. I decided to allow him to speak out loud just long enough to force him to tell the truth for the benefit of some of the bewildered believers who were with me in the session. Within a matter of a few minutes the demon confessed he was lying. Some of what it spoke is worth noting.

"Is he a true believer?" I asked.

"Yes," the demon replied. "He loves your Jesus just like you do."

"Why did you lie to him about his salvation?" I asked. "It's our nature to lie," it replied. "We did not want him to know that he is really a believer. That way we can mess up his life."

"You cannot take him to hell with you as you have been telling him," I said. "He has been cleansed from all sin by the blood of Christ and he is going to heaven, isn't that true?"

"Yes! Yes! We know it! We know it! We know he is going to heaven. We know we can't take him to hell, but we want to make his life a hell on earth," the evil spirit replied.

Thus the importance of the assurance of our eternal salvation. *We must understand once and for all that:*

1. *A Christian is still a Christian even if he is struggling with a serious sin problem in his life* (1 Cor. 5:1–5; 11:30–32; 1 John 2:1–2);

2. *A Christian is still a Christian even if he is struggling with a serious "world" problem in his life* (2 Tim. 4:10); and

3. *A Christian is still a Christian even if he is struggling with a serious demonic problem in his life* (Acts 5:1–10; 1 Tim. 5:9–15).

A hurting believer wrote me: "I am a conservative evangelical who has realized he has demonic problems. I've shared my problems with some of my conservative evangelical friends and they have cut off fellowship with me. They claim that Christians can't have demons. . . . Therefore I must not be a Christian. They were actually fearful of me. The rejection was very hurtful. Now I know it was partly Satan's influence that caused them to reject me."

The denial that true believers can have severe demonic problems can have devastating consequences on hurting believers. Any doctrine that undermines the faith and assurance of salvation of born-again believers must be rejected. Again I repeat: *A Christian is still a Christian even if he is struggling with a serious demonic problem in his life.*

A believer may be walking in the Spirit in most areas of his life and at the same time be defeated in one or more other areas of his life. That was the situation with many of the believers at Corinth and Philippi in Paul's day, according to the apostle's own words in 1 Corinthians 1:4–13 and 3:1–4 and Philippians 1:12–18 and 2:19–21.

Any Christian counselor or pastor who does any serious counseling knows this to be true. *The last thing one should do to weak believers is call into question their salvation in Christ.* Only on the basis of their relationship to Christ is there any hope of their victory over the evil spirits afflicting their life.

Finally, it is important to understand that spiritual warfare is a multidimensional sin issue that plagues all believers. As Christian soldiers, we continually combat evil on three fronts: the flesh, the world, and the Devil. It is time now to examine these battle lines in more detail.

13

What Is Happening to Me?
A Multidimensional Sin War

For as long as I can remember I have had a deep longing to know God. I knew a lot about Him, but I did not know Him personally. Unfortunately my Catholic church was weak at this point. It taught us about God. We learned about Christ. We followed the Stations of the Cross as they were marked out in the sculptured reliefs along each side of the church. This helped to engrave in our mind and emotions the steps of Jesus as He carried His cross through the narrow streets of Jerusalem to Calvary.

He did this for us. I loved Him for it. But how could I come to know Jesus personally? Unfortunately the priests and nuns who taught me didn't know either, or didn't know how to help me find Him. I wanted Him to become my personal Savior.

When I finally came to know Him personally, I was elated. Now He was mine. I was His.

I had always lived a "good" religious life. I had kept apart from "sinful" people. I did not shun them, but I refused to participate in their sinful ways. Everyone who knew me knew me as a good Catholic boy who did not "smoke, drink, cuss or chew, nor go out with girls who do," as someone has said.

Now that Jesus lived within me, I wanted Him to really live within me. I wanted to live a holy life. I read Saint Thomas à Kempis' classic book, *The Imitation of Christ*. Next to the Bible, it was my favorite devotional reading. I would do okay for awhile. Then before I knew it, imaginations towards things not pleasing to God would arise within me.

Then there was the world around me. Fortunately pornography was not in wide use when I was a teenager. How much compassion I feel for today's youth! They are forced to live in a world saturated with pornography. We adults have created a world whose sole purpose seems to be to stimulate everyone sexually, from kids to adults, everywhere, all the time. Then we wonder why kids get into trouble.

While not as flagrant in my little rural town, it was still there. The stimulus towards sin and self continually came against my mind from "the world." I tried to fight it off, but the struggle persisted.

There were also times when I seemed to be tripped up by supernatural forces stimulating me towards evil. At times they seemed to be stronger than God. I knew this was the Devil, but I didn't know how to fight him.

"Why, since God is my Father, Jesus is my Savior, and the Holy Spirit lives in me, can't I overcome sin?" I asked.

I didn't know at that time that we are at war. I didn't know what I now know, that *it is a multidimensional sin war.*

With this personal testimony, we begin a new section of our spiritual warfare studies. All we will be studying, however, rests upon the philosophical-theological foundations laid in prior chapters.

Past chapters stressed sin's origin in evil supernaturalism. Sin originated in the direct deceptive activity of Satan himself against God's angels, humanity, and especially the children of God. I did not know it at the time, but that is what was happening to me as a teenaged new believer.

We also have seen that sin has its source in the flesh and in the world. Sin arises from any one of these three sources or any combination of the three at the same time. That is what was happening to me, but I didn't know it.

THE HISTORICAL PERSPECTIVE OF THE CHURCH

Historically the church has seen the believer's sin war from this perspective. The believer's warfare with the flesh, the world, and the Devil has been recognized, written about, and preached from the pulpits of our churches for centuries. Why do I give such importance to this almost universally accepted fact?

First, because it is foundational to what we call sanctification, i.e., the process by which we learn to live as God's children in this sinful world. Paul writes to the Philippian believers about sanctification:

> Do all things without grumbling or disputing; that you may prove yourselves to be blameless and innocent children of God above reproach in the midst of a crooked and perverse generation, among whom you appear as lights in the world, holding fast the word of life . . ." (Phil. 2:14–16a)

Living as the apostle exhorts us is not easy. A kingdom-of-God lifestyle while living in the kingdom of Satan (the world) means spiritual warfare. Many believers become so discouraged (as I did) as they wrestle with the evil within them (the flesh), the evil that seeks to seduce them from without (the world), and the supernatural evil that assaults their minds from above (evil supernaturalism), that they begin to doubt their salvation. I did on occasion.

Sanctification Not Salvation

Second, as was mentioned in our last chapter, it is imperative that believers recognize the sin war in which they are engaged has nothing to do with salvation, only with sanctification.

The diagram on page 101 is an attempt to visualize this fact. At the top of the diagram we see the on-going conflict in the believer's mind with doubts, evil thoughts, desires for independence from a kingdom lifestyle, pride, lusts, materialism, fears, and various temptations. They have nothing to do with salvation. They are sanctification issues. They are in-house matters. They have to do with the child of God and his loving, heavenly Father who knows our every weakness. As the Psalmist wrote so long ago,

> Just as a father has compassion on his children,
> So the Lord has compassion on those who fear Him.
> For He Himself knows our frame;
> He is mindful that we are but dust. (Ps. 103:13–14)

Thus my title for the diagram: "The Christian's Warfare: A Multidimensional Sin Issue Relating to Christian Living."

At the bottom of the diagram is a visual representation of the theme of this chapter, indeed, of the entire book. Sin is personal; it comes from within, thus warfare with the flesh. Sin is social; it comes from without, thus warfare with the world. Sin is supernatural; it comes from above, thus warfare with evil supernaturalism.

Third, though the doctrinal fact of this multidimensional sin war is well known, its implications to the believer's struggles with sin are usually not dealt with in a systematic and holistic biblical manner. This I am attempting to do in this book.

Fourth, this multidimensional sin war is seldom dealt with from the perspective of a biblical world view. I have repeatedly affirmed the spiritual warfare dimension of a biblical world view. Spiritual warfare provides the all encompassing context in which God's self-revelation and redemptive activity is carried out and our Christian life is lived.

Figure 13.1
The Christian's Warfare:
A Multidimensional Sin Issue Relating to Christian Living

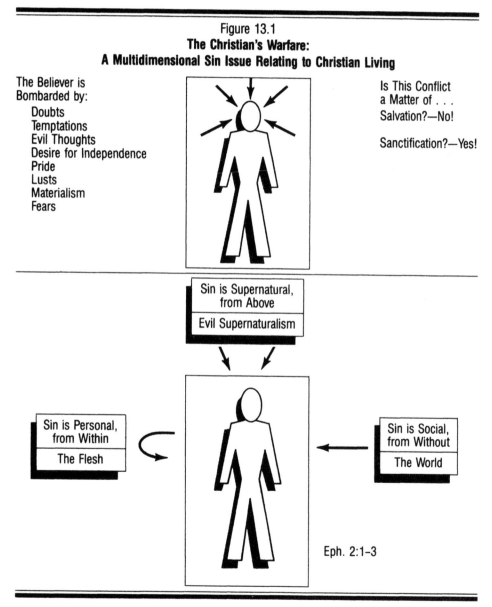

The Believer is
Bombarded by:
  Doubts
  Temptations
  Evil Thoughts
  Desire for Independence
  Pride
  Lusts
  Materialism
  Fears

Is This Conflict
a Matter of . . .
Salvation?—No!

Sanctification?—Yes!

Sin is Supernatural,
from Above

Evil Supernaturalism

Sin is Personal,
from Within

The Flesh

Sin is Social,
from Without

The World

Eph. 2:1-3

Warfare Between the Two Kingdoms

When I refer to spiritual warfare from this world view context I usually mean spiritual warfare in its original, more restricted sense as warfare between the kingdom of God and the kingdom of the Devil, not in its broader sense of the multidimensional sin war. We must realize this broader dimension exists only because spiritual warfare was first born in the cosmic realm.

For example, looking at the Genesis story of the pre-Fall lifestyle of our first parents, it is questionable whether or not Adam and Eve would have rebelled against the Word of God without the external deception of the serpent.

They were not plagued by the flesh. They were totally innocent of any internal stimulation towards sin. They did not live in the world. They lived in the paradise of God. They were evidently vulnerable only to the external deception to sin coming from above, from the Devil.

From the Fall until today, God's self-revelation and His redemptive activity occur in this spiritual warfare context. In what sense? Spiritual warfare in its broader or more narrow meaning? Both, but the primary focus must be on the narrower definition of warfare between the two kingdoms. After all, the other two (warfare with the flesh and the world) originated out of the warfare of the kingdom of Satan against the kingdom of God. Satan's deception gave birth to both the flesh and the world. He murdered the human race through deception (John 8:44; Gen. 2:15–17; 3:1f). He established himself as the god, the ruler of this world (John 12:31; 14:30; 16:11; 2 Cor. 4:3–4).

That warfare between the two kingdoms will continue until the eternal destruction of personal supernatural evil in the lake of fire (Rev. 20). Then and then only will evil be abolished from the experience of the children of God, forever. What a day that will be!

THE NEED FOR BALANCE

Since the words *spiritual warfare* automatically register in the minds of Christians in the narrower sense of warfare with Satan and his evil spirits, it is easy for us to drift into imbalance at this point. Traditionally, the church has dealt with the believer's sin problem primarily from the perspective of internal evil, the flesh. Some attention has also been given to the external evil, the world. Satan and his demons have been given some attention; yet since the church's world view traditionally has been fuzzy about the extent to which demons can partially control believers, this area of sanctification has not been developed to the extent of the first two, the flesh and the world.

We are now witnessing a deluge of literature on warfare with evil supernaturalism, however. The danger now is that we go to the other extreme of demonizing all sin in the believer's life. Satan and his demons thus become the primary source of humanity's present sin problem to such an extent that insufficient emphasis is given to the flesh and the world.

For these and other reasons it is crucial at this point to look at spiritual warfare as a multidimensional sin war. In future chapters I will examine the three dimensions separately.

Finally, the emphasis of the latter part of the book will be primarily upon the believer's warfare with evil supernaturalism, though the flesh and the world will always be considered. The usual channels of Satan's seductions of mankind, including believers, is through the flesh and the world.

WHICH IS WHICH?

While it is helpful to see our sin problem from three dimensions, it also is problematic. Sin is too dynamic (in the negative sense) to be compartmentalized. Sin energy is released against humanity from every dimension, continually. Thus, while concentrating on one of sin's dimensions, we must remember the other two are also active in every situation. Since the Fall, sin is multidimensional, never unidimensional.

If the stimulation towards sin comes from the flesh, it will immediately be reinforced by the world. Sin energy will also assault us from evil spirits reinforcing the evil arising from the flesh and the world. But if the stimulus towards sin comes from the world, the flesh will immediately respond. At the same time demonic powers will seek to influence our mind, emotions, and will to follow the evil allurements of the world. And if the sin energy bombarding us comes directly from evil supernaturalism, the flesh will favorably respond. The world will reinforce that response. All three dimensions are always active at the same time.

Often when I counsel Christians, they will express their confusion over this issue: "Does my problem come from the flesh, the world, or the Devil?" My answer is always, "Yes." I then explain that, according to Scripture, the major source of their problem may be one of the three in one situation and one or both of the other two in different situations. In every case all three dimensions should be dealt with even though the major emphasis may only be on one of the three levels presently causing the greatest problem.

We have already stated that the major sin focus of Scripture is on the flesh. It is interesting to note, however, in Ephesians 2:1–3 Paul ties man's flesh problem with the multidimensional sin problem we face. He writes,

> And you were dead in your trespasses and sins, in which you formerly walked according to the course of this world, according to the prince of the power of the air, of the spirit that is now working in the sons of disobedience. Among them we too all formerly lived in the lusts of our flesh, indulging the desires of the flesh and of the mind, and were by nature children of wrath, even as the rest." (Eph. 2:1–2)

The apostle begins with the affirmation that when we "were dead in your [our] trespasses and sins" (v. 1). Paul next reveals a threefold source of this sad spiritual state: the world (v. 2a), the Devil (v. 2b), and the flesh (v. 3a). Again, we fight a multidimensional sin war!

SATAN, THE PRIMARY SOURCE

Ultimately, as the late Donald Grey Barnhouse writes, Satan is the primary source of man's terrible sin problem. He writes of Satan's strategy of seduction with sin. Satan is "the author of confusion and lies," he says. He "has done one of his most effective bits of mystification in creating bewilderment even among many Christians, concerning his methods of attack." Barnhouse says "they are threefold. We do not know what student of the Word of God first coined the phrase, 'the world, the flesh and the devil,'" he says. "The oldest usage of this triple division of the field of attack is to be found in *The Book of Common Prayer* in a prayer for an infant, 'Grant that he may have power and strength to have victory, and to triumph, against the devil, the world and the flesh.'"[1]

C. Fred Dickason says the same thing: "The demonic use of the flesh and the world is obvious. Satan rules the world system and influences the flesh, his toehold in men's heart, to accomplish his rebellious and destructive purposes."[2]

D. Martyn Lloyd-Jones has written an amazing seven volume study on the *Epistle of Paul to the Ephesians*.[3] In volume 1 he comments on the power emphasis of Ephesians 1:19. He asks, "Why is this power essential?"

He answers, "Because of the power of the forces that are set against us." He continues with a lengthy discussion of the demon sin energy (my term) released against us directly by Satan and his demons and also indirectly through the world and the flesh.[4]

Of the world he says, "Nothing is so dangerous to the soul, because of its subtlety, as the worldliness which meets us on every turn. . . . This is surely the biggest fight the Christian church has to wage at the present hour. . . . But we not only have to fight the world but also the flesh." He then lists some of the sins of the flesh. Lloyd-Jones then comments, "Then there is the devil. I sometimes think that our failure to realize the greatness of God's power in us is due to the fact we have never realized the power of the devil. How little do we talk about him; and yet in the New Testament his activities are constantly emphasized. . . . the power of the devil is made terribly clear in the story of Adam and Eve. They are both perfect. Man was made in the image and likeness of God. . . . He was in Paradise—a perfect environment. He had never sinned, and there was nothing within him to drag him down—no lust, no corruption. . . . And yet he fell; and he did so because of the power and the subtlety of the devil." He then states that "nothing can enable us to stand against the wiles of the devil" but the power of God.

In closing this chapter on the believer's multidimensional sin war, I refer again to Ray Stedman's excellent book on spiritual warfare.[5] His first chapter is called "The Forces We Face." After reviewing Ephesians 6:10–13 he says it is clear that Paul's view of "the basic characteristics of life can be put in one word, struggles. Life," he says, "is a conflict, a combat, a continual wrestling." He then affirms that this is confirmed by experience. "We would like to think of ourselves as living in an idealistic world, where everything goes right and we can spend our days in relaxation and enjoyment." He affirms, "The Apostle Paul is not dealing with that kind of life. He is coming to grips with life as it really is now, and he says life is a struggle, a conflict, a battle against opposing forces."

Stedman inquires about the real source behind this warfare life. He identifies the source as demonic (Eph. 6:12). Recognizing the traditional Christian way of viewing evil's source as from the flesh, the world, and the devil, Stedman makes an interesting remark about the relationship between the three. "We often hear the idea, 'The enemies of the Christian are the world, the flesh and the devil,' as though these were three equally powerful enemies. But there are not three. There is only one enemy, the devil, as Paul brings out in Ephesians 6. But the channels of his indirect approach to men are through the world and the flesh."[6]

To some this may seem like an exaggeration. Yet, is it? The author admits the role of both the flesh and the world in our battle with sin. Yet he also affirms that the one true enemy is the devil who uses the flesh and the world.

This is totally consistent with the cosmic origin of sin itself and the satanic origin of human sin (Gen. 3:1f). It is also consistent with the believer's daily war with sin (1 Cor. 7:5; 1 Thess. 3:5)

Neil Anderson says something similar when he writes that "Satan is at the heart of all sin (1 John 3:8). He deceives people into believing a lie and counsels them to rebel against God."[7]

He usually does so, of course, through the flesh and the world. With this background we will look at each dimension of sin separately while still recognizing their interrelationship. We will begin with the believer's warfare with the flesh.

The Believer's Warfare With the Flesh

14

The Flesh, the Believer, and the Demonic

Psychologist Rodger K. Bufford in his excellent book, *Counseling and the Demonic* recognizes that the sins of the flesh "provide an avenue into demonic influence."[1] The following case study illustrates that fact.

Sins of the Flesh: Doorways to the Demonic

I was new in spiritual warfare counseling when the following incident occurred. As often happens when we discover a new dimension of spiritual reality, we tend to go overboard. We see everything through the lens of that newly discovered reality. This has probably occurred with most of us who have undergone a major paradigm shift in reference to the demonic dimensions of spiritual warfare counseling and ministry. It did with me.

A woman came to see me. She was under the care of a Christian psychologist. He was not making much progress towards her healing. Not wanting to interfere with the counseling being given, I asked her psychologist if he would agree that I counsel her from a spiritual warfare perspective and let him continue with his regular counseling procedures. He agreed.

I was doing all my spiritual warfare counseling with a small team. One of the most effective co-workers I had was Tom, a young man who had been one of the most severely demonized persons I had ever ministered to in the past.

Tom and I, with another helper, spent several hours with the troubled woman but made no progress. We were not even sure she was demonized. I tried my usual proven "methodology" of making contact with any demons which might be present, but to no avail.

We arranged for another counseling session a few days later. I was not able to be present because of other responsibilities. Tom and other team members ministered to her.

They began to probe into her background and discovered she was raised in a dysfunctional family. She had experienced terrible conflict with her mother, brothers, and sisters. It soon became evident she was filled with bitterness, even deep hatred, for all of them, especially her mother.

The team soon realized that regardless of what demonic activity might be attached to her life, her primary problem was the flesh. Filled with anger, pride, bitterness, and lack of forgiveness, she refused even to consider the possibility that her attitude towards her mother was sinful.

She refused outright to obey the Word of God in James 4:1–3 and 3:14–16. The team finally had to tell her that if she was not willing to humble herself before God and at least be willing to learn to forgive, even though she could not emotionally "feel" a desire to do so at the present, they could not help her. She got up and left, saying she was not coming back.

"Dr. Murphy," Tom said, "We cannot expect any demons which may be attached to her life to leave her when they have every right to be there."

I learned an important lesson from my junior partner that day. Our failure to be able to help that bitter woman helped me get back to a more biblical balance.

For the purpose of emphasis and analysis (theology) it is helpful to examine separately the role of the flesh, the world, and the Devil. Yet we must remember that the Bible does not make such sharp distinctions. It simply teaches us that spiritual warfare is being waged against the totality of our humanity, both as individuals and as members of social groups, and we are to learn to be faithful and victorious soldiers of the kingdom of God against the kingdom of evil.

Bufford makes some interesting comments about the sin war faced by all believers, the interrelationship between the flesh, the world, and the Devil, and how the flesh can open a life to demonic influence. After warning us that living for the things of this world, "sex, power, wealth, status, fame, influence and popularity" can lead to potential demonization, he says that

> central to all sin is a failure to love God fully and to submit ourselves to His divine will and guidance for our lives. To fail to submit is to side with Satan in adopting the view that we know better than God, and hence will decide for ourselves how to live our lives. Choosing Satan's side in the cosmic struggle between good and evil places us at risk of coming under the control of his demonic agents.[2]

Satan is always involved in sin. So are demons. Where sin flows, demons flow. They thrive on sin. It is their very life. They are sin personified.

In this and the following chapters we are going to concentrate primarily on warfare with the flesh, however. Yet sin is so deceitful, demonic deception often so complete, and the evil emanating from the world so overpowering, that the three cannot really be compartmentalized as I am doing here. I do so only for the purpose of emphasis and analysis.

WHAT IS THE FLESH?

The word *flesh* is used in both the Old and New Testaments. Yet the New Testament usage has greater theological significance and represents a more detailed development in God's explanation of humanity's sin problem than we find in the Old Testament. It is all there in the Old Testament, but in the New it is explained in more detail. Writing on the use of the word "flesh" in the Old Testament, R. K. Harrison says:[3]

The Old Testament theology of human personality . . . is of a dynamic order which emphasizes the psycho-physical unity of human nature. Although this "flesh" was regarded in the Old Testament as generally weak, there is no single element in Hebrew thought which corresponds to the New Testament view of the "flesh" as the central principle of fallen humanity. While the flesh for the Hebrews was frail, it was not regarded as sinful.

In the same volume, W. A. Elwell writes on the use of the word flesh in the New Testament.[4]

There are three basic ways in which the word *sarx* (flesh) is used in the New Testament. At one extreme are those places where no negative moral judgment is implied and the word flesh bears no negative connotation at all. At the other extreme are those places where a negative moral judgment is made and *sarx* becomes descriptive of man's baser nature or is defined as being simply sinful. Bridging the two extremes is a set of uses where *sarx* is not sinful per se, but tends in that direction.

William Vine lists 13 different usages of *sarx,* all of which would fit under Elwell's threefold classification.[5] For an almost exhaustive historical study of the word *sarx* (flesh), nothing surpasses the work of Eduard Schweizer in Kittel's *Theological Dictionary of the New Testament (TDNT).* He presents the use of the word during six historical periods. For one who wants an in-depth, complex study his work is exceptional.[6] Schweizer's study of the varied uses of the word flesh in the New Testament agrees with Elwell's views. So we cite Elwell's briefer comments:[7]

The flesh becomes the baser side of man defining either the impulse to sin itself or at least the seat of it (Rom. 7:18,25; 8:5b,12–13; Gal. 5:17,19; 6:8; 1 Peter 3:21; 2 Peter 2:10,18; 1 John 2:16. . . . An extension of this correlation of sin and flesh is seen where *sarx* is sin (Jude 23), or where by extension the word fleshly becomes an adjective meaning sinful, and qualifies other ideas. Hence one may have a fleshly body (Col. 2:11) or a fleshly mind (Rom. 8:7; Col. 2:18). . . . In this connection it is significant that Paul nowhere says the flesh will be resurrected; for him it is the body that will be raised to newness of life (see, e.g., 1 Cor. 15:44). This is because *sarx* connoted sin to Paul and the word *body* was a more neutral term. The flesh, man's fallen nature, will not be raised again. . . . It must be remembered that the mind may generate desires that are sinful too (Eph. 2:3), and that there is uncleanness of the spirit, as well as of the flesh. (1 Cor. 7:1)

Ray Stedman defines the flesh used in a morally negative sense as "the urge to self-centeredness within us, that distortion of human nature which makes us want to be our own god—that proud ego, that uncrucified self which is the seat of willful defiance and rebellion against authority."[8]

My own definition of the flesh is our defective humanness inclined towards self-centeredness, with its center in our sinful bodies which includes our mind, emotions and will.

THE FLESH AND THE SIN NATURE

The flesh with which we daily battle is not the same as the old self which once controlled our life but is now permanently crucified with Christ (Gal. 2:20). Before coming to Christ our life was dominated by our sinful nature inherited from Adam. We were separated from God and spiritually dead. This was the "old man" or "old self."

Jesus took our old man-self with him to the Cross. It died with him there. The apostle Paul affirms, "Knowing this, that our old self was crucified with Him . . ."

(Rom. 6:6). Paul could thus exhort the Colossians, "Set your mind on the things above, not on the things that are on earth. For you have died and your life is hidden with Christ in God" (Col. 3:2–3).

The old self is dead. As believers we have a new self that results from the life of Christ who lives in us (Rom. 6:5–8; 8:9; 2 Cor. 4:7–11; Gal. 2:20; Col. 1:27; 3:1–4). This helps explain why the apostle John is so emphatic that true believers are no longer slaves to sin. We, as believers, no longer practice sin. Why not? Because we are born of God (1 John 3:4–19).

To be "of God" (1 John 5:19) and to be "born of God" (1 John 5:18) means that our new nature comes from God. God's nature abides in us. "His seed abides in [us]; and [we] cannot sin [practice sin, vv. 7–8], because [we are] born of God" (1 John 3:9).

The apostle Peter tells us that through faith in God's promise of salvation in His Son we are "partakers of the divine nature, having escaped the corruption that is in the world by lust" (2 Pet. 1:4b). The apostle Paul, besides teaching this truth in his epistles, gives his own personal testimony: "I have been crucified with Christ; and it is no longer I who live, but Christ who lives in me; and the life which I now live in the flesh I live by faith in the Son of God, who loved me, and delivered Himself up for me" (Gal. 2:20).

The old "I" (the old self, the natural man) was crucified with Christ, Paul says. A new "I" has taken its place. That "I" is Christ who now lives in me. Because Christ lives in me in the person of the Holy Spirit, God lives in me in the person of His Son and the Holy Spirit (John 17:21–23; 14:16–18; Rom. 8:1–17; 2 Cor. 13:5; Gal. 2:20; 4:6; Eph. 2:19–22; Col. 1:27; 2:6–12). Therefore I am no longer a slave to sin. My new nature "naturally responds to God."[9]

As a believer I no longer walk according to the flesh, but according to the Spirit (Rom. 8:4). I am no longer "in the flesh but in the Spirit" because the "Spirit of God," "the Spirit of Christ dwells in" me (Rom. 8:9).[10] This is true even if I am not aware of it. That is why Paul says that when I become aware of who I am in Christ, I am to accept the fact that I am dead to sin, but alive to God in Christ Jesus (Rom. 6:1). All this is true because of the redemptive work of Christ on my behalf.

Does this mean that the sin problem is solved for the true believer? Can we no longer sin nor not be tempted to sin? Of course not. This would be contrary to both Scripture and Christian experience. As a child of God I still live in an unredeemed body. Though the Lord Jesus has purchased my new body with His blood, I do not have it as yet. It will not be mine until the Resurrection at His glorious second coming (Phil. 3:20–21; Rom. 8:18–25).

Until then, as long as I live on this earth, I live in a body which Paul describes as "the body of sin" (Rom. 6:6); "the body of this death" (Rom. 7:24); a "mortal body" (Rom. 8:11). He says I am to learn how, by the Spirit, to put to death the sinful deeds of the body (Rom. 8:13).

So my sin problem continues as long as I am in this world in this body. But the apostle Paul informs us that we are now able to put to death the deeds of the flesh since our old self in Adam was crucified with Christ (Rom. 6:1–23). We can receive as ours Paul's exhortation to believers at Rome:

> Do not let sin reign in your mortal body that you should obey its lusts, and do not go on presenting the members of your body to sin as instruments of unrighteousness; but present yourself to God as those alive from the dead, and your members as instruments of righteousness to God. (Rom. 6:12–13)

When Paul speaks of the members of my body he obviously means more than my material body. He means my mind, my imagination, my emotions, my will, and my physical body. God wants all of me yielded to Him to do His will in my life (Rom. 6:12–23; 12:1–2). Since I live in my body, if God truly has my body, He has all of me.

Until the bondage to the flesh is broken, however, effective deliverance is not possible for demonized believers. Where it does occur, it will not usually be lasting. *The expulsion of one group of evil spirits from a human life will usually lead to the entry of another group if the sin in the life to which the former demonic spirits had attached themselves is not removed.* The believer must begin to put to death the works of the flesh to become victorious in the sin war which involves him. If not, he will soon become a war casualty.

15
Walking in the Spirit
Galatians 5

OLD SELF, NEW SELF, AND THE FLESH

How is it possible that the flesh still has such a strong pull on the believer's life? How can the Holy Spirit cohabit the same body with the unholy flesh? We have already seen the Scriptures teach that the true believer is no longer in the flesh but in the Spirit (Rom. 8:1–9). How then does the flesh continue to operate in the believer's life alongside the Spirit? This is just as much an apparent contradiction as the cohabitation of the Spirit with a demon in the believer's body.[1] How can all this be possible? Lloyd-Jones suggests that

> My old self, that self that was in Adam, was an utter slave to sin. That self has gone, I have a new self, I am a new man. . . . I am not doing this or that, it is this sin that remains in my members that does so. Sin is no longer in me [in my new self in Christ], it is in my members only. This is the most liberating thing you have ever heard.[2]

"This sin that remains in my members," to use Lloyd-Jones' term, is called "the flesh" by the apostle Paul in Galatians 5:16–24. Neil Anderson, writing on the believer's warfare with this flesh, agrees. He says,

> The flesh is the tendency within each person to operate independent of God and to center his interests on himself. An unsaved person functions totally in the flesh (Rom. 8:7–8), worshiping and serving the creature more than the Creator (Rom. 1:25). . . . When you were born again, your old self died and your new self came to life. . . . [but] during the years you spent separated from God, your worldly experiences thoroughly programmed your brain with thought patterns, memory traces, responses and habits which are alien to God. So even though your old skipper is gone, your flesh remains in opposition to God as a preprogrammed propensity for sin, which is living independent of God.[3]

Who cannot identify with Anderson's words? I certainly can. Growing up in a home disturbed by alcohol, I developed a poor self-image. Because I did not receive adequate dental care, two extra teeth grew in behind my front teeth, forcing the two outer teeth forward. While not "buck-toothed," as the expression was used in those days, I saw myself that way. So I thought I was ugly.

I was an outdoor person, not a student. Since my mom was preoccupied with just keeping the family together, she had no time to correct my careless study habits. My more studious brother received almost straight "A's"; I got by on "C's" and "D's" with an occasional "B" thrown in. So I felt I was dumb.

When I committed my life to the lordship of Christ at 19 years of age, the Holy Spirit immediately called me into missionary work.[4] That meant college and seminary. I was terrified at the prospect of having to study in a context in which I could not get by with my no-study bluff. Already preprogrammed into thinking I was too dumb to succeed as a student, I went to Biola University only because God told me to go. At Biola I began to learn of the Christian life. God used the writing of L. E. Maxwell and Hudson Taylor to begin my freedom from the bondage of my failure preprogramming.

As I learned that Christ was my life, I began to have hope. As I learned to deny the flesh with its thought patterns, memory traces, responses, and habits which were alien to God, I began to change. I graduated *magna cum laude*. I found out I was not dumb. All I had to do was rest in Christ and *work* like a trouper.

The apostle Paul uses the word "flesh" *(sarx)* seventeen times in Galatians, perhaps his heaviest concentration of uses for such a small book. His uses cover all of the three New Testament uses of *sarx* previously described by Elwell.[5]

Galatians: Grace, Faith, and the Spirit

In his epistle to the Galatians, the apostle stresses that the Christian life is entered into only by grace through faith apart from the deeds of the law (Gal. 1:6—2:21; 3:6—4:31). It is lived only in the Holy Spirit, who is received by faith, again not by the works of the law or any other activity associated with the flesh (Gal. 3:1–5; 5:1—6:18).

In Galatians an intimate connection exists between grace, faith, and the Holy Spirit for both regeneration and sanctification as against the works of the law and of the flesh. Paul first speaks of the Spirit who is always associated with grace and faith in 3:1–5,13–14. Both regeneration and sanctification are in view.

> You foolish Galatians, who has bewitched you, before whose eyes Jesus Christ was publicly portrayed as crucified? This is the only thing I want to find out from you: did you receive the Spirit by the works of the Law, or by hearing with faith? Are you so foolish? Having begun by the Spirit, are you now being perfected by the flesh? Did you suffer so many things in vain—if indeed it was in vain? Does He then, who provides you with the Spirit and works miracles among you, do it by the works of the Law, or by hearing with faith?

> Christ redeemed us from the curse of the Law, having become a curse for us—for it is written, "Cursed is everyone who hangs on a tree"—in order that in Christ Jesus the blessing of Abraham might come to the Gentiles, so that we might receive the promise of the Spirit through faith.

We receive the Spirit by faith, not by the works of the law or any other activity of the flesh. He works in us and among us also through faith, not through any meritorious religious performance on our part. We begin our Christian life by faith in the Spirit who regenerates us, and live our Christian life in the Spirit who sanctifies us.

Galatians 5: Liberty Through the Spirit, By Faith

The believer enjoys not only freedom from the law as a means of salvation and sanctification, but freedom from the bondage of the flesh in *any* area of life. This theme of the believer's freedom is first mentioned by Paul in 5:1:

> It was for freedom that Christ set us free; therefore keep standing firm and do not be subject again to a yoke of slavery.

In an old but inspiring study on Galatians by Norman B. Harrison called *His Side Versus Our Side,* Harrison writes:[6]

> The Christian, born of God, is God's free-born man. He is His son, His heir; all that God has is his. . . . He has already "blessed us with all spiritual blessings in Christ"

(Eph. 1:3). These blessings include His unqualified favor, "justified from all things," the bestowal of His life, the gift of His Spirit, access to His presence in prayer—everything to be desired.

Christian liberty is a life so lived that these provisions of grace continue to operate. Saved by grace initially, we must be kept by grace continually. Life imparted by grace must be sustained by grace. Justified by grace (Rom. 3:24), we must be sanctified by grace. Standing in grace (Rom. 5:2), we must walk in grace. We must be taught, trained and disciplined by grace (Titus 2:11–14).

We are to grow in grace (2 Peter 3:18). We are to experience the riches of His grace (Eph. 1:7), not only now but eternally (Eph. 2:7). In the severest trial His grace proves itself sufficient for us (2 Cor. 12:9), and as we humble ourselves He keeps adding more grace (James 4:6). He calls Himself the God of all grace (1 Peter 5:10), able to make all grace abound toward us, that we may always have all sufficiency for all things (2 Cor. 9:8).

It is evident that God has a thorough-going program of grace. Grace set us free; grace sustains us in a continuous experience of freedom. This is Christian liberty, staying on His Side, in His favor, where His feeing grace continuously operates. In this freedom we are to "stand fast" at all costs.

Perhaps the various works of the Spirit who indwells each believer are all summed up in one expression in Galatians 5:5. It is "through the Spirit . . . by faith" that we live our Christian life. We do so waiting for the coming day of the King of Glory when the knowledge of the Lord will cover the earth as the waters cover the sea (Isa. 11:9). What a day that will be!

Galatians 5:16–25

Before beginning his contrast in Galatians 5:16–25 between the works of the Spirit and those of the flesh, Paul sounds a warning in verse 13: "Do not turn your freedom into an opportunity for the flesh, but through love serve one another."

Richard Longenecker in his superb commentary on Galatians says the word "opportunity for the flesh" means "a starting point," "a base of operations" and a "pretext" or "occasion."[7]

Longenecker makes two excellent comments about the Spirit and the flesh which will prepare us for our study of 5:16–25. First he says that "since the 'Spirit' and 'the flesh' are juxtaposed throughout the exhortations of 5:13—6:10, we may assume that just as Paul thought of the one as personal so he meant the other to be taken as at least semi-personified."[8]

What Is "the Flesh"?

Second, he comments on the meaning of *sarx*, the flesh, by saying that before Galatians 5:13—6:10, Paul used *sarx* mainly to refer to the merely human or purely physical. In this passage, however, *sarx* is defined ethically, and used in this way refers to "humanity's fallen, corrupt, or sinful nature as distinguished from human nature as originally created by God."[9]

To discourage ideas of anthropological dualism[10] that may arise from translating *sarx* as "flesh" in ethical contexts, various translators have interpreted *sarx* in a number of descriptive renderings.[11]

So there have appeared such translations as "physical nature" (AMŪT), "human nature/natural desires/physical desire" (GNB), "lower nature" (NEB), "corrupt nature" (KNOX), and "sinful nature" (NIV)—or more freely, "self-indulgence" (JB). . . . Probably the best of the interpretive translations are those that add the adjective "corrupt" or "sinful" to the noun "nature" (i.e., KNOX, NIV), thereby suggesting an essential aspect of mankind's present human condition that is in opposition to "the Spirit" and yet avoiding the idea that the human body is evil per se.

In conclusion to his discussion of this passage, Longenecker observes that "the Christian may choose to use his or her freedom in Christ either as 'an opportunity for the flesh' or in response to 'the Spirit.'"[12]

William Barclay aptly expresses the idea of *sarx* used in the ethical sense:[13]

The flesh is man as he has allowed himself to become in contrast with man as God meant him to be. The flesh stands for the total effect upon man of his own sin and of the sin of his fathers and of the sin of all men who have gone before him. . . . The flesh stands for human nature weakened, vitiated, tainted by sin. The flesh is man as he is apart from Jesus Christ and his Spirit.

All we have studied to this point is crucial to understanding Paul's description of the believer's warfare with the flesh which begins in Galatians 5:16. In that verse the apostle gives a command followed by a promise.

THE FLESH VS. THE SPIRIT

But I say, walk by the Spirit, and you will not carry out the desire of the flesh.

The command is "walk by the Spirit."

While it certainly is connected to what was said before (vv. 13–15), the exhortation to brotherly love, it also introduces what follows after. Verse 15 probably implies that the Galatians were deeply divided as a church. Indeed the nature of the epistle reveals a church split by the legalizers, probably Jewish Christians zealous for the Mosaic Law. Tensions must have been deep within the body of believers even as they are in so many churches today. Therefore, Paul tells them how to experience the brotherly love God wants to exist among them. It comes, he says, by "walking in the Spirit."

The Key Process: Walking in the Spirit

In reference to what follows, that is, the warfare between the flesh and the Spirit, Paul lays before them the same single secret to victory in that warfare: "walk in the Spirit."

Longenecker says:[14]

The word translated walk, *peripateo* (go about, walk around) appears frequently in Paul's letters and occasionally in the Johannine letters in the figurative sense of "live" or "conduct" . . . the figurative use of *peripateo* stems from the Hebrew *(halak)*, which is the repeatedly used term in the Old Testament for "walk" or "conduct one's life." . . . The present tense of the imperative *peripateite,* which denotes an exhortation to action in progress, implies that the Galatians were to continue doing what they were already doing, that is, experiencing the presence of the Spirit's working in their lives (cf. 3:3–5) and living by faith (cf. 5:5).

The way to victory over the flesh is thus a process, "living, walking, being led by the Spirit." The emphasis is on process, not crisis.

What About Crisis Experiences?

This is an important word for our day when so much emphasis is placed on a crisis experience or experiences with the Spirit as the door to sanctification, power in the Christian's life, and a unique level of Christian living out of which will flow all the other blessings promised to the believer. Certainly crisis experiences with the Spirit do and should occur. There are times when He "falls upon" believers both as individuals and groups. He comes "with healing in His wings." He visits His people leading to revival periods in which more is done for the kingdom of God in weeks and months than in previous decades.

We should all long for such visitations by God the Spirit. I do. We live in a dangerous hour, but also one of unparalleled opportunity to fulfill the redemptive mandate of taking the gospel to all the people groups on earth (Matt. 28:18–20). We will probably not complete the task without such divine visitations on a worldwide scale. In some places and churches it has already begun.

Genuine crisis experiences with the Holy Spirit are multiplying, especially in the Two-thirds World. In my overseas ministry with Christian leaders, I am continually humbled by the manifold gifts of the Spirit and experiences with the Spirit that God is giving to humble believers who read it in His Word, claim His promises by faith, and launch out in obedience to His commands.

One of my greatest concerns, however, is with an overemphasis on crisis experiences with the Spirit, leading from one spiritual high to another. Believers come together looking for these experiences. Emotions are often unrestrained, fired up by platform leaders who exploit the desires of the people for dramatic experiences with God that appeal to their emotional needs.

"God is going to visit us in an unusual way today, my brothers and sisters." (If the unusual happens in every meeting then it is no longer unusual!) "Let's raise our hands and voices to God! Let's all pray together that the Spirit will come upon us, that the slain of the Lord will multiply in our midst."

I have no problem either biblically, historically, or in contemporary Christian experience with a true visitation of the Holy Spirit which so overwhelms his people that they may enter into an almost trance-like state for a brief period of time. After all, it happened to Peter on the housetop in Joppa (Acts 9:9f; 11:5). It also has happened in most great visitations of the Spirit throughout church history. It has also happened to me.[15]

Crisis Experiences Cannot Be a Goal

But when this occurrence becomes a goal for our church meetings, we are in trouble. When this is sought and promises are made that the experience in itself will lead one to a higher level of Christian living for the future, I object. This is not what the Scriptures teach. Paul did not say, "Be baptized with or slain in the Spirit and you will not fulfill the lusts of the Spirit." He said, "Walk, live, be led by the Spirit and you will not fulfill the lusts of the flesh."

This is more process than crisis. The day-by-day, moment-by-moment life of faith in the indwelling presence of the Spirit, continual communion with and obedience to the indwelling Spirit—this is the secret of the normal Christian life. This alone brings the results God wants in our life. This is what the Holy Spirit Himself commands and promises through His apostle, "Walk in the Spirit [the command] and you will not fulfill the lusts of the flesh" [the promised result] (v. 16 NKJV). When crisis experiences are exalted at the expense of the daily process of walking in the Spirit, the flesh can and will still control.

A few years ago I was ministering for a month in Argentina, South America. One Sunday morning I was asked by a pastor to share the pulpit with an Argentinian leader deeply involved in the revival and spiritual awakening. Since the church was in the midst of an evangelistic outreach to its city, I spoke on evangelism.

The Argentinian brother who followed me spoke on the ministry of the Holy Spirit. His message was disturbing because he used an Old Testament passage totally out of context and took great liberties in making the passage say what he wanted it to say, violating what the passage was meant to say. It soon became evident that his goal was to lead the congregation into seeking a particular manifestation of the Spirit in their midst.

When the message was over he began to "work up" the people, saying God was going to slay them in the Spirit. He had them stand. Those who wanted God to bless them were to come forward, he would lay hands on them, and the Spirit would come. More than half of the 300 or so people present came forward. At the touch of his hands, down they went.

After the meeting had finished, the church pastor and I had lunch together. Being a guest, I said nothing about what had occurred during the morning service. The church was known to be open to all of the operations of the Spirit, so I assumed what had occurred was fully acceptable to my pastor brother. It was not my place to comment on an area of spiritual experience which is a point of deep controversy among believers worldwide. Besides, the operations of the Spirit must be judged from within, not from without. There is a given set of socio-cultural-spiritual factors which form the true context in which God the Holy Spirit always operates, and outsiders are *not* usually qualified to judge what is occurring in unusual moves of the Spirit.

However, in the middle of lunch the pastor said, "I am not happy with the brother's ministry during this morning's service. I intend to tell him so when I am alone with him."

"Why?" I asked. "Don't you believe in the validity of the Holy Spirit's coming upon His people, producing the type of phenomena which occurred this morning?"

"Yes, I do. The Holy Spirit is God. When He directly touches you, you can be overcome by His presence, just as we see in Scripture and church history. But we have passed the phase as a church when we need dramatic experiences with the Holy Spirit to reinforce our faith."

"Please explain to me what you mean," I asked.

"I believe when we are beginning to allow the Holy Spirit to do anything He wants with us as a church, God will often manifest Himself in a dramatic, visible manner. It is as if God is reaching out to us and giving us 'a hug' to encourage us. He is saying, 'I love you. I am here. Now walk in the obedience of faith.'

A Fleshly Craving for the Spirit?

"We went through that period. What happened to us is what too often happens in our churches. God manifests the presence of the Spirit in this 'felt' way. Selfish as we are, we begin to expect it to be repeated at the demand of our people. They come to meetings seeking this or that particular manifestation of the Spirit. If it doesn't happen they become discouraged. They feel that any meeting where dramatic power demonstrations do not occur are inferior to the meetings where they do occur.

"The result, in our case, was that we began to walk by sight, not by faith. The Lord spoke to us as leaders and told us to teach His people a life of faith and obedience and not become fixed upon any particular experience of His presence. What occurred today was a step backwards for us as a church."

For this pastor the issue was not whether or not power demonstrations of the Spirit were welcomed; rather, the issue was what *meaning* was attached to such manifestations. *Ironically, the craving for this or that manifestation of the Spirit can be fleshly, and it always is when crisis experiences are sought, but the process of walking in the Spirit is ignored.*

Walking in the Spirit Is the Goal

Writing about the exhortation, "walk in the Spirit," Longenecker says:[16]

Behind the individual believer Paul sees two ethical forces that seek to control a person's thought and activity; the one, the personal Spirit of God; the other, the personified "flesh." What, in such an ethical dilemma, does the Christian do? The promise of the Gospel, as Paul proclaims it, is that life in the Spirit negates life controlled by the flesh. In fact, that promise is stated emphatically by the use of the double negative *ou me'* ("no never") with the aorist subjunctive *telesate.*

Thus Galatians 5:16 may be translated in part, "Walk in the Spirit, and by no means will you perform the desires of the flesh." In the verse that follows (v. 17), the apostle addresses at least five issues related to the command and the promise of verse 16:

1. The rationale behind his dualism of the flesh and the Spirit: They are at war with each other within the life of the believer.

2. This warfare between the flesh and the Spirit is unceasing. Neither peace nor compromise is possible between the two.

3. The flesh is personified just as the Holy Spirit is a person. The flesh is pictured as having a life of its own, including mind, emotions, and a will. As such it engages in fierce warfare, struggling to overcome the Holy Spirit.[17]

4. The goal of each is the issue of control over the believer's life. The Spirit wars against the flesh to nullify its controlling power of evil in the Christian life. The flesh wars against the Spirit to nullify His holy control of the believer's life.

5. The battleground is found within the believer. His heart, his innermost being, is the battlefield on which the war is being fought.

This verse sums up the major problem of humanity from the Pauline perspective. Longenecker calls verse 17 a summary statement of Paul's "basic soteriological anthropology, which underlies not only what he said in v. 16 but also his whole understanding of humanity before God since 'sin entered the world' "[18] (cf. Rom. 5:12).

Barclay's free-flowing translation of verse 17 is excellent:[19]

> For the desires of the lower side of
> Human nature are the very reverse of
> The desires of the Spirit, and the desires
> Of the Spirit are the very reverse of those
> Of the lower side of human nature,
> For these are fundamentally opposed to each other
> So that you cannot do whatever you like.

Some may object to the use of the word *dualism* for what the apostle is describing here. The word is appropriate, however, if we understand it is a modified dualism. It did not begin this way at man's creation and it will not end this way at man's glorification. Besides, it is an ethical dualism, not cosmological or anthropological.

Before describing the fruit produced by the flesh (vv. 19–21) and those by the

Spirit (vv. 22–23), Paul sums up in verse 18 what he has been teaching. He does so in the context of the subversive efforts of the Judaizers to move believers away from the life in the Spirit to bondage to legalism.

They had begun to live the Christian life by faith through the Spirit (3:1–5) and had been "running well" (5:7). They had then become side tracked, however, into living by a set of legalistic standards. All they had to do was return to the Spirit-led life and he would remove the yoke of the law the Judaizers had placed upon their necks (v. 18).

Matthew Henry has the apostle Paul saying that

If, in the prevailing bent and tenour of your life, you be led of the Spirit—if you act under the guidance and government of the Holy Spirit and of that spiritual nature and disposition He has wrought in you—if you make the Word of God your rule and the grace of God your principle—it will hence appear that you are not under the law, not under the condemning, though you are still under the commanding, power of it. . . .[20]

I close this chapter repeating the words of the apostle in 5:13,16,18 in the *Amplified New Testament:*

> For you, brethren, were (indeed) called
> To freedom; only (do not let your) freedom be
> An incentive to your flesh and an opportunity
> Or excuse (for selfishness), but through
> Love you should serve one another. . . . But
> I say, walk and live habitually in the
> (Holy) Spirit—responsive to and
> Controlled and guided by the
> Spirit; then you will certainly not gratify
> The cravings and desires of the flesh—Of
>   human nature without God. . . . But if
> You are guided (led) by the (Holy) Spirit
> You are not subject to the law.

16

Moral Sins
Galatians 5

I was conducting a training seminar on Spiritual Warfare and Church Growth in Asia. During one of the sessions a young, Christian leader went into demonic manifestation. Since the man was otherwise a godly Christian leader, he was able to control the demons until the meeting was over.

My practice is never to deal with serious demonic problems with Christians in public if I can avoid doing so. Occasionally, demons come into manifestation in public, and some type of initial encounter may have to occur to bring the rebellious spirits under control. Since the man was a strong Christian and the demons fairly easy to control, I took him to a private building for prayer and ministry.

Several strong sexual demons had attached themselves to his life. While I do not usually use direct power encounter in dealing with demons attached to a Christian's life, I allowed it to happen in this case because I had to fly out of the country by dawn the next day and it was already late.

After certain sexual demons had revealed themselves, I forced them to retreat to the stomach of their victim so he had full control of his faculties. I then began a hurried process of pre-deliverance counseling, encouraging the brother to honestly tell me about his sexual activities from his childhood to the present.

Following the principle expressed by the apostle Paul in Ephesians 4:27b, "Do not give the devil a foothold" (NIV), I knew the activity of the evil spirits binding his life would continue until he recognized, confessed, and rejected the sins in his life that had provided the demonic footholds, what I call "sin handles."

Over the next few hours a sordid story of sexual bondage from childhood to the present unfolded. His greatest bondage at the moment was to pornography. Two of the ruling demons attached to his life called themselves Lust and Pornography. They had been around a long time but had gained stronger footholds in his life over the past few years through his weekly use of rented pornographic videos. So gross was the demonic activity in his life he would sometimes growl like an animal during sexual relationships with his wife. Worst of all, he had forced her to watch the videos with him to increase their sexual passions.

At first the videos revolted his lovely, godly wife. Fearful of losing her husband's love, however, she eventually accepted his demand that they view the videos together. In time neither she nor her husband could become sexually aroused by one another without the use of the videos.

Galatians 5:19–21: Four Sin Groups

Paul deals with bondage to sexual sins in Galatians 5. We will first examine the Pauline list of fifteen "deeds of the flesh" in Galatians 5:19–21. While they are classified different ways by different commentators,[1] I believe they fall into four primary groups.

First listed are *moral sins,* verse 19b. There are three, "immorality, impurity, sensuality." The King James Version lists four. *Moicheria* (adultery) is added to verse 19 alongside of *porneia*, literally "fornication," but more functionally translated "immorality." This probably was the work of a scribe who added *moicheria*.[2] It is not found in the oldest and best manuscripts.

Next the apostle lists two *religious sins*, "idolatry" and "sorcery."

Third, Paul enumerates eight *social sins*, beginning with "enmities" in verse 20 and ending with "envyings" in verse 21. I call them social sins because they are sins committed against others, as well as against God.

Finally, Paul lists two *sins of intemperance* or lack of self control: "drunkenness" and "carousings." The latter word is variously translated: "carousing" (NAS), "revellings" (KJV), "orgies" (NEB). The idea is that of a group out of control, usually under the influence of alcohol, drugs, sex, or even group religious cultic demonic rites or ceremonies.

Paul's list of the deeds of the flesh in this passage is not meant to be exhaustive. His statement in verse 21 "and things like these" attests to this. Also, the Scriptures elsewhere present other lists of the sins of the flesh different than this one, as in Matthew 15:19, Romans 1:24–32, and 1 Corinthians 6:9–10. Although no list is identical with the others, the list in Galatians is probably the most complete and systematic.

Dr. Ronald Y. K. Fung has produced one of the most outstanding commentaries on Galatians in print today.[3] It is part of the excellent series, The New International Commentary on the New Testament. His chart on the Greek words used in Paul's fourfold classification of "the deeds of the flesh" and the various way they are translated into English by some of the major English translations of the Bible is given on page 120.

The apostle begins verse 19a by saying, "Now the works of the flesh are evident." The noun *phaepos* here translated "evident" means "open to public observation" or "obvious."[4] The idea would be something so obvious one does not need the law to point them out.

Paul had expressed his concern in 5:13 that the liberty the believers enjoyed in Christ not become a pretext for "the flesh." Believers are to live by the law of love, itself the result of the Spirit's work in their lives. To believers who are living in, being led by, and walking in the Spirit these unholy practices should be obvious. This is evidently what the apostle is saying here.

Immorality

The first moral (sexual) sin mentioned by the apostle is *porneia*, properly translated "immorality" in the NAS.[5]

William Barclay comments:[6]

> It has been said, and said truly, that the one completely new virtue which Christianity brought into the world was chastity. Christianity came into a world where sexual immorality was not only condoned, but was regarded as normal and essential to the ordinary working of life.

Ridderbos says *porneia* refers to "illegitimate sexual intercourse in the widest sense of the word."[7] This is in harmony with what we have already said except at one point. The word "sexual intercourse" is too restrictive. One can be guilty of sexual sin without engaging in physical sexual intercourse. The New Testament reveals that sexual sins can be committed with the mind or imagination as well as with the body.

Figure 16.1
**The Works of the Flesh in Galatians 5:19–21:
Classification and English Translations**

	Greek	AV	RV	RSV	NEB	NASB	NIV
(a) Sexual sins (i)	[moicheia]	[adultery]					
	porneia	fornication	= AV	= AV	= AV	immorality	sexual immorality
(ii)	akatharsia	uncleanness	= AV	impurity	= RSV	= RSV	= RSV
(iii)	aselgeia	lasciviousness	= AV	licentiousness	indecency	sensuality	debauchery
(b) Religious deviations (iv)	eidōlolatria	idolatry	= AV	= AV	= AV	= AV	= AV
(v)	pharmakeia	witchcraft	sorcery	= RV	= RV	= RV	= AV
(c) Disorders in personal relationships (vi)	echthrai	hatred	enmities	enmity	quarrels	= RV	= AV
(vii)	eris	variance	strife	= RV	a contentious temper	= RV	discord
(viii)	zēlos	emulations	jealousies	jealousy	envy	= RSV	= RSV
(ix)	thymoi	wrath	wraths	anger	fits of rage	outbursts of anger	= NEB
(x)	eritheiai	strife	factions	selfishness	selfish ambitions	disputes	selfish ambition
(xi)	dichostasiai	seditions	divisions	dissension	dissensions	= NEB	= NEB
(xii)	haireseis	heresies	= AV	party spirit	party intrigues	factions	= NASB
(xiii)	phthonoi	envyings	= AV	envy	jealousies	= AV	= RSV
	[phonoi]	[murders]					
(d) Sins of intemperance (xiv)	methai	drunkenness	= AV	= AV	drinking bouts	= AV	= AV
(xv)	kōmoi	revellings	= AV	carousing	orgies	carousings	= NEB

The Battle for the Mind

As we have repeatedly mentioned, the real battleground is the mind, the imagination, the fantasy realm. The Scriptures are clear that immorality is first committed in the mind, the imagination, the fantasy realm, before it is committed with the body. In the Sermon on the Mount, Jesus taught:

> You have heard that it was said, "You shall not commit adultery"; but I say to you, that everyone who looks on a woman to lust for her has committed adultery with her already in his heart. (Matt. 5:27–28)

First we discover what Jesus did *not* say. He did not say it is a sin to look at an attractive woman (or in the case of women, to look at an attractive man). An attractive woman is attractive to any normal man.

What Jesus did say is that if one looks lustfully on a woman he is guilty of adultery (v. 28). This is immorality of the heart, of the mind, of the imagination. John Broadus comments that

> Jesus condemns not merely the outward act of sin, but the cherishing of sinful desire. Stier (says), "He who experiences at a first glance this desire, and then instead of turning away and withdrawing from sin (2 Peter 2:14) throws a second glance with lustful intent and in order to retain and increase that impulse, commits the sin."[8]

Living as we are in a world in which nudity, partial nudity and sexually stimulating dress style is rampant, the battle for mental purity in the child of God is more intense than ever. Those whose ministry involves continual travel and absence from one's spouse can be especially susceptible to such mental pollution.

For several weeks I had been traveling with a fellow missionary, holding training conferences for missionary leaders. We arrived in a major European city. After going through customs we were met by a European Christian leader who was to drive us to the site of our next conference.

We had to take an elevator to reach the underground parking lot. When we reached our floor the elevator doors opened and before our shocked eyes directly in front of the elevator was a row of small stores with a sign saying in English "Sex Shops." Below the sign, running the full length of the sex shops, stood life-size photos of beautiful but almost totally naked women.

My partner and I were so shocked we could not speak. The German brother had his back to the stores. He indicated that the fastest way to reach the car was straight ahead, which would have taken us past the sex shops and their alluring photographs. "Or," he said, "we can go another but longer way."

"Let's go the longer way," my traveling companion and I blurted out almost in unison.

As we walked away I said within me, "I reject all images of female nudity which have reached my mind. I reject all impure thoughts. I deny all sexual fantasies that want to impress themselves on my mind. I am a man of God and will not allow immoral thoughts a place in my mind or my imagination."

As I did this, I did not ask God's forgiveness for the sexual images that came against my mind. I had no power over them. I didn't place those sensual photos there, and I was not responsible for the images they naturally brought against my imagination. I was responsible only to reject them and not allow them any place in my mind. I did that and was thus free from any guilt before God.

There is great truth to the familiar saying, "We can't stop the birds from flying around our heads, but we can stop them from building their nest in our hair."

During one of his crusades a few years ago, Dr. Billy Graham said, "In any battle between the imagination and the will, the will loses out every time." What did he mean? He meant the battle has to be won at the beginning when wrong thoughts or images first reach the mind. If we entertain them in our imagination instead of rejecting them immediately, our will is not strong enough to overcome the inflamed imagination.

I often tell my students, "If you see me walking across the campus and suddenly I say, 'I won't accept that thought!' don't think I have lost my mind. I've just forcibly expelled some sinful thought or image which has come against my mind from the flesh, the world, or the Devil."

THE BOTTOMLESS PIT OF PORNOGRAPHY

One of Satan's primary instruments of sexual attack against the mind of humanity (usually men) in general and believers in particular is pornography. It exists in epidemic form in the U.S. and the Western world.

The word "pornography" comes from two Greek words of ancient vintage: *porne,* which originally meant a prostitute and is translated "harlot" in the New Testament. While it referred primarily to women prostitutes, it was also used of males. The second word is *graphe,* meaning a picture, a painting, or a writing. It covers all forms of external physical symbols which produce sexual arousal in those who are involved with them.

In the Western world and in many non-Western nations pornography is making inroads not only into our culture in general, but into our homes in particular. Christian homes are affected, also.

Once pornography was found primarily in sleazy stores "on the other side of the tracks." Now it is out in the open. Grocery stores offer soft core pornography of sexually stimulating pictures and stories focusing on nudity and normal sexuality, often right next to the checkout stands. Sexually explicit books, many with pictures of male and female nudity, are available for children as well as adults in most public libraries. The media, especially magazines, movies, videos, and T.V., promote nudity and illicit sexual activities at an alarming rate and boast that the pictures and stories will become more and more explicit in the months ahead.

Pornography, like prostitution, is not a victimless crime, as is often affirmed. Its victims are everywhere. It stimulates the imagination to commit mental adultery. It produces desires contrary to God's will for our life. It stirs the passions and sexual arousal, especially of men, which makes them temporarily potentially dangerous to women and to children.

While some "experts" deny this, the average man knows it is true. Many men, including Christians, have themselves been sexually stimulated by pornography and have been tempted to seek sex even with unwilling women or children. How much incest and rape is due to sexual arousal stimulated by pornography!

Pornography is a mind-imagination-fantasy game. It leads to the mental lusting after women condemned by the Lord Jesus in Matthew 5:27–29. It is an eight-billion-dollar-plus per year industry in the U.S. While inroads into the female portion of the U.S. population are now being made, it is primarily a male problem, particularly of single men.

Its negative impact on the male's view of women and the place of sex in the male-female relationship are devastating even according to many secular researchers. Pornography researcher Harriet Koskoff reports that

> Pornography feeds fantasies . . . by allowing men mentally to turn female flesh into putty. More exactly, pornography is an aid to masturbation . . . I think pornography has something to do with the laissez-faire society we live in . . . It's part of the "me, me, me, I am the center of the universe" mentality that has taken hold.

> Pornography is primarily about masturbation, whether it is mental or actual. The star of masturbation is also the director and the viewer. . . . Today, porn consumers go into a neighborhood video store and select one of 7,000 porn titles currently available.[9]

Another researcher adds:[10]

"Pornography is about the anatomical portrayal of sex. There is no room for human feeling . . . for two people sharing their deepest selves. If all (the viewer) has in his mind are images of people mating like barnyard animals, how will he ever learn that love electrifies sex?"

Dr. James Dobson, who was chosen to be part of the Attorney General's Commission on The Study of Pornography in the U.S. in 1986, has given a thorough overview of the pornography epidemic sweeping the U.S. in the August, 1986, edition of *Focus on the Family*.[11]

A Pastor Investigates

Rev. Bill Hybels, pastor of Willow Creek Community Church in South Barrington, Illinois, has written a shocking book on pornography entitled *Christians in A Sex Crazed Society*. Excerpts from his excellent book were printed in a cover article by *Moody Monthly* in April, 1989, entitled "The Sin That So Easily Entangles."[12] The article is thorough but shocking, especially as it concerns the inroads of pornography into our Christian homes. The following is taken from the article with permission of the publisher.

Hybels began to awaken to the inroads of pornography into the churches as he found himself counseling "godly" Christians, even church leaders, whose lives were being devastated by bondage to pornography. He was shocked to the core of his being at what he learned.

First, Hybels learned that *pornography has changed for the worse*. Hybels asks if his disturbing counseling experience with one of his church members who was in bondage to pornography was an exception: "Aren't we making too much hoopla over pornography?"

> I have hundreds of concerns more pressing than taking *Playboy* out of the hands of those who buy it occasionally. Besides, I viewed some of those airbrushed centerfolds when I was in junior and senior high school, and it didn't ruin my life. I'm happily married, with two wonderful children. What's the big deal?

> In the past few years, I have heard the cries of people claiming that pornography is proliferating and that we should do something about it. Area leaders even contacted me to help them close down the adult bookstores in our community. And all along I found myself asking, "Why all the drama?"

> One of the rudest awakenings of my life came when I researched this subject.

> I got copies of pornographic magazines, and I found out that the kind I used to sneak peeks at in high school doesn't even exist anymore. I couldn't locate one magazine

with partially clad women—the mild kind of pornography that was the standard 15 years ago.

Instead, I learned that today's mild form of pornography—the stuff we can buy in area convenience stores—contains photo layouts that defy the imagination, including pictures of women being bound and gagged, raped, whipped, and abused. Standard fare includes an array of multiple sexual partners in heterosexual, homosexual, and lesbian photo poses. The underlying theme is usually domination or violence.

The rougher magazines depict scenes of gang rape, torture, and bestiality. Some of the most popular magazines show men and women having sexual relations with children ranging in age from three to eight years. I was appalled and outraged.

And then I learned about the seedier side of the pornography industry—the adult bookstores. There are more adult bookstores in this country than there are McDonald's—20,000. They sell sex magazines and sexual paraphernalia, but their major attraction is the film booth. A police officer in my church infiltrated these bookstores and told me things not fit to print.

No, pornography isn't anything like it was 15 years ago. But what concerns me most is the damage it does to the people who get caught up in it.

Second, Hybels discovered that *pornography is addicting.*

When we indulge our sexual appetites and begin viewing explicit videos, movies, and magazines, we find that pornography is addicting. It makes us want more, more, more. And like alcohol and drugs, pornography shatters lives. This week I received a letter from someone in my church who is struggling with this addiction. He wrote:

"I am an emotional invalid. My addiction to pornography paralyzes my spiritual life, perverts my view of the world, distorts my social life, and destroys any possibility of God using me, and I just can't stop. Lust eats me up, yet it doesn't satisfy. Pornography promises me everything; it produces nothing."

Some time ago, I tried to help a woman whose husband was addicted to pornography. She brought in a phone bill of more than $300—he was making 20 to 30 dial-a-porn calls a night. He also had a stack of magazines four feet high and boxes full of pornographic films.

Those of us who have never been addicted to anything will never understand the intensity of desire that an addict feels. But we must be as understanding and as compassionate as we can be, because people who matter to God and who sit next to us in church have unintentionally crossed that invisible line. They are enslaved to a pattern of life that leads to heartache and ruin, and they don't know how to stop.

Third, Hybels understood that *pornography is degrading to women.*

Showing women being seduced, stripped, and handled like farm animals is a hideous assault on their dignity. Jesus elevated the role and dignity of women. So Christians are disgusted when a woman's dignity is assaulted in pornographic material.

But I'm even more concerned about the pornography's subtle assault on the nature and character of women. Pornography depicts women as having an insatiable appetite for sex. If there is a common thread that ties pornographic content together, it is the continual emphasis, made in dozens of ways, that even though women indicate they are not interested in a man's sexual advances, really they are. . . . There are thousands of men in our community who are addicted to pornography, who are wandering around in public places, convinced that all women are craving sex all day. If a woman resists, she really wants him to overpower her and take her forcibly.

Fourth, Hybels saw that *pornography undermines marriage.*

I know that many married couples in my church view adult videos to add some spice to their sexual lives. Initially, viewing pornography may excite and stimulate marriage partners. But it's not the initial results I'm concerned about.

I counseled with a woman recently who is a leader in her church. Her husband is an elder. The two of them began using pornography as a marital stimulus some years ago. She came to see me because her marriage is in a shambles.

God designed marital sexuality to flow out of the context of a loving and intimate relationship where nurturing, communication, serving, and tenderness go on. When those values are cultivated in a marriage, they arouse sexual interest. Sexual intercourse then becomes an expression of caring, of loving, a way of saying, "You matter to me. I love you and I want to communicate that to you tenderly."

Pornography short-circuits all of that. It reduces the sexual dimension of marriage to a biologically induced athletic event, and eventually there is no longer much emphasis on the loving part of marriage. Once that is drained out of a relationship, the heart and soul of marital sexuality is gone. The woman starts feeling used and abused, and the man starts feeling frustrated and empty.

A woman told me, "My husband and I can't have a sexual experience without pornography to get us started. But then we feel filthy and guilty and empty."

Fifth, Hybels found out that *pornography is devastating to children.*

Pornography inevitably falls into the hands of children (and teens) and often leads to misguided sexual experimentation. The results are shattering.

One woman said she has spent the past 20 years trying to recover from damage caused by her brother. He began viewing pornography as a 12-year-old and didn't know where to focus his sexual excitement, so he used his 10-year-old sister.

If pornography distorts the sexual perspective of adults, think what it must do to children who are incapable of making wise decisions about simple things, let alone something as complex as human sexuality.

Children become victims of pornography in another way. They fall prey to adults whose use of pornography has awakened in them a sickening interest in the sexual exploitation of children. A man from my church, in an unsigned letter, admitted that he is addicted to pornography and that he made advances toward a 12-year-old girl.

A group on the West Coast has this motto: "Sex before eight, before it's too late." Books on the market give explicit instructions to child molesters, describing in detail how to seduce children.

Producers and merchants of pornography are focusing their marketing strategy for the next wave of explicit materials on children between 12 and 17. Who's going to stop them?

In my worldwide ministry with Christian leaders I have ministered to hundreds with severe sexual malfunctions. In most cases their problems began either through being victims of sexual abuse in childhood or through bondage to pornography, usually beginning in adolescence or youth.

I would like to add to Hybels' observations about the threat of pornography to marriage by giving a recent case study.

During my spiritual life and warfare conferences, I try to be available for personal counseling with couples or individuals. I was counseling a handsome young missionary couple about various needs in their life. When the session was over, the wife tarried behind. She asked for and was granted a private counseling session with me the next day.

"I am having difficulty responding sexually to my husband," she confessed.

"Do you feel that you can identify the root of your problem?" I asked. "Yes," she replied. "I know when the problem began. Sometime ago I was rearranging his closet when I discovered some magazines hidden among his personal belongings.

"I ordinarily do not look through his personal things. I just accidentally found the magazines. When I opened them I was shocked to see they were filled with graphic pictures of beautiful women totally nude.

"I was stunned. I had never suspected he was interested in any other woman besides me. I was horrified and began to cry.

"As I looked again at the bodies of those fully endowed women, I went to the mirror and looked at myself. I could not help but cry out, 'My God, if that is what he wants from me, I can never satisfy him. I just don't have all that those women have to offer him.' I have never enjoyed sex with him from that time until now."

I cannot help but warn my male readers who are even casual users of pornography, this same thing could happen in your marriage. Probably 99 percent of the women in the world are not physically endowed as are the women willing to sell their bodies to the pornography industry. You threaten the intimacy of your marriage if you begin to superimpose such sexual fantasies upon your wife's role within your sexual union.

Michael J. McManus, author of the widely syndicated "Ethics and Religion" column, says the following about pornography:[13]

> Between 1960 and 1985, there has been a quadruple rise in the number of illegitimate children; the number of abortions has tripled; the number of divorces has tripled; there's been a 100-fold increase in child molestation. In my view, the reason for the rise can be traced to pornography. Pornography justifies taking off restraints.
>
> Man needs discipline in the sexual area just as he needs discipline to be a success in life.

There are cross-cultural dimensions to pornography. Some who do not have access to the printed page, pornographic videos and/or theaters, have their own form of potential pornographic enslavements. The young man who breaks a local taboo and regularly practices voyeurism in a tribal setting is involved in a local form of pornography as much as the one who has available pornographic literature, films, and porn shops within his culture.

Finally I would like to share another case study coming from one of my former students at Biola University, who wrote:

> I had been caught up in [pornography] since my childhood and was never able to become free, no matter how much I prayed or confessed. I had hidden this sin from everyone, I was so embarrassed and ashamed, I could not even confide in anyone, within or outside the church. I could only recently confess this sinful area of my life to my wife. I did not pursue the ministry because I could not resolve this addiction. I did not want to dishonor my Lord. I always feared I would be discovered. I am now grateful to say I am now free.[14]

Immorality, of course, involves much more than pornography. Yet in the battle for the mind pornography is one of the major open doors to illicit sexual stimulation of the imagination, what I continually call the fantasy realm.

An Appeal

I close this chapter with an impassioned appeal. If the reader has any involvement with pornography, break the habit now. Find a prayer-share-healing partner (James 5:16) who will pray with you and encourage you. Find someone to whom you can become accountable, who will check up on you, to whom you can go when temptations attempt to take control.

Your bondage will only increase if you do not stop now and get help now. If you are a casual user, cut off the practice now, completely. Guard what you see in movies and on T.V. and videos. Refuse to buy, look at, or read any sexually stimulating literature. The freedom you will experience is worth the initial struggle. "The Son of Man will set you free," and "you will be free indeed." I know. I personally enjoy that freedom. It is worth more than all the gold of Fort Knox.

17

The Age of Eros

In 1988 alone five of my pastor friends in northern California were caught in adultery. While this sounds almost unbelievable, it is true. All five were godly men. They were good pastors. They had lovely and loving wives.

All five had to leave their churches. Only one is back in the pastoral ministry today.[1] How many other fellow pastors have been or even still are involved in illicit sexual relationships but have not been caught as yet? Only God knows!

We are experiencing a worldwide plague of illicit sexual activities, even among Christians. The problem, of course, has been with us from the beginning. A look at illicit sexual activities in both the Old and New Testaments confirms this. The problem will continue until the believer's flesh is finally done away with at the coming of Christ. We are seeing new and disturbing dimensions of the problem around the globe, especially in the Western world.

Historical Perspective: Enlightenment Rejection of Revealed Ethics

From a human-historical perspective this is the predictable results of the Enlightenment of the eighteenth century. The Enlightenment rejected God and all normative ethics based on divine revelation. Individualism, human progress based on reason and not revelation, and total commitment to naturalistic science undermined religious and, particularly, Christian faith. All objective foundation for morality was removed. Whatever human beings enjoyed and found meaningful to their life was acceptable if it did not directly hurt other people.

The Enlightenment, in turn, gave birth to the triplets of naturalism, humanism, and materialism. These world views reject the objective reality of the supernatural or at least any direct involvement of whatever supernaturalism may exist in human life. They affirm man's capacity for self-realization through reason (rationalism) and the empiricism of the scientific method (scientism). All that exists is the natural world (naturalism). Man is thus alone in his universe (atheism).

Out of naturalism, humanism, and materialism has come nihilism, the view that all restrictive traditional values and beliefs are unfounded. There is no objective ground for truth, especially moral truth. Nihilism leads inevitably to the conclusion, consciously or unconsciously, that human existence has no objective meaning. As the only reality, we can live for personal satisfaction. Nihilism's motto is, "If it feels good, do it."

Either blatantly, especially through many of our educational institutions, or covertly, especially through the media, the present adult generation and the emerging generation of young people are being conditioned to believe the only restraints on sexuality are the consent of the persons involved and precautions against disease and unwanted pregnancy.

"We are sexual beings," it is claimed. "Why should not consenting persons be allowed to become sexually active as soon as they are able and desire to do so?"

As a result of this kind of thinking, the church which is supposed to change the world, is becoming changed by the world. As early as 1959 A. W. Tozer wrote that

The period in which we now live may well go down in history as the Erotic Age. Sexual love has been elevated into a cult. Eros has more worshipers among civilized men today than any other god. For millions the erotic has completely displaced the spiritual. . . . Tears and silence might be better than words if things were slightly otherwise than they are. But the cult of eros is seriously affecting the Church. The pure religion of Christ that flows like a crystal river from the heart of God is being polluted by the unclean waters that trickle from behind the altars of abomination that appear on every high hill and under every green tree from New York to Los Angeles.[2]

Randy C. Alcorn, whose book *Christians in the Wake of the Sexual Revolution* contains Tozer's quote, himself says,

In New Testament times, the sexual purity of God's people drew a sharp line dividing them from the non-Christian world. Prior to the sexual revolution, this was largely true of the Church in America. But things have radically changed. In *Flirting With the World,* John White draws these sobering conclusions: "the sexual behavior of Christians has reached the point of being indistinguishable from that of non-Christians. . . . In our sexual behavior we, as a Christian community, are both in the world, and of it."

Alcorn turns to a 1984 Gallup poll to substantiate White's claim. The poll discovered that churched and unchurched behaved alike on moral issues such as lying, cheating, pilferage—and sex. He reaches the sad conclusion that

It is increasingly difficult to discern where the world ends and the Church begins. . . . Like the frog that boiled to death by degrees, many Christian homes have been gradually desensitized to sexual sin. The result is predictable—immorality is more rampant among believers than ever before.[3]

Normal Human Sexuality and Victory Over Lust

I am a normal man with normal male sexuality. I have found that sexual temptations have not diminished one bit since I have passed fifty years of age. I used to have the idea that when I was older somehow sexuality would go on hold. I would be able to walk along the beach surrounded by women clad in their skimpy swimsuits and it would not have any impact upon me. I have found that this is not the case.

Years ago I was leading a Bible study with some of our younger missionaries from 1 Timothy 6:11 and 2 Timothy 2:22 where the apostle Paul admonishes us to "flee from these things"—"flee from youthful lusts."

I naturally had to touch on sexual lust. I suddenly remembered that an elderly gentleman in his eighties was with us. Since it was an informal setting, I stopped and said, "I am looking forward to the day when I am gray-headed like our brother and won't have to deal with sexual lusts."

Everyone laughed except our brother. Before I could go on he raised his hand for permission to speak. He said, "Young man, you will have that problem with you all your life."

Again, everyone laughed. I did not. I truly believed that "that problem" would disappear with age. Now that I am gray-headed I know what he meant. "Just because there is snow on the roof does not mean there is no flame in the fireplace."

Nevertheless, there is victory in Christ over sexual lusts and fantasy. One does not have to live in semi-mental-emotional bondage to sexual lusts even in our present age of sexual display.

When the apostle Paul said to flee from such lusts he meant just what he said. Men cannot be exposed to female nudity or semi-nudity without experiencing some form of sexual stimulation.[4] What is the answer? Simply this: As much as possible we must stay away from this type of sexual exposure.

This requires self-discipline, especially in our reading habits and television and movie viewing. We know what magazines, books, and programs contain sexually stimulating photographs, articles, and stories. We must refuse to buy, read, or view them. We must remember that the dangerous habit of looking, reading, buying, and lusting often leads to foiled marriages, disturbed children, broken fellowship with God, and shame before a world that expects Christians to live lives of sexual purity.

A Double Standard

The Bible *does* teach a double standard. There is a very high standard for Christians in general. There is an even higher standard for Christian leaders.

Martin Luther once said, "It is no small thing to stand before men in the place of God." That is what it means to be a Christian leader. Is that not what James meant when he wrote, "Let not many of you become teachers, my brethren, knowing that as such we shall incur a stricter judgment" (James 3:1)?

To my readers who are already Christian leaders or who aspire to Christian leadership, God requires more of you and me than He does of those he calls us to lead. We must count the cost. We must not aspire to Christian leadership unless we are willing to die to self, to fleshly lusts, to the pride of life (1 John 2:15–17).

If you are in bondage to any type of sexual sins, stay out of Christian leadership until you have a proven track record of victory over your problem. The idea that once you become a pastor, evangelist, Bible teacher, missionary or whatever, you will then be able to gain the victory and the holy life you yearn for is self-deception. It is a total illusion. The warfare with the flesh, with the world, and with Satan intensifies when you become a Christian leader, not lessens.

We must accept the responsibilities of Christian leadership. The battles are not won in the pulpit, on the platform, or from the podium, but in secret when no one is watching you.

What do you do with your eyes? Your hands? Your feet? Your mind? Your imagination when no one is watching you? No Christian leader ever fell into sexual sin without that sin first arising in his mind usually over and over again when no one was looking.

Of course there is forgiveness. That is a given. God always forgives His sinning leaders even when they have disgraced His name. But think, while you still have control over your mind, emotions, and body, of the shame you will bring upon God, upon yourself, your family, and the worldwide church by your self-centered activities! If you cannot live up to the demands and moral standards of the ministry, get out of the ministry. You don't belong there. You have heard the expression, "If you can't stand the heat, stay out of the kitchen."

My close friend and colleague, the well-known evangelist-Bible teacher Dr. Luis Palau, time and time again warns Christian leaders of what he calls "hanky pankyness" on the part of Christian leaders.

> Christian leaders often try to indulge in all they can get away with in border-line misconduct. They might not go to a prostitute or have an affair, but they will look at pornography. They will watch movies in hotel rooms which they would be

ashamed to watch at home with their wives. They will look and even touch and fondle and get sexually stimulated but stop short of outright immorality. This is sin. It has no place in the life of God's servant.

The Consequence of Sexual Sin for Leaders

During the years I spent as a full-time professor at Biola University, sexual falls on the part of male teachers with female students unfortunately occasionally occurred. One year two such incidents shocked the faculty. Both of the men were my friends. I, along with my fellow professors, had suspected nothing.

My wife, Loretta, has difficulty with this kind of misconduct on the part of Christian leaders. She is so pure of heart and so totally sincere and committed to God, to biblical standards and a holy lifestyle, and to me as her lover-husband, it always depresses her when a Christian leader falls sexually. After the above incidents occurred she said to me,

"Honey, I must ask you a question. It is not evidence of distrust but I must ask the question. I will preface the question with an observation about the Biola 'girls,' as you call them, who are in your classes. You as a man and their professor are very affectionate. You see them as 'girls,' like your two daughters, but they are not your daughters. Nor are they girls. They are fully developed women.

"You must be very careful when you counsel them. You must remember many of them are lonely and hunger for love. Many have not had a man in their life as a model. They can transfer their need for closeness to an older man, call it a father figure if you like, to you and it can become sexual without your or their being aware of it.

"Now, here is the question I want to ask. How can I be sure you will not become involved with one of these women or another woman in your constant travels? No one suspected your two fellow professors until they were caught. How about you?"

From my gentle, sweet, and quiet wife, that was really a bombshell of a question. Though her directness startled me, the question needed to be asked. In answering her, I was able to express how I deal with this issue in all of my ministry.

It is not something I do not think about. It is an ever-present danger which I have faced many times since I began my traveling ministry over forty years ago when I was only nineteen years old. I could have fallen sexually any number of times. The opportunities were there and they still exist. I said to Loretta,

"First, I know if I were to experience a sexual fall my relationship with God would be broken. Though He would forgive me, my relationship with Him would never be the same.

"How could I face God knowing what I had done? My heart is too tender before Him as it is. I cannot stand for any cloud to come between God and me. A sexual fall would undermine everything my spiritual life has been built upon. How could I pray? How could I have fellowship with Him if I so terribly betrayed Him?

"Second, I would personally have to leave the ministry. Others perhaps would not, but I would. I could not stand before God's people or the unsaved and preach what is not true in my life.

"I struggle with sin as all of us do. But sexual sin is always premeditated. There is always a point at which a man can resist and flee from sexual stimulation. No one just happens to fall into sexual sin. The sin has usually been floating around in one's imagination before one has occasion to act it out in physical experience.

"That is hypocrisy. How can I teach on victory in spiritual warfare if I am not walking in victory? How can I preach on holiness if I am not living a holy life?

"Third, I love you, totally. How could I face you as my wife if I did such a terrible thing? How could I look into your eyes, hold you in my arms, give to you and receive from you intimate love if I have been lusting after or having sex with another woman? You know me so well you would know it happened even before I told you. Besides, I love you so much it makes it that much easier to flee from the strange woman.

"Fourth, how could I ever face our two lovely daughters? If I failed them as an example of a godly, morally pure father, how could I ever again relate to them with a pure conscience?

"The same applies to our two sons. How can I help to influence them in their moral life in our immoral society unless I model before them a life of victory over sexual temptations? The same applies to our grandchildren."

Since that day Loretta has never brought up the question again. As she said, she had to hear it from my lips to be truly at peace. Since that day she has helped me counsel many men and women who have broken their marital vows. She knows we all carry the sinful flesh in our mortal bodies and are all capable of falling but she is at rest, trusting me to the Holy Spirit who has made my body His holy temple. It is to Him *I* also trust myself.

Choosing to engage in mental sexual pollution can and usually does lead to some kind of bondage, even demonic bondage. Figure 17.1, "The Continuum of Sin" (p. 134), illustrates how the wrong choices can lead to bondage.

Probably you feel you would never slip into immorality. All committed Christians should feel that way. So did the young woman whose story appeared in *Decision* magazine, January, 1988.[5] I trust it will serve as a sober warning of how vulnerable we all are to sexual temptation of both mind and body. Written by Maureen Grant, the article is called "I Was Not Immune."

> Our next-door neighbors were separating; Elaine had been having an affair with a business acquaintance. Two homes were broken—four lives would never be the same.
>
> "Well," I told my husband simply, "at least you'll never have to worry about your wife being unfaithful." Infidelity was the furthest thing from my mind.
>
> I naively thought that as a Christian I was safe from temptation. Nothing like that could ever happen to me! Little did I know that a few months later I would face one of the strongest temptations I had ever encountered in my 10 years as a Christian.
>
> A co-worker at the office, Doug, and I began to have an occasional cup of coffee together. I assured myself that there was nothing wrong with these "dates"—Doug was just a friend whose company I enjoyed. Yet I began to realize how much I looked forward to these meetings. The many compliments Doug gave me bolstered my ego. And soon I was telling him my personal problems and revealing confidences that should have been shared with my husband alone.
>
> Before I knew it, a fantasy developed in my mind. At first it happened occasionally, but it reached a point where my thought life centered on this man. I began mentally to rehearse details of an affair with Doug. Fidelity toward my husband looked colorless in comparison to the inviting relationship I could be having. To add to the temptation, Doug was suggesting meetings outside working hours.
>
> I struggled with conflicting feelings. I wanted to pursue the relationship and I wanted to remain faithful to my husband. Finally I confided in a trusted Christian friend.

Her advice was straightforward: "Run from the source of temptation." Quoting a verse of Scripture, she warned, "'Your adversary the devil, as a roaring lion, walketh about, seeking whom he may devour.' Resist Satan at all costs."

How foolish I had been to think that being a Christian somehow made me immune to temptation! I took her advice, even though it meant changing jobs. I knew that it would be difficult for me not to respond to Doug's attentions.

Next I realized that my thought life desperately needed changing. An affair happens in the mind long before it actually occurs. We read in God's word, "When lust hath conceived, it bringeth forth sin: and sin, when it is finished, bringeth forth death." Though it took self-discipline when a lustful thought entered my mind, I refused to let it linger.

How had I been spending my leisure hours? I thought of the trashy novels I read, the soap operas I watched where characters hopped from one lover to another, apparently suffering no ill consequences. Was this kind of entertainment meant for a child of God?

I reminded myself of a verse in Philippians: "Whatsoever things are true, whatsoever things are honest, whatsoever things are just, whatsoever things are pure, whatsoever things are lovely, whatsoever things are of good report; if there be any virtue, and if there be any praise, think on these things."

During the time I ordinarily spent watching television, I now started Bible study, something I had been neglecting. The verses I read provided spiritual strength, something to fall back on when tempted.

I examined my relationship with my husband. All too often we had been taking each other for granted! I reminded myself that my husband was a gift from the Lord, and I chose to make our marriage the most important relationship in my life.

I hesitate to think about the direction my life would have taken had I followed my selfish desires. How important that we adhere to the wisdom in Ephesians: "Put on the whole armor of God, that [we] may be able to stand against the wiles of the devil."

I was the main speaker at a major Christian conference center a few years ago. During the morning teaching session I spoke on "Spiritual Warfare as a Multidimensional Sin War." In one of the evening sessions I taught on the potential of demonic activity in the lives of Christians bound by sexual immorality to the point of sexual addiction.[6]

After that final session I had a late snack with John, the camp director.

"Ed," he said, "After hearing your sessions today, I have an idea what may be the problem in the life of the senior pastor where I was associate pastor before coming here. From what you have been teaching us I would suspect that the pastor is demonized," he said.

"I never say a person's problem is partially the result of demonization unless I actually make contact with demons in his life," I replied. "So if you will keep that in mind, I am willing to listen to the story. I can see you are deeply concerned about this pastor."

"I was the associate pastor of the church," John said. "It was and probably still is the largest and fastest growing church in the city. People come to Christ weekly during the church services. The pastor truly preaches the Word of God.

"One day a young married woman came to me for counseling. She was brokenhearted because she had been having an affair. God had brought her under such conviction she had already broken off the illicit relationship. She came to me for help.

"I ministered to her from the Word of God, assuring her of God's forgiveness and praying with her. Finally after one of the sessions she said, 'Pastor, the worst thing about this affair is the person with whom I have been involved is our senior pastor.'"

Figure 17.1
The Continuum of Sin
("an uninterrupted ordered sequence"—Webster)

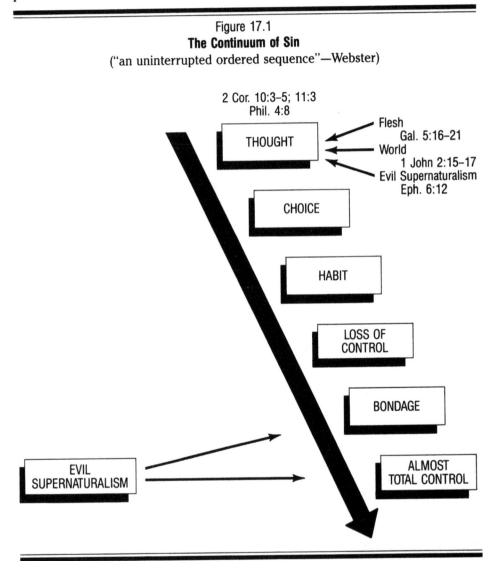

John was speechless. At first he thought the woman was lying, that perhaps she was infatuated with the pastor and was out to hurt him because he was unresponsive to her flirtations. But the more he counseled with her the more he became convinced of her sincerity.

Over the course of the months following this counseling session, several other women came to him with the same story. All had been having sexual affairs with the senior pastor.

John carefully investigated each case. He had to have irrefutable evidence with which to face the pastor. The pastor had a strong personality, and John knew his own ministry was in jeopardy if the pastor denied the charges. In time he had the needed evidence. Several of the women were willing to face the pastor with John and other church leaders.

John decided to talk with the pastor alone as the Scriptures teach. The meeting was very unpleasant. The pastor denied the charges. John asked him if he would deny the charges with the women present. He refused to see the women.

"I was really in a tight spot," John said. "If it had been just one woman that might be different. Perhaps it could be false accusation. While it seems unbelievable, before I left the church I had talked with about thirty women with whom the pastor had had sexual relations over the years. Since the pastor refused to confront any of the women face-to-face, I had to assume his guilt.

"I next followed the biblical procedure and took the matter to the church elders. They became furious with me. They said that God was blessing the church under the pastor's leadership. Therefore these stories could *not* be true.

"I begged them to at least look into the matter but they categorically refused. They were certain that people would not be coming to Christ and the church growing so rapidly, if the pastor were other than a holy man.

"Then came the final blow. The elders said I must leave the church since I was a carrier of malicious gossip.

"I had no choice but to resign. The pastor is still there and the church is still growing. After hearing your teaching this week I have begun to wonder if there might be a demonic dimension to his problem."

Of course there was no way I could judge just from the story I was told. Even if a strong demonic dimension to his sexual licentiousness existed, the pastor was still responsible for his actions. He was choosing to walk in the flesh in this area of immorality. To sin or not is a choice.

18

Homosexuality in Biblical Perspective

66 **I** hate my homosexuality!" The words exploded like small bombs in the quiet of the pastor's study. "I love the Lord and I want to serve Him! I know these homosexual desires of mine do not please Him. Please help me!"

The pastor listened intently to the handsome young man pacing the floor of the study and crying for help.

"I came to you," the young man continued, "because you are well known as an evangelical pastor and I thought you would understand my problem. Everyone else would damn me outright to hell, but I don't need damnation. I need someone to help me out of the hell of my homosexuality."

As the young man continued to pour out his anguish of desperation and frustration, the pastor shifted slightly in his chair.

"I've attended Bible school, but I simply can't enter the ministry with this hanging over me." The young man looked imploringly at the minister. "Please, I'm so confused. Will you help me?"

Did the pastor condemn the young man as others had? No! Instead, the pastor totally betrayed his ordination vows and the ethics of the counselor-counselee relationship and tried to seduce the troubled youth right there in his office!

Completely devastated, the young man fled. Badly damaged by this incident and on the edge of panic, he called me. I counseled him as much as I could by telephone. Finally he found a godly Christian counselor in his own city who is showing him the way to victory.

Too horrible to be true? No! This is a true story.

The second moral sin mentioned by the apostle Paul in Galatians 5:19 is *akatharsia* in Greek. Fung says its meaning is basically "uncleanness" as the KJV translates it.[1] The NAS translates it "impurity." It often appears in the New Testament with *porneia*, "immorality" (2 Cor. 12:21; Eph. 5:3,5; Col. 3:5).

Vine says the Greek word in this context means "uncleanness, impurity or filthiness in a moral sense."[2] It covers a wide variety of impure sexual practices, but I limit our study here to two areas, homosexuality and masturbation. I do so because of the prominence of these two impure sexual practices in our day among Christians and Christian leaders. We will start with homosexuality.

John White in his insightful book, *Eros Defiled: The Christian and Sexual Sin,* provides some of the most balanced teaching in print on Christians and sexual issues. His chapter on homosexuality is entitled "Two Halves Do Not Make One Whole."[3] I will return to White's ideas in a moment.

Homosexuality and the Bible

According to Scripture, homosexual activity of any type is sin and is strongly condemned.

It is first spoken of with reference to the cities of Sodom and Gomorrah in

Genesis 19. From the evil practices of the inhabitants of these two cities (v. 5f) the word *sodomite* has originated. It is used several times in the KJV of the Old Testament (Deut. 23:17; 1 Kings 14:24; 15:12; 22:46; 2 Kings 23:7; Job 36:14 margin). Most of the references refer to the abomination of male cult prostitution which was common among the pagan nations in contact with Israel and, in times of spiritual decline, was practiced by the Israelites also (Judg. 19:22; 1 Kings 14:24; 2 Kings 23:7).

Homosexuality is categorically prohibited by God in the Old Testament laws governing the sexual life of his people (Lev. 18:22; 20:13; Deut. 23:18). It is called an "abomination" five times in Leviticus 18 (vv. 22,26,27,29,30). In Leviticus 20:13 it is called "a detestable act." This is consistent with the root meaning of the word which means "to detest," "to hate," or "abhor."[4] It was so detestable a sin in the eyes of God that death by stoning was the punishment inflicted on its practitioners (Lev. 20:13).

The New Testament describes this sexual sin as one of the terrible consequences of humanity's rebellion against the lordship of God in Romans 1:18–32. In verses 26–28 the apostle writes:

> For this reason God gave them over to degrading passions; for their women exchanged the natural function for that which is unnatural, and in the same way also the men abandoned the natural function of the woman and burned in their desire toward one another, men with men committing indecent acts and receiving in their own persons the due penalty of their error. And just as they did not see fit to acknowledge God any longer, God gave them over to a depraved mind, to do those things which are not proper.

Homosexuality was as widespread during New Testament times as it was in the Old Testament era; thus Paul's references to it in Romans 1:26–28 and 1 Timothy 1:9–10.

John White writes that "Homosexuality is a problem common to both sexes. *Homo* means alike or equal to. It does *not* refer to maleness. Lesbianism is simply a word used to describe female homosexuality."[5]

Homosexual activity does *not* have its primary origin in the biological make-up of certain men or women. It is primarily learned behavior.[6] Whatever is learned can, with help if needed, be unlearned. Therefore homosexuals can unlearn this sinful sexual behavior just as heterosexuals who persistently commit immorality must "unlearn" theirs.

The Bible does not specifically deal with the social versus the biological origins of homosexuality. It simply presents it as sin and condemns its practice. Many secular authorities make it clear that no one is born homosexual, as many homosexuals affirm. In a thorough article called "The Homosexual In America" in *Time*, October 31, 1969, the writers affirm that

> The only thing most experts agree on is that homosexuality is not a result of any kinky gene or hormone predispositions—at least none that can be detected by present techniques. . . . The diverse psychological components of masculinity and femininity—"gender role identity"—are learned.

> "Gender is like language," says Johns Hopkins University Medical Psychologist John Money: "Genetics ordains only that language can develop, not whether it will be Nahuatl, Arabic or English.

> This does not mean that homosexuality is latent in all mature humans, as has been widely believed from a misreading of Freud. In American culture, sex roles are most powerfully determined in the home, and at such a young age (generally in the first

few years of life), that the psychological identity of most homosexuals—like that of most heterosexuals—is set before they know it.[7]

Homosexuality is not a different but acceptable lifestyle for human beings and especially not for Christians. In light of Matthew 5:27–30, homosexual fantasizing is sinful and all homosexual pornography must be resisted.

Homosexual conduct is completely forgivable along with all other sins, however. The Lord Jesus lists only one unpardonable sin, and it is not homosexuality (Matt. 12:31–32).

Christians with severe homosexual bondage need a support group to help them into freedom. Work with homosexuals reveals this need. Few homosexuals, even Christian ones, will make it alone. They need to confess their bondage to an understanding friend and support group.[8] Homosexual bondage both in the imagination and in practice is one of the most oppressive forms of sexual bondage known to man.

Homosexual Bondage in Biblical Times

Homosexuality was widespread in biblical times in both the Old and New Testament periods. Worst of all such activities were supported and encouraged by the nature-fertility cults and religions of the day.[9] While the fertility cults in their more "idealistic" form featured heterosexual cultic prostitution, it also included homosexual activities, along with bestiality and other almost indescribable sexual evils.[10]

John McClintock and James Strong write that the Hebrew word translated "sodomite" in the King James Version of the Old Testament

> was employed . . . for those who practiced as a religious rite the abominable and unnatural vice from which the inhabitants of Sodom and Gomorrah have defined their lasting infamy . . . This dreadful "consecration" [of the male prostitutes to the gods] or rather, desecration, was spread in different forms over Phoenicia (the land of Canaan), Syria, Phrygia, Assyria and Babylonia. Ashtaroth, the Greek Astarate, was its chief object. It appears also to have been established at Rome.[11]

Some of the converts from the pagan religions of Paul's day had been practicing homosexuals. Writing to the Corinthian church the apostle says:

> Or do you not know that the unrighteous shall not inherit the kingdom of God? Do not be deceived; neither fornicators, nor idolaters, nor adulterers, nor effeminate, nor homosexuals, nor thieves, nor the covetous, nor drunkards, nor revilers, nor swindlers, shall inherit the kingdom of God. And such were some of you; but you were washed, but you were sanctified, but you were justified in the name of the Lord Jesus Christ, and in the Spirit of our God. (1 Cor. 6:9–11)

In this passage Paul lists the sins common in the Gentile world of his day especially prevalent in Corinth and other centers of commerce and pagan religious shrines and temples. Ellicott writes that

> The mention of gross sensual sins (fornication, adultery and two words for homosexuality, "effeminate and homosexuals") in connection with idolaters point to the fact that they were particularly associated in the ritual of the heathen, which, of course, intensified the danger against which the Apostle warns the Corinthians.[12] (Rom. 8:13; Gal. 5:19–20; 1 Tim. 1:9–10; Titus 1:12)

The Greek word *malakos* translated "effeminate" has troubled commentators. All effeminate men are not homosexuals, just as all masculine women are not lesbians. Its contextual use here, however, would imply some gross form of sexual sin, probably involving non-heterosexual sexual sin.

Vine says it is used here "not simply of a male who practices forms of lewdness, but persons in general, who are guilty of addiction to sins of the flesh, voluptuous."[13] G. G. Findlay agrees, saying it signifies "general addiction to sins of the flesh."[14]

F. W. Grosheide takes a stronger stand, however. He says the words "effeminate men and abusers of themselves with men designate passive and active homosexuals respectively."[15]

The idea of fixed passive and active roles in homosexuality is a stereotype not compatible with the facts, John White says. Homosexuals can and do change roles at will.[16] However, although one cannot be certain that both *malakos* (effeminate) and *arsenokoitai* (abusers of themselves with mankind) refer to passive and active roles in homosexuality, the evidence would point in that direction.

Gordon D. Fee, writing in his commentary on 1 Corinthians, says that the evidence supports Grosheide's position. "Effeminate" probably refers to young men who sold themselves to older men as their mistresses, and to young cult prostitutes who took the more passive role. He supports the NIV which translates the words "neither male prostitutes nor homosexual offenders."[17]

No matter how we view some of these words, the widespread practice of homosexuality is probably referred to here twice (1 Cor. 6:9). This, with 1 Corinthians 5:9–11, would form the apostle's list of the sinful conduct the Corinthians were guilty of before coming to Christ.

William Barclay says the following about the word *pornoi*, translated "fornicators" in 1 Corinthians 6:9, "The word that is used for fornicators is an especially unpleasant word, it means male prostitute. It must have been hard to be a Christian in the tainted atmosphere of Corinth."[18]

Barclay records some interesting suggestions on the word *malakos* translated "effeminate" in the KJV and NAS. He translates it "sensualists" and has some insightful comments on "abusers of themselves with mankind" (KJV) and *arsenokoitai*, translated homosexuals (NAS):[19]

> We have left *the most unnatural sin* to the end—there were those who were *homosexuals*. This was the sin which had *swept like a cancer through Greek life and which, from Greece, invaded Rome*. We can scarcely realize how riddled the ancient world was with it.
>
> Even so great a man as *Socrates* practiced it; *Plato's* dialogue *The Symposium* is always said to be one of the greatest works on *love* in the world, but its subject is not natural but unnatural love. Fourteen out of the first fifteen Roman Emperors practiced unnatural vice.
>
> At this very time Nero was emperor. He had taken a boy called Sporus and had had him castrated. He had then married him with a full ceremony and took him home in procession to his palace and lived with him as wife . . .
>
> In this particular vice in the time of the Early Church *the world was lost to shame;* and there can be little doubt that that was one of the main causes of its *degeneracy* and the *final collapse* of its civilization.

Deliverance From Homosexual Bondage

The apostle begins 1 Corinthians 6:11 with the words "and such were some of you." Findlay says that "*kai tauta tines,* etc., means 'and these things you were, some (of you).' The neuter *tauta* is contemptuous, 'such abomination' were some of you."[20] Ellicott translates them "of such a description were some of you."[21]

Paul follows the bad news with the good by revealing God's fivefold transforming power which set them free from bondage to the terrible sins of verses 9–10.

First, he says, *"you were washed."* Matthew Henry explains this washing as referring to "the blood of Christ and *the washing of regeneration,* (which) can purge away all guilt and defilement."[22] Leon Morris concurs by saying that while many commentators see here a reference to baptism, there is nothing in the context to indicate it. He writes:[23]

> The verb *apelousasthe* . . . is in the middle voice, with a force something like, "you got yourself washed" (as in Acts 22:16). . . . The word may signify the kind of washing we see in Revelation 1:5: "Unto Him that loved us and washed us from our sins in His blood." The prefix *apo* points to the complete washing "away" of sins. The tense is past, the aorist referring to a decise action.

Second, and third Paul says *"you were sanctified, . . . justified."*

Matthew Henry calls this "a rhetorical change of the natural order," between sanctification and justification. I will return to this point in a moment.[24]

Fourth and fifth, the apostle says *their sanctification and justification came "in the name of the Lord Jesus Christ, and in the Spirit of our God."*

The use of "the name" in biblical times was much more complex than its similar use in the Western world. At times it can be a difficult concept to grasp. It takes W. C. Kaiser, Jr. seven double-columned pages in the *Zondervan Pictorial Encyclopedia of the Bible* to explain its use in Scripture and the culture of the biblical world.[25]

Perhaps Morris' short comment will suffice in reference to the name of Jesus and the Holy Spirit for now. We will examine the biblical concept of the name of our study of Acts.[26]

> The name brings before us all that is implied in the character of the Lord, while the full title "The Lord Jesus Christ" brings out the dignity of Him whom we serve. To this is joined the Spirit of our God. There is a power manifest in Christian living, and that power is not human. It is a divine power, given by the very Spirit of God Himself.

> It is curious that this reference follows that of sanctification. It may be that Paul felt that sanctification required special stress. . . . The God who has justified them will surely provide them with the power needed to carry through their sanctification.

Matthew Henry's comment is inspiring.[27]

> Sanctification is mentioned before justification and yet the name of Christ, by which we are justified, is placed before the Spirit of God by whom we are sanctified. Our justification is owing to the merit of Christ; our sanctification to the operation of the Spirit; but both go together. Note, none are cleansed from the guilt of sin but those who are also sanctified by His Spirit. All who are made righteous in the sight of God are made holy by the grace of God.

Thus there is hope for the homosexual. While homosexuality exerts an awful, disabling power over the lives of countless men and women, the justifying, sanctifying, transforming power "of the name of the Lord Jesus Christ and the Spirit of our God" is greater. I close this point with a beautiful extended quote from William Barclay:[28]

The proof of Christianity lay in its power. It could take the dregs of humanity and make men out of them. It could take men lost to shame and make them sons of God.

There is the most amazing contrast between the pagan and the Christian literature of the day. Seneca, a contemporary of Paul, cries out that what men want is "a hand let down to lift them up." "Men," he declared, "are overwhelmingly conscious of their weakness in necessary things." "Men love their vices," he said with a kind of despair, "and hate them at one and the same time." He looked at himself and called himself a *homo non tolerabilis,* a man not to be tolerated. Into this world, conscious of a tide of decadence that nothing could stop, there came the sheer radiant power of Christianity, which was indeed triumphantly able to make all things new.

While not minimizing the incredible binding power of homosexuality and homosexual fantasizing, I want to declare emphatically that God's power is available to all practicing homosexuals and to all those who are plagued by homosexual lusts. The God who made new creations out of homosexuals in Paul's day is in the same regenerating business today (2 Cor. 5:17).

A Modern Case Study

A very good friend was brought to Christ while she was a practicing lesbian. She was part of the street youth culture which characterized Hollywood in the 1960s. She had been faithful to her lesbian lover for five years. She told me the following story of her conversion and the gradual healing of her sexuality.

"A group of Christians were witnessing for Christ near Hollywood and Vine. As they shared the gospel I began to hunger to know God as they did. For the first time in my life I understood God's love for me. I was thrilled. God loved me, even me. Jesus loved me so much he gave his life on the cross for me, even me.

"I received Him on the spot and went home filled with peace. I sensed great joy at the reality of his love for me. Like the woman taken in adultery (John 8:1–11), He did not condemn me but forgave me. To me He spoke those immortal words, 'Neither do I condemn thee: go, and sin no more' (KJV).

"The people who led me to Christ did not know about my lesbian partner. They said nothing about homosexuality. As I went home, however, God spoke to my heart. I knew the union was unacceptable in His eyes. I knew I would have to break off the relationship if I were to live in His kingdom. Though it was one of the most difficult things I have ever done in my life, I did what I knew was God's will. My partner did not understand. She was heartbroken. I was too, but I left.

"I associated with the group of Christian young adults who had brought the gospel to me. In time I was able to tell them about my homosexual problem. They became my family and support group. I would not have survived if it were not for their support. They taught me the Word of God and how to pray and witness for my Savior.

"I went through an emotional storm for almost three years. I did not know how strong the homosexual emotions were in my mind, body, imagination, and my very being. Sometimes I did not know if I would make it, but by God's grace I did.

"I abstained from all sexual relationships. When the yearnings came upon me I would call out to the Lord for His strength and He was faithful. Also I shared with my Christian support group when the temptations became almost unbearable.

"God slowly began to change my sexual orientation. This meant he had to transform me totally, especially emotionally. Our sexuality is so interwoven with our emotions, our self-image, our mind, our will, that this transformation went to the very root of my personality.

"I realized my sexual orientation was not primarily biological. It was environmental, emotional, and the result of wrong choices I had made over a period of time. By God's grace I realized I could change to respond sexually to men, not to women. The change seemed to move through three overlapping stages.

"First I began to see women differently. They were my sisters, not my lovers. Gradually I began to lose the sexual drive towards other women.

"Next, I began to 'notice' men in a positive manner for the first time. Some of the brothers were so beautiful as men and as my close friends, I began to lose the negative male orientation that I had known before.

"Lastly, I began to feel sexual attraction towards men. This was a miracle. The thought of a sexual relationship with a man before this was as repugnant to me as a homosexual relationship is to a heterosexual man or woman.

"I didn't begin to fantasize having sex with every attractive man I met. That too would have been sinful. But I could now accept the fact that marriage to a fine Christian man would be acceptable. I began to look forward to that possibility as any 'normal' woman does.

"When this change began, I knew that I was truly a new creation in Christ. Sin had degraded me into something dishonoring to God. He gave my womanhood back to me. I love Him with all my heart."

Few practicing homosexuals are instantly set free from their homosexual orientation. To promise them this is to deceive them. It is both without biblical basis and contrary to the church's two thousand years of experience.

There are exceptions, however, especially if there is a direct demonic dimension to the homosexual problem. Even if the homosexual is demonized and homosexual demons are cast out of his life, the rebuilding of his or her sexuality is usually a process, not the result of a few deliverance sessions.

One important note brought out by my sister's testimony is the necessity of a support group if one is going to see the addiction of homosexuality broken in their life.[29] "Addiction thrives on isolation," says a former homosexual. "Once we establish a personal support system and we accept the grace of Christ, the power of any addiction will weaken, even that of homosexuality."[30]

My reborn, former lesbian sister in Christ lived for several years as a godly single young adult after her sexual transformation. In time an amazing thing happened. While actively involved in a ministry to emotionally damaged and disturbed people, a handsome Christian man became part of the ministry team with her. A few years ago they were married, and now they have several beautiful children. Both are continuing to be used by God to minister to needy people. What a reward for faithful obedience!

19

Homosexuality and Contemporary Ministry

The war with homosexuality is one of the most acute dimensions of spiritual warfare affecting the church today. The organized socio-political movement that has come to the forefront to force acceptance of open homosexuality upon society and the church is the so-called Gay Rights Movement.

As believers we must be fair to homosexuals. We must recognize that the Gay Rights Movement does not represent all of them. While exact figures would be almost impossible to come by, it is possible that many more homosexuals refuse to participate in this corrupt movement than those who do take part.

Most homosexuals or individuals who battle with homosexual lusts are not interested in flaunting their sexuality before the media and the masses. They are no more interested in parading down main street half-naked and engaging in shameful sexual actions in public than are heterosexuals. Thus they are people who merit our love, compassion, and gentle, but firm Christian witness.

The Gay Rights Movement, in general, is not a beneficial movement for confused homosexuals, however. It is a demonic movement. I am not affirming that all members of the movement are demonized. Many are, but not all of them. I am not affirming that all members of the movement are evil people. Many are, but not all of them. Some of their leaders may not be totally committed to unrestrained moral evil. Many are, but probably not all of them.

Finally, I am not denying that some members of the Gay Rights Movement are loving, kind, and compassionate people. Many of them are, but not all of them.

What I am affirming is that all of them are sinners whose damaged sexuality has almost become the focal point of their life. They are as enslaved to their distorted sexual drives as were the Nazis to their ethnic perversion as the Master Race. All of this shows evidence of manipulation by demonic forces.

Ronald Fung comments on the last of the group of three moral sins mentioned by Paul in Galatians 5:19. Since there is always overlapping when describing the four groups, and since his words are so appropriate to the unrestrained sexual misconduct characteristic of the Gay Rights Movement, I apply them to the subject at hand. Fung says:

> The sin of "indecency" (NEB) may represent and advance on "fornication" [immorality]; and "impurity," for it is vice paraded with blatant impudence and insolence, without regard for self respect, for the rights and feelings of others, or for public decency. Here precisely is why . . . indecency is such a terrible thing. It is the act of a character which has lost that which ought to be its greatest defense—its self respect, and its sense of shame.[1]

What a picture of the public image the organizers of Gay Rights Days and Gay Rights Parades seek to convey before the world!

I live in San Jose, California, only 40 miles from San Francisco. San Francisco, the "City by the Bay," is physically one of the loveliest cities in the world. Situated by the San Francisco Bay and the mouth of the massive Sacramento River and surrounded by lovely, green mountains, it boasts two of the most spectacular bridges in the world, the breathtaking Golden Gate Bridge and the splendid Bay Bridge. Its skyline both by day and night is beautiful beyond description.

Yet this gem of a city has unfortunately become one of the Gay Rights capitals of the world. Not only do some San Francisco public officials flaunt their homosexuality before the world, but its annual Gay Rights Day celebration and parade has become one of the most repugnant sexual displays in the USA.

The annual parade, with its semi-nudity and sensual street dancing before the television cameras, reminds one of Sodom in Genesis 19. The perversity of its sexual display is so sickening, a sensitive person cannot witness it without feeling physically and emotionally sick and spiritually sad and angry.

If heterosexuals were to do in public and on nationwide TV some of the evil the homosexuals engage in during Gay Rights Day they would probably be arrested. Because this brazen, shameless minority is so entrenched in San Francisco culture, public officials fear its wrath. Thus they are allowed to violate the public sense of decency without fear of serious repercussions.

Most of the leadership and members of the Gay Rights Movement seem to be persons who have lost their "self-respect," their "sense of shame," and any consideration "for the rights and feelings of others," as Fung pointed out. Such a movement for any so-called "cause" must be rejected.

The individual members are still the objects of God's love, however. Therefore they must be the subjects of our love. We must hate what they stand for without hating them as persons.[2]

They are all victims of multidimensional spiritual warfare. They are enslaved to the lusts of the flesh. They are carried along by the world which, confused as it is about right and wrong, supports them, applauds their expression of sexual freedom, and encourages their shame.

They are all controlled by the Devil, however. Sexual, rebellion, shame, self-hate, bitterness, and disease demons swarm in and around their movement, gleefully inspiring them to ever more flagrant and self-destructive vices. Not even the widespread agony of death by AIDS stops them in their mad journey towards self-destruction.

The present homosexual movement is making a tremendous effort to penetrate our churches and even the pastorate. Their targets are conservative evangelical churches. This is one of the most serious issues facing the church today.

At the time of this writing, the Southern Baptist Convention, the largest Protestant denomination in the USA, has successfully defeated the efforts of some leaders to allow Christian homosexuals to be admitted into the ministry. Three cheers for the Southern Baptists!

The Episcopalians have not fared that well, however. In 1990 they accepted into the ministry a practicing lesbian. In a television interview aired in June, 1991, President George Bush, who is an Episcopalian and evidently a genuine believer, expressed his opposition to this action. Three cheers for President Bush! Shame on the Episcopal bishops who ordained this woman!

At the time of writing (1991), the question of the acceptance of homosexual marriages and homosexuals in the ministry is to be finally decided upon by the Presbyterian Church, USA after years of intense controversy.

The Evangelical Lutheran Church in America is to be commended for its courage in expelling two San Francisco Lutheran churches in 1990 which defied denominational policy and ordained three practicing homosexuals to the pastoral ministry. The Rev. Joseph Wagner, Executive Director of the Church's Division for Ministry, said the denomination disagrees with those who contend ordination of homosexuals is a civil rights issue.

Wagner makes an excellent distinction between civil rights and ordination responsibility. In the *San Jose Mercury News,* January 10, 1991, he stated, "This Church champions the civil rights of all persons. But ordination is not a civil right. It is a privilege granted by the Church to those who meet its established standards." Excellent reasoning!

Perhaps one of the best summaries of the organized campaign of homosexual "Christians" to gain full acceptance as both members and pastors of Christian churches is found in one edition of *Pastoral Renewal.*[3] Though almost ten years old, it is not dated. The April, 1981, leading article is entitled "Christian Men and Homosexual Desires." One statement in this excellent article deals with the potential demonic dimension to homosexual bondage, a subject we will consider later in our study.

> It's important to pray with the man [the homosexual]. It is particularly important to pray for deliverance from the influence of evil spirits. Satan is very active in this area. Deliverance usually does not produce a change in desires, but it helps the man experiencing the freedom not to be ruled by them.

We must leave behind the repugnance of the Gay Rights Movement and return with compassion to those who battle with homosexual desires or have fallen into homosexual experiences.

While the church thrills at the testimony of adulterers, thieves, or even murderers who come to Christ, let a homosexual come into the light and often it is a different story. May we learn to love homosexuals with Christ's love, a love of understanding and compassion which is directed towards sinners like all of us.

I must reiterate that not everyone who has or is engaged in homosexuality is necessarily a homosexual. Dr. John White brings this out in his open confession of his own homosexual experiences as a child. The homosexual fixation that arose out of that experience accompanied him for years. He was never, however, a homosexual. Many persons who engaged in homosexual activities as children or young people are not homosexuals.

Usually such persons were led into these experiences by respected older persons or by peers with whom they engaged in sexual experimentation. Often these individuals will fear that they are homosexuals or bisexuals, while they are not.

Recently my wife and I were counseling a lovely young lady who was preparing for mission work. She was deeply troubled by a recent brief homosexual relationship she had been involved in. She was overseas working on a mission station. A careless mission administrator had placed her in an administrative task that was beyond her capabilities or experience. She worked from dawn until nightfall striving faithfully to carry out her duties. Soon she became physically and emotionally exhausted. She felt alone and very vulnerable.

An older woman working with her on the mission station would come into the young lady's room during evenings, supposedly to encourage her in her difficult job. Soon she began to hold her hand and hug her, supposedly out of concern for her welfare. The young lady at first was unaware of what was occurring, but as the hugging became more and more sensual, she tried to reject the lady's advances.

One night she was so weary, confused, and emotionally upset by her difficult job she did not resist the lady's fondling. Before she knew what was occurring they were involved in a homosexual act. She knew it was wrong, but once she was sexually stimulated, there was no turning back. She was too much in need of tender, touching love to stop.

This continued almost nightly for a period of time. One day the young lady went away from the mission base for rest and reflection. With horror and shame she "came to herself," to use her words, and realized the evil of what she was involved in from God's perspective. She wept in confession and repentance before God and recommitted her life, her body and all of its members, including her sexuality, to the lordship of Christ.

Shame and self-disgust overwhelmed her. She went to the lady and told her to keep away from her. When the lady refused and insisted they continue, the young girl had no recourse but to go to one of the mission leaders, confess her sin, and ask for protection from the aggressive older lady.

The older lady was dismissed from her mission work. The young girl voluntarily left, feeling unqualified to continue as a missionary. The emotional scars and shame continued for some time until the Lord met her in a wonderful manner and assured her of his forgiveness.

In time she applied to another mission as a career missionary. She felt she had to make them aware of her sin and trust the Lord for her future. One of the mission directors, knowing of my counseling ministry with troubled people, asked me to meet her. I asked permission for my wife to be with me, and it was granted.

It was not difficult to establish the fact that the young lady was not homosexual. Indeed, she was attracted to men in a normal way and repelled by even the memory of her brief, homosexual relationship. She was a lovely, Spirit-filled Christian, anxious to please the Lord. Also, while praying that some day God would send a godly man into her life, she had accepted her present singleness. She had learned important lessons through her past experience, however.

This was several years ago. She is doing well as a single missionary. She is part of a strong support group so that some of her needs for love and friendship are being met. Just because she became trapped in a brief, homosexual relationship by an aggressive, older woman did not make her homosexual. The same is true of many persons who have fallen into the same trap.

If the sympathetic reader wants to understand at even deeper levels the warfare a homosexual Christian can go through in finding wholeness in Christ read Don Baker's 1985 shocker, *Beyond Rejection: The Church, Homosexuality and Hope*. To better understand what the book is all about I quote from the book's foreword:

> "Homosexuals can't change."

> It's a lie that has permeated our society. It's accepted as a fact within many churches. Most tragic of all, many Christians who struggle with homosexuality have embraced it as reality.

> But the heart of the gospel is the hope of new life for all who seek it, including homosexuals. This is the story of one man's victory in embracing that new way of life.[4]

Frank Worthen, director of Love in Action and author of the foreword, describes the story the book tells as one of incredible discouragement and defeat, of a loving wife who clings to hope, of friends who gave sacrificially of themselves, and finally of "one man lifted from a tangled web of sin by the power and grace of God. . . . May this book be a beacon of hope to thousands of men and women who have been defeated by homosexuality—but who know in their hearts that Jesus Christ can set them free."[5]

Unfortunately, homosexual drives are also among the least understood and the least tolerated by the church.

The church is to love the most unloved. In the eyes of many believers, homosexuals (and child abusers) are to be detested. This attitude delights Satan and his evil spirits. For years they have been telling damaged people who battle with homosexual problems that the church hates them and will not receive them. Their job is not at all difficult. Many Christians become their duped allies, parroting Satan's lie that homosexuals are to be scorned and rejected.

In October, 1962, *Eternity* magazine published an article entitled "Homosexuality" by Dr. Lars I. Granberg, Professor of Psychology and Clinical Psychologist at Hope College. The subject was so controversial the editors did everything but apologize for even publishing the article. They wrote:[6]

> Several months ago, a Christian young man wrote us about his problem of homosexuality. A few months later, another man wrote us on the same subject; and still later, a missionary who was struggling with this problem wrote us.
>
> Gradually, we came to realize that this was a bigger problem than we had imagined. . . . We have refrained from discussing this subject for some time, and even now we are aware that we will be charged with sensationalism or crudeness for doing so. However, the problem of homosexuality—even in evangelical circles—cannot be denied.

While openness to the question of homosexuality among Christians and Christian leaders has certainly made some progress since 1962, we still have a long way to go. As a result, thousands of unchurched homosexuals avoid our evangelical churches like the plague. Believers with confused homosexual tendencies remain locked in their prisons of guilt and helplessness, not knowing where to go to find help.

While it would be inaccurate to affirm that all practicing homosexuals are demonized, as some brethren have done, the demonic activity in the homosexual movement is very strong.[7] Many individual homosexuals are demonized, some severely so—even Christians. All are in desperate need of finding the full freedom that is their birthright in Christ. May we be faithful in loving them with Christ's love, gaining their confidence, leading them to Jesus, and helping them to find a support group within all our churches!

20

Autosexuality

U ncleanness or impurity covers not only the practice of homosexuality, but also that of self-stimulation, otherwise known as masturbation.[1] Webster defines *masturbation* as the "stimulation of the genital organs to orgasm, achieved by manual or other bodily contact exclusive of sexual intercourse." There would probably be general acceptance among physicians and counselors on this or a similar definition of masturbation. The essence of the practice then would be bringing about orgasm by any means other than sexual intercourse.

Toward a Useful Definition

I have difficulty with this broad definition, however. That is why I prefer the narrower term "sexual self-stimulation." This definition emphasizes self-gratification, a form of narcissism. It is a totally self-centered sexual activity through self-stimulation to the point of orgasm. I also like Norman L. Geisler's word for this practice. He calls it "autosexuality."[2]

Webster's definition would mean that almost all married couples practice masturbation at different times in their married life when full sexual intercourse is not possible or advisable for one of the marriage partners for various reasons. It would also mean that some married couples regularly practice masturbation, particularly women who are not able to reach orgasm without manual stimulation by their mate. Often when this situation exists there is enough personal trauma without adding to it the idea that masturbation is being engaged in.

Psychologist Earl D. Wilson recognizes this reality in his excellent chapter on masturbation in his helpful book *Sexual Sanity*.[3] Wilson writes, "Masturbation is necessary for some couples in order to achieve maximum sexual adjustment."

When I counsel married couples who face this type of personal problem I never use the word masturbation to refer to their practice. I prefer the term "manual stimulation." Even though we live in an era of so-called sexual liberation, among sensitive Christians there is still shame connected with the word "masturbation." To heap that shame on an already troubled woman or man is unfair and unwise.

My definition of masturbation then would be the practice of self-stimulation to the point of orgasm by whatever means.[4] The focus is on self-stimulation. It is a form of self-sex involving a preoccupation with one's own sexual organs and orgasm. Most Christian authors I have read hold to a somewhat more flexible view of autosexuality than I do. However, they recognize many of its inherent dangers.

The Bible's Silence

The Bible says absolutely nothing about this practice. Psychologist Earl Wilson correctly observes:[5]

Masturbation, like many other topics of great personal and social concern, is neither condemned nor condoned in Scripture. In fact, I have not been able to find any direct scriptural statements about masturbation. Christians have not always been honest about this fact and have tried to give the impression that their opinions on the subject were fortified with biblical imperatives. Such is not the case.

He then cites the traditional Roman Catholic interpretation of Genesis 38:8–10.[6] Alcorn says it was from this text that masturbation became "labeled onanism after the supposed masturbation by a man named Onan," but a study of this passage reveals no autosexuality at all. Onan had sexual intercourse with the woman, but just as he reached the point of orgasm "he wasted his seed on the ground, in order not to give offspring to his brother" (v. 9). Alcorn continues saying, "The issue was Onan's disobedience in refusing to raise up children for his deceased brother, which he was bound by law and family loyalty to do."[7]

An Appeal to Scriptural Principles

In cases like this where the Bible is silent, we must be guided by broad Scriptural principles concerning sexual practices. Sexuality is a gift of God. It is not only necessary for procreation, but is the one act that in the most meaningful manner makes the man and woman "one flesh." Intercourse is a kind of marriage, Geisler says:[8]

> If it is outside a life-long commitment of love then it is a "bad marriage." In fact, it is a sin the Bible calls fornication (cf. Gal. 5:19; 1 Cor. 6:18). The first reference to marriage declares that man and woman become "one flesh" (Gen. 2:24), implying that marriage occurs when two bodies are joined. . . . Intercourse initiates a "marriage." If it is not engaged in with a life-long commitment of love, then it was an evil union, an act of fornication.

Geisler considers autosexuality to be generally wrong, and masturbation to be sinful "(1) when its only motive is sheer biological pleasure, (2) when it is allowed to become a compulsive habit, and/or (3) when the habit results from inferior feelings and causes guilt feelings." Geisler next makes an important statement, "Masturbation is sinful when it is performed in connection with pornographic images, for as Jesus said, lust is a matter of the interests of the heart" (Matt. 5:28).[9]

Finally Geisler writes that autosexuality

> can be right if it is used as a limited, temporary program of self-control to avoid sexual sin before marriage. If one is fully committed to leading a pure life until marriage, it may be permissible on occasion to use autosexual stimulation to relieve one's tension. As long as it does not become a habit nor a means of gratifying one's lust, masturbation is not necessarily immoral. In fact, when the motive is not *lust* but *self-control,* masturbation can be a moral act (cf. 1 Cor. 7:5; 9:25). . . . Masturbation used in moderation without lust for the purpose of retaining one's purity is not immoral.[10]

Problems of Autosexuality

I am happy with Geisler's first statements about the three ways that autosexuality is wrong. I have trouble with his (and other writers') permissiveness of autosexuality to release sexual lust. First, is autosexuality to become a substitute husband or wife? As any happily married person knows, once you enter into a life of deep sexual fulfillment with your beloved, it is even more difficult to suddenly cut it off because of sickness, forced separation, and death.

Second, is autosexuality the only way to avoid lust? Are there not other ways much more in harmony with Scripture with no danger of becoming habit forming as is true with masturbation? Earl Wilson and Randy Alcorn, while generally agreeing with Geisler, make some important observations which give balance to our subject. Wilson argues for the biblical emphasis on self-control by saying that if autosexuality was the road to take, why did not the apostle Paul say so in his teachings on sexual self-control in 1 Corinthians 7:8–9? Why did he not say if one cannot control his sexual drive let him masturbate? That is what many writers seem to be saying. Wilson says:[11]

> One answer seems quite obvious. Masturbation is not a means of self-control. It is often a lack of self-control. Sexual fantasy and masturbation allow a person to engage in mental sex with numerous people. This does not seem compatible with Paul's exhortation to have self-control which we read about earlier in 1 Corinthians 6:12–13. . . . We kid ourselves when we say we can't live without masturbation. That very statement borders on obsession. We need to face the fact that we are a pleasure-loving people and that masturbation is one way we choose to worship pleasure rather than God.

Wilson continues saying that the second major problem with autosexuality is its depersonalization and quotes the title of John White's outstanding chapter on autosexuality, "Sex on a Desert Island." White's entire argument against autosexuality as a legitimate sexual lifestyle is that sex is given by God to counteract human loneliness ("It is not good for the man to be alone; I will make a helper suitable for him," Gen. 2:18). Autosexuality, however, produces further loneliness. That which was made to bring a man and woman together for life is abused to produce the worst kind of loneliness and isolation.[12]

> Your sexual longings are associated with a deeper need—that someone should . . . bring your isolation to an end. . . . Masturbation is to be alone on an island. It frustrates the very instinct it gratifies.

Alcorn agrees with the general line of thought developed by Wilson and White. He concludes his chapter on autosexuality with two important items.[13]

One, "masturbation seems to be a natural part of adolescent self-discovery, particularly among boys." He warns Christian parents not to be upset if they catch their adolescent children masturbating. Nor should they threaten their children that masturbation will lead to insanity or some kind of physical or later emotional maladjustment.

Two, persons should not allow autosexuality to become "the focus of their life. The guilt, shame and self-hatred as well as anger against God for making sexual stimulation such a powerful force in human life can cripple a believer's life," he says.

If we have been guilty of this sin, it is forgivable. If we are in bondage to habitual autosexuality there is a way out. As all these author-counselors say, as one has chosen to masturbate, he can choose to stop masturbating. If the practice is obsessive and longstanding it may mean real spiritual warfare to stop, but in Christ we can stop. Alcorn, Wilson, and White suggest simple steps we can take to gain victory over this potentially obsessive habit.

Seven Reasons To Resist Autosexuality

I have other reasons why I take a firm stance against autosexuality. I do not accept it as "God's relief value for built-up sexual drive," a common expression among Christian leaders with whom I have discussed this issue.

First, *it is not necessary.* I have as strong a sexual interest as any man, but I do not engage in autosexuality. My ministry often has taken me away from my loving wife for months at a time. My intimate sexual relationship with my wife grows deeper, not shallower, with time. After over 40 years of marriage she is as desirable to me as ever, even more so. With maturity comes a deeper love for this marvelous woman that God has given me. I tell her continually that next to God himself, she is God's greatest gift to me.

When I am away from her, even when I am alone and desire her love, I do not engage in autosexuality. *I choose not to do so.* With this God-given self-control has come wonderful freedom and peace. There is no freedom nor peace in bondage to masturbation.

Second, *masturbation does not decrease sexual tension; it only increases it.* When you stop, your sexual tension will be taken care of by itself if you maintain an active life and disciplined physical exercise. Thus one will be tired each night and not need sexual self-stimulation to relax and sleep.

Third, *autosexual conduct usually involves sexual sin and lust in the fantasy realm* even though it may not be focused on any one person.

Fourth, *autosexuality fixates on one's own sexual organs and sexual desires, the opposite of a shared sexual relationship* with one's mate.

Fifth, *it is habit forming.* I am not saying that occasional self-stimulation will inevitably become an obsessive habit. Experience proves that is not so. No one, however, ever becomes bound by a habit which did not begin at a given point and continue with more and more frequency. This is the only way autostimulation can ever become a sexual bondage. Thus, the only sure way to avoid the possibility of habit and bondage is never to begin.

Sixth, *in almost every form of sexual bondage from promiscuity to homosexuality and pornography, autosexual stimulation plays a central part.* Probably all "sexaholics" are addicted to masturbation. To my memory, in every counseling case I have had with men or women who are in sexual bondage, masturbation has been involved. Some men and women cannot enjoy a normal satisfying sexual relationship with their mates but continually masturbate.

Finally, *there can be a definite demonic dimension to uncontrolled masturbation.* I have cast demons of masturbation out of the lives of sexually bound men and women. I am not saying that demons are directly attached to the lives of all those in bondage to autosexual practices, nor am I saying demons are attached to the lives of most persons addicted to such practices. I am saying that they can become attached to the life of anyone in bondage to this unwise sexual practice. Such persons need counseling, but they also need deliverance.

Bondage to masturbation is spiritual warfare. The desire may first come from within, warfare with the lusts of the flesh. It can also come directly from without, warfare with a sex-crazed world. Finally, it often comes from above, warfare with sexual demons who tempt us to unwise or illicit sexual activity (1 Cor. 7:5).

A fellow missionary with whom I often travel in ministry was experiencing increased sexual loneliness during his frequent absences from his wife. He had never practiced masturbation beyond a few experiences as an adolescent. As he shared his loneliness with two missionary friends, both were amazed that he did not try masturbation as a means of temporary relief while away from home. They both said they did. They affirmed it was God's relief valve for pent-up sexual desires.

My friend began to follow their advice, at first infrequently. Then it became more and more often, especially in the evenings while bathing or alone in bed. While it provided some relief, it actually made him feel very insecure. Mental images of what he was doing would cross his mind at the most inopportune times, often while he was praying and reading Scripture or preaching. He felt that he must stop. He did for a while; then the desire would come upon him stronger than ever.

Eventually he became quite disturbed by his lack of sexual self-control. His habit seemed to increase his sexual desires instead of decreasing them. One night while in bed the desire came upon him with the greatest intensity he had ever known. Suddenly he became aware of an evil presence in the room with him. He was only beginning to learn the demonic dimension of spiritual warfare, but he sensed it was Satan. He remembered James 4:7–8:

> Submit therefore to God. Resist the devil and he will flee from you. Draw near to God, and He will draw near to you.

He began to resubmit his sexuality and sexual organs to God, including his mind, his emotions, and his will. He then began to resist the Devil and his sexual demons, out loud. He took his position as reigning with Christ above all principalities and powers of evil. He claimed his victory through the one who had defeated Satan and his evil spirits on the Cross.

Within a few minutes the evil presence left. The uncontrollable sexual passion was now under control. He then drew near to the Lord in praise, worship, and thanksgiving. The Lord, as He promised, drew near to him (James 4:7–8). He did not masturbate that night. Though this occurred some twenty years ago he has never masturbated since then. Though he still travels in a worldwide ministry usually without his wife, he has had no problem with masturbation or even strong temptations toward masturbation since that day. Why risk bondage to sexual self-stimulation when freedom is ours in Christ?

21

Indecency

Can the tidal wave of explicit, visual sexuality have a negative, even dangerous, effect on an otherwise moral man? A fellow Christian leader and I were discussing this question. He told me the following story.

"It can, because it happened to me. I have always lived a very moral life both as a youth and as an adult. I stayed away from sexual sins as a teen even though they were so common among my peers. In fact, even though I was not yet a Christian, I tried to choose friends who had similar moral convictions.

"Now, I was attracted to girls like any other teenager. I had seen enough pictures of the female body to know how attractive it is, even though I stayed away from all forms of pornography. I knew pornography would only awaken desires that could not be fulfilled outside of marriage so it was a 'no-no' for me.

"One day a carnival came to our city. A group of us high school kids went to it to have some fun. We noticed a large group gathered in front of a small theater. Entrance was free, so we decided to go in. Soon some young women came on stage. They began to dance very sensually. We all laughed. Some of the crowd began to yell for the girls to 'take it all off.' To my surprise, they began to expose their bodies. All of a sudden I felt sexual arousal move through my body in a way I had never known before.

"The high school girls who were with us began to blush. Some were so embarrassed they got up and left. Others stayed, probably not knowing what to do. The boys were all enjoying it, and much to my embarrassment I have to confess I did also.

"Suddenly the girls stopped dancing. The announcer said that for a few dollars any of us could come behind stage to another theater where the young dancers would 'take it all off.'

"By that time I was so stimulated by what I had seen, I only wanted to see more. With the other guys I paid my money and went to the theater behind the stage. None of the girls joined us. I saw things I had never seen before. The dancers took everything off and danced naked before our lustful eyes. They were beautiful. I felt sexual desire like I had never experienced before. I didn't want it to stop. I yelled approval with the other guys and men in the theater.

"As I walked home alone in the dark I was still so sexually stimulated I did not know what to do. Suddenly the thought came to my mind that I would like to find a girl, any girl, and have sex with her.

"Thank God no young girl was walking those dark streets that night. While I am too gentle of a person to ever think of raping a girl, I don't know what would have happened if I had found one alone and available that night.

"That was the first and last time I ever allowed myself to be exposed to total female nudity outside of marriage. Don't tell me such exposure does not have a potentially dangerous effect on an emotionally healthy male. What if I had been a person more prone to violence or to domination of others? What if I had had a sister who loved me enough to do almost anything I asked? What if I had had a date with my girlfriend later that night? What if . . . ?"

Sexual stimulation for a man is a powerful force for either good or evil. Maintaining a truly moral life in today's sexually saturated culture is really spiritual warfare.

The last of the sexual sins with which we are at war which is mentioned by the apostle Paul in his list in Galatians 5:19 is *aselgeia,* in Greek. It is translated "lasciviousness" in the KJV, "indecency" in the NEB, and "debauchery" in the NIV. All this reveals a search in English for one word that best expresses the meaning of *aselgeia.*

William Vine says the word means "absence of restraint, indecency, wantonness . . . the prominent idea is shameless conduct."[1] It is used several times in the New Testament with Vine's idea of self-abandonment to vice, corruption, and unrestrained illicit sexual behavior without concern for the feelings of others. In Ephesians 4:17–19 Paul talks of people who

> walk in the futility of their mind, being darkened in their understanding, excluded from the life of God, because of the ignorance that is in them, because of the hardness of their heart; and they, having become callous have given themselves over to sensuality, for the practice of every kind of impurity with greediness.

What an indictment of the world into which Jesus came and the gospel first penetrated! It sounds like San Francisco, Los Angeles, Chicago, and New York City.

The word is used again in Romans 13:13. Paul writes, "Let us behave properly as in the day, not in carousing and drunkenness, not in sexual promiscuity and sensuality" (our word *aselgeia* also translated "sensuality" in Gal. 5:19, NAS).

Fung says, "the word is paired with 'debauchery.' The NAS accurately calls it sexual promiscuity from the Greek word which means bed, 'especially the marriage bed, here meaning illicit intercourse' and thus takes on the special nuance of sexual excess."[2]

While the apostle Paul was writing for us, he was primarily writing to the believers of his day. The verses, like those mentioned in Ephesians 4:17–19, describe the condition of the Gentile world of Galatia and all of the Roman Empire in Paul's day. Fung suggests that Paul begins his lists of sins with sexual sins because they were so prevalent in current society:[3]

> Such evidence has come not from Christian writers but from pagans who were disgusted with the unspeakable sexual immorality. Not surprisingly has it been said, "In nothing did early Christianity so thoroughly revolutionize the ethical standards of the pagan world as in regard to sexual relationship."

Fung's last words about the transforming impact of the Christian faith on the sexual standards of the pagan world stir me to the depths of my being when I consider the widespread sexual compromise with hypocrisy, adultery, homosexuality, and pornography among Christian leaders today.

As leaders they have, at least by implication, said with the apostle Paul, "Be imitators of me, just as I also am of Christ" (1 Cor. 11:1; 4:16–17). In Philippians 3:17 and Hebrews 13:7,17 Paul says all Christian leaders are to be the model for believers to follow. James warns, "Let not many of you become teachers, my brethren, knowing that as such we shall incur a stricter judgment" (James 3:1).[4]

Failure to exercise self-control and live in holiness in any area of the believer's sexual life is the main thrust of Paul's teaching in this passage.

What about men who coerce their wives to participate in sexual practices repulsive to the woman's usually more refined nature? It is prohibited. It is a sin against God and against one's wife. I have counseled many Christian men, among them Christian leaders, who have done perhaps permanent damage to their wives by this form of male sexual dominance.

I think of one outstanding Christian leader whom I have counseled on several occasions. He came from a dysfunctional family but married a beautiful, pure, gentle girl from a stable Christian family.

The man's sexual appetite was voracious. He not only wanted sex continually, but wanted his wife to be more passionate and do things that were repulsive to her. He began to rent the most blatant, X-rated videos of men and women practicing unrestrained sex. He compelled her to look at them. When my wife and I asked her why she submitted to it she said, "Because I love him and I was afraid of losing him." This is the most common reason given by this type of sexually abused wife.

Soon the videos became less repulsive to her. Eventually she became dependent upon the explicit sexual acts of the videos to become aroused. In time her self-image and her sense of female purity became so violated she went into a deep depression and almost committed suicide. Only God's tender grace and transforming power rescued both her and her husband from the pit into which they had pulled each other. Today they have fallen in love anew and enjoy a tender love life freed from the bondage to such sexual perversion.[5] Theirs was a long and painful recovery, however.

The above story involving the sexual abuse inflicted by an otherwise godly Christian leader on his wife sets the stage for a summary of a case study in this examination of the sexual sins listed by Paul in Galatians 5:19. It is called "Video Seduction," the confessions of a Christian leader who fell into the trap of video pornography. It appeared in *Moody Monthly* several years ago.[6]

The article retraces the path that took this Christian leader to the brink of an abyss of destruction. It began, innocently enough, with the gift of a video cassette recorder meant to be used to enhance his ministry.

At first, he and his family viewed only Walt Disney classics. But as he browsed for family movies at the video shop, an exciting selection of fast-action adventure movies caught his eye. So, in addition to the family-type movie, he chose one of a more "mature" theme for him and his wife to enjoy after the children went to bed.

He enjoyed the action in these films, but doubts nibbled at him when the actors swore, or the scantily clad actresses and actors engaged in scenes portraying sexual immorality. Most of these movies, rated PG, were 90 percent wholesome entertainment, however.

One day the suggestive picture and title on the carton lured him to rent an R-rated picture. Soon he was watching two of these movies every weekend, then mid-week, too. He observed that "although I continued my personal devotions out of habit, I knew that my reading of Scripture and prayer was a sham. My enthusiasm for teaching and preaching the Bible waned. I lost boldness in speaking on biblical commands against sexual immorality."

In spite of his determination not to view another R-rated movie, the sensuous titles and alluring pictures drew him to view these movies week after week. Only his wife's moral sensitivity and presence in the home kept him from renting the X-rated movies he yearned to see.

Then his wife went away for a weekend. At the video shop he justified his rental of the X-rated movie by rationalizing, "Perhaps as a Christian leader I should be aware of what the world is consuming."

But what he saw portrayed in the movie disgusted him. "What I saw was ugly," he says. "The film degraded men and women. The beauty of human sexuality as God designed it and as I had experienced it in marriage was absent. I felt empty, cheated, and defeated."

Shocked into realizing he was in danger of destroying his life and his ministry, that night he destroyed his video rental card, wrote a note of confession to his wife, repented before the Lord, and decided before God to stay out of video shops. Later, he made himself accountable to a respected pastor-friend to monitor his spiritual life.

He suggests the following to avoid misuse of a video recorder: Stay out of secular video shops; don't watch video movies alone; limit your viewing; cultivate God's attitude towards the things shown on video such as lies, bloodshed, and evil scheming; use the standard set by Paul in Philippians 4:8 when selecting films.

This is a powerful word of warning to all believers, a caution light to Christian leaders. The eyes are the gateway to our imaginations. Our imagination is a key to our life. "Be careful, little eyes, what you see."

Ours is a sexually polluted society. Sexual scenes and words which before were seen and heard only in "sleazy" sub-groups of Western society now enter our living room through television and videos.

Soap operas during the daytime; sexually explicit situation comedies in the evening; partial to almost complete nudity often accompanied by sexual violence against women on prime time television; Madonna and Cher on MTV[7] any hour of the day or night: Sex! Sex! Sex! We are being brainwashed into believing that "man cannot live by bread alone, but by every sexual act possible." Yet many "scholars" and "researchers" assure us that all of this has no real negative impact on children, young people, and adults.

"Normal" people can handle it without it affecting their moral values and their view of sex, marriage, and, especially, women, we are told. Only abnormal people are negatively affected by all of these sexually explicit sights, actions, and words.

Tell that to the girls and women raped by men and "boys" stimulated almost beyond self-control by the sexual pollution of films, television, videos, and pornography. Tell that to the wives and girl friends forced by their husbands and boy friends to witness explicit sex on rented videos. Tell that to the millions of men in bondage to pornography and autosexuality. Tell that to the adult survivors of sexual child abuse, perpetrated by their loved ones, trusted friends, and other authority figures inflamed by the exploitation of their sexuality by the media. If this occurs only with emotionally unbalanced people, then the U.S.A. is one of the largest mental institutions in the world!

Let us join Job and say, "I have made a covenant with my eyes not to look lustfully at a girl [woman]. Does He [God] not see my ways, and count my every step?" (Job 31:1,4, NIV).

> If my heart has been enticed by a woman,
>   or if I have looked at my neighbor's door
> then may my wife grind another man's grain,
>   and may other men sleep with her.
> For that would have been shameful,
>   a sin to be judged.

It is a fire that burns to destruction.[8]
It would have uprooted my harvest.
(Job 31:9–12, NIV)

I believe the beginning of victory in warfare with the sins of the flesh is found in Romans 12:1–2 and 6:12–14. God pleads through the apostle Paul,

Therefore, I urge you, brothers, in view of God's mercy,
    to offer your bodies as living sacrifices, holy and
    pleasing to God—
This is your spiritual act of worship.

Do not conform any longer to the pattern of this world,
    But be transformed by the renewing of your mind.
Then you will be able to test and approve what God's will
    is—
His good, pleasing and perfect will. (Rom. 12:1–2, NIV)

Therefore do not let sin reign in your mortal body
    So that you obey its evil desires.
Do not offer the parts of your body to sin
    As instruments of wickedness,
But rather offer yourselves to God, as those who have
    been
    Brought from death to life;
And offer the parts of your body to him as instruments of
    righteousness.
    For sin shall not be your master,
Because you are not under law, but under grace.
    (Rom. 6:12–14, NIV)

Yes, Lord, I choose to obey!

22

Religious Sins

After listing the sins a person can commit against one's own body, Paul turns his attention to sins against God. They are the two religious sins of idolatry and witchcraft or sorcery (NAS). These sins, even if entered into in ignorance, openly invite religious evil spirits into contact with the life of the individuals involved. We will have occasion to look at idolatry and witchcraft in a later section of our study. Here we will trace the biblical history and nature of these sins and examine them primarily as manifestations of the sinful works of the flesh.

IDOLATRY

The word idolatry comes from the Greek word *eidōlolatria.* It is a compound word, *eidōlon,* "idol" and *latreia,* "worship" or "service."[1] Fung says idolatry owes its meaning, if not its origin as a word, from these two words.[2] From his succinct treatment of the character of idolatry in his commentary on Galatians, I draw the following ten facts about idolatry that existed by New Testament times:

1. It was the "typical sin of the Gentiles."
2. It was completely "opposed to service of the 'living and true God' " (1 Thess. 1:9).
3. Its fundamental error was in giving "reverence and worship to created things instead of the Creator" (Rom. 1:25; cf. vv. 19–23).
4. "Idols" could refer to the images of the gods (Acts 7:41; Rev. 9:20) or the gods behind the images (1 Cor. 8:4,7; 10:19).
5. The term *idolatry* shares this "ambivalence of meaning." It could refer to the worship of the idol itself as a god or of the spiritual being represented by the idol. Both are idolatry and both are forbidden by God (Exod. 20:3–5). Both also invite evil religious spirits to make their presence known.
6. Paul regards idols as "mere nonentities, yet he recognizes that demonic forces lurk behind them, so that to take part in a pagan sacrificial feast is to become partners with demons" (1 Cor. 10:19–21).
7. Because of this demonic dimension to all forms of idolatry, Paul admonished believers to shun idolatry (1 Cor. 10:14; cf. v. 7; 5:11; Eph. 5:5; Col. 3:5).[3] If missionaries ignore or are unaware of this demonic dimension to idolatry, they will face serious problems both in the evangelization of idolaters and in leading the new converts to victory in Christ. Both power and truth encounter will have to occur.[4]
8. Sexual immorality and idolatry are strongly connected in the Bible. This is often true today as the phallic symbols in the temples of India indicate.
9. As a result, the typical idol worshiper in biblical times committed both a religious sin and a sexual sin whenever he participated in specific religious ceremonies. This was especially true when the religion featured cultic-ritual prostitution, like the worship of Aphrodite, the love goddess of Corinth.
10. In the broadest sense, "idolatry is the worship of anything which usurps the rightful place of God." Thus Paul speaks of "the ruthless greed which is nothing less than idolatry" (Col. 3:5).

Idolatry in the Old Testament

The Old Testament has much more to say about the idolatrous practices of the surrounding pagan world than does the New Testament. The idolatry of the New Testament was nothing more than a further development of what began in the ancient world. I will lean heavily on two masterful overviews of idolatry. The first is done by P. H. Garber in the *International Standard Bible Encyclopedia*.[5] The second was done by F. B. Huey, Jr., in the *Zondervan Pictorial Encyclopedia of the Bible*.[6]

Garber first looks at the word *idol*, then *idolatry*. Since we are approaching the subject from the biblical, not the comparative religion perspective, we will use many biblical references. Garber begins with a long list of the Old and New Testament words used to refer to idols and idolatry. There are some twenty-five Hebrew words used for idols and three or four used for idolatry. The New Testament confines itself to a few basic words for both idols and idolatry. We will look at the five most common ones.

First is *eidōlon*, the word more frequently used for idols and "several of its cognates." Second is *eidōlothyton*, used specifically for meats offered to idols. Third is *eidōlolatria*, the word we already looked at in Galatians 5:20. It is also used in Paul's well-developed polemic against idols and idolatry in 1 Corinthians 10:7–33. Fourth is the word *kateidōlos*. It appears only in Acts 17:16 in the context of Paul's difficult ministry in Athens. He found the city "full of idols."

Finally, there is the word *eikōns* used in Romans 1:23. Here is one of the apostle Paul's strongest condemnations of all idolatry and image worship. He says humanity in general "exchanged the glory of the incorruptible God for an image *(eikōns)* in the form of corruptible man and of birds and four-footed animals and crawling creatures."

Garber says one Hebrew word for idols is derived from *zana* which means "to have illicit intercourse. Its sexual connotations suggest the involvement of cultic prostitutes, a regular feature of Canaanite pagan worship (and later Greco-Roman cults)."

In the Old Testament, the dangers represented by idols and idolatry reflected the area of major concern by God and His appointed leaders. Even the strong prohibition against intermarriage with the pagan peoples in the land of Canaan was primarily because of the religious and moral corruption that this practice would and did bring into Israel.

The awful destruction of the cities and peoples of Canaan by the Jews which God commanded was essentially because of the total commitment of these peoples to idolatry and the unbelievable religious and immoral practices associated with it. Those practices included heterosexual and homosexual ritual sexual orgies and, most shocking of all, human sacrifice. The worshipers primarily sacrificed their own children. Contemporary Satanic Ritual Abuse (SRA) of children in modern Satanism and satanic cults widespread in the U.S.A. and other parts of the Western world seems connected with the popular revival of ancient paganism rooted in these ancient, evil practices.

Garber says the familiarity of the Hebrews with various forms of idolatry and foreign deities was due to various factors. One crucial factor was the pagan background out of which Israel itself sprang (Genesis 11—12:3). Abraham's family were idolaters, probably worshipers of Sin, the moon god. Some of its most important cultic centers were in Ur and Haran, the cities where Abraham was raised.

The second factor was the geography of Palestine in Old Testament times. Israel rubbed elbows with peoples totally given to polytheism and idolatry in some of the worst forms which have ever existed. The primary people were the Syrians, Phoenicians, Egyptians, Philistines, and the Canaanites. The latter included a wide variety of peoples whose names all ended in "ites" (Deut. 7:1) but were often summed up under the one name, "Amorite" (Gen. 15:16).

The Promised Land was located on the main caravan and military route from Egypt in the south to Mesopotamia in the north. The Hittites, Syrians, Babylonians, Assyrians, and Egyptians marched through the land of Palestine from one end to another for both commercial and military purposes. Coupled with Israel's 400-year sojourn in one of the most idolatrous nations in history, Egypt, this exposed the Jews to all forms of idolatry and religious syncretism.

As to Israel's battle with idolatry and idolatrous syncretism, there is no lack of material in the Old Testament. It begins in Genesis and continues through the minor prophets, especially Hosea, Amos, Micah, Habakkuk, and Zephaniah.

To the protagonists of Hebrew ethical monotheism the worst sins of God's people were idolatry and idolatrous syncretism, that is, combining the worship of Yahweh with elements of paganism. This almost always included ritual sexual activity of one type or another.

Israel's greatest sin was syncretism more than the outright rejection of Yahweh.[7] The nation worshiped other gods alongside of its worship of the true God. This syncretism included both the making of images of these gods, making images to represent Yahweh symbolically, and falling down in worship before them.

This is what occurred with the worship of the golden calf after the Exodus from Egypt (Exod. 32). When the calf was made, the leaders proclaimed, "This is your god [Yahweh], O Israel, who brought you up from the land of Egypt" (v. 4). All Israel knew it was Yahweh alone who had brought them out of Egypt. The calf then was to be an image or symbol of Yahweh.

The Decalogue (Exod. 20:3–5; Deut. 5:7) forbade the Jews from fashioning any images as objects of worship. They were not to "bow down to them or worship them" (NIV). Since it precluded making any image of "any likeness of what is in heaven" (v. 4), it precluded the making of any physical image or symbol of Yahweh himself. This did not preclude, however, the use of religious art. They were told to place cherubims over the Ark of the Covenant, but they were not to bow down before them or in any way venerate them (Exod. 25:18–22).

There seems to be no period in Israel's history when the people were free from the attraction of idolatry and idolatrous syncretism. It occurred in the patriarchal period (Gen. 31) and while Israel was in Egypt (Josh. 24:14; Ezek. 20:1–32; 22–23).

While they had left Egypt, Egypt had not left them. Just before they were ready to enter the Promised Land, their addiction to idolatry and the immorality that accompanied it led them "to play the harlot with the daughters of Moab." The Moabites invited them "to the sacrifices of their gods, and the people ate and bowed down to their gods. So Israel joined themselves to Baal of Peor and the LORD was angry against Israel" (Num. 25:1–3).

This was the climactic story of Israel's idolatry, immorality, and rebellion against God since the Exodus from Egypt. It was at this point that God judged the nation by keeping them out of the land until the entire rebellious generation except Caleb and Joshua had died in the wilderness (Num. 26).

Finally, just before the new generation was to enter the Promised Land under Joshua, Moses gave them his long farewell message (Deut. 1—33). An important part of that message was that they not make any image of Jehovah nor any image of any kind. Nor were they to intermarry with the nations of the land. Deuteronomy 4:15–20 and 7:1–6 are excellent examples of Moses' impassioned warnings:

Furthermore, you shall not intermarry with them; you shall not give your daughters to their sons, nor shall you take their daughters for your sons.

For they will turn your sons away from following Me to serve other gods; then the anger of the LORD will be kindled against you, and He will quickly destroy you.

But thus you shall do to them: you shall tear down their altars, and smash their sacred pillars, and hew down their Asherim, and burn their graven images with fire. (Deut. 7:3–5)

Moses stated further that any person who tried to seduce the faith of a Jew to lead them into idolatry or syncretism was to be executed (Deut. 13:6–16), and any Jew who worshiped any other god or served any god but Yahweh was also to be executed (Deut. 17:1–7). Huey writes that the Jews

did not obey the injunctions given by Moses to destroy the people completely, but settled down among them. They continued to worship the foreign gods they had brought from Egypt (Josh. 24:14,15,23) and also were enticed by the gods of the Canaanites after they settled in the land. (Judg. 2:11–13; 6:25–32; see also Judg. 17—18)[8]

The story of Israel's continual rebellion against God and compromise with idolatry and syncretism worsens in the rest of the historical and prophetical period of Israel's history. Samuel battled with it during his entire lifetime (1 Sam. 7:3–4). Garber writes:[9]

The tension between idolatry and the essential spirit of Israelite religion is reflected in the early prophetic protest of Samuel: "For rebellion is as the sin of divination, and stubbornness is as iniquity and idolatry" (1 Sam. 15:23). In this statement Samuel places disobedience to God and idolatry in the same category. In the final analysis idolatry was rebellion, for it constituted a violation of God's commands.

The brightest period was during the long reign of David. Yet his son Solomon, who began so well, in his old age was drawn into the worst forms of idolatry and paganism by his many women (1 Kings 11:1–9). He filled the royal gardens with the repulsive images of the gods of his wives and concubines. In judgment God wrenched out of his hand ten of the twelve tribes of Israel (1 Kings 11:11f).

Jeroboam became the leader of the ten separated tribes which were now called Israel. He too seemed to begin well (1 Kings 11:26–40), but soon erected two golden calves, one in Bethel and another at Dan, and forced the people of Israel to worship there instead of in the temple at Jerusalem (1 Kings 12:25—14:19). For the rest of Israel's history he came to be known as "Jeroboam, who caused Israel to sin."

Rehoboam, Solomon's son, was no better. He too caused Judah to sin (1 Kings 14:21–24). The writer reveals that under Rehoboam not only did Judah build for themselves high places and sacred pillars and Asherim [symbols of female goddesses, associated with fertility and sexuality] on every high hill, "but there were also male cult prostitutes in the land. They did according to all the abominations of the nations which the LORD dispossessed before the sons of Israel."

Ongoing and intense spiritual warfare characterized the history of Israel and Judah from then on to the time of the Babylonian Exile. Such spiritual warfare had been strong during their entire existence from the Exodus from Egypt, but now Israel became totally committed to the evils of the flesh, the world, and the Devil. All her leaders were evil, the most notorious being Ahab and Jezebel (1 Kings 16:29—22:40; 2 Kings 9).

Judah at first remained more faithful to the covenant. While some of her kings walked in the sins of Israel, others brought the people back to God, destroyed the idols, and abolished cult prostitution and child sacrifice. Most notable were the revivals under Hezekiah (2 Kings 18—20) and Josiah (2 Kings 22—23:28).

Yet these revivals came too late. Judah became as vile as Israel. God determined Judah too would go into Babylonian captivity (2 Kings 24—25) because of her idolatry, immorality, and rebellion against Him. This was Judah's final defeat in her long history of spiritual warfare.

During this period the prophets battled idolatry and its associated evils. First were the preaching prophets like Elijah and Elisha. Then came the writing prophets. From the eighth century B.C. on through the Exile they spoke and wrote the Word of God with boldness and passion.

Hosea denounced the stubborn spiritual and physical harlotry of Israel (Hos. 2:16-17; 8:4-6; 13:2). Amos spoke out against the Canaanite high places among the people and the image worship of God's people. Isaiah grieved over the idolatry of Israel.

Zephaniah "warned against the worship of astral deities, against Milcom, and against pagan superstitions (Zeph. 1:2-9)," says Huey.[10] "Habakkuk pronounced woes upon those who would worship a god made with their own hands (Hab. 2:18-19). No prophet fought the apostasies of Judah more vehemently than Jeremiah and Ezekiel. The latter fiercely denounced the sacrifice of children to the gods" (16:20-21).

Next came the post-exilic period: Ezra, Nehemiah, and Malachi strongly opposed any marriages of Jews with pagans. Those who had already done so had to put away their pagan wives. The people responded. They had finally learned the lesson of their past history. Writing of the intertestamental period, Huey states:

> In the 2nd century B.C., the Seleucid rulers of Palestine attempted to revive the worship of local fertility gods and the Helenistic deities. Antiochus IV Epiphanes (175—164 B.C.) issued an edict establishing one religion for all his subjects. He erected an altar to Zeus over the altar of burnt offering in the Temple at Jerusalem. He required the Jews to take part in the heathen festivals or be slain. His oppressive measures brought about the Maccabean revolt that resulted in a brief period of religious and political freedom for the Jews.[11]

Garber comments, "Never again were Jews to take idolatry seriously. Rather, idol worship became for them a matter of semi-humorous satire and ridicule (cf. Bel and Dragon)."[12]

Idolatry in the New Testament

The entire New Testament world was engulfed in idolatry and its accompanying sexual immorality. Temple prostitution was rampant. Some of the pagan religious rites were even more immoral than those of the Old Testament pagan nations including the Canaanites. Rome ruled the world, but Greek culture dominated. Greece had its pantheon of high gods and its innumerable lower gods and spirits. Rome took the Greek pantheon as its own and added its own maze of lower gods and spirits and those of all the peoples it conquered.

To this was added the cult of the emperor and the later mystery cults. Gods, goddesses, and spirits both bad and good were everywhere and indwelt everything. Religion ranged from polytheism and henotheism to animism and pantheism. As long as people also honored the gods of the Greco-Roman pantheon and venerated and later worshiped the emperor, people could believe what they wanted and do what they wanted in worship except perform human sacrifice. The Romans often killed whom and when they willed, but direct human sacrifice was not a part of their religious world view.

Coming as it did out of the fierce monotheism of post-exile Israel, the early Christian church, though born in such an idolatrous world, had strong monotheistic and anti-idolatrous roots. Therefore idolatry, though it existed and was always a threat, was not the threat that it had been to Israel before the Exile.

Church members living in heathen communities received their first warnings about compromise with idols from the early Christian leaders who met at the great church council of Acts 15 (vv. 26,29). Luke describes Paul's encounter with idolatry and paganism in Acts 13—20.

Paul had to address the problem of Gentile converts eating meat which had been sacrificed to idols in 1 Corinthians 8:1–13 and 10:14–22. While he denied that idols had any real existence in themselves (1 Cor. 12:2; Gal. 4:8; 1 Thess. 1:9), he knew that participation in their worship even in ignorance meant participating with demons (1 Cor. 10:20–21). Therefore he fully recognized the demonic spiritual warfare dimensions of idolatry.

The apostle John, too, warned believers against idolatry (1 John 5:21). The Book of Revelation has much to say about idolatry, both in reference to the churches and unbelievers.

Revelation 2—3 speaks about idolatry and Satan's dwelling among the churches of Asia. Revelation 9:20 says all unbelievers in one way or another are involved in the worship of "demons," and "the idols of gold and of silver and of brass and of stone and of wood, which can neither see nor hear nor walk," quoting Psalm 115:4–7. The same book warns against the worship of the image of the beast and promises glory to those who refuse to worship the beast or its image (Rev. 13:14–15; 14:9–11; 20:4).

As a final word, I quote F. B. Huey's *Why Idolatry Is Condemned in the Bible*.[13]

[Idolatry] denies the existence of the true God who created the world and mankind, and whose glory cannot be adequately captured in any tangible form. It is absurd that a person could carve an idol with his own hands and then be afraid of what he has made, or use it as an object of worship. . . . A visible representation of the deity tends to restrict a person's concept of God, for he will base his concept of God, consciously or unconsciously, upon the image or picture.

Finally, man becomes like that which he worships (Hos. 9:10). If his god is lifeless and cold, it can bring him no real hope or comfort. Only the true and living God can fulfill the hope of eternal life.

WITCHCRAFT OR SORCERY

Now we must look at the second type of religious sin Paul warns against and against which we war. The Greek word is a strange one. It is *pharmakeia,* translated "witchcraft" or "sorcery" in the NAS. Fung says originally it "meant the medical use of drugs."[14] Our English word *pharmacy* comes from this word. Vine says that "*pharmakeia* in English is pharmacy. It primarily signified the use of medicine, drugs, spells, then poisoning, then sorcery (or) witchcraft."

Vine then makes another observation. After stating that the word was later applied to witchcraft and sorcery, he says:

> In sorcery, the use of drugs, whether simple or potent, was generally accompanied by incantations and appeals to occult powers with the provision of various charms, amulets, etc., professedly designed to keep the applicant or patient from the attention and power of demons, but actually to impress the applicant with the mysterious resources and powers of the sorcerer.[15]

Ronald Fung parallels Vine's insightful words. He adds that the value of the books of magic arts that the Ephesian Christians burned "bore eloquent witness to the prevalence of such practices in those times (Acts 19:19; cf. 8:9–11; 13:8–10) in spite of the fact that sorcery was a serious offense in Roman law."[16]

It is difficult to find the best word for the practice Paul is condemning here. Most translations fluctuate between "witchcraft" and "sorcery" with the majority opting for sorcery. Perhaps the broader term "occultism" would be best as the practice in New Testament times covered most of what is done in the different branches of occultism today: sorcery, witchcraft, spiritism, divination, magic, spells, curses, and the mediumistic practices of contacting the spirits of the dead and astral or spirit projection.[17]

This activity of the flesh in the spirit realm covers at least nine areas:

1. Any form of spiritual practice which has as its goal making contact with the spirit world (with angels, spirits, the spirits [ghosts] of the dead, etc.) for selfish purposes, such as the "channeling" rage made popular by actress Shirley MacLaine.
2. To attempt the above even only out of curiosity.
3. To attempt to manipulate the spirit world to do one's bidding.
4. To attempt to gain knowledge from the spirit world outside of or beyond what God has revealed in His Word.
5. To gain power from the spirit world over one's own life, the lives of others, and/or over circumstances and events in this world.
6. To gain power from the spirit world to do good for one's self or for others such as healing, finances, or pleasures, or to do harm to others who stand in the way of the desired good one seeks.
7. To gain protection from good spirits against malevolent, evil spirits.
8. To contact the spirits ("ghosts") of the dead.
9. To contact or to serve Satan as over against the true God or the Lord Jesus Christ, whatever one's motive may be or whatever one's view of Satan's person and activity may be.

Sorcery includes the realm of magic (not sleight of hand); that is, the use of drugs, chants, and ceremonies which in themselves possess power to produce desired results or changes in people, circumstances or events, both black and white "magic."

If sincere believers break biblical norms in seeking spiritual experiences, even if they sincerely seek them from the Holy Spirit, they can become deceived by spirits who counterfeit the Spirit of God and the gifts of the Spirit (2 Cor. 11:4; Gal. 1:8; 1 John 4:1–4).[18]

23

Social Sins

The fine young pastor was seeing his church disintegrate before his eyes. The major problem centered around one highly gifted woman Bible teacher who had come to the small, struggling church about two years before. She appeared to be very sincere and was present every time the church doors opened.

"She said she wanted to help in a special way in a teaching ministry with the women of the church," the pastor said to me. "I was thrilled to have such a mature and gifted Bible teacher working with me. The women enjoyed her teaching and flocked to her class, but a strange thing happened. The elders and I noticed that the women of the church became increasingly restless and unhappy with the church and some with their husbands."

As they counseled the women they discovered two things. All the younger women had begun to resist their husband's leadership in the home. They wanted to control their husbands. All the older women began to lead their husbands away from the church to join other churches. Every one of the women showing these tendencies were members of that lady's Bible class.

The pastor did not know what to do. He had no direct proof the teacher was subverting the Christian homes and the church. He, with his elders, finally decided they would have to ask her to give up her women's Bible class. She refused.

The pastor was desperate. Every Sunday they were losing people either through families splitting up or families leaving the church. The elders, many of whose wives attended the Bible class, were afraid to act for fear of their wives. Most of them, however, supported the pastor in his desire to bring the issue before the church membership.

Since the woman was not a member of the church, she was not supposed to attend the membership meeting; but she came anyway. The men present were so afraid of their wives, the leaders could not get enough votes to force the lady to give up the class. So she continued to teach until no one was left. Then suddenly she disappeared. The pastor heard later she was doing the same thing in another church.

Distinctive Characteristics of Social Sins (Galatians 5:20)

While this is an extreme case, it is the sort of division Paul is dealing with in Galatians 5:20, where he begins to list what I call the social sins.

People commit them against one another. I also call them the Christian sins because they are so widespread among us and so widely tolerated by us. Many popular platform preachers and evangelists vehemently denounce the moral and religious sins. Yet the entire context of their lifestyle is that of bondage to these social, "Christian" sins.

Jealousy and envy too often fill them. They live in continual enmity and strife with other platform leaders whom they see more as their rivals than their brothers. They react with "outbursts of anger" to events and persons when things do not go their way. They constantly dispute and dissent with fellow believers. They have divided the body of Christ into endless factions centered around themselves, not the Lord Jesus Christ or the church at large.

The social sins form the most exhaustive list of the three and represent the most commonly practiced and accepted sins among us. In that sense they are most dangerous. While the moral and religious sins may have the greatest immediate negative impact on world evangelism, the social sins have perhaps the greatest long-range negative impact. They are emphasized almost a hundredfold more in the New Testament, especially in the epistles of Paul, than the other two groups combined.

The people of the world live in contention. We know or should know that only believers have the real solution for the desperate problems represented by broken interpersonal relationships among humanity. It is the peace of God found only in Christ.

What we refuse to acknowledge, at least in our lifestyle, is that we believers unfortunately usually behave as the world does in our interpersonal relationships. Probably the greatest single obstacle to world evangelism is the interpersonal conflicts among believers, particularly among Christian leaders.

Conflict began in the early church as evidenced by the epistles of Paul, Peter, John, and James. In their writings these men make constant reference to the negative interpersonal relationships between believers in the apostolic churches.

The Lord Jesus had said that oneness among his people would be the single most important factor leading towards effective world evangelism (John 17:18–21). Yet the Epistles constantly have to appeal for this oneness and correct the lack of it among God's people (Rom. 12—16; 1 Cor. 1—4, 6, 8—14).

I have classified the social sins mentioned by Paul here into three groups. They are sins of division, sins of bitterness, and sins of covetousness among Christians.

Divisions Among Believers (Galatians 5:20)

Admittedly all of the social sins produce division or are evidence of it among believers. Yet four are specifically that type of sin. They are "strife," "disputes," "dissensions," and "factions."

"Strife" and "jealousy" are the only sins in the list in the singular. We will see why later. The plural of the word translated "strife" here is found in 1 Corinthians 1:11, however, where it is translated "quarrels."

Paul uses the Greek word *eris* for "strife." Fung comments:[1]

> *Eris* is the "contentious temper" (NEB) which leads to "strife" (RV) and "discord" (NIV). Paul mentions it as a characteristic of pagan society (Rom. 1:29; cf. 13:13), but unfortunately it often gains entry into the church as well, causing quarrels and disrupting Christian fellowship (1 Cor. 1:11; 3:3; 2 Cor. 12:20).

Fung makes an interesting comment on the word *eritheiai* translated "disputes." He says it is the plural of *eritheia* which denotes "base self-seeking." The word is derived from *erithos*, "a hireling," and originally meant "working for pay." It came to acquire the sense of "canvassing" for office.

Elsewhere in Paul's letters it occurs in a context having to do with competing parties within the church (cf. 2 Cor. 12:20; Phil. 1:17; 2:3). Therefore it probably refers to the "selfish ambition" (NIV) which gives rise to rival "factions" (RV) and party "strife" (AV, cf. NAS).[2]

It is followed by two similar words, "dissensions and factions," all words with similar connotations. "Dissensions" translates *dichostasiai*. It is used in classical

Greek to mean "dispute, disunity, strife in general" and even "revolt" or "rebellion." It is the same word used by Paul in Romans 16:17 to warn the church against those who cause dissensions or divisions. It has a strong focus on those who cause parties, cliques, and disunity in general with the church.

The word for "factions" is *hairesis*. It is in the plural here and simply means "choices." As already stated, most of the words here are in the plural form, probably indicating they refer to a wide variety of ways of causing division within the church.

The singular, *haireseōs*, refers to a body of people who have chosen the same faith or position, like the party of the Pharisees in Acts 15:5 where it is translated "sect" in the Greek-English New Testament. Used in a negative context, as it is here, it means a faction (1 Cor. 11:19), in opposition to the official group, in this context, the church. Fung says that in this passage "the reference is to 'factions' (NAS), each exhibiting a 'party spirit' (RSV) and possibly engaged in 'party intrigues' (NEB). The KJV translates it 'heresies.'"

A New Period of Interpersonal Strife?

The church seems to move through periods of strife followed by some reconciliation and then new periods of strife. Where are we today? At the beginning of this century, the church moved into a period of terrible strife with the birth of the Pentecostal movement. From this movement subsequently arose all the present-day Pentecostal denominations. That early period was one of great strife between Pentecostals and the mainline Protestant groups out of which Pentecostalism emerged.

A period of reconciliation followed. The non-Pentecostal and independent churches, generally speaking, began to recognize that, in spite of what they considered to be errors in doctrine, the Pentecostals were God's people. The Pentecostal movement sparked a new era in evangelism, church planting, and world missions. In many countries the growth of Pentecostal-type churches has outstripped that of the older non-Pentecostal churches.[3]

Then when things began to settle down in the 1950s, a new spiritual bombshell dropped out of the sky: the Charismatic movement.[4] While this movement has great similarities with the Pentecostal movement, it has enough differences to classify it as a new movement. The Charismatic movement definitely is built upon the foundation laid by the Pentecostal movement, however, exactly as the latter is built upon the foundation laid by the Holiness movement of the nineteenth century.

Both the Pentecostals and the Charismatics have a wide-open stance concerning the function of all the gifts of the Spirit. Both believe that all (or almost all) of the gifts are still operative within the body of Christ today. The traditional Protestant and Roman Catholic view is that some of the gifts are no longer operative.

Two obvious differences exist between the Pentecostals and Charismatics. Both have caused some Pentecostals to be just as "skittish" about the Charismatics as are many traditional Protestants.

One, Charismatics usually have a more flexible view of the evidence of the baptism with the Holy Spirit. The traditional Pentecostal view is that the only true sign is speaking in tongues. Pentecostals distinguish between tongues as a gift of the Spirit and tongues as the sign of the baptism with the Spirit. While Charismatics believe in tongues, they do not usually see it as the only evidence of the baptism with the Spirit.

Two, the Charismatic movement sees itself as a revival movement cutting across all branches of Christendom, across Catholicism, Protestantism and even Pentecostalism. Thus it has not created official Charismatic doctrinal statements as have the Pentecostals and, of course, Roman Catholicism and the historical Protestant denominations. You can be a Charismatic and still hold to most, if not all, traditional Catholic, Protestant, or Pentecostal doctrines.

A Repeating Pattern

For years traditional Protestant writers and teachers have spoken out and written against the Charismatic movement as they had done earlier against Pentecostalism. With time mainline evangelicals began to look upon Charismatics with more tolerance and understanding as had occurred earlier with Pentecostals. Their zeal for God, their evangelism, their desire for a holy life gave evidence that God was working through the Charismatic movement in spite of what some saw as troublesome doctrinal errors within the movement.

Traditional Protestants, Pentecostals, and Charismatics began to work together, especially in evangelism and church renewal. Both Pentecostals and Charismatics began to serve as missionaries under outstanding non-Pentecostal-Charismatic mission boards.

Just when things seemed to settle down, another new spiritual explosion has occurred. It has originated, as was true for both Pentecostalism and the Charismatic movement (from a U.S. perspective) in California. The Third Wave has been born.[5] The Third Wave is the renewal movement now occurring among leaders within conservative evangelical churches who do not want to be Pentecostal or Charismatic. They want to be known as conservative evangelicals, yet are open to renewal by the Holy Spirit, including the operation of most, if not all, of the gifts of the Holy Spirit.

Whatever emphasis they may give to experiences with the Holy Spirit, they do not believe in a once and for all special baptism with the Holy Spirit additional to and subsequent to the Spirit's baptism which joins one to the body of Christ (1 Cor. 12:13). They will use such terms as "anointing" with the Spirit, "filling" with the Spirit, "empowerment" by the Holy Spirit, but not "baptism" of the Spirit. They also probably would accept the traditional conservative evangelical statement, "There is only one baptism but many fillings." They do give place to the so-called miraculous gifts, not just to the more traditional gifts.

I believe we are moving into a day of renewed strife within the body of Christ, especially in the United States, however. The Third Wave, for some evangelicals, has become the straw that broke the camel's back. Some have taken pen in hand and have written (and are still writing) books affirming that the full spectrum of the Spirit's gifts are not operative in the church today. What we are witnessing in these renewal movements, they declare, are counterfeits of the real gifts; some are demonic, and others are psychological or outright sham.

Guilt by association is now being revived after being dormant for so long. If you work with Pentecostals, Charismatics, and even Third Wavers, you are suspect. In the name of doctrinal purity, strife is again resulting from the speaking and writing ministry of some well-known traditional evangelical leaders.

Now a new division is being pushed. Mission boards which have opened their door to Pentecostals, Charismatics, and Third Wavers are threatened with the cut-off of financial support by the churches controlled by some of these preachers and Bible teachers. Unfortunately, a new hard-line position is being taken all in the name of the one who prayed that "they may all be one; even as Thou, Father, art in me and I in Thee, that they also may be one in Us; that the world may believe that Thou didst send Me" (John 17:21).

It is a sobering experience to read Jesus' and later Paul's words and then examine one's own life and ministry. *If I am a sower of strife, a leader of disputes, dissensions, and factions with the body of Christ, then at that point I am walking in the flesh, not in the Spirit.* All my declarations that I am only contending "for the faith which was once for all delivered to the saints" (Jude 3) are a total abuse of that verse. This is not what Jude had in mind when he wrote these words. Pentecostals, Charismatics, and Third Wavers are also defenders and advocates of true biblical faith.

Not only is the flesh involved in such attitudes, but also demonic spirits. They are the evil spirits behind most of the renewed divisions within the body of Christ. The Spirit is the Spirit of peace and oneness within the Body. The spirits are the spirits of division and disunity within the Body. Which spirit is influencing my life in my attitude towards brethren of different doctrinal or ecclesiastical persuasions?

24

Bitterness and Intemperance

A lovely young mother came to me because of serious problems with her young child. In our first session she showed evidence of severe bruising in her own life. As I carefully set the context in which she could feel free to open her heart about her own life, she suddenly cried out, "I hate my grandfather. I hate my grandmother. I hate my father. I hate my mother."

That was a lot of hate in one breath. Next to her husband and child, these were four persons she should love most in life.

"Why do you hate your grandfather?" I asked.

"Because he is sexually perverse," she replied.

"Why do you hate your grandmother?"

"Because she is as sexually perverse as my grandfather. They are both advanced in years; yet they talk about sex as if they were street kids."

"What did your grandfather do to you?"

She lowered her head on my desk and began to weep uncontrollably. I let her weep until she was ready to respond.

"I hate him because he has abused me sexually since I was a girl!" she cried out. Again she put her face in her hands and continued to weep.

I felt deep compassion for her but was very careful not to touch her in any way, even though she was only the age of one of my daughters. In my spirit, I felt she had deep, personal, sexual problems resulting from the abuse, and any physical contact on my part could be misunderstood. Besides, she was extremely beautiful and sexually attractive and I was not going to give any ground to the Evil One.

When she brought her emotions under control, she said, "My grandfather is so sexually perverse he used to set me on his lap when I was a little girl and fondle me. As I began to grow up, he did everything to me. Even now, though I'm married, he is always after me. When he hugs me I have to put my arms across my chest or he would touch me in a sensual way. I hate him. I hate him!"

"Why do you hate your grandmother?" I asked.

"She knows what my grandfather is doing. She seems to delight in what he does almost as much as he does. I hate them both."

"Why do you hate your father?"

Her eyes blazed with hate and rage. "I hate him for not protecting me from his father. He was supposed to be my protector, but he didn't protect me. When his father would hold me and touch me in an inappropriate manner, I would look at my father, pleading with my eyes for his protection, but all he did was either ignore me or laugh. I hate him! I hate him!"

Again she wept uncontrollably. When she had her composure she continued, "I also hate my father because he didn't show me love when I needed his love. He would hug and kiss me when I was a little girl, but when I began to grow up and needed his love, he never gave it to me. Therefore, I never knew male love that was not sexual."

Finally, I asked why she hated her mother.

"She is Mrs. Perfect. She is a well-known women's Bible teacher. She travels and speaks everywhere. She had no time for me when I needed her to be my friend and counselor. She is the same way today, Mrs. Perfect, and I am not perfect."

She then looked at me in puzzlement. "Dr. Murphy, what is wrong with me? Everywhere I go men stare at me and want to touch me. But they only want to touch me in a sexual way. Am I so dirty that men know what has happened to me? I don't want to be seen like that."

After several sessions with this young woman, I saw that some aspects of her problem needed more help than I could give her, so I brought in another counselor.

The time came when she was ready to face the issue of extending forgiveness to those who had hurt her so terribly. Her life had been characterized by interpersonal conflict with many authority figures. Her sense of betrayal by the authority figures who should have been her helpers was so deep, she distrusted all authority.

We had her make up a list of the names of the persons she hated, was bitter against, or had deep conflict with. To our amazement she returned for the next session with an 8½" by 11" sheet of paper with names on both sides!

She made a copy for me and my fellow counselor. When she was ready, she brought the names before God, one by one. She confessed her reactionary sin[1] (see Figure 24.1) against each of them and declared by faith she was now forgiving each individual one by one. When she came to the name of her grandfather, she skipped him and went on to other names.

I waited but she did not return to her grandfather's name. I knew he was the main one and felt she was avoiding the real emotional roadblock to wholeness. I said, "You skipped over your grandfather's name."

She stopped her praying and confessing and looked directly at me. "I am not ready for him yet," she bluntly replied, and went on. I made no more comment.

Finally, she came back to him. It was a terrible emotional battle. The very thought of him made her sob. She could hardly stand the sight of his name on her list. He was the one that had caused her the deepest pain. This marred relationship had affected almost everything in her life, including her relationship with her husband.

She wanted him punished, not forgiven. Finally she cried out to the Lord, forgiving this cruel man as the Lord had forgiven her. It brought about an emotional release the like of which I had never seen before. It proved the real key to the beginning of her emotional healing which occurred not all at once but over a period of several months.

Eight Ways to Deal With Bitterness

How do we discover and deal with the deep, often unconscious, roots of bitterness, shame, rejection, and like negative emotions that lie buried within most of us? I would like to share eight ideas.[2]

1. *Express these negative feelings instead of submerging and suppressing them.* If you are plagued by shame, rejection, low self-esteem,[3] anger, bitterness, or rage against others and against God, admit it.

This is what Dr. William Backus calls, "telling yourself the truth."[4] Say it, "I am angry with _____." "I feel rejected by _____." "I was sexually abused by my father-mother-brother-uncle-grandfather, etc." Whatever the truth is, tell it to yourself. Recognize what is going on inside of you.

Next, tell it to God. He already knows, but He is waiting to hear you tell Him the truth, even if you are angry with Him. David, Jeremiah, and other heroes of the faith became angry with God and not only told Him so, but they wrote it down for everyone to read.

Then, tell it to your James 5:16 prayer-share-healing partner. We will talk more about the need of such a helper later in our study.

2. *Accept your responsibility for your negative, hateful feelings.* I have had to do this over and over again. Others are not responsible for *our* reactionary sins. We are. This is the consistent theme of Scripture. People are always held responsible for their sins, even sins provoked by the unjust actions of others.

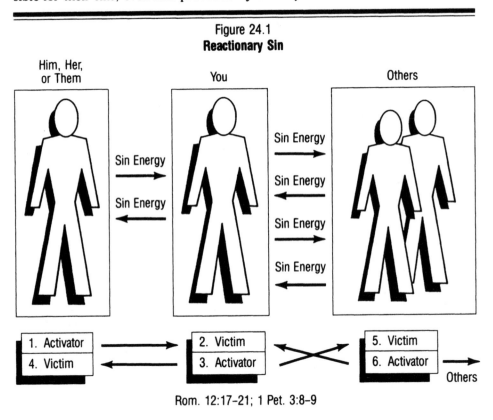

Figure 24.1
Reactionary Sin

Him, Her, or Them   You   Others

Sin Energy

Sin Energy

Sin Energy

Sin Energy

Sin Energy

Sin Energy

| 1. Activator | 2. Victim | 5. Victim |
| 4. Victim | 3. Activator | 6. Activator |

Others

Rom. 12:17–21; 1 Pet. 3:8–9

Key Insights
1. Sin builds up its own momentum—it reproduces itself.
2. I call this the "sin energy" cycle.
3. Hebrews 12:15 warns against this kind of sin.

In Ephesians 4:31—5:2b the apostle includes all believers, even those abused from childhood by others and those who may have been demonized from birth or even before birth. Those who hurt you have their own guilt, but it is guilt before God, not before you. You are not responsible for their actions. You are only responsible for your reactions to their actions.

3. *Confess your reactionary sin, if possible on at least three levels:* First, to the Lord: Accept by faith His faithfulness and righteousness in forgiving you your sins and His promise to cleanse you from all unrighteousness (1 John 1:6—2:1).

Second, to your James 5:16 prayer-share-healing partner: This way you are forced to verbalize to a trusted fellow human being what has been hidden within you most of your life. This not only opens the way for his effective prayer for you, but is therapeutic for you to bring the darkness of your inner life out into the light.

Third, wherever it is both necessary and possible, confess your feelings toward those against whom you hold such anger and bitterness (Matt. 5:22–24; 6:12–15; Mark 11:25–26; Matt. 18:21–35). If they were the perpetrators of some of the evil done to you, this provides them with the opportunity to face their sins, receive forgiveness, and be restored to life in Christ. At the same time it is not always possible and advisable to do so. This is where your counselor or James 5:16 partner can help you know what is profitable and what would do more harm than good.

4. *Ask yourself if you really want to be healed of your emotional bruising.* This may seem obvious, but it is not. Some have become so accustomed to their self-pity, anger, feelings of inferiority, rejection, they really don't want to change. For many, it has become an excuse for other sins which they do not want to abandon. They want to be whole, but not to pay the full price such wholeness demands.

5. *By faith choose to forgive all those who have hurt you.* Again this needs to be done by faith, by an act of the will in obedience to the Word of God. The emotions are not the key factor, because they change. The act of the will, "the obedience of faith," is stable. In time, the emotions may fall more in line with the will of faith. If not, it makes no difference. Your will has obeyed in faith the command of God. Someone has said, "Forgiveness is giving up the right to hate those who have hurt us." Without doubt this is the most difficult part of forgiveness.

A fifteen-year-old girl, the victim of years of incest on the part of her father, had come for counseling. As the Christian counselor brought up the subject of her need to forgive her father for the evil he had done to her, she reacted with anger against his suggestion saying, "Why should I forgive my father for ruining the first fifteen years of my life?"

The counselor wisely immediately replied, "If you don't, you will be allowing him to ruin the next fifteen years of your life."

What words of wisdom! The root of bitterness defiles many, Paul says. It especially defiles the one in whom the root is nourished (Heb. 12:15).

6. *By faith, choose to extend the redeeming love of Christ to the offenders.* By this I do not mean to try to win them to Christ. The offending party may already be a Christian. Sometimes they are well-known Christian leaders. Some are very effective soul winners.

While some may reject the possibility that perpetrators of such evil could ever be truly "born again" Christians, we have to accept the fact that some of them are. At least they have accepted Christ as Savior and have perhaps faithfully served Him except for this one dark area of their life.

When you forgive and can really pray for the salvation and transformation of those who have hurt you most, you are on the way to healing. God moves in answer to the prayers of His saints.

7. *Choose to forgive yourself and accept God's forgiveness for your sins.* Do not allow the Devil to accuse you any longer or to fill you with shame, self-rejection, a sense of dirtiness, or worthlessness.

Second Corinthians 2:6–7,11 is a key passage. Paul was afraid that the repentant believer at Corinth would fall short of receiving God's forgiveness and be swallowed up by too much remorse (v. 7). Paul felt this was about to happen unless the believers who had disciplined him now reaffirmed him and assured him of their forgiveness and love.

Often believers abused as children struggle to enter into the blissful peace that comes with the assurance of full cleansing and restoration. Guilt-plagued, they feel somehow partially responsible for what was done to them even though they know they were victims of the evil of others.

8. *Finally, break any inroads of Satan into your life which came through the abuse and the abuser.* Many child abusers are demonized, and the evil spirits attached to their lives often pair off and attach themselves to the lives of their victims. Or, they may ride the wave of reactionary sin and reinforce the victim's feeling of anger, shame, sense of worthlessness, bitterness, and rage. The believer, therefore, must learn to practice effective spiritual warfare (James 4:7–8; 1 Pet. 5:8–11).

In the lives of some people, the roots of bitterness, shame, rejection, and repulsion to others will not respond to the preceding suggestions; or if there is response, it may be superficial and not long-lasting. In almost 100 percent of such cases there has been very severe abuse in childhood, usually in preschool days. That abuse is either totally blocked from the memory of the counselee or strange, disconnected "flashbacks" of some early trauma occur. Unfortunately, this often seems to require an agonizing reliving of the pain-causing experiences so the memories can surface and be dealt with by the Spirit of God.

In the pastoral context such damaged people are often told that prayer and reading the Bible faithfully will bring the needed healing. This is an oversimplification. The healing does not usually occur either in a one-hour, laying-on-of-hands, healing service or in a brief counseling session. Occasionally it does, just as a person with a fatal disease may sometimes be instantly healed; but this is not the usual manner in which God heals.

The same is true with persons terribly damaged by prolonged situations of continual pain in childhood. In such a context, survival was possible only by some form of dissociation, or separating themselves totally from even the memory of such trauma. It usually requires a skilled and well-trained "healer" to help the counselee discover the root causes of his present problems.

We must ask God which counseling cases we should take and which we should refer. For every one I take, I refer many others to more skilled counselors who have the time, training, and experience to become God's healers to His bruised children.

Sins of Covetousness (Galatians 5:20–21)

The last group of social sins are two, "jealousy" and "envyings." I call them sins of covetousness.

"Jealousy" is *zēlos* in Greek. It is often used in a good sense in the New Testament as "zeal" (Rom. 10:2; Phil. 3:6; John 2:17; 2 Cor. 7:7). Fung says that whenever it is associated with *eris,* "strife," it has a negative connotation as here and in Romans 13:13, 1 Corinthians 3:3, 2 Corinthians 12:20. It represents jealousy.

According to Fung, jealousy is "a self-centered zeal which resents the good which another enjoys but is denied to oneself (cf. James 3:14, 'bitter jealousy') and may actively seek to harm the other person."[5]

"Envyings," *phthonoi* in Greek, is similar in meaning to *zēlos*. Fung says that "whereas *zēlos* can have the positive sense of 'zeal' as well as the negative sense of 'jealousy,' *pthonos* has only the ignoble sense of 'envy' (RSV) which regards another person with ill will because of what he has or is. This is not very different from *zēlos* as it is used here (cf. NEB, 'jealousies')."[6]

TWO SINS OF INTEMPERANCE

The Greek plural noun *methai* is translated "drunkenness" in the KJV, NAS, and most other versions (Gal. 5:21). The NEB translates it "drinking bouts" which captures well the meaning of the word. Fung says that while "the use of wine is in itself no sin (cf. John 2:10; 1 Tim. 5:23), excessive consumption in the form of 'drunkenness' (AV) and 'drinking bouts' (NEB) shows up repeatedly in catalogs of vices (Rom. 13:13; 1 Cor. 5:11; 6:10). In the last two passages the word used is *methysos*, a 'drunkard.'"[7]

The common practice in drunkenness is to get drunk at night after the day's work is done. The apostle Paul refers to this fact in his impassioned exhortation towards soberness of attitude on the part of believers in 1 Thessalonians 5:4–11.

On one occasion Paul had to correct the Corinthian church for allowing drunkenness at the Lord's table (1 Cor. 11:20–22). While this seems inconceivable, it is evidence of how widespread drunkenness was in the Gentile world in those days.

The New Testament expresses a strongly negative view towards "addiction to wine," that is, to alcoholic beverages, and drunkenness. The apostle Paul says the latter is "dissipation" (Eph. 5:18a, NAS). The word is *asōtia* in Greek, a compound of two words, *a*, "negative," and *sōzō*, "to save."[8] It is translated by various vivid words in different versions of the New Testament.

The KJV translates it "riot"; the RSV uses "debauchery." Beck translates it "wild living," while *The Emphasized New Testament* uses "dissoluteness." J. B. Phillips has one of the best functional translations: "Don't get your stimulus from wine (for there is always the danger of excessive drinking)." We are to be stimulated by the intaking of the Holy Spirit, Paul says, not wine (Eph. 5:18).

Fung, while commenting on Ephesians 5:18, makes reference to the Hellenistic cult of Dionysus, the god of wine with which the Ephesian Christians were only too familiar.[9] His ceremonies of worship degenerated into drunken festivals with the usual accompanying orgies. In Scripture drunkenness and immorality often go together (Gen. 9:20–27; 19:30–39).

The next word is another plural, *kōmoi* (Gal. 5:21). The NAS renders it "carousings," the KJV "revelings." Vine says it is "the concomitant and consequence of drunkenness."[10] Fung says it "is a natural companion of 'drunkenness' (cf. Rom. 13:13), a characteristic feature of the pagan way of life (1 Peter 4:3), and a concrete example of putting 'pleasure in the place of God' (so NEB, 2 Tim. 3:4, *philēdonoi*)."[11]

A functional equivalent in contemporary American youth culture would be "partying." Such parties with their drunkenness, loss of self-control, immorality, and the like, draw demonic spirits. I dealt with one lying, "partying" spirit who boasted he was going to transform hell into one riotous party and "dance on the flames."

This Is Not All

The apostle ends his catalog of the vices of the flesh with the statement, "and things like these" (Gal. 5:21). Fung says, as the list was prefaced by *hatina* (the kind of), it is climaxed by *kai ta homoia,* "and the like." Both expressions show that the enumeration is representative and not exhaustive.

Of the fifteen given here, Fung says the first three (immorality, impurity and sensuality) and the last two (drunkenness and carousings) are "sins committed in the sphere of the body, but the rest . . . might well be committed by disembodied spirits, this showing that 'the deeds of the flesh' are not necessarily physical or sensual, but embrace spiritual vices as well."[12]

Paul's closing statement, "of which I forewarn you just as I have forewarned you that those who practice these things shall not inherit the kingdom of God" (Gal. 5:21b), doesn't refer to an occasional act but to a lifestyle. He uses the participle *prassontes,* which should not be translated "these who do such things" (KJV) but "these who practice such things" (NAS).

Fung affirms that the participle "denotes not an occasional lapse but habitual behavior."[13] The NIV correctly translates the phrase "those who live like this."

There is no such thing as justification by Christ without regeneration by the Holy Spirit. As Fung says, "the Gospel which offers justification and freedom from the law through faith in Christ never gives the believers any liberty to turn that freedom into license to practice 'the acts of the sinful nature' (v. 19, NIV; cf. v. 13)."[14]

The apostle refers to inheritance of "the kingdom of God." The theme of the kingdom of God of Christ, and of heaven is the central theme of Scripture. As George Ladd says, "Modern scholarship is quite unanimous in the opinion that the kingdom of God was the central message of Jesus Christ."[15] I. H. Marshall agrees and says it means "the sovereign activity of God as King in saving men and overcoming evil, and the new order which is thus established."[16]

There seem to be three aspects of the kingdom revealed in Scripture: the kingdom which came with the coming of Jesus; the kingdom which continues to come in the ministry of the church; and the kingdom which is yet to come in the *parousia,* the second coming of Christ.

Our Lord's deliverance ministry was uniquely a kingdom ministry. Jesus said to the Jews that his ministry of binding the strong man and casting out demons was evidence that "the kingdom of God has come upon you" (Matt. 12:22–28).

An effective spiritual warfare ministry in the sense of victorious warfare against evil supernaturalism in the authority of Jesus' name is uniquely an evidence of the continuing coming of the kingdom of God. This is what brings joy to an otherwise difficult ministry.

The Believer's Warfare With the World

25

The Gospel and Culture

Syncretism as a Dimension of "The World"

"The church of Africa is like a river a mile wide but only an inch deep," someone has said. In recent conferences, the extent of the syncretism practiced by the church leaders in one African nation surfaced. I was compelled to teach over and over again from Joshua 24:14–23, where Joshua challenged God's people to make the decision whom they were going to serve, the true God or the no-gods (Gal. 4:8).

We were disturbed to find that many of the "godly" pastors and their wives present for the training conferences were double-minded. Although truly committed to Christ for the forgiveness of their sins and the assurance of eternal life in the coming kingdom of God, they still resorted to traditional gods, magic, and service to ancestral spirits, traditional good and evil spirits, and nature-cosmic spirits to meet daily needs. This was the "world" with which they continued to compromise.

Towards the end of the week after I had laid sufficient biblical foundation, I used Joshua 24:14–15, 23 to challenge the pastors and their wives to follow the Lord with their whole heart. I invited the leaders to demonstrate publicly their decision to "put away the foreign gods which are in your midst, and incline your hearts to the LORD" (v. 23). A number of the men stood up, making public their decisions to follow the Lord, completely rejecting all other gods. Some came forward for prayer and counseling.

None of the women responded, however. We had already discovered that usually it is the women who cling to the old gods and spirits and practice traditional magic. We also knew that culturally women would usually not respond in public where men are present.

During the afternoon session with the women, it was my wife's turn to teach. Loretta reviewed my teaching of the morning, gently but firmly pointing out that as pastors' wives they were often the most guilty of practicing traditional magic and serving the spirits for protection and blessings for themselves and their household.

We had been told that many of these women had magic strings tied around their waists and tied to the arms or feet of their children. Loretta challenged them to remove these magic strings and follow biblical teachings on healing, protection, and blessings for their daily needs.

Suddenly a spontaneous restlessness accompanied with a roar of protest swept throughout the group of women. Demons burst into manifestation everywhere, rejecting the teachings that had been given. Loretta was so startled she did not know what to do. She began to declare to the spirit world that Jesus was Lord and had total authority over all spirits and that His servants shared that authority over them. She silenced the spirits.

A godly YWAM leader who worked with them stood up and, speaking in their native tongue Chechewa, brought the women under control. They began to minister to those who wanted to follow the Lord fully.

A good number of women had become demonized through their homage to the spirits and practice of traditional magic. They needed to be set free. God was faithful and the teachers witnessed great victories. Not all the women responded, however. Yet these women hold the key to the real spiritual life of their families and churches.

Why do I use this case study to begin our study of warfare with the world? Syncretism is not only warfare with evil supernaturalism; it is also warfare with the world. The pastors' wives in this story were still in love with spirit magic, a major cultural feature of the world in which they lived. They needed to break with the world at this point.

As we focus on warfare with sin rooted in what the Bible calls "this evil world," we are looking at sin in its social dimension. William Vine defines the world from this social perspective as "the present condition of human affairs in alienation from and opposition to God."[1]

When we speak of human affairs we are forced to think of human societies. Each particular society becomes "the world" in which the members of that society live. For the believer that world becomes his spiritual enemy just as much as his flesh. This is what had occurred in the case of the African pastor's wives just mentioned. The social dimension of the believer's warfare, his warfare with the world, can become even more difficult for him to recognize and overcome than the personal dimension, his warfare with the flesh. The world is much more subtle than the flesh. It creeps up upon us unawares.

Though not easy to conquer, the sins of the flesh, more concrete and more recognizable, are easier to detect. This is not so with the world. As a result, most of us as believers are more worldly than we would like to admit.

Cultures, Religions, and the Gospel

Since every believer is part of a cultural group, many of the norms of that group become the sinful world of the believer. The self-centered lifestyle of the group relentlessly presses in upon believers to conform them to its mold. As citizens of the kingdom of God, believers are to recognize the intrinsic evil of many dimensions of their culture and resist their subtle entrapments.

Cultural Components and the Gospel: Neutral, Compatible, or Incompatible

Human cultures are *not* totally evil. While evil pervades all aspects of human life due to the Fall, human cultures in themselves are good for mankind in his present earthly state. They devise and enforce laws and values which make the survival of the group possible.

Human cultures are composed of various components, each of which exists in a given relationship to other components. Where there is harmony between those components, the social structure is relatively stable. Where severe disharmony exists, the continuation of the culture is threatened.

Generally speaking from a biblical perspective, there exist three different broad types of cultural components: those compatible with the Christian faith, those incompatible, and those neutral.

A people's style of dress, housing, food, and like cultural components are neutral. The gospel has nothing or little to say about them. People can become Christians and continue with those cultural components unchanged.

Many cultural components are compatible with the gospel. In fact some components of non-Western cultures are more "Christian" than parallel components of Western culture. Love for family, for example, female marital fidelity, love for and protection of children, respect for, love of, and care of the aged and handicapped, and acceptance of a simple lifestyle, are all cases in point. The gospel reinforces these good cultural components within the host cultures. It recognizes in them further evidence of God's general revelation which extends to all humanity.

Other cultural components, however, are not compatible with the gospel. At this point, the Christian message challenges the host culture and can upset the cultural balance. This is especially true when the culture is structured by a world view which clashes with a general biblical world view. This clash will occur even if the world view of that culture is a spiritualistic, or religious, world view. Religion, or its functional substitute, provides content to one's world view. As such, it lies at the very heart and soul of a culture.

Christianity is incompatible with any religion other than itself,[2] but non-Christian religions often provide the bridge over which the gospel crosses into a culture.[3] Just as often, however, religion becomes the major barrier to the acceptance of the gospel by a culture. Islam is a case in point.[4] Either way, when a culture or subculture responds to the gospel, dramatic cultural change often follows. The gospel will eventually challenge the "world" of that culture or subculture.[5]

Christianity is exclusive. It alone provides the one path to eternal life. Jesus Himself said:

> Enter by the narrow gate; for the gate is wide, and the way is broad that leads to destruction, and many are those who enter by it. For the gate is small, and the way is narrow that leads to life, and few are those who find it. (Matt. 7:13–14)

The gospel is authoritative and dogmatic. It will not compromise with evil or moral, social, or religious error. It lays down standards for both belief and conduct. Where these conflict with cultural components of the target culture, those components must eventually change or the culture will not become biblically Christian. The gospel challenges "the world" within the culture and the cultural "world" resists the gospel in continuous conflict. Thus each new generation must be brought to personal faith in Christ.

This is just as true with Western culture as in the rest of the world. In fact major components of Western culture are becoming increasingly incompatible with pure biblical Christianity. This is the world with which the Western church is at war.

Cultural Components: Making the Changes the Gospel Requires

Every major cultural component performs a function within the culture. If a major cultural component conflicts with Scripture, the people have a choice to make. From the perspective of the Word of God only one choice is permitted: The offensive cultural components must be rejected by the people and replaced by components compatible with the gospel.

The result will be both positive and negative. From a positive perspective the people will be pleasing God. From a negative perspective, they will be upsetting the equilibrium of their own culture. They will be producing a cultural void that cannot be left empty. It must be filled by a culturally relevant, functional substitute.

How are such functional substitutes to be discovered?[6] In mission work, the missionary can help the believers of the host culture recognize the function the offensive cultural components perform within their culture.[7] Together they must discover or create functional substitutes compatible with biblical truth but relevant to their culture to fill that cultural void. The role of the missionary and that of the people are both crucial in this matter. The missionary must *not* impose his cultural bias upon the host people in the name of the supracultural gospel.

When I say *supracultural* I mean "that which arises directly out of God's Word and is binding upon all cultures in contrast to that which is limited to or arises out of a given cultural context." For example, John 3:16 is supracultural, while 1 Corinthians 11:5–6,10,13–15 probably is primarily cultural.

Also, the missionary is only an advocate of culture change. He cannot produce the changes himself. As an outsider he will not fully understand the role of the offensive cultural components nor what will be the most acceptable functional substitutes. The changes must come from the people of the host culture themselves. They are the only true innovators. Only they will fully understand which functional substitutes will fill the cultural voids in question.

Since every culture is sinful, cultural changes must occur. For example, sexual and worldly lusts are always contrary to Scripture. Immorality is wrong in any culture, even if it presently seems to fulfill an essential function in that culture. Hatred and interpersonal conflicts, rivalries, and warfare between opposing people groups do not please God. He loves all people and equally desires their highest good. Vengeance is His prerogative (Rom. 12:18–21). Religion which does not submit itself to the lordship of Christ displeases God. If it does not result in compassion for the oppressed, the suffering, afflicted, and lonely, it is not "pure and undefiled religion in the sight of our God" (James 1:27).

Furthermore, Jesus is not one among equals or even just the best among other gods and spiritual beings who eventually lead to salvation and peace with God. He Himself affirmed, "I am the way, and the truth, and the life; no one comes to the Father, but through Me" (John 14:6).[8]

The Challenges of Syncretism

Syncretism is one of the major barriers to world evangelism facing the church today.[9] In many parts of the world people have become Christian without breaking with their pre-Christian fear of and obedience to the spirits or the "no-gods" (Gal. 4:8). This is especially true if the "version" of the gospel they received did not provide functional substitutes for the needs formerly met by the spirits or no-gods. Usually these needs are in the area of physical healing, fertility, blessings upon their work to provide for themselves and their families, help in their daily endeavors, and protection from real or imagined enemies.

Worst of all is when the church deliberately tries to combine the gospel with beliefs from traditional religions or spirit magic. A local newspaper printed the following excerpt in a story titled "Traditional Mayan Life Challenged: Evangelical Church, Catholics Compete":[10]

In the last decade, Catholic missionaries have worked hard to help the Indians combine elements of their traditional religion with Catholic teaching to convert the Mayans, who make up nearly half of the country's 9 million people. . . . Bishop Efrain Hernandez, secretary to Guatemalan Archbishop Prospero Penados del Barrios, says the Catholic Church is not trying to destroy indigenous beliefs, but simply mix two ways of thinking.

In the case of Guatemala the evangelicals were taking a strong stand against any form of syncretism. Thus the Roman Catholic clergy and the evangelicals took opposite points of view in the case at hand. We could wish all Protestants would follow the example of their Guatemalan evangelical brethren. Some Protestants have been just as compromising as the Catholics in the Guatemala story.

The early church was uncompromising in its declaration, "There is salvation in no one else; for there is no other name under heaven that has been given among men, by which we must be saved" (Acts 4:12). This must be accepted and declared by the people receiving the gospel or the result will be syncretism or Christo-paganism.

Living for self and not for the glory of God and the benefit of one's fellow man is never acceptable to God (Mark 12:29–31). Living in disobedience to God and His revelation in His Word and in the Lord Jesus is rebellion against His lordship. Men either create gods in their own image—idolatry, spiritism, spiritualism, mediumistic religions, animism—or make themselves to be God. Either way, they declare independence from the lordship of the one true God. As such they follow the world and live in a state of alienation from God.

This is the "world" found within all human cultures. This is the world which presses its non-Christian values against the mind, emotions, and will of all of us as believers, daily. With this world we are at war. It is our enemy because it is God's enemy. As we will soon see, it is also a demonized world. And this world flourishes in America.

The World, American Style

America offers a good example of the features of "the world" as they appear in Western, post-industrial cultures at the dawn of the third millennium. From a popular perspective, we follow Charles Colson who, in *The Body: Being Light in the Darkness*, calls the view of reality popular among many in America "the worldview of Donahuism."[11] This TV talk-show view of reality says, "Do whatever is right for you, and you are being faithful to whatever is true for you." The key idea, says Colson, is "that you—and only you—should decide what you want. No one else has a right to tell you what to do."

Those who advocate this lifestyle see it as "autonomy, liberation and freedom." It could better be described as moral decadence. It presents people as likeable animals who drift through life seeking self-satisfaction. Most defend few moral values since they say they believe in no moral absolutes.

What effect does this decadent view of life have on American culture? First, *it trivializes human experience by treating some shameful and selfish human acts as shameless and entertaining.*

Second, *it distracts us from facing the most profound questions of life,* such as the questions about true goodness and ultimate meaning and purpose in life.

Third, *it attacks virtues such as commitment, responsibility, and self-control, which sustain healthy families and societies.*

The evil inevitably resulting from the unrealistic lifestyle portrayed on television by Donahue and similar talk shows is reinforced by a diet of daily TV soap operas.

Here a credulous TV audience that seems to have blurred its perspective of right and wrong is mesmerized into approving acts that only increase our culture's moral crisis, and bringing devastation to us as a people.

If "Donahuism" is the popular term for this world view, a few technical terms better describe its true nature. One such term is *cultural relativism*. This view declares that ethical truths depend *only* upon the perspective of reality of the individuals and groups holding them. Truth is not absolute. Thus humans have no objective standard by which to evaluate their beliefs, values, and behavior. Right and wrong are determined in each situation by each individual and each group, not by divine revelation.

The result? Philosophical *nihilism*. This view denies that traditional Judeo-Christian values and beliefs rest on any rational foundation.[12] Humans thus exist without a purpose besides the purpose they invent for themselves.

Cultural relativism and nihilism encourage cultural *pluralism,* the condition in which no one world view or culture is held to be superior to another. Pluralism, in itself, is beneficial to this nation because it opposes the tyranny of one culture over others. Whether we speak of America as a cultural "melting pot," "stew," or "salad," we acknowledge that America's general openness to peoples of other cultures has strengthened our nation. This is the good news. Here is the bad news. Often cultural pluralism in the form of political correctness seeks to silence any clear witness to the Christ event. We can no longer assume that American culture is based upon and upholds Judeo-Christian values.

Because our culture increasingly opposes acknowledging the one true God as its ground of being, it strongly promotes the world view of *naturalism*. Traditional naturalism has, throughout the twentieth century, consistently affirmed that humanity, not God, is the center of the universe. Human life, for the moment, represents the zenith in a blind, purposeless process called evolution.

In essence, humankind came from nothing; lives for nothing but its own existence; has no predetermined future; and may someday be superseded by a superior form of life as different from the human species as humanity is from sheep, among the dumbest of mammals. Should this process continue, the new species also will cease to exist, be replaced by an even more sophisticated form, and continue the naturalistic cycle.

This view is still held in most of academia and, to a lesser degree, by the public at large. Today, however, we are witnessing the rise of a *neo-naturalism* that asserts the supremacy of nature as a whole. All nature is equal, according to neo-naturalism, so humanity should no longer be considered the center of the universe. "No surprise, then," Colson writes, "that Earth Day would get more attention than Easter." Or that David Brown, former executive director of the Sierra Club would write that "while the death of young men in war is unfortunate, it is no more serious than [the] touching of mountains and wilderness areas by mankind."

Colson observes that neo-naturalism "enshrines nature with its own mystique and breeds its own form of worship, which partially explains the spread of pantheism and the proliferation of bizarre New Age cults." Neo-naturalism makes relativism total: It is not possible to declare that one creature has more intrinsic value than any other; humans who evolved from nothing are nothing. Since they lack any inherent destiny, they can live as they choose. Thus there is no objective basis for human dignity; no logical reason to believe that we humans are intrinsically better than (or superior to) any other living thing.

It is perfectly logical therefore that activists fight for the right of endangered species—even insects—while not "blinking an eye at the abortion of unborn humans." Or as Ingrid Newkirk, president of People For The Ethical Treatment of Animals, puts it, "A rat is a pig is a dog is a boy."[13]

Ironically, neo-naturalism descends to a wild perversion, even a reversal, of Darwinism. The fittest who have survived now have to fight for the survival of species which cannot survive without their help, but can't think of themselves as in any way an inherently more valuable kind of being.

In the view of Scripture, neo-naturalists are persons who, while professing themselves to be wise, have become fools (Rom. 1:22; Ps. 14:1). Is it not foolish to fight for the survival of non-human protoplasm while describing yourself as "debased human protoplasm"? Is this view of human life worth dying for? Or, even living for?

Finally, the prevailing American (Western) world view is *utopian* and *pragmatic.* It is utopian because, if God is dead, then we are masters of our own fate. And since we are basically good, with time and increasing knowledge, we are only going to get better. It is certainly true that, in the twentieth century, we have advanced in science, technology, and the production of human knowledge more than in all previous centuries combined. Yet we find little evidence of human social and moral improvement. In this century, wars have been waged on a magnitude never known before. Brutal rulers subject their own people to untold misery. Stronger nations inflict genocide upon the weaker ones. Human beings are subjected to every conceivable form of horror. Murder, rape, incest, child abuse, greed, betrayal, bloodshed, and other evils threaten the very survival of society. Can this by any stretch of the imagination be called Utopia?

Colson states that pragmatism is the only philosophical system "made in America." With this philosophy, "Does it work?" has replaced "Is it right?" What are some of the natural consequences of this view?

- Abortion on demand: Whether or not a pregnancy and child works into a woman's or couple's life wins out over the life of the unborn child.
- No-fault divorce: If your marriage is not working, end it.
- Flight from ethics in business: If your profits are not what you wish, cheat! Lie!
- Disregard for the law: Break the law, but don't get caught!

In summary, Colson writes, "The 1960's adage, 'if it feels good, do it' has been updated for the 1990's, 'if it works, do it.'"[14] This is pragmatism at its worst.

This is the world with which we are at war. This is also the world to which we Christians have been called to bear witness to the eternal reality found only in Christ.

The World's Power, Its Character, Our Victory

Contradictory Attitudes Toward the World?

Many believers are puzzled by a seeming contradiction in God's attitude towards the world. The apostle John has Jesus declaring that God loves the world in John 3:16, while the apostle Paul declares God's negative view of the same world, as does the apostle John in his writings.

The most common word translated "world" in the New Testament is the Greek word *kosmos,* used over 200 times by the New Testament writers. The rest are about equally divided between *aiōn*, "age," and *oikoumenē*, "the inhabited world."[1]

Literally, *kosmos* means an ornament. Vine says it means "order, arrangement, ornament, adornment." From *kosmos* we get our English word, *cosmetic* (1 Pet. 3:3). How did a word meaning "ornament" develop into one meaning "the world"? Leon Morris suggests that the outstanding ornament is the universe, but to humanity the most significant part of that universe was the world in which they lived. A natural progression would be to regard the world as all of humanity, but this world at large crucified Christ. It is "not surprising that 'the world' in Scripture is used to mean 'mankind in opposition to Christ.'"[2]

Morris then makes an important statement which fits our study of the believer's warfare with the world well. He says the world becomes

> the sum total of the divine creation which has been shattered by the fall, which stands under the judgment of God, and in which Jesus Christ appears as the Redeemer. [The world is thus] in some sense personified as the great opponent of the Redeemer in salvation history.[3]

As such the world is also the great opponent of the redeemed in salvation history. This negative use of the word *kosmos* is unique to the New Testament. The word is not used this way in the Greek version of the Old Testament nor in Greek secular writings. Morris feels that "for John and for Paul the shattering thing was that the men who inhabit this beautiful and ordered universe acted in an ugly and unreasonable way when they came face-to-face with Christ"[4] (John 1:10; 7:4–8; 8:12, 23; 9:5; 12:31, 45–46; 14:17, 27–30; 15:18; 16:7–11, 20, 33; 17:6, 9, 13–18; 25).

Yet all is not hopeless. This world of human beings—shattered as they are by the Fall and living in hostility to God—is the object of God's most intense love. Did not Jesus say: "For God so loved the world, that He gave His only begotten Son"? Morris observes, "It is true that the world is not interested in the things of God, but it is not true that God reciprocates. . . . The whole work of salvation which God accomplished in Christ is directed to the world"[5] (John 1:29; 3:16–17; 4:42; 6:33; 6:51; 12:47).

Morris then points out that the success of Christ's saving ministry to the world is revealed in the references to the Lord's overthrow of Satan, the prince of this world (John 12:31; 14:30; 16:11). Thus, Jesus can affirm that he has overcome the world (John 16:33). This victory over Satan and the world by the Lord Jesus Christ does not alter the fact that the world basically opposed him, and still opposes him.

Perhaps God's relationship with the world could be called a love/hate relationship. God loves worldly men and women, the entire human race, sinful as it is and living its own life of separateness and rebellion against God. He has provided full pardon for the sins of the world in the Cross of His Son (2 Cor. 5:18–21).

God hates the world system, however. The world system also hates Him (John 7:7; 14—17). Its philosophies of life blind men to God's love and reinforces their sinful separateness from him. In this sense, we could define our enemy, the world, as the collective, social expression of the activities of our other two enemies, the enemy from within, the flesh, and the enemy from without, evil supernaturalism. Once again we see that both sin and spiritual warfare are multidimensional: warfare with the flesh, with the world, and with evil supernaturalism.

To better understand the evil power of the world in its warfare against the believer, we examine John's description of the world in 1 John 2:15–17 and two key references in Paul's letter to the Galatians.

1 John 2:15–17

The Command

John begins with a double command, "Do not love the world, nor the things in the world" (v. 15a). Wuest, in his comments on this passage, quotes Vincent as affirming that the double negative and the double usage of the word *kosmos* refers to the biblical view of the world as "the sum total of human life in the ordered world, considered apart from, alienated from, and hostile to God, and of the earthly things which seduce from God"[6] (John 7:7; 15:18; 17:9, 14; 1 Cor. 1:20–21; 2 Cor. 7:10; James 4:4).

He comments further saying, "much in this world system is religious, cultured, refined, and intellectual. But it is anti-God and anti-Christ," so it is understandable why John continues with the shattering affirmation "If anyone loves the world, the love of the Father is not in him" (1 John 2:15b).

The word for love here is *agape,* but without the unique Christian meaning given when it refers to God's love and the love of true believers, or self-sacrificing love. According to Wuest, in secular Greek the word means "fondness or affection for an object because of its value [to the lover]."

Wuest then states that, "This is how John is using the word here to refer to love for the world. It is a love of approbation, of esteem. Demas is said to have loved this present age. He found it precious and thus came to love it" (2 Tim. 4:10). Wuest next points out that the main verb in this sentence is a present imperative and speaks of "the act of forbidding the continuance of an action already going on."[7] The world was still precious to some of the Christians of John's day. Is it still precious to us in our day? I am afraid it is.

John then affirms that if one continues to regard the world or the things in the world as precious, it reveals that God is really not precious to that person.

Two Reasons Not To Love the World

John next gives two basic reasons why the Christian is to love God and his brother (1 John 2:5,10; 4:19–20) but is not to love the world. First, John says, love for the Father and love for the world are mutually exclusive. "If anyone loves the world, the love of the Father is not in him" (v. 15).

John Stott explains, "If a man is engrossed in the outlook and pursuits of the world which rejects Christ, it is evident he has no love for the Father"[8] (James 4:4; Matt. 6:24).

Next John points out the transience of the world as contrasted with the eternality of the one who does the will of God: "And the world is passing away, and also its lusts; but the one who does the will of God abides forever" (1 John 2:17).

Aspects of the World System

One's view of reality determines one's values. Four basic affirmations underlie the Christian's belief systems. These in turn determine both the Christian's values and the conduct that results from those values.

1. God has revealed Himself in human history as ultimate, absolute reality.
2. Because of God's self-revelation, the human race has a perfect and unchangeable foundation upon which to build its beliefs and its values and to which to conform its conduct.
3. Humanity cannot know true reality apart from a meaningful relationship with this self-disclosing God.
4. Without a relationship with God based on God's self-disclosure (primarily in the Scriptures and in His Son), humanity's beliefs will be flawed, their values distorted, and their conduct unwholesome. Tragedy will result and increase.

As we discussed in the last chapter, this traditional, historic biblical view of reality is being aggressively and persistently challenged and rejected in contemporary Western and American culture, even though these cultures ultimately owe their uniqueness to the biblical world view.

Yet Western culture seems adamant in progressively rejecting its own historic, theistic roots and abandoning itself to a lifestyle described in Scripture as the pursuit of "the lusts of the flesh, the lusts of the eyes, and the boastful pride of life." (1 John 2:16). In verse 15, John directs us not to love "the things in the world," thus giving us a fourfold description of "the things in the world," all it has to offer. He begins with "the lust of the flesh."

The Lust of the Flesh

As already examined, these lusts represent the personal dimension of sin, the warfare that wages within us (Gal. 5:17). The word *lust* literally means "strong desire" and can refer to good desire, even God's desire for us (James 4:5). It is usually used in Scripture with a negative connotation, however. Wuest says, "The lust of the flesh is the passionate desire or craving that comes from our evil nature."[9]

Slavery to the lusts of the flesh, John says, is really all there is "in the world." While often outwardly paying lip service to high ethical standards, the world is powerless to live by these standards. They are violated everywhere, by almost everyone, all the time. Of course, if the non-theistic view of reality is the correct one, there really can be no moral absolutes. One is really free to satisfy himself. That's what the media in most of the world tells us, daily.

This is not so for the church, nor for the Christian, however. We have moral absolutes given to us by God. He has caused them to be written in the Bible for our benefit. While the world shouts to gain our attention and to undermine our morals, all the believer is responsible to do and able to do is to say "No!" We are able to say "No!" because "those who belong to Christ Jesus have crucified the flesh with its passions and desires" (Gal. 5:24). This is how we win the battle against the lusts of the flesh which are daily stimulated to action by this evil world, Paul says. To the world and to the flesh we say "NO!" In contrast, to the Holy Spirit we say "YES!" (Gal. 5:16–17).

In his excellent appendix entitled "The Term Flesh in Galatians 5:24," Needham develops this truth in greater detail. He writes:[10]

A Christian is one who because he "is Christ's" has of necessity declared death to "in the flesh" life in terms of its passions and lusts. Since God has finished off the person I once was by the crucifixion of Christ I as a new man have made my declaration concerning the finishing off of my flesh.

In other words, God himself has already brought about the death of the old self, the old I, by union with Christ in his death. Paul declares this both in Romans 6 and in Galatians 2:20. Now, as a new person in Christ, I am able to say "no" to the lusts of the flesh. I am able to crucify the flesh with its passions and lusts.

For this reason, the believer is able to win the battle with the lusts of the world, also. Indeed, he is guaranteed victory over the lusts of the world because he is crucified to the world and the world to him (Gal. 6:14) and because he is born of God (1 John 5:4–5). By union with my loving Lord in His crucifixion I am dead to the world and its lusts and the world is dead to me. As Charles Spurgeon is said to have declared, "Come, world, with all your allurements. What can you do to me, a dead man?"

The Lust of the Eyes

John next describes the world as a system of activity energized by "the lust of the eyes." The former lusts, those of the flesh, come from within us. The latter, those of the eyes, come from without, from the world which surrounds us.

C. H. Dodd says that "the lust of the eyes refers to the tendency to be captivated by the outward show of things, without inquiring into their real value."[11] William Barclay carries this one step further, writing:[12]

It is the spirit which can see nothing without wishing to acquire it, and which, having acquired it flaunts it in the face of man. It is the spirit which believes that happiness is to be found in the things which money can buy and which the eyes can see.

The "lust of the eyes" became the downfall of many persons in Scripture. In fact, humanity's original sin was partially precipitated by just such lusts. Genesis says, "when the woman saw . . . it was a delight to the eyes . . . she took . . ." (Gen. 3:6).

We are all familiar with the sin of Achan. By his own confession things went well with him until "I saw among the spoil a beautiful mantle from Shinar and two hundred shekels of silver and a bar of gold fifty shekels in weight, then I coveted them and took them" (Josh. 7:21). "I saw . . . I coveted . . . I took."

And who does not know the story of the double sin of David, that of adultery and, indirectly, that of murder? It all began with the lust of David's eyes (2 Sam. 11—12).

The "lust of the eyes" continues to be a major stumbling block for Christians in general and Christian leaders in particular. One of the major problems with bondage to "the lust of the eyes" is lack of satisfaction. We obtain what our eyes have lusted for only to find that our appetite is not satisfied, so we look again and lust for more. The writer of Ecclesiastes wrote long ago that "the eye is not satisfied with seeing" (Eccl. 1:8). In Proverbs he says, "the eyes of man [are never] satisfied" (Prov. 27:20).

This is what is "in the world," John says, "the lust of the eyes." Wuest calls these lusts "the passionate cravings of the eyes for satisfaction."[13] What do we know of such passionate cravings? How guilty are all of us of the lust of the eyes? What do we do with our eyes when we are alone, when no one is watching us? If we obey God's Word in Romans 6:13 and present the members of our bodies "as instruments of righteousness to God" that will include our eyes. We will then begin to enjoy the victory over the world's attempts to captivate our eyes through lust.

The Pride of Life

John next reveals that "the things in the world" include "the boastful pride of life." Wuest says this phrase refers to "the vainglory which belongs to the present life."[14] He says the word *life* used here refers to that which sustains life like food, clothing, and shelter. The picture is that of the man and woman who seek a life built upon all that the world has to offer.

John Stott writes about "the boastful pride of life."[15]

> The pride of life is . . . an arrogance or vainglory relating to one's external circumstances, whether wealth or rank or dress, "pretentious ostentation" (Plummer), "the desire to shine or outshine others in luxurious living" (Ebrad).

A repulsive new theology has developed in our day to justify a luxuriant lifestyle. Its emphasis is on this-world prosperity, an "all this and heaven too" theology. "Something good is going to happen to you." "Seed money." "Name it and claim it." "God wants you to prosper." "Wealth is a gift from the Lord." "Health and wealth are always God's will for his children." "God owns the cattle on a thousand hills. He wants to share them with you. Visualize what you want. Speak the word of faith, and it will be yours."

Such a prosperity doctrine is possible only in an advanced middle-class economy. I would like to see its advocates proclaim it among the starving Christians of Africa, Asia, Latin America, and the thousands of true believers who are found among the homeless in the Western world.

This is *not* the supracultural gospel of Scripture with its emphasis on a simple lifestyle. It is a culturally distorted message based on faulty exegesis of a few Scripture passages twisted to advocate wealth and prosperity as the norm for all God's people. The prosperity message conflicts with Jesus' teaching in Matthew 6:19–21 and 19:16–26. It is contradicted by the apostle Paul's words in 1 Timothy 6:6–14 and Hebrews 13:5,13–14. In 1 Timothy 6:6–11 Paul writes:

> But godliness actually is a means of great gain, when accompanied by contentment. For we have brought nothing into the world, so we cannot take anything out of it either. And if we have food and covering, with these we shall be content. But those who want to get rich fall into temptation and a snare and many foolish and harmful desires which plunge men into ruin and destruction. For the love of money is a root of all sorts of evil, and some by longing for it have wandered away from the faith, and pierced themselves with many a pang. But flee from these things, you man of God; and pursue righteousness, godliness, faith, love, perseverance and gentleness.

Syndicated columnist Cal Thomas sums up the pride of life of much of American culture and the contemporary U.S. religious prosperity theology:[16]

> A moral alarm clock is going off in America, and not many politicians hear it . . . Our leaders—politicians, economists, technocrats and even preachers—have convinced us that more is better and much more is best. But increasing numbers of us do not like where we have been led. . . .

> Humility is one of our least taught and least appreciated character traits. You can't major in it at Harvard. You can't acquire it by mail, and it is virtually extinct in political, scientific and in much of contemporary religious leadership. No one would watch (on T.V.) "Lifestyles of the Poor and Humble." The rich and famous are who we want to emulate. Even some of the preachers have caught the disease and live like kings and not like the servants their Leader called them to be.

The cultural corruption that grips us is more dangerous than (enemy) missiles. Nations do not fail because of adversity. Nations fail because of prosperity and pride.

Drugs, crime, teen sex, AIDS and the rest are not a result of failed politics so much as they are the consequences of failed morals and of a politics that has been isolated from spiritual concerns.

Not even the preachers are safe from the cultural collapse. If we don't turn from our wicked ways and soon, that moral alarm clock . . . might turn out to be a time bomb.

Galatians 1:4

The apostle Paul expresses the New Testament view of the world and the Christian's relationship to that world in two passages in Galatians. The first is Galatians 1:4. There Paul writes that Jesus "gave Himself for our sins, that He might deliver us out of this present evil age, according to the will of our God and Father."

Paul uses *aiōn* in Greek to express the "world" here. Literally it means "age, a period of time." Vine writes, "It is marked in the New Testament usage by spiritual or moral characteristics and is sometimes translated 'world.'"[17]

Trench vividly describes the *aiōn*, the age referred to here by Paul as God's and the believer's mortal enemy. He writes that the *aiōn* represents

all that floating mass of thoughts, opinions, maxims, speculations, hopes, impulses, aims, aspirations, at any time current in the world, which it may be impossible to seize and accurately define, but which constitutes a most real and effective power, being the moral or immoral atmosphere which at every moment of our lives we inhale, again inextricably to exhale.[18]

Thus Paul asserts this age, this world, is evil. It threatens the believer's relationship to God so much that, while being forced to continue living in this world, the believer must be delivered from its power and its control.

Paul also says that this world is so totally evil that one of the major purposes of the redemptive work of Christ was to "deliver us out of this present evil age." Wuest says that the word translated "deliver" *(exaireō)* means "to pluck out, to draw out, to rescue, to deliver."[19]

The word strikes the keynote of the letter. The Gospel is a rescue, an emancipation from a state of bondage. The word here denotes, not a removal from, but a *rescue* from the power of the ethical characteristics of the present age.

Wuest comments on the Greek word chosen here by Paul to express evil, *ponēros.* He contrasts *ponēros* with another and more widely used word for evil in the New Testament, *kakos. Ponēros* is the stronger word for evil, revealing evil that seeks not only to express its own evil nature but also seeks to draw others into its evil web.[20]

The *kakos* man may be content to perish in his own corruption, but the *ponēros* man is not content unless he is corrupting others as well, and drawing them into the same destruction with himself. Satan is not called the *kakos* one but the *ponēros* one. This present age is described by Paul as *ponēros.* . . . This present age therefore is not content to perish in its own corruption, but seeks to drag all men with it down to its own inevitable destruction.

Galatians 6:14

Paul's second major reference to the world in Galatians is found in Galatians 6:14. There the apostle writes, "But may it never be that I should boast except in the cross of our Lord Jesus Christ through which the world has been crucified to me, and I to the world." The world (here, *kosmos*) is so evil, Paul is saying, that the only way of deliverance from its power is through a double crucifixion. The world has been crucified to us and we to the world.

The idea of being united with Christ in His death and in His crucifixion is a familiar teaching of Paul (Rom. 6:1f; Gal. 2:20; 5:24; Col. 2:20f; 3:1–4). In Galatians 6:14 the idea is the same, this time with focus on the world. "The world," Paul is saying, "strives to bring us into bondage to its declared values and philosophies be they secular or religious. We reject both. We are released from the world's point of view through our identification with Christ in his crucifixion. He died in our behalf unto the world's ways and we have been united with God in His ways. The world, in turn, no longer has any claims upon us. It is dead to us, crucified unto us."

John Eadie focuses his words on Paul's personal experience in Galatians 6:14, which is applicable to all believers:[21]

> Each had been nailed to the cross; each to the other was dead. Christ's cross effected this separation. It was the result of neither morbid disappointment, nor of the bitter wail of "vanity of vanities," nor of a sense of failure in worldly pursuits, nor of the persecutions he had undergone—scourging, imprisonment, hunger, thirst, fastings, and nakedness. By none of these things did he die to the world. But it was by his union with the Crucified One: death in Him and with Him was his death to the world, and the death of that world to him.

These are gripping words. They present to us the truth that we, as Jesus, are not of this world (John 15—17). He has set us free from bondage to this world. The longer I live my Christian life in this world and the more I counsel bruised and afflicted fellow Christians the more the words of Jesus in John 16:33 ring in my mind and heart:

> These things I have spoken to you, that in Me you may have peace. In the world you have tribulation, but take courage; I have overcome the world.

While living in this world, the world is not my true home. I am a citizen of the kingdom of God, not the kingdoms of this world. He has defeated this evil world in my behalf and brought me into His kingdom. Never in the world will I find true peace, but only in Him. In Him I can, daily, win the war with the world.

The World Is Passing Away

Lastly, John affirms that "the things in the world" are transitory. He writes, "And the world is passing away, and also its lusts" (v. 17a). If the world itself is passing away it is obvious that the things in the world will go the way of the world. Again he sums up the world and all it has to offer in one word, "lusts."

We know the world is "passing away" because we see its values destroying goodness, freedom, and even life itself. The pragmatism we discussed in the last chapter is called "vulgar relativism" by the well-known Christian writer, Michael Novak. Novak affirms that this world view "undermines the culture of liberty. If it triumphs, free institutions may not survive the twenty-first century." His reasoning? "An age wrong about God is almost certain to be wrong about man."[22] Ours *is* an age which is certainly wrong about God. And it is increasingly obvious that it is an age which is clearly wrong about man.

The late General Omar Bradley, one of the great heroes of World War II, put it this way: "We have grasped the mystery of the atom, but we have rejected the

Sermon on the Mount. The world has achieved brilliance without wisdom, power without conscience. Ours is a world of nuclear giants, but we are ethical infants. We know more about war than we do about peace, [more about] killing than living."

The lie about both God and man that permeates Western society—and the entire world for that matter—must be challenged by truth. In the final analysis, *Jesus Himself is the truth* (John 4:16). He came to bear witness to the truth. His Word is truth. This truth sets men free. But to bear witness to the truth to a world which has strayed from the path of truth, the Church must overcome the world as Jesus overcame the world. Too many of us have become so much like the world we have lost the right to speak of truth. As author John White states, "the world at present influences the Church more than the Church influences the world."

For a Christian to be overcome by "the world and the things in the world" is one of the greatest of all tragedies. He will find he has lived for that which is only transitory. When his life work is tried by fire, as the apostle Paul affirms it will, he will find that his work will "be burned up." True, "he himself shall be saved, yet so as through fire" (1 Cor. 3:13–15). Who wants to be saved that way?

This is the world with which we are at war. It is our enemy just as it is God's enemy. We must choose to be obedient to God and reject the deceptions of the world. Finally, we must never forget that the world's god is the devil (2 Cor. 4:4). This is a thoroughly demonized world.

Our Victory over the World

Is there victory over the world, or are we destined to passively allow it to conform us to its own mold? Yes, there is victory! Victory over the world is as much our birthright as is victory over the flesh and over the devil. That victory comes through Christ, of course, but in a way that differs from the specific means of victory over the flesh and over the devil. We win over the flesh, as we have seen, by putting its deeds to death and making no provision for its wrong desires. We win over the devil by resisting him, even as we submit ourselves fully unto the Lord.

With the world, however, we triumph neither by killing it (as we do the deeds of the flesh) nor by directly resisting it (as we do the devil). Instead, we detach ourselves from "this world," we ignore it. We win over the world by learning what it means to be *in* the world, but not *of* it. In Galatians 6:14, the apostle Paul testifies to this path of certain victory over the world through the cross of Christ:

> May it never be that I should boast, except in the cross of our Lord Jesus Christ, through which the world has been crucified to me, and I to the world. (NASB)

In Christ, believers are removed from life in "this world" (or "this present evil age" Gal. 1:4) and are transplanted into new life, the life of the age to come which is, in part, already here through Christ (Col. 1:13). Those who are in Christ, whom Paul would describe with himself as those who by faith are "crucified with Christ," receive by their new location in Christ a new relationship with the old world: In a word, they are dead to it. They have been crucified to it, and it to them. So we boom a hearty "Amen!" to Charles Spurgeon's flouting of the world: "Come, world with all your enticements. What can you offer to me, a dead man?"

Victory over the world is ours daily through continually choosing to practice obedient faith (1 John 5:5). If we walk in the obedience of the faith which overcomes the world, then our end will be the same as that promised by the writer: "the one who does the will of God abides forever" (1 John 2:17b).

PART THREE

A Survey of Biblical Teaching

Old Testament

27

Warfare in Paradise

Our study of biblical teaching on spiritual warfare begins with Genesis, the book whose name is Hebrew for "beginning," or more literally, "generation" or "family history."[1]

The primary purpose of Genesis is to provide the beginning of the history of God's elect nation, Israel. In so doing, Genesis 1 gives us the origin of the heavens and the earth; Genesis 2—11 tells of the creation of man, man's fall, and the origin of the nations; and Genesis 12—50 deals with the origin of Israel: the call of Abraham, the history of the patriarchs, the progenitors of the Hebrew race.

Genesis 1—11 gives us the necessary background to the call of Abraham and the beginning of the nation of Israel. These chapters also reveal the origin and early history of cosmic-earthly spiritual warfare in Genesis 3.

An unidentified cosmic being called the serpent introduces spiritual warfare into human experience. As we have repeatedly stated, this means that cosmic spiritual warfare had begun before Genesis 3. Genesis tells us nothing about the origin of that heavenly warfare. In fact the rest of the Bible primarily reveals it as a "given," a fact to be accepted with little or no explanation. We will have to be content with what the Bible says and be careful with speculations about what it does not say.

The Bible does say enough, however, to help us understand that a heavenly rebellion occurred among the angels of God, probably before man's creation and certainly before the Fall. This rebellion resulted in an on-going conflict between the kingdom of God and the kingdom of Satan.

The early disastrous progression of that conflict on earth is outlined in Genesis 4—11, forming the rationale behind God's new beginning with humanity in Noah and his family (Gen. 6–9). God will later start again when he calls one man, Abraham, out of the spiritual degradation, idolatry, polytheism, and gross immorality into which the human race has fallen. From the city of Ur of Chaldea God calls Abraham to Himself (Gen. 11:26—12:3). The rest of the Old Testament develops God's unique revelation of Himself to and through Abraham's descendants, Israel.

Commentator Gordon J. Wenham gives great attention to the world view clash Westerners experience with the early chapters of Genesis. Because we approach these chapters with our Western scientific mind-set, we expect Genesis to give us answers to the Bible-versus-science debate about the six days of Creation and like subjects. But Genesis 1—11, and especially Genesis 1—3, were written from a religious, not a scientific perspective:[2]

> The Bible-versus-science debate has, most regrettably, sidetracked readers of Genesis 1. Instead of reading the chapter as a triumphant affirmation of the power and wisdom of God and the wonder of His creation, we have been too often bogged down in attempting to squeeze Scripture into the mold of the latest scientific hypothesis or distorting scientific facts to fit a particular interpretation.

> When allowed to speak for itself, Genesis 1 looks beyond such minutiae. . . . Genesis 1, by further affirming the unique status of man, his place in the divine pro-

gram, and God's care for him, gives a hope to mankind that atheistic philosophies can never legitimately supply.

Genesis was written primarily to the people of its day and only secondarily to future generations. The teachings of Genesis had to meet the real and felt needs of the people to whom and for whom it was written or it probably would not have been written at all.

Genesis 1—11 shares a common spiritualistic world view with all Israel's Near Eastern neighbor nations. Many of the accounts in Genesis 1—11 are similar to accounts covering the same themes found in the history and mythology of Israel's neighbors.[3] Yet it is the differences between the biblical account and the pagan accounts that make Genesis 1—11 unique.[4]

While admitting that "Genesis and the ancient Near East probably have more in common with each other than either has with modern secular thought," Wenham says that the "similarities between biblical and non-biblical thinking . . . are overshadowed by the differences." One of these differences is man's place in the created order. According to Oriental mythology, man was created by the gods as an afterthought to supply the gods with food. Genesis 1 portrays man as the climax of creation, and instead of man's providing the gods with food, God provided the plants as food for man (Gen. 1:29).[5]

The same theme of the Lord's concern for man's welfare is very apparent in Genesis 2. Here He first creates man, then provides him with a garden to dwell in, with animals as his companions, and last of all, with a wife.[6]

> The ancient Oriental background to Genesis 1—11 shows it to be concerned with rather different issues from those that tend to preoccupy modern readers. It is affirming the unity of God in the face of polytheism, his justice rather than his caprice, his power as opposed to his impotence, his concern for mankind rather than his exploitation. And whereas Mesopotamia clung to the wisdom of primeval man, Genesis records his sinful disobedience. Because as Christians we tend to assume these points in our theology, we often fail to recognize the striking originality of the message of Genesis 1—11 and concentrate on subsidiary points that may well be of less moment.

George Ernest Wright, former Professor of Old Testament History and Theology at Harvard University, rejects the traditional critical position that Judaism passed through a series of predictable evolutionary stages from animism, to polytheism, to monotheism, and, finally, to biblical theism. Such a view, he says, fails to recognize God's supernatural intervention in the lives of His elect nation and fails to see the great difference in the Jewish view of God from the polytheism of the nations that surrounded them.[7] This insight is crucial to our Genesis 3 studies.

Six Significant Features of the Creation of Humanity

The purpose of man's creation is revealed in Genesis 1:26–31. We will not do an in-depth study but only touch on six major features of the story that directly relate to the Genesis 3 story of man's fall.

1. *God creates man in the image and likeness of God* (vv. 26a,27a). Debate continues over the exact meaning of man's creation in God's image and likeness.[8] We will not join that debate. We will, however, stress man's being made in the image and likeness of God. It is crucial to our understanding why the serpent sets out to seduce man into disobeying his Creator and heavenly Father.

Whatever the meaning of man as created in the image and likeness of God, Scripture states that only man is made in the divine image. This seems to be the one thing that separates man forever from all the rest of God's creation.[9]

Wenham helps us understand why the serpent interferes in the God-man relationship. He writes that man is

the apex of the created order. . . . The image of God means that in some sense men and women resemble God and the angels, though where the resemblance lies is left undefined in this chapter. The divine image does enable man to be addressed directly by his creator and makes him in a real sense God's representative on earth, who should rule over the other creatures as a benevolent king.[10]

No wonder God's enemy, the Devil, quickly makes himself man's enemy. When Satan understood—he is not omniscient and, like us, has to learn—the plan of God to make a creature more like God Himself than any other creature God had made, his primary strategy of defiance against the will of God then became to seduce God's man into unbelief and disobedience to the law of God. Since he could not attack God directly, he could now attack Him indirectly by attacking His in-the-image-and-likeness-of-God creature called man. This gives real insight into the mysteries of the Genesis 3 account of man's fall.

2. *God gives man total dominion over the earth* (1:26b,28c). So complete is man's lordship over the earth, he is to "subdue" the earth and "rule . . . over every living thing that moves on the earth" (1:26–28). How better could Satan war against the rule of God than by warring against God's ruler on earth?

3. *Man is made both "male and female"* (v. 27b).

4. *The couple is told to "be fruitful and multiply and fill the earth"* with their *progeny* (v. 28b). All Satan has to do to corrupt the entire earth, therefore, is to corrupt this one pair who will multiply and fill the earth with sons and daughters born in their image (5:3).

5. *God placed a special blessing upon the regal, God-like pair* (v. 28a). Derek Kidner comments that

to bless is to bestow not only a gift but a function (cf. 1:22; 2:3; cf. also the parting blessings of Isaac, Jacob and Moses), and to do so with warm concern. At its highest, it is God turning full face to the recipient (cf. Num. 6:24–26) in self giving (Acts 3:26).[11]

To seduce such a God-blessed pair in joining his rebellion against the rule of God would be Satan's greatest victory, perhaps even greater than his prior seduction of a large number of God's angels into throwing off the lordship of God (2 Pet. 2:4; Jude 6; Rev. 12:7–9).

6. *God states His pleasure in man and in all of His creation* (v. 31). Kidner quotes Karl Barth as saying, "It is a part of the history of creation that God contemplated His work and confronted it as a completed totality." Kidner remarks that

by His grace something other than Himself is granted not only existence but a measure of self-determination. And if the details of His work were pronounced "good" (4, 10, 12, 18, 21, 25), the whole is *very good*. Old and New Testament alike endorse this in their call to a thankful acceptance of things material (e.g., Ps. 104:24; 1 Tim. 4:3–5) as both from and for God.[12]

All of God's earthly creation is contemplated by God Himself as not only "good" but "very good" separately and collectively (vv. 4, 10, 12, 18, 21, 25, 31). Thus Satan has within his reach the ability to gain vengeance against the God he hates. If Satan can make bad and very bad what God sees as "good" and "very good," he will strike the most devastating blow against God since his successful corruption of a part of God's angelic kingdom.

WE BEGIN WITH A SNAKE

The words of Genesis 3:1 have probably aroused more discussion than most other verses in Genesis.

> Now the serpent was more crafty than any beast of the field which the LORD God had made. And he said to the woman, "Indeed, has God said, 'You shall not eat from any tree of the garden'?"

The first area of controversy centers around the identification of the tempter as a serpent or snake. Was it a snake as we know snakes today?[13] Did the animal first walk erect and revert to an animal crawling on its belly only after it was cursed by God?[14] The answers to these questions involve conjecture. The Scriptures do not say. It is therefore not important for us to know the answer. Without for a moment denying the historicity of the story, since we are dealing with historical symbolism, we become hopelessly sidetracked when we ask detailed questions about the symbols chosen by God and the writer of Genesis.

The original readers of the Old Testament did not usually raise the kind of questions about the text of the Bible that we raise. They understood the Old Testament to be God's chosen means to communicate what they needed to know to walk in obedience to God. They were not primarily speculative thinkers but more practical thinkers, while we tend to be more speculative than practical.[15] The Jews understood that in the Near Eastern cultural imagery, "Snakes were symbolic of life, wisdom and chaos . . . all themes that have points of contact with the present narrative," Wenham says.[16]

Wenham tries to handle the often repeated question, "Why did a snake appear and tempt the woman?" After listing some of the more common answers often given in response to the question as to why the writer wrote in symbolic language in general and with the symbolism of a serpent in particular, Wenham writes, "Within the world of Old Testament animal symbolism a snake is an obvious candidate for an anti-God symbol, not withstanding its creation by God."[17]

Wenham refers to Leviticus 11 and Deuteronomy 14 where the snake was counted as an archetypal unclean animal. He says, "Its swarming, writhing locomotion puts it at the farthest point from those pure animals that can be offered in sacrifice."[18]

> So for any Israelite familiar with the symbolic values of different animals, a creature more likely than a serpent to lead man away from his creator could not be imagined. The serpent Leviathan, mentioned in Ugaritic mythology, is also referred to in Isaiah 27:1 (cf. Job 26:13) as a creature destroyed by God, further evidence of the familiar association in biblical times of serpents and God's enemies.

Though some modern scholars like Jeffrey Burton Russell question that the writer of Genesis "intended to equate the serpent with the tool of Satan or Satan himself,"[19] it is not necessary to prove that he did to maintain the position that Wenham is advocating, a position with which I and most conservative biblical scholars agree totally.

In conclusion, I would affirm that the symbol of a talking serpent was meant by the writer of Genesis to communicate what the story reveals. The temptation to rebel against the lordship of God did not arise from within Eve and, later in Adam, but came first from without by a personal, probably supernatural, being who was dedicated to evil and sought to give birth to the rebellion of humanity against God.[20]

W. H. Griffith Thomas quotes one of the greatest biblical scholars of a past generation, Dr. James Orr, on Genesis 3. Orr gives an excellent overview of what we have been examining.[21]

> Temptation—consider its source. The practical character of the narrative is clearly seen in the reference to the serpent as the immediate cause of human sin. . . .
>
> There is no reference to the problem of how and when Satan sinned. The one point of stress is laid upon sin in relation to man, and we are taught very unmistakably two great truths: (1) That God is not the author of sin, and (2) that sin came to man from without, and was due to a power of evil suggestion and influence other than that which came from man's own nature.

The serpent is described as "more crafty than any beast of the field which the Lord God had made." The word translated *crafty* is literally "subtle." It is the Hebrew word *aroom* or *arum*. Calvin says it is the word by which the "Hebrews designate the prudent as well as the crafty. It is not agreed among interpreters in what sense the serpent is said to be *aroom* . . . Some, therefore, would take it in a good, others in a bad sense." Calvin takes it in the positive sense. He says the serpent is introduced with unique skills making it more "acute and quick-sighted beyond all others."[22]

> But Satan perverted to his own deceitful purposes the gift which had been divinely imparted to the serpent. . . . that gift which has proved so destructive to the human race has (probably now) been withdrawn from the serpent.

Personally I believe Wenham does the best job of handling this subject. He takes the middle ground by saying, " 'Now the snake was more shrewd than all the wild animals.' 'Shrewd' is an ambiguous term. On the other hand it is a virtue the wise should cultivate (Prov. 12:16; 13:16), but misused it becomes wiliness and guile" (Job 5:12; 15:5; cf. Exod. 21:14; Josh. 9:4).

With his great insight into Hebrew literature, Wenham comments about the writer's vivid description of the crafty serpent.[23]

> The scene opens with a circumstantial clause describing the snake as "more shrewd than all the wild animals of the plain which the Lord God had made." The rest of the scene is dialogue between the snake and the woman (cf. scene 5, vv. 9–13). Now, explicit characterization of actors in the story is rare in Hebrew narrative, so it seems likely that in noting the snake's shrewdness the narrator is hinting that his remarks should be examined very carefully. He (the serpent) may not be saying what he seems to be saying. Perhaps we should not take his words at their face value as the woman did.

THE SNAKE AND THE SIN

The writer of Genesis 3 begins the dialogue between the serpent and Eve in verse 1 with the words, "And he said to the woman. . . ." The serpent's speaking is another subject of endless controversy. I believe Keil and Delitzsch are correct when they affirm that the serpent, as is true of all other members of the animal kingdom, did not possess the power of speech when created by God. It spoke only because it was possessed by an evil spirit, that is, Satan, the Devil.[24]

The authors make three excellent points as to why Satan was not identified as the source of the temptation: first, because God did not want Adam and Eve to be able to blame Satan for their rebellion; second, because they alone are to blame for their sin. God ordained the testing of their obedience because it was necessary to their spiritual development and self-determination. Finally, God only allowed Satan to tempt them in the form of a creature not far inferior to God or an angel, but one inferior to themselves.[25] Thus, Keil and Delitzsch say, "They could have no excuse for allowing a mere animal to persuade them to break the commandment of God. For they had been made to have dominion over the beasts, not to take their own law from them."[26]

The writer of Genesis next describes Eve's actions after conversing with the serpent, "the woman saw that the tree was good for food, and that it was a delight to the eyes, and that the tree was desirable to make one wise" (v. 6). Wenham notes that now, in the woman's eyes,

> the forbidden tree was no different from the other trees (see Gen. 2:9), and she desired the enlightenment it would bring. Her covetousness is described in terminology that foreshadows the tenth commandment, ("thou shalt not covet"). "Delight" and "desirable" are from roots meaning 'to covet' (Deut. 5:21; cf. Exod. 20:17). When "she gave it to her husband with her, and he ate," the man associated himself with her sin (cf. 6:18; 7:7; 13:1). This last, decisive act of disobedience immediately preceded the description of the consequences.[27]

Adam was not present during Eve's deception by the serpent. The text is clear on that. Thus the emphasis of Scripture falls on the deception of Eve but not of Adam. If he had been present would the story have been different?

God had given the commands to Adam (Gen. 2:16–17). He evidently had passed them on to his wife. Yet when Eve quoted to the serpent the prohibition against eating of the tree of the knowledge of good and evil, she did not get it exactly right (3:3). Why, is impossible to say.

God's words to Adam in verse 17 seems to be proof that Adam was not present during Eve's deception by the serpent. He is charged by God for listening to his wife, not for listening to the serpent. Since he was placed by God as head over God's earthly creation he is held responsible for his disobedience. This is consistent with all biblical teaching that the human race sinned in Adam, not Eve.

Francis A. Schaeffer affirms that the battle is lost or won in the mind. He says, "The flow is from the internal to the external; the sin began in the thought world and flowed outward. The sin was, therefore, committed in the moment that she believed Satan instead of God."[28]

Schaeffer also notes how easily Eve was able to persuade Adam to join her. He says, "Temptation is hard to resist when it is bound up with the man-woman relationship."[29]

Two great drives are built into man. The first is his need for a relationship with God, and the second his need for a relationship to the opposite sex. A special temptation is bound up with his sexual drive. . . . While what happened in the Garden of Eden was a space-time historic event, the man-woman relationship and force of temptation it must have presented to Adam is universal.

THE IMMEDIATE EFFECTS OF HUMANITY'S SIN

The immediate effects of the sin of Adam and Eve are at least sevenfold.

First, there is shame.

"Then the eyes of both of them were opened, and they knew that they were naked" (3:7a). Many commentators attempt to spiritualize these words saying they refer primarily or even exclusively to shame in the presence of God.[30] Thus their nakedness and guilt as they stand before God is spiritual.

While the latter is true, that is not what verse 7 is saying, because the last verse of chapter 2 also speaks of their nakedness: "And the man and his wife were both naked and were not ashamed" (2:25).

What a difference between the man-woman relationship before and after the Fall! As we look at the words in 3:7, we have to ask if they knew of their nakedness before. When Adam looked upon Eve did not he see her nakedness and vice versa?

The shame, however, is evidence of the immediate corruption of their total personality. They now look upon each other with soiled eyes. The emotional grid through which visual stimulations reach their mind is defiled. Their conscience now tells them it is not right for them any longer to be continually naked in each other's presence.

Until verse 7 Adam and Eve were together, naked without shame before each other and before God. They were so pure of mind and heart as God made them and so much one flesh in their marital relationship that they were as innocent as naked little children who frequently play together with no sense of shame.

Derek Kidner says that

the Serpent's promise of *eyes . . . opened* came true in its fashion (and cf. 22), but it was a grotesque anti-climax to the dream of enlightenment. Man saw the familiar world and spoilt it now in the seeing, projecting evil onto innocence (cf. Titus 1:15) and reacting to good with shame and flight. His new consciousness of good and evil was both like and unlike the divine knowledge (3:22), differing from it and from innocence as a sick man's aching awareness of his body differs both from the insight of the physician and the unconcern of the man in health.[31]

This is an apt analogy. Before they were well; now they are sick. They project evil into all innocence. That was the immediate price of eyes opened by Satan, to see what they were not meant to see. Kidner follows with another insightful observation.[32]

The *fig leaves* were pathetic enough . . . but the instinct was sound and God confirmed it (v. 21), for sin's proper fruit is shame. The couple now ill at ease together, experienced a foretaste of fallen human relations in general. There is no road back. . . . God's way is forward, for when the body is redeemed (Rom. 8:23) and love is perfect we shall not be back in Eden but clothed with glory (2 Cor. 5:4).

Leupold writing on Satan's promise, "Ye shall be as gods," comments, "What a sorry godlikeness, if we may use the paradox, and what a pitiable achievement on man's part."[33]

Second, there is separation from God.

They seek to hide themselves from His presence (v. 8). The sense of separation from God did not come until they directed their faces away from each other and towards God. They had forgotten about Him up until now. He, however, had not forgotten about them. As was evidently His custom,[34] God came to share His presence with His children.

Leupold says God, of course, was fully aware of what had occurred. When He came to the man and his wife, instead of rushing out to be in His presence as they had done in the past, they hid from Him among the trees of the garden as if tree leaves could block His penetrating sight. How confused are the self-deceiving hearts of sinful men!

Third, there was a lack of honesty before God (v. 10).

Leupold says that

> the first words of fallen man lie before us, . . . a compound of half truth, evasion and attempted deception. So dreadfully altered has man become, the admission that he is afraid at hearing God's voice is the only true thing about this statement. . . . Here is one of the most telling indictments of the viciousness and supreme sinfulness of sin.[35]

Fourth, Adam blames others.

First he blames his wife (what's new under the sun?). Next it is his circumstances. Ultimately he blames God Himself for the terrible effects of his sin. Adam says, "The woman whom Thou gavest to be with me, she gave me from the tree, and I ate" (3:12).

The divine inquest has been very brief, God firing three disarming questions at Adam (v. 9b,10). Adam is left truly naked before the all-seeing eyes of God. Leupold says, "He that aspired to godlikeness now stands a shamefaced culprit without a word of defense left. The lame reply that he does make causes us to blush for him. It is a reply that offers further evidence of the complete corruption and contamination of all of man's nature by sin."[36]

Fifth, there is immediate judgment upon the man and his wife, separately and then as a unit (vv. 16–24).[37]

Sixth, there is the forced separation of the man and the woman from the Paradise of God (vv. 22–24).

God expresses sadness over man's miserable state (v. 22a). Some have claimed that those words are a form of sarcasm on the part of God. Nothing could be further from the truth. As Keil and Delitzsch affirm, "Irony at the expense of a wretched tempted soul might well befit Satan, but not the Lord."[38] Leupold says sadness might be the best word to describe the emotions of God as He speaks these words.[39]

God then expels the damaged pair from the Garden of God (v. 24b). Keil and Delitzsch write of the symbolism involved here:[40]

> Had (mankind) continued in fellowship with God by obedience to the command of God, he might have eaten of [the tree of life], for he was created for eternal life. But after he had fallen through sin into the power of death, the fruit which produced immortality could only do him harm.

Immortality in a state of sin is not the *zoe aionios* [eternal life] which God designed for man, but endless misery, which the Scriptures call "the second death" (Rev. 2:1; 20:6 and 15; 21:8). The expulsion from Paradise, therefore, was a punishment inflicted for man's good, intended, while exposing him to temporal death, to preserve him from eternal death.

God placed both a cherubim and an ever-moving flaming sword to bar any re-entrance to the Garden of Eden (v. 24). Cherubim seem to be the highest ranking beings in the angelic hierarchy. They are revealed as surrounding the throne of God (Ezek. 1:22f; 10:1; Rev. 4:6). They stand in the immediate presence of God and are especially active with Him in judgment, as here. Leupold quotes K. W. Well as saying, "They are representatives and mediators of God's presence in the world" (Ps. 18:10). Leupold continues,

> The root from which the word may be derived would suggest that the word as such means "a brilliant appearance" . . . How these marvelous beings appeared was well remembered by the Israelites at least, for they seemed to require no further description when they were told to make two cherubim and otherwise to use the figures of cherubims for ornamental purposes [in the tabernacle], cf. Exod. 25:18; 26:1.[41]

The flaming sword is usually pictured as being in the hand of the cherubim, but that is not what the passage says (3:24b). The two were evidently separate, the sword moving in every direction without the intervention of the cherubim. All this is powerful symbolism.

Verse 24a uses a strong word: "So He [the LORD God] drove the man out." What a shame! The pair who were made for the garden and the garden for them are forced out, expelled. Leupold says that "Divine goodness aimed to make man feel his altered state very keenly; first blessed fellowship, then harsh expulsion."[42]

All this because of sin! All this because Eve listened to the voice of the serpent and Adam listened to the voice of Eve! Neither bothered to listen to the voice of God. They are the first human victims of defeat in spiritual warfare. They are war casualties. What terrible things soon follow this defeat!

Seventh, the existence of on-going spiritual warfare is revealed (v. 15).

So important is this subject and so crucial to the entire course of cosmic-earthly spiritual warfare, I save Genesis 3:15 for the next chapters.

28

Enmity Between the Seeds
Genesis 3:15

The seventh immediate effect of the Fall is the revelation of ongoing spiritual warfare. It is based on Genesis 3:15, perhaps the most important verse in the story of the Fall. Though these words did have immediate implications for Adam and Eve, they are primarily a prophecy of ongoing spiritual warfare between humanity and the serpent. The strongest focus is on conflict between the seed of the woman and the seed of the serpent. That warfare will continue until the seed of the woman finally crushes the head of the serpent. In the process, the serpent will painfully bruise the heel of the seed of the woman.

While God interrogates Adam and Eve as to the cause of their disobedience (vv. 11–13; of course, He already knew), when He turns to the serpent, He does not interrogate him at all. He pronounces judgment upon him for his terrible evil (vv. 14–15). In fact, though the serpent is revealed as a unique creature with mind, emotions, will, and the faculty of speech (vv. 1–5), he never speaks again in the story before us. God does not allow him to speak; does not even question him. He only passes judgment upon him.

In contrast to Adam and Eve, no forgiveness, mercy, or redemption is extended to the serpent. Calvin says, "He does not interrogate the serpent as He had done the man and the woman because, in the animal itself there was no sense of sin, and because, to the devil He would hold out no hope of pardon."[1]

We have already established that the original recipients of Genesis were people with a firm belief in the existence of evil, invisible, supernatural spiritual beings that were both desirous and capable of influencing human actions towards evil. They would immediately know that such a being is represented by the serpent.

All the nations of the Near East surrounding Israel had a highly developed demonology.[2] The assumption of some scholars that the Jews had no developed demonology or Satanology until the period of the Exile may be partially true, but it does not mean that they were not vividly aware of the existence of a devil and demons.[3]

Wenham correctly states, "The Jews knew well that the serpent was either a symbol of a fallen spirit being later called Satan by them (Job 1:6; 2:1; 1 Chron. 21:1) or that the animal was controlled or possessed by that evil spirit in bringing about man's fall."[4]

R. Payne Smith, writing in *The Ellicott Bible Commentary*, comments on God's words to the serpent in verse 14a, "because you have done this . . . ."

"The outward form of the condemnation is made suitable to the shape which the tempter had assumed; but the true force and meaning, especially in the last and most intense portion of the sentence, belong, not to the animal, but to Satan himself."[5]

THE SNAKE IS CURSED

One part of the curse falls only upon the animal (v. 14). "Cursed are you more than all cattle." Then, he is cursed "more than every beast of the field" (v. 14).[6] Why are cattle singled out? The Hebrew word is *behemah* which simply means "animals." Since, in the second part of the curse, the beasts "of the field" are singled out *(chayyath hassadheh,* "the wild beasts,") it is assumed the former means domesticated animals which directly serve man, and the latter the undomesticated or wild animals.[7]

Then God says, "On your belly shall you go." As already mentioned many commentators see in this expression the suggestion that, before being used by Satan to deceive man into rebellion against God, the serpent had legs, feet, or paws, and walked somewhat erect.[8] R. Payne Smith rejects this view:[9]

> But such a transformation belongs to the region of fable. . . . The meaning is that henceforward the serpent's crawling motion is to be a mark of disgrace, and to Satan a sign of meanness and contempt. He won the victory over our guileless first parents, and still he winds in and out among men, ever bringing degradation with him, and ever sinking with his victims into deeper abysses of shame and infamy.

Smith's mixture of application first to the reptile and then to Satan is characteristic of most commentators; and not without reason, for Satan is the principle agent of man's fall, not the snake.[10] Leupold quotes St. Chrysostom who said that "God destroys the instrument that brought His creature to fall 'just as a loving father, when punishing the murderer of his son, might snap in two the sword or dagger with which the murder had been committed.'"[11]

"Dust shall you eat all the days of your life" is a parallel thought to the above. The serpent's diet didn't change any more than did his means of locomotion. Since he had tried to exalt himself above the stars in down-playing God to man, he is now brought down to the dust. The serpent doesn't actually eat dust, but his condition of eating from the dust in which he crawls is to all of creation a sign of how God has cursed the serpent of old, Satan and the Devil (Rev. 12:9). Leupold says, with these words "the higher agent that employed the serpent" is brought before us in preparation for what follows in verse 15.[12]

GENESIS 3:15

All that we have been considering has now prepared us to examine one of the most well-known, but controversial, passages of Scripture, Genesis 3:15.[13] There have been two extremes among commentators in writing on this verse. Some see in it a type of mythology or allegory. Others view it literally.

The mythological-allegorical approaches would see it as a non-historical story written to explain mysterious aspects of reality. In ancient literature this approach was often used to explain man's conflict with the animal kingdom, especially with serpents. It was used to explain the origin of natural evil, and man's conflict with his fellow man, and the ongoing conflict between good and evil, or all at the same time.

Those who follow the literal approach insist on a pre-Fall snake or other animal which *possibly* walked erect and had powers of mind, emotions, and will, including the powers of speech.[14] For this reason, they affirm, Eve was not startled by the talking snake. She had seen him before, perhaps had even conversed with him. At the same time, it is affirmed, the story primarily refers to Satan and his seduction of Eve who, in turn, tempted Adam.

Thus we have a double-faceted interpretation. Those who hold to this two-level view develop both dimensions. This view was common in earlier commentators. The position taken by all the commentators and Old Testament scholars used in this book rejects the mythological-allegorical view and holds to a more moderate double-faceted view. This is my position, also.

Thus, this is an *historical account*. It all happened just as recounted in Genesis. The suggestion towards rebellion against the lordship of God came from outside of man. It came through the one who is here called the serpent, but later called Satan in the Old Testament (1 Chron. 21:1; Job 1:6–12; 2:1–7; Ps. 109:6 [perhaps]; Zech. 3:1–3).

This is also a *pictorial account*. The crafty, talking snake is a picture of the one later called "the serpent of old who is called the devil and Satan" (Rev. 12:9). Whether or not he is a literal snake is not important to the story. Most conservative commentators, however, believe it was a literal animal controlled by Satan.

Man made in the image of God had the Word of God to guide him when he faced temptation. Thus he possessed an intuitive, but not experimental, insight into evil. Furthermore, he had full freedom of the will. Even the strictest Calvinist would accept this fact for pre-Fall man. He had every capacity to "resist the Devil" and obey God.

Four Purposes of the Story of the Fall

The writer of Genesis gives us the story for at least four purposes:

1. To reveal that solicitation towards rebellion against God came from outside of man.
2. To teach that man is responsible before God for his disobedience.
3. To warn us that ongoing spiritual warfare will exist between humanity and Satan.
4. To encourage us with the truth that God will provide full redemption through the "seed" of the woman.

The only way man would have fallen is for external, personal evil, already in existence, to insert doubt about God and His Word through deception into the mind of man. Man's situation in God's Paradise was too perfect for his innocent, but untested, nature to give birth to such unbelief. The process had to begin outside of man.

Some point to the self-deception of Lucifer as an argument against this assumption. Somehow evil had to arise within his innocent nature or he would not have fallen. Others take a different view of this decision towards evil that arose from within Lucifer. In order to test Lucifer's free will, God himself would have had to plant the idea of evil in Lucifer's mind. This way Lucifer could choose either to accept evil or reject it.

This latter view is impossible. God cannot do that which is contrary to His nature. God cannot do evil nor tempt His creatures to do evil and still be God. Thus James writes, "Let no one say when he is tempted, 'I am being tempted by God'; for God cannot be tempted by evil, and He Himself does not tempt anyone" (James 1:13).

Evil, therefore, could not have been planted in the heart or mind of Lucifer by God.[15] It had to be a capacity possessed by Lucifer from his creation, and perhaps also possessed by the angels, though this is less certain since Lucifer evidently attempted to deceive all of God's angels, being successful with only a limited number of them. This self-originating nature of supernatural evil, then, did not exist in man, the creature made "in the image and likeness of God" as it evidently did in Lucifer.

Immediately after speaking of God's judgment upon the snake, Calvin, writing on Genesis 3:15a, says that

> we must now make a transition from the serpent to the author of this mischief himself. . . . God has not so vented his anger upon the outward instrument as to spare the devil, with whom lay all the blame. . . .

> I therefore conclude, that God here chiefly assails Satan under the name of the serpent, and hurls against him the lightning of his judgment. This he does for a twofold reason: first, that men may learn to beware of Satan as of a most deadly enemy; then, that they may contend against him with the assured confidence of victory.[16]

The controversy over the meaning of these profound words in 3:15 has endured for centuries. Yet among most conservative Old Testament scholars there is now a general unanimity of position with disagreement dealing only with details concerning this spiritual warfare prophecy. The areas of the greatest concerns, however, have to do with the meaning of these words to Adam and Eve themselves and to believers down through the ages.

We begin with noting some of Matthew Henry's thoughtful comments on this passage. Henry deals first with the serpent as the enticer to sin. "Here," he says, "the serpent is laid under man's reproach and enmity. He is to be forever looked upon as a vile and despicable creature, and a proper object of scorn and contempt."

Henry points out that God's sentence against the serpent

> is much fortified by that promise of God to his people, *"Thou shalt tread upon the lion and the adder"* (Ps. 91:13), and that of Christ to his disciples, *"They shall take up serpents"* (Mark 16:18), witness Paul, who was unhurt by the viper that fastened upon his hand.

> Observe here, The serpent and the woman had just now been very familiar and friendly in discourse about the forbidden fruit, and a wonderful agreement there was between them; but here they are irreconcilably set at variance.[17]

Henry then switches from the snake to Satan. He says, "This sentence may be considered as leveled at the devil, who only made use of the serpent as his vehicle in this appearance, but was himself the principle agent."

Then he observes, "A perpetual quarrel is here commenced between the kingdom of God and the kingdom of the devil . . . war is proclaimed between 'the seed of the woman and the seed of the serpent.' "[18]

The issue for man is whom will he serve, God or the anti-God, Satan? "No man can serve two masters," Jesus declared (Matt. 6:24). Yet how many try to do so! If we are not "gathering with Him," Jesus said, we "are scattering abroad." If we are not "for Him," Jesus said, we are "against Him." If we are not serving him, we are serving the Devil. If we are not the children of God, we are the children of Satan.

Henry says that "A gracious promise is here made of Christ, as the deliverer of fallen man from the power of Satan." He then makes an interesting point, seldom observed by commentators:[19]

> Though what was said was addressed to the serpent, yet it was said in the hearing of our first parents, who, doubtless, took the hints of grace here given them, and saw a door of hope opened to them, else the following sentence upon themselves would have overwhelmed them. Here was the dawning of the Gospel day. No sooner was the wound given than the remedy was provided and revealed.

Genesis 3:15: Three Prophecies of Christ

Henry then mentions three things concerning Christ which he sees coming out of Genesis 3:15:[20]

> (1) His incarnation, that He should be *the seed of the woman,* the seed of *that* woman; therefore His genealogy (Luke 2) goes so high as to show Him to be the son of Adam, but God does the woman the honor to call Him rather her seed, because she it was whom the devil had beguiled, and on whom Adam had laid the blame. . . .

This is a significant statement. In biblical and ancient reckoning of lineage it is usually the lineage of the man that is mentioned (cf. 5:1f). In this case, God passes by Adam and speaks of the seed of the woman, Eve. It is also startling to note that the rest of the Genesis account stresses more the exuberant faith of Eve than of Adam (4:1f).

Eve was the one who was deceived by the serpent. Eve in turn persuaded Adam to follow her in sin. As a result, Eve was also the first of the two to be judged by God.

After the Fall, Eve's repentance was perhaps the deepest. She became a woman of faith. She probably believed the promised seed would be born to her in her lifetime and that he would crush the head of the Evil One, the Great Deceiver. It is her seed, not Adam's, which God said would finally undo what she first caused to be done. Interesting, is it not, that it is the seed of Eve which will take us out of the first Adam and place us in the second Adam (1 Cor. 15:45–49)!

Matthew Henry comments, "He [Christ] was likewise to be the seed of a woman only, of a virgin, that He may not be tainted with the corruption of our nature; He was sent forth, *made of woman* (Gal. 4:4), that this promise might be fulfilled."[21]

The question as to whether or not the recipients of the book, though men and women of great faith, understood from 3:15 the Virgin Birth of the promised redeemer would be impossible to answer. What matters is that they had faith, and that faith, like that of Abraham, was counted unto them for righteousness (Rom. 9:11).

Matthew Henry continues:

> (2) His sufferings and death, pointed at in Satan's *bruising His heel,* that is, His human nature. . . . It was the devil that put it into the heart of Judas to betray Christ, of Peter to deny him, of the chief priests to prosecute him, of the false witnesses to accuse him, and of Pilate to condemn him, aiming in all this, by destroying the Savior, to ruin the salvation; but, on the contrary, it was by death that Christ destroyed him that had the power of death (Hebrews 2:14).

> Christ's heel was bruised when his feet were pierced and nailed to the cross, and Christ's sufferings are continued in the sufferings of the saints for His name. The devil tempts them, casts them into prison, persecutes and slays them, and so bruises the heel of Christ who is afflicted in their afflictions. But, while the heel is bruised on earth, it is well that the head is safe in heaven.

These are challenging words. One has to appreciate Matthew Henry's devotional, yet biblical handling of Genesis 3:15. He continues with excellent comments on the seed of the woman crushing the head of the serpent.[22]

> (3) His victory over Satan thereby. . . . *He shall bruise his head,* that is, [the seed of the woman] shall destroy all his politics and all his powers, and give a total overthrow to his kingdom and interest. Christ baffled Satan's temptations, rescued souls

out of his hands, cast him out of the bodies of people, dispossessed the strong man armed, and divided his spoil: by his death, he gave a fatal and incurable blow to the devil's kingdom, a wound to the head of this beast, that can never be healed. As his gospel gets ground *Satan falls* (Luke 10:18) and is *bound* (Rev. 20:2). By his grace, he treads Satan under his people's feet (Rom. 16:20) and will shortly cast him into the lake of fire (Rev. 20:10). And the devil's perpetual overthrow will be the complete and everlasting joy and glory of the chosen remnant.

Generally speaking, Matthew Henry's overview of Genesis 3:15 represents the position of most conservative Old Testament scholars and commentators. He mentions the meaning of these words to both Adam and Eve and to future generations. He also implies that their full meaning cannot be really understood except in light of the New Testament. He then applies these words to the needs of believers of all ages.

We will scrutinize the Messianic import of Genesis 3:15 next.

29

The Messianic Promise
Genesis 3:15

Martin Luther said about Genesis 3:15: "This text embraces and comprehends within itself everything noble and glorious that is to be found anywhere in the Scriptures."[1] The Old Testament saints understood Genesis 3:15 as messianic. While some critical commentators reject the messianic implications of Genesis 3:15, this is the view of all conservative Bible scholars.[2] It is the only view which fits the entire thrust of Scripture.

Hamilton's discussion is very critical (in a positive sense), but well balanced. He affirms that the translators of the Septuagint seem "to have had a messianic understanding of the verse." This is an important admission. Wenham never seems to fail in giving a balanced, reverent interpretation of Genesis. He says the word translated *enmity* is really *hostility* in Hebrew.[3]

> Both this context and other passages suggest that long-lasting enmity is meant (cf. Num. 35:21–22; Ezek. 25:15; 35:5). The human race, "her offspring," and the serpent race, "your offspring," will be forever at loggerheads. Those who had been in league against their creator will from now on be fighting against each other, a motif that reappears in the tower of Babel story (11:1–9). It is not simply a case of God versus the snake in perpetuity but is mankind versus the snake as well (cf. Isa. 11:8).

Wenham raises the textual problem. "The translation of this curse is extraordinarily problematic, because the root 'batter, crush, bruise' occurs only here and in two other difficult poetic passages: Ps. 139:11; Job 9:17. There is a similar root which sometimes means 'crush,' e.g., Amos 2:7."[4]

How are we to understand the "bruising" (NAS) of the serpent's head and the "bruising" (NAS) of the heel of the seed of the woman?

"The majority view is that the sense is the same in both passages," Wenham says. "A minority prefers to see a word play between two different meanings, the woman's seed 'crushing' the serpent, and the serpent 'craving' the man's heel (so Cassuto, Kidner, Procksch; Vg. Tg)."

Rather than try to resolve the issue, Wenham lets it stand as is. He wisely states that despite the long discussion over the issue

> etymology makes little difference to the understanding of the passage. Close attention to grammar and context is more important. The imperfect verb . . . implies repeated attacks by both sides to injure the other. It declares lifelong mutual hostility between mankind and the serpent race. Of more moment for interpretation is the question whether one side will eventually prove victorious in the battle, or whether the contest will be never-ending.

Tactically, the serpent has the disadvantage. Since he now crawls on his belly—definitely a lowering of his sights—he can only strike the man's heel. The man, towering above, can crush the serpent's head.

Wenham again:[5]

Once admitted that the serpent symbolizes sin, death and the power of evil, it becomes much more likely that the curse envisages a long struggle between good and evil, with mankind eventually triumphing. Such an interpretation fits in well with 4:7 where Cain is warned of sin lurking to catch him, but is promised victory if he resists.

With this quote Wenham answers his own question about who wins the long struggle. God wins. We win in Him. He then tells us the oldest Jewish interpretation yet discovered sees Genesis 3:15 as messianic, also, and with "King Messiah" winning the battle.[6]

Certainly the oldest Jewish interpretation found in the third century B.C. Septuagint, the Palestinian targums (Ps-J., Neof., Frg.), and possibly the Onqelos targum takes the serpent as symbolic of Satan and look for a victory over him in the days of King Messiah. The New Testament also alludes to this passage, understanding it in a broadly messianic sense (Rom. 16:20; Heb. 2:14; Rev. 12), and it may be that the term "Son of Man" as a title for Jesus and the term "woman" for Mary (John 2:4; 19:26) also reflect this passage (Gallus; cf. Michl). Certainly, later Christian commentators, beginning with Justin (ca. A.D. 160) and Irenaeus (ca. 180), have often regarded 3:15 as the Protoevangelium, the first messianic prophecy in the Old Testament.

Let me sum up the general messianic interpretation of 3:15 held by most conservative biblical scholars.[7] We begin with R. Payne Smith. He comments on what he calls "the perpetual enmity between the serpent and man" and the two seeds:[8]

We have here the sum of the whole matter, and the rest of the Bible does but explain the nature of this struggle, the persons who wage it, and the manner and consequences of the victory. Here, too, we learn the end and purpose for which the narrative is cast in its present form.

Smith then outlines the relationship of Adam and Eve to God before the Fall, stressing all the benefits God gave to man in the Garden and how he fellowshipped with his beloved pair daily. Smith then says humanity will prevail in this sinister conflict, but not unscathed. Mere human strength will not afford him his triumph, "but by the coming of One who is 'the Woman's Seed'; and round this promised Deliverer the rest of Scripture groups itself."[9] If the last phrase of Genesis 3:15 were to be omitted,

all the inspired teaching which follows would be an ever-widening river without a fountain-head. But necessarily with the fall came the promise of restoration. Grace is no after-thought, but enters the world side by side with sin. Upon this foundation the rest of Holy Scripture is built, till revelation at last reaches its corner-stone in Christ.

Frances A. Schaeffer calls his chapter on Genesis 3:15 "The Two Humanities." Commenting under the subheading, "Thy seed and Her Seed," he writes, "It is important to emphasize that the seed here is considered personal, 'he.' The one who is promised here is a person. A person will bruise Satan's head, and in doing so will be wounded."[10]

Schaeffer points out that the male is the one considered to have the seed, so the reference to "her seed" is peculiar in Semitic languages. "Is it possible that this way of speaking already casts a shadow of the Virgin Birth? Does it suggest that when the Messiah was born, he would be the seed of the woman and that in his conception there would be no male seed?"[11] This is frequently suggested by evangelical scholars. It is not universally held to be true, however. Either way, Messiah was virgin born.

Schaeffer then compares Genesis 3:15 with Hebrews 2:14. Noting that "Jesus fulfilled the promise in Genesis 3:15, for it is the Messiah who is to be bruised, and yet, in the bruising, destroy the power of death and the devil. By this death, he would 'deliver them who through fear of death were all their lifetime subject to bondage' (v. 15)."[12] This substitutionary note to the death of the Messiah portends the overcoming of the results of the Fall. Schaeffer continues to discuss this substitutionary aspect by tying Isaiah 53:10 to Genesis 3:15. Note, Schaeffer says:

> *He shall see his seed.* It is in this sense, therefore, that God has given Jesus children. Romans 16:20 also ties in with Genesis 3:15. Speaking to the Christians in Rome, Paul writes, "And the God of peace shall bruise Satan under your feet shortly." The reference is to the second coming of the Lord Jesus Christ when God himself shall bruise Satan under the feet of the Christians.[13]

Schaeffer's discussion has been to prove that "Christ is the seed of the woman in Genesis 3:15." As a result of his redemptive work, Christ has a seed, and that seed shall contend with the seed of Satan. Christ is to be "the *second Adam* and the *second founder* of the race."[14]

Taking all we have seen thus far and adding a few ideas we can summarize the teachings of Genesis 3:15 as follows:

First, there will be mutual hostility between Satan and the woman (v. 15a).[15]

Second, God established this enmity, not the serpent nor the woman: "I will put enmity" (v. 15a).

Third, the woman here must stand for the entire human race, not just the female gender. Genesis 3:20 can be used for confirmation. The woman is called Eve, "living or life," because "she was the mother of all the living." As Adam was the representative man, Eve is the representative woman. This is in keeping with the Hebrew view of humanity. All future generations are said to be "in the loins" of their fathers (Heb. 7:9–10). How about "in the womb" of their mothers, also?

A case can be made from Genesis 3:15 and from history for Satan's unique hatred of women, however. Women contain within themselves the key to the very existence of the race. Every human being born since the Fall, including the man Christ Jesus, was born from the womb of a woman.

Furthermore, whether or not Satan understood it, the one who was to crush his head would be born of a woman. The Incarnation would come through the Virgin Birth (Luke 1:26–38; Gal. 4:4; Rev. 12:1–6, 13–17). Thus Satan's historic and continuing attempts to corrupt and destroy womankind take on greater significance than we normally give.

Fourth, this mutual hatred will be carried forward by the two twofold seeds (v. 15b).

I believe the diagram on page 211 is harmonious with later biblical teachings and confirmed by encounters with Satan and his evil spirits in the course of Christian history, life, and redemptive ministry.

He (the seed of the woman) will bruise the head of the serpent (Satan). When the apostle Paul takes this concept and applies it to the Christian life in Romans 16:20, he selects a stronger verb. He uses *suntribō*, which, according to William Vine, means "to shatter . . . break in pieces by crushing." The same verb is used for "bruising of a reed, Matthew 12:20; . . . the breaking of fetters in pieces, Mark

5:4; the breaking of an alabaster cruse, Mark 14:3; an earthen vessel, Revelation 2:27 . . . of the eventual crushing of Satan, Romans 16:20."[16]

A Bifocal Focus

The words focus primarily on the crushing of the serpent's head which has already occurred historically in the Christ event, i.e., the redemptive activity of the Lord Jesus Christ (Matt. 12:22–29; Acts 10:38; Col. 2:13–15; Heb. 2:14–15; 1 John 3:8b).

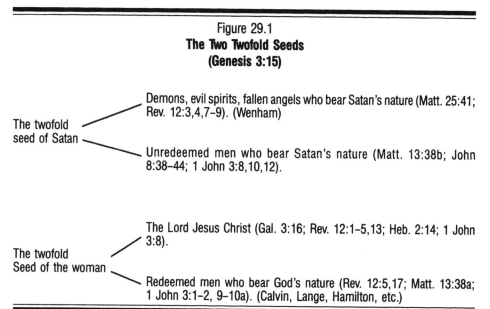

Figure 29.1
The Two Twofold Seeds
(Genesis 3:15)

The twofold seed of Satan

Demons, evil spirits, fallen angels who bear Satan's nature (Matt. 25:41; Rev. 12:3,4,7–9). (Wenham)

Unredeemed men who bear Satan's nature (Matt. 13:38b; John 8:38–44; 1 John 3:8,10,12).

The twofold Seed of the woman

The Lord Jesus Christ (Gal. 3:16; Rev. 12:1–5,13; Heb. 2:14; 1 John 3:8).

Redeemed men who bear God's nature (Rev. 12:5,17; Matt. 13:38a; 1 John 3:1-2, 9–10a). (Calvin, Lange, Hamilton, etc.)

Thus, while our foe is a powerful, awesome supernatural foe, he is already a defeated one. If there exists a single key to victory in warfare with evil supernaturalism, it is that God through the Lord Jesus Christ, His Son, has already totally defeated Satan and his seed in our behalf (John 12:31–32; 16:11 with Luke 10:18), and in behalf of all humanity (2 Cor. 5:18–21; John 3:16).

How demons fear and resist this truth! They will fight it with all of their being when spoken in faith and authority by the child of God (Eph. 3:10 with Rev. 12:11).

A secondary focus of the words deals with the "Christian" or the "Church" event. By this I refer to the ongoing crushing of the head of the serpent by the people of God. Is this not implied in Romans 16:20, Matthew 16:18–20, and Matthew 18:18–20? While the context (in Matt. 18:18–20) describes interpersonal conflicts among believers, the principles have this wider application.

We crush Satan's head in our own life as we resist him and submit to God (James 4:7). We crush his head in the lives of others through intercession and as we bring Christ's life, love, and healing power into their bruised lives.

In the context of warfare with the spirit world, this means our powerful foe is first defeated by our Lord and then by us, His sons and servants.

The greatest compliment demons ever paid to me—and I do not seek compliments from them—has occurred when I bring them under control and they do not want to obey me, but finally have to.

"Why do you have to obey me?" I occasionally ask.

"Because you are the Lord's servant," they reply.

And such we are! But we are also His sons.

If there exists a second key to victory in our warfare with evil supernaturalism, it is this: Jesus has committed to us His authority over Satan and his seed (Luke 10:19; Acts 16:18; 1 John 5:18–19; Rom. 16:20).

How demons hate and fear this truth spoken in faith by the mouth of God's seed (Eph. 3:10 with Rev. 12:11). They will fight it fiercely until made to submit. Then they will fearfully admit it to be true.

This secondary crushing of evil supernaturalism also involves the agony of direct participation in spiritual warfare and Warfare Praying, deep intercession in the context of spiritual warfare (Eph. 6:10–20; 1 Peter 5:8–11; Rev. 2—3 and 12:7—13:7). There is no effective spiritual warfare without pain. Jesus Himself said, "In the world you have tribulation. . . . But," He continued to say, "I have overcome the world" (John 16:33b). He also said, "Do not be afraid, little flock, for your Father has chosen gladly to give you the kingdom" (Luke 12:32).

In the process of being crushed, Satan will painfully but not mortally wound the heel of the seed of the woman (v. 15d). This too has a primary and secondary focus. The primary focus is on the satanic source of the afflictions and sufferings of the Lord Jesus Christ while he lived on earth. This began with the wilderness temptation and continued until his death on the Cross.

It is interesting to see the satanic source of the betrayal, agony, and death of the singular seed of the woman, the Lord Jesus (John 13:2 and 27; Luke 22:47–53). In this event, the stupidity of Satan is revealed. He "shot himself in the foot," so to speak. By taking Jesus to the Cross, Satan and his entire kingdom of principalities and powers were totally defeated (Col. 2:14–15; Heb. 2:14–15). Is this the deeper meaning of 1 Corinthians 2:6–8? I believe it is.

The secondary focus of these words has to do with the most agonizing aspect of our life and redemptive ministry, the demonic source of the afflictions and sufferings we face in our personal life and ministry (2 Cor. 2:11; 10:3–5; 11:3; 12:7; Luke 22:31–32; Eph. 6:10–14a; 1 Thess. 2:18; 3:5; 1 Pet. 5:6–11).

This is clearly spelled out in Revelation 2—3. All seven messages to the seven churches are formed within the context of spiritual warfare. First we have the conflict promise: "To him who overcomes" (2:7; 2:11; 2:17; 2:26; 3:5; 3:12; 3:21). This is followed by even more graphic descriptions of sufferings at the hands of the spirit world (2:9–10; 2:13–16; 2:20–25; 3:9–10; 12:17; 13:7). Paul's words in 1 Thessalonians 2:18 and 3:5 also take on new meaning. Furthermore, this gives new significance to verses like Philippians 1:29, Colossians 1:24, and 2 Timothy 1:7–12 and 4:1–8.

There is no redemptive ministry apart from warfare sufferings. The dual wounding of the seed of the woman by evil supernaturalism is part of the mystery of God's plan. This was true of the wounding of the Son of God (John 19:10–11; Isa. 53:4–6 and 10a; Acts 2:22–23 and 36), and continues to be true of the wounding of the sons of God (Acts 4:27–31; 2 Thess. 3:3; 1 John 5:18; Luke 10:19 with Luke 22:31–32; Job 1—2).

As we well know, however, in their crushing by Jesus as the Seed of the woman, Satan and his demonic hosts were not annihilated. They still exercise authority over those who do not know Christ (2 Cor. 4:3–4; Eph. 2:1–3; 1 John 3:10; 5:19). They are also allowed under the sovereign will and control of God to war against the children of God (1 Cor. 7:5; 2 Cor. 2:11; 11:3; Eph. 6:10–18; 1 Thess. 2:18; 3:5; James 4:7–8; 1 Peter 5:8–11; 1 John 2:12–14; Rev. 12—13).

We face afflictions and sufferings as God's servants as we live for our Lord in the enemy's territory, this evil world (Gal. 1:4). It is our privilege to say with the apostle Paul:

"Now I rejoice in my sufferings for your sake [for our fellow believers who look to us as a model of steadfastness in the midst of suffering], and in my flesh I do my share on behalf of His body (which is the church) in filling up that which is lacking in Christ's afflictions" (Col. 1:24).

The word translated *afflictions* here is never used of the Lord's atoning sufferings but of the general afflictions He faced on earth as the God-man. These afflictions come from two personal sources, evil men and evil supernaturalism. In a mysterious sense, there seems to be a predetermined "quantity" of sufferings necessary to bring the church, Christ's body, to its fullness in Christ.

Jesus began filling that sufferings quota. We continue with similar quota sufferings. The sufferings come from men. They also come from bearing a fallen body in a fallen world. Above all, however, they come from the serpent and his seed, the demons.

The rest of Scripture is the unfolding of that suffering, bruised-heel lifestyle of the people of God. Until the Lord returns in his glory and Satan and his angels are cast into the lake of fire (Matt. 25:41; Rev. 20:14–15), our heel will be continually bruised by the serpent and his seed. We will also continue to crush the serpent's head, however. In that process we will always be victorious, even in defeats and if necessary, in death (Rom. 8:35–39). In the end, the Lord Himself will finish crushing the serpent's head (Rev. 19:20; 20:10). Amen!

30

The Beginning of Warfare Between the Two Seeds
Genesis 4:1–8

In Genesis 4 we discover the first in a series of encounters between the two opposing seeds. As God calls to Himself a people for His name, He can only call them out of the fallen family of Adam, all of whom are in bondage to "the god of this world," Satan. Some will respond to God's will. They will become the seed of the woman. Others will reject God's call. They will become the seed of the Serpent. This will divide the human race into two warring families, or seeds, the children of God and the children of the Devil.

In rage and hatred both against God and the elect of God, Satan will war against the family of God. God's children will become the object of the hatred of the "no-family of God," those still fallen in Adam who remain as the seed of the serpent.

Cain and Abel

Most of the time the invisible supernatural personalities who are the demonic seed of Satan will not be seen. What are seen are the human agents through whom they operate (Eph. 6:12). In Genesis 4 Cain is one of those "sons of disobedience," the beginning of the evil line of the seed of Satan. Satan will make war with the first saints through his seed, in this case Cain. That is why we begin with him.

I express the mutual hostility in the above manner because in such stories the hostility is more on the part of the seed of the serpent than vice versa. It is usually occasioned by a negative reaction on the part of the human seed of Satan to the righteous lifestyle of the human seed of the woman. The godly life of God's people provokes jealousy, anger, and resistance on the part of evil people. It can become open hatred. The seed of the righteous are often made to suffer and die at the hands of the unrighteous seed. That is exactly what happens in the story before us.

Cain and Abel can be seen as the first representatives of the two warring seeds spoken of by God in Genesis 3:15: the seed of the serpent, Cain, and the seed of the woman, Abel.

After the Fall, the first parents proved to be a godly couple. Two of their three sons whose names are given in Genesis 4—5 evidently walked in the faith of their parents. Eve joyfully cries out after the birth of her firstborn, Cain, "gotten one," "I have gotten a man child with Yahweh."[1]

Leupold's comment on 4:1 is worth noting:[2]

In this phrase lie both thankfulness and praise; thankfulness at deliverance from pain and danger [as this was the first child born of a woman, without doubt the curse of 3:16 is in view], praise that Jehovah is manifesting His grace and faithfulness in giving a son. So the use of the name "Yahweh" should be observed. Apparently, then, since the name stresses His gracious faithfulness, Eve praises God that He who promised victory to the seed of the woman actually lets the (seed of the woman) be born. Nothing indicates whether Eve did or did not anticipate that this very seed, Cain, should personally crush the serpent's head. But in any case, she had a token of Yahweh's fidelity.

Adam and Eve were present when the curse and promise of 3:15 were spoken by God to the serpent. What we see in 4:1 is evidence that Eve never forgot those words. Her first and third sons were probably named in light of 3:15.

She was wrong about Cain, however. How deep must have been her disappointment when Cain turned out to be more the seed of Satan (1 John 3:12) than the promised seed of the woman! What tragedy she experienced as the first mother! She sets the pattern for godly women through the ages who have seen a special son turn away from God. How great is their suffering!

Verse 2a refers to the birth of the younger brother, Abel. No explanation is given as to why he was called Abel ("breath") as there was for Cain.[3] As Cain was the firstborn, much importance is attributed to his birth.

Wenham points out some of the privileges of the firstborn in biblical cultures (Gen. 25:32; 27:1–40; Deut. 21:15–17). He observes, however, that in the Old Testament God uniquely seems to call the second born, usually even before their birth. Examples are Isaac in place of Ishmael; Jacob in place of Esau; Ephraim not Manasseh; David, the youngest of Jesse's sons, as over against the older sons. He feels that there are hints here (vv. 1–2a) "that Abel is the elect younger brother."[4]

Scene 1: Verses 2b–5

Verse 2b–5 represents the first scene, Wenham says. It is all narrative. Cain and Abel are the main actors. Yahweh does not speak. Abel's occupation is mentioned first, then Cain's. But Cain's offering is mentioned before Abel's.

Much has been made of Abel's offering being accepted and Cain's rejected because Cain brought the "fruit of the ground," while Abel brought an animal (blood) sacrifice. This does not seem to be the point of the story, however. Grain offerings or other offerings of the fruit of the ground were not only later revealed to be acceptable but commanded by the law of God.[5]

Why was Cain's offering not accepted, while Abel's was?[6] The two most common explanations are, one: the different motives of the two brothers, motives known only to God (Heb. 11:4); two, the different attitudes toward worship by the two sons. Wenham calls this latter view "the commonest view among commentators, ancient and modern."[7]

A look at the description of the offerings seems to support this view. "Abel . . . brought of the firstlings of his flock and of their fat portions" (4:4). "Cain brought an offering to the LORD of the fruit of the ground" (v. 3). There is no mention that it was "the first fruit of the ground" as the law later required, but only that it was the fruit of the ground.

The fact they brought sacrifices at all reveals that Adam and Eve understood how to worship God since the Fall. They understood the need for sacrificial offerings and had correctly taught their children to do so.

Abel did as he was taught, but Cain did as he thought. As a result Moses says, ". . . the LORD had regard for Abel and for his offering, but for Cain and for his offering, He had no regard" (vv. 4b–5a). God first responds to the person of each son before He does to their offerings. Evidently the different inner attitudes of obedience, faith, and true love for God made the difference.[8]

Both sons were raised in the same home by the same godly parents (it is interesting that Eve's faith is more prominent than Adam's in chapter 4) under identical circumstances. Both were taught to worship. Both were taught to present offerings to the Lord. The heart of one, Abel, was inclined toward God, on pleasing him, by faith. The heart of the other, Cain, was inclined towards himself, on doing as he pleased.

Cain's reaction in verse 5b to God's rejection of his offering is described in strong words. First, Cain was "very angry." Next "his countenance fell." Then he became "crest fallen and depressed."[9]

We are not told how the brothers knew God's reaction to their offerings, but God did let them know. Cain is not confused about why he was not accepted. Instead he is furious, both at God and his brother. He falls into a deep despondency triggered by self-pity and deep anger. Wenham says that, in Scripture, being "very angry" is often a prelude to homicidal acts (cf. 34:7; 1 Sam. 18:8; Neh. 4:1; cf. Num. 16:15; 2 Sam. 3:8).[10] It certainly was so with Cain. Calvin writes:[11]

> Moreover, in the person of Cain is portrayed to us the likeness of a wicked man, who yet desires to be esteemed just . . . Such persons truly, by external words, strenuously labor to deserve well at the hands of God; and, retaining a heart wrapped in deceit, they present to Him nothing but a mask; so that, in their laborious and anxious religious worship, there is nothing sincere, nothing but mere pretense. When they afterwards see that they gain no advantage, they betray the venom of their minds; for they not only complain against God, but break forth in manifest fury, so that, if they were able, they would gladly tear Him down from His heavenly throne. Such is the innate pride of hypocrites.

Scene 2: Verses 6–7

Scene two begins with God's response to Cain's anger and depression (4:6–7). God's recorded response to Cain is very helpful in understanding what was occurring in Cain's life from God's all-knowing perspective. God is shown as being willing to forgive Cain and to accept him into His family. At the same time, the record of God's response in verse 7 is one of the hardest verses in Genesis to translate and interpret.[12]

God begins with two direct questions: "Why are you angry? And why has your countenance fallen?" There is great compassion on God's part in asking these questions. He, of course, knew the answers to both questions. His purpose seems to be to give Cain the opportunity to reflect on the real reasons for his anger and sadness.

This view is further strengthened by God's third question in verse 7. "If you do well, will not your countenance be lifted up?" Others translate it: "Is there not forgiveness if you do well?"[13]

While objections can be raised about forgiveness being earned through well-doing, this too is beside the point. The point is, Cain has done evil. He knows it and God knows it. God wants to forgive him, to accept him, but he must first recognize and confess his sin. If he does, God invites him to Himself. God has not arbitrarily accepted Abel as over against Cain, as some commentators affirm. God has a heart big enough for both of them. Cain must recognize his wrong and come to God with a sincerely repentant heart and God will forgive and accept him. I believe Cain's repentance motivates all three of God's questions, but especially this last one.

God follows His three questions with a strong warning and an exhortation or promise. All evidence God's grace toward Cain. "Cain, it is not yet too late," God is saying. "You too will be accepted by me just as I have accepted your brother, Abel."

Cain's Sin and Evil Supernaturalism

Next is the strong warning. In it we discover some of the spiritual warfare dimensions of Cain's sin problem. "And if you do not do well, sin is crouching at the door; and its desire is for you."

This is a powerful word. It is also the first appearance of the word sin in the Bible and lends insight about the nature of sin itself. Sin is personified, given independent life as if it were an animal or even a serpent lurking in the doorway of Cain's house, ready to destroy him. Keil and Delitzsch say, "The feminine (for sin) is construed as a masculine, because with evident allusion to the serpent, sin is personified as a wild beast, lurking at the door of the human heart, and eagerly desiring to devour his soul" (1 Peter 5:8).[14]

Hamilton says that the Hebrew word for sin here is connected with the Akkadian word "demon, *rabisum*."[15]

> In Mesopotamian demonology the *rabisum* (demon) could be either a benevolent being that lurks at the entrance of a building to protect the occupants, or just the opposite, a malevolent being that lurks at the entrance of a building to threaten the occupants.

Wenham refers to an article by Ramaroson who translates the warning in verse 7, "If you do not do well, the croucher (demon) is at the door."[16]

I believe this position is accurate. It is certainly the New Testament view. The apostle John refers to Cain's sin problem as being satanic (1 John 3:12). Was Cain demonized?

Wenham then adds, "Here then sin is personified as a demon crouching like a wild beast on Cain's doorstop."[17] In this we discover the spiritual warfare dimension of Cain's sin problem. Of course Cain's sin came from within him, the problem of the flesh. It did not come from outside him, from the world, however. The world to Cain was not yet evil. The evil world was really only born with his sin, not that of Adam and Eve. He is the first "worldly" man revealed in Scripture.

The dominant power of evil revealed in this story is evil supernaturalism. Personified sin was present in Cain's life (v. 7). John says that, as believers are "of God" (1 John 5:19), so Cain was "of the evil one" (1 John 3:12). He belonged to Satan as we believers belong to God. As the believer shares the life of the God who indwells him, Cain shared the life of Satan who indwelt him. This was probably not yet true at the stage of sin in his life when God first spoke to him (vv. 6–7), but it became true immediately afterwards. God warned Cain that the demon of sin was outside waiting to "possess" him. It had its "desire" set upon him. Hamilton translates these words, "Its urge is toward you."[18] In his refusal to respond to God's warnings, he probably allowed that demon into his life, becoming demonized.

God's warning here is a word of grace towards Cain. God knew where Cain was heading and stepped in to warn him. He was saying, "Stop, Cain! Turn back. You are heading for disaster." God then continues his attempt to stop Cain. He says "but you must master it," i.e., the personal demon of sin crouching at his door.

Keil and Delitzsch share a beautiful quotation from another commentator called Herder:[19]

> God talks to Cain as a willful child, and draws out of him what is sleeping in his heart, and lurking like a wild beast before his door. And what He did to Cain He does to everyone who will but observe his own heart, and listen to the voice of God.

What was Cain's immediate response? Stony silence. Leupold observes, "There is something ominous about Cain's silences. He is not reported to have thanked (God) for the warning, or to have repented of his jealousy, or to have mended his ways. A stubborn silence seems to have been all he had to offer.[20]

Anticipating verse 8, he says,

Cain's sin in reference to his brother was primarily jealousy culminating in hatred, a sin that seems comparatively weak and insignificant but which carries possibilities of great development within itself.[21]

Anger, bitterness, and lack of forgiveness are some of the most dangerous sin handles in a human life. Thus Paul's impassioned warnings (Heb. 12:15; Eph. 4:26–27; 5:29–6:2; Col. 3:8–17). Cain is experiencing this in the story before us. Leupold comments:[22]

Now the account proceeds in a drastic manner to show what possibilities for development lay in the sin which had by this time fastened itself strongly upon man. Possibilities for evil that no man would have suspected lay hidden in sin. All of a sudden it breaks forth and displays to the full its vicious nature and terrible curse.

Scene 3: Verse 8

Scene three is found in verse 8, revealing Cain's negative response to God's questions, His promise, and His strong warning found in verses 6–7. Wenham calls it "the central theme, with Cain and Abel the only actors. The awfulness of the deed is accentuated by the stark brevity of the description and the twice-repeated 'his brother.'"[23]

Cain murders his believing, godly brother, Abel.[24]

Hamilton writes that

the reason Abel is murdered is because of an unchecked envy and jealousy on Cain's part. Rather than accept God's decision, he rejects the one God has accepted. But this reaction only exacerbates Cain's dilemma. He has eliminated Abel, but what will he do with God?[25]

Leupold writes that

the first murder was fratricide. Sin could hardly have displayed more drastically the potentialities that lie in it. In the second generation it has already grown to the proportions of murder. Clearly, the term "seed of the woman" (3:15) must suffer modification. Here already is a clear instance how "the seed of the woman had already (in part) become the seed of the serpent" (Keil).[26]

Scene 4: Verses 9–14

Scene four is found in verses 9–14. This scene, like the second, is a dialogue between the Lord and Cain. In verses 6–7 Cain's replies are unrecorded, if he replied at all. Here they are given in full. Wenham says the divine interrogation of Cain and the subsequent pronouncement of curses resemble "the similar treatment of Adam (cf. 4:9 and 3:9; 4:10 and 3:13; 4:11 and 3:14, 17; 4:12 and 3:17–19). Many of the key words of chapter 3 appear here too: 'knew,' 'guard,' 'cursed,' 'land,' 'drive.'"[27]

We bring our commentary on Genesis 4 to an end with the last part of verse 8, "Cain rose up against Abel his brother and killed him." Keil and Delitzsch write,

Thus the sin of Adam had grown into fratricide in his son. . . . Cain was the first man who let sin reign in him; he was "of the wicked one" (1 John 3:12). In him the seed of the woman had already become the seed of the serpent; and in his deed the real nature of the wicked one, as "a murder from the beginning," had come openly to light: so that already there had sprung up that contrast of two distinct seeds within the human race, which runs through the entire history of humanity.[28]

With this story the ongoing spiritual warfare between the two seeds, the two kingdoms, has begun. Spiritual warfare has broken out in full force. The rest of the Bible only traces what we have seen here and what Keil and Delitzsch have called "two distinct seeds within the human race, which runs through the entire history of humanity."

The seed of the serpent bruises the heel of the seed of the woman. Unrighteous Cain murders his righteous brother Abel (1 John 3:12). The world has never been at peace since.

31

The "Watchers" of Genesis 6 and the Call of Noah

A s soon as we begin to study Genesis 6:1–8, a long list of questions confronts us:

Who are the "sons of God" (vv. 2a,4b)?

Who are the "beautiful daughters of men" (v. 2)?

What was the nature of the relationship of the "sons of God" with the attractive "daughters of men" (vv. 2,4)?

Why does the Holy Spirit resist their relationship (v. 3a)?

What does it mean that man is "flesh" (v. 3)?

What is the meaning of man's "days" as 120 years (v. 3b)?

Who were the "Nephilim . . . on earth in those days" (v. 4a)?

What do the Nephilim have to do with the "sons of God," "the daughters of men," and the children born to them (v. 4b)?

Who were "the mighty men who were of old, men of renown" (v. 4b)?

What was their relationship with the Nephilim (v. 4a)?

What was their relationship with the sons of God (v. 4b)?

What was their relationship with the daughters of men (v. 4c)?

How is all of this related to the total depravity of the human race described in verse 5?

How do we understand God's becoming "sorry that He had made man on earth, and He was grieved in His heart" (v. 6)?

What did man do to become so morally and spiritually gross, perverse, and hopeless that God chooses to utterly destroy all men except Noah and his family?

Let me first answer two questions that have nothing to do with spiritual warfare. First, the 120 years probably refer to the time between the call of Noah and the destruction of the world by the Flood, not the lifespan of future generations. The fact is, Noah himself lived 950 years (Gen. 9:29). His sons and grandsons continued to live for hundreds of years—not just 120 years (Gen. 11:10f).

God Repents?

Second, God's repentance and sorrow for having made man is a problem to many. "What does Genesis 6:6 mean when it describes God as having 'repented'?" Walter Kaiser asks. He says this is especially difficult in light of Numbers 23:19, which states, "God is not a man that He should lie, nor a son of man, that He should repent."[1]

Kaiser answers by pointing out that in other passages "both affirmations are made about God. God repented and God never repents" (1 Sam. 15:11,29). Obviously two different things are in view. The answer seems to be at least threefold.

1. God's character is not changeable as is man's. He is always consistent with Himself. Thus, He never repents.
2. God is not a machine. He is a true person possessing perfect mind, emotions, and will. Therefore, He can become sad. He is always saddened by evil. Thus, He does repent.

    This is but another in a long series of anthropomorphisms in Scripture. God describes Himself or is described in human terms. We find this all through Genesis and the rest of the Bible.

3. While God is omniscient, He created moral, responsible beings who possess the power of choice. Therefore, in Scripture God is often described as responding in human-like actions to the choices His creatures make. This is what is occurring in the story before us.

Spiritual Warfare Questions

Most of the remaining questions relate to spiritual warfare. We will begin with what is probably the most controversial question: "Who are the sons of God spoken of in verse 2 who enter into evidently unrestrained sexual relationships with the daughters of men?"

Wenham says that

> 6:1–8 falls into two paragraphs—vv. 1–4, divine/human intermarriage ["divine" in the sense of supernatural or nonhuman, not as being God], and vv. 5–8, intimation of total destruction—which conclude the whole section 5:1—6:8, "the family history of Adam." Though 6:1–8 appears to have little connection with the preceding genealogy, it is in fact closely integrated with it.[2]

We will say little about the connection between Genesis 6:1–8 and Genesis 5:1–32.[3] All we need to know is that Genesis 6:1–8 is not an isolated story. It records the total degradation and apostasy of the family of Adam, leading to God's judgment of man in the Flood. What a contrast with 4:25–26!

The writer introduces 6:2 after making two important statements in 6:1: "When men began to multiply on the face of the land," and "daughters were born to them." What is he trying to tell us?

First, the statement "when men began to multiply on the face of land" points back to God's original command that man "multiply and fill the earth" (Gen. 1:28), and to man's relationship with "the land" (Gen. 2—4). In other words, there has been a vast population explosion. Men cover the face of the land. This is exactly what God wanted to occur (1:28).

Second, "and daughters were born to them." Daughters or women have only been mentioned in passing (4:17–26; 5:2–4,7f). The writer has been tracing the male descendants of the sons of Adam, not their daughters. Here the women are finally given their place.

Verse 2 hints that something has gone astray, however. Three things are specified. One, the sons of God see the beauty of "the daughters of men." In itself there is nothing wrong with that. Two, they take wives for themselves. At first this seems acceptable. Three, they take "whomever they choose." Here is the hint something is wrong.

They see! They choose! They take! That sounds like male exploitation of women. It also sounds like polygamy. It could imply rape or forced concubinage, with women being forcibly taken into harems. *What is happening here?*

WHO ARE THE SONS OF GOD?

The verse does not tell us. Thus it becomes one of the most problematic in Genesis. Difficulties begin with the first questions, "Who are the sons of God?" "Who are the daughters of men?" "What did the sons of God do to and with the daughters of men?"

With the first question, "Who are the sons of God?" we must begin. This is the most difficult question of all. G. H. Livingston asks, "To whom does this title refer—to pagan deities; to pagan rulers; to angels or to descendants of the lineage of Seth?"[4]

Pagan Deities?

Most commentators affirm that there are three main lines of interpretation offered by modern exegetes. Livingston, however, affirms a fourth, the view that the sons of God refer to pagan deities. We will look briefly at that view before examining the three more popular ones.

Livingston says that among pagans there "are mythological stories which go back to the Hurrians (ca. 1500 B.C.) which tell of nature deities who engage in illicit relations among themselves, and in some instances with humans. Is this passage a remnant of such a story?"[5] He next mentions that while "most Old Testament scholars affirm that erotic mythology is not a normal feature of the Old Testament, others claim that here we have an exception. The Old Testament writer altered an ancient myth and, with embarrassment, set it forth as a basis for God's judgment in the form of a flood."[6]

Livingston himself rejects this view, as do most commentators.

The three common views are: One, the sons of God are rulers, an early royal aristocracy; two, the sons of God are angels; and three, they are the godly line of Seth. The daughters of mankind are then seen as women from the ungodly line of Cain.[7]

Human Rulers?

We will look briefly at the first view. This view affirms that the sons of God were members of the leadership (princes and kings) among men. Their royal power soon corrupted them. They took into their harems sexually attractive women from all social classes.[8] Their sin would be polygamy, at best. While many—perhaps most—of the women consented because of the luxurious life they were brought into, others would have been compelled by their families to respond to their ruler's demands. Often the girls were probably too young to know the full implications of such a lifestyle. For some women this probably meant rape, forced concubinage, or kidnapping for sexual exploitation. In time they became as corrupt as their exploiters (v. 5).

Whatever be the case, like boastful Lamech before them, (4:19,23–24) and sexually addicted King Solomon after them (1 Kings 11:1–13), these kings sexually abused the women. While this is the position of Orthodox Judaism, Keil and Delitzsch say it can "be dismissed at once as not warranted by the usages of the language and as altogether unscriptural."[9]

Fallen Angels?

The main views held among the majority of Jewish commentators and Christian scholars until today, are the second and third views already mentioned. Let's examine each separately. First there is the view which affirms that the sons of God are fallen angels (watcher angels, as we will soon see) and the daughters of men are human women. This position does not mean that the women were raped or abducted by the fallen angels, say the commentators. Indeed, the opposite seems to be true. The women gave themselves to the angelic beings to be their sexual partners, probably with the full consent of their families. This makes the picture of human depravity so terrible that it justifies God's decision to destroy the human race (vv. 7,13).

Wenham accepts this position while admitting, "Given the variety of ways in which the 'sons of God' has been understood, it is hard to know which sense is correct—angelic, royal, or traditional Sethite."[10]

The Tradition of Watcher Angels

C. Fred Dickason—who does not hold to this view—says that the names given to angels in Scripture reflect either their nature or their function within the angelic kingdom. One name which reveals the ministry function of one group of angels is that of "watchers." Dickason says the name "denotes angels as supervisors and agents under God employed by Him in control of world government. They may be involved in decision making and execution of decrees that affect world affairs"[11] (Ps. 89:5–7; Dan. 4:13,17,23; 7:9–16; I Kings 22:19–23; Ezek. 1:4).

It is possible that this is the class of angels described here as "the sons of God" who entered into illicit sexual union with women. It is also possible they are the territorial spirits which are the subject of much research and power encounter evangelistic efforts today[12] (Dan. 10:13,20; Rev. 2–3; 17).

The name "angelic watcher" is found in Daniel 4:13,17,23 in Scripture. It was very common in Jewish apocalyptic and some non-canonical Christian literature. In Daniel 4 each is described as an "angelic watcher, a holy one." Together with God they form a heavenly council under God, involved in major decisions affecting the earth (v. 17). When they are described as being in motion, they are always seen "as descending from heaven" to earth (vv. 13,23). Thus they partly control the affairs of men on earth.[13]

Russell describes the activity of Watcher angels as God's divine council. Using ancient Middle Eastern tradition, not the Bible, he writes of an angelic rebellion under Semyaza who evidently was the leader of the Watchers. Russell believes Semyaza later becomes Satan or the Devil.

A large number of the Watchers in turn rebelled against the lordship of God under Semyaza—Satan, Russell affirms. Their primary act in declaring their independence of Yahweh was to descend to earth, probably in human form, to lust after mortal women.

They take as sexual partners all the women they want. Their children become demigods, evil creatures, with great strength and supernatural abilities. This leads to the degradation of the human race. The Watchers, in turn, are punished by God, and the human race comes under God's judgment in the Flood, Russell says.[14] Thus Russell does an excellent overview of the fall of Satan and his angels. His views lend support for the view that angelic-sexual exploitation of women is indicated in Genesis 6.

As already mentioned, Wenham also holds to the angelic view of Genesis 6:1–4.[15] He says that modern scholars who accept this view advance various reasons for supporting it.

First, elsewhere in the Old Testament (Ps. 29:1; Job 1:6) "sons of God" refers to heavenly, godlike angelic creatures. Second, in 6:1–4 the contrast is between "the sons of gods" on the one hand and "the daughters of man" on the other, not between one group of the sons of men versus another group of the daughters of men.

The alternative interpretations presuppose that what Genesis 6 really meant was that "the sons of some men" married "the daughters of other men." The phrase "sons of God," is, to say the least, an obscure way of expressing such an idea.

It is made the more implausible by 6:1 where "man" refers to all humanity. Also, "it is natural to assume that in verse 2 'daughters of man' has an equally broad reference, not a specific section of the human race." Finally, he points out that "in Ugaritic literature 'sons of God' refers to members of the divine pantheon, and it is likely that Genesis is using the phrase in a similar sense."[16]

Wenham then makes an important observation about the nature of the sexual sins involved.[17]

One must look behind the specific terms used to discover the reason for the condemnation in this case. . . . Here the fault of the daughters of man lies presumably in their consenting to intercourse with 'the sons of the gods.' . . . The girls' fathers would also have been implicated, since, if there was no rape or seduction, their approval to these matches would have been required. The obvious avoidance of any terms suggesting lack of consent makes the girls and their parents culpable, the more so when the previous chapter has demonstrated that mankind was breeding very successfully on its own.

Wenham further supports the angelic view by saying, "This story may also be . . . a polemic against the fertility cults which often included sacred marriages between the gods and men." He points out the Old Testament prohibition against mixed crops, mixed clothing, and crossbreeding of species and intermarriage with non-Israelites. Therefore "unions between 'sons of the gods and human women' would be especially odious."[18]

The Line of Seth?

The third position is that "the sons of God" refer to the godly line of Seth. "The daughters of men" would then refer to the apostate line of Cain. The sin would be the breakdown of the godly line by intercourse with the godless daughters of Cain.

Can the Question Be Answered?

Wenham, an English scholar, says this view, "for a long time the preferred Christian exegesis, again because it avoided the suggestion of carnal intercourse with angels, has few advocates today."[19] Evidently this traditional view is not very popular among evangelical scholars in Great Britain, but it is in the U.S.A. In fact, it is probably still "the preferred Christian exegesis" in the United States and Canada, as well as other parts of the world where American missionaries have labored.[20]

If these writers do not hold strongly to the Sethite view, they take a neutral position, presenting both the angelic and the Sethite views, but not stating a preference between the two.[21] I find myself among their number. I am not certain which is the better view. I like Kidner's position that "the main point of this cryptic passage is that a new age has been reached in the progress of evil, with God's bounds overstepped in yet another realm."[22] He then outlines the support for both the angelic and the line of Seth views.[23]

If the [angelic] view defies the normalities of experience, the [Sethite] defies those of language, for while the Old Testament can declare God's people to be His sons, the normal meaning of the actual term "sons of God" is "angels," and nothing has prepared the reader to assume that "men" now means Cainites only.

Kidner ties the angelic view to the New Testament record.[24]

Possible New Testament support for "angels" may be seen in 1 Peter 3:19, 20; also in 2 Peter 2:4–6, where the fallen angels, the Flood, and the doom of Sodom form a series that could be based on Genesis, and in Jude 6, where the angels' offense is that they "left their proper habitation." The craving of demons for a body, . . . offers at least some parallel to this hunger for sexual experience. . . . More important than the detail of this episode is its indication that man is beyond self-help, whether the Sethites have betrayed their calling, or demonic powers have gained a stranglehold.

This is excellent insight by Kidner. While we have great difficulty understanding this passage, evidently the original recipients of Genesis did not. What they understood by verses 1–2 unfortunately has not been passed on to us. Our understanding of Genesis as a book, which is written to a people who knew fallen spiritual beings could take on human bodies to engage in illicit sexual relationships with human beings, would incline me towards the view of the sons of God as fallen angelic beings. My objections to this view, however, are all but insurmountable to me because of my research, my counseling with demonized people, and my experience with them in dealing with sexual demons.

Sexual Demons

Demons which specialize in having sex with human beings, both male and female, are very common. They have been known and written about for centuries. They are called *incubi* and *succubai*. The former take on the male sexual role and the latter the female. While incubi and succubai spirits do engage in full sexual relationships with humans, they do not produce sperm, and are thus incapable of procreating children and producing a race of beings half demon and half human.

Russell mentions this problem. He says, referring to the view of the theologians of the Middle Ages who dealt with this phenomena: "Though having no body himself, the devil may assume a body in which he can (for example) have sexual intercourse, though neither as incubus nor succubus can he engender offspring."[25] I agree with Russell at this point. To me this makes the angelic view much more improbable than the Sethite view, in spite of difficulties with the latter.

While I am strongly inclined towards the Sethite position and away from the fallen angel view, like Wenham, I have difficulty with its way of interpreting both "the sons of God" and "the daughters of men." I also have difficulty believing the original recipients of the book would get that position from the text alone. Thus, we are probably left with an unresolvable question.

A New Age in the Progress of Evil

I believe Kidner is right when he states, "with this cryptic passage a new age has been reached in the progress of evil," and "more important than the detail of this episode is its indication that man is beyond self-help, whether the Sethites have betrayed their calling, or demonic powers have gained a stranglehold."[26]

I would like to add to Kidner's excellent observations. Not only is man "beyond self-help," but he has become so depraved that he is beyond divine help. He is now so totally demonized (my view) and so given over to "the lust of the flesh and the lust of the eyes and the boastful pride of life" (1 John 2:16), that he is beyond hope of ever responding to the striving of God's Spirit (6:3,5–7). Like Ephraim of a yet future day, he is totally "joined to idols" (Hos. 4:17). Thus, God declares in verse 3, to paraphrase Hosea 4:17b, "He is beyond help, let him alone."

Human civilization in Noah's day reached a state of total depravity never known before and never known since. All men in all cultures have become like the future cities of Sodom and Gomorrah. God cannot find even ten righteous men to cause him to hold back the total, universal destruction of the human race. He found only eight in Noah's family: Noah, his wife, three sons, and three daughters-in-law (Gen. 7:1,7).

Judged on the basis of upcoming studies in this book on how demons latch onto sin areas in human lives, a race of men—including men, women, and their victimized children—like those described in Genesis 6 would be universally demonized. The one joyful exception is Noah and his family.

Now we must deal with three other related matters. First, the immediate effect of the unlawful cohabitation described in verses 1–2 upon God Himself (v. 3); the fruit of the unnatural cohabitation, whatever it was (v. 4); and, the long-range effect of all the evil described in verses 1–4 upon a holy and righteous God (vv. 5–8).

The Immediate Effect on God

We begin with the immediate effect upon God of the disgusting promiscuous and unnatural cohabitation described in verses 1–2. First, God says, "My Spirit shall not strive with man forever" or, "shall not remain in man forever," the literal translation.[27]

While the exact meaning of the verse may be difficult to discover, the general meaning is not, and that should be good enough for all of us. Hamilton observes that

> the word about the divine displeasure comes between the cohabitation scene (v. 2) and the reference to the children produced by the union (v. 4). By placing the verse where it is, the author is making the point that this forbidden union itself is offensive to Yahweh, rather than the fact that such a union produced (hybrid) offspring.[28]

In other words, the offense is so horrendous it is unforgivable. God will withdraw His Spirit from His former relationship to humanity. Keil and Delitzsch interpret God as saying, "My Spirit shall not rule in men forever; in their wandering they are flesh."[29]

Calvin's notes are very helpful at this point.

> Moses . . . introduces God Himself as the speaker. For there is greater weight in the declaration when pronounced by God's own mouth, that the wickedness of men was too deplorable to leave any apparent hope of remedy, and that therefore there was no reason why he should spare them.

Calvin continues, saying that "God had not been impelled by the heat of His anger into precipitation, nor had been more severe than was right; but was almost compelled, by necessity, utterly to destroy the whole world, except one single family."[30]

Verse 3b gives the crucial rationale behind the statement of God's "giving up" on the existing race of men, including the line of Seth (except Noah's family). The verse says, ". . . because he also is flesh." This is really an amazing statement. It almost anticipates the later New Testament usage of the word "flesh" (*sarx* in Greek) in a moral—or better—immoral sense.

Wenham says, "Flesh is one of the most significant anthropological terms in the Old Testament. Its basic meaning is 'flesh,' 'body.' Sometimes 'flesh' refers to man's moral weakness and propensity to sin" (cf. Gen. 6:12).[31] This is New Testament language, but not totally unknown in the Old Testament, Hamilton states.[32]

Thus, in God's use of "flesh" here we have a preview of the highly developed New Testament use of flesh. We now know from the New Testament's advanced teachings that if men fail to maintain the flesh crucified with Christ, they open the doors of their lives to demonic entrapment (1 Cor. 7:5; Eph. 4:27; 1 Tim. 3:6–7; 4:1; 5:14–15). This, on a worldwide scale, is what happened in Genesis 6. The result was the total demonic bondage of the race to evil spirits. The final result was the judgment of the Flood (6:13—Gen. 9). This to me is the only possible interpretation of this unique story of angelic-human evil.

The Identity of the "Nephilim"

The next subject we must consider as it relates to the spiritual warfare motif of Genesis 6 is the reference to "the Nephilim" and "the mighty men who were of old, men of renown" (v. 4). These are somehow related to the events of verses 1–2 as the same sin of the sons of God with the daughters of men is retold in the middle of verse 4. Their lives and those of the sons of God and daughters of men are somehow related.

The best explanation to the relationships involved seems to be the simplest. While the sins of the sons of God and the daughters of men were occurring, other disturbing events were taking place on earth at the same time. One, the Nephilim were then on earth. Two, "mighty men who were of old, men of renown" were also making their impact felt on the world.

Who were the Nephilim? One thing is certain. They were not the progeny of fallen angels and mortal women—half demon and half human. While a popular view, it is totally without biblical support. The proof is that the Nephilim appeared again hundreds of years after the Flood in Numbers 13:33. Yet, the Nephilim on earth in Genesis 6 were all destroyed in the Flood. Thus, they must have been a class or type of human being who could emerge again any time after the Flood. That is exactly what occurred.[33]

Hamilton says the word "Nephilim" means "fallen ones."[34] Leupold says it means "to fall apart, to attack,"; i.e., "robbers, attackers or bandits who struck fear into the heart of men."[35] He quotes Luther as saying they were "tyrants" who were "on the earth already at the time when the Sethites commingled with the Cainites," but also that they continued after that sad confusion.[36]

Leupold then connects verse 4a with the rest of verse 4. He says that while the Nephilim were on the earth the line of Seth intermingled with the line of Cain. Finally, he says, the mighty men were these Nephilim. In their own eyes they were "the heroes of antiquity, or the men of renown (Heb. men of the name)." They scared everyone else to death, however. "They achieved a reputation the world over by violence, but a reputation better deserving of the term notoriety. The world certainly did not in those days, even as it does not now, esteem godly men highly. Only the wicked were renowned or had a name."[37]

Finally they are identical with the "giants" who frequently appear in the biblical record, W. B. Wallis says.[38]

Everything in verses 1–4 is meant to be the rationale for what follows in verses 5–8 and beyond: God's total displeasure with the entire human race because of their almost undescribable perversity and His decision to destroy all humanity except Noah and his family.

Verse 5 reveals what God saw. Verse 6 reveals how He "felt" about what He saw. Verse 7 reveals His decision to take action in light of what He both saw and felt. Verse 8 reveals God's recognition that there was one man and his family whom he could behold with favor.

Thus, on carrying out his decision of verse 7, God would spare this man and begin anew with him. Here was a man worthy of becoming the second father of the race made in God's image and likeness. Here was the new "Adam." His name was Noah.

Major Spiritual Warfare Lessons From Genesis 6:1–8

Regardless of what position one takes concerning the more difficult aspect of this story (we have outlined the major ones, but not all the problems commentators have with this passage), the major spiritual warfare lessons are clear. One, since the Fall "every intent of the thoughts of (man's) heart was only evil continually," the result is "the wickedness of man was great on the earth" (v. 5). Humanity is now capable of sin in any form (Gal. 5:19–21). Humanity is involved in a sin war.

Two, this war is a multidimensional sin war. Man battles with his flesh (v. 3). He battles with the world (vv. 1–7). He battles with evil supernaturalism (vv. 1–4 in light of 4:7). He totally loses this multidimensional sin war.

The world was now a world of "Cains" (4:4 with 6:1–7). Like Cain, it had become "of the evil one" (1 John 3:12). Without doubt, this was the most demonized generation of human beings ever to live on earth. Thus God must totally destroy them and begin again with the one man who, like Seth whose descendant he was, "called upon the name of the LORD" (4:26).

One man had learned to put to death the passions of his flesh. One man had learned to resist victoriously the external stimulus of perhaps the most wicked world system ever to exist on this earth. One man had learned to "resist the devil" and see him flee.

Most important of all, he helped his wife and three sons to do the same. His sons, in turn, found young women not yet totally depraved by evil. They led them to know Yahweh as their Lord and formed God-fearing ideal homes.

Nothing is said about Noah's sons having borne children before the Flood. It is possible that they did, however. Since small children are not held responsible for sin even though they possess a sin nature (Rom. 4:15; 5:13), they would not be counted as unjust, especially since they were raised in such a God-fearing family. Thus, it can be affirmed no matter how corrupt is the environment in which we are forced to live, God has given to all of us the necessary weapons of our warfare in order to walk in victory (2 Cor. 10:3–5; Eph. 6:10–20; 1 Pet. 5:8–11).

32

Spiritual Warfare From the Flood to the Call of Abraham

T he rationale behind God's drastic decision to destroy "all flesh" (Gen. 6:13) is summed up in verse 5:

> Then the Lord saw that the wickedness of man was great on the earth, and that every intent of the thoughts of his heart was only evil continually.

The outward actions resulting from the evil mindset of the heart of pre-Flood humanity are revealed in six graphic statements in Genesis 6, either supplied by the writer or spoken by God Himself.

1. Illicit sexual activities prevailed (vv. 1–2).

No matter which of the three interpretations of "the sons of God" and "the daughters of men" one may choose, illicit sexuality is the focus of these two verses. In time this sexual exploitation corrupted the women and eventually their offspring. When the sexual revolution had become worldwide, the full description of the total perversity of the age was revealed.

2. The wickedness of man was great on the earth (v. 5a).

3. "Every intent of the thoughts of his heart was only evil continually" (v. 5b).

4. "The earth was corrupt in the sight of God" (6:11a,12). Corruption is the dominant word mentioned three times in these two verses.

5. "The earth was filled with violence" (6:11b,13b).

Violence and general wickedness were evidently the results of the total corruption of humanity. The most repulsive form of this violence and corruption seems to have been sexual. The selfish exploitation of women seems supported by two other statements.

First, though all males followed these evil sexual practices, the Nephilim seem, in time, to have become initiators of this unrestrained sexual evil.[1] Second, these mighty men of renown were known not for their goodness, but rather for their evil. As Calvin says, "The giants, then, had a prior origin; but afterwards those who were born of promiscuous marriages imitated their example."[2] Evil reproduced itself in more evil. Children followed the licentious behavior of their parents until all humanity, except Noah and his family, were beyond hope of repentance.

It is this world which God sees as totally worthless and unredeemable. God then declares His purpose to annihilate mankind totally from the face of the earth, with the exception of Noah and his family (6:13,17). The Flood soon follows (6:14—5:22).

Chapter 9 records the Noahic Covenant. Chapter 10 lists the lineage of Noah and his three sons. We will not give attention to these two chapters. We will, however, return to chapter 10 in a moment. Chapter 11 records the beginning of the second phase of corruption, which engulfs the human race after the Fall—the events surrounding the Tower of Babel, or Babylon (11:9).

THE TOWER OF BABEL

The Tower of Babel, indeed Babylon itself, takes us right into the arena of terrible spiritual warfare. Both the Tower and the city are symbols of religious humanism, idolatry, polytheism, and defiance of God. Babylon had been mentioned in 10:10. The writer now explains the origin of the name—confusion (11:9) as he describes the efforts of humanity to defy God and to deify themselves.

It helps us to follow the chronological flow of the early chapters of Genesis to know something about the time which elapsed between the Flood and Babel. Calvin believes it was about 100 years.[3] He arrives at this conclusion by computing the years recorded in Genesis 10. (Wenham says over 300 years.)

This means that Noah and his three sons were alive during the events described in Genesis 11:1–9 if there are not large gaps in the genealogies listed in chapter 10.[4] They were probably not part of the rebellious group mentioned in chapter 11, however. This group had journeyed east to Shinar (11:2), that is, to Babylon.[5]

Nimrod

Genesis 10 gives us the origin of Babylon in one man called Nimrod. His personal character became the character of the nations of that area, even until today—Iran and Iraq. Genesis 10:8–12 talks of him as "Nimrod . . . a mighty one on the earth" (v. 8). He is one of the most famous but enigmatic men named in the Old Testament. Not only was he called a mighty hunter but also the great city builder who built Babylon and Nineveh (vv. 10–11). He was one remarkable personage!

Because of the seeming impossibility that one man could accomplish all that is listed here, some suggest Nimrod is the expression of a series of god-kings in this area who defied the Lord. His name would support this conjecture. It means "we shall rebel."[6]

Israel's relationship with Mesopotamia, Assyria, Canaan, and Egypt formed the most important socio-cultural and religious relationships in her entire history in the Old Testament. Mesopotamia in general and Babylonia in particular are synonymous in the Old Testament with human culture separated from the true God, founded upon human pride, world domination, polytheism, henotheism, demonism, and animism.[7]

For this reason I believe the scholars who take a more negative view of Nimrod and his exploits are correct. He built Babylonia and Assyria, Israel's most horrendous persecutors in later days. He established the idolatrous culture out of which God found it necessary to call Abraham in order to build His elect people, Israel.

Two more things are important about Nimrod. He is the man of rebellion of Genesis 10—11. He becomes a new Cain, a murderer and rebel against God. As "a mighty one upon the earth," he became the "mighty hunter." What he hunted were not animals, but men.[8]

Leupold says that the word about his being a mighty hunter by itself might be taken to refer to hunting animals were it not for the phrase "in the sight of Yahweh . . ." He says, "man's little hunting exploits are hardly sufficient to rouse the wonder and admiration of the Almighty. Besides, in this case the name of Yahweh is used, i.e., the God of mercy and covenant."[9]

Thus Leupold states that since Nimrod's exploits in conquering peoples and building two powerful anti-God and anti-Israel empires is the focal point of his hunting exploits, it is the hunting of men which is in question. He is an Old Testament antichrist figure.

Calvin says Moses describes him as "a furious man—he violently seized his prey—he approximated to beasts rather than to men. The expression 'Before the Lord,' seems to me to declare that Nimrod attempted to raise himself above the order of men." He became the prototype of later god-kings.[10] This is important to the lifestyle picture Joshua later gives of the fathers of the nation of Israel.

Nimrod is described as the builder of Babel (10:10). This leads to the story of the Tower of Babel (11:1f). Wenham says that Babel was the manifestation of man's "desire to displace God from heaven, to make a name for one's self rather than allow God to do this."[11]

The Sin of Babel

Again this supports our spiritual warfare interpretation of the sin of Babel leading to God's judgment. Satan, "the god of this world," building on the corrupt flesh of man (his pride) and his worldly ambitions, was the spirit behind the Tower of Babel. Wenham says, "Throughout Scripture Babylon is seen as the embodiment of human pride and godlessness that must attract the judgement of almighty God."[12] It is also the symbol of the rejection of the true God and the creation of god systems which are created by men to meet their own selfish wants.

Therefore the story before us in Chapter 11:1–9 is not encouraging. While those who journeyed east to Shinar did not constitute all of humanity, the judgment against Babel seems also to have been against all humanity. Human languages were confused. They were scattered "abroad over the face of the whole earth" (11:9). It was from descendants of this group that God called Abraham and formed the elect nation of Israel.

One thing is certain, however, using this story as representative of the spiritual and moral conditions of humanity in general, things were bad. Forgotten were the lessons humanity should have learned from the judgment of God against man's sinfulness in the Deluge. Unfortunately, though God gave the human race a new beginning with Noah, the human heart was still the same. The warfare with the flesh and the world and the Devil continued. As man became more and more preoccupied with himself and negligent of God, the old sin patterns soon surfaced again.

Wenham wisely comments that "the tower of Babel story is the last great judgment that befell mankind in primeval times. Its place and function in Genesis 1—11 may be compared to the fall of man in Genesis 3 and the sons of God episode in Genesis 6:1–4, both of which triggered divine judgments of great and enduring consequences." The same type of divine judgment occurs in this story also.[13]

The social system established in Babylon is revealed in verses 3–4. It was thoroughly humanistic. They were not interested in God's name, but in their name.[14] As Calvin remarks:[15] "To erect a citadel was not in itself so great a crime; but to raise an eternal monument to themselves, which might endure throughout all ages, was a proof of headstrong pride, joined with contempt of God . . . they wage war with God."

"They wage war with God." They devised a social structure—their world—at war with God. This is both the flesh and the world at war with the law of God written on human hearts. As we will soon see, it also had demonic overtones.

Hamilton says the Tower was the predecessor of the Mesopotamian *ziqqurat* or ziggurat. He says it is

a temple tower. Toward the end of the last century, the discovery of Esagila, the great temple of Marduk in Babylon, suggested this particular edifice as the source behind the biblical narrative. The ziggurat of this temple was called *E-temen-an-ki*, "house of the foundations of heaven and earth." Rising 300 feet above ground, with two sanctuaries in it, it was believed to have been built by the gods. This background makes the assertion of 11:5 very interesting: "it was built by earthlings."[16]

M. J. A. Horsnell calls the Tower of Babel and the ziggurat "major temple complexes. Others have seen it as the throne of the deity (cf. Isa. 14:13)."[17]

Thus there is little doubt that the Tower had a religious as well as a human function. Hamilton says the Tower was a temple tower. It was not only an expression of man's pride (the flesh) with the purpose of gaining the esteem of other cultures (the world). It was also dedicated to foreign gods (evil supernaturalism). If so, Genesis 11 is a passage dealing with spiritual warfare from the perspective of multidimensional sin.

While there is nothing in the account which speaks of foreign gods, building the Tower was man's attempt to make himself God or equal to God, Hamilton, Wenham, and Calvin affirm. Hamilton quotes P. C. Calderone as saying that "the builders of the tower of Babel (Gen. 11:4) . . . in some way are rebelling against God and trying to be like Him."[18]

Building the Tower was a repetition of humans deceived by Satan's first great lie (Gen. 3:5). While Satan's tactics might change, his goal is always the same: to lead humanity to rebel against the lordship of God and to serve Satan by seeing himself as his own god or by serving false gods.

The Call of Abraham

The next great incident in Genesis is the call of Abraham (12:1–3). God called him out of the land of the Chaldeans, i.e., Mesopotamia (11:28). Thus from the very heart of the land of idolatry and polytheism, God begins again. He calls one man—probably an idolater—Abraham (Josh. 24:2) to Himself (Gen. 11:26—12:3).

It is not our purpose to make a study of the life and family of Abraham. We must look at God's purpose in calling him, however. Genesis 12:1–3 incorporates at least four major elements into Abraham's divine call:
1. a call to a new land (v. 1);
2. a call to be the father of a great nation (v. 2);
3. a call to great blessings from God Himself (v. 2);
4. a call to be a blessing to "all the families of the earth" (v. 2b–3).

We know the land was the land of Palestine, or Canaan. The great nation was the nation of Israel. The blessing of God was to be His covenants with Abraham and His nation, Israel. The blessing Abraham was to be to "all the families of the earth" was God Himself manifested through Israel to all humanity. All, of course, would ultimately focus on the Messiah, the Son of God, our Lord and Savior.

To accomplish this, God must first call Abraham out of the pit of idolatry and polytheism in which he was involved (Gen. 11:26; Josh. 24:2–3). Hamilton comments on Genesis 11:27–32, noting that some of the names of Abraham's family members are associated with moon worship.[19]

The possible connection of Terah (Heb. *terah*) with the word *Yareah*, moon and *yerah*, lunar month, if substantiated, would suggest that Abram's family and ancestors were worshipers of the moon. One suggestion is that Terah means *Ter*, i.e., the divine brother or protector (Heb. *'ah*), *ter* being a dialectal variant of *shr*, a South Arabic term for the moon. *Sarai*, Sarah, is the equivalent of *sarratu*, queen, an Akkadian translation of a Sumerian name for Ningal, the female partner of the moon-god Sin. Milcah is the same name as the goddess Malkatu, the daughter of Sin.

Laban (Heb. *laban*) means white, and *lebana*, the white one, is a poetic term for the full moon. In addition, both Ur and Haran were thriving centers of moon worship; thus it is probable that the theological milieu in which Abram lived for a good bit of his life was one in which the cult focused its adoration on moon worship.

Next, God must strengthen Abraham to be able to live in the land of Canaan, a land also totally engaged in idolatry and polytheism. In God's plan was a 400-year exile for Abraham's descendants in the land of Egypt (Gen. 15:13–16). His descendants would then take the land, and through their godly lifestyle all the nations would come to know the one true God.

The rest of the Old Testament is the story of that plan in progress. It is often a sad story of failure upon failure in following Yahweh, the true God. Israel would have only one major battle during the entire Old Testament period. It was the battle with the other gods, i.e., the "no-gods" (Gal. 4:8; Eph. 2:12).

During their lifetime, the great patriarchs Abraham and Isaac and their families lived in the midst of the polytheism and idolatry of Canaan but remained true to God. To a limited extent, so did troublesome Jacob. During and after the sojourn in Egypt Israel went the opposite direction, however. Even after the Exodus, the nation continued to serve the gods of their fathers—the gods of Mesopotamia. They also continued to serve the gods of Egypt. Above all, they went after the gods of Canaan right up to the time of the Babylonian exile. This was Israel's major area of spiritual warfare. It was a war that Israel continually lost (Josh. 24; Judg. 2–21; 1, 2 Kings).

THE EXODUS

The Exodus story found in Exodus 3—12 records the greatest series of power encounters in all the Old Testament. As A. A. MacRae says,[20] Exodus describes

one of the few periods in biblical history when God chose to work a substantial number of miracles . . . the purpose of a miracle is to show that a greater than human power, namely the power of God, is involved, and to establish God's authority in the presence of doubt or apostasy.

There are three groups of miracles in Exodus. By *miracles* I mean demonstrations of God's power in either working with forces He had already established in His universe or directly intervening and rearranging the course of nature. The biblical words for miracles refer to either process. Both are miracles because God is directly involved, using them as signs of His presence.

The first are pre-Exodus miracles. They occur with Moses, starting with the burning bush and continuing until the beginning of the contest with Pharaoh. The second are the ten plagues, and the third are miracles God performed in the wilderness journey.

Exodus Power Encounters

Without doubt, Exodus records the greatest series of miracles in any forty-year period of history in all of Scripture. As we will see in this study, the miracles, which become power encounters with the gods of Egypt, are the most spectacular in all of Scripture.

First, the entire story from Exodus 3—12 must be seen as an encounter, a contest, between God and the gods of Egypt. This is the way God himself describes the plagues against Egypt in Exodus 12:12: "For I will go through the land of Egypt on that night, and will strike down all the first-born in the land of Egypt, both man and beast; and against all the gods of Egypt I will execute judgments—I am the LORD."

This is how Moses understood the whole Exodus story as he declared in his great hymn of praise which he evidently taught to the sons of Israel in Exodus 15. He says, "Who is like Thee among the gods, O LORD? Who is like Thee, majestic in holiness, awesome in praises, working wonders?" (v. 11).

When he reported the story of the Exodus to his father-in-law, Jethro, the priest of Midian, what was Jethro's response? Exodus 18:9,11 tells us. "And Jethro rejoiced over all the goodness which the LORD had done to Israel, in delivering them from the hand of the Egyptians. . . . 'Now I know that the LORD is greater than all the gods; indeed, it was proven when they dealt proudly against the people.'"

So Moses, Jethro, and God Himself saw the entire Exodus story as a series of power encounters by which God made fools of the gods of Egypt. Even the magicians of Egypt, in the midst of the contest, cried out to hard-hearted Pharaoh, "this is the finger of God" (Exod. 8:19).

God hit Egypt with a series of ten plagues, power demonstrations on God's part. All struck directly at the nature gods of Egypt. They had one overall, primary purpose: to cause Egypt, Pharaoh, and Israel as well, to know that "the Lord, He is God" (6:1–8; 7:5,17; 8:10,19; 9:14,29; 10:1–2; 14:17–18; 15:1–18). The last one, the death of the firstborn, had the additional purpose of bringing God's direct judgment upon Egypt and its proud demi-god leader, the Pharaoh.

When Moses was first commissioned by God to go to Egypt and bring out his people, God told him that Pharaoh would not listen (Exod. 3:19), but God would stretch out His hand with all His miracles, which He would do (Exod. 3:20).

Just before Moses left for Egypt he received his first indication that the job would not be easy. God told Moses:

> When you go back to Egypt see that you perform before Pharaoh all the wonders which I have put in your power; but I will harden his heart so that he will not let the people go.

> Then you shall say to Pharaoh, "Thus says the LORD, 'Israel is My son, My first-born. So I said to you, "Let My son go, that he may serve Me;" but you have refused to let him go. Behold, I will kill your son, your first-born.'" (Exod. 4:21–23)

God, then, is giving Moses an overview of the slow process of the contest. He also says it will not be over until God has killed Pharaoh's firstborn son. Certainly, God had set out to punish this proud, idolatrous, demonized nation. He had also determined to strike down Egypt's god-king.

With Aaron as his prophet, Moses first goes to the Hebrews in bondage. Exodus 4:30–31 records: "and Aaron spoke all the words which the LORD had spoken to Moses. He then performed the signs in the sight of the people. So the people believed; and when they heard that the LORD was concerned about the sons of Israel and that He had seen their affliction, then they bowed low and worshiped."

The signs were certainly the same signs indicated by God in 4:1–9, the rod turning into a serpent; the hand which became "leprous like snow" then was restored again "like the rest of his flesh"; water from the Nile turning to blood as it was poured out upon the dry ground.

While not recorded in the early chapters of Exodus, it is later recorded that during the Egyptian bondage the Jews began to worship the gods of Egypt. Nevertheless, they evidently kept their historic faith alive from generation to generation (4:5, 31). God, however, had lost His power in their eyes. He was a God with less power than the power gods of Egypt. To bring them back to the true God, historic theology alone was worthless. They needed God to demonstrate that His power was greater than the power of all the gods of Egypt. On seeing the power demonstrations, the people believed (v. 31a). Then when they heard "the theology" after the demonstrations of power, "they bowed low and worshipped" (v. 31b), perhaps for the first time in hundreds of years.

Moses' first request for permission from Pharaoh to let Israel go was a total failure (5:1ff). Moses felt defeated. He wished he had never "volunteered" (Exod. 3:10—4:17) for the job (4:10–13). This is exactly what God wanted to happen, however (4:21).

Anatomy of a Power Encounter

The power demonstrations began with the next contact between Moses, Aaron, and Pharaoh (6:1f). God set the stage when He said, "Now you shall see what I will do to Pharaoh; for under compulsion he shall let them go, and under compulsion he shall drive them out of his land" (v. 1).

Pharaoh, without knowing it, had already established the challenge, an essential part of any true power encounter. He had mockingly declared, "Who is the LORD that I should obey His voice to let Israel go? I do not know the LORD, and besides, I will not let Israel go" (5:2). God answers Pharaoh by saying, to paraphrase, "Now you are going to find out just who I am when you see what I will do to you and to all of Egypt. You will become so terrified of Me, you will drive Israel out of the land" (6:1).

We cannot examine in detail each of the ten plagues. I have listed them on the chart below.

Figure 32.1[21]
The Plagues of the Exodus

	Plague No.	Plague	Plague No.	Plague	Plague No.	Plague	Structure
First Set	1	blood	4	flies	7	hail	Moses appears before Pharaoh in the morning at the river
Second Set	2	frogs	5	animal pestilence	8	locusts	Moses "comes before" Pharaoh
Third Set	3	gnats	6	boils	9	darkness	Moses does not appear but uses only a symbolic gesture

(F. W. Bush, *ISBE* 3:879.)

From the beginning God had warned Moses, "I know that the King of Egypt will not permit you to go, except under compulsion" (3:19). God repeats this word after Moses' first "failure" (6:1).

Next we have God's promise-threat concerning Pharaoh, "I will harden his heart so that he will not let the people go" (4:21).[22] This, too, was spoken before Moses and Aaron even arrived in Egypt. Exodus repeatedly records that Pharaoh "hardened his heart" (8:15) or, simply, that his "heart was hardened" (7:13).

Thus, after Moses' failure in 5:1ff, God tells his servant the battle plan he is following. In doing so, he clearly states "But I will harden Pharaoh's heart that I may multiply My signs and My wonders in the land of Egypt" (7:3). This all fits into his dual purpose of declaring to all that "I am the LORD" (6:29) and judging Egypt and its gods (12:12).

God himself issued the power challenge to the gods of Egypt. While Pharaoh responded with his own challenge (5:2), God initiated it. He was going to judge "the gods of Egypt" (12:12). In doing so, he allowed the magicians to gain certain advantages at first. They matched power with power and miracle with miracle with Moses and Aaron. They made their rods become serpents also (7:11); they turned water into blood (7:22), and had frogs come up on the land of Egypt just as did Moses and Aaron (8:7).

Then, they totally failed, beginning with the plague of insects (8:18–19). They tried once more with the plague of boils. Again they failed (9:11). With this they gave up. They then joined Moses' and Aaron's "team," begging hard-hearted Pharaoh that he let Israel go (8:18–19; 10:7f).

This is the only record of a power encounter in all of Scripture where the servants of the no-gods are allowed to duplicate the power demonstrations of the servants of God for a period of time. While in the long run it only served to intensify the final power demonstrations and to magnify the absolute power of God Almighty, it must have been unnerving to Moses and Aaron.

The story does raise very controversial questions about the power of Satan and his demons to perform creative miracles. I leave this matter to the experts. God allows evil supernaturalism to work with the existing powers of nature and to manipulate them towards their evil and deceptive purposes. Thus they can cause storms, illnesses, and all kinds of damage, as the Scriptures clearly reveal. In the end time, the Antichrist will evidently possess greater miraculous powers than ever witnessed before on the part of evil supernaturalism. He will come "in accord with the activity of Satan, with all power and signs and false wonders, and with all the deception of wickedness" (2 Thess. 2:9–10), similar to the encounter told me by my friend Dr. Petros Octavianus of Indonesia.

A Modern Power Encounter

Dr. Octavianus was challenged to a power encounter by a pagan power worker, one of the most famous in all of Indonesia.

Dr. Octavianus told me he never lightly responds to serious challenges to power demonstrations like this one. Power encounter is part of his ministry, working as he does with folk Muslims as animistic as they are Muslim. But in power encounters to which the public is to be invited, he is very cautious. He seeks the mind of God before giving his answer. God told him, he said, to proceed.

When the day of the public power encounter arrived, the demonized power man took the initiative. Before hundreds of people he singled out a nearby dog. He said, "To show you the power of my gods I will take the life of that dog without touching him. Can your God do that?" Pointing at the dog he gave a command and the animal dropped dead in its tracks. The multitude was astonished. Without hesitating, Dr. Octavianus walked right up to the power worker and pointing at him, said, "My God does not arbitrarily take life. He came to give life. He wants to give life to you also. In the name of the Lord Jesus Christ I take away all of your demonic power."

Instantly the magician fell to the ground, unconscious. The multitude thought he was dead. Dr. Octavianus knelt down beside the lifeless form of the power worker and touched his head. Instantly he revived. Right there on the ground he came to Christ. Later, long golden needles had to be removed from his legs. These were the physical power amulets of his demons. Embedded below the surface of the skin, they emerged miraculously on their own through prayer.[23]

We are all familiar with the rest of the Exodus story. By the power of God, God took His elect people out of Egyptian bondage. The elect nation of Israel was born on that day.[24]

THE CONTINUING ENCOUNTERS WITH THE "NO-GODS"

The next major spiritual warfare sections of the Old Testament all unite under one common theme. It is an area of warfare that became the greatest problem Israel faced in all of her history, the encounter with the no-gods of the pagan nations surrounding Israel after Israel's entrance into the Promised Land.

Preparation Through Joshua

In Joshua 24, God's man, Joshua, knows he will soon die and leave the fickle nation he has led since the death of Moses. He knows these people too well. He knows they are still sensual, worldly, and wide open to religious spirits which deceive their followers by first meeting most of their selfish physical and emotional needs.

Joshua wants to bring them to a fresh encounter with God. Through Joshua as His prophet, God speaks to them with power and deep conviction (24:2f), recounting their history. In verses 14 and following, Joshua himself comes to the forefront as God's prophet. He concludes the first portion of this parting discourse with "therefore," and begins the final part of his challenge with a threefold command: "fear the LORD"; "serve Him in sincerity and truth"; and "put away the gods which your fathers served" (v. 14).

We want to concentrate on this third command.

The foreign gods (vv. 15,20,23) are of three types and form the major spiritual warfare force set against Israel till the end of the Old Testament era. There are "the gods which your fathers served beyond the River" (vv. 2,14–15); there are the gods of Egypt (v. 14); and there are "the gods of the Amorites in whose land you are living" (v. 15). While they had different names in different places, there was enough similarity and even interchange of foreign gods, so that what we say about one group applies equally to the others.

The Gods Beyond the River

The river was the Euphrates (v. 2). Thus the gods were the gods of Mesopotamia, the land of Babylon. This reference takes us back to Genesis 10—11. In Genesis 10, the writer records the generations of Noah's three sons, Shem, Ham, and Japheth. All the nations of the biblical world are traced to the three lines of these three sons in Genesis 10—11. The peoples of Babylon (Mesopotamia) are traced to Ham (10:6–14), as are the Canaanites (v. 11–20), and the Egyptians— "Mizraim" is another name for Egypt . . . and other peoples (v. 6).[25]

Many of the people listed here were important to Israel in her later history. However, it is uncertain exactly which peoples they were, but their general area is usually identifiable.[26] I will mention only those who will be important in Israel's later history and the spiritual warfare context of that history. The four in verse 6 are important, "Cush," "Mizraim," "Put," and "Canaan."

One, "Cush" lies to the south of Israel and is identified with Ethiopia, following the Septuagint. But "it probably covers a variety of dark-skinned tribes (cf. Jer.

13:23) living beyond the southern border of Egypt. Most of Cush's descendants listed in the next verse seem to be located in Arabia," Wenham says. This also includes Seba, which some think referred to Sheba from where came the famous Queen of Sheba of Solomon's day (1 Kings 10:1–13).[27]

Two, "Mizraim" should be translated "Egypt," because it is the Hebrew word most used for that nation. Most of us are not aware of the terrible bondage of the Israelites to the gods of Egypt, both while they were in Egypt and also afterwards.

Three, "Put" is a little more difficult to identify with certainty but there is general agreement that it represents Libya. Hamilton concludes his discussion, saying, "Except for Ezekiel 38:5 the LXX [Septuagint] translates Put in the prophetic passages as Libyans."[28]

The strange thing is that the Canaanites are identified with Ham rather than with Shem since they are clearly related to the Israelites, who are descendants of Shem (11:10f). Canaan as used here, Wenham writes, would "include the various people that inhabited the territory of modern Israel, Lebanon and part of Syria." A more precise definition follows in verses 15–19.[29]

Finally, in the more precise genealogy of Genesis 11:10–31 the direct connection is made between Shem and Abram. Abram was born and raised in the idolatrous demonic-prideful-anti-God land of Mesopotamia. This is the point picked up with great force and passion by Joshua in Joshua 24:2–3,14–15,19–20.

We are now ready to examine Israel's warfare, first with the gods of their fathers, the gods of Babylon.

33

Warfare With the Gods

The Mesopotamian Pantheon of Gods

The gods "on the other side of the river" still appealed tremendously to the Israelites poised for conquest of the Promised Land. The Mesopotamian pantheon offered a god or goddess for every conceivable situation. Among the most important were Anu, Enlit, and Ea, the three principal cosmic deities, and Sin, Samas, and Ishtar, the three astral deities, all with their consorts, or sexual partners. Ishtar was the most important female deity. "She was the morning and evening star (Venus), goddess of sexual love and fertility—goddess of war—goddess of passions."[1] She was soon to be merged with Asthoreth, the principal Canaanite goddess.

Other prominent deities included Adad, Dagan (called Dagon in Judg. 16:23–30; 1 Sam. 5:2–10; 1 Chron. 20:9–10; and Jer. 50—52), Ninurta, Nergal, Marduck (the biblical Marduk, Jer. 50:21), and Ashur. All had consorts.[2] Dagan (biblical Dagon) was apparently a fertility god and the chief god of the Philistines.[3]

Second, while these were the most prominent gods, they were by no means all. Horsnell says, "Over three thousand deities were known altogether, many only by name from god-lists or from theophoric personal names."[4]

Besides being polytheistic and henotheistic the religion of Mesopotamia included a fanatical search for protection from hordes of demon spirits which "attacked people with distress and diseases."[5] Elaborate rites of exorcism were developed with official priestly exorcists. Cult prostitutes, mostly female, tended many shrines. Sexual encounters among the gods and goddesses were common. The king and the principal cult priestesses reenacted these sexual encounters in special ceremonies. So did the common people, especially during religious festivals.[6]

According to Babylonian "theology," human spirits survived death and could return and trouble the living. They had to be appeased, also. Divination and magic were essential to the cults. Amulets were worn as protection against demons and angry human spirits. Images were treated as if they were alive.

Finally, Mesopotamian religion was animistic. The entire universe pulsated with life, and "every phenomenon was embodied with living power, its numen . . . various numena were worshiped as divine and eventually personified as anthropomorphic, superhuman, immortal beings, resulting in naturalistic polytheism."[7]

According to Joshua, the fathers, including Abraham himself,[8] revered these gods "from ancient time." At the same time the stories of the Deluge and the Tower of Babel and the only true God must have been in the memory of many of these Semitic peoples. Noah and Shem were still alive. Shem outlived Abraham! While nothing more is said about them, they were probably living at not too great a distance from the Chaldeans. Where else would they have gone?

Now, four hundred years after Abraham, Joshua challenges the patriarch's descendants:

> Now therefore, fear the LORD and serve Him in sincerity and truth; and put away the gods which your fathers served beyond the River and in Egypt, and serve the LORD.

And if it is disagreeable in your sight to serve the LORD, choose for yourselves today whom you will serve: whether the gods which your fathers served which were beyond the River, or the gods of the Amorites in whose land you are living; but as for me and my house, we will serve the LORD. (Josh. 24:14–15)

Thus Joshua is concerned about three god systems threatening the purity of the Israelite's worship of Jehovah: the gods beyond the river; the gods of Egypt; and the gods of the Amorites in whose land they now lived, i.e., the Canaanites.

As we have seen, their fathers had been born and raised in the immoral, syncretistic, demon-ridden culture of Ur of the Chaldeans. While in Egypt they came into contact with people from these and other pagan lands. They fell back into the worship of the gods their fathers had abandoned when they were brought to faith in the true God (v. 14).

The Gods of Egypt

Their biological fathers were Egyptian-born, however. The land of Egypt was filled with gods and goddesses. W. S. LaSor says there were thirty-nine gods and goddesses widely worshipped in Egypt. Many were in animal form, in human form, or "in human form with animal heads." More than this, the Egyptians regarded all nature as personal. "Even the fiercest and most deadly of animals, i.e., the cobra, the scorpion, the crocodile, and the hippopotamus, were creatures connected with some god or king."[9]

In addition, both male and female nudity was common in their religious shrines and art work, all which had religious significance. I, myself, have been embarrassed to the point of speechlessness after innocently walking with my wife into some of the most famous Egyptian ruins depicting life-sized figures, both male and female, their sexual organs grossly exaggerated. When one realizes that the Jews, as slaves, had to build many of these buildings and were surrounded by such vivid "pornography" year after year, it is no wonder that, with their faith in God shaken after years of slavery, they gave in to the sensual excitement of the pagan religions of Egypt and later of Canaan.

The Gods of the Amorites

Next in Joshua's concern are the gods of the Amorites, "in whose land you are living" (v. 15). The word *Amorite* here includes all the peoples of Canaan, many of them listed in verse 11. Thus they were the Canaanites, the ones I call the "ite" peoples. Where did they come from? What were their religious practices that were so appealing to the flesh of the Israelites?

The best summary of Canaanite religion is given in Judges 2:13 and 3:7. After the death of Joshua and "the elders who survived Joshua, and had known all the deeds of the LORD which He had done for Israel" (Josh. 24:31), the people "forsook the LORD and served Baal and the Ashtaroth" (Judg. 2:13). They "forgot the LORD their God and served the Baals and the Asheroth" (Judg. 3:7). The entire Canaanite religious system centered in this god-goddess pair.

The origin of the Canaanites is given in the table of the nations in Genesis 10. Canaan was a son of Ham (Gen. 10:15–19), Wenham remarks, "The relevance of Canaan to Israel explains the amount of detail included here."[10] Hamilton calls him the second [after Ham] most productive ancestor in the Table of Nations.[11] The list of the people of Canaan is not complete nor does it mean they are all ethnically related to Ham or Canaan. Many scholarly commentators point out the basis of the descent is not always ethnic, but geopolitical, cultural, religious, and linguistic.

Joshua's Demand for a Break With the Gods

The Canaanites scattered everywhere (Gen. 10:18–19). They became a constant thorn in the flesh of the Israelites. Wenham says that "the Canaanites are often viewed in the Pentateuch as *the* sinful nation who deserves God's wrath."[12] Joshua forcibly demands that they break with their bondage to the base Canaanite religious practices (Josh. 24:15,23). What was he insisting that they forsake?

First, they were to forsake Baal, the most prominent of the Canaanite gods. The name *Baal* means "owner, master, lord, or husband." While El, the common Canaanite-Hebrew name for the creator of all, was the supreme God of their theology, Baal and Ashtoreth were more important to the actual life of the land and the people. Baal had risen to the place of almost universal prominence during the first millennium B.C.

Baal began as the god of weather. In a dry land like Canaan, this soon gave him the place of prominence. Life could not function without him. It was natural next to see him as the god of fertility. A. E. Cundall says that Baal and the many local Baals were really one god. They were the great cosmic nature god. They (as "he")

> controlled fertility in agriculture, beasts and mankind. It was highly important to gain their favor.... This led to the adoption of extreme forms in the cults, including the practice of ritual prostitution (Judg. 2:17; Jer. 7:9; Amos 2:7) and child sacrifice (Jer. 19:5).... In the process of time Baal became the region's chief deity.[13]

The myth of the dying and rising god was reenacted during the Canaanite New Year Festival. It was directly connected to the fertility cycle and the corresponding sexual fertility rites. Cundall says that this myth "was attended by the appropriate response from the worshipers, culminating in the grossly sensuous rites accompanying the sacred marriage, in which ritual prostitution of both sexes was a prominent feature."[14]

Second, they were to forsake Ashtoreth, their most important goddess. Ashtoreth was formerly the consort of El, but as this ancient god faded, Ashtoreth, his sexual partner, was slowly transferred over to Baal. Thus Judges 2:13 and 3:7 link Baal and Ashtaroth (2:13) and Asheroth (3:7) together (these are different names for the one goddess, Ashtoreth).

Baal also had another goddess consort, Anath or Anat. She was called "the virgin." Anath was perhaps a virgin to others but not to Baal, for she "was both consort and sister to Baal and shared his several adventures."[15] Here is incest and polygamy among the gods.

This mother goddess—in the queen of heaven tradition of which Ashtoreth (Asthtart, Athtart, Asheroth, Astarte, or Ashtoreth)[16] played the key female role was universal throughout the Near East, going back as far as "the fourth millennium B.C." according to W. White, Jr.[17]

The sexual practices associated with her cult were so repulsive to Jewish leaders that the Greek LXX [Septuagint] and other Old Testament texts commonly mutilated her name by supplanting

> the original vowels with those of another usually derogatory word ... (like) the vowels for "shame" were infixed, thus any magical power or ascription of praise to the pagan deity was forever prohibited from the biblical texts.[18]

White says that "the worship of the mother goddesses in the Near East and elsewhere in the world is evidenced by the frequency of small fertility figurines excavated from sites as early as the Lower Paleolithe Period."[19]

In the earliest written documents from Mesopotamia, she is first called Inanna and later Isthar. Both were consorts of leading male gods. White says, "Inanna was the consort of the shepherd god Dumuzi (Hebrew, *Tammuz;* see Ezek. 8:14) for whom she wept at his seasonal death."[20] As mother goddess, Inna-Isthar-Ashtoreth forms a vital part of the fertility rites.[21]

White comments that "This sexual aspect of the worship of the mother goddess appears to have carried over into every culture of the Near East where the cult was practiced." He then comments on the annual reenactment of the marriage of Dumuzi and Inaana-Ishtar which features sexual intercourse between the King (in Babylonia) and a temple priestess-prostitute.

Ashtoreth-Isthar was well known among the Egyptians, also. Her name has been found in Egyptian inscriptions. Regarding a letter among the remains of Pharaoh Amenophis III (1405–1357 B.C.), White writes that

> the name of the goddess is glossed with the descriptive phrase, "Istar, Queen of Heaven." . . . In time, cuneiform literature utilized the name Istar as a general noun for "goddess." . . . In the Syria-Palestine she is depicted in art with Egyptian garments and attributes.

Thus the Jews were familiar with the cult before leaving Egypt. When they reached the Promised Land (Canaan), they found it filled with shrines to Baal and Ashtoreth. She appears frequently in the Ugaritic tablets from Ras Shamra. White says, "Her comprehension in the minds of her devotees reached extraordinary heights of poetry and drama, some aspects of which were later sublimated by the Hebrews to the worship of Jehovah."[22]

As a result, Israel was constantly drawn to the Baal-Ashtoreth cults, especially the sexual aspects of the cult. White in great frankness says, "Throughout history the Jews were constantly tempted to worship this pagan goddess and attend her rituals, and it was this forbidden practice which finally led to Israel's captivity and the seventy years in Babylon."[23] But that captivity was centuries in the future when Joshua issued his challenge in Joshua 24.

The people responded positively to his call to put away the foreign gods which were presently in their midst. A search of their tents and possessions would have revealed household gods, or seraphim. Also, they were already secretly serving Baal, Ashtoreth, and the other Canaanite gods and spirits.

Joshua also realized they were living in a land in which "the iniquity of the Amorite" was now complete (Gen. 15:16). This reference from Genesis is very important. It is found in the context of one of the greatest of all Abraham's face-to-face encounters with God. Abraham had just returned from his deliverance of Lot. God meets his faithful servant in a vision and says,

> Do not fear, Abram,
> I am a shield to you;
> Your reward shall be very great. (Gen. 15:1)

Abraham complains that he is still childless (15:2–3). God promises him a son, born of his own loins (vv. 4–5). Verse 6 says, "Then he believed in the Lord; and He reckoned it to him as righteousness." The writer states that God told Abraham that his descendants would be slaves in a strange land for four hundred years. Then God promises:

> But I will also judge the nation whom they will serve; and afterward they will come out with many possessions . . . .
>
> Then in the fourth generation they will return here, for the iniquity of the Amorite is not yet complete. (Gen. 15:14,16)

This amazing revelation from God deals with three incredible future events: the four-hundred-year Egyptian bondage (v. 13); God's judgment upon Egypt (v. 14); and taking with them the spoils of Egypt in the Exodus (v. 14).

Then God gives the only reason for this four-hundred-year wait until the Promised Land would finally be given to the descendants of Abraham. God says, "for the iniquity of the Amorites (Canaanites) is not yet complete" (v. 15). Hamilton comments that "this last half of the verse articulates the idea that the fixing of times is conditioned not on necessity but on morality. This commentary on the immorality of the indigenous population of Canaan also establishes Joshua's invasion as an act of justice rather than aggression."[24] Kidner adds, "Until it was right to invade, God's people must wait, if it cost them centuries of hardship. This is one of the pivotal sayings of the Old Testament."[25]

Returning to Joshua 24, we can say that at the time Joshua was speaking, the Amorites had not been exterminated as God had commanded, though their iniquity was now complete. This was Joshua's worry. Instead of exterminating the Amorites, the people compromised with their gods. Jehovah was different than the gods they were used to. He was in a class by Himself. They found it difficult to relate to Him. He was just too holy for such a sinful people.

One cannot escape forming the impression the people followed God because they were afraid of Him, not because they truly loved Him. In their response to Joshua, it is the newly revealed power of God that is their main focus, not His compassion and gentleness. Joshua knew this. He knew how attractive the Canaanite gods were. They made no moral demands. In fact, drunkenness, orgies, and all types of immoral partying was part of the way they "worshipped" these human-like gods and goddesses. Thus, Joshua becomes even more direct. He answers the people in Joshua 24:19–20:

> You will not be able to serve the LORD, for He is a holy God. He is a jealous God; He will not forgive your transgression or your sins. If you forsake the LORD and serve foreign gods, then He will turn and do you harm and consume you after He has done good to you.

The people were persistent, however. "No, but we will serve the LORD," they responded (v. 21). Joshua had no choice but to take them at their word. He stated,

> You are witnesses against yourselves that you have chosen for yourselves the LORD, to serve Him. And they said, "We are witnesses."

Things go very well for a number of years. Joshua 24:31 states,

> And Israel served the LORD all the days of Joshua and all the days of the elders who survived Joshua, and had known all the deeds of the LORD which He had done for Israel.

But Judges 2 tells the rest of the story. It is a prelude of the history of Israel for centuries to come:

the sons of Israel did evil in the sight of the LORD. . . . So they forsook the LORD and served Baal and the Ashtaroth. (Judg. 2:11,13)

The battle with the gods of the land which we have described in this chapter had just begun. If Joshua spoke these words about 1400 B.C., then that battle would go on for about 1000 years or more, until the return from the Exile in about 457–440 B.C. The Jews were slow to learn the horrible consequences of serving foreign gods. When they did finally learn, however, they never again forgot that "the Lord, He alone is God." They really only suffered one major failure after that. It occurred at the foot of the cross outside of Jerusalem in the year 30 A.D. That was, for Israel, the greatest moral-spiritual failure of their centuries of spiritual warfare.

34

The Low Point in Spiritual Warfare

Human Sacrifice

Before looking at the nadir or lowest point to which the demonic religions of the Old Testament world had sunk, two remarks must be made about Israel's understanding of the demonic activity found in pagan religious practices. First, not all Israelites at all times recognized they were involved in direct encounter with demons as they related to the gods and idols of the peoples of the Promised Land. Their understanding waxed and waned in relation to the closeness of their walk with Yahweh, the true God. Second, their view of the spirit world was always filtered through their view of the absolute sovereignty of God. Israel could not conceive of Satan or his seducing spirits being able to work among believers without the direct permission of God.

Satan and the spirits could do what they wished with the pagans since they were actually worshipping them anyway. They understood that "the things which the Gentiles sacrifice, they sacrifice to demons and not to God" (1 Cor. 10:20).[1] But when it came to disturbing a child of God directly, they had first to obtain direct permission from God (Job 1—2). The Jews also knew that in some cases God Himself sent evil spirits to punish His disobedient children (1 Kings 22:19–23).

When God Sent an Evil Spirit: 1 Kings 22

The 1 Kings 22 passage has disturbed commentators for centuries. To even begin to understand what is occurring it must be seen in its context. Wicked King Ahab is at war with Syria (22:1f). Jehoshaphat, king of Judah, pays him a visit (22:2). Up until now he has been an excellent king (2 Chron. 17). His only major mistake, one he committed twice, was seeking a close relationship with the kings of Israel. God rebuked him through the prophet Jehu for his alliance with Ahab, but forgave him (2 Chron. 19:1f). He did not forgive him when he repeated this sin with King Ahaziah of Israel (2 Chron. 20:35—21:1).

Ahab wants God to sanction his plan to go to war with the Syrians (1 Kings 22:5f). He assembles his 400 false prophets who give him the go-ahead word (22:6,10—12). Jehoshaphat does not trust them. He asks for a true prophet (v. 7). Ahab says there is one but he hates him because he does not support the king's evil policies (v. 8). At Jehoshaphat's insistence Ahab sends for him (v. 9).

When Micaiah arrives, he decides to go along with the deception, telling Ahab to go to war and promising he will win (vv. 13–15). Ahab knows he is toying with him and asks for the truth (v. 16). He gets it (vv. 17–23). Micaiah suffers for his integrity (vv. 24–28).

Micaiah has a vision. In that vision God is declaring His plan to take the life of Ahab, perhaps the most wicked of all Israel's wicked kings (v. 19f). In that vision, first we see Jehovah, the LORD (v. 19a). Next is His heavenly council standing on His right and left. These evidently represent the council of the Watcher angels already referred to. The Lord asks the best strategy to lead Ahab to his own defeat. There is general disagreement in the council (v. 20). Suddenly a "spirit" comes forward. He offers to be a "deceiving spirit in the mouth of all his [Ahab's] prophets" (v. 22a). His offer is accepted by God (v. 22b).

Micaiah interprets the vision to the two kings and evidently before all the lying prophets. He says, "the LORD has put a deceiving spirit in the mouth of all these your prophets; and the LORD has proclaimed disaster against you" (v. 23). Needless to say, this did not make Micaiah very popular with King Ahab and his prophets (vv. 24–28).

How is this passage to be understood? Once again, the problem is a world view problem.[2] Filtered through the Jewish view of the spirit world already mentioned, there is no problem. What Micaiah described in his vision occurred as he describes it. In his description, he resorts to anthropomorphism. God is seen as a king seeking advice of His council of wise men. He is also seen as Lord even over the evil spirits. Since His people are involved (Ahab was the leader of one group of God's people), the lying spirit must obtain God's permission to cause the death of Ahab. The permission is granted because it fits God's plans.

As Matthew Henry says, "It is not without the divine permission that the devil deceives men, and even thereby God serves His own purpose."[3]

Finally, the New Testament provides us with the needed balance at this point. Satan and his demons are fully developed personalities with mind, emotions, and will. Like the men they inspire towards evil, they can scheme against God's people, attack and afflict them, defeat and even kill the children of God (1 Thess. 2:18; 3:5; Rev. 2:10; 12:17; 13:7). Yet, the child of God who puts on the full armor of God and learns spiritual warfare is protected from serious injury by the Evil One. Satan's freedom in the evil he does against God's people is still subject to God's sovereign will. Sin and unbelief on the part of the believer, however, opens him to direct satanic-demonic attack (1 Cor. 7:5; 1 Thess. 3:5; Eph. 4:27).

The Demonic Practice of Child Sacrifice

As we continue with the Old Testament encounter with the spirit world we must now examine the most horrible dimension of demonic religious activity among Israel's neighbors, the practice of child sacrifice. I do this for three major reasons.

First, child sacrifice was commonly practiced not only among the pagan Canaanites but in all probability among most of the major people groups whose inhabitants worshipped the same or similar gods as the Canaanites.

Second, in most major periods of apostasy, Israel fell into the darkness of this horrible practice. Thus it was a major feature of Israel's terrible defeat in its warfare with the spirit world.

Third, child sacrifice has resurfaced in our day in Satanism, satanic cults, and in many witchcraft cults now flourishing in America and other parts of the Western world. It also still exists in some areas of the Two-thirds World.

There are dozens of references to child sacrifice to the gods in the Old Testament. There are none in the New Testament. Roman law, which dominated the New Testament world, did not permit human sacrifice. Unfortunately for the thousands of human beings—mostly children—sacrificed to the gods and the spirits during the Old Testament era, no such laws existed. If they did exist, they were not enforced. E. E. Carpenter lists the key phrases used in the Old Testament which refer to child sacrifice.[4] The phrase used most frequently is "cause to pass over" followed by one or more of the following phrases: "to Molech" (Jer. 32:35); "through the fire" (2 Kings 16:3; 17:17; 21:6; Ezek. 20:31); or the combination of "Molech" with "through the fire" in 2 Kings 23:10; "burnt offerings" (Judg. 11:31; 2 Kings 3:27); and "caused their sons, whom they bore to Me [God is speaking], to pass through the fire to them [the idols] as food" (Ezek. 23:37).

In Ezekiel 16:21; 20:26 the verbal form "cause to pass over" is used alone, "but the meaning is clear," Carpenter says. It means "you slaughtered My children, and offered them up to idols by causing them to pass through the fire" (Ezek. 16:21).

Then we have "burn in the fire to [the god]" (Deut. 12:31; 2 Kings 17:31; Jer. 7:31; 19:51); and "offer it up as a burnt offering," also referring to child sacrifice, in Judges 11:31, the story of the daughter of Jephthah, and in 2 Kings 3:27, the story of the oldest son of the king of Moab.

Carpenter notes that the common Hebrew word for sacrifice, zabah, is used in Psalm 106:37, for "they even sacrificed their sons and their daughters to the demons." Again, the Old Testament clearly recognizes the truth of 1 Corinthians 10:20, "the things which the Gentiles sacrifice, they sacrifice to demons and not to God." When the Jews imitated these practices and sacrificed their children to the gods or even to Jehovah, they too were actually sacrificing to demons. The same, of course, is true in religious child sacrifice today.

In Ezekiel 16:20 and 23:39 we again have zabah. In the first case the verse says, "Your sons and your daughters whom you had borne to Me . . . you sacrificed them to idols to be devoured" (Ezek. 16:20). In the second case it is, "for when they had slaughtered their children for their idols" (Ezek. 23:39). In both cases the charges were being brought against rebellious Israel and Judah.

It should be pointed out that the Israelites became involved in this heinous practice primarily in their days of war and apostasy. This practice was prohibited and strongly condemned by God at every period in Israel's history, from Genesis to Malachi.

Carpenter surveys the practice of human or child sacrifice in the ancient Near East. He points out that the practice was widespread in Mesopotamia, Phoenicia, and in Africa; especially in Phoenician Carthage. The Phoenicians were Canaanites who migrated to North Africa. Human/child sacrifice was also practiced by the Chinese, Celts, Aztecs, and Mayans; in Sardinia, Sicily, Tunisia, and probably other places.[5]

Lawrence E. Stager and Samuel R. Wolff, in a recent report on ancient child sacrifice, note that the Phoenician cemetery in Carthage, North Africa, dedicated exclusively as the repository of the burnt bones of child and animal sacrifices, "is the largest cemetery of sacrificed humans ever discovered. Child sacrifice took place there almost continuously for a period of over 600 years" from about 400 B.C. to the third century A.D. It probably began about 800 B.C., however.

Tertullian (160–225 A.D.), the great church father from Carthage, writes about this horrible practice continuing even in his day. He calls it "the evil activity of Satan causing his servants to sacrifice their own children to him." He then writes that

in Africa infants used to be sacrificed to Saturn [Satan]. . . . Yes, and to this day that unholy crime persists in secret. . . . Saturn did not spare his own children . . . their own parents offered them to him, were glad to respond and fondled their children that they might not be sacrificed in tears.[6]

Stager and Wolff further say that the biblical name Tophet, taken from Jeremiah 7:30–32, is the name used to refer to all such places of sacrifice and repositories of the remains of children sacrificed to the gods. Tophet names a location in the Valley of Ben-Hinnom on the south side of ancient Jerusalem where ritual sacrifice-by-fire took place:

> "The people of Judah have done evil in my sight," saith the Lord. . . . "They build the high place of Tophet, which is in the Valley of Ben-Hinnom, to burn their sons and their daughters in fire. Such a thing I never commanded, nor had in mind." (Jer. 7:30–32)

Biblical references connect the Tophet to Baal worship:

> They rejected the commandments of the Lord . . . and served Baal. They consigned their sons and daughters to the fire (2 Kings 17:16–17; see also Jer. 32:35).

In 2 Kings 23:10 and Jeremiah 32:35, we find strong suggestions that Tophet was also associated with the Canaanite god Molech.

> The Jerusalem Tophet was dismantled by King Josiah in the seventh century B.C. "[King Josiah of Judah] defiled Tophet, which is in the Valley of the son of Hinnom, that no man might make his son or daughter pass through the fire for Molech." (2 Kings 23:10)

> Whether this was its first destruction and whether it was thereafter rebuilt, we cannot be sure.

> These Biblical references have led modern scholars to call by the name Tophet the huge cemetery of sacrificed children at Phoenician Carthage, as well as similar precincts at other Phoenician sites in Sicily, Sardinia and Tunisia.[7]

The cemetery at Carthage is between 54,000 and 64,000 square feet. It may contain as many as 20,000 urns with the remains of the children sacrificed, plus bones of animals also sacrificed.[8] Some urns contained the charred remains of two to three children. Their ages ran from the earliest days of birth to six years of age, evidently all from the same family. Thousands of additional urns were lost when the Romans destroyed the cemetery in 146 B.C. While unlawful, the practice of child sacrifice continued.

The Phoenicians established Tophets in many of their leading cities and trading centers. For centuries the Phoenicians were the great merchants, traders, sailors, and craftsmen of the biblical world. In 900 B.C. the Phoenician king, Hiram of Tyre, provided King Solomon with the necessary materials to build the great Jewish temple. Phoenicians also were the sailors of Solomon's fleets (1 Kings 5:1ff; 7:13–45; 10:11,22).

The Case of Abraham and Isaac: Genesis 22

The first mention of the subject of human sacrifice in the Bible is in Genesis 22. There God commands Abraham to offer up his promised son, Isaac (vv. 1–2) in one of the most dramatic, controversial stories in the Old Testament. Abraham was probably well acquainted with the child sacrifice of Mesopotamia and of some of the tribes in the land of Canaan where he lived. He knew it was wrong. He also knew God would somehow intervene, even if it meant God would have to raise his son from the dead (vv. 5–8). "God will provide for Himself the lamb for the burnt offering, my son," (v. 8) is the key phrase. It was spoken in answer to Isaac's question, "Where is the lamb for the burnt offering?" (v. 7).

The writer of Hebrews provides us with new insight into Abraham's faith as he responded in obedience to God's strange request that he offer Isaac in sacrifice.

> By faith Abraham, when he was tested, offered up Isaac; and he who had received the promises was offering up his only begotten son; it was he to whom it was said, "IN ISAAC YOUR DESCENDANTS SHALL BE CALLED." He considered that God is able to raise men even from the dead; from which he also received him back as a type. (Heb. 11:17–19)

Carpenter says that Abraham was startled by Yahweh's demand, but not unfamiliar with the requirement. The sacrifice does not occur, however. The story, as it stands, rejects human sacrifice. Instead it both stresses Abraham's faith and demonstrates Yahweh's ability to provide an approved substitute sacrifice. Carpenter states that "Genesis 22 thus indicates that human sacrifice was not approved in the time of Abraham, Israel's most remote ancestor."[9]

In Leviticus 18:20, God forbids child sacrifice, equating it with profanation of His name. Leviticus 20:2–5 declares that anyone who practices child sacrifice, i.e., "who gives any of his offspring to Molech," is to be stoned to death. That man and his family would have their name cut off from Israel "for playing the harlot with Molech," God says (v. 5). God goes so far as to say if others knew of the man's sin and did not have him executed, they too would come under the same curse (v. 4–5). What more powerful warning against, and condemnation of, the practice could ever be given!

Deuteronomy 12:29–31 has Moses talking with Israel about the conquest of the Promised Land. Moses says God will cut "off before you the nations which you are going in to dispossess, and you are to dispossess them and dwell in their land" (v. 29). He next says Israel must "beware that you are not ensnared to follow them" (v. 30). He then lists some of the abominable acts which the inhabitants of the land were guilty of which caused God to have them destroyed (vv. 30b–31a). The worst act of all, God says, is "they even burn their sons and daughters in the fire to their gods" (v. 31b).

The historical books contain the greatest amount of references to child sacrifice in the early books of the Old Testament. References occur in most of the books from Judges to 2 Chronicles. Judges 1—2:10 reveals Israel's failure to destroy the Canaanites. Chapters 2:11—3:8 reveal their apostasy and God's decision not to drive out the rest of the remaining evil nations as he had promised. This was because of Israel's continual disobedience. They fell into idolatry and immorality, God says, especially in the worship of the god and goddess pair, Baal and Ashtoreth.

The Baal-Ashtoreth connection was the most vile form of pagan worship imaginable, as we have already discovered. It involved religious prostitution, orgies, and child sacrifice. The child sacrifice at Carthage was also devoted to this god-goddess pair, Baal and Ashtoreth. In Carthage they were known as Baal-Hammon and Tanit. Tanit was the same as Ashtoreth.[10]

In Judges 3—21 the battle with the spirit world goes on. That these chapters reflect an ongoing power encounter is clear in the account of Gideon recorded in Judges 6:1–35. There Gideon, in true power encounter style, destroys the altar of Baal and his companion Asherah (vv. 25–27). The people are so angry they decide to kill Gideon (vv. 28–30). Gideon's father, Joash, defends his son: "Let Baal defend himself if he is what he claims to be" (see vv. 31–32). It is amusing reading.

One case of child sacrifice in Israel has to do with Jephthah (Judg. 11:1–40). She was not a child, but a daughter of marriageable age. It is a tragic story of zeal for

God, cursed by syncretism.[11] The vow Jephthah took was totally contrary to the law of God (vv. 29–40). The response of the daughters of Israel to the sacrifice of Jephthah reveal the writer's and the nation's negative view of Jephthah's action (vv. 37–40).

First Kings, 2 Kings, and 2 Chronicles contain terrible stories of child sacrifice among the pagans but especially among the Jews. Isaiah, Jeremiah, Ezekiel, Amos, Micah, and others refer to this abominable practice.[12]

We are witnessing a terrible revival of child mutilation and sacrifice in our day. Later in our study I give a major case study of my deliverance and counseling ministry with a missionary who is an adult survivor of Satanic Ritual Abuse in which her Satanist father attempted to offer her in sacrifice to Satan.

We are also witnessing an organized satanic conspiracy to refute the accounts of child sacrifice in the U.S. and other parts of the Western world. This is a satanically inspired cover-up. Dozens of children have come forth testifying how they were tortured into submission to wicked satanic leaders. They also were made to participate in the sacrifice of other little children to Satan.

Adults converted to Christ from Satanism and satanic cults have told horrible stories of child sacrifice. Major television news programs have given shocking revelations of the practice. Adult survivors have appeared on talk shows telling the horror of child sacrifice which they witnessed or were forced to participate in as children and young people, even as adults. The books by Wilder (1992) and Friesen (1991) document these horrors. Other references in the bibliography at the end of this book and in the chapters on child abuse tell where more information can be obtained.

The revival of paganism in America will only increase unless a nationwide Christian revival occurs to break the back of this demonic evil. In the meantime, let us use every weapon at our disposal to help save our children from this ultimate evil.

35

Of Kings and Prophets

All pagan religion is a power game.

Dr. Arthur Mouw was a pioneer missionary with the Christian and Missionary Alliance in Borneo. His entire ministry among the Dyak tribal people of Borneo is a story of faith, suffering, power demonstrations, more sufferings, and more power demonstrations. All was done by God through the unpretentious steps of obedience of Mouw and mostly of his converts.

The gospel, under Mouw's ministry, had divided the Dyak tribal people. Some followed the missionary while others continued with the power-magic indigenous religious leader. While Mouw was away a village chief called the heads of the village and all the people together.

"We have always followed the spirits of the hills, the rivers, and the jungles till the Jesus people came to live among us," he said. "We are now divided as a people. Who is God? The spirit-man says the gods and spirits of the forest, rivers, and mountains are the true gods. The Jesus people say Jesus alone is God. Today we are going to know who is God. I will set up a contest of the gods. Whichever god meets the challenge, he is the god we will follow."

The leaders and the people agreed. The chief then set the stage for the ordeal. He took the traditional power worker to one of the biggest long houses. It was about 30 feet or more tall and 100 feet long. He called for a leader of the Jesus people. A young believer was put forward. This in itself was unusual for their culture: the older, wiser, respected religious practitioner paired against a young man, and a new believer at that. The chief gave a fresh egg to each of the men.

"The god who is the true God will preserve the egg of his servant. We will all follow the God who reveals His power. You each are to throw your egg over the house. The true God will not allow his egg to break."

The magic power worker went through his magic power rituals. He then hurled his egg over the long house. The elders stood on the far side to observe the results. It smashed into a thousand pieces.

The young man lifted his heart to God. "Show yourself to be the Lord, the Creator of heaven and earth. Show to all the people that Jesus is Your Son. Show to everyone that we are Your servants and that we speak Your Word in Your Name."

He hurled his egg over the long house. It fell to the other side and bounced like a rubber ball without a single crack in the shell.

"The Jesus God is the true God!" the chief shouted. "We will all follow him." And they did.[1]

Dr. Mouw's story took place in the twentieth century, but its overtones echo power encounters that reach back into the Old Testament, where God commands Israel to have no gods before Him. The major focus of the first part of the Ten Commandments (Exod. 20:1–17) is upon the person of God (vv. 1–3). The commandments were given to a people whose past and present history engulfed them in the world of polytheism, idolatry, and evil spirits. Consequently, the second focus of the Ten Commandments is on the no-gods (Exod. 20:3–5). Thus the Ten Commandments are placed in a spiritual warfare context.

Next, God follows with a unique curse upon all who "hate Me" (vv. 5–6). This hatred of God occurs in the context of warfare with the no-gods. If one hates God by serving the no-gods, God will not only judge him, but will extend this judgment upon future generations, onto "the third and the fourth generations of those who hate Me" (v. 5b). This is a unique curse. It is repeated over and over again throughout the Old Testament, always in the context of serving the no-gods.

This following of the no-gods and its subsequent divine curse is often called generational sin, inherited sin, and familial sin. It is one of the major causes of demonization in the lives of people till today.

The Case of King Saul

The books of 1 Samuel through 2 Chronicles are filled with direct or indirect references to spirit world manifestations. The power encounters between God and Dagon, the Baals and Ashteroth in 1 Samuel 5—7 are fascinating reading, filled with possibilities for deeper study. Perhaps the single most important story in this book which relates to the people of God and evil spirits is the story of King Saul (1 Sam. 9–31). I continually use his life as a case study of a man of God who becomes demonized because of serious personal sin.

Saul's Positive Spiritual Qualities

We need not begin with Israel's demands for a king so they could be "like all the nations" (1 Sam. 8:5). We will begin with Saul himself. Saul began well. During his first two years he is a man of God, humble, zealous for the honor of God and the salvation of His people. First, he is elected by the sovereign choice of God as prince over God's people (9:15–17; 10:1). From the very beginning he reveals his true humility (9:20–21; 15:17).

Second, Saul is transformed by the Spirit of God. He was made "another man" (10:6). He was given a "new heart" (10:9). The Spirit of God came upon him mightily (10:6,10). He prophesied under the power of God's Spirit (10:10). All who knew him before his conversion were amazed at his spiritual transformation (10:11–12). Third, he displays an amazing trust in God to glorify him as His appointed king. He refuses to exalt himself (10:15–16,22–24).

Fourth, he reveals his zeal for the name of Yahweh and the salvation of His people in his victory through the power of the Holy Spirit over the Ammonites (11:1–11). Fifth, he refuses to take vengeance upon those who opposed him. He chooses to glorify the Lord instead (11:12–13). Sixth, because of Saul's exemplary conduct, all Israel reaffirms its covenant with God (11:14–15). Saul brings the whole nation back to God. Here is a king after God's own heart who will bring nothing but blessings to the people of God, it would seem.

Saul's Slide to Disobedience

The complex, confusing story of his gradual but persistent, prideful disobedience to God is described in three steps:

The first errant step is found in 1 Samuel 13:9–12. Saul assumes Samuel's role as God's priest and prophet. Samuel sees Saul's action as rebellion against the word of the Lord God. He pronounces judgment upon the nation because of Saul's disobedience (vv. 13–14).

The second backwards step is revealed in 14:24–46. Here we find an unholy mixture of self-assertion and zeal for God. He reaches the point of willingness to kill his own son, Jonathan, in the name of the Lord. He is an extremist, a religious fanatic.

The third and most serious evidence of a declining spiritual life is disclosed in

15:1–35. Saul's self-centeredness and pride lead him to rebel openly against the word of the Lord. His confession and repentance are not true brokenness for sin against God. He is rejected by both God and Samuel.

The final evidence of Saul's pride and rebellion is his growing jealousy of David. He is an egomaniac. He goes into rages. He repeatedly attempts to kill David (18:7–17; 19:1,8–11). Saul's persistent pride and rebellion against God and His word finally push him across the fine line between the operations of the flesh and the world[2] and those of demonic spirits. He becomes demonized.

Up to now his sin has had its origin in the flesh and the world. From now on it will be fully multidimensional, the flesh, the world, and demons (16:14; 18:10–11; 19:9).[3]

The result? Saul at times becomes irrational in his thinking and conduct (18:10–11). Yet he continues to seek God. He is again filled with the Holy Spirit (19:18–24). Saul's case is indeed strange. He is filled with the Holy Spirit, "mightily" twice (10:6–13; 11:6). This filling is similar to the New Testament focus on filling as empowerment for service (Acts 2:4f; 4:8,28–31; 9:17–22). He then begins his fall due to pride. The climax is reached with "the Spirit of the Lord" departs from Saul, and an evil spirit from the Lord terrorizes him (16:14).

Ralph W. Klein marks the difference between the Holy Spirit coming upon Saul repeatedly and the statement concerning David that "the Spirit of the Lord came mightily upon David from that day forward" (16:13).[4]

The "evil spirit from the Lord" also comes and goes (16:14–23; 18:10; 19:9). His departure in one case (16:14–23) was due to David's musical ministry to Saul on his harp. The result was, "Saul would be refreshed and be well and the evil spirit would depart from him" (16:23).[5] This was not always successful, however. In fact in the next two cases David's presence and music only agitate Saul and probably the evil spirit within him (18:10f; 19:9). The latter has been my experience with evil spirits also.

Yet, with all of this the Holy Spirit again comes upon Saul giving him the ability to prophesy (19:20–24). Again, I repeat, Saul's is a most unusual case. To go into depth to deal with his complex life would require more pages than I can give in this chapter.

Saul's Demonization

Saul's demonization seems to move through progressively worsening stages.

Stage one. At the beginning, his demonization is more mild. He has periods of normality. Probably, the purpose of these was to bring him to true repentance (1 Sam. 16:14–23; 1 Tim. 1:20).

Stage two. His demonization becomes very intense. He at times becomes irrational (1 Sam. 18:10a). He is destructive in his interpersonal relationships: first with his own daughters, then he tries to kill Jonathan. Finally, he again seeks to murder Jonathan's best friend and God's anointed, David (18:10,11; 19:9–17; 20:30f).

Stage three is revealed in 1 Samuel 28. Without denying his faith in the Lord, Saul slips into occultic, mediumistic practices. He becomes involved with the medium of Endor.

I have seen this occur on many occasions, especially with believers in Africa and Asia. They are Christians. They love the Lord. In a desperate attempt to get power or hidden knowledge, they resort to spirit power practices. Like Saul, they usually end up demonized.

For Saul, this desperate act was precipitated by the death of Samuel and God's final rejection of Saul as the leader of His people (25:1; 28:6). As the Philistines gather for a final battle with Israel, Saul becomes desperate.

"When Saul inquired of the LORD, the LORD did not answer him" (28:6). Showing the paganism which lay under the surface of many believers of his day, he seeks for a medium to bring up the spirit of Samuel. In this case God causes Samuel to appear, even surprising the medium (28:7–12). Samuel rejects Saul's appeal for help. He reminds him of the occasion of his first major wilful rebellion against the word of God (28:16–18).

Samuel pronounces judgment upon Saul. His life will be taken the next day. Israel will be defeated by the Philistines (v. 19). Saul had sinned unto death (28:19; 31:1–6; see 1 Cor. 5:1–5; 1 Tim. 1:19–20 with 2 Tim. 2:17–18; 1 John 5:16–17; 1 Cor. 11:27–32). Saul dies severely demonized, but maintaining his faith in God to the end. Saul was not an apostate. He did not become a Solomon and serve foreign gods. He was disobedient. He sought hidden knowledge from a medium as tens of thousands of erring believers, including Christian leaders, have done after him. Thus he will be in the kingdom of God. He did not go to hell but into the abode of the righteous dead (28:19).

Using only the biblical text one cannot refute the position I have taken that Saul was a true believer. He fell, as thousands after him have done, through pride. We are reminded again of the four P's that plague many Christians and especially Christian leaders: power, position, pleasure, and possessions. All are evidences of the sin of pride.

Saul died as a severely demonized believer. Even when he was demonized, the Scripture records that "the Spirit of God came upon him also, so that he went along prophesying continually" (1 Sam. 19:23). He is truly a mystery man.

Ahab and Further Evil

First Kings records the evil of the kings of Israel and Judah who led God's people into unbelievable idolatry, polytheism, child sacrifice, immorality, and demonism. The most notorious, of course, was King Ahab of Israel and his evil wife, Jezebel. The story of Ahab is a striking case study of a leader among God's people who gives himself to be controlled by a powerful woman pagan spirit practitioner from among the Canaanites, Jezebel.

The writer records that Ahab "went to serve Baal and worshiped him" . . . "he erected an altar for Baal in the house of Baal, which he built in Samaria." "Ahab also made the Asherah." "Thus," God says, "Ahab did more to provoke the LORD God of Israel than all the kings of Israel before him" (1 Kings 16:29–33).

It is remarkable these verses are immediately followed by another reference to pagan child sacrifice, the sacrifice of the two royal sons of Hiel of Jericho (v. 34).

THE CONFLICT WITH THE GODS UNDER THE NON-WRITING PROPHETS

First Kings 18 records the most famous power encounter in all of Scripture, that between the prophet Elijah and the "450 prophets of Baal and 400 prophets of the Asherah" (v. 19ff). I will give a running commentary on the incident.[6]

God had repeatedly commanded Israel not to become involved with the gods of Canaan. The people failed, over and over again. They served these gods, particularly Baal and Asherah. That is the context of the story before us.

Elijah's Challenge: 1 Kings 18

The type of story recorded in 1 Kings 18 is called in missiology, a challenge or ordeal. It is very common in power encounters between God and the no-gods and even within the religions of the no-gods, themselves. The entire story is one of the outstanding examples of literary satire in the Bible (vv. 21–40).

First, we have Elijah's challenge to God's rebellious people (v. 21f). A paraphrase of his words in verse 22 would be "At this moment on this hilltop I stand alone with God."

Second, Elijah sets up the "ordeal" (vv. 23–24). It is accepted by the people. One wonders if the pagan prophets wanted this to happen! It is doubtful.

Third, the intensification of the satire is described (vv. 25–29). Animal blood sacrifice is involved, a common feature in animism (vv. 25,26a). The intensity of the religious fanaticism of the pagan prophets is graphically revealed (vv. 26–29). They continue from morning till the hour of the evening sacrifice, the ninth hour, or 3:00 P.M.

Fourth, Elijah acts to reformulate the faith they had abandoned. He rebuilds the partly destroyed "altar of the LORD" (v. 30). This symbolizes a return to the historical point when God first called them as a nation. It is a return to the faith of their fathers from which they had strayed. It is an act of rededication.

We next notice the aggressive steps taken by Elijah:

He dramatizes the situation with all physical factors set against him (vv. 32–35). He waits till the right moment, the time of the evening sacrifice, as a further reminder of the faith they have abandoned (v. 36a). He then declares the motive for the ordeal or challenge and that he acts only in the name of the Lord (v. 36b). Next, Elijah prays, publicly (v. 37). He goes "out on a limb," so to speak. God has to answer or Elijah is revealed as a false prophet. Then God would be no different than Baal and Asherah. Power encounters provoked by God's servants are acts of great faith.

Then the climax of the action is reached in verse 38. God answers with fire in the most dramatic way possible. The divine fire consumes Elijah's sacrifice. It burns up "the wood and the stones and the dust." It even "licked up the water that was in the trench" (v. 38).

Finally, the purpose of power encounter and trial by ordeal must always be kept in view. It does not serve just to validate the authority of God's servant, though that, too, usually occurs. It is meant *to lead people to a verdict, to a decision.* We find that in verse 39: "and when all the people saw it, they fell on their faces; and they said, 'The LORD, He is God; the LORD, He is God.'"

A summary of what has occurred would be:

The issue: God's people had left Him for the "no-gods."
The ordeal: The true God will vindicate His name and that of His servant.
The reformulation of the faith (vv. 30–32).
The motive (v. 36–37).
The climax (v. 38).
The verdict (v. 39).

The verdict results in a people movement leading to two acts: the altar of the Lord is rebuilt (vv. 30–32a); and the false prophets are put to death (v. 40).

CONFLICT WITH THE GODS AMONG THE WRITING PROPHETS

I will give one classic story of power encounter among the writing prophets (Isaiah through Malachi are the writing prophets; Abraham, Samuel, Elijah, Elisha, and others like them are often considered the non-writing prophets). The passage is Isaiah 57:1–21.

In the story Isaiah speaks and God speaks. It is difficult to know when one begins, leaves off, and the other begins.

First is described the sufferings of the unnamed "righteous man" (v. 1a). He could represent Isaiah himself. More likely he represents all the righteous in Judah who remain true to God. They are suffering at the hands of the apostate Jews and possibly some of the pagans of the land. Some were even killed for their faith (vv. 1b–2). This is the concept of "againstness," another key power encounter concept. It is the "for and against" motif found all through Scripture and church history.

Second, the opposing pagan cult is described exactly like the Canaanite cults we have already examined (v. 3f). It is led by a woman (v. 3). This, too, is common. She is a sorceress, who leads the people into sexual orgies. She is herself a cult prostitute (v. 3). The ones called the "sons" of this woman are the Jews who are involved in the cult with her.

Third, the Jews involved were totally given over to the cult. They were in rebellion against Isaiah and the righteous men who were trying to turn them from their apostasy. The rebellious Jews were using mockery ("jest"); verbal defiance ("open wide your mouth"); ridicule ("stick out your tongue"); and deceit. They were both deceived and, in turn, were deceivers (v. 4).

Fourth, the religious orgies ("inflame yourselves") were carried out in the sacred groves spoken of all through the Old Testament (v. 5a). What was done was done in the open and in groups. This was a key cultural feature of this abomination.

Fifth, near to the oaks were the Tophets (if the burial also took place there) where they sacrificed their children to the gods. This was done in wadis (small ravines) and in openings in the rocks (v. 5b), where the flame would not burn the "luxuriant" trees. The children were first killed by stabbing with a knife. Then their bodies were offered as burnt offerings to the gods.

This is Canaanite religion at its worst. It is also Jewish apostasy at its lowest point. In such practices demonic powers are present. Probably almost all, if not all, of these occult, satanic worshippers were severely demonized.

Sixth, stones were involved (v. 6a), usually of five types. One, a sacred stone was often set up. Idols or images of Baal and Astarte were placed on the stone. Two, altars were constructed of stones. Incense, libations, even the children's blood were offered upon the stone altars. Three, stone monuments to the gods or goddesses were often set up.[7] Four, stones as phallic symbols were common. Five, any unusual stone, rock, or rock formation was looked upon as either filled with impersonal power, or as the dwelling place of spirits.

The second part of Isaiah 57:6 makes it clear the stones were considered sacred. The stones themselves received the libations to the gods and spirits poured out upon them. Also, the grain offerings were placed upon them to be burned or left there for the gods to use (v. 6c).

Seventh, the groves were located on mountain tops or high places (v. 7a). Pagan ceremonies occurring on "high places" are very prominent in the Old Testament. There are dozens of references to them, especially in the historical books. The first references are in the Pentateuch, however. The one in Leviticus 26:30 provides the context for all such future references. There God warns Israel of the consequences of disobedience to his laws. He says, "I then will destroy your high places, and cut down your incense altars, and heap your remains on the remains of your idols; for My soul shall abhor you."

There, on the high places, "you have made your bed," Isaiah says. This probably refers to cult sexual practices including prostitution and ritual sexual acts. Did this also involve Satanic Ritual Abuse, as in today's revival of paganism? This is difficult to say. Some of the cult prostitutes were given to this form of prostitution by their parents as adolescent children and perhaps even before. So SRA could possibly have occurred. The high places were also the places where their sacrifices were offered.

Eighth, some sort of symbol of the deity seems implied in verse 8a, "and behind the door and the doorpost you have set up your sign." This may have been a secret, magical symbol hidden behind doors or in a concealed place in a doorpost. The individual would return to that magical symbol or spirit sign to gain new power. All pagan religion is a power game.

Ninth, all this was done by God's people "far removed from Me," the Lord says (v. 8b).

Tenth, the sexual perversions of this cultic system are again mentioned (v. 8c). They were evidently the most prominent feature of the cult. This is seen in several features here. One, there is the prior reference to "inflame yourselves among the oaks" (v. 5a). Next is "you have uncovered yourself" (v. 8c). This is followed by the reference to their "bed" (v. 8c).

Also we find "you have made an agreement for yourselves with them," that is, the temple prostitutes (v. 8d). Then we have, "You have looked on their manhood" (v. 8d). Was this a phallic symbol? Or was this homosexual prostitution? The latter is a strong possibility (see Deut. 23:17).

Eleventh, they exported their practices to others, far and wide (v. 9). In doing so, they were leading themselves and those they enticed to follow their wicked ways "down to Sheol," that is, to death (v. 9b).

Twelfth, the next verse seems to imply this unrestrained evil lifestyle wore them out. It was personally costly. Yet they continued with it, renewing their strength but only for continued evil (v. 10).

Thirteenth, God says they were liars and had so totally forgotten God that they did not give him a thought when worry and fear gripped their hearts. They simply went back to their decadent practices. Their "deeds" and "righteousness" are of such a perverted sort: it brings them no profit, only shame (vv. 11–12).

Fourteenth, God challenges and warns the rebellious Jews, "When you cry out, let your collection of idols deliver you" (v. 13a). God then contrasts himself with their gods who are so unstable "a breath will take them away." In contrast God is a faithful refuge (v. 13b).

Finally, God promises that if they humble themselves and come back to Him, He will forgive, bless, and restore them. If not, they will never find peace (vv. 14–21).

What a remarkable passage of Scripture! How deep, however, was Israel's involvement with evil spirits in the days of Isaiah![8] A similar picture is found in Jeremiah and several of the other prophets who wrote just before and during the time of the Exile.

The Case of Job

There remain other significant Old Testament stories with a strong spiritual warfare motif. The story of Job and Satan's attack upon him will be referred to several times in our New Testament studies. The main focus of Job 1—2 is the direct role Satan has in the sufferings of this man of God. Satan is behind all the sufferings and losses suffered by Job.

The attacks are varied. First is the attack through evil men (1:13–15). Second is a natural disaster that destroyed all Job's sheep and killed all but one of his servants. The surviving servant called the disaster "the fire of God" (v. 16). Yet it did not come from God but from Satan.

The third is another attack from hostile men, in which Job's camels are stolen and his servants killed (v. 17). The fourth is another natural disaster which kills all of all his sons and daughters (vv. 18–19).

Satan, not God, is involved in all these tragedies suffered by Job. Satan manipulates evil men, this we have always known to be true. Is he also the direct cause of all natural disasters, except those which are clearly sent by God to judge sinful men? Most tragic of all is the sudden death of all of Job's children. Can Satan take the lives of the children of God's children? According to Job's story, Satan can do all of the above, but only with God's permission.

In Job 2, it is Job himself who is attacked. Satan is given permission to cause all manner of physical evils to befall him, short of taking his life. God tells Satan "Behold, he is in your power, only spare his life" (2:6). His life is spared but not the life of his children. Most good parents would gladly give their life for that of their children. There are great mysteries here yet to be pondered.

When we come to Satan's attempts to accuse Joshua the high priest in Zechariah 3:1–4, God immediately stops him (v. 2). Evidently God only allows some of his faithful servants to be accused and abused by Satan but not others. God is sovereign in all things, even in His handling of Satan and evil.

The Case of Hosea

Most of the remaining major spiritual warfare passages in the Old Testament are dealt with elsewhere in our studies. I will, however, close this chapter with the Book of Hosea. It is a good summary of God's polemic with Israel and Judah for their flagrant "harlotry" in forsaking the Lord. Hosea gives a most thorough and heart-rending picture of the apostasy of God's people. The main focus is on the nation's harlotry with the idols of the land and with Baal in particular.

The word *harlot* is mentioned ten times, the word *harlotry* nine, an unusual concentration of references for a book of its size. The book primarily has spiritual harlotry in view even when it refers to the prophet's harlot wife. In addition are the six appearances of the word *lovers,* again with spiritual adultery in view. *Idols* are mentioned seven times; *Baal* and *Baals* seven times.

Some key verses are: "I will punish her for the days of the Baals when she used to offer sacrifice to them" (2:13a). Israel is accused of following " 'her lovers, so that she forgot Me,' declares the LORD" (2:13b). "Ephraim is joined to idols; let him alone," God says (4:17). Next God says, "The men themselves go apart with harlots and offer sacrifice with temple prostitutes" (4:14b). "They play the harlot continually" (4:18).

God then follows with, "My people consult their wooden idol, and their diviner's wand informs them; for a spirit of harlotry has led them astray" (4:12). "For you have played the harlot, forsaking your God. You have loved harlots' earnings on every threshing floor," that is, in ritual sexual harvest orgies (9:1).

"They came to Baal-peor," God continues, "and devoted themselves to shame, and they became as detestable as that which they loved" (9:10). "Israel made the sacred pillars," or phallic symbols (10:1–2).

Most amazing are God's cries of both love and lament for his wayward people. He promises that they will return to Him as the result of the terrible punishment He must allow to fall upon them. "How can I give you up, O Ephraim? How can I surrender you, O Israel? . . . My heart is turned over within Me. All my compassions are kindled" (11:8). What a loving God we have!

This concludes our spiritual warfare overview of the Old Testament. Much yet remains to be said. The New Testament will build upon and greatly expand what we have discovered in the Old Testament. If we seem to have a scarcity of direct references to Satan and demons in the Old Testament, the opposite is true in the New Testament. The Gospels truly present a picture of demons everywhere.

PART FOUR

A Survey of Biblical Teaching

New Testament

Jesus Encounters the Devil and Demons

36

The Temptation

Modern Scholar Boldly Reaffirms Existence of Devil[1]

The Old Testament emphasizes the person and absolute sovereignty of God. Historian Jeffrey Burton Russell writes that "in pre-exilic Hebrew religion . . . the Devil did not exist. The Hebrew concept of the Devil developed gradually, arising from certain tensions within the concept of Yahweh."[2] In light of our studies of Genesis 3, we would have to question the statement that in "pre-exilic Hebrew religion the Devil did not exist." Indeed the Devil did exist even if he was called the serpent, not the Devil. Otherwise the Genesis story would not be a truthful rendering of the world view of Patriarchial or pre-Patriarchial Hebrew culture.[3]

In an interview with *Christianity Today,* Russell clarifies the above.[4]

> In the Old Testament there is a tension between the idea that the Lord is absolutely powerful, that everything that happens is the will of the Lord, and the idea that there are spiritual forces obstructing or battling the work of the Lord. . . . It is not until the intertestamental period that Satan really comes forth as a very powerful and independent personality.

That the early Jewish world view did include spiritual forces obstructing or battling the work of the Lord is clear from Genesis 3 through Malachi. That these forces were not described with the detail and clarity with which they were later treated by the Jews in the intertestamental period is no problem to those who believe in progressive revelation. One does not have to possess the latest description of a reality to experience it in its fullness. Russell himself implies this in this affirmation:

> The fact that the Devil is not fully developed in the Old Testament is not a ground for rejecting his existence in modern Jewish and Christian theology. That would be the generic fallacy; the notion that the truth of a word—or a concept—is to be found in the earliest form.[5]

When we come to the New Testament we do discover a somewhat highly developed Satanology and demonology. Russell says that in the New Testament

> the powers of darkness under the generalship of the Devil are at war with the power of light . . . Christianity has the virtue of taking the problem of evil seriously. . . . The conflict between good and evil stands at the center of New Testament Christianity.[6]

Russell then systematically criticizes all attempts at dealing with the problem of evil without taking into account the personal Devil and his kingdom of fallen angels. He strongly criticizes the continual attempt by Christian theologians and writers to play down, even to dismiss, the reality of a personal Devil. He criticizes all attempts to dismiss all Christian dualism. He does the same with the demythologizers who try to remove both the miraculous and the demonic from Scripture. The demythologizing approach towards the Devil is a position impossible to support historically or in its contemporary outworking. According to Russell, students of Christianity are fortunately now turning away from this unprofitable approach.[7]

It is refreshing to read the words of a prominent historian as he criticizes any attempt to remove the Devil and evil supernaturalism from their central position in Christian theology. It is also refreshing to find a scholar of Russell's repute who so fully recognizes the centrality of cosmic-earthly spiritual warfare to salvation-history. When Western Christians remove their monistic eyeglasses which see God directly involved in all evil which falls upon believers and unbelievers, and begin to see the Devil as directly involved, we will begin to more effectively live and minister within a biblical world view.

There exists an almost universal agreement that Satan was originally an angelic creature, probably of the rank of Michael the Archangel. Before the creation of man, he rebelled against the lordship of God, taking about one-third of the angels of God in rebellion with him. While demons universally will affirm that they were deceived into rebellion by Satan, it is nowhere stated how Satan (Lucifer?) could be deceived in the first place. This is another given in Scripture.

Clinton E. Arnold says that "The Bible never explicitly addresses the origin of evil spirits or their ruler, Satan. The biblical writers are far more concerned about the *fact* of their existence than with speculations about how they rebelled against God."[8]

JESUS AND THE DEVIL: THE SYNOPTIC GOSPELS

Satan's opposition to Jesus, and Jesus' need to face the Devil in terrible combat and His total victory over him concern Matthew, Mark, and Luke.

Baptism and Temptation

Both Jesus' baptism and His conflict with the Tempter are tied in directly with the beginning of Jesus' public ministry (Matt. 3–4). Mark and Luke join Matthew in beginning our Lord's public ministry with these two interrelated events. "Immediately," Matthew tells us, "the heavens were opened, and he [evidently John] saw the Spirit of God descending as a dove, and coming upon Him, and behold, a voice out of the heavens saying, 'This is My beloved Son, in whom I am well-pleased'" (3:16–17).

What a way to begin His ministry! He is baptized by John in the Jordan, evidently in public. The heavens open. God the Father speaks for all to hear that this one is His "beloved Son" and that the Father is already "well-pleased" with Him, even before He begins His public ministry.

We would expect Him, filled with the Holy Spirit (Luke 4:1) to begin His public ministry of preaching, teaching, healing, and casting out of demons right away. Instead, Matthew tells us

> Then Jesus was led up by the Spirit into the wilderness to be tempted by the devil. And after He had fasted forty days and forty nights, He then became hungry. And the tempter came and said to Him . . . . (Matt. 4:1–2)

Now we are in another world. Before Matthew is through with the story, "the tempter" is called "the devil" (4:5,8,11) and Jesus calls him "Satan" (v. 10). We are face-to-face with spiritual warfare of the most intense magnitude. Jesus, the Son of God, meets the Devil, Satan and the Tempter, face-to-face in true mortal combat.

In His public baptism, Jesus commits Himself to do the will of the Father who was already well pleased with Him (Matt. 3:13–17). In His private encounter with the Tempter, He reveals that the major focus of His ministry will be against Satan, the ruler of this age. To win men from Satan's kingdom to God's, He must first personally, as a man, overcome the Devil's power.

Jesus, though divine as a person, will not function at all on the level of His divinity. He will function only at the level of His humanity. That is what the wilderness temptation is all about. Satan is allowed again to resist God in man and to attempt to destroy God's purposes for the man whom God made in His own image. Man, in the person of the God-man, is also given a second chance to face and resist that temptation. This time the Second Man will obey God and win the war with sin and Satan. He will not fail as did the first man in his encounter with the Evil One.

We will primarily use Matthew's account and go to the other two only when necessary. Mark's is the briefest of the three. The only distinctive feature is his statement that, during the temptation, Jesus "was with the wild beasts" (1:31). This was mentioned probably for at least two reasons.

One, to reveal that it was a true "wilderness" (Matt. 4:1; Mark 1:12; Luke 4:1). It was a lonely, dangerous place. He was alone, without the comfort of the presence of other human beings. Kenneth Wuest says:[9]

> The region abounded with bears, jackals, wolves, foxes, leopards and hyenas. Expositors suggest that this description is "not merely pictorial or intended to hint danger, rather to indicate the uninhabited nature of the place; no supplies obtainable there, hunger therefore a part of the experience." Alford commenting on this says, "Perhaps the being with the beasts may point to one form of temptation, that of terror, which was practiced on Him." The first Adam fell into sin in an environment that was perfect and harmonious. The Last Adam maintained His sinlessness in an environment that was hostile.

Jesus is to be seen here as the Last Adam and the Second Man in contrast to the first Adam and the first man (1 Cor. 15:45–47). Adam, the representative man, was seduced into disobedience by the Devil. Jesus as the new representative man, the Last Adam and the Second Man, is to face the same temptation from the same source. Jesus was to undo the tragedy of Adam's fall, but it was to be more difficult for Him than it was for Adam.

Adam was tempted in the garden of God where all his needs were fully met. He had food, shelter, the companionship of his wife, and the presence of God. The animals there were all his friends. Here we see Jesus in a hostile context, however.

There He is alone, without food, and probably without adequate shelter. His only companions are wild animals who did not live at peace with humanity.

The wilderness in Jesus' day was also considered as the abode of demons (Matt. 12:43). John Broadus, commenting on Matthew 12:43 says, "It was a prevailing Jewish idea that evil spirits especially frequented desert or desolate places. See Tobit 8:3, Baruch 4:35. . . . The imagery . . . is favored by this passage and Revelation 18:2."[10]

Since Jesus is to penetrate the very abode of evil supernaturalism, it is fitting that it should be symbolized by the wilderness. There Satan rules. All of the environment is conducive towards fear and danger from the spirit world. Especially is this true when one is without food and shelter for a long period of time. In these circumstances a human being is even more defensiveless. He is exhausted. His mind does not function well and his emotions are out of control. His will and resolve are at their lowest. He is most susceptible to any offer of relief. This is the context in which Jesus finds Himself in the wilderness as He braces for the Devil's attack.

Matthew says, "Then Jesus was led by the Spirit into the wilderness to be tempted by the devil" (4:1). The "then" here is like a "therefore" in other passages. It takes us back to the preceding story. In this case what precedes is Jesus' baptism in water and anointing by the Holy Spirit. Mark makes it even clearer. He writes "immediately the Spirit impelled Him to go into the wilderness" (Mark 1:12).

Matthew next says, "And after He had fasted forty days and forty nights, He then became hungry" (v. 2). Both Mark and Luke add their descriptions which help us to see what was going on during these forty days and nights before the last three temptations by the Devil recorded by Matthew and Luke.

Mark writes, "He was in the wilderness forty days being tempted by Satan; and He was with the wild beasts, and the angels were ministering to Him" (Mark 1:13). Taking these words in their most natural sense, they would imply that He was being tempted by the Devil during the entire forty-day period.

Luke writes that Jesus was "in the wilderness for forty days, being tempted by the devil. And He ate nothing during those days; and when they had ended, He became hungry. And the devil said to Him . . ." (Luke 4:1b–3a). Again the natural interpretation would be that He was being tempted by the Devil during the entire period. Though not all commentators are agreed, it seems the final three temptations came at the end of the forty-day temptation period when He began to feel the full impact of His prolonged fast and Satan's continual, oppressive temptations.

Kenneth Wuest points out that the word "being tempted" in Mark 1:13 is a present tense participle speaking of continuous action:[11]

> Satan tempted Messiah constantly during the forty days. The three temptations which Matthew records at the end of the forty day period of temptation, merely indicate the additional intensity of the temptations as the period of temptation closes. Satan was attempting his worst, seeing that he had but a short time left.

C. L. Blomberg summarizes the four main approaches to this account found among biblical interpreters.[12] There is first a "parenetic or psychological view in which Jesus' temptations represent the three main categories of human temptations (cf. 1 John 2:16, 'The lust of the flesh and the lust of the eyes and the pride of life'; cf. also the three appeals of the tree of the knowledge of good and evil for Eve in Gen. 3:6)." Second is the "Christological approach, which stresses the obedient nature of the son of God."

Third is the "messianic interpretation, in which Jesus is tempted to reject the way of the cross in favor of following the more political, nationalistic hopes of his countrymen." Finally is the "salvation-historical option in which Jesus obeys the commands of God that Israel had disobeyed in the wilderness wanderings, thus proving Himself to be the true representative of Israel." Blomberg says, "None of these views necessarily excludes the others." I agree. I would say all four are in view.

Temptation One

The first temptation enticed Jesus to meet His desperate physical needs outside of God's will.[13] Both Matthew and Luke connect this temptation to Jesus' terrible hunger (Matt. 4:2b–3; Luke 4:2b–3). Both record that the Devil assails Jesus with this particular temptation as proof of His Sonship with God the Father, "If you are the Son of God . . ." (Matt. 4:3 and Luke 4:3). We are not to see the "if" as an expression of doubt on Satan's part as to the Lord's true nature. The doubt lies in another area. Satan well knew who He was. Broadus says Satan invites Jesus

> to establish the fact by a miracle and in order to intimate that He certainly has the right to satisfy His hunger. "Son" is by its position in the Greek, emphatic. God's ordinary creatures may suffer, they cannot help it; but if thou art his Son, it is unworthy of thee thus to suffer, and unnecessary—"speak, that these stones may become loaves." It does not follow on this view, that Satan fully understood what was involved in Jesus' being God's Son; and this ignorance will account for an attempt otherwise not only audacious but absurd.[14]

Jesus had legitimate physical needs that unmet would eventually lead to death. Satan is saying Jesus could and should provide Himself with food by exercising His divine powers. The rashness of this suggestion cannot be exaggerated. Jesus is the Son of God become the Son of Man. As such, He is to function as a man, not as God or a demigod. He is not to be a man some of the time and God at other times.

The moment Jesus begins to function as God, He ceases to be the Last Adam. He ceases to be identified with us in our temptations and sufferings. While He is always God, He will never function by His divine attributes while He lives among men (Phil. 2:5–11). Thus Satan not only reveals his evilness, he also reveals his ignorance of the true implications of the Incarnation.

Also, even if Jesus were allowed, so to speak, to use His creative attributes so He could turn the stones of the desert into bread, He would not do so. Why? Because it was God the Holy Spirit who "drove" (KJV), "impelled" (NAS) Him into the wilderness (Mark 1:12), not the Devil. The word translated "drove" and "impelled" is the Greek word *ekballō*. Wuest says it means "literally, to cast forth, with the suggestion of force (*ek*, 'out'; *ballō*, 'to cast'); hence to drive out or forth."[15] Wuest says Mark's word is "stronger than Matthew's *anagō*, 'was led up,' and Luke's *agō*, 'was led.'" It was used in our Lord's expulsion of demons in Mark 1:34 and 39.

He was in the wilderness because God the Holy Spirit sent Him there. Not that He was reluctant to go "into so wild a place," says A. B. Bruce.[16] But the Spirit filled His mind with the prophets' vision to be alone with God, meet His adversary head on, and reach out to sinful, burdened men with the message of the kingdom of God. Since God compelled Him to go there, He wilfully went. Since God impressed upon His mind the need to fast the forty days and nights of the temptation, He did so. He also knew His Father would sustain Him.

A. B. Bruce says, "Those few touches of Mark suggest a vivid picture of a spiritual crisis: intense preoccupation, instinctive retreat into congenial grim solitudes, temptation, struggle fierce and protracted, issuing in weakness, calling for preternatural aid."[17]

Jesus gives only one word of response to Satan's first temptation. "It is written, 'Man shall not live on bread alone, but on every word that proceeds out of the mouth of God' " (Matt. 4:4). Such direct quotations from Scripture, are *rhema,* a portion of the Word of God brought to the mind by the indwelling Holy Spirit which becomes God's answer to Satan's present line of temptation. This will later become the famous "sword of the Spirit, which is the word of God" of Paul's spiritual warfare teachings in Ephesians 6:17.

Satan himself will try to wield this same sword of the Spirit in the second temptation (v. 6). As always, he will misapply the divine truth and will be sharply rebuked by Jesus for doing so. Jesus will again quote God's Word to silence the adversary's misuse of that word (v. 7).[18]

While Satan failed in this first temptation with Jesus, he knows *this approach is effective against believers.* He still begins his assault against our minds in the natural, physical realm. "If you are a son of God you have physical needs which must be met. Here's the logical way of meeting those needs. Do it." And we do it. We become selfish. We become worldly, living for creature comforts. We adopt a lifestyle with a success orientation primarily measured by power, position, pleasure, and possession. We even create a power, position, pleasure, and possession *theology* to support our attempts to turn stones into bread for selfish purposes. We are one of the most bread-seeking generations of Christians ever to live on this earth.

Broadus suggests that during the forty days in the wilderness Jesus had been meditating on Israel's forty years in the wilderness. Deuteronomy records Moses' reviewing Israel's wilderness experience just before the people crossed the Jordan into the Promised Land. As the representative man, Jesus is also the representative Jew. In His forty days in the wilderness He too is being tested by God through Satan as Israel was in their forty years of wanderings. Whereas Israel continually failed, refusing to believe God's Word, Jesus chooses to believe and obey. The sword He uses against Satan's attacks is choice nuggets of God's Word from Deuteronomy (4:4,7,10).

Temptation Two

Matthew writes, "Then the devil took Him into the holy city; and he had Him stand on the pinnacle of the temple, and said to Him, 'If you are the Son of God throw Yourself down . . .' " (4:5–6a). Much has been written about Jesus being carried physically by Satan from the wilderness back to the city of Jerusalem and placed on "the pinnacle of the temple." Did this occur in time and space or simply in Jesus' mind? The two views are: one, this literally happened in the physical realm;[19] two, it all occurred in the realm of the mind.[20]

A. B. Bruce compares the latter view to the experience of Ezekiel being carried by the Holy Spirit "by a lock of my head" from Babylon to Jerusalem. Ezekiel tells us that it all occurred in a vision (Ezek. 8:3).[21] This possibly occurred here.

It is the *meaning* of the temptation that counts, not the details of how it came to pass. Even in seeking for the main thrusts of the Devil's temptation we encounter problems, however. Many commentators see a twofold temptation: one, for Jesus to prove His trust in God by an irrational act; two, for Him to do so in public to gain the loyalty of the multitudes.[22] Others see only that Jesus is tempted to test God's promise of protection by exposing Himself to life-threatening danger. While the former has interesting possibilities,[23] I believe our Lord's reply in verse 7 gives the answer, "You shall not put the Lord your God to the test." Jesus saw one temptation.

In contrast to the first temptation appealing to Jesus' physical needs, the second tempted Him towards religious fanaticism. As Calvin expresses it, Satan:

> exhorts him (Jesus) to indulge in a foolish and vain confidence—to neglect the means which are in his power—to throw Himself, without necessity, into manifest danger—and, as we might say, to overleap all bounds . . . to induce Christ to make trial of His divinity, and to rise up, in foolish and wicked rashness, against God.[24]

Jesus is to lay aside His common sense and act as if He were a totally spiritual being, not an embodied spiritual being living in a world governed by natural laws created by God which are to be carefully observed in the course of one's life. He is to cast aside all God-given instincts toward averting danger and cast Himself into a totally religious world. He is to expect direct divine intervention whenever He wanted it and according to His views of how God should operate on His behalf. This would be a miracle-on-demand lifestyle.

Jesus saw through this deception towards fanaticism; He saw it was putting God to the test to see if He was truly with Him, but He did not slip into fanaticism and the quest for miracles on demand to prove the presence of God in His life. While God does confirm by miracles, it is only on His terms. Sometimes He works miracles, but more often He does not. We obey in either case and God gets all the glory, not us. This is a needed lesson in our day of Christian showmanship.

Temptation Three

In the third temptation, Satan lays aside the subtle approach he used in the first two. Now, in desperation, he throws all caution to the wind. He is losing ground. Frantic to succeed, he comes to the heart of the matter. Satan wants Jesus to pay him homage, tribute, honor, and service, if only for a moment (Matt. 4:9). In return he will give to Jesus what Jesus rightfully should possess, "all the kingdoms of the world, and their glory." "Jesus can rule them," Satan promises. Of course, He can only do so side-by-side with Satan who actually owns them all (vv. 8–9 with Luke 4:6).

First, "the devil took him to a very high mountain" (v. 8). We must resist the peripheral concerns dealt with by many commentators as to whether or not Satan actually moved Jesus bodily through space and what mountain is involved. Those concerns only accommodate our humanness. To see all the kingdoms of the world, one is naturally pictured as looking from the top of a high mountain. Commentators are also divided about how to view Satan's boast that "all the kingdoms of the world, and their glory" have "been handed over to me, and I give it to whomever I wish" (Luke 4:6). Jesus did not refute Satan's claim. That in itself is not proof He accepted the claim. The temptation does not focus on Satan's claim, but on Jesus' response.

Others state that Satan is, by nature, a liar (John 8:44). He never can deliver what he promises. He will promise us "the world" if he can but gain some control over our life. While this is true, it is also true that there is often truth in Satan's lies. This makes his lies that much more deceitful and dangerous.

On three occasions Jesus Himself described the Devil as "the ruler of this world" (John 12:31; 14:30; 16:11). Satan presently rules the kingdoms of this world, not God. While God is always God and as such He ultimately rules over all, He allows Satan and evil men to rule until the coming day of His kingdom when their rule will be abolished and His will be established forever. As Broadus says:[25]

> The claim which Satan here implies that he possesses the control of the kingdom of the world and their glory is not wholly unfounded . . . . The Scriptures speak of him as the prince or god of this world (John 12:31; 14:30; 16:11; 2 Cor. 4:4). As to the precise nature and limitations of this power we are not informed; but it has been committed to him (Luke 4:6), and the Revelation of John teaches that it shall one day be withdrawn.

Most critical commentators agree with Broadus. A. B. Bruce goes so far as to say that Luke's addition of "It has been handed over to me" was "added to guard against the notion of a rival God with independent possessions and power."[26]

As to who handed these kingdoms over to Satan there are also two views: One, Adam did when he sinned. He switched his loyalty from God to Satan. Thus the God-given control to man over the earth is transferred to Satan. Two, God gave Satan the rule over the world as a result of the Fall. Which is true? In a sense both are true. This is immaterial to the point of the story: Will Jesus respond to Satan's offer of a painless shortcut to world dominion, or will He choose the Father's road, the Calvary road?

Broadus well sums up the appeal behind the phrase, "if you will fall down and worship me" (Matt. 4:9): falling down is "the usual posture in the East, whether for adoration or for homage." If all this is implied is homage paid to Satan, that automatically means worship.[27]

> The tempter proposes that Jesus shall recognize the worldly power which Satan is allowed to exercise, and shall conform his Messianic reign to existing conditions by acknowledging Satan's sovereignty. Jesus was in fact to reign over this world, yet not as successor or subordinate to Satan, but by utterly overthrowing his dominion.

Jesus' Response

What did Jesus do? He overcame the temptation with two final words, first one of stern rebuke (v. 10a), then one of total commitment (v. 10b). He spoke the rebuke forcefully and probably vocally to Satan himself, "Begone, Satan." It is "Get thee hence, Satan" in the KJV, "Away with you, Satan" in PHILLIPS.

James Morrison records Jeremy Taylor as saying that this is "a word of indignation and of castigation and of dismission. . . . The Lamb of God was angry as a provoked lion, and commanded him away, when his demands were imprudent and blasphemous." He then comments, "The victory is achieved. The Second Adam has not fallen and will not fall. For 'it stands written.' Our Lord wields His favorite weapon. It is the sword of His mouth. It is too *the sword of the Spirit.*"[28]

Jesus concludes His dismissal of Satan and His word of total commitment to God and His worship, homage, and service. "For it is written, 'You shall worship the Lord your God, and serve Him only' " (v. 10b). Later when Jesus is asked which is the greatest commandment, He will answer, "You shall love the LORD your God with all your heart, and with all your soul, and with all your mind. This is the great and foremost commandment" (Matt. 22:37–38). Here Jesus becomes the supreme example of that totally consuming love.

Matthew then records, "The devil left Him . . ." (v. 11). Luke adds his own unique ending to the temptation account: "And when the devil had finished every temptation, he departed from Him until an opportune time" (Luke 4:13).

A. B. Bruce says this phrase implies that similar temptations recurred in the experience of Jesus.[29] Geldenhuys agrees.[30]

> In every possible way that he could think of he assailed the Saviour, but without avail. So he departed when vanquished, but not for good. Again and again he renewed his attacks on Jesus on suitable occasions (cf. 11:13 and Mark 8:32–33), even through Peter.

Geldenhuys then points to Gethsemane and the Cross as the ultimate of temptations.[31]

> But it was especially when the Lord on the eve of the crucifixion wrestled in Gethsemane that Satan attacked Him . . . with all the power and savagery of hell in a desperate attempt to overcome Him before He finally triumphed in His death on the cross over all the powers of darkness and confirmed His victory through the resurrection and ascension.

The subtle threefold deceptions Satan tried with Jesus he continues with us. In our Lord's case, he totally failed (John 14:30). With us, he too often succeeds. If we can but learn from our Lord's example! We all have legitimate human needs for food, shelter, and all the rest. Everything depends on how we go about meeting those needs and where such needs fit into God's priorities for our life, however (Matt. 4:4).

We all need and want God's supernatural activity in our life. We are willing, if necessary, to place our lives in danger in His will. I, with my entire family, have faced many life-threatening situations in our mission work. At times I wondered if I should not leave violent Colombia, South America, where my wife, my children, and I had our life threatened more than once. One enraged man fired a pistol at me point blank, three times, but his bullets could not find their mark. God's angels were with me and with my family.

Every time I contemplated leaving for greater safety, I had to respond to only one question, "Were we in Colombia in God's will?" The answer was "yes." Therefore we could rightfully claim Psalm 91:11–12:

> He will give His angels charge concerning you . . . they will bear you up in their hands lest you strike your foot against a stone.

Finally, we are all tempted daily concerning the focus of our homage. Do we love the Lord our God with all our heart, soul, and mind, and our neighbor as ourselves? (Matt. 22:37–40).

Having met the test of the temptations, Jesus is now ready to enter into His proclamation, healing, and deliverance ministry. Satan failed personally to dislodge Jesus from His obedience to the Father's will. Perhaps if Satan opens the pit of demons to allow them almost to smother Jesus with their vile presence, they can do what Satan himself failed to do.

37

In the Synagogue
Mark 1

Ⅰf we had only the case of Satan's assault against Adam and Eve and the account of his first major attack against Jesus, we would have enough to discover almost every major aspect of Satan's strategy of deception. There would be one element that would be missing, however. It is Satan's ability to launch systematic, well-organized, and non-ending assaults against any number of human beings at the same time, through his vast army of co-workers, "co-devils" in that sense, evil spirits.

As we look at Jesus and the demons in the Gospels, we see Jesus living and ministering in a world of such systemic evil supernaturalism. Satan and his demons are at war with mankind and with Jesus, and Jesus has declared war on them. This is what George E. Ladd had in mind when he wrote that Jesus' ministry was that of "attacking the dominion of Satan and delivering men from the power of evil."[1]

> God's kingdom in Jesus' teaching has a twofold manifestation: at the end of the age to destroy Satan, and in Jesus' mission to bind Satan. . . . In some way beyond human comprehension, Jesus wrestled with the powers of evil, won a victory over them, that in the end of the age these powers may be finally and forever broken.

JESUS' FIRST ENCOUNTER WITH DEMONS

Mark 1 records Jesus' first public encounter with demons in the gospel narrative, the deliverance of the demonized man in the synagogue of Capernaum (1:21–28).

The Setting (1:21–22)

The deliverance occurred in Galilee, in the city of Capernaum, on the northwestern shore of the Sea of Galilee, a beautiful spot even today. According to Matthew 4:12–17, Jesus settled in this city. It was his home whenever he was in Galilee. It was the city of Simon Peter and his brother, Andrew (v. 29).

The deliverance took place in the synagogue of Capernaum while Jesus was teaching. It was a common practice for gifted laymen to be allowed to teach in the synagogues in Jesus' day. Since Jesus is later called *Rabbi*, "teacher," Jesus evidently became a noted teacher in the synagogues. The most striking feature of Jesus' teaching was the authority with which he taught (vv. 22,27).[2]

A Demonic Goes to Church (1:23f)

Mark writes, "And just then there was in their synagogue a man with an unclean spirit." Luke's description of his case is unique in Scripture. He says the man was indwelt "by the spirit of an unclean demon" (Luke 4:33).

The synagogues were the local churches of those days. What kind of people go to church? Primarily, religious people. Generally speaking, all believe in God and in Christ. They are there because they want to be where the people of God meet and where their needs will be met. Here worshippers engage in prayer and praise. Here is where the Bible is taught.

It was no different in our Lord's day. People went to synagogue on the Sabbath because they wanted to go, especially in Gentile cities like Capernaum. While it is impossible to say what proportion of the city was made up of Jews or of Gentiles, Galilee was called "Galilee of the Gentiles" (Matt. 4:12–15). The Jewish communities were always close-knit in cities like Capernaum. Almost all of the Jews attended synagogue each Sabbath.

Why do I place such emphasis on this fact? Because this man was probably a believer, not an unbeliever. Even if he was a God-fearing Gentile or a proselyte, in all probability he was a believer or he would not be there.

R. Alan Cole says that Capernaum

> was the proud city of unbelief, compared with which Tyre and Sidon would fare well in the day of judgment (Matt. 11:23–24). It is a strange commentary on the spiritual situation in Capernaum that a demonic could worship in their synagogue with no sense of incongruity, until confronted by Jesus and apparently with no desire to be delivered from his affliction.[3]

The statement that the man apparently had "no desire to be delivered from his affliction" comes from ignorance of how demons and the demonized operate. Demons do not usually announce their presence to their victims. Unless the individual is born demonized, the demons slip into a human life at a specific point of trauma or sin. They do not want to be discovered and are angry when they are, as this demon was (vv. 23–24). The afflicted individual is not usually aware he is demonized and will remain ignorant of his true condition until one or more of three possible circumstances produce a change in the demon's hitherto incognito activity within the life of his victim.

First, the demon may be forced into manifestation by a man of God who operates with authority in the spirit realm. This can occur in public ministry as it did here.

Second, the victim begins to suspect part of his personal problems may be demonic. This usually occurs when the individual begins to receive teaching on the demonic realm.[4] He begins to pray and do spiritual warfare in a manner quite different from the sterile, matter-of-fact manner it is carried on by the average believer. When this occurs the demons may begin to make their presence known to intimidate the believer or in fear or anger or both.

Third, the demonic affliction becomes so bad and the victim so emotionally, spiritually, and often physically injured and incapacitated (see Mark 5:1f) that the demons can make their presence known to their victim. Their purpose in doing so is to increase their victim's pain. That is why they are called "evil spirits."

With this in mind, let's return to our story. We can use a touch of what I like to call sanctified imagination to make the story more real and to better understand what probably occurred.

Both Peter and Andrew were hard-working men who were members of this synagogue. When they asked permission for their friend Jesus from Nazareth to teach, it was readily given. Jesus took the scroll from the hand of the synagogue attendant and read some of the well-known Messianic passages from Isaiah. He explained that the day of God's visitation had come to Israel. The satanic, demonic bondage of mankind was going to be broken. The good news of God's redemption from the guilt, penalty, and power of sin was at hand.

All of a sudden the demonized man was filled with fear. He could not continue looking at the eyes of Jesus. Jesus' eyes burned him. They seemed to glow with the white heat of God's holiness, making the man feel uncomfortable.

What is happening to me? he thought. *I feel deep anger within me towards this Jesus. I don't want to listen anymore. His words are upsetting me. I feel anger, rage, fear, almost terror within me.*

Something inside of me is rising up in protest against Jesus and is taking over. I can't resist any longer. What is wrong with me?

All of the above occurred within a matter of seconds. Suddenly a demonic personality emerges from within the man, forcing the body of his victim to his feet and screaming out at Jesus, using the man's vocal cords, interrupting Jesus' teaching: "What have you got to do with us, Jesus from Nazareth? Have you come to kill us? I know who you are—you're God's holy one" (v. 24, PHILLIPS).

Something like the above could have occurred that Sabbath in Capernaum. It was not, as Cole assumed, that the man was unconcerned with his demonic condition. As is true of most demonized persons, he probably did not know he was demonized. As to the sad "spiritual situation in Capernaum that a demoniac could worship in their synagogue with incongruity until confronted by Jesus," this too is not unusual. It is more the norm than the exception.

Such people will probably be found in most all of our churches, even strong evangelical ones. Mark records that Jesus, after leaving Capernaum, "went into their synagogues throughout all Galilee, preaching and casting out the demons" (v. 39). This type of ministry is needed in our churches today, worldwide. These may be shocking words. If they are it is because we have too often read Mark 1:39 filtered through the grid of too many theological presuppositions. Thus these words have lost their real impact on our lives.

Cole says it well:[5]

> The immediate result of Christ's preaching was not harmony, but division and strife, exactly as He later warned (Matt. 10:34). This strife might be concealed in the minds of the congregation, but was made plain in the outcry of the demoniac.

Demons do what demons do, not what we think they can or cannot do. If we are going to avoid being ignorant of the schemes of our enemy (2 Cor. 2:11), we dare not stipulate which schemes are acceptable to them or dictate to the God who allows them to operate in our midst.

The Demonic Discourse (1:24)

The demon appears to begin with a question, which as we will soon see, is not a true question at all: "What do we have to do with you, Jesus of Nazareth?" The literal translation is "What to us and to thee, Jesus Nazarene?"[6] This is not a question. According to Webster, a question is "a way of seeking for information or testing one's knowledge." The demon was not seeking for information nor was he testing Jesus' knowledge. Frightened and angry, he was protesting the disturbing, threatening presence and teaching of Jesus, the Holy One of God.

The demon wanted Jesus to go away and leave him alone. He and his companion demons had held their victim in bondage for years, inflicting upon him deep, inner pain—up until now. They had probably afflicted him with "floating guilt," a strong sense of rejection, and a feeling of worthlessness and hopelessness.

They "loved" the sheer, sadistic joy of seeing their host suffer and of being the primary source of his suffering. It was the "joy" of gradually increasing their con-

In the Synagogue 273

trol over more and more areas of his life until he literally moaned from within, cried when he was alone, and most joyful of all, cried to God in vain.

Now this Jesus they had been warned about by their master, Satan, was in *their* synagogue. They were forced to listen to him expound the threatening message of the kingdom of God. They had to look at him. They had to endure "His eyes (which) were like a flame of fire" (Rev. 1:14). His eyes, His words, and His personal presence brought unbearable pain into their immaterial being. Since they were embodied in their victim, he too felt that pain and was confused by it all. They were terrified by what they were enduring in Jesus' presence.

Finally, they could contain their pain and rage no longer. They exploded into protest. "Get out of here, Jesus, you cursed Nazarene. We want nothing to do with you." Now they had blown it. Now everyone, including their victim, knew the true source of the man's problem. He was demonized.

If only the demons had shut their mouths and endured the rest of Jesus' kingdom teaching, they would probably have been left where they were in the life of their victim, because Jesus did not hunt down demons. He did not launch a spiritual warfare campaign on behalf of demoniacs. He did not provoke them into manifestation and cast them out as a central focus of His ministry.

He only dealt with them when their victims came for help or the demons tried to impede His redemptive ministry. He dealt with them when His presence caused demonic stirrings in the life of their victim either in a group setting or a one-on-one contest.

The demon follows with a second apparent question, a declaration of fear, anger, helplessness, and protest. "Have you come to destroy us?" "Have you come to kill us?" PHILLIPS paraphrases His words. I follow with my own paraphrase, based on similar experiences with demons. Here are actual quotes of demons protesting my interference.

"You are seeking to destroy us." "You have come to take her away from us." "You hate us as we hate you." "We don't like what you are doing. Get away and leave us alone. We were doing okay until you showed up."

"Haven't you caused us enough trouble? Why are you bothering us? We weren't bothering you." "Why do you care about this man? He is not worth anything anyhow." "You have more things to do with your time than coming here and messing us up." "Get the (expletive) out of here and leave us alone."

Puzzling Pronouns: "We" to "I"

There is an interesting change of pronouns in the demonic speech recorded here. This is also common in serious demonization. Mark begins by saying the man had "an unclean spirit" (v. 23). The spirit, however, begins speaking in the first person plural, "we," in verse 24a. He continues with "us" in verse 24b. He then switches to the first person singular "I" in verse 24c. When the demon leaves the man in verse 26, Mark uses the singular again, "the unclean spirit."

This has puzzled commentators. They are not sure what the switch implies. William Lane in his commentary on Mark gives two possibilities. First, "it is natural to find a reference to all of the demonic powers who shall be destroyed." Thus Lane believes this demon possibly speaks in behalf of the entire kingdom of evil supernaturalism.[7] Guelich holds the same view.[8] Wuest has the demons saying, "What do we demons have in common with you, holy one of God?"[9]

Nothing in Scripture or experience with demons would deny this possibility. I doubt that this is what is happening, however.

Second, Lane says, "It also is distinctly possible that the demoniac identifies himself with the congregation and speaks from their perspective. Jesus' presence entails the danger of judgment for all present."[10] This seems highly unlikely because the protest by the demons reveals a judgment not applicable to mankind. Demons are unredeemable. No provision has been made for their redemption, while it has been for the people in the synagogue; and the demons knew the difference.

There is a third more plausible position: The demon is speaking for all the demons who indwell this man. He speaks as their representative, and possibly, as their leader. The support for this position is at least twofold. One, the next time Mark records any detail of our Lord's one-on-one encounter with a demon this is exactly what occurs (Mark 5). There the demon switches from the singular pronouns, "I," "me" and "my" to the plural pronouns "we" and "us." When Jesus speaks to the demon, He first speaks to "him," then He speaks to "them." In this case the explanation for the switching is given to us. In response to Jesus' question, "What is your name?" Mark writes, "And he said to Him, 'My name is Legion; for *we* are many' " (Mark 5:7–13, italics mine).

Two, contemporary experience with the demonized reveals that probably all serious cases of demonization involve multi-invasion. One or more ruling demons will speak for all who are under their immediate control. Often there will be more than one ruling demon. At times they are not even aware of each other's presence.

The "unclean spirit" continues his protest. After saying that Jesus had come to destroy them, he connects this destruction with Jesus person as "the Holy One of God" (v. 24). In the Gospel records several references to demonic speech refer to their day of destruction and torment. In Mark 1:24 we have the words used here, "Have you come to destroy us?" In Mark 5:7, we find "do not torment me." Those words are repeated in Luke 8:28. The words recorded in Matthew 8:29 are, "Have You come here to torment us before the time?"

These are strong words. In Mark 1:24, Mark uses *apollumi*. Vine says it means "to destroy utterly, i.e., to perish." He says, "the idea is not extinction but ruin, loss, not of being but of well being. It is used in Matthew 10:28 and related passages of the destruction of the lost in hell."[11]

The word used by the demon(s) in Mark 5:7, Luke 8:28, and Matthew 8:29 is *bansanizo*. Vine says it means "to torment. It is used consistently of the sufferings of the lost in the lake of fire, both of man, Satan and demons."[12] Whatever may be a person's belief about the judgment to come, the demons confess to its reality. The demoniac confession, "I know who you are—the Holy One of God" is not a confession of submission but of truth and defiance.

Demons will lie about the true nature of the Lord Jesus to their victims. They are so determined to keep people from Him, there is no limit to their lies about Him. They will deny His deity. They will say He is evil. To those with sexual malfunctions they will say everything from the lie that Jesus will rape them to the lie that He wants to have sex with them. They will say He was deceived, even, that He was Himself demonized. But when demons are in His *presence,* though they may express their hatred and fear of Him, they spontaneously confess His deity, lordship, holiness, redemption, and His role as their coming judge. In deliverance ministry, they can be made to confess that Jesus has defeated them and their master, Satan. That is what is occurring here, in similar incidents in the Gospels, and in Acts 16:17.

Jesus' Response to the Demoniac

Next we see Jesus' reaction to the demonic outburst. *First, He "rebuked" the demon* (v. 25a). Wuest says there are two words used in the New Testament which mean to rebuke. The first is *elencho*. This is a rebuke "which results in a conviction of sin and sometimes a confession of sin on the offender's part." The second is *epitimao* which means a rebuke "failing to bring the offender to acknowledge his sin." Wuest writes that the latter

> is used by Mark, for Satan, the fallen angels, and the demons. They are incorrigible. They refuse to be convicted of their sin. . . . They will not acknowledge it nor repent. This is just another illustration of the meticulous accuracy of the Bible writers in the choice of words as guided by the Holy Spirit.[13]

Second, He commanded it, "Be quiet" (Mark 1:25). The KJV translates it "Hold thy peace." Goodspeed says, "Silence!" PHILLIPS has Mark writing, "But Jesus cut him short and spoke sharply to him, 'Hold your tongue.'"

The word is *phimoō*. Wuest says it literally means "to close the mouth with a muzzle, to muzzle." It is used "metaphorically, to stop the mouth, make speechless, reduce to silence. Martin Luther translates it from the German by 'shut up.'" Wuest says that "Shut your mouth" is the equivalent idiom of that day for our expression today.

> From the latter we can gather something of the attitude of God towards Satan, the fallen angels, the demons, because of the enormity of their sin. The verb is in the imperative mood and the aorist tense, issuing a sharp command to be obeyed at once. The same holds true of the command, "come out!"

Wuest then follows with his own unique translation directly from the Greek of verse 26, "And Jesus rebuked him, the rebuke not resulting in any conviction or confession of sin, saying, 'Shut your mouth and come out of him at once.'"[14] This is the only way to converse with demons. Shut their mouths!

Just a note of application to any ministry with demons and demonics today. We do not want to injure the victim of demonization further. The best way of not injuring them is to help them get free of the demons afflicting their life, once it has been accurately diagnosed that their problem is demonic or partly demonic. That determination made, there must be no quarter given to the demons. Demons are totally evil. There is nothing, absolutely nothing, about any of them deserving of our pity or compassion.

Here we see Jesus as our example of love and hate. He loves the demonized man. He sets him free from the demons attached to his life. He hates the demons. He cannot even bear their voice, even though everything they are publicly announcing about Him is true. When He speaks to them He displays neither love, compassion, nor even common courtesy. He tells them, "Shut your mouth."

The Demon's Response

The reaction of the evil spirit to Jesus' command is threefold according to Mark 1:26. First, he overpowered his victim for the last time in an outwardly violent manner. He threw him onto the ground. He wracked his body with convulsions (v. 26a). This is a horrible scene. The man is wallowing on the ground as if in an epileptic fit. Anyone who has witnessed such a demonic attack knows how terrible it can be.

Why did Jesus let it happen? I don't know because the Scriptures do not tell us.

He could have forbid it from occurring, if He had chosen to do so. I usually do. Occasionally, however, it happens so quickly that I do not have time to forbid the demonic abuse. Most of the time it can be stopped almost instantly, but not always.

In contemporary deliverance accompanied by visible power encounters like these, demonic reactions will differ with different people just like we discover in the Gospels and Acts. While we may become upset when demons produce gross reactions like the ones recorded in the Gospels and Acts, we should not be too concerned about it. If it happened that way with Jesus it will probably happen that way at times with us.

Luke records the incident this way: "And when the demon had thrown him down in their midst, he came out of him without doing him any harm" (Luke 4:35). Mark says the unclean spirit, after "throwing him into convulsions," then "cried out with a loud voice, and came out of him" (v. 26). Wuest says the word "to convulse" signifies spasms. It is a term used by doctors for stomach spasms. He says this was no doubt vindictiveness on the demon's part in protest at being ordered out of the man. He is correct, I believe.

The word for crying "out with a loud voice" here (see Acts 8:7) means "a screech," according to Wuest who translates the verse, "And when the unclean spirit had torn him with convulsions, he screeched and came out of him."[15]

As terrible as it all appears, it did not cause any injury to the man. Doctor Luke carefully observes that the demon went out "without causing him any harm." That is what is important. It may have looked and sounded bad, but it was not half bad after all. Let's be careful in judging others when demons repeat what Jesus allowed to occur here. While I may try not to allow demons to do this, if they do, I am not to blame. Neither is Jesus. The demons are.

The Crowd's Response

"They were all amazed," Mark records (1:27). They did not necessarily believe, but they were amazed. "What is this?" they asked. Did anyone answer their question? Did they find the answer themselves by further reflection? They had heard Jesus' sermon. Then they should have known the answer. "What is this?" however, probably means "Who is this?"

"A new teaching!" they exclaimed. This was observation number one. They had never seen nor heard anything like this before. "A new teaching (accompanied) by authority," was observation number two. "He commands even the unclean spirits and they obey him," is observation number three. These three observations should have led them at least to a partial answer to the question, "What" or "who is this?"

They then spread the word, everywhere. This was the beginning of the early phase of Jesus' ministry. It is often called "The Period of Popularity." Lane says, "the disturbance of men by God had begun."[16] Wuest says the amazement of the synagogue crowd focused on our Lord's authority over the demons.[17]

> Our Lord has the hosts of Satan under his absolute power at all times. Unwilling and incorrigible as they are, He can command them at will, and they obey Him. Satan always operates on a limited tether. To the synagogue crowd, the most astonishing thing was that the demons obeyed Him.

What a story! What a way to begin His ministry!

38

Among the Tombs

Mark 5

Joachim Jeremias in his book on New Testament theology called *The Proclamation of Jesus* emphasizes Jesus' ministry in the gospel of Mark as overcoming the rule of Satan.[1] He says "the Gospel of Mark depicts Jesus' exorcisms as battles." Jeremias gives preeminence to Jesus' dramatic personal separation from the contemporary Jewish view of demons which saw them as "individual beings in one sense, operating on their own. Thus their detailed lists of the names of demons."[2]

Jeremias says, "Jesus changed all that. He stressed the connection between the appearance of the demons and Satan. He expressed this connection with a variety of pictures." First, "Satan appears as a commander of a military force" (Luke 10:19) *dunamis*. "Next he is seen as ruling over a kingdom (Matt. 12:26; Luke 11:18; *basileia*); the demons are his soldiers (Mark 5:9)." He is seen as master of the house and the demons as his servants (Matt. 10:25).[3]

DELIVERANCE OF THE GADERENE DEMONIAC

The deliverance of the demonically battered man in Mark 5 is dramatic evidence of this battlefield focus. In the introduction to his study of Mark 5, the late Dr. Merrill F. Unger says, "The fact that confronts us in all demonization is that demons are in control [partial control] of the demonized person. This is true of course of *all* degrees of demonization, including mild, moderate and severe invasion."

Unger then comments on severe demonization:[4]

But in the severest cases the control is much deeper and more domineering and enslaving. The number of demons may be more, their wickedness greater, their strength more terrible, and their entrenchment in the life more binding. All of this is dramatically illustrated by the demonized man of Gadara (Mark 5:1–20; Luke 8:26–32).

Alfred Edersheim in his characteristic style speaks of the archaeological site of Gerasa against the plains of Gennesaret on the east side of the Sea of Galilee. He writes of the tombs in the limestone hills and caves of the steep bluff over which the pigs ran to their own destruction into the sea (Mark 5:13).[5]

Perhaps his greatest contributions, however, are his understanding of the often enigmatic and confusing blending of the two personalities (the human and the demonic) in the body of the demonized, and his understanding of the cultural accommodation of the demons. In this story demons embody an evidently Jewish man. While the fact of his Jewishness is questionable to some, that does not change the point. The Gentiles had similar views. We will assume his Jewishness, however.[6] The demons behave exactly as they would be expected to behave dwelling within the person of a first-century Jew. There is a cultural dimension to their words and actions.

While satanic-demonic activity is supracultural, it is also cultural. Demons "learn" the culture of their victims and act in a somewhat predictable manner within the context of their culture. In doing cross-cultural spiritual warfare teaching and counseling, I always try to learn as much as possible about the spirit world as it operates within each local culture. While this is crucial to modern cross-cultural ministry, it is just as crucial to the interpretation of the spirit world from Scripture and the application of that interpretation to the contemporary world.

We do not have a book or even a portion of a book in the Bible which gives us a general outline of the supracultural dimensions of the activity of evil supernaturalism. Therefore, as Dickason often points out, we must have contemporary experience and case studies to learn what demons often do and do not do in a given contemporary context. This cannot be determined beforehand from Scripture alone, as many dogmatically affirm. Some dimensions of biblical demonology can be discovered by carefully examining the biblical accounts such as this amazing story in Mark 5. I say some dimensions, and that's all.

This is only one case study limited to one man's problems with demons. It is also the most severe case of demonization of an adult male given in Scripture. Therefore we cannot, using the inductive method of biblical interpretation[7] and from only one case, draw conclusions about how demons *always* operate in human lives and how they always should be dealt with. We can only come up with valuable insights as to their activity in this one particular case of severe demonization and how Jesus dealt with them.[8]

To draw more universally applicable conclusions, we have to examine every case recorded in Scripture and all the biblical teachings on demonic activity in the biblical world. With this truth foundation before us, we then can begin to examine both extra and post-biblical demonic activity as well as contemporary demonic activity, worldwide.

The Setting (5:1–2)

The setting, Mark 5:1–2, focuses on the boat trip to "the country of the Gerasenes, verse 1 with 4:35–41, and the demoniac among the tombs, verse 2. The important part of the setting is the presence of the demoniac among the tombs. Mark tells us he was "from the tombs," he had "an unclean spirit," and he "met" Jesus. I like the way Barclay writes about the man dwelling among the tombs.[9]

> It was a part of the lakeside where there were many caves in the limestone rock, and many of these caves were used as tombs in which bodies were laid. At the best of times it was an eerie place; as night fell it must have been grim indeed.

> Out of the tombs there came a demon-possessed man. It was a fitting place for him to be, for demons, so they believed in those days, dwelt in woods and gardens and vineyards and dirty places, in lonely and desolate spots and among the tombs. The demon-possessed man dwelt in the haunt of demons.

> It was in the night-time and before cock-crow that the demons were specially active. To sleep alone in an empty house at night was dangerous; to greet any person in the dark was perilous, for the person might be a demon. To go out at night without a lantern or a torch was to court trouble. It was a perilous place and a perilous hour, and the man was a dangerous man.

Mark next says the man had "an unclean spirit" (v. 2). Mark uses "unclean spirit," "demons," and "spirits" interchangeably in his gospel.[10] The demoniac "met" Jesus (v. 2c). This does not mean the man was there waiting for Jesus.

Verses 3–6 explain what the writer has in mind. Mark next follows with a detailed description of the demoniac. Edersheim says that

> we must . . . remember the confusion in the consciousness of the demonized between their own notions and the ideas imposed . . . by the demons. It is quite in accordance with the Jewish notions of the demonized, that . . . he should feel as it were driven into the deserts, and that he was in the tombs. . . . It was characteristic of the demonized, that they were incapable of separating their own identity being merged, and to that extent lost, in that of their tormentors. In this respect the demonized state was also kindred to madness. . . . The demonized speaks and acts as a Jew under the control of a demon. Thus, if he chooses solitary places by day, and tombs by night, it is not that demons really preferred such habitations, but that the Jews imagined it and that the demons, acting on the existing consciousness, would lead him, in accordance with his preconceived notions, to select such places.[11]

The Demoniac's Actions and Their Interpretation

Guelich adds that "the man's home among the tombs bespeaks his ostracism from society and corresponds to his possession by an unclean spirit, a being often thought to dwell among the tombs."[12]

Is this true today? Generally speaking, no. In some cultures this may be true, because the cultural view in that society is similar to that of the Jews. In some parts of India the severely demonized reportedly dwell among the tombs to eat the flesh of the recently buried.

Some commentators use this passage to teach that three of the key symptoms of demonization are isolation, uncleanness, and withdrawal from human contact, but this is not necessarily true. The extreme anti-social behavior revealed here is only characteristic of *some* of the most severely demonized. A condition resembling madness would only be true of *some* cases of very severe demonization. Most of the demonized, while struggling with problems, some of them very severe, do *not* act like madmen.

Furthermore, demonization and true mental-biological-neurological problems are not identical. While they have certain things in common, there are marked differences. The two conditions can go together, however. Edersheim remarks that "the Jews did not hold that all physical or even mental distempers were due to demonization."[13] Neither did Jesus nor the early Christians. They knew the difference and treated each differently. So must we.

Mark says that "no one was able to bind him anymore, even with a chain" (5:3b). In verse 4 he amplifies this statement with details ending with "no one was strong enough to subdue him." From this some affirm another symptom of demonization is unusual strength. Again this is not necessarily so. It depends on other factors such as the severity of the demonization, the type of demons present, and the expectations of the demons, the demonized, and those who are in relationship with him. Some demoniacs become violent and display great strength only when the demons are in manifestation. Others may display anger not accompanied by violence and superhuman strength. The hidden factors in each case are so complex and individualized that we must be careful not to generalize.

The gospel writer next says that he "was constantly night and day, among the tombs and in the mountains" (v. 5a). Mark follows this, saying he was "crying out." Wuest says the word cry out is *krazō* and means "an inarticulate cry, a shriek" or "a scream" (v. 5b).[14] Many declare this to be another symptom of demonization.

In some very severe demonizations approaching dementia this may occur. In most cases, even severe cases at least in the U.S., this does not occur.

When something like this does occur, it is usually due to four possible factors or any combination of the four. First, extremely wild demons are in full manifestation, usually protesting some interference in their activities. Second, they are threatening their victim or others. Third, they are leaving their victim with one last loud scream (Mark 1:26; Acts 8:7). Fourth, it is the demonized person who is crying out in agony or anger against his misery and the demonic tormenters, not the demons.

Mark next says he was "gnashing himself with stones" (v. 5c). The word "gnash" is *katakoptō*. Vine says it is an intense form of *kata*, "down," with *koptō*, "to cut by a blow." He says it means "to cut in pieces."[15] Wuest says it means "to cut oneself up in the sense of gashing, hacking, or cutting one's whole body so as to leave it covered with scars."[16] The poor man was evidently cut all over his body.

The Demoniac's Response to Jesus' Presence

Next we discover the demoniac's initial response to Jesus' presence (vv. 6–7 with v. 2d). When he was at a distance from Jesus he recognized Him. Instead of running away from Him, as we are told the demonized will usually do, he ran straight to Jesus and "bowed down before Him" (v. 6). We are frequently told that another symptom of demonization is repulsion in the presence of Jesus. "Demons want no contact with Jesus or His people. That's why demonized people stay away from Christians. They will never go to church," we are assured. This is not necessarily true.

Why then did the demoniac run and throw himself at Jesus' feet? I suggest several possible answers. One, I don't know nor does anyone else because the Bible doesn't tell us. Two, according to Mark whenever the unclean spirits beheld Him, they would fall down before Him crying out confessions of His divine person. "You are the Son of God" was the most common spontaneous confession (Mark 3:11). Jesus even had to "earnestly warn them not to reveal His identity" (3:12).[17] Something here needs further exploration. There is a deep mystery in this seemingly contradictory reaction of demons to His presence. They fear Him; yet they seemed compelled to pay Him homage.[18]

Three, since whenever demonic speech is recorded, that homage is always in the context of a spontaneous confession of His deity, lordship, and His role as their future judge, it is probable that their confused response to Him is because of their overwhelming fear that He will punish them now, before "the time." After all, they had no idea when the appointed "time" would arrive. In deliverance ministries today they do the same. They will even confess that their master, Satan, is a deceiver who is destined to burn in the lake of fire with them. They will confess that Jesus has defeated him and them. Just as we are discovering here in Mark, they will not confess Him as their Lord, but they will confess that He is the Lord.

Four, there is always the possibility it is the demonized man himself here who is so strongly drawn to Christ. As the poor, bruised, and tormented victim fights off any demonic interference to his being drawn towards Jesus, the demons are "caught," so to speak. They can't stop him. Wherever their victim goes, they go too. Often in the blazing glory of Jesus' holiness, they come into full manifestation confessing in fear who He is and what He is going to do to them. They appeal to Him to leave them alone and plead that He would not torment them before the time.

The Demons' Speech

First is the defiant question-protest: "What do I have to do with You . . .?" (Mark 5:7a). Cole remarks that the demon's first question-protest is "What is there in common between you and me?" What an insightful comment by a demon!

Next we find his confession of Jesus as "Son of the Most High God" (v. 7b). Alan Cole remarks about this and similar outbursts of confession of Jesus' divine person. He writes, "Strange that the insight of evil into the nature of Christ should be so clear and instantaneous while ordinary men were so slow to see His Godhead (vv. 6–8)."[19]

All this occurred as the man and his demons ran to Jesus and fell at His feet. Cole remarks:[20]

> They ran and did their homage all unwillingly, confessing at once the vast gulf between them, and the searing effect that Good has on evil. A better reply to the Pharisaical accusation that the Holy Spirit resting on Christ and the spirit of evil were fundamentally one (Mark 3:22) could hardly be found: here was evil itself refusing to acknowledge the Christ as in anyway akin to itself.

Finally, we have another defiant protest, "I implore You, by God, do not torment me!" (5:7c). This is what Wuest calls an "oath" formula.[21] Guelich says these words further reveal the desperation the demons feel in the presence of Jesus. He writes, "The demoniac betrays his clear awareness of his inferior position and the futility of his situation (Gnilka, 1:204) by desperately 'adjuring' Jesus not to 'torture' him."[22]

> The demoniac adjures Jesus by the God whom he has just recognized to be Jesus' father! Thus, the man's response to Jesus further demonstrates the unclean spirit's confused desperation before Jesus. . . . He has met his match and simply desires to negotiate a settlement.

Guelich then states:[23]

> Finally, Jesus' superiority over the unclean spirit is expressed by the demoniac's fear of "torture." Many find here a latent reference to an apocalyptic expectation of the final judgment as in Matthew 8:30 (so Lohmeyer, 95; Taylor, 280; Grundmann, 144). Others find simply a fear of "punishment" or banishment from the spirit's "home," as supported by the context (e.g., 5:10–13; Haenchen, 193; Gnilka, 1:205).

Mark records that Jesus had spoken first to the demons before all the demonic speech we have already examined had even occurred. Mark says, "For He had been saying to him, 'Come out of the man, you unclean spirit!' " (v. 8). This is the *only occasion* in the Gospels in which demons do not immediately obey Jesus. In all other cases "He cast out the spirits with a word" (Matt. 8:16). Many commentators have problems with this part of the story.[24] Barclay, as usual, sees no problem.[25]

> We shall not even begin to understand this story unless we see clearly how serious a case of demon possession this man was. It is clear that Jesus made more than one attempt to heal this man. . . . Jesus had begun by using his usual method—an authoritative order to the demon to come out. On this occasion that was not successful.

Barclay is right. Other commentators try to avoid the problem. Barclay suggests that Jesus demanded the demon's name because in that era it was supposed that knowledge of a demon's name gave power over that demon.[26]

I like the first part of Barclay's position, but not the part about knowing the name of a demon to get authority over it. This is not what Jesus had in mind. Such a view is magic. What Jesus is doing is what most deliverance ministers do. He requests information from the demon to know better what is occurring in the life of the poor man.

Someone asked John Wimber why Jesus asked the demon his name. In his characteristic style, John answered, *"Because Jesus wanted to know his name."* Perhaps Jesus asked the demon's name because he knew there was an unusual concentration of demonic power residing in this man's life which he had never encountered before. He wanted to know exactly what was going on inside of him. Guelich agrees. He does not think that Jesus asked the demon his name as a way of gaining control over him but to gain more accurate knowledge about the condition of the man:[27]

> Instead of granting Jesus control over the demon(s), the question and the response reveal the extent of the man's domination. On the one hand, this verse explains his uncontrollable behavior in 5:3–4 in terms of the power "legion." . . . On the other hand, the ready submission of the man to Jesus in 5:6 accents Jesus' power over this extensive force of the demonic.

Legion is "a term referring to a unit of Roman soldiers, about six thousand strong," Hurtado says.[28] It does not necessarily imply there were exactly 6,000 demons inside of him. It probably means only what the demons say next, "for we are many" (v. 9c). Barclay adds an interesting historical-cultural note. "Later 2,000 swine will plunge over the cliff to their death. . . . If there is a ratio of one demon per swine, the number must have been 2,000 or more. That is a lot of personnel in one human body. No wonder his condition was so desperate."[29]

Hurtado makes an excellent spiritual warfare comment:[30]

> Legion also has the effect of making the scene like a battle between the powers of evil and Jesus, who comes in the name of the kingdom of God. This imagery is likely intentional, for already Jesus has described His exorcisms as assaults upon Satan's strongholds. (See 3:23–27.)

The Demons' Request

The demonic request has two parts: that Jesus not send them "out of the country" (Mark 5:10); and that he not send them "into the abyss" (Luke 8:31). The idea of not sending them out of the country is not without parallel in Jewish literature, Lane notes.[31] A. B. Bruce mentions the Jewish negative view of "the country" of the Gerasenes and the entire area of the Decapolis (vv. 1,20), the ten cities which worked together as a miniature European Common Market. He quotes a Jewish writer as saying, "Decapolis, beloved by demons, because full of Hellenising apostate Jews."[32]

Again experience with deliverance reveals the territorial nature of some demons. They are often comfortable where they are and do not want to be sent to other places. I don't have problems with that, however. I just send them to where Jesus sends them.

Luke's addition about their plea that they not be sent to the abyss (Luke 8:31) is worth looking at. It is the word *tartarus*. It is found seven times in Revelation as the place of demons. It is a place of confinement for them, and, at one period, even for Satan, awaiting their expulsion into the lake of fire (Rev. 20:1–3). It is evidently not a place of torment. Demons do not want to be sent to the abyss for they will then be rendered inactive except for some that will evidently be let out at a future date (Rev. 9:1f).

In the early days of my deliverance ministry, I consistently sent demons to the abyss, based on this passage. I, like others, received criticism for attempting to handle demons that way. Almost simultaneously several strong evangelical leaders who were also involved in a deliverance ministry switched to the command, "Go to where Jesus sends you."

They do go where He sends them. Most of us believe, however, that Jesus sends them to the abyss or pit. As in those days, so today, they beg not to be sent there.

Mark does not record any response by Jesus to the demonic plea. Instead he tells of the demons' third fearful response to Jesus' presence (Mark 5:11–12). They asked to be sent into a nearby herd of swine.[33]

Jesus' Response

Next is Jesus' response to the demons' request. Matthew writes, "Begone" (Matt. 8:32), and they were gone (Mark 5:13). Mark and Luke say, "He gave them permission." This was followed by the destruction of the swine resulting in what the demons feared most, their disembodiment (v. 13b). Guelich's explanation is excellent:[34]

> Like the description of the unmanageable man in 5:3–4, whose behavior "Legion" helps explain, 2,000 uncontrollable swine demonstrate the immense power of the forces that had taken control of their victim. . . . The death of the swine vividly depicts the destructive nature of these evil forces.

Hurtado adds an additional note. He says the swine episode reveals not only the destructive power of the demons but also the authority of Jesus.[35] That is partly what such power encounters were meant to be (Matt. 12:28).

The Demons' Expulsion

We note that the demons were terrified that Jesus was going to begin their torment now. "It is not yet time," they protest in Matt. 8:29. They were filled with fear. Next we discover that the demonic emotions run from to screaming defiance (Mark 5:7a), to angry acknowledgement of His divine sonship (v. 7b). This is anger mixed with sheer terror to the point that they begged Him in the name of God not to begin their awaited, future torment now.

"Torment" is *basanizō*. Wuest says it is used for ways "to test metals," "to test by torture" and "to torture," the latter being its use here.[36] "Not now! Not now!" they exclaim. Their confused minds sought first to overpower or intimidate Him by defiance (v. 7a); then by arrogance (v. 7b); then by refusal to obey His commands to abandon their home, their victim's body (v. 8). Finally they try to intimidate Him with the sheer force of numbers arrayed against him (v. 9), "We are Legion—we are many, . . . too many for you!"

Failing in all this and sensing in His calm presence that the torment of expulsion from their victim is coming, they begin to maneuver for compromise. "Don't send us out of the country, we have been given this territory to rule (v. 10). Also don't send us into the abyss" (Luke 8:31).

Before Jesus can even answer, they spot the swine herd. "Animal bodies are better than no body," they say among themselves. "We can go to the swine as our first step. Then, when Jesus leaves, we can transfer back to our present human home or find another one." This is demonic self-talk. It failed.

"If you are going to cast us out," or "we know you are going to cast us out" (Matt. 8:31); "how about the swine? We promise we will not resist any longer if you will please just send us there. We promise we will never again torment another human being. We will just live in the swine. What do you care about swine, anyhow?"

Jesus then lets them go into the swine. The translation "go!" in the KJV (Matt. 8:32); as if it were a command initiated by Jesus; is not accurate. "Begone" of the NAS is much better. It is the verb *hupagō* in Greek. Vine says it means "to go away or to go slowly away, to depart, withdraw oneself often with the idea of going without noise or notice."[37] A. B. Bruce calls this "Christ's laconic reply 'begone.'"[38]

Mark and Luke use *epitrepō*, "to permit, to give leave."[39] This conveys the idea that Jesus acquiesces to their frantic appeal for some sort of compromise. He lets them go out of the man, the most important being in the story, to the swine, the least important beings in the story.

The Man's Deliverance

The horrible, unbelievable prolonged torture and pain of the man immediately ceases. For the first time in perhaps his entire lifetime, he is now free. He is human again. He is free to go home. "Be it ever so humble, there is no place like home." Think about it: home! No more wilderness and tombs, but home!

He is also free to think his own thoughts. He is never again to be tormented to the point of insanity by demonic thoughts so mingled with his own he could not tell the two apart.

No one who has never suffered the agony and confusion of the intrusion of foreign thoughts, or voices into their mind can fully understand the living hell this represents to a human being. Whether it be the internal voices of demons, alter personalities or related internal voice disorders, or the external voices of schizophrenia or related brain disorders, to live in such a condition is to live in a madhouse.

He is now free to love Jesus and to serve Him. Perhaps at no point is his transformation more radical than at this point. He unknowingly served the demons. He had to give them homage, out of sheer terror. Now he only wants to be with Jesus as his voluntary bondslave forever (v. 18).

All of this leads to the disembodiment of the demons. Either they were left on earth to seek other victims or they ended up in the abyss. I hope the latter was what occurred.

The Death of the Swine

Next we have the death of the swine (v. 13). This produces a serious negative impact on both the swine keepers and the public (vv. 14–17). Was this an unlawful action on Jesus' part? "It represents the destruction of other people's property," some complain.

Let's answer the last objection first. Jesus did not destroy another's property. The demons did. There we go again blaming Jesus for the Devil's evil! Now to the second objection, that of cruelty to the animals. R. A. Cole says, "We know so little in this realm that we do well to tread reverently: It may be that such an outward sign was required in this case to convince men of the reality of the expulsion."

"It is sometimes half-humorously suggested," Cole adds, "that, if the owners of the pigs were Jews, . . . this was . . . a punishment to them as well. But it seems unlikely that the Lord would take such pains to punish a breach of ceremonial law."[40]

William Barclay adds his comments about those who criticize Jesus for allowing the death of the swine:[41]

We do not, presumably, have any objections to eating meat for our dinner, nor will we refuse pork because it involved the killing of some pig. Surely if we kill animals to avoid going hungry, we can raise no objection if the saving of a man's mind and soul involved the death of a herd of these same animals. . . .

This is not to say that we need not care what happens to God's animal creation, but God loves every creature whom His hands have made, but it is to say that we must preserve a sense of proportion; and in God's scale of proportions, there is nothing so important as a human soul.

I like Stier's comment as quoted by John A. Broadus. "The question of why our Lord permitted the demons to enter the swine is already answered by another question. Why had the Lord permitted them to enter the man?"[42]

The Response of the Locals

Mark next records the saddest part of the story, except for the sad condition of the man himself before his deliverance. It is the response of the local inhabitants to Jesus, to the death of the swine, and to the former demoniac (Mark 5:14–17).

The immediate response of the swine herders is not unusual, however. They flee to report the incident to the inhabitants of the city and countryside (v. 17). Wuest says the word "ran away" *(pheugō)* means "'to flee away, to seek safety by flight.' The implication is that the swine herders were filled with terror at what had taken place as well as the tragedy of the sudden destruction of and loss of a herd of two thousand hogs."[43]

The sad scene begins with the response of the multitude who came to see for themselves what had occurred. Mark records their reaction. They observed the man who had been demonized not, as we have in the NAS and NKJV, "demon-possessed" (v. 15). He is sitting down, not running wild as before. He is clothed, no longer naked (Luke 8:27). He is in his right mind, not insane as before. He is still clearly recognizable as "the very man who had had the legion."

What was their response? Mark says "and they became frightened" (v. 15b). What an unbelievable response! No one ran up and asked the man what had happened to him. No one embraced him with tears of joy that this man who had suffered as few others in their community was now completely whole and healed. No one lifted their hands and hearts with him in thanksgiving to God for the final end to his unbelievable terror and agony.

Then the swine herders add to the brief report they had already given (v. 16). This was probably directed to the owners of the swine. It was the custom for many swine owners to mix their smaller herds and put them in the care of one group of herders like the men in this story.

This is followed by the rejection of Jesus by the people (vv. 16–17). A. B. Bruce comments:[44]

The eyewitnesses in further explanations to their employers now connect the two events together—the cure and the catastrophe . . . The owners draw a natural inference: the cure caused the catastrophe, and (v. 17) request Jesus, as a dangerous person, to retire.

Next we see the healed man's first recorded response to Jesus since his healing (v. 18). A. B Bruce says Jesus had probably planned on staying for several days in the region. His rejection produces the immediate response on His part to leave the area. As He was "getting into the boat," Mark says, the healed man approached Him, asking to become His disciple (v. 18).

What a contrast in the response of different persons to the same events! The people were more concerned with the loss of the swine than the healing of their fellow man. The man is more concerned with Jesus than with the reactions of his townsmen. He saw Jesus as Savior. They saw Him as a threat.

Mark follows with Jesus' final word to the former demoniac. It is beautiful, indeed. Jesus denies his request to leave the Decapolis to become Jesus' disciple, but he commissions him to evangelism (v. 19). In most healing cases Jesus forbids those he cures to give public witness to what he had done for them. Here he does the opposite. Why?

The text does not say, so we cannot be certain. We can propose, however, that it is because this Gentile area needs to hear of God's love. What better evangelist than one of their own who had been transformed by Jesus' touch?

Mark concludes the story with the former demoniac testifying throughout the Decapolis and the public's response (v. 20). He did exactly what Jesus told him to do. He reported everywhere what great things the Lord had done for him and how He had mercy on him (v. 19). He also interprets Jesus' person correctly by saying that Jesus is the Lord (vv. 19–20).

While the deliverance of the Gerasene demoniac did not result in the immediate conversion of the observers, it did lead to the evangelization of the Decapolis by the delivered man. Jesus did not set the agonized man free from demonization with direct evangelistic purposes in mind, however. He healed him, as Jesus Himself declares, because He had mercy on the bruised man (v. 19).

We are not through with the story of the inhabitants of the region of the Decapolis, however. John Hunter, the British Bible teacher, says,[45]

> Finally, we have the verses in Mark 7:31–37 which tell of Jesus' return to Decapolis. Notice the contrast in the reception. The first time they begged Christ to go away— this time they brought to him other sufferers . . . .

> In Mark 7:36 we find that the ordinary people of Decapolis followed the example of the healed demoniac. They went around telling of the wonderful things Christ had done. What a glorious finale there is! "He hath done all things well: he maketh both the deaf to hear and the dumb to speak." (Mark 7:37)

Contemporary Reflections

When we are dealing with a realm about which we are ignorant, we must be slow to criticize just because we are uncomfortable with some of the things that often accompany deliverance ministry. This is not grounds for rejection. For example, true believers having demons is a biblical abnormality. But if the reality reveals the abnormality to be true, I must deal with the reality. I must not further damage the victim, possibly driving him to total despair and even suicide, by rejecting his claims to true faith in Christ.

Let me cite an experience I had while suddenly counseling a troubled young man. He had been sent to a mental health counselor because of antisocial behavior. I led him to Christ. Then, as I continued talking and praying with him, he went into severe demonic manifestation. He had been in the occult and still had strong occult demons indwelling his life although he had received Christ.

I had a difficult time. After several hours we were able to expel some of the most vile, rebellious unclean spirits from his life. He was not yet totally free, however.

He later wrote a letter to one of the women who ministered to him with me. In the middle of the letter, a demon took control of his writing. The handwriting, grammar, and vocabulary radically changed. The demon began to pour out its hatred for the lady calling her a "bitch" and things too vile to write. He then began to pour out his curses upon me. Finally, he wrote about the victim, saying, "He belongs to us from childhood. His whore of a mother gave him to us before he was born. We will finally win this battle. We will get him back to the psychologist. He will tell him he is crazy. Then we will have him again."

The demon's claim that the man was given to them "before he was born" and "from childhood" is disturbing. Later ministry with this man proved these claims to be true.

What if I had rejected the possibility that he could still have demons even after he had received Christ? I tremble to think of the suffering he would have endured, had I not proceeded with the deliverance counseling (which continued for several months).

What demons can do, they do. I must deal with reality, not merely with theory. Hurting people are more important than theological presuppositions.

The Apostolic Church Encounters Demons

39

Foundations and Lessons From a Failure

Mark 9

THE GOSPELS AND THE REST OF THE NEW TESTAMENT: PROPERLY UNDERSTANDING THE ROLE OF EVIL SUPERNATURALISM IN EACH

We have four primary groups of documents which record the experience of the disciples of Jesus with the world of evil supernaturalism: the Gospels, the Acts of the Apostles, the Epistles, and the Book of Revelation. In all four Satan and demonic powers have an important place. In the Gospels the disciples begin their deliverance ministry observing Jesus as he deals with the spirit world. Soon they themselves encounter demonic resistance to their invasion of Satan's kingdom in the name of their Lord and in the power of the kingdom of God. Theirs is a kingdom ministry. The result is power encounter between the two kingdoms.

After the Gospels: Diminishing Encounters With the Demonic?

As we look, however, at the disciples and the spirit world as recorded in Acts, the Epistles, and Revelation there seems, at first sight, to be a diminishing of their encounter with evil supernaturalism from that recorded in the Gospels. This apparent abrupt change is often used to question the revival of ministry to the demonized the church is experiencing worldwide in our day.

The primary difference is that while Jesus confronts demons continually, His disciples seem to give demons little place in their minds and ministry after the Lord's resurrection and ascension. It is claimed that Satan has some place, but not demons, and so the disciples did not give importance to direct ministry with the demonized. Neither should we in our day, we are told. "I want nothing to do with this ministry," one Christian leader wrote. "The redemptive work of Christ defeated the spirit world once and for all. So I have no place for them in my ministry."

Finally, it seems evident that the emphasis on the spirit world in general and demons in particular is so different in the Acts, Epistles, and Revelation, it is as if the disciples ministered in a different world after Pentecost.

There is some truth (mixed with obvious error) in making these distinctions between the place of evil supernaturalism in the Gospels (the Synoptics) and the place given to the spirit world in the rest of the New Testament. This is really what we should expect for two reasons: *First, the coming of Christ was the invasion of the kingdom of Satan by the kingdom of God in the person of the King.* He came as a man (the God-man), but it was the King of Heaven who came and the Enemy knew it.

As we have seen, both Satan and the demons openly and consistently declared Jesus to be the Christ, the Holy One of God, even the Son of God, in the gospel accounts. This initial invasion, as is always true when the Enemy knows the invasion is coming, provoked perhaps the most open and intense opposition by Satan and demons to God's kingdom in history. This alone would explain why so much of Jesus' ministry involved personal direct confrontation with the spirit world, especially with Satan's agents of evil, the demons.

Second, in His redemptive event, Jesus totally defeated the kingdom of evil supernaturalism, once and for all. While neither annihilated nor bound, the spirit world is already defeated. The early disciples understood they were still involved in a terrible war, but to them it was a war with an already defeated foe. That makes all the difference in the world as to how one both sees and engages the foe. *This difference alone would account for all the differences between the warfare with the spirit world in the Gospels and the rest of the New Testament.*

The Prominence of Evil Supernaturalism in the New Testament Apart From the Gospels

We must correct the common error, however, which declares that the spirit world is not as prominent in the later New Testament documents as it was in the Gospels. Nothing could be further from the truth. The sheer *volume of references* to the world of evil supernaturalism is impressive in the rest of the New Testament. There are actually more verses which refer to the spirit world in the Acts, Epistles, and Revelation than in the four Gospels combined (see Figure 39.1).

There are more references to the spirit world in the Acts, Epistles, and Revelation than there are for what are often considered more major doctrines of Scripture. For example, the Gospels represent just over 40 percent of the content of the New Testament. The largest concentration of references to the spirit world seem, at first sight, to be found in these first four books of the New Testament.

The word "seem" is carefully chosen. In this case what seems to be true is not true, however. There are about 150 references to the spirit world in the Gospels, but there are about 178 such references in the rest of the New Testament. The Gospels form the foundation to the Acts, the Epistles, and Revelation. The latter seldom extensively repeat what was taught in the former. The rest of the New Testament takes these foundational teachings for granted.

Besides, most of the case studies of warfare with the spirit world in any one of the synoptic Gospels are the identical stories repeated in the other two. Even the accusations in John that Jesus was demonized are evidently repetitions of the same accusations brought against Him by the Jewish leaders which are also found in the Synoptics.

Figure 39.1
Direct References in the New Testament to the Spirit World

Matthew	Mark	Luke
4:1–11,24	1:12,13,21–28,32–34,39	4:1–13,33–37,41
6:13	3:11–15,22–30	6:18
7:22	4:15	7:21,33
8:16,28–34	5:1–20	8:2,12,26–39
9:32–35	6:7,13	9:1,37–43,49–50
10:1,25	7:24–30	10:1–20
11:18	8:33	11:14–26
12:22–30,43–45	9:14–29,38–40	13:10–17,32
13:19,24,28,37,39	16:9,17	22:3,31–32,53
15:21–28		
16:18–23		
17:14–21		

John	Acts	Romans
6:70	5:3,16	8:15,38–39
7:20	8:7,9–11,18–24	16:20
8:44,48–52	10:38	
10:20–21	13:6–12	
12:31	16:16–19	
13:2,27	19:12–20	
14:30	26:18	
16:11		
17:15		

1 Corinthians	2 Corinthians	Galatians
2:6–8	2:4–11	1:6–8
5:5–7	4:4	4:8,9
7:5	6:14–17	5:19–21
10:7–21	11:3–4,12–15	
	12:7–10	

Allowing for such parallel accounts probably reduces in half or more the number of the individual accounts of conflict with the spirit world found in the Gospels. In that sense there is a true balance in the teachings recorded in the Gospels and the other books of the New Testament about the spirit world. *In fact there are more separate references to the spirit world in the rest of the New Testament than there are in the Gospels.* There is no question that the gospel writers saw the spirit world as the very context in which they and Jesus lived and ministered. So did the later New Testament writers, however.

It is commonly stated that in the rest of the New Testament there are more direct references to the Devil than there are to evil spirits. Is this observation accurate? We will find that it is not. In Acts there are four references to Satan and eight to evil spirits. The picture in Revelation is mixed. In Revelation 2 and 3 Satan and his intimate relationship with the churches of Asia and the territory where the churches are functioning is prominent. Nothing is said about demons. In the rest of Revelation the picture continually switches, until, we discover that overall in Revelation there is an equal focus on evil spirits as there is on Satan.

How about the assumption that in the Epistles Satan is much more prominent than the demons? To my amazement when I read through the Epistles looking for

Ephesians	Colossians	1 Thessalonians
1:21	1:13–17	2:18
2:2	2:6–15,20	3:5
3:10		
4:26,27		
6:10–20		
2 Thessalonians	1 Timothy	2 Timothy
2:1–12	1:20	1:7
3:3	2:14	2:14–26
	3:6–7	3:1–17
	4:1–3	
	5:9–15	
Hebrews	James	1 Peter
2:14–18	2:19	3:22
	3:13–18	5:8–11
	4:1–8a	
2 Peter	1 John	2 John
2:1–22	2:12–14,18–23	1–13
	3:7–12	
	4:1–6	Jude
	5:18–21	1:6–9
Revelation		
2:9–10,13,24	13:1–18	18:1–24
3:9	14:9–11	19:2,20
9:1–21	15:2	20:1–10
11:7	16:2,13–16	21:8
12:1–17	17:1–18	22:15

every reference by name to Satan and evil spirits, I came out with an entirely different picture. There are actually a few more references to the demons by name than there are to Satan, about 39 for Satan and 41 for evil spirits (see Figure 39.2).

I am not saying that the importance of a subject in Scripture is directly proportionate to the number of times it is mentioned. That would be a totally inaccurate assumption. Those who criticize the contemporary emphasis on the spirit world follow that fallacious line of reasoning, however.

While demonic activity seems to dominate the Gospels, Satanic activity is also prominent in the Gospels. For every two references to demons in contact with Christ or His disciples there is at least one reference to Satan.

There are actually a few more references to demons and demonized persons, entities, or movements in the Epistles than there are to Satan. This is usually overlooked. Thus the assumption that while demons have prominence in the Gospels, Satan has that role in the Epistles, is proven to be false if sheer number of references is considered.

The book where demonic activity is most prominent in the New Testament is not one of the Gospels, but the Book of Revelation. Satan and his evil spirits are mentioned about 86 times in Revelation. This is more than in the gospel of Matthew which is almost twice the length of Revelation.

The Acts, the Epistles, and Revelation do not give prominence to the deliverance ministry of the apostles and Christians in general, that is true. In the Gospels that dimension of spiritual warfare ministry was prominent in Jesus' life and, to some degree, in that of the disciples. We want now to examine that ministry.

Figure 39.2
Quantity of References in the New Testament to Satan and to Evil Spirits

	Satan	Evil Spirits
Romans	1	4
1 and 2 Corinthians	7	7
Galatians	0	5
Ephesians	6	3
Colossians	5	5
1 and 2 Thessalonians	3	3
1 and 2 Timothy	6	4
Hebrews	1	0
James	1	2
1 and 2 Peter	2	2
1 and 2 John	6	5
Jude	1	1
Total	39	41
Gospels	48	102
Acts	4	8
Revelation	29	57
Total	120	208

The Deliverance Ministry of the Disciples in the Gospels

There are various references to the deliverance ministry of the disciples in the Gospels. First and foremost is the commission of the twelve to a deliverance ministry. It occurs in Matthew, Mark, and Luke. The twelve are commissioned in Mark "to preach, and to have authority to cast out demons" (Mark 3:14–15). In Matthew they are to cast out demons, preach the kingdom of heaven, heal the sick, and raise the dead (Matt. 10:7–8). Luke does not mention raising the dead (Luke 10:1–2).

The primary feature in the apostolic commission to ministry is casting out demons, however, not healing nor preaching. This fact would not be of such importance if it were not for the centrality of encounter with demons in the ministry of Jesus. Since the apostles' ministry is an extension of Jesus' own ministry, the two become compatible. It also reveals an understanding by the synoptic writers of the importance of such power encounters to the redemptive program of God.

Guelich's comments on Mark 6:7 and 13 are appropriate here:[1]

> The task of casting out unclean spirits is the only specific task mentioned at the outset. It reappears in the brief summary in 6:13, which indicates the importance that Mark attached to this part of the mission. It also shows how integral the mission of the Twelve was to Jesus' own ministry, since Mark introduced Jesus public ministry with an exorcism (1:21–27) and adds exorcisms to several earlier summaries. (1:39; 3:11; cf. 3:22–29)

Larry Hurtado says that "the defeat of evil spirits was for Mark *the representative deed* showing the authority of Jesus and the nature of the kingdom of God."[2] Thus the conferring of this authority upon His disciples was the sign, or at least one of the signs, of their union with Him in His ministry. Is it any less so today?

The entire account of the apostolic commission to their ministry by Jesus focuses on their encounter with the demonic realm. Mark records, "And He summoned the twelve and began to send them out in pairs; and He was giving them authority over the unclean spirits" (Mark 6:7). This is followed by a report of the ministry that they carried out. In contrast to the singular commission to exercise "authority over the unclean spirits," the apostolic ministry reported by Mark is fourfold: They preached, they cast out many demons; they healed the sick (vv. 12–13); and they "taught" (v. 30). The focus, however, is still on their deliverance ministries.

A second passage would probably indirectly refer to the apostolic deliverance ministry. It is found in Mark 9:38–40 and Luke 9:49–50, where the apostles meet a man who is casting out demons in Jesus' name and they forbid him because, in their words, "he was not following us" (v. 38c). The implication would be he should have joined them in their deliverance ministry. He would have thus been acceptable as a deliverance partner. Jesus rebuked their organizational pride at that point (vv. 39–40).

We see then that a deliverance ministry was an essential part of the apostolic commission to mission. This will be better understood as we examine the one account of their inability to bring about the deliverance needed.

Deliverance Failure: The Lessons Learned

In the technical sense the church did not begin until Pentecost; yet, since it began with the apostles, I consider their deliverance ministry prior to Pentecost to be the beginning of the deliverance ministry of the apostolic church. To understand the extent of that deliverance ministry it will be profitable to examine their one recorded major failure to effect release for a demonized person. It is the case of the severely demonized child as recorded in Matthew 17, Mark 9, and Luke 9.

By Jesus' own confession the apostles were dealing with a serious case of demonization as we will soon see (Matt. 17:21). In addition I want to single out two things about the apostolic deliverance ministry implied by this story. (We will use the Mark 9 account of the story primarily.) One, deliverance was part of the normal course of their ministry, even if it is only mentioned a few times in the Gospels. Both the disturbed father and the crestfallen apostles looked upon effective deliverance of the demonized as a normal part of apostolic ministry. Two, deliverance was such a normal part of their ministry everyone, including the apostles themselves, were perplexed as to why, in this case, the demon did not respond to the apostles' authority.

We begin the story with the glory of Jesus on the top of the mount of transfiguration (Mark 9:1–13). Next we see the shame of the disciples at the foot of the mount of transfiguration (v. 14–18).

We follow with the direct connection between Jesus' deliverance ministry and that of His disciples as seen by an outsider. It is established in the use of "you," Jesus, and "they," His disciples, in verses 17 and 18. The father bringing his demonized son to the disciples was considered bringing him to Jesus, the man implies. They are "Jesus men."

A Severely Demonized Child

Verses 17–18 also give a vivid description of the severity of the demonization tormenting the little child. He "had a spirit," the father says. "Had" here is the word *echō*, the most common Greek word for "to have" in the New Testament. Unfortunately, the NAS fails to translate the verb. Instead it engages in theological speculation by rendering *echō*, "have" by "possess." If possess was what the writer had in mind he would have used an entirely different Greek word, *ktaomai, katecho,* or *huparchō*, for example, not *echō*. The NKJV correctly translates the verb as "has a . . . spirit." The spirit made him "mute" (NAS, NKJV), not "dumb" (KJV). Here a specific biological impediment is due directly to demonic activity, not to a physical defect. This still occurs today.

In one incident I was ministering to a young man who was continually sick. Many demons were identified and cast out. I then came across one who called himself Fever.

"What is your purpose in his life?" I asked.

"To make him sick," he answered.

When Fever went out, the man stopped getting sick. Not that he never became sick again—we all do; but the continual sickness that had plagued him before was immediately gone.

The spirit in Mark 9 was also a "seizing" spirit, an epileptic-type spirit. It continually caused the child seizures. It dashed him to the ground, causing him to foam at the mouth and grind his teeth. After convulsing him for awhile, it then caused him to stiffen out (v. 18). These are all common symptoms of epilepsy or similar biological disorders.

This was not biological epilepsy, however. There was evidently nothing biologically wrong with his brain and nerves. This was demonic. It is interesting to note when this foul spirit went out, he gave him one more epileptic-like attack, on the way out (v. 26). The boy was not hurt by this violent exodus of the spirit, however (v. 27).

The other gospel writers add further dimensions to his physical-mental abuse by this filthy demonic creature. Matthew adds that he was "a lunatic" and that he was "very ill" (Matt. 17:15). The word lunatic is *selēniazō* in Greek, literally, "moon struck." It is translated both "epileptic" and "lunatic" in the New Testament. According to Vine, "Epilepsy was supposed to be influenced by the moon."[3]

Selēniazō is used only by Matthew (4:24; 17:15) in the New Testament. In 4:24 it is used for biological epilepsy in direct contrast with the demonization mentioned in the same verse. The New Testament world knew the difference between the two illnesses. We would do well to follow their example.

Luke adds that he was the "only boy" of the heartbroken father (Luke 9:38) and that the spirit "mauls him" and that it "scarcely leaves him" (v. 39). The spirit caused him suddenly to "scream" (a mute spirit can scream, Mark 9:17,25–26).

What an awful group of words and expressions describing the spirit's attempts to destroy the boy!

Three of the most common New Testament names for evil spirits are also used here: "spirit" (Mark 9:17,20); an "unclean spirit" (Mark 9:25; Luke 9:42); and a "demon" (Mark 7:18; Luke 9:42). In addition, Jesus addresses him as a "deaf and dumb [mute] spirit" (Mark 9:25).

The fact that the spirit made him both mute and deaf further intensifies the sheer horror of what this little boy was suffering. Also, the spirit had indwelt him from "childhood" (v. 21). The Greek word for "childhood" used here is *paidion*. It is used of infants just born as well as older children.[4] In all probability he was demonized from infancy. It also helps understand the agony the father was facing.[5]

Furthermore, it intensifies our utter contempt for and holy hatred of demons and their filthy, brutal kingdom. Again this is why I, personally, along with many of my colleagues, are willing to bear the bruises and attacks from many critical brethren that this crucial ministry to the demonized always brings with it. The price is not too much to pay to help release God's little ones as well as brutalized adults from the agony of severe demonization.

This story and the one in Mark 5 represent the most extreme cases of demonization recorded in Scripture. In Matthew the father says, "He often falls into the fire, and often into the water" (17:15). In Mark he says, "It [the demon] has often thrown him into the fire and into the water to destroy him" (9:22). This was not attempted suicide, but attempted murder. The distraught father says in Luke that the spirit "scarcely leaves him" (9:39). What a living hell for the little one and for his father!

In Jesus' private pre-deliverance counseling ministry with the father He seeks information from the boy's father. Then He publicly frees the child (Mark 9:25–27). Next we see the inquiry by the apostles as to the cause of their failure in bringing about the child's deliverance (vv. 28–29).

Reasons for Failure

I will mention only a few reasons for their failure.

One, they were not operating in the right spirit (using that word in a non-technical sense) to face perhaps the most serious case of demonization recorded in the Gospels. The sheer horror of what the demons were doing to the little child perhaps from birth exceeds anything like it in Scripture.

Why do I say they were not in the right "spirit"? Verse 14 tells us they were disputing with the scribes. That is not the best context in which to begin a major deliverance ministry. I can never forget the only serious failure (to date) in my deliverance ministry. I was under continual criticism from a group of theologians and Christian psychologists for diagnosing demonization with seriously troubled Christians. I decided to invite some of them to participate with me in a deliverance counseling session to judge for themselves what I was doing. I will never again repeat that mistake.

My deliverance team and I were ministering to a severely demonized woman. We had already seen groups of demons leave her life, but we knew she had more. She was not difficult to help into freedom, so I felt the critics would be able to learn (and I too could learn from them) by participating in the next counseling session with the troubled woman.

Only one psychologist showed up, however. He was a friend of mine but very critical of this dimension of my ministry. I decided to allow the demons to come into controlled manifestation for his benefit. In this woman's case, all the demons already expelled were the type which wanted to come forward. They were always vocal and intimidating if I did not bind them into silence.

We were about to begin with a session of prayer when my psychologist friend noticed a young, attractive woman on the team. He reached over and took her hand. Holding it tightly, he said, "What a privilege to hold the hand of such a lovely young woman. I don't often get that privilege." The lady was embarrassed but didn't know what to say. I was shocked beyond words. We were all disturbed by the levity and carnal attitude of the psychologist, but tried to go on with the session.

I began to pray with my eyes open. I saw the evidence the demons had surfaced within the woman. Their evil presence was visible in her face, especially her eyes. The psychologist, if he was even looking, probably saw nothing. I knew the demons were there, so did my team members and the victim. The control demon only spoke once, in a soft voice directly to me. My team members could also hear what he said. The psychologist was behind me, so I don't know if he could hear. He made no reference to hearing or seeing anything except the lovely lady team member.

"You are trying to destroy us." That was all. The silence for the next two hours meant, "We are not going to cooperate. We don't have to. The flesh of some here gives us grounds to stop what you are trying to do." Anyone who has had years of ministry in deliverance knows what one person with a carnal, sensual, critical and unsympathetic spirit can do in a ministry with deeply entrenched demons.

This was evidently the type of situation the disciples faced with the demonized boy, only in their case the problem was with themselves. If the human spirit of those affecting the deliverance is not in tune with the Holy Spirit, deliverance can come to a halt.

Two, the disciples were facing a difficult "kind" of spirit they had never faced before, Jesus says in Matthew 17:21. The word "kind" used by Jesus here is *genos* in Greek. Vine says it means "family, race, kindred, generation, kind, or class."[6] It was the type that would come out only by prayer and possibly fasting (Mark 9:29 with Matt. 17:21).

James Morrison comments that though they had received power to cast out demons, "the power was not absolute. . . . Its exercise was conditional." He then refers to Jesus' statement in Matthew 17:20 that *they failed because of their little faith.*[7]

> He did not mean to say that His disciples were absolutely unbelieving. They were not. They had belief. But there was so much remaining unbelief. There was, as it were, the company of two armies within them. There was conflict. And now it was faith and anon, it was *unbelief,* that prevailed. . . . Their faith . . . had difficulty maintaining its ground in the conflict.

As one of the church fathers affirmed, "They had fallen out of faith." That is an insightful word.

Morrison says of Matthew 17:21, "This kind of demons, of which we have here a specimen . . . is a kind that are peculiarly subtle, malicious, and powerful."[8] The story brings us face-to-face with the perplexing problem of stubborn demons which are often hard to remove from the life of their victim. Why are some deliverance cases so difficult to work with?

Forces Making Some Cases Complex

As is true of most of the "why" questions dealing with the spirit world, there is no hard and fast list of answers one can present. The solution is as complex as are individual demons, individual human victims, and the whole area of demonization itself. First and foremost are all the often hidden, complex, and unknown pieces of the puzzle which represents the history of the victim. One crucial area is the victim's family heritage, including all the events leading up to the victim's conception, birth, and early home life or lack of it.

Next are the unique life experiences of the victim up to the moment of attempted deliverance, both what he himself has done and what has been done to him and the circumstances involved. Much also depends also upon the type and class of demons being dealt with. Scripture, history, and contemporary experience verify that some demons and groups of demons are more difficult to deal with than others.

Then there is the question of the degree of control the demons are exercising in the life of the victim at the time of deliverance. (We will look at this important issue in some detail later in our study.) The demons in the Mark 9 story were strongly attached to the life of their helpless child victim. Such demons are usually difficult to expel in one deliverance session. Also, besides the strength of their attachment, if we are dealing with very strong and very "bad" demons, the process can be even slower. This is what the apostles were facing with the little boy in Mark 9.

Finally, we have the word of Jesus in Matthew 17:21, for which Morrison's comment is appropriate: "The faith that would be victorious in a contest with the subtlest and most powerful of demonic agencies would need to give itself much both to prayer and corporate self-denial."[9]

40

The Success of the Seventy
Luke 10

The most detailed report of successful deliverance ministry by the Lord's disciples in the Gospels is the story of the seventy in Luke 10:1,17–19. It all begins in verse 1 where the seventy are given their missionary commission. Jesus sends them out "two and two ahead of Him to every city and place where He Himself was going to come" (v. 1). Though not specified in verse 1, the central focus is on deliverance ministry (Mark 6:7,13; Luke 10:17–19).

In Mark 6 the apostles simply reported to Jesus "all that they had done and taught" (Mark 6:30). But in Luke we are told what the seventy had done and, by implication, what they had taught. It is summed up in one triumphant acclamation, "Lord, even the demons are subject to us in Your name" (10:17).

This report is important because it is the only specific report of the ministry accomplished by the Lord's disciples after being commissioned. Also it is consistent with the focus on demonic encounter and deliverance in the continuation of the ministry of Jesus to which these seventy "lay disciples" were commissioned. Even more important, it settles the question of where the immediate authority for deliverance really lies—in the deliverance ministers.

The ultimate authority, of course, lies in Jesus, but the immediate authority lay in them and they knew it. Thus they declare, "The demons are subject to us, in your name." In other words, "Lord, we are doing what you gave us authority to do," they affirm. "The demons recognize our authority to exercise your authority against them. The result is they are forced to obey us."

Jesus' Joyful Response

Jesus' response was immediate, exhilarated, confirming, affirming, and cautious. First it was *immediate*. "And he said to them," Luke says. He did not ask any questions. He just responded immediately to their ecstatic ministry report (v. 18a). Second, it was *exhilarated*. There is joy in his words, "I was watching Satan fall from heaven like lightning. Behold, I have given you . . ." (vv. 18b–19a).

Luke next records, "At that very time He rejoiced greatly in the Holy Spirit, and said, 'I praise Thee, O Father, Lord of heaven and earth, that Thou didst hide these things from the wise and intelligent and didst reveal them to babes. Yes, Father, for thus it was well-pleasing in thy sight" (Luke 10:21).

Norval Geldenhuys comments on the Lord's exhilaration.[1]

> From these words it appears that the Saviour rejoiced in the fact that God in His wisdom, omnipotence and love has so arranged matters that insight is given into the redeeming truths of the kingdom not to those who are self-exalted and wise in their own esteem (as so many Pharisees and scribes were at that time) but to those like His faithful disciples who in childlike simplicity and humility feel their utter dependence on the Lord and accept without intellectual arrogance the truths revealed by God through Him.

Geldenhuys then concludes, "Jesus makes the contrast not between educated and uneducated but between people with the wrong and self-sufficient attitude and those with the right and childlike attitude."[2]

Third, it was *confirming.* "I was watching Satan fall from heaven like lightning," Jesus declares. What does this mean? Commentators offer various suggestions. I suggest two. One, Jesus was saying, "Amen! What you are saying is true. The demons are subject to you in my name. That is what I have been telling you." Two, Jesus actually saw Satan fall from heaven like lightning. Whenever I am asked what this verse means I usually answer very kindly, "It means Jesus saw 'Satan fall from heaven like lightning.' That is what it means."

Before the intervention of the kingdom of God into the kingdom of Satan, Satan seemed to rule without serious competition. While God was always at work in His universe, Satan was allowed to rule somewhat as king. He ruled in the heavenlies over a vast kingdom of evil spirits. He ruled almost unhindered on earth, his spirits having free access both to heaven and earth.

Christ came to bring that rule to an end (Matt. 12:28–29). He began the dethronement of Satan in His redemptive event as the God-man. As Lord ruling in heaven at the right hand of God, He continues the breakup of Satan's kingdom through His church. Finally, He will fully accomplish the destruction of Satan's kingdom when He returns as King of Kings, and Lord of Lords (Rev. 19:11—20:15).

In the occasion before us, Jesus looks up. He sees in a vision, so to speak, the sudden fall of Satan from his place of rule and authority. He directly connects that fall of Satan to the deliverance ministry of the seventy. That is the immediate context in which these unique words are spoken. Leon Morris affirms that this is the preferred interpretation of Jesus' words here.[3]

> In the mission of the seventy, Jesus saw the defeat of Satan, a defeat as sudden and unexpected (to the forces of evil) as a flash of lightning. To the casual observer all that had happened was that a few mendicant preachers had spoken in a few small towns and healed a few sick folks. But in that Gospel triumph Satan had suffered a notable defeat.

Jesus here, in the Holy Spirit, sees laymen, not apostles, dethroning the perverse principalities and powers of Satan at the word of their command and in the name of their Lord. Jesus is overcome with joy and satisfaction. In verse 18, he says Amen!

Norval Geldenhuys supports this position.[4]

> When Jesus utterly rejected the temptations of the devil (4:1–13), the victory over his power had already been won. Throughout the Saviour's public ministry this victory was revealed in the liberation of those possessed of the devil and in other manifestations of His power. And especially in the grand offensive by the seventy against the might of Satan it could plainly be seen how Satan had already lost his exalted position of power. Satan is a conquered enemy, and where action is taken in the name of Jesus, the Conqueror, victory is gloriously assured.

This is an excellent word. It is a teaching that has application to all who, in the name of Jesus, are called upon to face the entrenched focuses of darkness both in individual lives and in the territorial expansion of the gospel as in this story.

Striking a Balance

Yet there is a desperate need of balance to this type of power ministry. Jesus' response is cautious. After greatly encouraging his obedient disciples He brings them back to earth by speaking of their redemption in heaven. In Luke 10:20 He says, "nevertheless, do not rejoice in this, that the spirits are subject to you, but rejoice that your names are recorded in heaven." Geldenhuys comments:[5]

> From the original it appears that by this verse Jesus meant that the disciples must not seek their permanent ground for joy in the fact that the demons are subject to them, but in the fact that through the grace of God their names are written in the heavenly registers—they have been enrolled among God's elect. The fact of their redemption is the all-surpassing boon conferred upon them.

The Promise of Delegated Authority

Next, his response is *affirming*. He takes them one step further in their faith and redemptive spiritual warfare ministry. "Behold, I have given you authority to tread upon serpents and scorpions, and over all the power of the enemy, and nothing shall injure you" (Luke 10:19).

This is without doubt one of the greatest gems found in the precious collection of promises of delegated authority in all of Scripture. With what can we compare it? We will look at this promise from a sixfold perspective.

1. *The source of the promise.* "Behold, *I* . . ."

Someone has said the value of any promise is directly proportionate to the authority of the one who gives it. The "I" is the Son of God whom God the Father has "appointed heir of all things, through whom also He made the world." He is the one who is "the exact representation of His nature." He is the one who "upholds all things by the word of His power" (Heb. 1:2–3). Thus he can later affirm, "All authority is given to me in heaven and on earth" (Matt. 28:18).

2. *The assurance of the promise.* "I *have given* you . . ." is not future, it is now. The verb is in the perfect tense *(dedocha)*, an action completed. They already have the authority promised. Jesus "repeated, ratified and enlarged their commission. . . . They had employed their power vigorously against Satan, and now Christ entrusts them with greater power."[6]

3. *The gift of the promise.* "I have given you *authority* . . ." The KJV translates the Greek word used here, *exousia,* and the word *dunamis,* used of Satan later in the verse, by "power." The NKJV and all the more modern translations correct this error. "*Dunamis* power is might and ability, while *exousia* is right to act."[7] The enemy has might and ability. The believer has the right to act. He has delegated authority.

The illustration of the police officer and the semi-truck is often used to point out the difference. The mighty semi-truck comes rolling down the street. As the semi approaches an intersection a policeman steps forward, a gnat in comparison to the mighty truck. Suddenly he raises his hand in a signal which means "Stop!" The semi squeals to a stop.

The truck has power, terrible power behind it. It could crush the police officer and continue on its course without even slowing down, but it has no authority to do so. It does not possess the right to act. The police officer does. True, he has no power. What power is there in one hand with five little fingers? However, the authority of the city, the state, and even the nation stands behind him. That delegated authority brings the power of the truck under its control.

"Behold," says Jesus, "I have given you *authority* over all the *power* of the enemy." No wonder Jesus chided the apostles for their "falling from faith," which rendered them without authority before the power of the demons indwelling the life of one little boy (Matt. 17:14–21)!

4. *The opposition to the promise.* It is summed up in three words, "serpents," "scorpions," and "the enemy." The authority over serpents and scorpions could be a reference to the serpent of Genesis 3:15. He is the one who will later be called "the enemy." Even more probable, however, is to see it as a reference to the serpents of Psalm 91:13, one of the greatest of the many spiritual warfare Psalms.[8] E. H. Plumtree, writing in Ellicott, agrees saying the reference is to these serpents of Psalm 91:13 which are "symbols of spiritual power of evil."[9]

"The enemy" is used several times by Jesus in the Gospels to refer to the Devil himself. In Matthew 13 he is called, "his enemy" (v. 25); "an enemy" (v. 28); and "the enemy . . . is the devil" (v. 39). The enemy we face is the singular Devil. All our other enemies are but extensions of his evil power.

In spite of all appearances to the contrary, the enemy is neither omnipresent, omniscient, nor omnipotent. Thus he needs his serpents and scorpions, that is, his angels, demons, and evil spirits. There are evidently billions of them. Since they are everywhere, this makes it appear as if Satan himself is everywhere. In the sense that demons are also devils, possess the devil's nature, he, in them, is everywhere at the same time. Thus the relationship between serpents and scorpions with the enemy in this verse is an anticipation of Ephesians 6:10–12.

5. *The extent of the promise.* "I have given you authority over *all the powers of the enemy.*" While it is obvious what Jesus is saying here, the verse is also capable of misapplication in many ways.

There can be *misapplication in method.* Believers have used this verse to go demon hunting, but the promise is to be seen primarily within the context of the missionary mandate. "I have sent you out to continue my redemptive ministry," Jesus is saying. "The Enemy will oppose you. When he does, I have given you full authority over all his power which he will bring against you."

There is the *misapplication of oversimplification.* Believers are told they can dethrone the principalities and powers which have ruled both geographical and socio-cultural units of humanity for centuries in a weekend spiritual warfare conference. This is self-deception. While our enemies are already defeated they are not dead, not even sickly. Satan is described as the still-active "god of this world" by the apostle Paul years after the Lord's death, burial, resurrection, and ascension (2 Cor. 4:4). Our enemy, though defeated, is still at war with us. He fights until he is forced to withdraw, but it is not a permanent withdrawal. He regroups! He goes on the offense! He continues to prowl about seeking for every possible channel through which he can return (1 Peter 5:8f).

Then there is *the potential abuse of faith and power* which can become brazenness and pride. "I can handle it. God has given me authority over the enemy. Let them come. I am ready for them." We must avoid a spiritual power trip, just as we are to avoid a worldly power trip. This is neither a war with toy soldiers, nor is it a mock battle. It is a dirty, hellish, and painful war with a defeated foe who has not as yet accepted his defeat. There have been and will continue to be many Christian causalities.

Finally there is the *misapplication based on fearfulness.* "I don't like serpents and scorpions," people complain. "While Jesus has given me authority over the Enemy, I don't want to mess with him. Those who do get into trouble. I have enough trouble as it is without looking for more. If I leave Satan alone I expect him to reciprocate and leave me alone also."

6. *The consolation of the promise.* "Nothing shall injure you." Is this really true? Yes and no. I say no because all of God's people who have stood and continue to

stand against the Enemy have been and are still being hurt by him; often very painfully. We must remember it was the battered warrior, the apostle Paul who wrote, "From now on let no one cause trouble for me, for I bear on my body the brandmarks of Jesus" (Gal. 6:17).

I say, yes, it is true. In our warfare, while we will be "cast down, but not destroyed" (2 Cor. 4:8–9). "We are more than conquerors through him that loved us" (Rom. 8:37, KJV). "God always leads us in His triumph in Christ" (2 Cor. 2:14). Matthew Henry writes that Christ has given us "defensive power" as well as "offensive authority."[10]

This then, was the spiritual warfare ministry of the twelve apostles and the larger band of seventy disciples in the Gospels. Next we will see what probably amounts only to the tip of the iceberg of their continual deliverance ministry as recorded in the Acts of the Apostles.

41

Beginnings in Acts
Acts 2, 4

All of the warfare case studies given in Acts focus on Christian leaders in their encounters with Satan and his demons. Without doubt "lay people" experienced such encounters also, but Luke focuses only upon leaders. In light of the scriptural portrait of Satan in his hostility against the children of God, though he will not be mentioned by name until Acts 5, he is present from the beginning of Acts to the end.

SATAN'S STRATEGY AGAINST THE EARLY CHURCH

My friend Dr. Arthur Glasser, Dean Emeritus of the School of World Mission at Fuller Theological Seminary, sees a fourfold spiritual warfare strategy of Satan against the early church in the early chapters of Acts.[1]

Strategy one, Satan tries to stop the evangelistic outreach of God's people. In Acts 4:1–4 the Jewish Council apprehends, imprisons, and interrogates Peter and John for preaching and effecting the healing of the lame beggar at the Beautiful Gate of the Jewish temple (3:10 with 4:7). Luke notes that the causes of the opposition were that they were "teaching the people" and "proclaiming in Jesus the resurrection from the dead" (v. 2). The Jewish leaders dared not physically abuse the apostles because they feared the people, however (vv. 21–22). They simply warned them not "to speak or teach at all in the name of Jesus" (v. 18).

The opposition to the church's preaching, teaching, and power ministry flares up again in Acts 5 with more serious consequences. This time the entire apostolic band is imprisoned (v. 17). The immediate cause is a series of power encounters through God's servants against Satan and evil spirits plus the general power ministry of the apostles (4:30–37), especially Peter (5:1–16).

The apostles are tried by the full Jewish Council or Senate (5:21,27), who are furious at the apostle's disobedience to their prior command not to teach "in this name" (v. 28). When Peter and the eleven boldly defend themselves, the angry Council decides to execute them (v. 33). Only through the intervention of Gamaliel are the apostles' lives spared (vv. 34–40a), but they are beaten and ordered "to speak no more in the name of Jesus" (v. 40c). This is the fourth time the name of Jesus is used as a power concept in Acts (v. 31). The apostles disobey the gag order and the Devil suffers his first recorded defeat in Acts.

Strategy two, Satan tries to contaminate the spiritual life of the church's members. Acts 5:1–10 contains probably one of the most well-known and controversial stories in the New Testament, the strange behavior and deaths of Ananias and Sapphira. Satan attempts to gain power over the church through corrupting the life of one of its prominent church families. While the strategy fails, it fails only because God directly intervened and caused it to fail. Since that day, this has been one of Satan's most effective strategies to halt or hinder the impact for good of the church on the world. Here the Devil suffers his second defeat (vv. 12–16).

Strategy three, Satan attempts to divide the fellowship of the church. The background context here is the increased explosive growth of the church (5:42—6:1a). Satan tries to divide the church by taking advantage of its success in evangelism and church growth. With more people come more problems. He wants to bring failure through their successes.

Acts 6:1b shows us that the mono-cultural Jerusalem church has become bi-cultural. The church is now made up of two different cultural groups, "the native Hebrews" and "the Hellenists." The immediate cause of the potential church split is the tension between the two groups resulting from the alleged discrimination on the part of the apostles in their direction of the social welfare program of the church. The Hellenistic widows were evidently being bypassed in favor of the Hebrew widows.

With the discrimination problem, action had to be taken. The apostles responsible for the distribution of the welfare program (Acts 4:36–37) accepted the responsibility for the problem. In their response, "It is not desirable for us to neglect the word of God in order to serve tables" (6:2), we discover that the social program had created problems too big for them to handle.

The apostles acted wisely and solved the immediate problem as revealed in verses 2–6. Increased church growth resulted (v. 7a). The gospel spills over into a new cultural group, the priestly (v. 7). Thus the Devil was dealt another defeat.

Strategy four, the Devil then uses his last strategy. He stirs up the political leaders to do what the Jewish leaders had not been able to do. King Herod strikes out at the church leadership (12:1f), first by executing the apostle James (vv. 1–2). According to verse 3, Herod must have taken this step with certain trepidation. In the past the apostles had enjoyed great favor with the Jewish people (4:16,21; 5:26). Evidently that favor had eroded by Acts 12. The Jewish people "were pleased" at Herod's execution of James.

The second step was the arrest and imprisonment of the apostle Peter (12:3–4). Herod was going to put Peter on public trial, not execute him privately as he had done with James (v. 4b). Evidently Herod wanted to use this incident both to enhance his position with the Jewish public and to stir the smoldering opposition against the Christians into flaming resistance. Then, in time, he could arrest and execute the entire leadership of the church without fear of opposition from the Jewish people.

The plan would probably have succeeded if God had not stepped in by sending his jail-breaking angel to release Peter from prison (vv. 6–10). When the angel is through with Peter, he next pays a visit to King Herod. This time the results are disastrous for the arrogant king. He dies "eaten by worms" (v. 23). The result? "But the word of the Lord continued to grow and to be multiplied" (v. 24). The Devil is defeated again.

Little Deliverance Ministry in Acts?

Just because demons are not often mentioned does not mean the apostles and early Christians were not involved in deliverance. They probably were. Why then is so little attention given in Acts to this more overt dimension of spiritual warfare when it is so prominent in the synoptic Gospels? While no certain answer can be given, I share a few suggestions.

1. It would be just as appropriate to ask why the apostle John in his gospel never mentions Jesus' deliverance ministry while the Synoptics do. Does his silence mean it was not occurring? If we believe the Holy Spirit directly guided all

the Bible writers in their writing, then we have to believe He led John with different purposes in writing his gospel than the other three.[2] For example, he does record some of Jesus' teaching on Satan not found in the Synoptics (John 8:31–59; 12:31; 14:30; 16:11; 17:15). The same thing applies to Acts. The Holy Spirit did not choose to have Luke record the full power encounter deliverance ministry of the apostolic church.

2. The pattern of ministry to which Jesus trained His disciples would naturally continue throughout their lifetime. It is nowhere rescinded or changed. It is evidently to be understood that when demons appeared opposing their ministry, they dealt with them exactly as they had been taught.

3. All of the deliverance "sessions" recorded in the Gospels occurred in public and with the demons in full manifestation. While there were probably specific reasons for this, they are not listed. This does not mean there was not private deliverance ministry going on all the time. There probably was. Since Jesus' deliverance ministry was a sign of the kingdom and His unique authority (Matt. 12:28–29), He did it in public. Since the disciples' ministry uniquely extended His, the same would apply to them.

4. Demonic encounters are recorded as occurring several times in the ministry of the disciples in Acts. They were all public manifestations of demons (Acts 5, 8, 16, 19).

5. The Acts records many rapidly growing evangelistic and church-planting movements often accompanied by healings and other miracles and, at least in Samaria, by the massive exodus of demonic spirits (Acts 8:5–13). When a people movement occurs in the context of power demonstrations by the Spirit of God, demons often leave, en masse, on their own. One-on-one deliverance sessions are not usually necessary.

6. One aspect of Luke's style in Acts in recording specific evangelistic, church-planting strategies is to give one major overview of that strategy. He may follow it with another brief reference to the strategy. After that he does not repeat it again. In similar circumstances we are to understand that similar things occurred.[3]

7. If it is asked why the Acts (and the Epistles) do not make any reference to apostolic teaching about how to work with the demonized, the answer is the familiar one of the silence of Scripture. I don't know, because the Bible does not say.

We can raise a related question, however. Why do not the Gospels make any reference to Jesus teaching His disciples how to work with the demonized? We see Jesus doing deliverance. We see Him commissioning the disciples to a deliverance ministry. We even see the disciples doing deliverance ministry. But we have no teaching by Jesus to the how of a deliverance and power encounter ministry. We must assume that it was done, that the disciples did the same thing, and that they, in turn, would have trained others in the same manner.

8. Of this we are certain, Jesus did deliverance, as did the apostles, the seventy, and the leadership of the apostolic church (Acts 5, 8, 16). The frequency or infrequency of references to it is not a valid indication of its importance.

Uninhibited Evangelism

The first three chapters of Acts reveal the apostles filled with the Holy Spirit and evangelizing uninhibited in Jerusalem. Satan used every strategy at his disposal to stop the church in its church-planting ministry. According to Luke's record in Acts, the main apostolic witness centered on at least two powerful "evangelistic crusades," to use a modern term, separated by a period of effective teaching and personal witness. These "crusades" began with miracles.

The first, in Acts 2, started with a blast of wind like that of a cyclone. It filled the city of Jerusalem. The sound drew multitudes to the Upper Room (Acts 2:1–6a). This was immediately followed by the miraculous gift to the disciples of the languages represented by the crowd which had gathered (vv. 4–11). The response was first, honest inquiry, "What does this mean?" (v. 12); and second, ridicule, "They are full of sweet wine" (v. 13).

Peter with the eleven stood up and proclaimed the gospel (vv. 14–36). Evidently, the Spirit brought the people to the place of great openness to the gospel. Their response was, "Brethren, what shall we do?" (v. 37). Peter gives the answer (vv. 38–40). About three thousand respond. They believe, are baptized, and are added to the 120 (v. 41).

The Jerusalem church thus grew from 120 to 3,120 in one day. This is called "church growth"! It is also called "power evangelism."[4] A period of intense teaching for the new converts and continued power evangelism followed. The growth of the new church daily was nothing short of spectacular (2:42–47).

Next, God set the stage for another effort in power evangelism. This time it came through the power healing[5] of the lame man at the entrance of the Beautiful Gate of the temple (Acts 3:1–26). Even more spectacular church growth resulted (4:4). About five thousand additional men came into the church.

F. F. Bruce tells us the phrase is "*ton andron*, 'of the men' as distinct from women and children, not *ton anthrōpon*, 'of the men' in the sense of human beings."[6] Why are only men mentioned? Possibly because this was a male-oriented society, or because these men probably represented heads of households. If so this could have been an influx of at least 15,000 or more people.

The First Opposition

This was too much for the Devil to accept. He must have been beside himself in rage. Thus he did all he could to stop the expansion of the church through his control over the Jewish leaders. When the Jewish leaders call Peter and John before them for examination in Acts 4, they ask two interesting questions. Both fit our spiritual warfare overview of Acts.

A Question of Power

First, "by what power, or in what name, have you done this?" (v. 7). Notice that the leaders were not questioning the authenticity of the miracle. In fact they bitterly complained that "a noteworthy miracle has taken place through them is apparent to all who live in Jerusalem, and we cannot deny it" (v. 16). R. J. Knowling says the question implies that they are accusing them of using some magical name or formula for the performance of the miracle like that which occurred in Acts 19:13.[7] What was done by Peter and John was outside the acceptance of Judaism at the time. The healing, therefore, was looked upon as magical or demonic in origin.

The word "power" here is *dunamis*. Walter Wink says *dunamis* had two primary uses in the New Testament. Its first use was for "miracles." After that it is used primarily to denote spiritual entities or attributes, as we will see later in our studies. He says the reference in Acts 4:7 is actually to an "evil spirit."[8] These Jewish leaders, as they had consistently done in reference to Jesus (Matt. 12:24), were accusing Peter and John of performing spirit magic. The miracle, they insinuated, was demonic in origin. They wanted Peter and John to admit this and give them the demonic source or power formula behind the miracle.

A Question of Name

Second is the question about the "name" behind the miracle (v. 7c). "Name," or *onoma*, is also a power term.[9] It was so in the world of contemporary biblical cultures, including Jewish culture. It also had the same connotation as used by Jesus and the early church.In the pagan world the name of something or someone had magical significance when used in a spiritual sense. The magical papyri, as we will see later in our study, contain lists of power names and advice on how to use them. In pagan exorcisms to know the name of the spirit was supposed to give one some control over that spirit.

The use of the name of Jesus in power ministry was fundamental to Christian power concepts. It was divorced from all magic by the early Christians, however. Hawthorne, writing on the use of "name" in Scripture, says that it would be incorrect in the Old Testament to see "names" as just "an identity tag" as is true in contemporary Western culture. He writes, "The name of a person sometimes revealed his character, his personality, even his destiny. In fact, a person's name was often considered to be but an expression, indeed a revelation, of his true nature."[10]

The author then speaks of the relationship between speaking one's name over or in reference to a person, thing, place and ownership over the object named.[11]

> It becomes clear . . . that "to call one's name over" a people or a place is an idiom that . . . declares that they now belong to him. They are now under his authority and protection. (2 Sam. 12:28; Ps. 49:1; Isa. 4:1)

> This idiom is especially significant when used to describe the relationship of Yahweh to the people of Israel. They are called by His name. They are His peculiar possession, subject to His rule and under His protection and care. (2 Chron. 7:14; Isa. 63:19; Jer. 14:9; 15:16; Dan. 9:19) They are His people.

In the New Testament, the use of "name" continued unchanged, except for a few more elements coming out of Greek culture.

Understanding the Council's Questions

These facts help us understand the meaning behind the council's question to Peter and John (4:7), the use of the name of Jesus by the apostles in the healing of the lame man (3:6 and 16), and the continued use of His name (4:10,12,30; 5:41). Finally this information throws light on the council's constant references to Jesus' name and objections against the continuous evangelistic ministry in the name of Jesus (4:17–18; 5:28 and 40).

Hawthorne points out that

> statements made about God in the Old Testament are now made about Christ in the New Testament (cf. Heb. 1:7–12). The most frequent name for God in the Old Testament, *Yahweh,* (LXX *Kyrios,* "Lord") now becomes the Church's favorite name for Christ.

> The Church's earliest confession of faith in Christ was in all likelihood, "Jesus is Lord" (cf. Rom. 10:9; Phil. 2:9–11). Thus, all that can be said about the name of Yahweh. . . . are said about the name of Jesus Christ. (Acts 4:17; John 14:1; 1 Cor. 1:2)[12]

Jesus' disciples prophesied in His name (Matt. 7:22); cast out demons in His name (Luke 10:17); performed miracles in His name (Mark 9:39)—they did everything in His name. By using this expression, it became evident that the disciples spoke and acted like Jesus, in His place and with His authority, as did the prophets of Yahweh in the Old Testament (see Acts 4:7–10).

Wink writes on the biblical concept of power and powers, good and evil. As a power term, *onoma*, "name," in the New Testament is used most often of Jesus as Lord or Christ (97 of 226 uses), Wink says. It is associated with God's name 44 times, "always with the sense of the totality of God's power and being."[13]

He also states that seven times "name" represents the essence of satanic evil, all in Revelation. As used of the beast or harlot (Rev. 13:1,17; 14:11; 15:2; 17:3,5), "it crystallizes the inner reality, the moral degeneracy and political brutality of the Roman Empire." He says when used of the king of the locusts, "it encompasses etymologically his function: he is the 'angel of the bottomless pit; his name in Hebrew is Abaddon, and in Greek he is called Apollyon,' that is, Destroyer (Rev. 9:11)."

Here in Acts the rulers *(archontes)*, elders, and scribes ask Peter and John, "By what power *(dynamei)* or in what name *(onomati)* have you done this?" In defense, Peter responds, "There is no other name *(onoma)* under heaven that has been given among men, by which we must be saved" (Acts 4:12). Jesus' name, in short, has become the Name of names; "on His thigh He has a name written, 'King of kings, and Lord of lords'" (Rev. 19:16).

Wink's next comment is correct.[14]

> When . . . Jesus is given "a name which is above every name," that is *kyrios* (Phil. 2:9–11), and is exalted far "above every name that is named" (Eph. 1:21), this . . . must include every power with a title, every authority invested with an office, every incumbent with a role, whether divine, diabolical, or human. Like Colossians 1:16, then, the term *onoma* (name) points us toward the most expansive understanding of the Powers possible.

Now we can understand the seriousness behind the question of the Jewish Council in Acts 4:7 and their frantic efforts to disallow the continued use of the name of Jesus (Acts 4:17–18; 5:28,40). They must at all cost stop the release of the supernatural energy that flowed from that name, *Jesus*.

We also now understand why, when this command is broken by the disciples, the council members "were so furious they wanted to kill them" (Acts 5:33, PHILLIPS). We also understand why the disciples used the name of Jesus as a channel for the release of God's miraculous power. The name of Jesus and the person of Jesus are, for all practical purposes, one and the same (3:6,16; 4:8–12,30; 5:41).

While the council saw the power and name of Jesus as magical or demonic, the disciples saw it as the name and person of God, the Lord, the Son. While the council saw his name as a satanic attack against the kingdom of God, the disciples saw it as God's kingdom attacking the kingdom of Satan. That name is the power source behind the kingdom of God.

Evidently because of their fear of the people, the Jewish Senate released Peter and John from prison. A great miracle had taken place. A well-known Jewish lame man had been healed through the mediation of Peter and John (4:13–16). Yet these men had to be stopped. The Senate concluded they could accomplish this by frightening the two men (vv. 17–18). When Peter refused to agree to their terms for release, all they could do was threaten them and let them go, anyway (4:21).

The Church's Bold Request

The disciples meet with the church. They pray that God will "extend [His] hand to heal, and signs and wonders take place through the name *(onomatos)* of Thy holy servant Jesus" (4:30). God answers with power (v. 31a). They continue to speak the Word of God with boldness (v. 42). And "with great power the apostles were giving witness to the resurrection of the Lord Jesus, and abundant grace was upon them all," Luke tells us (v. 33).

What can we say about the church's request, asking God to do miracles, praying that He would extend His "hand to heal and signs and wonders take place through the name of Thy holy servant Jesus"?

One, we say that true miracles result from God's direct intervention in the normal operations of the laws of His universe. His power momentarily sets aside "natural" laws in order to accomplish specific purposes. The Acts of the Apostles records many such incidences of direct divine intervention. John Bright calls these miraculous acts "the signs of the kingdom."[15] The most common "formula" to describe God's miraculous activities in Acts is miracles, wonders, and signs, any combination of the three, or any two of the three.

The prayer for miracles in Acts 4 focused particularly on healing (v. 30). This is understandable for at least three reasons. One, most of the disciples had witnessed and participated in Jesus' healing ministry. Two, they were commissioned by Jesus to this ministry along with their deliverance ministry. Three, prayer for healing was culturally relevant to the Jews.

William Barclay has written, "If a Jew was sick he was more apt to go to the rabbi than to the doctor; and he would most likely be healed."[16] Miracles of healing are just as relevant and just as needed today among suffering people who have little or no medical help. Furthermore, it is with the purpose of meeting the needs of God's sick people that our Father has given the "gifts of healings" to his church (1 Cor. 12:9).

Finally, in deliverance-power encounter ministry miracles continue to occur. While often denied, not only is a deliverance ministry a healing ministry, it is also a miraculous ministry. The binding demons have both the grounds, the rights, and the power to continue to partly own their victim. The victim and the demons are all a part of this world over which Satan rules as god.

By the authoritative command of the deliverance minister (this can be the victim himself through self-deliverance), the demons are forced to release their control over their victims. The power of the kingdom of God, the Holy Spirit and, often the angels of God, directly intervene to break the power of the kingdom of Satan at that point. This is a true miracle. This is true power encounter.

With this beginning study of some of the spiritual warfare dimensions of the apostolic ministry discovered in Acts, we are now ready to examine the six major accounts of encounters with demons in the apostolic church as recorded in Acts.

42

Ananias and Sapphira
Acts 5

The story we are about to examine is probably one of the best known in the Book of Acts. It has to do with a church family headed by Ananias. His wife Sapphira is mentioned, but nothing more is known about the family. Evidently they did not have children living at home with them.

The incident occurred soon after the Jerusalem church emerged from the persecution centering on the healing of the lame man in the temple (Acts 4).[1] The church emerged from that attack stronger than ever (4:31–33). Acts 4:32–37 records the efforts by the early Christians to meet the social needs of its members. The actions taken would indicate that the church had grown rapidly, bringing both the wealthy and the poor into its membership. The passage pictures a unified body of believers who loved and cared for each other. The more prosperous members readily sold some of their properties to help meet the needs of their poorer brethren. What a marvelous group to be associated with!

It is in this bigger context of unity, love, and compassion that we meet the Christian household that was not quite Christian (Acts 5:1f). I do not mean to affirm that Ananias and Sapphira were not true Christians. They probably were. There is nothing to indicate the contrary. In a context like this, we are expected to take them as true believers unless told the contrary. When I say they were "not quite Christian," I mean they did not act like Christians in the incident at hand. While their brethren were occupied with the real needs of others, Ananias and Sapphira were preoccupied with their own felt needs.

The immediate context of the story is the acclaim given to Barnabas. True to his lifestyle as the "Son of Encouragement," he had sold a tract of land and "brought the money and laid it at the apostles' feet" (4:36–37). Evidently the attention this sacrificial act had brought to Barnabas disturbed Ananias and Sapphira.

While Peter deals with both husband and wife, he places the blame primarily on Ananias (5:3–4). Verse 2 says, "with his wife's full knowledge." This implies that Ananias originated the plan, shared it with Sapphira, and she went along with it. The major responsibility belongs to Ananias as the head of the household and then upon Sapphira for not speaking out against her husband's hypocrisy.

The Couple's Status, the Dramatic Situation

I want to make three comments. First, as mentioned above, there is no support for the view that Ananias and Sapphira were unbelievers. Their sin of hypocrisy has been committed by millions of Christians, perhaps by all believers, including the reader and the writer, at one time or another.

Second, the story should be interpreted in light of the larger context. To use a modern expression, the "in thing" to do at that time was to sell one's property and give the proceeds to the local church (v. 1–2; 4:34–37). That's what all the prosperous but "committed" Christians were doing. "If we don't do this we will not be considered spiritual," Ananias and Sapphira perhaps reasoned. Since everyone was talking about Barnabas' sacrificial gift, and Ananias and Sapphira wanted everyone to speak well of them, they had to do something impressive. So they joined the movement to "sell your property and give it to the church by way of the apostles' feet" within their local church.

The problem is they didn't feel they could afford to pay the price required to be part of the "in group." Thus they agreed to sell the property but give only part of the sale price to the church while telling everyone the part they gave was the total price (vv. 1–2).

Third, there have always been Ananiases and Sapphiras in our churches. They want to belong to the "in group." If everyone is talking about body life, that's what they'll talk about. If the emphasis is on conversational prayer, they are the greatest conversational pray-ers in the church, at least in public. If the Holy Spirit is awakening His people to the truth about spiritual gifts, they'll discuss the gifts. If the emphasis is on discipleship, they'll talk about how many people they are discipling. If it's on being "slain in the Spirit," they will be slain more than the rest. If it's on spiritual warfare, they'll come to church dressed in the armor of God.

But they are not sincere. They are not genuine, because they are not willing to live totally under the lordship of God. If the Ananiases and Sapphiras are able to work their way into leadership in our churches, our churches are in trouble. The problem people in many of the churches are not so much the carnal Christians who know they are carnal, but the carnal Christians who want to be known as spiritual. They are the functional equivalents of the first-century Ananiases and Sapphiras.

The Gift of Distinguishing Spirits in Operation

Ananias and Sapphira made the mistake of failing to recognize that the church belongs to Jesus Christ. He knows even the thoughts and intents of a person's heart. To protect His church from deceitful activity, the Spirit of Christ gives the gift of "distinguishing of spirits" (1 Cor. 12:10).

This seems to be the one protective gift given to the church. What happens when this gift is not recognized and in operation? What would have happened in the Jerusalem church if the gift was not recognized or accepted?

Perhaps it was during one of the church meetings in which believers presented the proceeds of the sale of their properties "at the feet of the apostles" that Ananias made his public move. Using our imagination, we can almost see the smile of satisfaction on his face as the people in the congregation respond to the sacrificial love gift presented by this outstanding head of household. Perhaps he was about to return to his place in the congregation when Peter called him back. As he looked at Ananias, Peter knew exactly what had happened. Exercising the gift of the distinguishing of spirits, Peter points out the dual source of Ananias' sin (vv. 3–4).

First, he says, it came from Satan, the Adversary (v. 3).[2] Second, he says, it came from within, from Ananias' heart (v. 4). The combination produced the sin problem Peter is dealing with in the life of Ananias, and later in Sapphira (vv. 3–11).

In sinning against Christ's church he had sinned against God, Peter says (vv. 3–4, 9). The local church is part of Christ's body. Sin against His body is sin against Him. This should caution us in our relationships with fellow believers.

Finally, every believer faces this same adversary, daily. We can be destroyed by him if we fail to walk in obedience to the Lord Jesus (James 4:6–11; 1 Pet. 5:8–11). The experience of Ananias is a warning to all. Without doubt many disobedient Christians have been delivered "to Satan for the destruction of his flesh, that his spirit might be saved in the day of the Lord Jesus" (1 Cor. 5:5; 1 Tim. 1:18–20 with 1 Cor. 11:23–32; James 5:19–20; 1 John 5:16–19).

Results of Divine Judgment

The sixfold result of God's judgment on this sinful Christian family is spelled out. First is the physical death of Ananias (v. 5); Sapphira died with her husband because she was part of the plot (v. 10).

Two, great fear came upon the church and the general public (vv. 5,11). This was a wholesome fear producing reverence towards God and stimulating believers to holiness and away from careless, hypocritical living.

Three, unusual manifestations of God's power through the apostles followed (vv. 12,15–16). Once again this was in direct answer to their prayer in Acts 4:29–31.

Four, a seemingly contradictory reaction on the part of the public occurred (vv. 13–14). Those who had thought of becoming Christians but wanted nothing to do with full commitment drew away from the church in dread (v. 13a). Those with sincere hunger for God and spiritual reality rejoiced in what they saw and heard, and came into the church in increasing numbers (vv. 13b–14).

Five, the greatest numerical growth to date resulted (v. 14). This is the only instance in the New Testament of the use of the plural "multitudes." It would indicate crowds surpassing those of Acts 2—4. The size of the Jerusalem church by now must have been staggering. The response to the gospel even spread to "the people from the cities in the vicinity of Jerusalem" (v. 16). Once again, Satan's efforts to stop church growth backfired.

For the first time it is specifically stated that women were coming into the church in great numbers (v. 14). As already mentioned, Acts 4:4 speaks only of men and Acts 2:41 speaks of "three thousand souls." The presence of women probably means the church was now centered in family units. True women's liberation has its roots in biblical Christianity.

Six, a movement of power evangelism led by the apostle Peter occurred. It featured mass healings and mass deliverance (vv. 15–16). This was the most important result of all.

Not Demonization, but Satanic Manipulation

This story of the hypocrisy of a church family has become the point of considerable controversy in our day. Much of the problem centers around the question of the possible demonization of some Christians. When this issue is raised we all approach the story with different theological presuppositions.

Those who affirm that true believers cannot under any conditions of sin become demonized dogmatically declare that Ananias and Sapphira were not true believers, or they affirm that if they were believers in the past, at this point they no longer are. They have "fallen from grace." Others who do not accept the possibility that true believers can ever lose their salvation probably affirm they were never really converted in the first place.

Those who are not concerned with the question of the possible demonization of some sinning believers usually affirm they were true believers. In truth they had sinned against the Spirit of God. There is nothing in the story to indicate they were not Christians.

However, that is not the point of the story. Luke is giving us neither a case study of true believers who become demonized nor one of false Christians who managed to gain some prominence in the church at Jerusalem. It is the story of a church family manipulated by Satan so he (Satan) can gain entrance into the life of the church at Jerusalem. That is what it is all about. It reveals how terrible are the sins of hypocrisy, deception, lying, and scheming for a place of prominence among believers.

It also reveals, again, that Christ is head of His church. He knows exactly what is occurring in His churches (Rev. 2—3), good, and bad. He will, when He desires to do so, step in and directly judge willfully sinning believers. He will even take their life when He deems it necessary. This is a very sobering story!

There is no need to try to cause Ananias and Sapphira to lose their salvation. It is enough that they lost their lives because they opened their hearts to the lie of the Enemy without sending them to hell, also.

The main reasons why some commentators and preachers affirm that Ananias, at least, was not a true believer focus around the words of Peter to him and the actions of God against him. Peter asks him, "Why has Satan filled your heart to lie to the Holy Spirit?" (v. 3). It is the matter of Satan's filling of the heart of Ananias that causes such problems.

"Fill" is the Greek word *pleroo* which Vine says means "to make full, to fill to the full." Among its various usages he says is the figurative use of filling "the hearts of believers as the seat of emotions and volition, John 16:6 (sorrow); Acts 5:3 (deceitfulness)."[3] It certainly indicates a strong control over the heart of the person at the point of reference. It is the same word used for the filling of the Holy Spirit in Ephesians 5:18.

True believers do sin and sin terribly, just as did Ananias and Sapphira. They lie, deceive, steal, commit adultery, are filled with rage, shame, rejection, even bitterness and hatred. They are not supposed to act this way, but they do. It is a biblical abnormality, but a vivid reality.

My former pastor, the late Dr. J. Vernon McGee, after going through this sad story in his dramatic Texan style, stopped and asked, "How many of you have ever been guilty of hypocrisy, deception, lying, and pride since becoming believers? Raise your hand if you have."

He paused to allow the honesty of believers to help them overcome their pride. Most of us raised our hands.

In his characteristic style he said, "Man! What a crowd of evil people I'm ministering to today. By looking at the hands raised, if God judged everyone today the way he did Ananias and Sapphira, I would not have anyone left to preach to. But that's all right. Come to think of it, I wouldn't be here either because I've done all of these things myself."

Insightful words. "He that is without the sin of Ananias and Sapphira let him be the first to send Ananias and Sapphira to hell." No one steps forward.

William Barclay wisely says that

the Bible refuses to present an idealized picture of anything. . . . There is a certain encouragement in this story, for it shows us that even in its greatest days the Church was a mixture of good and bad. We do well to remember that if the Church were a society of perfect people there would be no Church at all.[4]

There is the problem of God's judgment upon the sinning couple (vv. 5–10). "God would never do this to one of his own children, only to those who do not love him," we are told. Who says so? Paul tells us in 1 Corinthians 11:30–31 that God was doing so on a regular basis, if we may put it that way, in the church at Corinth. God will often use Satan to bring about just such a fatal judgment, Paul tells us

(1 Cor. 5:5; 1 Tim. 1:18). We will do an in-depth study of these passages at a later time.

Satan can gain partial control over the hearts of believers who wilfully sin. It is probably continual, planned, wilful sin that we see in this story. All who are involved in counseling troubled believers run into this problem all the time.

I am not affirming that demons had entered into the body of Ananias or Sapphira. I do not know if they did or did not. It doesn't really matter. Demons become attached to the lives of people. Sometimes they are clearly inside of them; other times they seem to come in and then leave as they did with Saul in the Old Testament. Oftentimes they seem to only hover around people. Wherever that person goes, a demonic "cloud" seems to go with them.[5]

The Scriptures are not preoccupied with defining these issues. They are not obsessed with the spatiality issue, that is, exactly where the demons are, inside or outside the human body?

Again, this is a world view problem. We Westerners have a list of philosophical, theological presuppositions which we impose upon Scripture whenever we have difficulty handling certain unpleasant experiences or concepts, even though we have no clear word from God to support our bias.

Demons can often exercise almost as much partial control externally as they can internally. As we deal with them *they* know where they are, even if we do not. We resist them or fail to resist them in the same way, no matter where they are.

The Case of Sylvia

I was counseling with a Christian leader who had left the ministry because of serious struggles in her Christian life. She was a godly woman who truly loved the Lord, but she was almost totally defeated in her personal life, and she felt like a hypocrite trying to teach others. Fortunately, she found an excellent Christian counselor who recognized in her the symptoms of severe sexual child abuse.

In the process of the counseling, Sylvia began to have flashbacks of her early childhood. She had not been able to remember what had occurred in her childhood years before the age of twelve. In time it became evident she was not only sexually abused as a child, but was the victim of Satanic Ritual Abuse.[6] This had so damaged her she had never been able to function normally as a wife, mother, and Christian leader.

Victims of severe SRA always turn out as dysfunctional persons to one degree or other. They are also almost always demonized. More often than not, they end up with Multiple Personality Disorder (MPD). Sylvia was discovered to be a multiple. Dozens of alter personalities began to appear in her life. Some of the "alters" did not act like normal alters, however. The counselor began to suspect they were demons, trying to pass as alter personalities. The counselor knew how to handle alters, as difficult as that is. She did not know how to handle demons, however. She sent Sylvia to me.

Over the course of many hours of pre-deliverance counseling, I too discovered evidence that Sylvia was another in a shocking surge of victims of SRA now exploding into the light in the U.S. As an SRA victim, I knew she would probably be demonized. She was. It was not long before the demons began to appear. They were, as usual, furious with me for discovering them. They were angry and helpless as I began to expel them from their victim's life.

The demons had been very subtle in the way they manipulated Sylvia's life. With the presence of alter personalities, they were even more deceptive and difficult to identify. I was dealing with one of the ruling demons. He was angry with me for "messing up" (his words) the skillful way they had been able to manage her life by manipulating her alter personalities. They had deceived her in three major ways. First, they confused her mind. The demons would allow her just enough freedom to cause her to think she was somewhat in charge of her life. Then when all was apparently going well, they would begin to speak to her again. They would imitate her own "thought" voice, telling her how evil she was; that God did not love her; that she was useless and deserved to suffer. This was the inner agony which caused her to leave her Christian ministry and seek help.

Next, they hid behind the alter personalities existing incognito within Sylvia. All her alters were either demonized or so afraid of the demons that they would give in to them to keep from being abused by them.

As we will see later in our study, alter personalities and demons are not the same. Alters are fragmented parts of the host personality. Demons are alien personalities who seek to live within the body of human beings. They are not part of the host personality but spiritual invaders. Like dangerous germs and viruses, they enter where they do not belong.[7]

Here I must inject an important observation. The presence of evil spirits and even alter personalities within a life do not necessarily lead the individual into a sinful lifestyle. Such persons may lead a sinful life, just as do human beings who are not demonized or multiples; often they do not.

As I was dealing with the chief demon, Deception, he boasted how he deceived Sylvia and her counselor. He could come and go in Sylvia's life at will. He could "park himself" outside the door of the counselor's office. The counselor did not know he even existed. Then as Sylvia left the counselor's office, he could reenter her through the permanently open door he had to her life. This in-and-out internal demonization versus external demonization (he still demonized her from outside because he ruled all the demons inside her life) game made it almost impossible to deal with him in her life.

It was when I was in the final phase of forcing him to expose the rest of the demonic activity remaining in Sylvia's life that I found he was the type of demon who worked both from within and from without. Since he had her so brutalized, confused, and preprogrammed to accept him as a part of her own personality, he could come and go at will. As I dealt with him, I found no reason for disbelieving his story. I had heard of it happening in the experience of other counselors.

I do not know where Satan was as he filled Ananias' heart to influence him towards his actions of independence from the will of God. God knew. Satan knew. Peter knew, but neither he nor Luke are concerned with informing us.

We will look at the next recorded story of spiritual warfare-deliverance ministry in Acts in the following chapter. It focuses on the ministry of the deacon-evangelist, Philip, in Samaria.

43

Philip's Ministry at Samaria and Peter's Encounter With Simon Magus
Acts 8

The greatest demonstration of power evangelism recorded in Acts, perhaps in the entire New Testament, occurred not through the ministry of an apostle, but through that of a deacon, a layman. Philip was one of the deacons among the seven chosen by the church at Jerusalem (Acts 6:1–7).

Philip and most of the other Hellenistic leaders fled from the persecution under Saul (8:1), but wherever they went they preached the Word (8:4). The persecution drove Philip to the city of Samaria.[1] The presence of widespread demonization in the city (v. 7) indicates a city which had given grounds to evil spirits. In light of the magic-demonic activity of Simon, the main spirit practitioner there, the spirit-world problem in Samaria probably involved deceiving, religious spirits with their accompanying spirits of immorality and physical illness.

Philip's remarkable mass power evangelism ministry (vv. 5–8) was, without doubt, directly tied in with the person and activities of Simon, known in later Christian history as Simon Magus, or Simon the Magician (vv. 9–24). More is said about Simon Magus than about any other person in Acts outside of the apostles. His influence did not end with Acts. F. F. Bruce says, "Simon the sorcerer, or Simon Magus (as he is usually called) plays an extraordinary role in early Christian literature."[2]

B. F. Harris shows real insight into the power encounter and spiritual warfare dimensions of this story and in Acts in general. Writing under the subheading of "Christianity and Magic in Acts," he says that Luke gives us "a recurring motif in Acts [of] the conflict between Christianity and the magical practices which were so prevalent in the Greco-Roman world of the first century."[3]

ANTIMAGICAL POLEMIC IN THE GOSPELS AND ACTS

D. E. Aune in his excellent article on magic in the *ISBE*[4] says that the magic of the New Testament Greco-Roman world was divided into four major categories according to purpose: protective or apotropaic magic, particularly against dreaded diseases; aggressive and malevolent magic; love magic and magic aimed at acquisition of power over others; and magical divination and revelation. Erotic magic, magic revelation, and magic to gain control over others were the most popular.

Aune says that Jesus and the early Christians were persistently charged by both Jews and pagans with practicing the magical art.[5]

The controversy centered on the performance of miracles of healings and exorcism. Jesus and the early Christians claimed that they were agents of God, while their opponents charged that they were rather agents of evil spiritual forces. These charges were serious enough to require refutation. Consequently, a vigorous antimagical polemic permeates the four Gospels and Acts, and traces of it can be found in the remainder of the New Testament as well.

Aune then mentions that this antimagical polemic is strong in the Gospels. It is reflected in "the Beelzebul pericope (Mark 3:22 par. Matt. 12:24; Luke 11:15f). Beelzebul is apparently a name for Satan." His opponents see Jesus as being indwelt and controlled by Beelzebul. They accuse Him of practicing magic. Matthew 10:25 suggests that "Jesus' opponents may have actually nicknamed Him 'Beelzebul.' This charge and all that it implies are refuted in the following pericope (Mark 3:23–30 par.)."[6]

In John's gospel, Jesus is accused of having a demon three times (John 7:20; 8:48–52; 10:20f). In the eyes of His accusers, He was a false prophet whose powers to perform miracles came from Satan. The accusation that Jesus was an impostor or deceiver (Matt. 27:63; John 7:12, 47) can be understood in this light. He is accused of practicing magic, and since false prophets and magicians were subject to the death penalty "according to the Deuteronomic code (Deut. 13:5; 18:20), Jesus' Jewish opponents may have used these ancient laws to justify His execution."[7]

The gospel accounts of the temptation of Jesus (Matt. 4:1–11 par. Luke 4:1–13; cf. Mark 1:12f) likewise express an antimagical polemic. Aune points out that only Satan's offer of the kingdoms of the world to Jesus can be considered a messianic temptation. "The accounts of the other two temptations should be understood as depicting Jesus' rejection of conventional magical means to attain His goals. Such feats as turning stones to bread and flying through the air are commonly claimed by magicians."[8]

King Herod's hearing about Jesus' miraculous deeds (Mark 6:14–16) further reflects the charge that Jesus practiced magic. "John the Baptist is risen from the dead, and therefore these powers are at work in him" (v. 14) demonstrates the view that

> those who died violent deaths were thought particularly susceptible to postmortem control by magical practitioners (cf. Lucian Philopsendes 29; Tertullian Apol. 23: PGM, IV, 333, 1914, 1950: LVII, 6); thus Jesus is here accused of performing wonders by gaining control of the restless spirit of John the Baptist.[9]

Aune then turns to our book, Acts. He declares that the author of Luke—Acts "appears to have been exceptionally well informed regarding the techniques and technical terms of Greco-Roman magic. This is most evident in three important passages: Acts 8:9–24; 13:4–12 and 19:11–20." The Acts 8 passage deals with Simon Magus; that of Acts 13 deals with Elymas the sorcerer, and that of Acts 19 deals with the seven Jewish exorcists.

Finally, Aune says that

> all these passages describe contests between Christians with miraculous powers and magicians whose powers are derived from incantations and the control of malevolent supernatural forces. The author of Acts carefully demonstrates the superiority of Christianity in each of these encounters.[10]

Religion and Magic

Since we are going to encounter spirit magic in Acts a word must be said about the relationship between religion and magic. Magic is usually opposed by organized religion. At the same time, it is an essential part of most pagan religious practices and is accepted by the religious institutions of the day. The practitioners see them as religious, not magical. All these spiritual powers or practices are magical, however, even though they occur in a religious context. It is not possible to draw clear lines of distinction between them.

Christianity and biblical Judaism are strongly antimagical. The Old Testament had strong words to say against all magical practices. In a technical sense, magic is defined by any practice that functions *ex operer operato*, that is, that has power in itself: there is power just in the performance of the act itself; it will work if it is done by the right person, in the right manner, and in the right circumstances. A moral or immoral lifestyle on the part of the magician has nothing at all to do with the power of magic performed.

Magic can either be spoken or acted out. Thus it is often held that magic becomes manipulative and coercive, while religion is based on the attitude of supplication and veneration. The former always works if done in the prescribed manner by the authoritative persons. The latter depends on the will of the god or spirit and the faith of the petitioner.

While these distinctions are helpful, they are not always consistent. Much of religion is magical, even some activities done in the name of Christianity. The Roman Catholic repetition of the same prayers over and over again or the Protestants' excessive, almost endless emotional outbursts of "Amen! Hallelujah! Praise the Lord!" come close to being magical at times. Any Christian religious "formula" like these for gaining spiritual power is a form of Christian magic if not "Christian" occultism.

With this background we can now begin to appreciate the antimagical, antipagan, and antisatanic nature of Acts 8, 13, 16, and 19. Commenting on all these accounts, B. F. Harris says, "In all these incidents Luke shows an awareness of the 'principalities and powers' which lay behind the magician's actions."[11]

As in Acts 5:15–16, so in Acts 8: The demons leave their victims en masse. There is no reference at all to what some commentators call an "exorcism formula," such as, "I command you, etc." The power of God is present to act. It is not magic. Nothing is done or said by the messenger of Christ that produces the exodus of the demons. The messengers themselves probably do not know what is going to occur any more than the people do.

Usually these releases of God's power to heal the sick and to free the demonized do not produce visible demonstrations as we see occur in Acts 5 and 8, however. The Acts of the Apostles do not attempt to record everything the apostles did in every city and in every circumstance as we have repeatedly stated. Acts does pull back the curtain enough times, however, to let us know that power evangelism, including healings, encounters with evil spirits, and deliverance from demons is going on.

THE MINISTRY AT SAMARIA

In Acts 8 we encounter screaming demons (v. 7). When these demons went out, evidently en masse, during Philip's public ministry in Samaria, it must have been awful to behold. The noise level must have been terrible. The scream of one demon can be unnerving to the inexperienced observer or deliverance minister.

If you want to hear screaming demons today, go to an outdoor crusade in Argentina led by Rev. Carlos Annacondia.[12] It is the closest thing to Acts 8:7 I have ever seen. When my friend Annacondia decides it is time to challenge Satan and the demons to a power contest, you better be ready. In fact, God help you (reverently speaking) if there are any demons still in your life.

Down go the demonized people, sometimes by the hundreds. It is not a pretty sight to see nor sound to hear. Demons scream in protest. Human faces contort in a way that is anything but pleasant. Trained assistants make their way through the crowd (you stand for three hours in Annacondia crusade meetings). They take the demonized, demons still screaming in protest, to the "intensive care" tent where they are led to Christ (not all choose Christ) and set free from the demons.

Provoking demons to public manifestation is not the only approach, however. Annacondia's Argentine contemporary Rev. Omar Cabrera (also my friend) binds evil spirits before his meetings and does not allow them to manifest during public ministry. I also use this approach and forbid demons to scream. If they don't obey, I shut them down. They usually respond with minimal resistance.

Simon the Magician

Luke's description of Simon the Magician (Acts 8:9–10) notes three things. First, he had been "practicing magic" in their midst. Second, he claimed to be someone great (v. 9b). This fits the power position ambitions of magicians. They want to gain power over others and position in the community. Simon had gained that and more. Third, he was declared to be "the Great Power of God" (v. 10b). In Greek it is literally "the power of God being called great" or "the power of God which is great."[13]

Harris says inscriptions have been found on which magicians have applied the name of gods to themselves. The "Aramaic original suggests 'in the power of the God who is called the Great.'" This would imply a "combination of the Greek Zeus (most High God) and the Hebrew Yahweh (power was a rabbinical synonym for Yahweh). Simon's reputation is emphasized in order to show the dramatic changes now brought about."[14]

Alexander Whyte in his characteristic sermonic style says that

> Samaria, where Simon Magus lived and carried on his astounding impositions, was a half Hebrew, half heathen country. . . . There was something positively sublime about the impudence and charlatanry of Simon Magus, until he was actually feared and obeyed and worshiped as nothing short of some divinity who had condescended to come and take up his abode in Samaria.[15]

Philip's message in Samaria was "the kingdom of God and the name of Jesus Christ" (v. 12), the power and authority message that breaks demonic bondage. The response was evidently city-wide. Even Simon was converted and baptized with the others (vv. 12–13). Much has been written as to whether or not Simon was truly converted. No one would even raise the question if it were not for his later response to Peter's powers and Peter's answer to his response (vv. 14–24).

Simon followed Philip, observing his incredible power ministry. He was constantly amazed (v. 13). While he formerly had power, he had nothing like this. If he pretended to be a "divine man,"[16] he knew now that he was not. Philip was that kind of man, however. Simon had now discovered the reality of God's power.

He realizes he wants this genuine God-power in place of his former demonic power. So when he sees Peter impart the Holy Spirit to needy people, he wanted this even more than healing-deliverance power. This is a power-conscious man who lived in a power-conscious world. The man of power was the man of the hour. His power hour had once come. His power hour had now gone. He wanted his power hour to begin again. Is this out of the norm for a recently converted, power-religious practitioner? I don't think so. How could Simon be expected within a few days of his conversion to be a mature Christian, living as he was in a Christian power-context movement?

There is nothing abnormal at all for one living in such a power context. It is not right, but it is normal. There is nothing in this story that gives us the right to damn this former pagan sorcerer to hell. Peter did not. He still held before him the hope of freedom from his present bitterness and bondage to iniquity (v. 22).

It is to Simon's credit that he did not stomp off, angry, frustrated, and rejected when Peter rebuked him. Many of us would have. Instead, he pled with Peter to pray for him that he be forgiven and not come under God's judgment. Isn't that what verses 22–24 imply? What is so evil about that?

This was both an understandable and a wise request in light of Simon's present state of knowledge. Peter has the power of God operative in his life. If anyone's prayers for Simon would be effective, Peter's would. We have to believe that Simon responded to Peter's words. There is nothing in the text to indicate the contrary.

J. B. Phillips' translation of Peter's words to Simon in verses 20–23 are powerful. He has Peter saying,

> To hell with you and your money. [*These words are exactly what the Greek means. It is a pity that their real meaning is obscured by the modern slang usage,* Phillips writes in a footnote.] How dare you think you could buy the gift of God? You have no share or place in this ministry for your heart is not honest before God. All you can do now is repent of this wickedness of yours and pray earnestly to God that the intention of your heart be forgiven. For I can see inside of you, and I see a man bitter with jealousy and bound with his own sin.

I can think of a lot of people I know, many of them Christian leaders, to whom these words would be appropriate. On occasion I know they have been appropriate to me.

Many critical, historical studies of Simon, of "Christian" Gnosticism, and of Gnosticism in general, declare that this dislike of Simon is totally without historical justification.[17] A lot of it is associated with the writings of Justin Martyr and the apocryphal writings called the Acts of Peter.

Alexander Whyte helps apply what I have been saying somewhat in defense of Simon Magus. It is also a warning to all of us potential Simons. Whyte writes that

> it may be in sorcery and witchcraft like that of Simon Magus; it may be in the honours of the kingdom of Heaven like the sons of Zebedee; it may be in preaching sermons; it may be in making speeches or writing books; it may be in anything you like, down to your child's possessions and performances; but we all, to begin with, give ourselves out to be some great one. Simon Magus was but an exaggerated specimen of every popularity-hunter among us.

> There is an element and first principle of Simon Magus, the Samaritan mountebank, in all public men. There is still a certain residuum of Simon left in order to his last sanctification in every minister. . . .

> Popularity was the very breath of life to that charlatan of Samaria. He could not work, he could not live, he could not be converted and baptized, without popularity. And there is not one public man in a thousand, politician or preacher, who will go on living and working and praying out of sight, and all the time with sweetness, and contentment, and good-will, and a quiet heart.[18]

With a new twist to what I have already said, "He that is without any trace of Simon Magus still within him, let him cast the first stone."

44

Paul's Encounter With Elymas and the Spirit Medium of Philippi
Acts 13, 16

Paul's first recorded encounter with a Simon Magus-type religious power worker is in Acts 13:4–12.[1] It has certain similarities with Acts 8 and many dissimilarities. It is disappointing to examine many of the studies in scholarly works on Elymas, Simon Magus, and like spiritual power workers described in the New Testament. Words like *frauds, superstitious,* and *charlatans* are continually used to refer to these magicians and their magical lore. Too often it is implied that their powers are reducible to trickery or the great credulity of the people.

While the latter is often true, it is usually only a small part of the truth. Most, if not all of these men were demonized by religious, deceiving spirits. While fraud was often present, so was direct demonic activity. They were called magicians, but not in the popular use of that word in the Western world today.

The Greek word is *magos.* It can be translated "magician, sorcerer, wizard, enchanter, astrologer" or simply "wise men" (Matt. 2:1f). F. F. Bruce explains how the term was used in the ancient world:[2]

> The magi were originally a Median priestly caste, but in later Greek and Roman times the word was used more generally of practitioners of all sorts of magic or quackery. The latter sense is required here; a Jew, even a renegade Jew (as this man was), could not have been a member of the magian priesthood.

POWER ENCOUNTER PROVOKED BY A MAGICIAN

Luke calls Elymas "a Jewish false prophet" (Acts 13:6b). As a Jew he knew the truth of the living God but had apostatized and immersed himself in Eastern religion. He was "false" not because none of his prophesies came true, but because he had abandoned the truth of God and had become, in Sir William Ramsay's words, "a man skilled in the lower and the uncanny arts and strange powers of the medium priests or *magi.*"[3] He mixed religion with science and magic until the dividing line between the three no longer was clear in his own mind.[4]

Such men exercised great influence over both the rulers and the masses of the biblical world. Ramsay comments that

> it is certain that the priests of some Eastern religions possessed very considerable knowledge of the powers and processes of nature; and that they were able to do things that either were, or seemed to be, marvelous. . . .

> It is natural that the Magician's knowledge and powers should have made him a

striking and interesting personality; and a person like the proconsul, keenly interested in nature and philosophy, would enjoy his society.[5]

Bruce also unfortunately uses the word *quackery* which gives the impression that all these practitioners were pretenders, false, fakes, and frauds.[6] Some were, but not all. Both Simon Magus and Elymas or Bar-jesus were not dealt with by the apostles as pretenders, but as genuine magical operators in possession of real supernatural powers coming from Satan.

A true power encounter, provoked by Bar-jesus, occurs when he listens to Paul. The satanic powers operating in the life of Bar-jesus grew angry. They would not allow the power of the Lord Jesus in Paul to go unchallenged; nor would the authority of the Lord Jesus in Paul make peace with the satanic forces operating in Bar-jesus.

A Son of the Devil

An objection may be raised against the statement that the power of Bar-jesus was satanic. Yet Paul's words in verse 10 seem conclusive in this matter. The apostle calls Bar-jesus a "son of the devil" and the "enemy of all righteousness." Paul never speaks this way to common unbelievers. He also accuses him of endeavoring "to make crooked the straight ways of the Lord." He was without doubt thoroughly demonized, both deceived and a deceiver (2 Cor. 4:3–4; 1 John 4:1–6; Titus 3:3; 2 Tim. 3:13).

Here another power encounter occurs. Paul calls the magician "a son of the devil," not just because he opposed the gospel, as most commentators affirm. Otherwise Paul would have been calling everyone who opposed him sons of the Devil. Paul rebukes him with such strong words because he was an embodiment of satanic, religious evil opposing the faith (v. 8). Thomas Walker, a missionary who has written the best commentary on Acts from a missionary perspective, says, "Those powers of darkness . . . which lay behind his [Elymas's] system, strove hard to stem the progress of the Gospel."[7]

The story here is similar to the "for and against" motif of religious encounter already discussed in our Old Testament studies. I. Howard Marshall understands this:[8]

> The superior power associated with the *teaching* of the Christian missionaries astounded the procounsel to such an extent that he was prepared to believe their message. . . . [but] Luke tells the story more to show how Paul overcame the power of magic than to indicate how a Roman governor was converted.

So central is this issue of the power encounter between the gospel and the demonic religious systems of the Greco-Roman world as illustrated in this story that Elymas became more important to Luke than to the governor.

The governor was just one man. Elymas represented a spiritual kingdom of deception and a terrible syncretism of Yahwehism and paganism. As the spirits indwelling him seek to stop the movement of the gospel, Elymas must be stopped in his tracks. Sir William Ramsay caught this truth when he wrote that

> Bar-jesus represented the strongest influence on the human will that existed in the Roman world, an influence which must destroy or be destroyed by Christianity, if the latter tried to conquer the Empire. Herein lies the interest of this strange scene; and we cannot wonder that to Luke, familiar with the terrible power of that religion, the Magian seemed the prominent figure round whom the action moved.[9]

The Masquerade Uncovered

The encounter itself is described in Acts 13:8–11. Elymas or Bar-jesus stood in open resistance to the apostles. Luke states, "that he . . . was opposing them, seeking to turn the proconsul away from the faith" (v. 8). One ancient text expands Luke's words saying, "Bar-jesus stood forth in opposition to them, seeking to divert the proconsul from the faith because he was listening with much pleasure to them."[10]

Luke leaves his readers with many unanswered questions. He clearly indicates that the opposition was an open and vociferous attack against the apostles, accompanied by outright denial of the truth of their message.

Elymas contradicted Paul and Barnabas to their face, evidently in the governor's palace where, by the latter's personal request, Barnabas and Paul came to present the gospel. This helps explain the sharpness of Paul's rebuke of Bar-jesus, the sternest words Luke ever attributes to the great apostle.

Paul "filled with the Holy Spirit, fixed his gaze upon him" (v. 9). The stress was on the fixed intensity of the gaze. Through that spiritual gaze Paul saw into the very center of the man's being, discovering the true source of power in Bar-jesus, Satan himself, probably represented by an evil spirit or spirits (Eph. 6:10–12).

In dealing with demonized persons contact with demons is often made through direct, intense eye contact. Through experience one can learn to detect the change that comes over a person's eyes when the demons have come up to take temporary control of the victim. Demons will often cry out in fear or anger at the brightness as a Spirit-filled Christian stares intently at them.

This is what is happening in the story before us. Through Paul's gaze the authority of Christ within him was revealed. Perhaps Paul's eyes were like those of his Master, "a flame of fire" (Rev. 1:14). The demons inside Bar-jesus would have immediately recognized that authority. Filled with the Spirit, Paul spoke to Bar-jesus, "You who are full of all deceit and fraud, you son of the devil, you enemy of all righteousness, will you not cease to make crooked the straight ways of the Lord?" (v. 10).

The word "deceit" is *dolos*, meaning "a snare or a bait," Vine says.[11] Bar-jesus was out to trap men, to snare them, to bring them under Satan's control. This is the exact description of Satan's ministry Paul gives in 1 Timothy 3:7 and 2 Timothy 2:26.

The second word is "fraud," the Greek word *padiourgia* meaning "ease of working or easiness in doing anything, also laziness, wickedness and facility in doing wickedness."[12] Paul is accusing Bar-jesus of being so accustomed to evil that it had become natural and easy for him.

Next Paul calls him a "son of the Devil." Devil, of course, is the Greek word *diabolos* which means "slanderer." Bar-jesus was Satan's child, his servant. Thus he was slandering God, God's people, and God's truth. He was so controlled by the Devil that he was as much a child of the Devil as Paul was a child of God. As Christ was the source of Paul's life, Satan was the source of Bar-jesus' life. "You enemy of all righteousness," is Paul's next accusation against him. Bar-jesus masqueraded as "an angel of righteousness," as does his master, the Devil (2 Cor. 11:13–15).

Finally, Paul describes the man's teaching as making "crooked the straight ways of the Lord." He was deliberately distorting and perverting God's truth in order to turn the governor away from God. It was not just that Bar-jesus was deceived.

He had also become a deceiver (2 Tim. 3:13). The deceptive nature of his master, Satan, had become his nature.

From Light to Darkness

The temporary judgment pronounced upon him is described in verse 11. He was struck blind for a season. The punishment symbolically corresponds to the offense. He wilfully turned his eyes away from God's light. He wilfully believed a lie and lived in darkness. He wilfully sought to lead other men from the light into the darkness in which he was dwelling. So God struck him with darkness.

The judgment was only temporary, however. Vine says the expression "for a time" means "a time suitable for a purpose."[13] Only God knows the meaning and duration of that purpose. The church father Chrysostom remarks, "The apostle, remembering his own case knew that by the darkening of the eyes the mind's darkness might be restored to light."[14]

The judgment was immediate, but it came in stages (v. 11). First, "a mist" came upon him. This is the word *axlus* and it occurs nowhere else in the New Testament. Vine says it means a "dimness of the eyes." He states that in its use here it becomes the "outward and visible sign of the inward spiritual darkness which would be his portion for a while and punishment for his resistance to the truth."[15]

It soon turned to absolute darkness, to blindness. Walker notes that "This word also was used by Greek physicians in a technical sense. The whole description is graphic. There fell on Elymas a mist, which gradually deepened into total darkness and blindness."[16]

This is the end of the record. Paul and his team now leave Cyprus and begin their incredible ministry through Asia Minor, eventually reaching Greece.[17]

THE YOUNG SPIRIT MEDIUM OF PHILIPPI

Paul's next recorded direct encounter with the spirit world is perhaps the best known. It is his encounter with the demonized slave girl of Philippi (Acts 16:16–18), the only case in Acts where an individual is freed from demons outside of the context of a people movement to Christ.

The incident occurs sometime after Paul and his team began preaching at the riverside prayer meeting outside of Philippi. F. F. Bruce says, "Day by day as the missionaries went to the place of prayer, she followed them through the streets of Philippi, advertising them aloud as servants of the most high God."[18]

The girl, controlled by a spirit of divination, practiced fortune telling (v. 16). The Greek word "divination" here is the word from which we get our English word "python." Thus she was called a "pythoness." The name was used to refer to persons supposedly indwelt by the spirit of the Greek god Apollo, associated with the giving of the famous Greek oracles. Apollo was worshipped as the Python god at the shrine of Delphia in central Greece. The girl's "involuntary utterances were regarded as the voice of the god, (thus) she was much in demand by people who wished to have their fortunes told," Bruce says.[19]

She cried out after Paul and the others saying, "These men are bond-servants of the Most High God, who are proclaiming to you the way of salvation" (v. 17). This can be understood in at least three ways. First, the expression "Most High God" was commonly used by both Jews and Gentiles to refer to the Supreme Being. Salvation was commonly sought at the time through the Greek mystery religions and other pagan cults. Thus there is nothing necessarily salvific in her cries.

Second, demons recognize the Lord Jesus and spontaneously declare Him to be the Son of the Most High God. Third, demoniacs are not totally controlled by the demons who have invaded their lives. Thus this cry could represent the little girl's confused cry of desire to know "God the Most High." Knowling says that

> the account may point to that disturbed and divided consciousness so characteristic of the possessed; at one time the girl was over-mastered by the evil spirit who was her real *kyrios* (lord), at another time she felt a longing for deliverance from her bondage and . . . she associates herself with those around her who felt a similar longing for some way of salvation.[20]

My personal ministry with demonized persons would incline me towards one or both of the last two explanations. Demonized people, when the demons are not in manifestation, will often seek help from men of God.

Instantaneous Deliverance, but Immediate Consequences

Whatever the case, this poor girl was a slave to the demons which controlled her and to the men who owned and exploited her. She was just a little girl. The Greek word used to describe her is *paidion*. It refers to a young girl or female slave.[21] Her condition must have been pitiful. The frenzied cries of the girl are singled out by Luke in verse 17. The word "crying out" is commonly used to describe the cry of demonized persons (Mark 1:26; 3:11; 5:5, 7; Luke 4:41).

It was when Paul reached a high point of annoyance that he cast the demon out of the girl (v. 18). The word "annoyance" is *diaponeou*. It is a forceful word in Greek. It is used only here and in Acts 4:2 where it describes the agitated state of the Jewish leaders when they found Peter and John teaching the people about Jesus and the resurrection from the dead. Knowling says it contains the idea of grief, pain, and anger, all together.[22]

As the Lord Jesus took no pleasure even in the truthful declaration of demons, so Paul refuses to allow the demonized girl to continue advertising his presence. He commands the spirit to leave the body of its victim (v. 18c). The deliverance was "in the name of Jesus." This is the biblical "formula" used all through Acts for one who stands as the representative of the Lord. Her deliverance was "at that very moment" (v. 18)—instantaneous.

Since the girl was a slave, she was forced to practice divination for her masters. With the exodus of the demons, her spirit powers were all gone. Her masters became enraged with Paul and prevailed upon the masses and the authorities to punish him and Silas, accusing them of political insurrection, religious proselytism, and treason against Rome (vv. 20–21). Richard B. Rackham in his old, but excellent commentary on Acts points out that the most serious part of the accusation was the last part, treason against Rome.[23]

> It was in these last words, "being Romans" that the sting lay. The rumor of disloyalty to the sacred name of Rome was enough to rouse up the mob of Romans in the market place as one man; the hint of treason would cast magistrates and all alike into a panic. There was then no time for legal proceedings; prompt measures had to be taken, and to satisfy the people as well as themselves the magistrates gave orders for him to be stripped naked and beaten . . . on the spot. In the panic and tumult it would have been useless to plead their citizenship, and Paul and Silas bowed their backs to the rods.

Paul and Silas were placed in the care of the chief jailer, a Roman probably with the rank of centurion (Acts 16:23). He was ordered to put them into the most secure area of the inner prison, reserved only for the most dangerous prisoners

(vv. 23b–24). He carried out his orders to the letter, even clamping their feet in stocks.

Several additional facts about the story fit our spiritual warfare emphasis. One, this is the only occurrence of the word *puthōn*, translated "divination" in the New Testament. Vine says that

> the word was applied to diviners or soothsayers, regarded as inspired by Apollo. Since demons are the agents inspiring idolatry, 1 Corinthians 10:20, the young woman in Acts 16:16 was possessed by a demon instigating the cult of Apollo, and thus had a spirit of divination.[24]

Two, the Greeks associated ventriloquism with pythonism, attributing the power to demons. Because of this Ramsay calls the girl a ventriloquist.[25] This is not the case, however. The ability to project one's voice so that it appears to come from another person or object is ventriloquism. When another being and evil personality speaks out of the mouth of a human being often producing strange sounds or a different voice than that of the individual, that is demonism. That is what was happening with the slave girl. Knowling clears up the matter. He says that "this power of ventriloquism was often misused for the purposes of magic."[26] Thus many came to associate it with spirit activity.

Three, the matter of why Paul put up with this demonic activity for a period of time is indeed a mystery. Paul seems to have tried to avoid the girl so as to be able to continue on with his teaching ministry in the city and by the riverside. Finally the noise and confusion became too much to bear. He became greatly annoyed and expelled the religious spirit (v. 18).

Evidently there is the right and wrong time to handle demons. Paul knew that Jesus did not send him out to hunt down demons and expel them, but to preach and teach the gospel. When demons interfered with this ministry he did expel them, however.

On one occasion, while counseling a traumatized believer, a powerful demon suddenly exploded into manifestation. It caught me totally off guard. The quiet, gentle person was suddenly transformed into a screaming, evil being. It all happened so quickly I pulled back, a wave of sudden fear vibrating through my already weary body.

"Look at you! Look at you!" the evil spirit screamed. "You are afraid! You are afraid! Your entire body is trembling," it mocked. I instantly replied, "My knees may be trembling (they were), but that has nothing to do with what is going to happen here. It is the authority and power of the Lord Jesus, the Holy Son of God who abides within me, that will expel you through my word, fear, trembling, and all. He is the one with whom you have to deal. Shut up!"

Instantly the demonic mocking subsided. Within a short time the demon was more afraid of me than I had been of him. He recognized I knew the source of my authority and power over him. He was deathly afraid of the Lord Jesus in me.

Four, there was the exodus of the spirit of divination. Luke tells us, "And it came out at that very moment." Further evidence of that is found in what is recorded next. "But when her masters saw that their hope of profit was gone . . . (v. 19).

Divination for Profit

Religion was big business in Philippi. Everybody had their own gods, spirits, and idols. There were temples and priests everywhere. Luke describes Philippi as "a leading city of the district of Macedonia, a Roman colony." It was the first major city associated with the important port of Neapolis. "Here the great Ignatian Way, a Roman road linking the Adriatic with the Aegean, reached its eastern terminus," Bruce says.[27] Thus there was constant travel in and out of the city. The little girl, probably an adolescent or young teen, had been sought and bought by these shrewd businessmen because of her strange gifts. Philippi needed a fortune teller, they reasoned. What an opportunity to serve the needs of the public and make a lucrative financial profit at the same time (v. 19)!

They perhaps found a small room in one of the many buildings in the heart of the city out of which she worked. They put the girl there and widely advertised her presence. What could be more appealing than a pretty, innocent little girl possessed by the famous Apollo python spirit? When inquired of—for a good price—the girl would go into a semi-trance. While at times her utterances were unintelligible, she eventually gave a personal word to each inquirer, depending on their request. She was not gifted at contacting the spirits of the departed as did others. Her specialty was divination, telling the future to her inquirers or answering their questions concerning their personal, social, and business life.

This gives us a good background as to why Luke says, "But when her masters saw that their hope of profit was gone, they seized Paul and Silas and dragged them into the market place before the authorities" (v. 19).[28]

I was dealing with a former occult practitioner whom I had only recently led to Christ. While some of his demons left when the Holy Spirit came into him, the majority of them did not. He had too many open doors into his life which had to be closed before they would leave.

In the deliverance I allowed the demons to come into controlled manifestation. This was helpful in the training of the deliverance team working with me. None of them had any prior experience with the demonized. Many powerful occult demons surfaced, several of them associated with the man's addiction to heavy metal rock music. They all had the potential of extreme violence and I had to continue working from my authority base in Christ. Finally the control demon came into manifestation. His name was Divination, and he was a terror. He was arrogant and defiant, filled with hatred and rage against me. He also hated his victim and spoke of him in the most degrading manner.

The young convert had little control of himself during the entire deliverance session. When Divination came up, the young man fought back into control, warning me not to "mess with this one."

"He is too powerful. He can kill you," he warned. "When this one is up I have awesome power. I can point at objects in a room and move them around at will. I sometimes do this in my bedroom. He is so dangerous he can make the walls of this building fall in upon us. Please let him alone."

"Jim, if we back down now we will be defeated," I said. "We have to deal with all of them, including Divination. I am not afraid of him. The angels of God are here with us, and they will protect all of us from his power. I want you to allow me to call him back up."

He gave his consent. When Divination came up, he caused Jim, who had been lying on a couch in the church office, to sit up straight. He turned and looked defiantly at me. He laughed and began to tell me of his power. I shut him down. His boast of power stirred me to provoke a power encounter. There was a glass filled with water on the other side of the room. I pointed at it and said,

"Divination, I have taken away all your power by the authority I have in Jesus

Christ. I am his servant. My Master has defeated your master. He has given me authority over you.

"See that glass of water? If you have the power you boast of, I challenge you, make that glass move. I won't let you move it, but go ahead. Try and make it move."

He did. First he just stared at the glass. Nothing happened. Next he pointed at it. Still nothing happened. He had not spoken a word. Then he began to go through weird movements with his arms and hands, like karate moves. Still nothing happened. He yelled. He jumped up and down, waving and commanding the glass to move. It remained where it was.

Suddenly he looked at me with total surprise in his eyes. He looked back at the glass and began his ravings and wild body movements again. Still nothing happened.

He turned to me and said, "You have killed me!" With that, the demon left without any more protest.

Something similar may have occurred with Paul and the demonized slave girl at Philippi. More important, here, as elsewhere in Acts, God's power through Paul overcame direct demonic opposition, and the liberating gospel continued its spread.

45

Idolatry at Athens and Corinth

Acts 17, 1 Corinthians 8—10

Paul's next ministry in a heavily demonized city was at Athens (Acts 17:15–34). The city, full of idols (v. 16) and full of philosophers (vv. 18–32), was also full of idle people, people with too much leisure time on their hands. Luke says, "Now all the Athenians and the strangers visiting there used to spend their time in nothing other than telling or hearing something new" (v. 21). Paul had never faced such a city before.

Paul did not like to be alone in ministry. Committed to team ministry, he finds himself alone (vv. 15–16a) with free time on his hands in a city not in his plan of evangelism. He was only waiting there for Silas and Timothy to join him so that together they could press on towards Corinth, his primary evangelistic target in Greece (vv. 15–16 and 18:5). Paul's sensitive spirit was deeply stirred by the total bondage to idolatry he discovered as he toured the city. This disturbed him more than the arrogance and resistance of the philosophers.

A Brief Look at Athens

The center of Greek culture, architecture, learning, and religion in the ancient world, Athens was the most celebrated city of ancient Greece.[1] In addition, this capital of the Greek province of Attica was the intellectual and university capital of the entire Roman Empire, excelling Rome itself. Most important for our study, Athens was the metropolis of Greek mythology. Its importance both as a religious and philosophical center cannot be overestimated. As Paul wandered its streets, "he could appreciate its learning; he could admire its beauties; but most of all, he could pity its spiritual blindness and mourn over its idolatries."[2]

Paul continues his usual synagogue strategy, but evidently with little success (v. 17). He also preached in the famous Athenian Agora. Because business was conducted there—slaves bought and sold, and goods offered for sale—it was called a marketplace (v. 17). Paul followed the method of Socrates and other Greek philosophers and reasoned in the Agora every day (v. 17).

Paul in the Midst of the Athenian Philosophers

The two competing Greek philosophical schools are mentioned. The Epicureans, the followers of Epicurus (341–270 B.C.) who had taught philosophy in Athens for some thirty-five years, proposed that pleasure is the chief goal of life; not necessarily sensual pleasure, but "a life of tranquility, free from pain, disturbing passions, and superstitious fears (including in particular the fear of death). They did not deny the existence of gods, but maintained that the gods took no interest in the life of men."[3] They were philosophical materialists who denied the existence of life after death. They held strictly to an atomical world view, asserting that even the human soul and the gods were composed of material atoms. The Epicureans were utilitarians, holding to happiness as the goal of life.

The other group was the Stoics, followers of the philosopher Zeno (340–265 B.C.), who also had taught in Athens. Holding a spiritualistic world view, they affirmed that the greatest end of life was human self-sufficiency. The greatest good was to remain unaffected by either good or evil. One must rise above all the changing circumstances of life. The Stoics were the idealists, stressing moral attainment and the importance of duty. The world view of the Stoics was spiritualistic. They held to the spirituality of man and the existence of God. They were pantheists, however, believing man was part of the universal spirit which was God—or better, god. They were first-century "New Agers."

Paul's Sermon on Mars Hill

Verse 19 says the philosophers took Paul to the Areopagus saying, "May we know what this new teaching is that you are proclaiming?" Paul was not on trial. As Harrison says, "The court of the Areopagus was the council which had oversight of the educational, moral and religious welfare of the community."[4] Ramsay says that to this council Paul was only "one of the many ambitious teachers who came to Athens hoping to find fame and fortune at the great center of education." The Council of Areopagus had the authority to "appoint or invite lecturers at Athens, and to exercise some order and morality."

This is why Paul was taken to the Areopagus, Mars Hill. In Athens, lecturers enjoyed great freedom to speak. The scene described in verses 18–34 seems to prove that the "recognized lecturers could take a strange lecturer before the Areopagus and require him to give an account of his teaching and pass a test as to his character."[5]

Paul respectfully began his message (v. 22) by declaring that his hearers were "very religious in all respects." He then fixes his attention on one of their objects of worship which bore the inscription "to the unknown god." Taking advantage of this point of reference from within their own culture, he states that this God, whom they have been worshipping in ignorance, is the very God he proclaims to them (v. 23).

He next talks about God as the One who has made Himself known in nature, that is, by natural revelation (vv. 24–29). The Creator is transcendent (v. 24a), separate from His creation. This was directed to the Stoics. The Creator is also immanent (vv. 25b, 27–28), personally involved in His creation. This was directed to the Epicureans.

The purpose of God's loving care for humanity was that men might find God, Paul affirms (v. 27). Anyone who seeks God in this way will find Him, for "He is not far from each one of us" (v. 27). Harrison points out that Paul's strong emphasis on God as the Creator of all things runs cross-current with the Greek ideas about God. The Greeks held to an eternal physical universe. Everything made by the gods was made out of preexistent materials. In contrast, the Hebrew-Christian view is that God alone is eternal; everything else was made by Him out of nothing (Heb. 11:3).

Paul's message began to rankle his listeners. In a city replete with the temples and shrines, Paul says God does not make His abode in humanly constructed temples. In affirming that all men were made by the same God and are therefore equal in God's sight, Paul "struck a blow at the Athenian pride of native origin."[6]

Paul finishes his message by stating that in the past God allowed men to go their own way, but now He commands that they repent and change their attitude towards Him, themselves, and their fellowman. Paul startles his listeners when he says God has set a definite day in which He will judge all men on a righteous basis (v. 31a). This was something new to them, for the Greeks had no place for an eschatological judgment, a time when God would step directly into the affairs of men and hold them accountable to Him for their lifestyle.

Paul then presents his proof that this day of righteous judgment is coming. It is seen in the historic event that has recently occurred. God raised a man from the dead who is going to be the judge of all men. That is the undeniable proof that a future resurrection will come in which men will given an account before God (v. 31b).

This was too much for his listeners. The courtesy with which they had first received him had worn thin (v. 32). Harrison says:[7]

> Paul could have furnished evidence of Christ's resurrection (cf. 1 Cor. 15), but his audience was in no mood to hear him out. His allusion to the resurrection was too much for their prejudiced minds to receive.

The idea of a resurrection was repudiated by all schools of Greek thought. Being materialists, the Epicureans completely rejected an afterlife. Being pantheists, the Stoics rejected the bodily resurrection.

Some began to sneer, unable to conceal their disdain for Paul and his message. Others tried to maintain the appearance of courtesy for which the Athenians were famous. They simply excused themselves saying, "We shall hear you again concerning this." Whether or not they were sincere, Luke does not say.

However, some believed. Dionysius was a member of the Council of the Areopagus, Luke says (v. 34). According to Athenian practice, to be part of this council he had to be a highly respected man, at least sixty-five years old, a former high official, wealthy, and come from a prominent Athenian family. Damaris probably was a God-fearer, converted during one of Paul's synagogue messages at which women would be present (women were not allowed in the Areopagus). There were others with them.

No mention is made of the establishment of a church in Athens. Neither is there any record of a later visit by Paul to shepherd this flock, nor of Paul's dispatching team members to visit them. Yet "according to the patristic fathers of a later time, especially by Origen,"[8] a church was planted there. One gets the feeling that Paul was not very impressed with the spiritual climate of Athens and the indifference of the proud Athenians.

Bondage to Idolatry

Paul started his message with the most startling thing about the Athenian's idolatry and polytheism. For fear they would offend some unknown god, they had erected an "object of worship" with the inscription, "To an Unknown God" (v. 23). Paul did not overlook what modern tourists today overlook when they visit the ruins of this majestic city. The artistic splendor of Athens was first religious; that is, idolatrous before it was artistic.

Kenneth F. W. Prior, a university lecturer and English churchman, has written a book called *The Gospel in a Pagan Society.*[9] In it, he tries to see the idolatry of Athens as Paul would have seen it as a Christian Jew. He ties Paul's view of the idolatry of Athens with his blunt statement (1 Cor. 10:20–21) about idolatry and demonization. Paul was deeply concerned about the demonic bondage which idolatry brings to the idolaters. He says Paul's attitude (1 Cor. 10:20–21) was not only Christian, but Jewish. Paul was nurtured with the view that idolatry was demonic. Even the worship of Jehovah in physical form was idolatry and forbidden by God.[10]

> This was the attitude inherited by the New Testament Christians from their Jewish predecessors and which they took with them as they evangelized in the Greek cities. It accounts for the way that Paul and Barnabas recoiled in horror when they themselves became the objects of idolatry at Lystra by a crowd that had been carried away with unthinking enthusiasm by the spectacle of Paul healing a cripple.

To Paul, and to all Christians, idols were usurping the place that belonged to God and Jesus alone. As Michael Green has written, "It would be pointless to preach Jesus as Lord if He were merely to be thought of as an addition to an already overcrowded pantheon."[11]

Also, the Christians would reject all idolatry because idolatry had long been associated with gross forms of sexual immorality and perversion. This was true in Athens and Greek religions in general.

Blaicklock notes that

> perhaps the Christian can still touch the edge of that deep sensation [that Paul saw in Athens] only in the revolting presence of the phallic images. Some fragments, vast and intricately carved on Delos, reveal the gross mingling of carnality and religion which stirred the wrath of the Hebrew prophets, and which evoke a Christian disgust. The sculptured sensualities of some Eastern temples stir the same nausea. Athens must have had examples enough of this base use of Greek art.[12]

Athens probably was Paul's most vivid encounter with idolatry in the New Testament to date. He will face it again at Corinth and Ephesus. Not long after this experience, he wrote Romans 1:18–32 and 1 Corinthians 10:20–21. In 1 Corinthians 10:20–21, he reveals fully the severe demonic dimension of idolatry and polytheism. It does not matter that there is no reference in Acts to any encounter with demons while Paul was at Athens. He knew they were there exactly as he knew they were there in all the pagan cities where he preached of the one God and the one mediator between God and man, the Lord Jesus.

Since Paul's teachings on the demonic dimension of idolatry and polytheism given in 1 Corinthians are the most complete in all of his epistles, I want to turn to that epistle. Paul's teaching in 1 Corinthians reflects the world view with which he approached all his ministry, even in Athens.

Idolatry and Demons in 1 Corinthians 8—10

His most famous teachings in 1 Corinthians 10:20–21 must be seen in complete context beginning in 1 Corinthians 8: "Now concerning things sacrificed to idols" (v. 1a). This takes us back to 7:1a, "Now concerning the things about which you wrote . . ." The inference would be that the matter of food offered to idols was the second major issue on which they sought his help, along with the question about marriage dealt with in 1 Corinthians 7.

There were two views held by the Corinthians concerning the matter of meat offered to idols. Some felt the believer has liberty in Christ to do anything not prohibited by God's law. Others felt that in some things new laws of prohibition should be created. Believers should have nothing at all to do with idols and their meat.

Paul corrects both views by expounding broad principles instead of enacting a new system of laws. These principles can then be applied to each situation. Each situation can be examined in light of the bigger principles. The main focus of 8:1 is on the principle of love versus the trust of each group in the superiority of their knowledge. Thus, his apparent diversion from the immediate problem of idols and their sacrifices (vv. 1b–3). "We must avoid the tyranny of knowledge which destroys true love among believers," Paul is saying. This is a needed warning for today as much in Paul's day.

At Corinth idolatry was just as widespread as at Athens (vv. 4–13; 10:1–3). Gordon D. Fee says that

> the religious expression of Corinth was as diverse as its population. Pausanias describes at least 26 sacred places (not all were temples) devoted to the "gods many" (the Roman-Greek Pantheon) and "lords many" (the mystery cults) mentioned by Paul in 1 Cor. 8:5.[13]

Commenting further, Fee says, "Vice and religion flourished side by side. Old Corinth had such a reputation for sexual vice that Aristophanes (ca. 450–385 B.C.) coined this verb *korinthiazō* (= to act like a Corinthian; i.e., to commit fornication)."[14]

Commenting on this religious-moral problem, F. F. Bruce writes, "The difficulty which even Christians had in resisting the influence of this particular Corinthian characteristic is plain to the readers of Paul's epistles to the Corinthians."[15]

In 8:4 Paul says:

> As concerning therefore the eating of those things that are offered in sacrifice unto idols, we know that an idol is nothing in the world, and that there is none other God but one. (KJV)

Some believers had been so accustomed in their past life of associating the gods with the idols and the pagan festivals with food sacrificed to the gods, they were defiled by eating meats offered to idols. Fee says that

> in both cases Paul does not allow reality to the "gods" of idolatry. What he does rather is to anticipate the argument of verse 7, that such "gods" have subjective reality for their worshipers; that is, they do not objectively exist, but they do "exist" for those who have given them reality by believing in them. Hence, there are indeed "gods many" and "lords many."
>
> In chapter 10 he will again deny that a "god" is involved; what the Corinthians have not taken seriously is that pagan religion is the locus of demonic activity, and that to worship such "gods," is in fact to fellowship with demons.[16]

Leon Morris also sees Paul responding to and even quoting the words of the stronger brethren—in contrast to the weaker brethren mentioned in verse 7, believers who felt it was all right to eat meat which had been offered to idols, even if it meant eating it in the temples.[17] Their arguments were twofold.

Probably verse 4 is a direct quote by Paul from these brethren. "There is no such thing as an idol," the Corinthians were saying. The gods they are meant to represent do not exist. "There is no God but one"; therefore, there was no problem in eating meat which has been sacrificed to idols; that is, to the gods represented by the idols, since they do not exist. One can even participate in the pagan feasts in the temples themselves (v. 10). Since the gods really don't exist, they cannot harm us. Paul will later strongly reject participation in the pagan feasts in the temples as worship of demons (1 Cor. 10:19–22).

Paul's answer in chapter 8 to the stronger believers gives a part—but only a part—of his views of idols and the gods of idolatry. He will agree with their basic premise and even expand on it, giving one of the most beautiful and profound theological statements about *theos*, God, in the New Testament. Its focus will be on God as Father and Jesus Christ as the one Lord. Paul will then correct the selfish views of these same stronger brethren (8:1–9, 23).

After spelling out this wonderful Christian view of God as God and Lord, in contrast to the gods and lords of polytheism and idolatry, Paul warns them that not all believers can handle contact with foods offered to idols and participation in the feasts, which Paul will later say is to be avoided at all cost (1 Cor. 10:12–22). Idols and gods are still a problem to the weaker Christian. In Christian love we do not want to hurt their walk with God, he says (vv. 8–13).

Leon Morris puts it this way:[18]

> Paul has been speaking of that knowledge which enables a man to regard an idol as a thing of naught. Now he makes the point that such knowledge is not universal among Christians. There are some weaker brethren who have not risen to this knowledge. From their pre-Christian days they were so accustomed to thinking of the idol as real that they could not completely shake off such thoughts. It is like the situation in the modern mission field, where some converts find it very hard to rid themselves completely of a belief in witchcraft.

In verses 10–12 we find the warning. Paul is saying, "The consequences of you strong exercising your rights over the weak is wrong. You boast, you want to build him up in order to strengthen him to be able to eat meat offered to idols and even dine in an idol's temple. This is because you know the idol is a non-entity and he should know that too.

"But are you really building him up to stand? I say you are building him up to fall. You are strengthening him all right, but you are strengthening him to violate his conscience. Thus you are bringing spiritual disaster to the brother for whom Christ died.

"This is wrong and should be stopped; you are sinning against these brothers. When you sin against them, you sin against Christ."

In verse 13, Paul explains how he handles such issues of Christian liberty and the weaker conscience of other believers. "Here is how I personally handle questions which affect my brother in Christ. First, I recognize he is my brother, not just an impersonal, almost non-entity, out-there individual. I love him as my brother.

"I have to deal sternly with the 'I' in my life. Here is the decision I have made concerning the 'I' for my brother. I will only do and allow in my life what builds up my brother. I reject all that will cause my brother to stumble. As I will tell you later, 'Be imitators of me, just as I also am of Christ'" (11:1).[19]

In chapter 9, Paul continues speaking to the same general issues, setting forth the same basic principles of love for and service to our brothers in Christ. Morris remarks, "Paul has been dealing with people who asserted their rights to the detriment of others. He has told them that this is wrong. He now proceeds to show that he himself has consistently applied this principle. He practices what he preaches."[20]

Paul begins chapter 10 with an appeal to history, leaving behind his personal testimony. Paul knows where he is heading in his discussion of Israel's troubled history. He has not forgotten the immediate problem of idols and idolatry. Thus, in the list of Israel's sins he mentions idolatry (v. 7a). He will expand on the idolatry of Israel and its accompanying immorality in verses 7b–8.

The references to idolatry and immorality as seen together in Israel's experience all refer to the terrible episode described in Exodus 32 relating to the golden calf incident. Paul quotes from this chapter in verses 7–8:

> And do not be idolaters, as some of them were; as it is written, "The people sat down to eat and drink, and stood up to play." Nor let us act immorally, as some of them did, and twenty-three thousand fell in one day.

Here we see ritual sexual immorality. The people are worshipping the golden calf and presenting offerings to it. As they do so, they sit down to eat (the question of eating in the idol's temple, 1 Cor. 8:10), then they rise up to play. This was sexual play, Paul says in 1 Corinthians 10:8; they committed immorality at the idol's table and were judged for it. This is further brought out by Paul's second Old Testament reference, Numbers 25, the idolatry and immorality with Baal at Baal-Peor. In that narrative, idolatry, cultic meals, and immorality are mentioned.

Gordon Fee writes about Paul's careful choice of words here, all from Exodus 32 and Numbers 25. He says that Paul, using Exodus 32,

> chooses that portion of the narrative which specifically indicates that the people ate in the presence of the golden calf, thus, along with 8:10 and 10:14–22, specifically identifying the idolatry as a matter of cultic meals in the idol's presence. . . . The final verb, "and they rose up to play," is probably also to be understood as part of this concern. . . . in this case (both in the LXX and in Paul) it almost certainly carries overtones of sexual play. . . . Furthermore, in the example that follows, eating in the presence of the idol and sexual play are specifically joined in the Numbers narrative (25:1–3). Thus for Paul this verb leads directly to the example of sexual immorality that follows, which is also expressed in the context of cultic eating.[21]

In verse 8, Paul ties the Old Testament example to the situation in Corinth. Fee suggests that it is not a general prohibition against sexual immorality that Paul has in mind. He dealt with that in 6:11–12. Here it is cultic immorality, that is, immorality involved in the feasting and revelry of idol worship. The proof?

First, the Old Testament event referred to (Num. 25:1–9) specifically relates the sexual immorality with eating in the presence of the Baal of Peor. Second, the prior text (v. 7) alludes directly to eating before idols joined with sexual play. Third, Fee says "in the prohibition against prostitution in 6:12–20, Paul deliberately reapplies the 'temple' imagery of 3:16–17 to the Christian's body that was being 'joined' to a prostitute."[22] Fourth, Fee says that

> every other mention of "idol food" in the New Testament is accompanied by a reference to sexual immorality (Acts 15:29; Rev. 2:14,20). Moreover Revelation 2:14 has the same allusion to Numbers 25:1–2. It is highly probable, therefore, that in each case these two sins really belong together, as they did in the Old Testament and pagan precedents; and they go together at the meals in the pagan temples.[23]

Paul lists other sins of Israel. He soon returns again with a warning which reveals idolatry has been in his mind during his entire discourse, "Therefore [in light of all I have written] flee from idolatry" (v. 14). With verse 14 Paul brings us back to his concern about involvement with idolatry by the Corinthian Christians first mentioned in 8:1. Fee says that

> the basis of Paul's prohibition is twofold: His understanding of the sacred meal as "fellowship," as the unique sharing of believers in the worship of the deity, who was also considered to be present. His understanding, based on the Old Testament, of idolatry as a locus of the demonic.[24]

Paul's appeal in verse 14 is "both abrupt and absolute," Fee says. In verse 15 Paul writes to show how logical it is. They had boasted in their superior knowledge. Now Paul says, "I appeal to your wisdom. You judge what I say." As Fee brings out, it does not mean they are to judge of the rightness or wrongness of his argument, but rather that "they are to judge for themselves that Paul is right."[25]

The point is that as they participate in the sacred meal, that is, the Lord's table, they have fellowship *(koinōnia)* with Christ, who is present in the meal with them. In the same way, demons are present in the occult meals they have been participating in. Therefore, when they participate, they are in fellowship with demons (vv. 16–21). This is a serious, sobering thought.[26]

In verse 19 Paul gives the application of the argument of verses 16–18. He begins with a rhetorical question, "What do I mean then?" He then divides his own question into two parts. One, are "the things sacrificed to idols . . . anything"? Two, is "an idol . . . anything"? The grammatical construction of both questions demands "No!" as an answer. The meat sacrificed to idols is meat, that is all. The idol is a non-real entity. "On that we are all agreed," Paul is saying.

"But," Paul is saying (vv. 20–21), "there is something here that you have missed. Just because an idol is not a god does not mean spiritual beings are not involved in idol worship and idol feasts. They are. Demons are involved in both.

"I don't want you to be involved with demons. If you do, you will actually be having *koinōnia* with these demons. If you do that, you cannot any longer have *koinōnia* with Christ. The two are mutually exclusive."

Fee makes an important statement concerning the connection between idols and demons in the Old Testament. He says in verse 20, "Paul is not implying reality to idols. Rather, they are to understand idolatry in terms of Old Testament revelation. The sacrifices of pagans are offered to demons, not to a being who might be rightly termed God."[27] Fee remarks that

> Israel in the desert had rejected God their Rock for beings who were no gods, indeed who were demons. Although the Old Testament itself contains no theological reflection on this understanding of idolatry, almost certainly it was the natural development of Israel's realization that the "mute" gods of the pagans did in fact have supernatural powers. Since there was only one God, such power could not be attributed to a god; hence the belief arose that idols represented demonic spirits.[28]

This is a crucial affirmation by Fee, one that applies two ways. Just because the Old Testament does not contain a systematic theological study on the demonic powers behind the idols and gods does not mean they did not know they were there. The same applies to the New Testament view of the spirit world in Acts and the Epistles. The writers and the early Christians knew Satan and the demonic spirits were behind the evil and the power of the idolatrous, polytheistic, and magical religious systems of the Greco-Roman world. This was true even though with few exceptions (1 Cor. 8—10 being the major one) they did not deal in detail with this already well-known and universally accepted fact. Fee points out that

> Paul's point is simple: These pagan meals are in fact sacrifices to demons; the worship of demons is involved. One who is already bound to one's Lord and to one's fellow believers through participation at the Lord's table cannot under any circumstances also participate in the worship of demons. . . . One is not merely eating with friends at the pagan temples; one is engaged in idolatry, idolatry that involves the worship of demons.[29]

Verse 22 brings Paul's argument begun in 10:1 to a conclusion. He says in 10:1, "For I do not want . . ." He repeats that strong exhortation again in verse 20b, "I do not want you to become sharers in demons." That is followed by the emphatic statements, "You cannot," twice in verse 21. Does this mean that no one can do both? That would be an impossible conclusion because that is exactly what they were doing.

What is Paul saying then? He is saying, "What you are doing is not acceptable to God. Stop it right now!" That leads to his two questions in verse 22, "or do we provoke the Lord to jealousy? We are not stronger than He, are we?"

The answer to the first question is "yes." The answer to the second question is "no." The last question about being stronger than the Lord implies judgment by God if they continue their present flirtation with demons and fellowship with the Lord. As Fee remarks, "God's jealousy cannot be challenged with impunity. Those who put God to the test by insisting on their right to what Paul insists is idolatry are in effect taking God on, challenging Him by their actions, daring Him to act."[30]

In verses 23–33 Paul again uses his own testimony to continue his argument that liberty must not be exercised at the cost of brotherly love. In the midst of this he also tells them, so great is the consciousness of the relationship of idols with meat sacrificed to them, the believer should refuse to eat such meat even in the homes of unbelievers, if their host informs them the meat has been sacrificed to idols (vv. 27–29a). Not only are we not to give offense to our fellow believers by eating such meat, we are not to cause an unbeliever to stumble by our exercising of our proclaimed freedom in Christ.

In everything we seek first the glory of God, and next we seek to give no offense "to Jews or to Greeks or to the church of God" (v. 32). Why? Because we are to live for "the profit of the many, that they may be saved" (v. 33). The glory of God, the building up of my brethren, and the salvation of the lost are to be the guiding principles for judging myself in the exercise of my liberty in Christ.

Corinth was to Paul and the early church what a mission field is to the church today. So was Cyprus, all of Asia, Greece and Europe. All were centers of idolatry, polytheism, animism, pantheism, ancestral veneration, witchcraft, sorcery, and divination with their accompanying immorality and spirit magic.

I have often read biblical commentators who affirm that little is said about idolatry in the New Testament in contrast to the Old Testament, and it was not a real problem in the Gentile churches. Nothing could be farther from the truth. What we find here reveals that idolatry was a real problem at Corinth and in all of Paul's churches. If we are consistent with our professed view of the inspiration of the New Testament, what Paul wrote to the Corinthians was applicable to all believers under similar circumstances. The principles outlined—not the specific situations—are supracultural. They transcend the local cultural situation and apply to all believers at all times and in all parts of the world.

When we are willing to admit that *all this formed the universal socio-cultural context of the New Testament world,* we will begin to understand that *power encounter in the spirit world was going on all the time,* even if only occasionally mentioned. Especially was this true, as it is today, in the missionary expansion of the church. While we are only given occasional glimpses of it, and occasional instructions about its reality, we are to understand that *the problem was universal in these early days of Christian mission, just as it is today.*

Fee sums up by saying that

what Paul is finally forbidding is any kind of relationship with the demonic. How that translates into modern Western cultures may be moot; probably what most Western Christians need to learn is that the demonic is not as remote as some of them would wish to believe.[31]

The believers at Athens, Corinth, and the other mission field cities in the Greco-Roman world where Paul and the other early Christians planted churches must have faced this issue daily. As this epistle circulated among the churches, they would apply Paul's words to their own very similar situation.

In my own experience as a missionary teacher, these passages come alive when I am teaching believers in Asia, Africa, Latin America, and Oceania in a way they often do not in the West. The views Paul expresses in 1 Corinthians are supracultural. They applied to every context in which Paul ministered and the believers lived in the first century. They have applied in every century. They apply equally today. I wonder how many among us are having fellowship with the Lord and demons at the same time, and like the Corinthians, don't realize it.

46

The Nature of Power Encounters

No overview of Paul's encounter with the spirit world in Acts would be complete without a study of his ministry at Ephesus. Though there is no direct evidence that the apostle was involved in personal encounters with demons or demoniacs while at Ephesus, there is indirect evidence that such did occur. We will deal with that as it occurs in the text.

Paul made at least two personal visits to the city of Ephesus (Acts 18:19–21; 19:1—20:1). At the end of his third missionary journey he met with the elders of the Ephesian church at Miletus. Because of the docking schedule of his ship and his hurry to reach Jerusalem before the Passover, he was not able to return to the city itself (Acts 20:16f).

Paul's first contact with Ephesus was made while he was returning to Jerusalem and Antioch of Syria at the end of his second missionary journey (Acts 18:19–21). Fortunately, the ship made a stop in Ephesus. Paul began with his usual synagogue strategy, evangelizing Jews and God fearers (18:19). In Ephesus he discovered an amazingly responsive Jewish population. The Jews asked him to stay longer (18:20). While he did not consent, he promised, "I will return to you again if God wills" (18:21). As a token of his good faith, he left Priscilla and Aquila there to continue the ministry he had begun in the synagogue.

Paul left Ephesus for Jerusalem, then traveled to Antioch of Syria. He returned to Ephesus as soon as he could. This was the beginning of his third missionary journey (18:22–23). During this time, contrary to Paul's practice, he seems to have been alone. He left his team members behind in Asia and Europe to provide oversight for the young churches. In this story, Luke was at Philippi, Silas and Timothy at Corinth, and Priscilla and Aquila at Ephesus. Evidently Priscilla and Aquila were gifted primarily in personal evangelism.

Then Apollos arrived. A Jew of the Diaspora residing in Alexandria, he would soon emerge as an outstanding evangelist, teacher, and theologian. Apollos was a man of outstanding abilities, an "eloquent man" (v. 24). The word means a man of outstanding learning, one who could express himself with beauty, grace, and great persuasiveness. Evidently versed both in Greek philosophy and the Hebrew Scriptures, he was both a philosopher and a theologian. He also was "mighty in the Scriptures." "Mighty" is a word we have met before, *dunamis*. It means unusual power. Apollos, like Paul, had developed his own synagogue strategy (vv. 25–26a). Because of his unique combination of Greek and Hebrew scholarship, he was better equipped to convince Jews and Greeks than any of Paul's contemporaries.

Luke describes his meeting with Aquila and Priscilla in verse 26a. Perhaps Priscilla and Aquila expected another Old Testament reading which would reflect the general misunderstanding among the Jews that the Messianic promises had been fulfilled. What a surprise when Apollos began to teach "accurately the things concerning Jesus"! The only fault they could find in his teaching was his lack of stress on Christian baptism, an essential part of Christian preaching. This they soon corrected (v. 26).

PAUL'S RETURN MINISTRY IN EPHESUS (Acts 19:1—21:1a)

Ephesus was the capital of the Roman province of Asia, its largest and most important city. Four trade routes converged there. It ranked with Alexandria and Syrian Antioch in importance to Rome. A cosmopolitan city with a large Jewish, Greek, and Roman population, it served as a Roman political, military, and commercial center.

The majority of the people were Asiatics, however. As such, they were animists paying homage to evil spirits and wrapped up in the cult of Artemis, patron goddess of Ephesus and all of Proconsul Asia. The temple of Artemis, one of the wonders of the ancient world, was located in Ephesus. So great was the attraction of this temple served by hundreds of priests and priestesses, it drew people from all over Asia (19:27).

As a center of Greek culture, Roman law, and pagan religion, Ephesus was second only to Rome in the Empire. Paul seemed to view it as a second Rome, a pagan power standing against the power of the gospel. Ephesus attracted Paul as Athens did not. The power encounter he faced there was probably the most dramatic of his entire ministry.

Paul returned to his synagogue strategy in Ephesus (v. 8f). This resulted in his longest synagogue ministry recorded in Acts, lasting for three months (vv. 8–9). This was in addition to his first ministry in the same synagogue, followed by that of Priscilla and Aquila and finally, by Apollos (Acts 18:18–26). No synagogue in Acts opened its doors to such a prolonged evangelistic ministry as this one in Ephesus.

From the beginning, Ephesus is revealed to be a city uniquely responsive to the gospel. Paul evidently faced no opposition to his preaching for the first three months (v. 8). Soon the familiar reception-rejection pattern set in, however (v. 9a). Yet in Ephesus evidently only a hard-core minority of Jews resisted the message. The opposition became entrenched. Luke says the resistant party became disobedient. The Greek word means "to refuse to be persuaded, to be obstinate."[1] Unbelief is usually an act of the will more than a decision based upon careful evaluation.

This group also "spoke evil of the way." "Spoke evil" is a strong word in Greek meaning "to curse."[2] As a result, Paul rejected the unbelievers and began a new phase of ministry (v. 9).

School-House Evangelism

When the synagogue closed its doors to Paul's teaching, he separated the church from the synagogue (vv. 9–10). There was no organized violence on the part of the Jews to hinder Paul's continued ministry as occurred in other cities, however (v. 10). He rented the school of Tyrannus and continued his teaching without interruption (v. 9). The stage was now set for a people movement to Christ unrivaled in the Gentile world.

This is the first time in Acts that it is recorded that Paul used a school as a church building, a center for evangelism, and a training school. These were private schools usually located in the center of major cities, in park-like areas similar to the Agora of Athens. The schools usually functioned only in the morning from dawn to about 11 A.M. This was also the regular morning work schedule for an Asiatic city. Several hours of "siesta" followed. F. F. Bruce writes that more people would be asleep at 1 P.M. than at 1 A.M. But Paul, after spending the early hours of the day at tent making (cf. ch. 20:34) devoted the hours of burden and heat to this more important and more exhausting business, and must have infected his hearers with his own energy and zeal so that they were willing to sacrifice their siesta for the sake of listening to Paul.[3]

Paul's strategy was successful. Luke records, "And this took place for two years, so that all who lived in Asia heard the word of the Lord, both Jews and Greeks" (v. 10).

Power Encounter

By now the reader probably has a general understanding of how I have used the term *power encounter*. It is in increasing use today, especially in missionary circles where the power dimension of evangelism and even sanctification is so strongly stressed.

Spiritual warfare and power encounter are not synonymous. While we cannot have a power encounter without the broader context of spiritual warfare, we can have spiritual warfare without power encounter. In other words, all spiritual warfare does not imply power encounter. Power encounter is unidimensional. Spiritual warfare is multidimensional warfare with the flesh, the world, and evil supernaturalism. Thus power encounter can really only exist by very definition in the context of warfare with evil supernaturalism.

Even in warfare with evil supernaturalism, power encounter does not always occur. This distinction is very important. Unfortunately many excellent spiritual warfare writers and practitioners refer to spiritual warfare and power encounter as if they were one and the same.

How do we define power encounter? Some confuse power encounter with evangelism, Christian living, miracles, signs and wonders, and even casting out demons. "Evangelism always involves power encounter in the sense that it is the bringing of men and women from the power of Satan to God," it is affirmed.[4]

Is this true? Yes and no. Evangelism is always the bringing of men and women from the power of Satan to God, and in that sense is a type of power encounter. Yet *power encounter must be something special or unique,* or it has no meaning at all. In that sense the answer must be "no."

Does power encounter always occur in evangelism? That is the key question. The answer is "no." In some evangelistic situations power encounter occurs and in others it does not. Otherwise power encounter would only refer to the Devil's general opposition to evangelism which occurs in every evangelistic situation. But power encounter in an evangelistic context must be more than the general opposition of Satan to people coming to Christ. Power encounter is a more intense, a more open resistance on the part of Satan which leads to a spiritual showdown, a spiritual "OK Corral" type of encounter between the good guys, reverently speaking, and the bad guys. Thus it is best to say, "Evangelism always involves spiritual warfare and occasionally it also involves power encounter."

Power encounter is sometimes equated with Christian living. "There is a sense in which the whole Christian life is a power encounter."[5] Is this true? Again, *yes* in the sense that Satan will resist every believer at each step of advancement in his Christian life: *no* in the sense that this resistance does not always involve power encounter. It always involves spiritual warfare, but not power encounter. Therefore it is more accurate to affirm, "The whole Christian life involves spiritual warfare and will occasionally involve power encounter."

Casting out demons always involves power encounter, even where truth encounter is the approach used. It is not true, however, that power encounter always or primarily involves casting out demons.[6] There is continuing power encounter occurring both in the spirit world and on earth which does not involve casting out demons.

Finally, power encounter is sometimes equated with miracles, signs, and wonders. In his article "Testing the Wine From John Wimber's Vineyard," Tim Stafford says Wimber has broadened the concept of power encounter to "any event where the kingdom of God confronts the kingdom of this world." "The battle," Wimber says, "is marked by signs and wonders, particularly healings and exorcism as in Jesus' ministry."[7]

The first part of this definition is both too broad and too narrow. The word "confronts" needs to be qualified. If by "confronts" he means a unique crisis point, then this definition is partly acceptable because while there is continual confrontation between the two kingdoms, all such confrontations are not power encounters. It would be better to call this spiritual warfare, not power encounter.

It is also too narrow. It limits power encounter "to this world." Power encounter also occurs within the spirit world, in the heavenlies, not just on earth (Rev. 12:3–9).[8] It is also too limited because there is continual power encounter occurring within the kingdom of evil supernaturalism itself.

Power encounter occurs without the occurrence of miracles, signs, wonders, healings, and exorcisms, which are always visible. Power encounter is often visible. Besides, miracles, signs, and wonders occur outside of the context of spiritual warfare and power encounter. God acts in miraculous power with a wide variety of purposes, not just within the context of spiritual warfare and power encounter.

What Is Power Encounter?

Power encounter is a crisis point of encounter in the on-going spiritual warfare between the two supernatural kingdoms, the goal of which is the glory of God or of a no-god and the obedience of men to God or to the no-god. It is a crisis point in contrast to an on-going state, not synonymous with either evangelism or Christian living, though it can occur in both. It is a crisis point in the on-going spiritual warfare process and occurs in the context of the continual conflict between the kingdom of God and the kingdom of Satan.

The ultimate goal of each power encounter always focuses on humanity, even if it occurs only in the cosmic, invisible realm and even if men do not seem to be directly involved. The ultimate issue of this universe is the glory of God. Just because He is God He must be glorified as God now and forever. The second issue in this universe is, Who is going to be God to humanity, the true God or Satan, the no-god? In other words, who is man going to obey?

Finally, and this will take us back to the power encounters of Acts 19, power encounter occurs on the Christian level and on the non-Christian level. The Christian level, for lack of a better word, of power encounter is the level in which the people of God are directly or indirectly involved. The non-Christian level of power encounter occurs among the no-gods themselves. Each competes with the other for power and prominence.

I will close with four observations. First, the release of supernatural power operating on the basis of spiritual authority can flow directly from God Himself or from the no-god itself with no human involvement. Second, it can flow directly through God's angels or from the no-god's angels according to God's or the no-god's purposes.

Third, it can flow through God's servants or the no-god's servants. The flow of supernatural power based on the Christian's delegated authority can be initiated by the believer himself (Luke 10:17). Every believer involved in this type of ministry acts in blind faith totally dependent upon God's power being released through him and around him or he fails.

This is a great adventure of faith, but it can often be very frightening. Recently I was conducting a spiritual warfare training seminar in a local church. The second day a troubled teenager met me as I was about to begin the next session. He was visibly under demonic attack. He had been walking to the church when suddenly he could not move. Some of the other believers coming by saw his plight and brought him on to the church.

I inquired to know if he was a true believer. He was. In front of the pastor and the elders, I laid hands on him and rebuked the disabling power of evil binding his life. Instantly he was able to walk. He rejoiced in God's power and love. That was a small power encounter. The power of God was released as I spoke His word of defeat to the spirit world. The evil paralyzing power was broken, immediately.

Four, it can flow directly through God's angels and God's human servants at the same time. It can do the same through the angels and servants of the no-gods. I was ministering deliverance to a fine Christian young man. He had been raised in a Christian home, but he became bitter against God and his family in high school and in early college, and had fallen into deep sin. On drugs, he was a rock musician addicted to heavy metal rock music.

Recently he had come back to the Lord. He was a deeply sincere but troubled renewed believer. He went into demonic manifestation as he heard my lecture on spiritual warfare. Over the course of many weeks, I had several deliverance sessions with him. During one of the later sessions we made contact with the chief demon, Kill.[9] When Kill was up for the last time he threatened me, both aloud and in the victim's mind.

"Dr. Murphy, he is going to kill you. Be careful! He is going to kill you," the young man cried out.

"He is not going to touch me," I replied. "Lord, I ask you to release the power of your protecting and ministering angels right now and break the killing power of this filthy demon."

Immediately, Kill became paralyzed. He could not touch me. Within minutes, he gave up and went out of the young Christian.

I have had this happen on several occasions when wild, uncontrollable demons were present in a deliverance session. To this date, I have never been injured in spite of both their threats and their power to carry out these threats. This is true power encounter.

With this background we are now ready to examine the power encounters revealed in Acts 19. There are at least three. All are on the non-Christian level. We will take them one by one in the next chapter.

47

Power Encounters at Ephesus
Acts 19

Paul's ministry in Ephesus (Acts 19:11–20) included at least three power encounters. They probably occurred fairly close together and evidently towards the end of his two years of ministry there (v. 10). The first gives birth
to the second (vv. 11–13). The second gives birth to the third (vv. 14–17). The third
brought multitudes to Christ (vv. 17–20) and produced a serious revolt within the
city which could have led to Paul's death (vv. 21–41). Knowing something of the
cultural milieu of Ephesus helps us understand better what Paul faced there.

THE RELIGIOUS-SOCIAL MILIEU OF EPHESUS

Ephesus was a main center for magical practices for all Asia Minor during the
first century of the Christian Era.[1] When we speak of magic in the Western world
we usually have in mind illusion or sleight of hand. Magicians in our culture continually affirm "the hand is quicker than the eye." This definition of magic is probably the most common in Western culture.[2]

The magic in Scripture was totally different. It involved the use of means (as
charms, spells) believed to have supernatural power over natural forces, magic
rites and incantations, such as the casting of spells. This is the type of magic which
prevailed in the biblical world during the Old and New Testament eras.[3]

Clinton Arnold, Assistant Professor of New Testament at Biola University and
Talbot School of Theology, has written a masterful study of Ephesians from a spiritual warfare perspective called *Ephesians, Power and Magic*. It serves as the foundation for our study of the spiritual climate of Ephesus during Paul's era. He quotes
various scholars' depictions of Ephesus:[4]

> B. M. Metzger states, "Of all ancient Greco-Roman cities, Ephesus, the third largest
> city in the Empire, was by far the most hospitable to magicians, sorcerers, and char-
> latans of all sorts." O. Meinardus concurs: "Perhaps even more than Pisidian An-
> tioch, Corinth, and Antioch-on-the-Orontes, this city of traders and sailors, of
> courtesans and rakes, swarmed with soothsayers and purveyors of charms."

Arnold states that the reputation of Ephesus as a magical center partly derived
from the fame of the "Ephesian Letters" or *Ephesia grammata*. The letters, first
mentioned as early as the fourth century B.C. in tablets discovered on the island
of Crete, focus around the use of six magic terms: *askion, kataskion, liz, tetraa,
damnauenuez,* and *aisia*.

These terms were used to ward off evil demons and could be written amulets
or spoken charms. At first it was held that the bearer or user of the grammata had
personal access to supernatural power. Soon, however, the grammata were themselves transformed "into active and powerful beings" or spirits, even demons, to
do good to those who possessed them and evil to others.

While the Ephesian grammata evidently did not originate in Ephesus, they became connected to the city probably because of their close association with Artemis of Ephesus (vv. 23–35). Arnold notes that

the Ephesian Letters are not the only evidence of magical practice in Ephesus and western Asia Minor. A whole magical apparatus has been discovered at Pergamum. . . . A magical amulet with Jewish characteristics was found in the area around Ephesus.

Additional amulets were reportedly discovered between Smyrna and Ephesus, also bearing Jewish characteristics. It is also interesting to note that Ignatius' only use of the word mageia occurs in his letter to the Ephesian congregation (Ign., Eph. 19:3): with the coming of Christ "all magic was dissolved."[5]

New discoveries of magical materials in the Greco-Roman world have added greatly to our understanding of how this magic was believed to work, and how widespread magical practices were in the biblical world. One indication is Caesar Augustus' order for two thousand magical scrolls to be burned in 13 B.C. By that time the waning personality of the Olympian gods were being replaced by magic, the mystery cults, and a rapid rise in astrological belief; and the Roman government did not want the power of magic possibly undermining its own.

F. F. Bruce also deals with both Ephesus as a center of magic and the Ephesus *grammata* in his excellent book, *Paul: Apostle of the Heart Set Free.*[6]

The phrase "Ephesian writings" *(Ephesia grammata)* was commonly used in antiquity for documents containing spells and formulae like the lengthy magical papyri in the London, Paris and Leiden collections or small amulets (like the mottoes in Christmas crackers) to be rolled up and placed in small cylinders or lockets worn around the neck or elsewhere about the person.

The syncretism of those days was simply incredible. The spirits were given Jewish names, Egyptian names, and Greek names. The whole Greco-Roman world was a mixture of all that seemed appealing and powerful from every spirit source possible. It was magic and religion fused into a world of spirits, gods, magicians, priests, temples, amulets, and images.

Summing it all up, Arnold says, "The magical papyri are therefore extremely valuable in reflecting the language and beliefs of a great number of the common people in the Hellenistic world."[7]

Arnold then states that we now understand why Paul gives his most profound and complete study of the spiritual powers operative in our universe and on earth against the people of God in his Epistle to the Ephesians. He writes that

The epistle was written to an area famed as the center for magical practices in western Asia Minor; presumably (and according to Luke), many converts came into the church forsaking a background of magical practices. It is then certainly conceivable that the epistle could be concerned with addressing issues arising in the community related to the former (or, perhaps continuing) practice of magic on the part of some of the converts.[8]

In other words, Paul stressed spiritual warfare in Ephesians because his converts needed help at this point. This is contextualization. That Paul does not repeat this teaching in other epistles does not mean it was not intended for all believers. Ephesians was probably a circular letter meant for the believers in Ephesus and all of Asia Minor. While spirit magic was concentrated in Ephesus, all churches in the Gentile Greco-Roman world were planted in cities where spirit-demon magic power was a part of the religious context.

Finally, even though the power encounters at Ephesus seem unique, similar encounters could have occurred in other cities where Paul planted churches in the Greco-Roman world. In fact, Paul himself made reference to power demonstrations occurring through his ministry in several of his epistles. Paul says in 2 Corinthians 12:12, "The signs of a true apostle were performed among you with all perseverance, by signs and wonders and miracles." Paul also wrote to the Romans of his ministry "in the power of signs and wonders, in the power of the Spirit; so that from Jerusalem and round about as far as Illyricum I have fully preached the gospel of Christ" (Rom. 15:19). Paul considered these demonstrations of God's power not only as the credentials of his apostolic ministry (2 Cor. 12:12), but also as necessary to plant churches in cities opposed by the spiritual powers of evil. Power encounter evangelism was the norm for him, part of his work to "fully preach the gospel" (Rom. 15:19). Are cities today any different?

Miracles or Magic?

We have discovered that Luke, who wrote Acts, is as critical of spirit magic as was Paul. Yet he records in Acts 19:11–12 that "handkerchiefs or aprons [the sweat bands and work aprons used by Paul, Vine and F. F. Bruce say][9] were even carried from his [Paul's] body to the sick, and the diseases left them and the evil spirits went out" (v. 12). Luke seems so astonished by this phenomena that he introduces the story by saying that "God was performing extraordinary miracles by the hands of Paul" (v. 11).

Why does he write this way? Again, we cannot be sure because he does not tell us. How was this extraordinary healing-deliverance ministry through physical objects associated with Paul's body affected? Again, we cannot say because Luke does not tell us.

There seem to be only two broad possible approaches to this controversial subject. One, this was a conscious activity on the part of Paul. He allowed or even encouraged the practice of taking these sweat bands and work aprons which had contact with his body to the sick and the demonized for their healing.

Two, this was an unconscious activity on Paul's part. He probably did not know at first that it was occurring. Daily he found his sweatbands and work aprons missing. Soon he heard that third parties were taking them to the sick and the demonized with the results Luke records.

Which of the two approaches is the correct one? Again, we cannot say for sure because Luke does not tell us. In light of Paul's antimagical teaching I would lean towards the latter position as the better. Paul himself did not believe objects associated with his physical body automatically possessed divine power to heal and break demon bondage. That would have been spirit magic. It also would have been contrary to all of biblical teaching concerning how God's power operates. It is not the power person's body that distributes divine power but the God who indwells the power person.

R. J. Knowling says that Paul was evidently carrying on both an extensive healing and deliverance ministry in conjunction with his preaching and church planting in and about Ephesus. He writes that "those who could not be reached by the hands of the apostle" were reached and healed by the personal objects that "had been in contact with the body of the apostle."[10]

Verse 11 in the Greek is literally "and powerful deeds, not the ordinary, God did through the hands of Paul." "Through the hands of" is an idiomatic expression which simply means that Paul was the channel through which the healing powers of God flowed. Thus Luke is *not* affirming that Paul laid his hands on the items, even though that is still a *possibility*, especially if one takes the position that Paul was consciously involved in the entire process.

In either case, Luke stresses that neither Paul's hands nor the articles were inherently powerful; neither were magical. It was the gracious power of God that healed and delivered. Given the place that magic held in this culture, we may see here God's accommodation in the way He expresses His power to the expectations of a people in a specific place and time.[11]

R. J. Knowling suggests that "we may perhaps see a possible appeal to the populace, who would recognize that the charms and amulets in which they put such confidence had not the same potency as the handkerchiefs and aprons of the apostle."[12]

The same occurred with Jesus (Luke 8:43–48) and with Peter (Acts 5:15–16). God is God. What God does, He does. Who are we to fight against God? If in His great love for people bound by demonic religion and spirit magic, He accommodates for a time to their view of how spiritual power operates, as in this example of physical objects associated with the power person, who are we to fight against God? We must not, however, profane the extraordinary aspect of these miracles of God by trying to reproduce them on demand, thus challenging God's sovereignty and merchandizing His power as some are doing in our day.

A word as to why I call these "powerful deeds not the ordinary," as a form of power encounter is in order. In the New Testament world, sickness was often looked upon as coming from spirits. While the people were aware that illness was caused by organic malfunctions, accidents, and disease, they also knew that many sicknesses involved evil spirits. Therefore, if they could find a healer or exorcist whose familiar spirits had greater power than the afflicting spirits, they could be healed. In the case of demonization, it was the same. One had to find an exorcist with power over the power of the afflicting spirits. It was just that simple.

With this background we can understand how the healings and the deliverances God wrought through the sweat bands and aprons of Paul were power encounters, especially in the minds of the people. That is the key. What did the public see in these occurrences?

At first they probably saw Paul only as another power worker, whose spirit—"Jesus"—was simply more powerful than the spirits they feared. But as they heard Paul's preaching (cf. vv. 18,20), many would understand that Jesus was not a spirit whom Paul manipulated to do his bidding, but the only Son of the one true God, before whom all other spirits are in subjection. Paul, consequently, was merely the weak human channel through whom the exalted Lord Jesus Christ revealed His power, and the result of these works of power was not the exaltation of Paul, but of the name of the Lord (v. 17).

Paul and the Sons of Sceva

That the other power workers in the city misunderstood Paul's power is what Luke is trying to illustrate for us in the second power encounter, the confrontation with the seven sons of Sceva (Acts 19:13–17). It results from "the powerful deeds, not the ordinary" we have been considering and should not be separated from this immediate context. Other exorcists heard about this power which was connected to Paul and his spirit, Jesus (v. 13). They carefully noted his power formula "the name of the Lord Jesus" (v. 13). Evidently more individuals were being delivered in Jesus' name by Paul than we are informed of, situations similar in some ways to that of the slave girl at Philippi. This selectivity of reporting is in keeping with Luke's style.

Hellenistic Jewish Exorcism and Magic

The most prominent group of exorcists who tried to tap into Paul's Spirit power were the Jewish exorcists (v. 13). Why are Jewish exorcists mentioned instead of Asian ones? Arnold's answers provide relevant insights into the Jewish syncretism we have already discovered at Samaria (Acts 8) and Cyprus (Acts 13):[13]

> Numerous strands of evidence point to the fact that the Judaism of the Hellenistic period had been heavily permeated by contemporary magical beliefs. H. D. Betz finds such a great amount of evidence that he can assert. "Jewish magic was famous in antiquity."
>
> M. Simon, followed by Goodenough and Charlesworth, saw three features which characterized Jewish magic: (1) a great respect for Hebrew phrases which seemed to some Jews to have magical power; (2) a sense of the efficacious power of the name; and (3) an overwhelming regard for angels and demons.

F. F. Bruce also refers to the popularity of the Jewish exorcists in the Greco-Roman world:[14]

> Among practitioners of magic in ancient times Jews enjoyed high respect, for they were believed to have specially effective spells at their command. In particular, the fact that the name of the God of Israel was not to be pronounced by vulgar lips was generally known among the pagans, and misinterpreted by them according to regular magical principles.

Commenting on verse 13, Bruce notes that the name of Jesus proved so potent in exorcism that Jewish exorcists began to use it too. The use of the power name of Jesus in Jewish exorcism became so widespread it was later strongly denounced in rabbinical writings.

The group of Jewish exorcists singled out by Luke are described as the seven sons of Sceva, a Jewish Chief Priest. Bruce says he was probably not a Jewish Chief Priest but

> more probably "Jewish Chief Priest" was his own designation of himself, set out on a placard, and Luke would have placed the words within quotation marks had they been invented in his day. A Jewish Chief Priest would enjoy high prestige in magical circles, for he was the sort of person most likely to know the true pronunciation of the Ineffable Name. It was not the Ineffable Name, however, but the name of Jesus that his seven sons employed in an attempt to imitate Paul's exorcism.[15]

Power Encounter Between the No-gods

The power encounter here is unique to the New Testament, perhaps to the entire biblical record, because it was not between God and the no-gods, as is usually the case. It is an encounter between the no-gods and the no-gods. The demons in the demonized person physically attacked the demonized Jewish exorcists. If someone objects to my description of the seven sons of Sceva as demonized, then he does not know the spirit world. All spirit-world practitioners of this type are demonized to one degree or another. That is how they get their powers.

The Jews had their own exorcists, Jesus tells us (Matt. 12:27).[16] Origen and Justin Martyr tell us the Jews were successful in this ministry only when they cast out demons in the name of the God of Abraham and Isaac and Jacob, and unsuccessful when they adjured in the name of kings, prophets, and patriarchs.[17]

The men in this story were not legitimate Jewish exorcists. however. They were spirit magicians, occult practitioners who happened to be Jews. They were after power names wherever they came from. Their successes in exorcism—and they had to have them to stay in business—had to come from demonic powers attached to their own life.

In this case the demons residing in the demonized person go to war with the demonized occult practitioners. They beat them. They strip their clothes off them, sending them fleeing out of the house "naked and wounded" (v. 16).

Satan Against Satan, Demons Against Demons?

"But this cannot happen," some would affirm. "This would be Satan divided against Satan (Matt. 12:25–26). Demons will not turn against demons." Who says they won't? Demons have turned against their fellow demons for ages. In Matthew 12:25–26, Jesus is not affirming that Satan's kingdom is a unified kingdom. All He is saying is that He could not, as "Beelzebub the ruler of the demons" (vv. 24 and 27), engage in a ministry of destroying his own kingdom. Satan is not going to commit suicide. Jesus is saying that by the power of the Spirit of God through His deliverance ministry, the kingdom of Satan is being systematically destroyed (vv. 28–29).

The deduction from this doctrine that demons will never turn against or even cast out their peers does not follow. In fact, it contradicts Jesus' own words earlier in this same gospel (Matt. 7:21–23). Demons will cast out demons to enhance the power of demons. Demons in demonized exorcists will expel the demons in other persons to enhance the control of the exorcist over the person or persons in question. They will do so by brute force and in utter hatred for other demons. This principle of demons expelling demons to enhance the control of demons occurs continually within animistic societies. The entire kingdom of Satan among animistic, polytheistic, idolatrous, and occultic people is built on this duality.

Shaman vs. Sorcerer

There is always a positive and a negative religious practitioner among animistic people. The positive practitioner, called a shaman, a witch doctor, a healer, a magician, a medicine man, or the like, operates through demonic powers usually resident within him or her. The negative practitioner is considered a sorcerer, a witch doctor, or a magician, skilled in the black arts. He may be a formal sorcerer where his role is recognized beforehand, or an informal one. He may be involved only in the particular sorcery under question. It is a complex social phenomenon.[18]

The positive practitioner is welcome in his community. Not so with the negative practitioner. The community fears, even hates, the practitioner who practices sorcery and black magic in their midst. Yet when they want to curse enemies, they often seek out a sorcerer. Again, it is a complex social phenomena.

When black magic or sorcery occurs in a community, usually manifested through unusual sicknesses, crop failures, and other bad events, the shaman must discover its source and break the evil spirit power. That evil spirit power is released through the sorcerer. If the shaman's spirits are stronger than those of the sorcerer, the evil will be lifted. The spirits who have caused the evil will be forced to submit to the authority of the spirits working through the shaman. If the sorcerer's spirits are stronger, it can go the other way. A battle between spirits is the result. It can go on for days. The outcome is never certain.

I remember hearing a missionary tell the story of being present in a village during such a spirit battle. A respected village leader suddenly became demonized through sorcery. The shaman was called in and he began his exorcism. When all the ceremony, magic, and incantations had run their course with no benefit to the victim, the shaman did an amazing thing. He laid down on the ground right next to the demonized man. Soon he was in a trance. Suddenly the spirits within the shaman began to speak out loud against the spirits within the demonized man. The spirits within the man began to speak back. The verbal argument went on for a long time.

"What are you doing here?" the shaman's spirit asked.

"I have been sent here, and here I plan to stay," was the reply.

"I don't want you to stay. I want you to go out of him and don't come back."

"No, I won't go and you cannot make me. I am stronger than you are and you can't make me leave."

"Yes I can, and I will. You are hurting my people by being in this man. He is a leader in this village and we need him. Get out and don't come back."

On and on it went. After several hours the spirits in the demonized man began to weaken. Finally, they left, quite suddenly.

While this may appear strange to us, it is strange neither to the spirits nor to the people who live in this kind of world. Again for Westerners, this is a world view problem.

The successful shaman or exorcist came out of this battle with an assured place of control over the community, much stronger than ever before. Thus the control of demons is enhanced either by cooperative demons, or in this story by strong demons casting out weaker ones.

This can even occur where demons do not work together voluntarily but only through the brute force of superior demons working against them. I told the story of Thadius in chapter 8. When I asked Thadius if he was sad that the stronger or control demon Liar had been expelled from the victim's life, he arrogantly replied,

"No! Because now I am in charge."

If Thadius had been in a stronger position he probably would have expelled or domineered Liar himself so he could become the "boss." This type of civil war is common among demons.

Satan's Kingdom Is Divided

Returning to Acts 19, we see that the power encounter revealed in verses 15–16 was an encounter within the kingdom of evil itself. The arrogance, defiance, and hatred of the demons were turned against their fellow demons, or at least, against the human beings who were serving Satan's kingdom. In this sense Satan's kingdom *is* a divided kingdom and his house will not stand. As we do deliverance ministry, we can count on that internal division within the kingdom of darkness and use it to help advance the kingdom of God.

In the case of these Jewish exorcists, the demons reveal their stupidity. They "shoot themselves in the foot," to use a common saying. If they had only shut their arrogant mouths and cooperated with their fellow demons working through the sons of Sceva, they would have hurt the cause of the gospel in Ephesus. Instead, they became directly responsible for turning the spiritual warfare within the city towards the kingdom of God. This power encounter resulted in the most destructive defeat of the kingdom of Satan in the history of Ephesus, all instigated by the stupid evil spirits themselves (vv. 17–20).

The People Movement Power Encounter

Multitudes of people in Ephesus publicly rejected the spirits and the no-gods by confessing their former bondage to them and then defying the no-gods by burning all their power objects. Everything which had tied them to the service of the no-gods was destroyed. Luke gives special emphasis to their magic books, probably including magical texts, adjurations, formulas, protection rituals, curses, incantations, and similar written magic-power symbols. This is a power encounter people movement to Christ perhaps unparalleled in the biblical record. Also unparalleled is the inclusion of great numbers of former magic-occult practitioners (v. 18).

Marshall comments that

> the story and presumably others like it became known among both Jews and Greeks in the area, and the effect among a superstitious people was to cause both fear and praise for the name of Jesus.

> In a situation where people were gripped by superstition, perhaps the only way for Christianity to spread was by the demonstration that the power of Jesus was superior to that of the demons, even if those who came to believe in Jesus were tempted to think of his power and person in ways that were still conditioned by their primitive categories of thought.[19]

His use of "superstition" is unfortunate. Yet the essence of his observations are correct. F. F. Bruce also writes that

> these converted magicians renounced their imagined power by rendering their spells inoperative. Many of them also gathered their magical papyri and parchments together and made a bonfire of them. . . . On this occasion fifty thousand drachmae's worth of such documents went up in smoke. (The public burning of literature as an open repudiation of its contents can be paralleled both from antiquity and from more modern times.) The powers of darkness were worsted, but the gospel spread and triumphed.[20]

What is described in verses 17–20 probably occurred over a period of time with the greatest demonstration of defiance of the spirits probably coming about suddenly.

Verses 21–22 reveal the impact of the people movement through power encounter on the apostle Paul. The church is now so strong with its own leaders, Paul feels he can now fulfill a long-standing desire. He can go to Rome and from there to Spain (Rom. 15:22–24). One more major incident at Ephesus must first be recorded, however.

The Role of Artemis Worship at Ephesus

The encounter led to the rapid spreading of the Word of the Lord among the people (v. 20), making great inroads into the religious-economic life of the city. Demetrius the silversmith (v. 24f) gathers "the members of the employers federation (as we would call it) in order to organize a protest demonstration," I. Howard Marshall says.[21] The reason was, as Marshall affirms, that "throughout Ephesus and its neighborhood many of the worshipers of Artemis were turning to Christianity, and no longer believed in idols made by human hands."

The result was great danger to the silversmiths' business. People converted in a power encounter like that described by Luke do not buy idols. Demetrius knew this. He decides to appeal to the unique role the craftsmen played in the cult of Artemis (vv. 26–27). Marshall says that

> the ordinary people might not be too concerned that Demetrius was going out of business, but they might well take to heart the possibility that *the temple of Artemis* might lose its position in popular regard, and, even more, that the *goddess* associated with Ephesus but drawing worshipers from all over the world, might be dethroned from her position.[22]

This introduces us to the very heart of the power-religious-magic-pagan context of Ephesian life, the presence of the great temple of Artemis and the worldwide worship of the great goddess in this her protector city (vv. 27,36).

From Clinton Arnold's excellent study of Artemis we learn the following:[23]

1. The temple of Artemis at Ephesus was one of the seven wonders of the ancient world.
2. The Ephesian Artemis, or Diana, was worshipped more widely by individuals than any other deity known in the Asian world.
3. The dissemination of the cult was aided by a strong missionary outlook by its devotees as well as an annual month-long festival held in her honor.
4. The temple wielded tremendous power through its function as a banking and financial center.
5. The cult also obtained a sizable income from the large amount of property owned in the environs of Ephesus. Through economic means the religion of Artemis was therefore a crucial factor in the daily lives of the people.
6. Unsurpassed cosmic power is attributed to her. To those who called upon Artemis she was Savior, Lord, and Queen of the Cosmos.
7. As a supremely powerful deity she could exercise her power for the benefit of the devotee in the face of other opposing "powers" and spirits.
8. Artemis was also a goddess of the underworld. Thus she possessed authority and control over the multiplicity of demons of the dead as well as the demons of nature and of everyday life.

Arnold concludes his discussion of the place of Artemis in Ephesian life by saying that

> few New Testament scholars have referred to the Artemis cult as relevant to the background to Ephesians, much less as relevant to the teaching on the hostile "powers." Most scholars quickly dismiss seeing any reference to the Artemis cult in Ephesians since neither the name "Artemis" nor specific and unique details of the cult are mentioned. This may prove to have been an erroneous assumption. I would tentatively suggest that an understanding of the cult may also give some insight into why the author emphasized the "powers" in Ephesians. It may also be helpful in understanding one of the terms for the hostile "powers."[24]

The power term Arnold has in mind is *kosmokratōr* translated "world forces" in Ephesians 6:12 (see chapter 51). Arnold's words provide good background to our study of spiritual warfare and Ephesians.

The story of Paul's dramatic ministry in Ephesus only begins with Acts 19. While the incident with Demetrius and the riot that followed (vv. 23 ff) would be interesting to examine, it does not add to our knowledge of warfare with the spirit world except to see another case of men using religion for personal profit.

If this were all we had in the way of references to encounter with the spirit world, it would be enough to reveal that the apostolic church *lived* in the context of spiritual warfare and power encounter, including delivering the demonized from the evil spirits which held them in bondage. We have much more, however. We have the rest of the New Testament. We will continue in our study by surveying the Epistles and Revelation. We will find that Paul's Epistle to the Ephesians both connects to what we have seen in Acts 19 and culminates the New Testament understanding of the church's role in the continuing conflict with the powers.

Spiritual Warfare in the Epistles and Revelation

48

Galatians, 1 and 2 Thessalonians

ESTABLISHING THE PERTINENT BACKGROUND FOR INTERPRETING THE NEW TESTAMENT EPISTLES AND LETTERS

The Gospels and Acts portray the life and ministry of Jesus and His disciples in narrative form. They reveal Jesus and His followers in specific contexts involving other people, God, Satan, and the demons, as we have seen.

In the words of Luke, the Gospels record some of what "Jesus began to do and teach" (Acts 1:1). While Luke has his Gospel specifically in mind, what he writes is true of all four Gospels. In the words of Jesus Himself, the Gospels reveal the coming of the kingdom of God and the initial overcoming of the kingdom of Satan through His life and ministry and that of His disciples. They, like Jesus, both preached the gospel of the kingdom and ministered in kingdom power, overthrowing the kingdom of Satan (Matt. 4:23 with Mark 1:14–39; Matt. 12:28; Luke 9:1–2 with Mark 3:14–15; 6:7–13, 30; Luke 10:1–24).

The presence of the kingdom of God and the disciples' ministry in the power of that kingdom does not diminish with Jesus' death, burial, resurrection, and ascension. In fact, it increases even as Jesus had promised (John 14—17). Thus the language of Acts 1:1 and the record of Acts 2—28 reveal that while the Gospels disclose what Jesus *began to do and teach* Himself and through His disciples, the Acts (and the Epistles, as we will soon see) disclose what Jesus *continues to do and teach* through His church by the power of the Holy Spirit. They reveal the kingdom of God in direct conflict with and continuing to displace the kingdom of Satan in the remaining years of the first century. Thus prominence is given in Acts to the kingdom of God (1:3; 8:4–8, 12; 14:22; 19:8; 20:24–25; 28:23, 31) and to kingdom power ministry.

We have examined selected instances of Jesus's ongoing conflict with the powers of evil in the life of the early church in our studies on the Acts. Now we turn to the Epistles, a section of the New Testament which portrays in quite different ways various dimensions of the life of the early believers. While every book in the New Testament was written primarily for believers, the Epistles have as their subject "how to live the Christian life and carry on a Christian ministry" in varied circumstances in the first-century world. The Gospels and Acts share this purpose as well. We call the first four books *Gospels,* "good news," primarily because they show and tell the good news of the salvation brought by Jesus. They are uniquely a record of salvation history. As narratives, the Gospels and Acts tell the story and give a wealth of pictures of Jesus and His disciples particularly in evangelistic and mission action.

The Epistles, in direct contrast, are not narratives; they do not aim at showing us one event after another, such as we see on television in a nightly news broadcast. Instead, the Epistles are devoted to specific comments on specific items of the news, interpreting what the good news means for believers living in specific social and cultural contexts. Thus the difference, for example, between Paul's writing to the Ephesians and the Colossians and his writing to the believers at Philippi.

The Epistles are more like divinely inspired editorial comments inserted into a news broadcast, so to speak. In them we find no stories told directly and completely; instead the specific experiences of the believers receiving an epistle are part of the background of the epistle. In other words, Paul contextualizes his teachings in all of his epistles to meet the specific needs of the specific churches located in a specific social, cultural, and religious context.

Thus, whenever we read any portion of the Epistles and seek to interpret its meaning, we must take what it says on the surface and add to it what we believe its background is in order to arrive at its meaning, at correct interpretation. Commentaries and Bible dictionaries help us know something about a text's background and are thus very helpful. I used many of them in writing this book.

This discussion is very important to our study of spiritual warfare and the spirit world in the Epistles, because our ideas about their background, both generally and specifically, greatly influence how we interpret each epistle.

On the surface, several of the Epistles seem not to deal with spiritual warfare as often or in the same manner as do the Gospels, particularly the synoptic Gospels, and the Book of Acts. They do not contain close-up descriptions of evil spirits being cast out or of disobedient believers being slain by the Holy Spirit (as in Acts 5). They do not describe in any detail any of the kinds of power encounters we have discussed in previous chapters on Jesus and the apostolic church. Without doubt, deliverances from evil spirits and power encounters were going on continually; such were part of the context in which the churches were planted, but no specifics are given.

Also, nowhere do the Epistles directly discuss any teaching on the possibility of the demonization of Christians or their deliverance. Yet I believe we seriously misunderstand the Epistles if we read them and conclude that they do not reflect exactly the same spiritual warfare world view described close-up and vividly in the Gospels and Acts. Yet many who oppose aspects of spiritual warfare as I describe them in this book do so because they claim that what I am describing is biblical only if the Epistles also teach through instruction and exposition exactly the same content as the Gospels and Acts teach through narrative.

All of this underscores again the importance of reading the Epistles with an adequate sense of the background that is pertinent to them, that is, the spiritual warfare context in which the early churches lived and had their being. By their very nature, the Epistles assume that those to whom they are sent know the background needed (indeed they live in that context!) and therefore do not need to be instructed again, for example, in the reality of encounter with the spirit world. Yet we, two thousand years removed from the time in which the Epistles were written, must work at moving from the text itself back to a specific social, cultural, and religious background against which the text can only be properly interpreted and understood. This type of exegesis is challenging, important, and best left to gifted Bible scholars, whose work I draw upon in all of my Scripture studies in this book.

I have one major concern with Western Bible scholarship, however. Very often it focuses on discerning what is the specific background and content of an individual epistle, while failing to include in that background pertinent dimensions of the social, cultural, and religious context common to all New Testament churches. The resulting "background" used for interpreting that epistle is thus too narrow, and it conflicts with the general background of the New Testament world. We all admit that this more general background (which, made most general, becomes a world view) to the New Testament is dramatically pictured for us in the Gospels and Acts. I am arguing that the world view of these books, particularly their general view of spiritual warfare and the range of activities involved in encounter with the spirit world, must be presupposed as a crucial part of the background scholars construct in order to interpret the Epistles.

When this world view is not presupposed, it is all too easy for mentions of evil supernaturalism in the Epistles to be interpreted from the perspective of the world view of modern interpreters. If encounters with evil spirits, such as are depicted in the Gospels and Acts, are not part of the experience of these interpreters, would we expect them to relate mentions of Satan in the Epistles to the range of activities depicted in Acts if: One, they do not presuppose the world view of Acts as part of the Epistles' background; and two, they resist on theological grounds the notion that such activities were part of life for the believers to whom the Epistles were addressed?

Similarly, when modern interpreters approach the Epistles presupposing the world view of Acts as part of the Epistles' background and suspending for at least the moment any theological resistance to implications that result from looking at the Epistles through the world view lenses of Acts, should we be surprised if they relate mentions of evil supernaturalism in the Epistles to the more fully developed pictures recorded in the Gospels and Acts?

From a historical perspective, we simply must set the Epistles within the world view and against the background of the Gospels and Acts. The Epistles are addressed to groups of believers who, for the most part, became believers in Christ during the period covered by the Acts. For instance, those believers who received 1 and 2 Thessalonians from the hands of Paul were the very ones who became Christians during the evangelistic activities of Paul and Silas recorded in Acts 17. This is even more dramatically true with the Epistle to the Ephesians. Similarly, those to whom Galatians, Philippians, 1 and 2 Corinthians, and Colossians were addressed were themselves Christians as a result of Paul's missionary work described in Acts and that of his disciples. For these, power encounter and spiritual warfare were an essential part of their life and ministry.

To repeat, we do not read the Epistles and the references in them to evil supernaturalism rightly if we sever them from the general background supplied by Acts. Of course this does not mean that any and every reference to Satan or evil powers necessarily refers to any one specific dimension or manifestation of evil super-naturalism. It does mean that such even passing references to the reality of Satan, demons, principalities, and powers and their influence will mean something far different to one who links those mentions to the activity described repeatedly in the Gospels and Acts than to one who treats such mentions in almost total isolation from the general spiritual warfare context of the world in which all of the Epistles were written. Commentators who tend toward isolating the world of the Epistles from the world of the Gospels and Acts will more than likely interpret those references strictly within their own limited world view. There, the reality of evil supernaturalism is rarely, if ever, recognized or understood as it was recognized and understood in the world of the Acts of the Apostles. However, one who is involved in contemporary encounters with the spirit world and who is a gifted and faithful biblical interpreter will more readily look at such references through the "eye-glasses" of the biblical world and not through the lenses of a Western world view.

It simply will not do for one to interpret the Epistles primarily through a world view that, while "Christian" in the traditional sense, is yet fully influenced and corrupted by the blending of rationalism and empiricism that is the legacy of the Enlightenment and of naturalistic science. These traditions and their theological offspring either resist or have difficulty in understanding the experiential reality of supernatural evil that surfaces through the synoptic Gospels, the Acts, and is present also in the Epistles, if one has "the eyes" with which to see them. We must discipline ourselves to allow the aspects of the Bible's world view which most clash with ours to be fully present when we read the Bible, and this includes the Epistles. Otherwise, to use an illustration, we will be like a club which meets faithfully in the library to read the plays of Shakespeare. We will enjoy all that the theater of the mind can offer us, but miss the grandeur of the actual experience of the stage production, the true setting in which the plays were intended to be performed and to be understood.

With this approach in mind, we now turn to the Epistles. In this section, we treat only those texts that help disclose dimensions of spiritual warfare, particularly those that point to dimensions which some today find controversial and to dimensions which can help us learn to fight the good fight of faith as it was understood by the early church. For those important texts, such as Galatians 5, which are discussed elsewhere in the book, the reader is simply referred to those locations.

Because of space limitations, my presentation will be brief and only suggestive. There is a wealth of ore to be mined from the Epistles about the world of supernatural evil. What I have space to present will barely tap into the lode. I hope my study will inspire others to do the deeper dig and go for the gold, so to speak.

Finally, some case studies which are included are not intended as perfect parallels to the biblical text. They are provided, however, as a voice of contemporary experience which often illustrates one application of the general thrust of the text in question.

Now we turn to those books that reflect the historic experience of the earliest believers over a period of years, of dealing with a foe who is already defeated by the Son of God and progressively so by the sons of God. In them we hear a dominant note: the believer's victory over all the malevolent powers through the Christ event, through the armor of God provided for the believer, and through intercessory prayer, our major weapon against the powers of evil. Perhaps Paul's words in Romans 8 best sum up the believers' victory over the spirit world, a view that undergirds and is expressed in all of the Epistles:

Who shall separate us from the love of Christ? shall tribulation, or distress, or persecution, or famine, or nakedness, or peril, or sword? As it is written: For Thy sake we are killed all the day long; We are accounted as sheep for the slaughter. Nay, in all these things we are more than conquerors through him that loved us. For I am persuaded, that neither death, nor life, nor angels, nor principalities, nor powers, nor things present, nor things to come, nor height, nor depth, nor any other creature, shall be able to separate us from the love of God, which is in Christ Jesus our Lord. (Rom. 8:35–39, KJV)

THE EPISTLES AND LETTERS OF PAUL

Through his letters, Paul expounds the greater part of the major doctrinal truths that make up the Christian faith, including the truths concerning spiritual warfare in general, and the spirit world in particular. Paul has more to say about evil supernatural powers and warfare with evil spirits than any other New Testament writer. As far as direct teaching is concerned, he probably says more than all the others combined, except for the Gospels and Acts. Except for Ephesians and Colossians, we will study Paul's epistles in the probable order in which they were written, not in the order we presently find them in the Bible.

GALATIANS

Galatians was probably Paul's first letter, perhaps even the first of all the New Testament books.[1] Paul probably wrote to the Galatians while on his first missionary furlough in Antioch of Syria. The most polemic of all his writings, Galatians records his battle with the Judiazers, a delegation of whom had gone to Galatia and were undermining the faith of the churches (Gal. 1:6f).[2] Paul is battling for the very survival of the churches, for "the truth of the Gospel" (Gal. 2:5,14).[3] This was spiritual warfare at its zenith. False teaching can be demonic in origin (1 Tim. 4:1).

In his anxiety and ever aware of Satan's deceptive tactics, Paul sounds an alarm: "even though we, or an angel from heaven, should preach to you a gospel contrary, let him be accursed" (Gal. 1:8). Paul is pulling out all rhetorical stops. We can almost sense an all-night prayer vigil behind these words as the determined apostle will not, cannot, let the Galatians slide into demonic false teaching.

Yet this is more than rhetoric. Fallen angels do teach a different gospel through false prophets (teachers and deceived believers). Paul warns of this fact in many of his epistles (see Rom. 16:17–20; 1 Cor. 8—10; 2 Cor. 2:11; 4:2; 10:1f; 11:1–4; 13—15; 2 Thess. 2:1f; 1 Tim. 1:18–20 with 2 Tim. 2:14–26; 1 Tim. 4:1f; 6:3f; 2 Tim. 3:1f with Titus 1:10f).

Frederic Rendall, writing in the *Expositor's Greek New Testament,* says that Paul "desires to impress on his disciples that the controversy is not between one teacher and another, but between truth and falsehood: no minister of Christ, not even an angel, can alter the truth in Christ."[4] The battle between truth and error was one of the major dimensions of spiritual warfare faced by Paul throughout the years of his ministry. It underlies all of his critique of those who distort the true gospel of grace.

Within this struggle, why the reference in Galatians 1:8 to "an angel from heaven"? Cole suggests that Paul may be using "angel" to show them "the possibility of Satan himself appearing as an angel of light to deceive them. It was on the hearing of a false gospel, a gospel without a cross, that the Lord said, 'Get thee behind me, Satan'" (Mark 8:33).[5] While all deceivers are not necessarily demonized, Paul saw all deception as being, ultimately, demonic (1 Tim. 4:1; 2 Tim. 3:13).

Paul's final references to the spirit world in Galatians are in 3:1 and 4:3–9. While *3:1 is uncertain,* 4:3–9 is clear. Paul twice here mentions "the elemental things of the world" (vv. 3,9). (This is the Greek word *stoicheia.*) The NEB correctly interprets the verse "we were slaves to the elemental spirits of the universe." Paul next refers to their former life when they were "slaves to those which by nature are no gods" (v. 8).

Both expressions refer to the world of evil supernaturalism. We will save our study of Paul's first expression, "the elemental things" *(stoicheia)*—Paul calls them "the worthless elemental things" in 4:9—for our study on principalities and powers in Ephesians and Colossians. Paul repeats almost the exact words in Colossians 2:8,20.

His reference to their former slavery to the no-gods is a powerful expression. It takes us back to our studies from 1 Corinthians 8—10 where Paul dealt with the gods of paganism (see chapter 45).

According to Paul in Galatians 4:1–9 both the Jewish Christians who were in danger of turning back to the *stoicheia* of the law and the Gentiles who served the *stoicheia* of the no-gods were serving demonic powers and not God. Paul's great concern is expressed in these verses and in many similar ones in his other epistles.

Finally in Galatians, Paul treats the believers' warfare with the flesh (5:16–21,24), and warfare with the world (1:4 and 5:11–14), the multidimensional perspective on spiritual warfare which we have already examined in chapter 13.

1 AND 2 THESSALONIANS

It is almost unanimously agreed that the next two extant epistles which Paul wrote were 1 and 2 Thessalonians,[6] both written about 50 A.D.[7] to the believers who became Christians during his ministry in Thessalonica recorded in Acts 17.

1 Thessalonians 1:5–9

Paul's first reference to the spirit world in 1 Thessalonians occurs at 1:5–10. First he reminds the believers that the gospel did not come to them in word only, but also "in power" (v. 5).

We do not know if "power" referred specifically to power encounters, since Luke's record in Acts 17 to the planting of the church in Thessalonica is silent about the matter! Since evangelistic preaching accompanied by unusual power demonstrations often included power encounters, we would be on safe grounds assuming such also occurred in Thessalonica. Given the way the way the Holy Spirit was working in Philip (Acts 8), in Peter (Acts 5,9—10), and in Paul (Acts 13, 16, 19), it is probable that the Spirit worked in much the same way at Thessalonica, where believers had turned "from idols to serve a living and true God" (1 Thess. 1:9). As we have already seen (chapter 47), idolatry and demonic activity go together. Thus we can assume that some kind of power encounter defeating the demons behind the no-gods occurred at Thessalonica as part of these believers' conversion. Their conversion resulted not only in "joy of the Holy Spirit" (1:6), but also "in much tribulation," a common result whenever the Gospel confronts evil powers.

1 Thessalonians 2:18

The next reference to the spirit world is 1 Thessalonians 2:18. This is Paul's first reference to Satan in his Epistles, as well as his first reference to defeat by Satan in his evangelistic endeavors.

Paul is writing with the memory of his sufferings at Philippi and his hasty retreat from Thessalonica to Athens still fresh in mind. Thus the letter to the believers in Thessalonica mentions that they too "endured the same sufferings at the hands of your own countrymen" as other believers were experiencing (2:14). All of this gives Paul occasion to reflect with them upon the opposition of Satan which, until now, has stopped him from returning to them.

While Satan and the evil powers are described in the New Testament as already defeated, it is an "already, but not yet" defeat. They are bound, but as one theologian expressed it, they are bound by a long rope. That rope Paul knew extended as far as Thessalonica and to Corinth, from where he wrote this epistle.

In the Old Testament, God's enemies are portrayed primarily as men and nations, while in the New Testament they are seen as the hostile spiritual powers who work through men and nations opposing God, His kingdom, and His people. These enemies, as we have seen repeatedly, are high-level, invisible cosmic powers which operate in human history. Thus, as George E. Ladd says, the victory over them can only "be won on the plane of history."[8]

This conflict of powers—that of the gospel and that of opposition to it—forms the background to Paul's words in 1 Thessalonians 2:12–16. The mighty destroying, binding, delivering, and building kingdom power of God was at work among the Thessalonian Christians, but as always, there was also strong opposition in the heavenlies. Paul knew a return visit to Thessalonica would have furthered this kingdom work, but so did Satan. So Satan stopped Paul in his tracks; he hindered his plans to return to Thessalonica: Paul says, "we wanted to come to you—I, Paul, more than once—and yet Satan thwarted us" (v. 18).

Verse 18 reveals profound truths about the conflict in the spirit world which occurs uniquely in the lives of those who seek to spread God's truth to the world and those who are in need of that truth. Commenting on verse 18, Bruce observes that Satan's "main activity is putting obstacles in the path of the people of God, to prevent the will of God from being accomplished in and through them."[9]

The Reality of Satan's Power

Satan stopped Paul from doing what Paul knew was the will of God. Is that possible? According to Paul, it is. Most of us have difficulty with this dimension of spiritual warfare. We try to ignore it, or we water it down until Satan is seen almost as already bound in the pit and completely unable to effectively oppose believers. Our preachers often tell us, "God is sovereign. He always does His will in heaven and on earth. Neither man, nor the Devil, nor demons can ever interfere with His will. Therefore as long as we are walking in the Spirit, Satan cannot successfully resist us when we are in God's will. To do so would be to successfully resist the will of God. This God would never permit."

This sounds pious, but it fits neither the teachings of Scripture nor the experience of God's people. It certainly is a "truth" unknown to the apostle Paul according to this passage. Though we are protected from serious or total defeat while we walk in the Spirit (if we walk in the flesh he already has a stronghold in us), we can and will suffer setbacks. That is what Paul is explaining here. He was in the midst of a serious setback, and he didn't like it.

If we become super-spiritual and call such setbacks the will of God, we deceive ourselves. We do not deceive God, nor do we deceive Satan. Indeed, he must be delighted when we clean up his dirty work by calling it the will of God. While we are taught to rejoice *in* everything we are not taught to rejoice *because* everything is the will of God. We are to rejoice because even when God's will is not being done, we are sharing in Christ's sufferings for His body's sake, not because the work of Satan is really the work of God. Let's not try to eliminate the mystery of evil by calling it "good."

How do we handle the supernatural opposition against us when we know we are in the will of God? The answer is simple to say, but hard to do! We stay where we are, serve faithfully, and suffer. We continue to serve and to suffer until, if necessary, we die. That is what Paul did (2 Tim. 4:7–8). So did Peter (2 Peter 1:12–15). So have many of God's saints from the beginning until now (Heb. 11:32–40). At the same time, God's Holy Spirit sustains us with joy (1 Thess. 1:6; Rom. 5:1–5).

1 Thessalonians 3:5

The final clear reference to Satan's warfare against the children of God in this Epistle is found in chapter 3. It naturally flows from what Paul has just said about Satan's hindering him and his team from returning to Thessalonica. He writes,

> For this reason, when I could endure it no longer, I also sent to find out about your faith, for fear that the tempter might have tempted you, and our labor should be in vain. (3:5)

Notice the steps in the development of this verse.

1. Paul could not handle waiting any longer to find out if the saints had survived in Thessalonica. (See v. 1a for the same phrase.) PHILLIPS translates these words, "when the suspense became unbearable."

The deep emotion in these words reveals an anxiety to the point of impatience. Paul must take a prescribed course of action to get release. The pressure had reached the breaking point. He could not continue suppressing his anxious feelings, especially when the power of the enemy was involved.

2. To relieve the anxiety, Paul sent Timothy to find out about their present state (vv. 1–4). While Paul speaks of the sending of Timothy as a personally costly move, his love for them was stronger than his personal needs.

3. His real concern was for their faith: not for their faithfulness, but for their very Christian faith, Leon Morris says.[10]

4. The real cause of this concern was his profound understanding of both the strategy and the power of Satan. Paul calls him here, "the tempter." This title is used of Satan only here and in Matthew 4:3. This is the first of the two occasions that Paul will refer to Satan's strategy as that of tempting the people of God. The second one is in 1 Corinthians 7:5.

5. Paul knew the Tempter was able to totally turn them from their faith due to the very things Jesus warned of in his parable of the sower (Matt. 13:18–23). He comes directly to the point. He says that he sent Timothy "to make sure that the tempter's activities had not destroyed our work" (PHILLIPS).

F. F. Bruce's comments in reference to "lest the tempter should have tempted you" that the "aorist *epeirasin* here implies successful temptation, temptation which had succeeded in overthrowing their faith. The clause expresses apprehension over what might be discovered by Timothy on his arrival."[11] Bruce continues, commenting on "and our labor should be in vain." He says it would be in vain "if the Thessalonians' faith collapsed."[12]

These are sobering words. Indeed, they are even shocking. Our traditional evangelical theology of our enemy is that he is so totally defeated, so totally without power against us, he is not allowed by God to destroy the faith of new Christians or of older Christians, for that matter. Evidently Paul saw it differently.

Here in Thessalonica we have new believers recently converted out of demon worship (1:9 with 1 Cor. 10:21–21). The Holy Spirit has come in power into their lives with full conviction of faith. They receive the word with much tribulation and with much joy in the Holy Spirit. They have become examples to all the believers in Macedonia and Achaia. From them the Word of God has begun to be "sounded forth" everywhere. Their faith has been demonstrated. They live with the great hope of Jesus' return (1:5–10). Yet they are still new believers. They are still in grave danger. The persecution against them has grown significantly (1:6 and 2:13–16 with 2 Thess. 1:4–10).

Thus Paul becomes apprehensive. Time and again he tries to go to them. Each time Satan is able to "break up the pathway" before him. Paul cannot reach his beloved friends. Finally he writes them and tells them of his fears. He really only has one fear, that Satan has succeeded in turning them from the faith. Matthew Henry also states that Paul was concerned that the "tempter had tempted them and prevailed against them, to move them from the faith."[13]

Thus we must honestly face the fact that we have an enemy who is capable of, and allowed by God to, undermine the faith of the people of God. No wonder Paul later speaks of our need to not be ignorant of Satan's schemes. If we are, he is able to take advantage of us (2 Cor. 2:11). The fall of Christians all around us, including Christian leaders, is ample proof that our defeated adversary is still capable of unleashing terrible attacks against the children of God, especially in the context of evangelism.

2 THESSALONIANS

2 Thessalonians 2:1–12

F. F. Bruce says that "If any section can claim to be described as the (body) of this letter, it is 2:1–12 [where Paul discusses the "man of lawlessness"]. This is not only the most distinctive feature of 2 Thessalonians, it probably represents the purpose of the letter. What precedes leads up to it and what follows leads on from it."[14]

This epistle is the *only* book in the Bible whose focus is primarily on *Satan's future, final efforts to control, deceive, and rule mankind* through his own "christ," the Antichrist, "the man of lawlessness." Those who minimize the place Paul gives to supernatural evil would do well to reconsider their position. This is an essential part of Paul's world view, and in 2 Thessalonians it is the central teaching.

When we consider Paul is writing to new believers in 1 and 2 Thessalonians and that he says he is putting in writing what he had taught them in person during the few weeks he was with them, we are amazed. We usually reserve these teachings for mature Christians. Yet they form the subject of his teaching to new converts (2 Thess. 2:5).

Paul's teachings in this epistle about the spirit world all focus on the coming "man of lawlessness" (2 Thess. 2:3–10), called the Antichrist by John (1 John 2:18 and 22; 4:3; and 2 John 7). Here are instructions so profound that biblical scholars still struggle for full understanding of these teachings. Yet again, Paul taught them to brand-new converts (2:5).

This is new teaching about the spirit world. Jesus taught his disciples about the last times, of false prophets (Matt. 24:11), of the Abomination of Desolation foretold in Daniel (Matt. 24:15), and of a proliferation of both "false christs and false prophets." He said deceivers would "arise and will show great signs and wonders, so as to mislead, if possible, even the elect. Behold, I have told you in advance" (Matt. 24:24–25). All this teaching is associated with his second coming (Matt. 24:3–31).

Yet, Jesus did not speak as Paul does here and John does later about one particular Antichrist. (For John's discussion of the Antichrist, see chapter 52.)

Jesus first indicates that antichrist-like beings will come and John is the last to write about them (him). Yet it is Paul, early in his apostolic ministry, who gives the first detailed teachings about this evil one here in 2 Thessalonians 2:3–10.

As we examine Paul's description of this "man of lawlessness" (v. 3), he is seen as the personified embodiment of deceptions through counterfeit spirit power demonstrations which Jesus warned would come. He also perfectly fits John's description of both the Antichrist and the beast, the latter in the Book of Revelation.

The Day of Christ

Paul begins chapter 2 with a request that the believers not be troubled by the report that the day of Christ had already come (vv. 1–2). He then takes the believers back to his former teachings in his first epistle about the second coming of Christ and, "our gathering together to Him" (v. 1b with 1 Thess. 4:13–18).

The Second Coming is also a key teaching in the two epistles. All of his teachings about Satan and the man of lawlessness here in 2 Thessalonians are related to the Lord's coming, His *parousia.*

Paul uses three principal words for the Lord's second coming: *epiphaneia,* literally "a shining forth"; *apokalupsis,* "unveiling, a revelation or appearing"; and *parousia,* "coming and presence."[15] The latter is Paul's favorite word here in 2 Thessalonians for the Lord's coming. He will also use the same word for the coming of the "man of lawlessness," as we will soon see.

In his excellent commentary on 2 Thessalonians, Leon Morris says that

> Paul had spoken a good deal about the second coming at Thessalonica, but it is clear that not all of his teaching had been grasped. New converts, full of enthusiasm, perhaps emotionally unstable . . . as yet imperfectly instructed in the deep things of the faith, not unnaturally went astray in some points in this important, but intricate, subject.[16]

Morris then comments that "Paul had had occasion to refer to the *Parousia* in his first letter. This, however, did not clear away all doubts. He felt, accordingly, that he must deal with the subject again."[17]

Morris makes an interesting observation about our major difficulty in interpreting what Paul is saying here about both the *parousia* of Christ and the man of lawlessness. "It is a supplement to his oral preaching. He and his correspondents both knew what he had said when he was in Thessalonica. There was no point in repeating it. He could take it as known, and simply add what was necessary to clear up the misunderstandings that had arisen."[18]

Regarding false teaching, I must add that later Paul will affirm that the widespread deception which will characterize the Last Days will come about through believers who "will fall away from the faith, paying attention to deceitful spirits and doctrines of demons" (1 Tim. 4:1). Thus the true source of all such deceptions and false teaching is demonic, Paul is saying.

This is the kind of future, Last-Days deception Paul is warning about here in 2 Thessalonians 2. He outlines in broad strokes the course the spiritual deception will follow (v. 3ff). He says it will bring ever increasing and ever more powerful demonic spirits. All prepare the way for the appearance of the man of lawlessness himself (v. 3).

His coming, Paul says, will be at the climax of a period of widespread deception. Deception is Satan's main strategy. That deception will produce "the apostasy." This apostasy, or falling away, will prepare the way for the final arrival of the man of lawlessness.

Leon Morris' comments here are outstanding. He says, "Paul is desperately anxious that his friends do not fall into error. 'Let no man beguile you in any wise' is not only an exhortation, but a reminder of the folly of being led astray in this way."

Morris then points out the evidences which prove the day of the Lord has not yet come. There must first occur the great apostasy already mentioned, the worldwide "falling away" from the faith (v. 3a). This will lead to the appearance of the man of lawlessness (v. 3b). Neither has taken place yet. Therefore, the Day of the Lord has not yet occurred.[19]

There is some difficulty about our understanding of both the falling away and the coming of "the man of lawlessness." What is beyond doubt is that Paul expected his allusions to be so clear to the Thessalonians that they would see the folly of their error and return to spiritual "sanity" in the matters under consideration.

Morris says that Paul "speaks of the rebellion coming 'first.' But he does not say what it is to precede." He then states that there "can be no doubt [that the KJV] is correct in supplying 'it will not be,' with 'it' referring to the day of the Lord."

The Man of Lawlessness (or Sin)

Arising out of this falling away is the appearance of the man of lawlessness (v. 3b; "sin," NKJV). Morris says that lawlessness must be understood as, "failure to conform to the law of God, and this is what sin is (cf. 1 John 3:4). In the last resort sin is the refusal to be ruled by God. . . . The individual in mind is seen against the background of the rising of Satan against the power of God."[20]

Morris says it is a grave error to identify this lawless one with historical figures of the past. The man of lawlessness "is an eschatological personage," he states. Paul says he will not appear until just before the Lord returns. Thus it is foolish to search history for his identify. He is yet to come.

Morris then says that Paul, in speaking of this figure being "revealed," indicates that the man of lawlessness will "exist before his manifestation to the world. It may also point us to something supernatural about him. This would be natural enough, from his close association with Satan."

Morris next states that the man of lawlessness is

further described as "the son of perdition" a description which Jesus applied to Judas Iscariot (John 17:12). This type of genitive has a Hebraic twist. It denotes "characterized by" the quality in the genitive (cf. Isa. 57:4). So here it means that the Man of Lawlessness will certainly be lost. As Moffatt put it, he is "the doomed one."[21]

In verse 4 Paul says this evil one "opposes and exalts himself" above all gods and passes himself off, in the temple of God, as being God. What an incredible series of statements!

The word "oppose" is from the word family for the word Satan, "adversary." It stresses the satanic evil which characterizes the person of this son of perdition. He sets himself against God, Paul says (v. 4). This is a present participle, indicative of a continuous attitude, Morris says. It is no passing phase.

Morris then comments that "the second participle (also present continuous) deals with the exalted position the Man of Lawlessness arrogates to himself. He puts himself in the highest possible place." Supreme political position is not enough.[22]

> He insists on having the place reserved among all mankind for the supreme object of worship. He demands religious veneration. More exactly, he insists that no god nor anything bearing the name of God, nor any object of worship whatever should be allowed pride of place. The Man of Lawlessness must be first of all.

The man of lawlessness next takes a further step. He claims he is God. Morris says, "The climax to all this is the explicit claim to deity. He is to sit in the temple proclaiming himself to be God."

It is difficult to know exactly what is the "temple of God" referred to here by Paul. Paul and his readers evidently understood (v. 4b). Morris tells us that the temple refers to an inmost shrine, and not the temple as a whole. "It is not that he enters the temple precincts: he invades the most sacred place and there takes his seat," Morris says. "His action is itself a claim to deity, and the verb 'setting himself forth' may imply an explicit claim in so many words (several translators render 'proclaim') . . ." Finally, Morris affirms this means that he will actually "take his seat in a formal way in a sanctuary . . . in some material building which will serve as the setting for the blasphemous claim to deity which the Man of Lawlessness will make as the climax of his activities."[23]

Commenting on the debate over the identification of "the restrainer," (v. 6) Morris says that although Paul's readers knew what he was talking about, we do not, and it is best we acknowledge our ignorance. "The important thing," says Morris, "is that some power was in operation, and that the Man of Lawlessness could not possibly put in his appearance until this power was removed."[24]

Finally, there is the phrase in verse 6, "in his time," that is, the man of lawlessness can only come in his time. The idea is that *God is in control of all.* He alone determines when this man will come. Thus the man of lawlessness will be revealed only when God permits. He is not to be viewed as one acting in complete independence.

This entire passage reveals the sovereignty of God. He is in control, even when evil seems to have complete control. Here is God Himself outlining the course of evil, Satan, demons, and the Antichrist from Paul's day until the Day of the Lord.

Evil is strong. It will only wax stronger as the day for the appearance of the man of lawlessness begins to draw near. God's hand is seen in the entire process. "Evil will not pass beyond its limits," Morris says. "God's purpose, not that of Satan or his henchmen will finally be seen to have been effected."[25]

Evil: For How Long?

What a comforting word. Even as I write I am seeing evil at work in the lives of people very dear to me. I cry out, "Why, God? Why? Where is your power? I have prayed for years for these loved ones, but you do not answer! Where are you, God? When will evil finally come to its end?"

I also see evil flourishing in my city, my state, my nation, and my world. Deception, corruption, fraud, and selfishness abound. Hurting people are subjected to increased pain by power and position people, in local and national government, business enterprises and public officials.

Then there is abortion on demand. Millions of little ones are tortured and killed before they can even be born. AIDS and cancer strike down both the just and the unjust. Why? For how long?

Decent men and women lose their jobs and their homes. They live in cars, under bridges and on the street. Why?

Millions of my fellow men and women suffering from depressive illness are expelled from hospitals and forced to live on the streets. They live in their own bodily filth, too disturbed to care for themselves. They are exposed to the natural elements and to public disdain. They are rejected and neglected by the most prosperous nation in history, a nation of selfish consumers, too busy to give them more than a passing notice. Why? For how long?

Even our evangelical churches are totally preoccupied with their own programs. Their focus is on "meeting the needs of our own church family." Meanwhile, those who are homeless through no fault of their own (they are not bums and panhandlers who prefer to live on the street) and heads of households, who find themselves without jobs, without sufficient income to pay their bills, go destitute. Why? For how long?

There is enough wealth and God-given ingenuity in the churches of America to help these people of pain towards the road of recovery. This, along with the good will of concerned men and women outside of our churches, plus government programs are enough to start many of the destitute toward the road of self-sufficiency. The truth of the matter is these people are not high on the priority list of churches, or local or federal welfare institutions. Why?

And what about evangelization—of our cities and of the world? Why do we as churches have so little time or concern for any but ourselves? Why can we not unite as one body for intercession and warfare praying to reach even our own cities for God? Have we as leaders usurped God's headship over His churches? Why? For how long?

Finally, I cry, "God, where are you when evil spreads even among your churches? Where are you when evil engulfs our land and our world? Things are getting worse instead of better. Why, God, why? For how long?"

Then when I am alone with Him, I open His Word and I discover where He is in the midst of this ocean of evil, both human and supernatural. He is where He always is. He is working His mysterious will and His will shall be done even if, temporarily, for now it is *not* being done. I realize now His will is always good, even when He allows evil, seemingly, a free course.

His will is good even when I hurt; even when my loved ones, family and dear friends, hurt until we all cry; even when my community and my nation calls evil good.

Evil is allowed by God to run its mysterious course, but, as the song says, "Our God Reigns." As the Scriptures say, the mystery of evil *must* be allowed to work, but *only* until God declares, *"Enough!"* Evil will then be no more. Lord, please hurry that day.

2 Thessalonians 2:8–10

In light of all this, verses 8–10a are crucial to our study. Here Paul speaks of two appearings: First the lawless one, then the Lord.

When the Lord appears, he "will slay (the Lawless One) with the breath of his mouth and bring (him) to an end by the appearance of his coming." This will be the beginning of the final solution to evil.

The Antichrist (John's name for him) is revealed to be in direct allegiance with the activity of Satan. He comes with "all deception," Paul says, received from its source in the supreme deceiver, Satan.

All through our spiritual warfare study I have been striving to maintain balance. While we must look at Satan and his demons as Paul does here, they are not the focus of Scripture. Above all stands God, His Son our Lord, and the Holy Spirit our Helper. Though Paul refers over and over again in this chapter to the person and career of the lawless one, his focus is on the sovereignty of God. Better yet, his focus is on the God who is sovereign.

Morris observes that as Paul "contemplates the happenings of the end time it is not with the eager eye of one who seeks to trace out the course of events and follow the progress of the Man of Lawlessness. Rather, he looks with joy on the revelation of the mighty hand of God."[26]

This is a crucially needed balance today in all teaching on evil and spiritual warfare. God is the only God. Jesus is the only Lord. Satan is a no-god. He is a defeated no-god in spite of the incredible power to do evil which he still possesses.

Let's trace the divine order of events leading up to the destruction of the lawless one in "the supreme moment of history," to use Morris' words. This is revealed in verse 8.

Paul says first, "the Lord will slay him." Second, all He needs to slay him is "the breath of His mouth." Third, He will do so "by the appearance of His coming" (v. 8). The Thessalonians need not fear, "however illustrious evil men might be. Even the most outstanding of them all would be far outshone by the Lord of these lowly believers when He returns," Morris comments.[27]

Paul does not underestimate the man of lawlessness. He is vicious and he is powerful. But "his confident assertions of the last couple of verses spring from recognition of the splendor and the power of the Lord Jesus, not from any failure to appreciate the power of the opposition," Morris says.[28]

In verse 9, Paul refers again to the lawless one's coming. As we have seen, this is the same word used for the second coming of Christ in verse 8. The man of lawlessness will come with his own splendor and power from Satan. He is Satan's representative. Morris says that the verse:

> strongly suggests that we are confronted with a parody of the incarnation. The Man of Lawlessness is not simply a man with evil ideas. He is empowered by Satan to do Satan's work. Thus he comes "with all power and signs and lying wonders."[29]

Powers, signs, and wonders are the three words used all throughout Scripture for God's works of power through the Lord Jesus and his people. "They are probably used for that reason," Morris says. "They help us to see the counterfeit nature of the ministry of the Man of Lawlessness."

Paul says these are lying, or false signs, however, referring to all three power words used here. It is not that the miracles are counterfeit, as if there is no real miracle at all. These are genuine miracles. They are counterfeit only because they come not from God but from the no-god who tries to do the works of God to deceive those who want to be deceived.

Paul next turns to the effect of the deception energized by the man of lawlessness upon the unbelieving. As he does so he gives us thorough insight into the nature of unbelief and unbelievers. He also writes from the perspective of God's sovereignty. Paul says:

1. Those deceived will "perish" (v. 10a).
2. They perish because "they did not receive the love of the truth so as to be saved" (v. 10b).

Morris states that " 'Truth' here, (vv. 10b–12) . . . is intimately related to Jesus (cf. Eph. 4:2; 'as truth is in Jesus'; John 14:6, 'I am . . . the truth'). More particularly it is the saving truth of the gospel."[30]

This fact is very prominent in the entire passage. Receiving the truth means receiving salvation. Rejecting the truth means damnation. This truth should have been received with warm affection, but these men rejected it.

Paul then speaks not just of the truth but of "the love of the truth." This is an expression found only here in the Bible.

Paul says the attitude of the people he is describing is away from all the things of God, and therefore away from the truth of God. Morris states that they "gave the truth of God no welcome (this is the force of the word rendered 'received'; see on 1 Thess 2:13), that truth of God, which is expressed in the love which brought about the gospel," he says. This is a willful act. It expresses the attitude of their heart. It leads to eternal negative consequences. They will be judged for their attitude and resultant actions.

Morris says that verse 10 "concludes with a clause of purpose which emphasizes the magnitude of the gift these men rejected. Other men love the truth with a view to their salvation. It was this upon which those who perish had turned their backs."[31]

2 Thessalonians 2:11–17

Paul says in verse 11a, "For this reason . . . ." He looks back at all that he has said. Because men do not hold to the truth, they will perish. Because they do not love the truth, they allow themselves to be deceived. As a result they will not be saved (v. 10). They will perish with the man of lawlessness (vv. 8 and 10).

Finally, with this negative background in view, the apostle says that God will now step in and begin the judgment of rebellious men. God's initial act is a hard one to understand at first. God himself will "send upon them a deluding influence so that they might believe what is false," i.e., a lie (v. 11).

This is Paul's first purpose clause in this section. This also is the second time he uses the word "false" in these verses. Morris describes it as "an energy unto delusion."

This is one dimension of my concept of "sin energy." In this case it means that God Himself will send a power which will influence them to believe a lie. "The last expression is really 'the lie,' " Morris says. "It is not just any lie that these people accept, but Satan's last and greatest effort: the lie that the Man of Lawlessness is God. They refused to accept the truth and they find themselves delivered over to a lie."[32]

This view of evil is important for a thoroughly biblical perspective. From all we have seen one could possibly get the impression "of a contest in which Satan on the one hand, and God on the other, make their moves, but with God somewhat the stronger," as Morris says. He corrects this by affirming that "Paul has a much grander conception. God is using the very evil that men and Satan produce for the working out of His purpose."[33]

God is at work. He is not making evil men more evil. He is but judging wicked men for their evil by confirming them in their evil. God has the right to do this, because He alone is God. These men actually believe they are acting freely to defy Him. So do Satan and the evil principalities and powers at work in the world. But their acts of defiance are the very vehicles of their own judgment. Unfortunately for those who allow deceiving spirits to deceive them, they too will be judged as deceived and deceivers. It is no small thing to allow lying spirits access to our minds and hearts.

Finally, with verses 13–15 Paul turns away from the unbelieving. He again returns to his beloved saints at Thessalonica. Everything he has written has been with them in mind. He now speaks to them in terms unparalleled in Scripture, all with the purpose of providing comfort and assurance to these beloved battle weary believers.

First, he says that God chose them "from the beginning for salvation through sanctification by the Spirit and faith in the truth" (v. 13). Wonderful words! Next Paul says it was to this destiny that God called them "through our gospel, that you may gain the glory of our Lord Jesus Christ" (v. 14). Wonderful words! They are meant to be words of assurance to the Thessalonians and *to us who believe* as they did. I believe. Do you?

"It was necessary to deal with the Man of Lawlessness and his detestable enormities," Morris writes, "but Paul's real interest lay elsewhere. The advent speculations of his Thessalonian friends had made it essential for him to say enough to set them right. That done he turns to a more congenial subject, the divine choice of the Thessalonians to salvation."[34]

That divine choice includes all believers. We were all chosen in Christ "before the foundation of the world," Paul says in Ephesians 1:4. Here it is the same. God "has chosen you [and us] from the beginning for salvation through sanctification by the Spirit and faith in the truth" (v. 13b). What a passage of Scripture this is!

It is one of the most comprehensive spiritual warfare passages in the New Testament, because it traces the course of the warfare between the two kingdoms until its final outcome in the appearance and destruction of Satan's most vicious of servants, the "man of lawlessness." The *men* of lawless are to be destroyed with the *man* of lawlessness, Paul declares.

According to the Book of Revelation, next comes the eternal judgment of Satan himself. He is cast into the lake of fire (Rev. 20:10–15). This is followed by the saints of God, with God and "the Lamb" forever, in the City of God, the New Jerusalem (Rev. 21—22). Hallelujah! The Devil is defeated! Our God reigns!

It is fitting that Paul close this spiritual warfare passage, not with the man of lawlessness, but with God's family (vv. 13–17). It is the same note with which John closes the Book of Revelation and thus, the entire Bible. John has Jesus saying,

"I, Jesus, have sent My angel to testify to you these things for the churches. I am the root and the offspring of David, the bright morning star."

This is followed by the response:

And the Spirit and the bride say, "Come." And let the one who is thirsty come; let the one who wishes take the water of life without cost. (Rev. 22:16–17)

This is the final outcome in the warfare which we are all involved in, every moment of our life, knowingly or unknowingly. To God be the glory! The final victory is absolutely sure. We win the war. Hallelujah! The Devil is defeated! Our God reigns!

49

1 and 2 Corinthians, Romans, and the Pastoral Epistles

1 CORINTHIANS

Paul's fourth epistle was sent to the church at Corinth about 54–55 A.D., some three years after planting the church in the city. He had evidently written an earlier letter to them which is lost. He mentions it in 1 Corinthians 5:9f.

Since we have dealt in depth with the question of idolatry using Paul's teachings in 1 Corinthians 8—10 (in chapter 45), we can go directly to Paul's first mention of the spirit world.

1 Corinthians 2:6–8

Some see Paul's reference to "the rulers *(archontes)* of this age" in 1 Corinthians 2:6–8 as a possible repetition of his use of similar expressions in Ephesians 6:12 where they refer to the evil spiritual forces which govern the human rulers of each age. While not generally accepted by commentators, this is a real possibility. I would lean towards that position because we have Paul's clear teachings about the spiritual powers behind human rulers in Ephesians and Colossians.

Of course, human rulers crucified "the Lord of glory," but who is called the ruler *(archōn)* of this age (John 12:31; 14:30; 16:11; Eph. 2:2)? Satan. Who are the rulers, the authorities, the world rulers of this darkness (Eph. 6:12)? Demons. Who filled the heart of Judas to betray Jesus to the human rulers (John 13:2,27)? Satan.

In deliverance ministries demons readily confess to exactly what Paul is affirming here. They and their master, Satan, drove evil rulers to crucify the Lord of glory. They did not know God's plan, that through His cross Jesus would defeat them. If they had known "they would not have crucified the Lord of glory." (See Isa. 24:21–22 and our studies in Ephesians and Colossians.)[1]

1 Corinthians 5:1–5

The first undisputed reference to the evil spirit world is in 1 Corinthians 5:1–5. The setting is Paul's attempt to deal with a major moral problem in Corinth which has been reported to him (v. 1). Gordon Fee writes that in a "culture where one could matter-of-factly say, 'Mistresses we keep for the sake of pleasure, concubines for the daily care of the body, but wives to bear us legitimate children,' moral failure could be expected."[2]

Paul had to address this question often in all the Gentile churches (cf. 1 Thess. 4:1–8; Col. 3:5–7; Eph. 5:3–13). Yet Corinth seems to have been in a class by itself. From other passages in Corinthians (1 Cor. 5:9f; 6:12–20; 7:2f; 10:8; 2 Cor. 12:21), we learn that sexual immorality of the most flagrant type had been part of the Corinthians' previous lifestyle. In all probability many continued in that lifestyle after coming to Christ.

While the church knew of this sin, they had done nothing about it, but Paul says they should be in mourning. The offending party must be disciplined. If the man does not repent, he should be removed from their midst (v. 2). Paul wants decisive action taken—by the church in a gathered assembly, where both he and the power of Christ are present by the Spirit. In that type of gathering the church is to "put the man back out into the sphere of Satan for some form of 'destruction' that has his salvation as its ultimate goal."[3]

This brings us to a new dimension of spiritual warfare not yet dealt with in our study: committing a sinning believer to Satan for the destruction of his flesh. His spirit will "be saved in the day of the Lord Jesus," Paul affirms (v. 5). This means he was a true believer. This is a family disciplinary action against a disobedient child of God, not an act that has as its goal the commitment of an unsaved person to eternal separation from God. Since the church has failed in its responsibility in this matter, Paul himself has initiated the action (vv. 3–5). *Satan will be used by God* to accomplish God's goals of discipline with his erring child.

Some affirm that the destruction of the flesh means the destruction of his sinful nature. On being expelled from the church, the man will begin to see the "hell" which is life in the flesh lived in the world of godless men. This world is the world over which Satan reigns as its god. Satan the no-god will so oppress the wayward, lonely brother, he will see his sin. He will repent and return to the fold.[4] Others say the destruction of the flesh simply means physical death. Satan will be allowed to take his life, not necessarily within a day or two of the church's action, but soon.[5]

I take the latter view. First, the believer's sinful flesh will *never* be destroyed until we are with the Lord. Second, how can Satan do for the sinful believer what God himself cannot do: destroy our sinful flesh before the Resurrection? Third, Paul elsewhere speaks in a similar manner of believers who have made shipwreck of their faith in 1 Timothy 1:19–20. The two men here are also "delivered over to Satan so that they may be taught not to blaspheme." As at Corinth, Paul has in view remedial punishment.

Finally, the premature death of disobedient believers has already occurred in the case of Ananias and Sapphira (Acts 5:1f). Satan was also involved with their problem, in their case, inciting them toward evil. Also, Paul has already referred to more than one believer at Corinth who had experienced God's judgment by His taking their lives prematurely (1 Cor. 11:30). It would seem natural, then, that the Corinthian believers would understand the judgment of 5:5 to be similar to that described in 11:30.

While differences over these two points will always exist, this should not cause us to miss the part Satan plays in the extreme discipline of God's sinful people: *Satan is actually carrying out the will of God.* Again, this is a consistent Scriptural theme involving "the mystery of iniquity," as Paul calls it. God often takes what Satan means for evil and uses it for good. In this case Satan, as the Destroyer (Rev. 9:11) is either ignorant of God's purpose in allowing him to take the life of the disobedient believer or too evil to care or both. When he can do evil he does it without taking into account the long-range consequences of his actions. He is an awesome foe in his evil, but a pitiful foe in his ignorance.

1 Corinthians 7:5

The next reference to Satan is 1 Corinthians 7:5. Paul, writing about the sexual relationship of husband and wife, warns of unwise sexual abstinence. He says:

Stop depriving one another, except by agreement for a time that you may devote yourselves to prayer, and come together again lest Satan tempt you because of your lack of self-control.

Paul had a realistic view of human sexuality. He knew that sexual love in marriage is very important. Thus, even in godly pursuits like prayer and fasting there must be a limit set on abstinence for married couples. Also, it should only be by mutual agreement.

Satan also understands the power which is human sexuality. How effectively he stimulates it toward his evil purposes! He uses sexual temptation against the most godly of believers. It is one of his most effective weapons of destruction.

Finally, the combination of sexual lusts arising in our flesh with sexual stimulation bombarding us from the world sets the stage for sexual demons to attack our minds, imaginations, emotions, and eventually our will. We must walk carefully in such a sensual world, always practicing Philippians 4:8. As we saw in our study of Galatians 5:19 and will yet discover in future chapters, Satan has successfully damaged and destroyed Christian homes and even Christian leaders through sexual sin. Husbands and wives, guard your sexual life in light of the principles carefully laid down by Paul in this passage!

Turning next to Paul's detailed arguments about idolatry and the direct demonic dimension that it entails, we have already seen that the apostle says involvement with this dimension of occultism means direct involvement with demons (1 Cor. 10:20–21). The reader is referred to the discussion in chapter 45.

1 Corinthians 12:1–3

Paul does return again to idols, however, in, of all places, 1 Corinthians 12:1–3. In chapters 12—14 he gives his most detailed teachings about the gifts of the Spirit. What has that to do with idols? Let me quote verses 1–3.

Now concerning spiritual gifts, brethren, I do not want you to be unaware. You know that when you were pagans, you were led astray to the dumb idols, however you were led. Therefore I make known to you, that no one speaking by the Spirit of God says, "Jesus is accursed"; and no one can say, "Jesus is Lord," except by the Holy Spirit.

The literal meaning here would be "spiritual things," not "spiritual gifts." The word Paul commonly uses to refer to a spiritual gift is *charisma* or the plural, *charismata*. He uses that word in the rest of this chapter and also in chapters 13—14. He begins his teaching here on spiritual gifts with a different word, however. It is *pneumatikos,* an adjective used as a noun. It can best be translated "spirituals" or "spiritual matters." Why does Paul use this strange construction?

We can see first that verse 1 refers to questions the Corinthians themselves have raised about the spiritual manifestations which were occurring in their midst. Some were exercising dramatic spiritual gifts, but others did not operate with such gifts. Because of this, placing the word "gifts" after "spiritual" seems acceptable, while it would perhaps be more accurate to supply the word "manifestations" instead of "gifts," just as Paul himself does in verse 7.

I make this point because spiritual *manifestations* occur in all religions. *Spiritual gifts,* the gifts of the Holy Spirit to His children, occur only among true Christians. Where the Holy Spirit is in operation, we call spiritual manifestations, "spiritual gifts," or "gifts of the Holy Spirit." They are the *charismata.* When the spiritual manifestations come from other spirits, they are false spiritual gifts. All such false gifts or manifestations of supernatural origin are demonic.

In verse 2 Paul talks of their days in paganism-occultism. The idols they served were dumb idols, he says. Paul here uses two strong phrases to describe the Corinthians' former relationship to these idols. First, they were led astray to the dumb idols. Morris says this word is often used of leading away a prisoner or condemned person (see Mark 14:44; 15:16).[6]

Who led them astray to wherever they were being led? Satan, through his demons, of course. I say this not only because this is what Paul has already stated (1 Cor. 8—10), but also because it fits what he is trying to say about "spirituals." Spirituals, that is, spiritual manifestations, are not all of God. That is why Paul is soon going to attempt to put in order the house of the Corinthians, which was in a chaos caused by these very spiritual manifestations.

Paul has a larger concern here than just teaching about the various gifts. He sets forth a pagan example—the idols—against which they are to understand both inspired utterances and the significance of tongues. If so, then it seems probable that what is in view is their former pagan experiences of ecstatic or inspired utterances, including prophesies, tongues, and revelations. "Although neither verb on its own necessarily implies this, the unusual compounding of the verbs, with emphasis on the Corinthians being acted upon by others (implied in the two passive verbs), seems to lead in this direction," Fee says.[7]

Demonic spirits are involved in at least two ways, Fee says:

1. In their pagan past they experienced demonic tongues, ecstatic utterances, prophecies, revelations, and the like. This regularly occurred in the pagan temples. Probably many of the converts themselves had been formerly involved.

2. Demonic spirit utterances, which they took as coming from the Holy Spirit, were still occurring in their midst, probably even in their church services. These utterances were evidently blasphemous against the person of the Lord Jesus. This seems to explain Paul's unusual words in verse 3, "Therefore I make known to you, that no one speaking by the Spirit of God says, 'Jesus is accursed'; and no one can say, 'Jesus is Lord,' except by the Holy Spirit" (1 Cor. 12:1–3; see 1 John 4:1–3).

We are witnessing a worldwide renewal in the manifestation of spiritual gifts in our day. This is encouraging. While many do not accept it as a genuine work of God, most Christian leaders do. Even men like the late Dr. Merrill Unger, who was not at home with any of the more ecstatic gifts, strongly affirmed that what we are seeing is a genuine work of renewal by the Holy Spirit.[8]

That is only one side of the coin, however. The other side is the real issue Paul is touching on here. All spiritual manifestations are not from the Holy Spirit, even what appears to be Christian manifestations. When the Holy Spirit is operating, He always produces a certain sound about Jesus. His words eventually always equal "Jesus is Lord." When the other spirit abides in or comes upon a person and that person speaks out, an uncertain sound comes out. This is especially true concerning the person of Jesus as Lord, Paul is saying.

This much seems clear. As we read these verses, however, we must be very careful we do not oversimplify what can occur. Demons, when in manifestation and face-to-face with Christ, always tell the truth about His person. They do not deny either His incarnation or His lordship. Demons will not confess Jesus as their Lord, however.

When Paul says, "No one can say, 'Jesus is Lord' except by the Holy Spirit," this seems to be a confession-submission formula. It is the cry of a human heart or of an angel who falls before His majesty and submits life and lip to His lordship. On the other hand, when a person stands up and speaks in the voice of a spirit which denies the absolute lordship of Jesus or speaks evil of Him, that spirit is demonic. That is true even if the person is a Christian and seems to be praying and praising in tongues.[9]

One more thing could be involved here. It is possible, even probable, that these demonic expressions attacking the lordship of Christ were occurring *during their church meetings*. This is why Paul absolutely forbids public tongues without public interpretation by proven believers with proven gifts of interpretation (1 Cor. 14:27–33).[10]

While I was teaching and speaking with my dear friend Tom White at the first Congress on Evangelism for the Soviet Union in 1990, a priest came forward for prayer. As we talked with him, we became disturbed both with his actions and with some of his statements. We decided to have a time of prayer with him. Instantly he broke out in harsh, rasping tongues. Feeling very uncomfortable with his tongues, we stopped him and asked some of our Russian friends to quiz him about his relationship with the Lord Jesus.

Suddenly he began to yell. He was uncontrollable. He was demonized. Later we found out he was a "Christian" occult practitioner, a Rasputinian-type minister who was disturbing the churches in the city with his evil practices. He had come to the session on spiritual warfare to disturb. Among other possible supernatural abilities, he had received the manifestation of tongues, but not from the Holy Spirit.

This, then, was part of Paul's concern for the spiritually gifted believers of Corinth.

2 CORINTHIANS

We next examine Paul's reference to the spirit world in 2 Corinthians. They are frequent (2 Cor. 2:4–11; 4:3–4; 6:14–18; 10:3–5; 11:3–4,13–15; 12:7–10). Some are very complex, requiring much more extensive commentary than space permits in this book. I begin with 2 Corinthians 2:4–11.

2 Corinthians 2:4–11

Before examining Paul's words in verses 4–11, I want to begin with a difficult counseling experience. A few years ago a Christian friend of mine confessed to me a homosexual encounter with another Christian leader. It was a one-occasion incident for both of them. Both had repented and had asked forgiveness from each other. Neither man was a homosexual, but because of reasons too complex to mention here, both men struggled with homosexual fantasies.

When he confessed his homosexual fall, he was so filled with shame he was suicidal. His body shook with wave after wave of shame and remorse. As I began to pray with him, he suddenly went into demonic manifestation. It was then we discovered he had been demonized since childhood, especially by sexual demons directly related to homosexual abuse he had suffered as a child.

In a situation like this, one faces a series of dilemmas demanding difficult decisions:

1. Does my friend tell his co-workers or keep his confession confidential? We decided to keep his story confidential.
2. Does he tell his wife? She is so sensitive to sexual matters he felt she could not handle the problem at least for the present. He would not tell her now

of his fall but would tell her in time if God clearly indicated he should do so.
3. He was so filled with shame and remorse, he felt unworthy to continue in the ministry. If he left the ministry his wife and children and friends would have to know why. We decided he should continue in the ministry for the present, if he felt secure in doing so. Why?

First, his problems were of demonic origin, i.e., his demonization from childhood. Second, he had lived a morally pure life up to and after that one fall. Third, he had been seduced by the other Christian leader. While my friend was responsible for his actions, he did not initiate the encounter.

We decided he could continue in the ministry, but under certain conditions. He was to be accountable to me for the immediate future. He would seek professional counseling immediately if his problems continued.

According to 2 Corinthians 2, something like this was going on with a believer in the church at Corinth. Paul had dealt with many of the Corinthians' problems in the letter we call 1 Corinthians. The present issue had to do with a man in the church who felt like the Christian leader I have described. His situation was worse, however. His sin was known to the entire church. He was under church discipline (2 Cor. 2:4–11).

Either the man in question is the same man Paul dealt with in his first epistle, the one who had been guilty of incest (1 Cor. 5:1—8:2), or he is a different person, one guilty of rude and critical behavior towards Paul himself. If so, it probably occurred during the recent visit by Paul to the church (2:1).[11] No one can be certain which view is the correct one, since Paul does not tell us. It was clear to the church whom Paul had in mind. We don't have to know to grasp the teachings given here.

I want to begin by focusing on verse 11. Paul writes,

In order that no advantage be taken of us by Satan; for we are not ignorant of his schemes.

These words form the conclusion to Paul's encouragement that the Corinthian believers forgive the repentant man, whoever he was. Thus the apostle pleads in verses 6–8, according to *The Amplified New Testament*.

For such a one this censure by the majority [which he has received is] sufficient [punishment].

So [instead of further rebuke, now] you should rather turn and [graciously] forgive and comfort and encourage [him], to keep him from being overwhelmed by excessive sorrow and despair.

I therefore beg you to reinstate him in your affections and assure him by your love for him.

Then the apostle concludes (after more comments in verses 9–10) with his rationale behind his appeal for forgiveness to be extended to the offender,

To keep Satan from getting the advantage over us; for we are not ignorant of his wiles and intentions.

To best grasp some of the impact of these words, we need to see them in light of several of Paul's important statements in verses 6–8. First, the offender's punishment has been sufficient. He needs no more (v. 6a). Second, the majority of the church had participated in this punishment (v. 6b), whatever it consisted of. Third, their duties towards the man now are to forgive, comfort, and encourage him. All three are necessary (v. 7a).

Assurance of forgiveness is the first need of this and every repentant believer. Only in that way could he continue in the church. Also only in this way could he finally accept himself and be able to accept God's forgiveness and their forgiveness. *Comfort* was the second need. He was so filled with shame and remorse that he was unable to function normally as a human being and a church member. Then he needed *encouragement*. They were to help relieve the deep depression he was in. Fourth, there was another and more serious danger they must face in his case, however. "Overwhelmed by excessive sorrow and despair" (v. 7b), implies that he could become suicidal.

When Paul warns here (v. 11) of Satan's schemes as they apply to the erring believer (Satan also had his "wiles and intentions" for the church in general), he could be implying at least two things. One, Satan set out to hinder the man's Christian life through his sin. Two, now that the man has repented, he wants to destroy his life.

In other words, Satan's first plan, his "roaring lion" tactic, failed. The brother has repented and broken off his sexual relationship with his father's wife—assuming that 1 Corinthians 5:1 is the background for the story. "Now we face Satan's angel-of-light approach," Paul says. "Satan will now try to imitate the convicting ministry of the Holy Spirit to entice our brother to self-destruct. Suicide is now a terrible possibility to him.[12]

"You must act, now! Assure him of your love, now! Comfort him, now! Encourage him, now! Please tell him that I also forgive him. I love and respect him. If you fail at this point, Satan will take advantage of us."

Along with our brief study of the specific case Paul is dealing with here we must ask ourselves what happens when believers and churches are ignorant of Satan's schemes? What does Paul say will happen?

Satan will "take advantage of us" Paul says (v. 11). This is why the Scriptures, both in precept and in case studies, outline in such detail Satan's deceptive schemes. Knowing Satan's schemes helps us to foil his plans against us and God's church.

Now we know how to reply to the continual barrage of statements by well-meaning brothers who tell us, "Don't focus on Satan's schemes. That will lead to devil phobia. All we need to do is focus on the person of Christ and he will protect us from all the schemes of the enemy. Isn't that what John tells us in 1 John 5:18?" (We will deal with 1 John 5:18 in a future study.)

Though I am not implying that Paul is dealing with the case of a demonized believer in this story, I must express anger with the cruel unfairness of many critics who undermine ministry to demonized Christians on this point. They claim that if Christians can be persuaded that they are demonized they will absolve themselves of responsibility for their wrong choices and can continue sinning. But this is absolute nonsense. I have never counseled a sincere believer who wanted to be demonized to escape responsibility for his sins. That would be like a person with a stress-related migraine headache wanting to be persuaded he had a brain tumor to escape his responsibility for his self-inflicted stresses leading to the migraine.

We dare not be ignorant of Satan's schemes against our churches and our own Christian life. Christian leaders are especially obligated to learn the world of evil supernaturalism. They must learn what demons really do, not what we say they do, or cannot do; nor must they be afraid of the demons as too many are.

It is difficult to say but it must be said: Western Christian leaders are the most resistant to teaching on the spirit world which takes them beyond the comfort zone of their unchallenged theological presuppositions. This is true within all branches of Western Christendom, from Roman Catholics and historic Protestants to Pentecostals and Charismatics. Two-thirds World Christian leaders are usually far ahead of Western leaders and much more open to change at this point. Perhaps this is one reason why their churches are rapidly growing while Western churches are rapidly declining. As Paul says elsewhere, "Consider what I say, for the Lord will give you understanding in everything" (2 Tim. 2:7).

2 Corinthians 10–13

Chapters 10—13 counter another one of Satan's major schemes, deception. We have seen deception as a key weapon of evil several times throughout this book. Here its specific goal is to undermine the credibility and spiritual authority of the apostle Paul. Paul portrays his role with the Corinthians as that of betrothing them to Christ (11:2); the undermining of his leadership through deception will corrupt the believers and lead them to receive "another Jesus," "a different spirit . . . a different gospel," in short to break their engagement to Christ (11:2–4).

While Paul was away from these believers, other ministers who thought themselves to be spiritually superior to the apostle gained acceptance within the church at Corinth. They apparently projected an attractive mix of qualities that won the allegiance of a significant number of believers there. These ministers spoke with eloquence (10:10–11; 11:5–6), were bold and quite dynamic in person (10:1–2, 9–11), may have claimed special authority from the "mother church" at Jerusalem (11:22), bore glowing letters of recommendation attesting to their effective ministries (10:18; 12:11; 3:1; 5:12), and testified to wondrous experiences of spiritual power and rapture (11:18 with 12:1–6, 11–13).

None of these qualities (if true) in and of itself would have been bad. But Paul's opponents boasted about them and compared themselves with Paul in such a way that he came out looking rather lame and ineffectual—in a word, weak. This putdown of Paul seized misunderstandings that developed between Paul and the congregation and misrepresented them as clear evidence that Paul was fickle (10:2; 11:10–11) and that he played favorites among his churches (11:7–11; 12:13)—in short, that he was not a truly spiritual or powerful leader (11:5; 12:11–13).

2 Corinthians 10:3–6

Paul's strategy for disarming this false interpretation of him and his apostolic ministry is a fascinating study in its own right.[13] Here I stress his portrayal of the battle for the mind that occurs—even for believers—particularly when deception is the enemy's weapon:

> For though we walk in the flesh, we do not war according to the flesh. For the weapons of our warfare are not carnal but mighty in God for pulling down strongholds, casting down arguments and every high thing that exalts itself against the knowledge of God, bringing every thought into captivity to the obedience of Christ, and being ready to punish all disobedience when your obedience is fulfilled. (2 Cor. 10:3–6, NKJV)

In denying that he walks "according to the flesh," Paul denies that his method of spiritual warfare is likewise merely human and carnal. Instead, his weapons of warfare are spiritual, "mighty in God." What are these weapons? Here Paul does not get more specific than referring to the various ways God's power works through him: not only in "signs and wonders and mighty deeds" (12:13), but also in faithful endurance through affliction and humiliation (11:23—12:13) and in apostolic correction (13:1–10). (We will explore a more detailed description of the believer's resources for spiritual warfare when we study Ephesians 6, chapter 51).

The target of his warfare here is deception, described as "strongholds,"[14] "arguments," "every high thing that exalts itself against the knowledge of God," "every thought" not now obedient to Christ (10:4–5). It is important to notice that deception involves erroneous ideas or ways of evaluating things, ways of thinking. These ways of thinking are false; here specifically because they are based on a false understanding of what characterizes a true minister of Christ (not a culturally and religiously appealing style, as the "false apostles" had, but faithfulness to the gospel). They are arrogant because they exalted certain stubborn preferences and desires above the truth of the gospel. And they are destructive because they prepare the way for "false apostles, deceitful workers" to abuse believers (11:13–21).

Thus the "strongholds" and "arguments" to be overcome by God's power are, in general, human evaluations, like Peter was guilty of (Matt. 16:21–23). They are ways of thinking and evaluating that are false, arrogant, and destructively disobedient. Here such strongholds of evil refer specifically to the attack on Paul's legitimacy as an apostle, but they include as well any form of reasoning, any attitude, and any way of thinking that "exalts itself against the knowledge of God," or "misbeliefs." Misbeliefs are beliefs that are untrue about oneself, others, or circumstances. They can become demonic strongholds against one's life, family, church, etc. It is important to note that these ways of thinking can become strongholds within a church through carnal leadership (whether clergy or laity); but of course, the ultimate source for all such deception is Satan (11:14–15).

2 Corinthians 12:7–10

Part of Paul's defense both of his ministry and of the truth of the gospel itself includes a proper understanding of what constitutes power and weakness in light of the gospel. He has been found wanting in the eyes of the culturally and religiously pretentious Corinthians, deceived as they were through strongholds of misbelief, because they do not see him as a powerful enough leader. Because their notion of power is idolatrous, Paul defends himself by showing that what they saw in him and despised as weakness is instead, in light of the gospel, the way God has chosen to manifest divine power.

It is with this context that we come to one of the most mysterious passages in the New Testament concerning the world of evil spirits and a Christian leader, 2 Corinthians 12:7–10. Here Paul recounts an exceptional visionary experience (something quite popular, it seems, with the opponents and their following in the church) and its painful results:

> And lest I should be exalted above measure by the abundance of the revelations, a thorn in the flesh was given to me, a messenger of Satan to buffet me, lest I be exalted above measure. (12:7, NKJV)

Scholars disagree as to what precisely this thorn was *(skolops tē sarki)*.[15] But I prefer one view offered by R. G. V. Tasker, which understands the expression to denote "something malignant . . . embedded in the [physical] flesh." Specifically, as the verse asserts, I believe Paul struggled with a continuing affliction that, while allowed—even willed—by God, was demonic in origin.

A reason why God would will, or even allow such an affliction emerges from considering Paul's temptation to be proud. Paul had received personal revelations from God perhaps as had no one else in the New Testament (12:1–4,7), and Paul himself knew of the temptation to pride that would come from others exalting him too much because of his having such experiences, or from his exalting himself. To Paul, humility is one of the greatest graces in the Christian life, and pride one of its greatest detriments. Pride is the root cause of all sin in heaven and earth.[16]

Thus the thorn "was given" to Paul. Clearly God is in view as the giver here; Satan is only the instrument, not the initiator of the action. The thorn, God's gift and solution to Paul's temptation to pride, was "a messenger of Satan," evidently a demon, since *angelos* is the Greek word for "messenger" or "angel."

A negative reaction to such a statement demonstrates ignorance of the spirit world. It reveals a lack of understanding of how demons, with God's full permission—even at His direction—can afflict the life of the most faithful, Spirit-filled believer. It also reveals difficulty in appreciating how God uses demons to accomplish mysterious, divine purposes in the lives of His children.

The effect of this affliction was to "buffet" the apostle, a term that, according to W. E. Vine, signifies striking with clenched hands or fist.[17] The NEB translates the word "to bruise me," and PHILLIPS grasps the imagery here by translating "to harass me." Harassment wears on the nerves, the emotions, and on the body, becoming oppressive and wearisome. Frustration, anger, loss of sleep, a sapping of strength and shortening of patience—this is what was happening to Paul.

Paul entreats the Lord three times for release. He does *not* resist the demon, or reject it, or command it. Instead, he addresses God, because God was *ultimately* responsible for this affliction, even as Paul was *initially* responsible, and Satan was *immediately* responsible.

Paul's experience points out the necessary balance to be struck in properly interpreting Scriptures such as Luke 10:19, Ephesians 6:16, 2 Thessalonians 3:3, and 1 John 5:18. These promises of victory over evil and the Evil One point toward both an ultimate victory and a progressive victory, one that we reach only after enduring faithfully satanic attacks, terrible struggles, sufferings, and afflictions in the present.

God first answered Paul's requests in the most effective and drastic response possible to pride-based, hidden sin: "No!" (12:9a). God's second answer was the promise of grace: in other words, "Though the demon will continue to work, I [God] will continue sustaining you by my grace." Interestingly, pride seems to be the only thing that directly hinders God's grace in our lives (cf. James 4:6,10; 1 Pet. 5:5–6). Thus God's provision for Paul included the "No" that checked the apostle's pride and the "Yes" that sustained him in fruitful service to God's glory. The "No" of discipline brought continuing weakness (12:9c); the "Yes" of grace brought power—purely divine power, able to be channeled through a vessel now prepared to be God's instrument and not exalt himself.

We are all aware of the craze for spiritual power among zealous Christians today. Does this desire originate in God, or in the flesh or the world? If Paul's experience is the model, what is the terrible price to be paid for becoming channels of uncorrupted divine power? Sufferings—terrible, agonizing, even demonic sufferings; not exactly what the power-crazed are seeking today.

Having received God's answer, Paul exults in all the forms of weakness God allows him to experience (these are primarily forms of public shame, felt keenly in a world whose main cultural values were honor and shame; cf. 11:23–33; 12:20–21;

4:8–11), because these are the situations through which God chooses to manifest His power. The greatest of these is, of course, the cross of Christ. While His work as the substitutionary sacrifice for all sin is His work alone, we who, along with Paul, wish to be channels of God's redemptive power in our world must first submit to the specific forms of the weakness of the Cross which God assigns to us. The strongholds of deception (10:4–5) against which Paul fights in these chapters are precisely a view of divine power and a view of what it means to be a "powerful leader" which reject anything having to do with an ongoing experience of Cross-weakness and which seek instead nothing but resurrection power on demand (cf. Matt. 16:21–25).

Paul's experience does not pit Cross-weakness against resurrection power; but it does establish the gospel relationship between the two: power manifested in and through weakness. Wherever religious people reject weakness, the power of which they boast and for which they crave is surely corrupted by carnality. Such a way of thinking is a stronghold needing to be pulled down. Only through increasing weakness does increasing power come—not exactly what the spiritually power-hungry of today are seeking.

A. W. Tozer summarizes the significance for us and for Paul of the "thorn in the flesh" in these words: "It is doubtful that God can use a man greatly, until He has hurt him deeply."

ROMANS

Paul's view of the spirit world as revealed in Romans, written soon after he wrote 1 and 2 Corinthians, is profound in quality if not extensive in quantity. He does not refer to Satan and his demons often in Romans, but when he does his teaching is helpful.[18]

Romans 8:15

Twice in our study of Romans 8 we encountered the spirit world. We first saw the spirit of slavery leading to fear mentioned in verse 15. We took this to be an evil spirit or evil spirits in general. Their work is to keep the unredeemed in bondage. They use fear. The unredeemed fear God in a negative sense. They do not want to live under His lordship or that of His Son. They prefer slavery to the spirit of this world. They fear losing control over their life. Unknown to them, they have already lost that control. While believing they are free and doing their own will, they actually are bound by this spirit of slavery and are doing its will (Eph. 2:2).

The same evil spirit(s) of bondage and fear seek to exercise control over the lives of Christians, also. In Romans 8:15 Paul says when we came to Christ, we did not receive the spirit of slavery leading to fear; we received the Holy Spirit.

If a spirit of slavery leading to fear is operating in our life, there is something wrong. The ideal is the Spirit of God who bears witness to our spirit that we are the children of God. Thus a Christian who lives in continual fear of anything, especially that he is not a child of God, is allowing a spirit other than the Holy Spirit to be in control at that point in his life. This does not necessarily imply demonization, though it may. It only means the wrong spirit is influencing the believer's life at that point. He needs to be set free from that other spirit, the spirit of fear.

Finally, in 8:15 Paul uses "again" because before coming to Christ we all lived in bondage to the spirit of slavery leading to fear. In Christ that spirit should have been exorcised, so to speak, from all of us. It can come back again, however. I have dealt with many fear spirits disturbing Christian lives.

We have received the "Spirit of adoption," Paul says. That Spirit continually tells us we are part of the family of God. Later Paul states that the Spirit even tells us we are God's heirs and fellow heirs with Christ (v. 17). He is the Spirit that enables each and all of us to cry out, "Abba! Father!"

As Paul ends his symphony of testimony to our conquering life in Christ, he lists many of the major enemies which are trying to hinder our lives as God's sons (v. 35). He then states we "overwhelmingly conquer through Him who loved us." Among these enemies he lists at least three spiritual beings or, more accurately, groups of evil, cosmic level spiritual majesties who seek to do us harm. They are angels, principalities, and powers (Rom. 8:37–38). They are totally ineffective in their efforts to "separate us from the love of God, which is in Christ Jesus our Lord," he affirms (v. 39; see chapters 10 and 11).

Romans 16:17–20

On one more occasion Paul returns to these spiritual-cosmic enemies. This time he bypasses the fallen angels, principalities, and the powers and speaks of the Evil One himself, by name. He calls him Satan, the Adversary (Rom. 16:20). To get the full impact we must examine this verse in the context of a recurring theme in Paul's epistles, one we have dealt with many times: deception.

Here in Romans 16:17–18 he warns:

> Now I urge you, brethren, keep your eye on those who cause dissensions and hindrances contrary to the teaching which you learned, and turn away from them.

> For such men are slaves, not of our Lord Christ but of their own appetites; and by their smooth and flattering speech they deceive the hearts of the unsuspecting.

These men are deceivers because they themselves have been deceived (1 Tim. 4:1f; 2 Tim. 3:13). They cause dissension in the church (Acts 20:28–31). They are evidently both power people and position people. The great danger of these teachers is that "by their smooth and flattering speech they deceive the hearts of the unsuspecting," Paul says. These men are skilled, not only in carefully choosing their words in order to deceive, but also careful in their manner of presentation. They skillfully and eloquently reason their way through their arguments. Thus they leave many people convinced of the correctness of their views. They win converts. Paul says they are deceivers, however. They thoroughly beguile the hearts of the unsuspecting. James Denney says unsuspecting means "guileless, suspecting no evil, and therefore liable to be deceived."[19]

Verse 20 is the key verse here, however. In verse 19 Paul speaks of wisdom "in what is good" and innocence "in what is evil." In so doing, he is evidently referring again not only to the evil men of verses 17–18 (see Eph. 6:12), but to the evil spirit who operates through them (2 Cor. 11:3–4,13–15; 1 Tim. 4:1f). Thus he says in verse 20, "and the God of peace will soon crush Satan under your feet."

This, says John Murray, is a clear reference to Genesis 3:15, the crushing of the head of the serpent by the seed of the woman. In this case, the seed of the woman is the church at Rome. God does the crushing. He does it under their feet, and he will do it soon. Murray says that "it is God who bruises Satan and establishes peace in contrast with conflict, discord, and division. He is, therefore, the God of peace."[20]

Murray then writes of the fight of faith. He says that "the final subjugation of all enemies comes within the horizon of this promise (cf. 1 Cor. 15:25–28). But we may not exclude the conquests which are the anticipations in the present of the final victory (cf. 1 John 2:14; 4:4)."[21]

In this verse Paul is saying that God is the only one who can truly bring peace to troubled believers because he is called "the God of Peace."[22] His major focus on presenting God here as the God of peace has to do with the activity of Satan, who is the true source of division and deception among the people of God. He alone takes away the peace God wants in our churches. Disunity is one of his most effective weapons against the church. It quenches the Spirit of peace. Thus in verse 20 Paul focuses on Satan himself. The only way peace can be restored or maintained, he says, is for God Himself to "crush Satan under your feet." What a verse! It takes us all the way back to the *protevangelium* of Genesis 3:15. God had promised that the seed of the woman, the Lord Jesus Christ, would crush the serpent's head. Here Paul latches onto that promise.

When Paul wrote Romans 16:20, Jesus had already crushed the head of Satan. Yet it still is necessary that God continue to crush him. It will be necessary in the eschatological future for God to do it again. That time it will be forever, however (Rev. 20:10). God will crush Satan but he will not now do it directly, as He did through the Christ event and as He will do in the future (Rev. 20:10). Now, He does it indirectly through the saints. Satan is to be crushed "under your feet," Paul says.

A quote from John Calvin beautifully ties together these three dimensions of the defeat of Satan. His comment is based on Romans 16:20.[23]

What follows, God shall bruise Satan, &c., is a promise to confirm them, rather than a prayer. He indeed exhorts them to fight manfully against Satan, and promises that they should shortly be victorious. . . . He then promises ultimate defeat, which does not appear in the midst of the contest . . . he does not speak only of the last day, when Satan shall be completely bruised; but as Satan was raging, as it were, with loose or broken reins, he promises that the Lord would shortly subdue him, and cause him to be trodden, as it were, underfoot. Immediately a prayer follows,—that the grace of Christ would be with them, that is, that they might enjoy all the blessings which had been procured for them by Christ.

Lord, may the day of Satan's final crushing come soon. In the meantime, may your churches learn to crush him under our feet! Amen.

THE PASTORAL EPISTLES

First and 2 Timothy, along with Titus, have been called the Pastoral Epistles since the 1700s.[24] They evidently were given that title because they are written to two pastors and deal with the life of local churches from a pastoral perspective. Not all agree the title fits the books, however.

Kenneth S. Wuest notes that "their contents revolve around three main subjects: false teaching, directions for church polity and adherence to the traditional doctrines of the Church." He then observes that "they are just as authoritative and helpful in the twentieth century local church, and as well adapted to meet its problems, as they were in the first century Church. . . . These epistles should be the handbook of every pastor in the administration of the affairs of the local church."[25]

1 Timothy 1

In two of the three pastorals, Paul deals with the activities of the spirit world as he instructs his leader, Timothy, in the affairs of church life.[26]

Paul first mentions the spirit world in 1 Timothy 1:18–20. These verses form the climax of the first chapter, a passage dedicated to the problem of false teachers within the church of Ephesus (v. 3f). Paul was probably writing from Macedonia, possibly from Philippi, about 65 A.D. The letter was written between Paul's first and second imprisonments (after his epistle to the Ephesians). Paul had evidently recently been in Ephesus with Timothy.

Given the confused spiritual nature of that large city, it is no wonder that religious teachers rose up in the church teaching error. Paul had warned the elders sometime before that this would happen after his departure (Acts 20:29–35). Paul said these problem teachers would come from outside the church: "savage wolves will come in among you, not sparing the flock" (v. 29); and from within it: "and from among your own selves men will arise, speaking perverse things, to draw away the disciples after them" (v. 30).

Both 1 and 2 Timothy reveal that Paul's predictions had already come true. The two letters make continual reference to deceived and deceiving teachers. Whether or not they were demonized, they were instruments of Satan in his war against the church at Ephesus.

First Timothy 1 reveals a strong spiritual warfare motif. After his usual greeting (vv. 1–2), Paul goes directly to the problem of false teachers and the need to teach teachers to teach the truth (vv. 3–11). He follows with his personal testimony of God's grace in his life (vv. 12–16). He ends with a magnificent burst of praise to God (v. 17).

Next Paul addresses himself directly to pastor Timothy (v. 18f). First Paul lovingly but firmly speaks directly to Timothy as a spiritual warrior and encourages him to "fight the good fight." Guthrie says the language of the charge Paul gives Timothy is military style. "It conveys a sense of urgent obligation. Timothy is solemnly reminded that the ministry is not a matter to be trifled with, but an order from the commander in chief."

In Guthrie's words, Paul continues the "military language; 'war a good warfare' as he assures his young lieutenant that the several prophecies confirming his calling will provide inspiration for the conflict that lies ahead."[27]

Paul next tells Timothy to keep faith and a good conscience (v. 19a). Guthrie comments:[28]

> Faith and a good conscience are three times conjoined in this Epistle (cf. 1:5 and 3:9), showing the inseparable connection between faith and morals. We need not restrict faith here to "right belief." It appears to epitomize the spiritual side of the Christian warrior's armor.

In the same verse Paul speaks of men who "have rejected and suffered shipwreck in regard to their faith" (v. 19b). Guthrie says that here "Paul's chief concern is to warn against the peril of neglect of conscience. The verb . . . *apōtheō* ["put away" in the KJV] implies a violent and deliberate rejection."[29]

While Paul begins his teaching using hope, faith, and love in chapter 1, faith early becomes the dominant word-concept. This is because he immediately begins his teaching-correcting focus referring to false teachers. He then spotlights two of the most dangerous false teachers, Hymenaeus and Alexander (v. 20).

A sincere youth filled with love for God and the truth as he saw it, Bill belonged to a church which placed a strong emphasis on certain spiritual experiences which led to power in life and ministry. He had "gone down under the power," he said, and had received powerful gifts from God.

He told me he had powers of precognition. He could read people's minds. He often knew future events in people's lives before they happened. While somewhat disturbed by this gift—that's what led him to seek me out—he felt it was from God. He was also one of the most sought-out Bible teachers in his group of believers, he said.

As I talked with him I knew these gifts were *not of God*. While God does give His people direct insight into people's needs and occasionally insight into possible future events,[30] such insights are not to give a person power and control over the lives of others, as this young man was using them.

That first counseling session with him is one I will never forget. As is so often the case, he came from a dysfunctional family. His parents separated while he was an adolescent and he had to live with his grandparents. They did not know how to affirm or support each other or their grandson. Bill grew up feeling unloved, rejected, and unaccepted. He also felt guilty for his family breakup though he had nothing to do with it.

Being part of a power-and-gift-driven group of believers coupled with his dramatic experiences with the Spirit had become his avenue of self-acceptance and acceptance by others. His "gifts" also gave him power over others, even though he was not fully aware of that fact.

After hearing his story I suggested we pray together.

It wasn't long before he was disturbed in his praying. He was blocked by inaudible words in his mind saying, "This is nonsense. This is crazy. Don't listen to this guy. He is nuts. He wants to take away your power. Get out of here."

He stopped praying and told me what he was hearing. I then began to lead him in a prayer of total commitment to the lordship of Christ over his spiritual life, his gifts, and his present and future ministry.

He began to pray, but suddenly stopped. He couldn't go on. As I looked at his face, it was twisted in obvious internal struggle. Something held him and he was trying to fight it off. Suddenly a voice spoke out, at first very low and very slowly, "I . . . won't . . . let . . . him . . . say . . . that . . . ."

Then louder this time, "I . . . won't . . . let . . . him . . . say . . . that."

Then louder and with great anger, "I WON'T LET HIM SAY THAT. HE BELONGS TO US. WE GIVE HIM POWER. THAT'S WHAT HE WANTS. LEAVE US ALONE. WE HATE YOU. YOU CAN'T HAVE HIM. HE IS MINE! HE IS MINE! HE IS MINE! THE HELL WITH YOU!"

I shut the angry spirit down. After a few counseling sessions Bill was totally free from the deceiving spirits.

Is this what Paul is dealing with in the case of Hymenaeus and Alexander? The problem with them, however, is, unlike Bill, they were too stubborn, deceived, or deceitful to allow Paul or others to deal with them. They refused to accept doctrinal correction. They did not want the spirit source of their gifts and teaching ministry to be tested. Thus Paul had to take the drastic action he describes in 1:20a. He delivered them over to Satan.

It is often assumed that the two men were apostates. This does not seem to be the case. Paul delivered them to Satan like he did the man at Corinth, not to send them to hell, but with remedial purposes: that they be taught not to blaspheme (v. 20b). What does Paul mean when he says he delivered Hymenaeus and Alexander "over to Satan, so that they may be taught not to blaspheme"?

Most commentaries connect this expression with the similar one in 1 Corinthians 5:5, and rightly so. What Paul meant by the expression there is probably what he has in view here (see chapter 49). Guthrie has a good word for us here:[31]

The concluding clause "that they may learn not to blaspheme" shows clearly that the purpose was remedial and not punitive. However stringent the process, the motive was mercy, and whenever ecclesiastical discipline has departed from this purpose of restoration, its harshness has proved a barrier to progress. But this is no reason for dispensing with discipline entirely, a failing which frequently characterizes our modern churches.

1 Timothy 3

Paul's next important reference to the spirit world is in 1 Timothy 3, one of the most shocking, disturbing, yet sobering treatments of the potential power of the spirit world over Christian leaders in all of Scripture. Here Paul writes about the person, qualifications, and conduct of bishops (vv. 1–7) or overseers, pastors, elders—the words are used interchangeably in the New Testament—and deacons (vv. 8–10,12–13; see Paul's message to the pastors of Ephesus in Acts 20:17–35).

In doing so he makes thirteen statements about what a pastor must be and do and what he must not be and do. In the midst of the negative statements, the "nots," he mentions the spirit world:

> . . . and not a new convert, lest he become conceited and fall into the condemnation incurred by the devil. (v. 6)

The "nots" in question here are a "not" of maturity and a "not" of character and conduct. The "not" of maturity is not to put a young, immature Christian in pastoral leadership.

I just told the story of Bill. He was what Paul calls here a "novice," which comes from the word *neophutos*. Vine says it means "newly planted . . . a new convert, neophyte, novice, 1 Tim. 3:6, of one who by inexperience is unfitted to act as a bishop or overseer in a church."[32]

We look next at the "not" of character and conduct. It focuses around the word "pride" or "puffed up" (v. 6).

"Puffed up" here is *tuphoō* in Greek. It means "to raise a smoke, to emit smoke," Wuest says.[33] That is a good metaphor for one who has a lot to say but little substance. This attitude can draw evil spirits like the dunghill draws flies. Sooner or later, this type of pastor will fall, the apostle says.

Paul continues with a shocking statement. He warns that pastors, through pride, can fall into the condemnation incurred by the Devil. This is almost too terrible to fully grasp. Each reader can use his own imagination to seek to understand what this warning implies.

Paul's next warning is even stronger. He says the pastor must not be a man with a poor reputation among those outside the church. Why? Paul answers, "So that he may not fall into reproach and the snare of the devil" (v. 7). The language here is almost too vivid for us to accept. We tend to look for ways to weaken this warning about pastors being snared by the Devil.

First, let's look at why Paul ties this in with the opinion of the pastor by those outside the church. Newport J. D. White writing in the *Expositor's Greek New Testament* says that Paul's words here are "one of the many proofs of his sanity of judgment." He continues saying that while they are "outside the church" they "have the law of God written in their hearts; and, up to a certain point, their moral instincts are sound and their moral judgments worthy of respect."[34]

White notes that there is

something blameworthy in a man's character if the consensus of outside opinion be unfavorable to him no matter how much he may be admired and respected by his own party . . . Thus to defy public opinion in a superior spirit may not only bring discredit on oneself and on the church, but also catch us in the devil's snare.[35]

Again Paul warns us that the Devil is directly involved in the life of pastors and churches. He faithfully attends church. He continually visits behind the closed doors of the pastor's office and home. He knows everything that is going on in both the private and public life of pastors.

In the warning before us Paul says, "So does the public!" They see the character flaws in the pastor's life, especially if he is a high visibility, Christian leader. They heap scorn upon Christians and churches who tolerate leaders whose life is not above reproach, and they begin to reproach Christians and Christian leaders in general.

What a description of the church today! When I look at and listen to many of the high visibility platform performers and their wives who present themselves as the prophetical voice of my Master's church today, I blush with shame. I want to run away and hide. The public laughs us to scorn. They see through the sham and hypocrisy. The Devil is delighted. This is just the trap he has set before the leader. The leader falls. Thus we have another Christian leader snared by and in bondage to the Devil at this point.

No pastor is automatically protected from the Wormwoods just because the Holy Spirit is in his life. The Holy Spirit is not a spiritual vacuum cleaner, automatically sucking up and expelling all the evil and evil spirits which may co-inhabit the temple of a person's body once He comes in to dwell. He lives in us with all the garbage of natural and supernatural evil and begins the on-going process of cleaning us out. This is what the Bible calls sanctification or holiness. While He doesn't like what He finds, He does not run away and hide because He finds it.

One Christian leader who came to me for help was battling with lust. When I first mentioned that demons of lust are occasionally involved in cases like this, he was shocked. Yet, while his theology would not permit this to be true, his experience told him otherwise.

He had tried everything else. Why not be open to the possibility his theology was not based on either correct interpretation of Scripture or valid experience? He allowed me to lead him in Warfare Praying and probing. Within minutes we were in contact with sexual demons that had been in his life since childhood, secretly damaging his relationship with his wife and inflaming him with fantasy desires for other women.[36] God set him free in that one session.

I am not affirming that all leaders who have fallen into "the snare of the Devil" are demonized. Most probably are not. All, however, are bound by the Devil at the point of direct contact where they were ensnared.

1 Timothy 4

Paul says more about false teachers demonically deceived and deceiving demonically in 1 Timothy 4:1. He writes, "But the Spirit explicitly says that in later times some will fall away from the faith, paying attention to deceitful spirits and doctrines of demons."

On first reading this verse seems more like a prediction for the future with no bearing on Paul's day or that of the church of Ephesus. While it does look to the future, its construction implies the problem already existed. Commentators see these verses two ways. First, the demonically deceived persons spoken about here, like those spoken of in 1 Timothy 1:3 and 2 Timothy 2:14, are teachers. The other view is that they are the victims of these demonized teachers. They have fallen away through responding to the spirits working through the demonized teachers.[37] I believe both are probably in view. We can make several observations with some degree of certainty. The origin of the apostasy described here is directly demonic. The persons involved are deceivers, without doubt, but they, in turn, were first deceived by the spirits.

The danger of any deception is directly proportionate to the seriousness of the matter about which one is deceived and how thorough is the deception. In this case the deception has eternal consequences: it could not be more serious. In this case the deception is complete: it could not be more dangerous. The deception takes doctrinal form. It is systematically organized so as to appeal to the minds of those who are the target of the spirits of deception. The deception causes the unwary to fall away from the faith, Paul says. The definite article is placed before the word *faith*. This then is apostasy, not just doctrinal error.

One cannot be an apostate from the Christian faith unless one has first embraced that faith. The apostasy begins as the unwary give heed to deceitful spirits. These spirits of error stand in direct contrast to the Holy Spirit (v. 1a). The deceiving teaching comes from the evil spirits. These are not Spirit-given doctrines, but spirit-given doctrines. Thus no two systems of doctrine could be farther apart in spite of the deceptive ability of the spirits to make them look similar.[38]

Paul then focuses on just one aspect of the form of spirit-given doctrinal error of his day (vv. 3–5). We have here "incipient Gnosticism with its dualistic view of matter (the physical world) which found its climax in the heretical teachers of the second century," Guthrie says.[39]

We seem to be living in the beginning of this fulfillment of predicted last days of demonic deception. The fastest-growing, pseudo-Christian demonic movement today is the New Age movement, a refined form of spirit world deception now infiltrating not only the world, but also our churches. Satanism, satanic cults, and some branches of witchcraft are the more gross manifestations of the same spiritual deception sweeping our land today. Hinduism, Islam, and materialism as a religion are rapidly growing worldwide. All this is possible evidence that we are in the *last* of the Last Days.

1 Timothy 5

Paul's next section deals with potential demonic problems in the life of women. They, too, are Christian leaders. The story is found in 1 Timothy 5:9–15.

In 5:3–8 the apostle is writing about Christian widows in general.[40] Beginning with verse 9 he speaks of widow leaders, a select group of elderly women evidently financially supported by the church. They had special duties in the church reserved only for certain of the oldest widows, not for younger ones.

In contrast to the elderly widows of verses 9–10, the widows of verse 11 are specifically called "younger widows." Wuest says the word "young" as it is used here simply means young, not just under sixty years of age (v. 9). These young women need to be cared for by the church; yet they are never to be put into the special ministry order along with the older widows because the latter take vows of celibacy which younger women should not do.

The reference to marriage in verse 11f is not meant to speak negatively of a widow's natural desires for remarriage. Paul has something else in mind. He is speaking of younger widows who really want to remarry. Yet, because they are in dire financial need, they want to join the group of full-time widows supported by the church. "No," Paul says. "When the right man comes along, they will desert their post and get married. Don't take any younger women into the order of celibate widows."

In verses 14b and 15, Paul returns to his warnings in chapter 3 about potential demonic involvement in the disorderly life of Christian workers, in this case women. Paul expresses his concern that Christian widows who are involved in special service to the church must be careful not to give the enemy an occasion to bring the church into reproach. He says this has already happened. He goes so far as to say that some women leaders have already turned aside "to follow Satan" (v. 15).

The word translated "enemy" here is *antikeimai,* which means "to lie opposite, to be set over against," Vine says. He comments that "the present participle of the verb with the article, which is equivalent to a noun, signifies an 'adversary.' "[41] Here the word can be taken for either men or the supreme adversary mentioned in the next verse, Satan, or both. In the latter sense, which is probably what Paul has in mind, it would be Satan in opposition to the church. He is seeking to cause scandal in the church, one of his most successful tactics.

Verse 15 takes what we have just written about verse 14 and directly applies it to the Devil and his control over the women mentioned in verses 11–13. The NEB comes right to the point: "For these have in fact been widows who have taken the wrong turning and gone to the devil." Depending on how far into sin they have gone and the circumstances in which they are living in sin,[42] some of them *could* have become demonized. I have personally dealt with women who are.

With this we bring to a close Paul's references to the spirit world in 1 Timothy. As we turn to 2 Timothy, the spiritual warfare motif continues, especially in relationship to Christian teachers.

2 TIMOTHY

Someone once remarked that 2 Timothy is the saddest of all Paul's epistles. Paul is in prison. He knows his end is near. He is tired and lonely. In his own words, written to the Philippians a few years before, he is longing to depart and be with Christ, for that is much better (Phil. 1:23). Paul writes of the joys of his Christian life and ministry (Phil. 1:1–12). Part of Paul's joy is found in the faithfulness of his beloved son Timothy to whom he addresses this his last letter. No man was more faithful to Paul and to Christ than Timothy (Phil. 2:19f).

We will look primarily at 2 Timothy 2:26. The context is again doctrinal error (v. 14f). He even mentions (v. 17) one of the same men, Hymenaeus, first mentioned in 1 Timothy 1:20. Thus Hymenaeus was still alive and as bad as ever. His deliverance over to Satan—whatever it was—that he learn not to blaspheme was unproductive. It failed. Again Paul knew failure in spiritual warfare just as we all do (see 1 Thess. 2:18; 3:5).

Here are Christians—teachers who are teaching doctrinal error. Here the errors are specifically mentioned as having to do with confusion concerning the Resurrection (v. 18). The words "gone astray" in verse 18a is the verb *astocheō,* "to miss the mark." Paul uses it here and in 1 Timothy 1:6 and 6:21. He writes that these men denied a future resurrection.

Guthrie says that this

shows the serious extent of their error, for this is a basic element of Christian faith, as Paul so forcibly brings out in 1 Corinthians 15. In fact, 1 Corinthians 15:12 shows that at Corinth some were denying the reality of the resurrection altogether, and the present allusion must be similarly understood.[43]

He next states that by "treating the resurrection as a spiritual experience, these teachers had planned to dispose of it. No wonder they overthrow the faith of some, since Christianity without a resurrection ceases to be a living faith."[44]

Here are Christian teachers in bondage to Satan (v. 26b). First, they are ensnared, trapped by the Devil. This involves strong control over their mind, emotions, and will. This is the third time Paul uses this expression in the Pastorals (1 Tim. 3:6; 6:9). Not only are they trapped, but Satan is holding them captive. Guthrie writes,[45]

> Graphic words are used to describe the reclamation of the devil's captives. That they may recover themselves (ananēphō) means literally "that they may return to soberness" . . . as in the case of intoxication the devil's method is "to benumb the conscience, confuse the senses and paralyze the will."

Guthrie next states that "the metaphor becomes mixed when the snare of the devil is introduced (see 1 Tim. 3:7; 6:9). . . . The devil is portrayed in a double role. He is both intoxicator and captivator of men's minds. The second vivid verb, zōgreō (taken captive), means 'to catch alive'; it is used elsewhere in the Greek Testament only in Luke 5:10 where it occurs in Jesus' promise to Peter that he would catch men."[46]

While there has been some debate about whose will is involved in verse 26, God's or the Devil's, Guthrie says the context indicates it is the Devil's will, not God's will. He remarks that "it is impossible to have Paul saying the devil holds them captive to do God's will. It is the devil's will which they are doing, and that is Paul's point."[47]

We were in a tiny jungle village where a small church was flourishing. A Christian school there was directed by a beautiful, Colombian young lady, a recent graduate from Bible school.

The former church pastor, a modern Hymenaeus, still lived in town. Seduced by lying spirits, he was teaching doctrines of demons. The believers had expelled him from his pastoral position. In time, however, due primarily to his amazing "gifts" including healings and miracles, he was able to work his way back into leadership. Soon the faithful but less gifted pastor was forced out of his pastoral role. The miracle man took over.

Months went by. The church grew. The man of spiritual power drew people from the surrounding communities. Soon he had the fastest growing church in the entire jungle area. One Sunday, the people gathered for worship. The power pastor did not show up. When they went to his house, he was gone. So was the lovely, faithful school director. The miracle worker had seduced her both spiritually and sexually. The elders found out that she had been his mistress for some time.

The former faithful pastor returned to pick up the pieces. In time it was discovered that the power man had overpowered even more women. Half a dozen of the young girls in the church were pregnant. The "power" worker was the father of all their illegitimate children. What a shipwreck Satan makes of the life of deceived men and women, even Christian leaders, who refuse to be governed solely by the Word of God (2 Tim. 2:15)!

50

Colossians and Ephesians

COLOSSIANS

Colossians, along with Ephesians, contains some of the most profound teachings on the believer's warfare with the powers found anywhere in the New Testament. Both would validate C. S. Lewis' claim "Enemy occupied territory, that is what this world is. Christianity is the story of how the rightful King has landed and is calling us all to take part in a great campaign of sabotage."[1]

Because Ephesians and Colossians cover similar issues in spiritual warfare and because Ephesians deals with those issues in greater depth, we will save our major study of their common themes for our studies in Ephesians. Colossians does, however, have its own unique contribution to make on the warfare between the church and high level cosmic evil principalities and powers. It was written about the same time as Ephesians, being one of the prison epistles.

Colossians was written to combat what has come to be called "the Colossian Heresy," about which there is no end of debate among commentators.[2] Bruce says that although we have no formal exposition of the Colossian heresy, we may reconstruct it with fair accuracy from Paul's treatment of it.[3]

The main focus of the heresy was on the activity of high level, evil cosmic spirit powers. The Jewish element was the belief these personal powers originally gave the Jewish law. United with Jewish legalism, keeping of sabbaths, and asceticism, this became the Jewish side of the Colossian heresy. The Hellenistic element was the belief that these principalities and powers were the dominant elemental spirits of the universe. They were the lords of the planetary spheres. They were held to be part of the divine essence.

Christ was inferior to these principalities and powers, it was held. He had to relinquish "successive portions of His power to these planetary lords as he passed through their spheres; one after the other, on His way to earth," Bruce says. Also, Christ was believed to be inferior to the powers because they caused His suffering and death.

Finally, all of this "was presented as a form of advanced teaching for the spiritual elite." Christians were told they must pursue various steps toward "progressive 'wisdom' (Greek *sophia*) and 'knowledge' (Greek *gnōsis*) to explore the hidden mysteries by a series of successive initiations until they attained perfection *(teleiōsis)*," Bruce says. This has been called incipient Gnosticism.[4]

With this background it is not difficult to see why the message of Colossians fits well into our spiritual warfare study. Paul's emphasis on Christ alone and salvation found only in Him also becomes more meaningful. His stress on Christ as Lord over the principalities and powers becomes significant. So does his statements that this syncretism brings men under bondage to demonic powers.

The focus of the entire epistle centers on combating those doctrines of demons. Carson says that since Paul has only one answer to the erroneous teaching and "that is the Person and work of Christ," we get the

high Christology of the Epistle. In His Person Christ stands supreme and unique. He is no emanation of deity, for in Him the fullness of the Godhead dwells. He is the beloved Son. He is the image of the invisible God. Thus in virtue of His divine nature He is above and beyond every angelic power.[5]

Colossians 1

O'Brien calls verses 15–20 of chapter 1 "the majestic hymn about the lordship of Christ."[6] The interesting thing for our study is the focus on the Lord Jesus as Lord over all the powers (vv. 16,20).

In verse 16 Paul writes (or sings):

> For by Him all things were created,
> both in the heavens and on earth,
> visible and invisible,
> Whether thrones or dominions
> or rulers or authorities—[7]
> All things have been
> created by Him and for Him.

O'Brien gives an excellent word about this beautiful, Christ-exalting verse.[8] He says that "lest there should be any doubt as to the superiority of the Son to other spiritual beings Paul stresses that He is not only the agent of the creation of the visible world, but also of the invisible world of heavenly beings." He next states that these "beings who comprise both the angels of God and also the devil and his angels—Paul uses synonymous terms here without giving a precise classification— are all alike due to the creative power of the Son, and so are subject to His control." He then declares that in "fact He is not only the agent, but the very goal of their creation. They exist with a view to His glory, and so are subservient to His eternal purpose."

What majestic words! What need is there, then, of cosmic spirits or angels to work on our behalf, when we are complete in Christ? This becomes Paul's theme in 2:2. He speaks of the mystery of God which is "Christ Himself." Nowhere else in the entire New Testament are so many and so powerful descriptions of our blessed Lord heaped together, so to speak, in one tiny book.

Colossians 2

With all this great Christological teaching as his foundation, Paul then begins to warn in more detail about the demonic teaching with which they were struggling. He focuses on four primary sources of danger, all involved in the Colossian heresy.

First, he warns of the danger of "philosophy" (2:8a). This is the Greek word *philosophia*. The particular "philosophy" at Colossae was, as we have seen, a mixture of Jewish and Greek esoteric-mystic ideas. To this they had added Christ and Christian ideas. The result was a confusing hodgepodge of Greek, Jewish, and Christian concepts, a terrible syncretism, similar to that still faced by the church of Asia today.

Second, he warns of "empty deception" (2:8b). The grammatical construction of the sentence reveals that Paul is saying the philosophy they were being seduced by was "empty deception." Philosophy as a way to God is insufficient, empty, and deceiving (see 1 Cor. 1:18–31).

Third, he warns of "the tradition of men" (v. 8c). Again the focus goes back to philosophy. It is of human, not divine, origin. Thus it is totally ineffective to help them live lives pleasing to God. O'Brien says Paul exposes it as "a hollow shame, having no true content, seductive and misleading."[9]

Finally he warns of "the elementary principles of the world."[10] Literally, it is "according to the elements (*stoicheion,* "one of a row, or series"[11] "of the world and not according to Christ" according to the *Greek-English New Testament.* This is another strictly Pauline concept. Assuming Paul wrote Hebrews, he uses it again in Hebrews 5:12 in a positive but also in a critical sense. There it refers to "the elementary principles of the oracles of God."

In Galatians 4:3,9 Paul uses the phrase exactly as in Colossians, but also, as in Colossians, in a totally negative sense. The "elementary things" (called "things" in Galatians, "principles" in Colossians) are "weak and worthless," Paul says (Gal. 4:9). They are part of the world system. Worst of all they hold one in spiritual bondage, he states (Gal. 4:3). They cause one to be enslaved all over again (Gal. 4:9). Thus, they are demonic. They come from the no-gods (4:8).

This is the sense in which Paul uses "the elementary principles of the world" in Colossians, also. Thus, though Colossians was written years after Galatians, Paul still holds the same unchanged negative view of these worldly, binding, enslaving, demonic "principles" of the world (Col. 2:8,10).

What occurred with the Galatians years before is now occurring with the Colossians, but even worse. They have relapsed into slavery to the high-level, evil cosmic principalities and powers of evil which control the unholy mixture of philosophy and religion found at Colossae. It is a demonically controlled, mystical, religious system which will separate them from Christ.

O'Brien takes the commentators to task who see the *stoicheia* as simply ideas or "principles." He says that Paul speaks of them in a "rather personal fashion (at Gal. 4:3,9 they seem to be conceived of as angelic powers), and in contexts where other personal beings or forces are referred to (at Colossians 2:10, 15, demonic principalities desire to exercise their tyranny over men)."[12] As a missionary I have had to help contemporary, Colossian-type believers recognize and break similar bondage.

This deception is the kind the believers at Colossae were experiencing. Paul wrote to warn them. But he also wrote to teach them that all the wisdom and power they sought was already theirs in Christ "in whom are hidden all the treasures of wisdom and knowledge" (2:3). Indeed, "in Him all the fulness of Deity dwells in bodily form," Paul tells them (2:9).

The phrase "in bodily form" was directed against one of the most dangerous errors of the mystery—semi-Gnostic—spiritual pursuits in which they were entangled. That was a negative view of the human body. Because of this, the resurrection of the body was denied. It is probably with this in mind that Paul stresses so strongly the Lord's bodily resurrection in 2:12–13 (see 1 Cor. 15:1f).

As Paul brings his critique of the mystic practices at Colossae to a close, he mentions the work of God in Christ which dealt the first blow to the believers' fear of and bondage to principalities and powers. He says two things. One, the debt we owed to the broken law of God has been "nailed . . . to the cross" (2:14). God, in Christ, not only canceled out the debt we owed, He has even destroyed the certificate containing the record of our sin-debt (v. 14a).

Two, the power of the principalities and powers over us has been removed (v. 15). O'Brien says God did the above because, quoting F. F. Bruce, the possession of this "damning indictment kept us in their grip." He next comments on v. 15b: "Having divested the principalities and powers of their dignity and authority on the cross, God exposed to the universe their utter helplessness." He then says "by putting them on public display God exposed the principalities and powers to ridicule." Finally he remarks, "this open manifestation of their being divested of dignity and authority only serves to demonstrate more clearly the infinite superiority of Christ."[13]

With this as his truth base, Paul then begins a long section outlining some of the practical steps they must take, first to free themselves from bondage to "the elementary principles of the world" (2:16–23), then to be totally Christocentric (3:1f), and finally to live out in their daily life the fullness of Christ (3:18f). All believers *are* free from the fear of bondage to all demonic principalities and powers.

This book, along with Ephesians, expresses Paul's deepest insights into the dangers the religious spirit world present to the children of God and the great treasures which are ours in Christ. May we learn to be believers who are totally committed to Christ and "the mystery of Christ" for which Paul was in prison when he wrote (4:3). May we also understand that, in spite of their incredible might, these evil cosmic powers have been totally defeated by Christ in our behalf (2:9–23).

EPHESIANS

Paul's Epistle to the Ephesians is one of the great theological masterpieces of the ages, even from a non-Christian perspective. Our study of the planting of the church at Ephesus in Acts 19 is the background against which this epistle must be interpreted. We discovered that Ephesus was the center of all of Asia Minor of occultism, spirit magic, and the worship of the goddess Artemis. Demonic powers saturated the city and surrounding regions. This helps us understand why Ephesians contains a greater number of references to spiritual power and the spiritual warfare with these evil cosmic powers than any other book of its size in the New Testament.

Ray Stedman in a Bible study on Acts 19 entitled "Off Witchcraft"[14] describes Ephesus in the following manner. It was

> a city in the grip of superstition, fear, demonism and darkness. It was a city devoted to sex and to religion—in other words it was the San Francisco of the Roman empire . . . it was a center for witchcraft, superstition, demonism. A weird mixture of black arts, worship of demons, astrology, occult practices of various kinds . . . (which) filled this city with priests, magicians, witches, warlocks and quacks of every kind.

The Ephesian Christians were converted to Christ out of a terrible atmosphere of demonic bondage. Some continued their occult involvement even after they came to know Jesus as Savior. When the power encounter with the sons of Sceva occurred, the picture began to change (Acts 19:13f). The new converts began to break with their occult-magical practices. Acts 19:18 tells us "Moreover many of those who had become believers came and openly confessed that they had been using magical spells" (NEB). This is the language of *power encounter.*

In Ephesians Paul combines teaching on *power encounter* with *truth encounter.* As was Paul's custom, he contextualizes his teachings to fit the life situation of those to whom he is writing. Arnold refers to the *Zeitgeist,* the cultural atmosphere of the city and the age concerning the spirit world.[15] "One of the distinctive traits of the early Jewish *Zeitgeist* is the fear of demons." Arnold quotes Charlesworth on the demonology of the Pseudepigrapha:[16]

> The earth is full of demons. Humanity is plagued by them. Almost all misfortunes are because of the demons; sickness, drought, death, and especially humanity's weaknesses about remaining faithful to the covenant. The region between heaven and earth seems to be almost cluttered by demons and angels; humanity is often seen as a pawn, helpless in the face of such cosmic forces . . . .

Arnold comments that "the Pseudepigrapha thus accurately represents the *Zeitgeist* of Paul's time and also for the composition of Ephesians."[17] This is another important clue to Paul's focus on the spirit world in Ephesians.

Ephesians 1

Paul begins with his inspiring portrait of believers as the elect of God. This is *truth encounter,* which must always accompany power encounter. In the apostle's teaching on election, he enters the spirit world in his references to the heavenlies (1:3, 20) and to "the summing up of all things in Christ" (v. 10).

He also comes forth with his first power concepts. The first is his reference to the Holy Spirit (vv. 13–14, 17). As Arnold says, "Ephesians highlights the role of the Holy Spirit, who is frequently represented as the agent of divine power . . ."[18] (see also 2:18, 22; 3:5, 16; 4:3–4, 30; 5:18; 6:17–18). Thomas H. McAlpine quotes Ernst Kasemann who says that

> any version of Christianity is incredible which, while professing belief in the Holy Spirit, fails to carry His power and victory into every deepest hole and corner. What our world needs everywhere today is this exorcism of its demons. For it is only when the heavens open and the Spirit descends that God's good creation comes into being and continues in being.[19]

Paul begins his entrance into the cosmic realm where demonic powers are centered in verse 3. He writes that God "has blessed us with every spiritual blessing in the heavenly places in Christ." God's blessings are "in the heavenlies," *en tois epouraniois.*

This problematic expression is used only by Paul in the New Testament, five times in Ephesians (1:3, 20; 2:6; 3:10; 6:12).[20] Lincoln says that

> It is the spiritual world above . . . seen in the perspective of the age to come, which has been inaugurated by God by raising Christ from the dead and exalting Him to His right hand (1:20) . . . Yet, since heaven is also still involved in the present evil age, there remain hostile powers in the heavenly realms (3:10; 6:12) until this consummation of the age to come.[21]

This is the first spiritual warfare suggestion in Ephesians. At first, verse 3 appears to have no relationship with spiritual warfare. When we read about "the heavenlies" again in 1:20, 3:10, and 6:12, we realize it does. In this context the expression "in Christ" refers to our being "incorporated into the exalted Christ as . . . (our) representative, who is Himself in the heavenly realm," Lincoln summarizes.

We are in Christ. Positionally, Christ is exalted to the Father's right hand, in the heavenlies. Since we are seated with Him, we too, positionally, are in the heavenlies, co-regents with Him over the powers (2:6). The rulers and authorities which oppose both Christ and us are located in the same heavenlies. From there they wage war against us (6:12). As the church we are to declare to these evil spirit authorities "the manifold wisdom of God" (3:10), Paul says. God's wisdom enthrones Christ as Lord of the universe and brings believers into union with Christ, empowering us with Christ's fullness (1:23; 2:6; 3:10, 6:10–20).

Who said spiritual warfare is only a peripheral aspect of God's redemption plan in the Epistles? Here is spiritual warfare, at the heart, so to speak, of God's great plan of salvation history in Christ. Here is Christ exalted in the heavenlies. Here is also the believer exalted with Him in the heavenlies. Here also are demonic powers warring against Christ and His church in the same heavenlies. Here is the church on earth and in the heavenlies declaring the wisdom of God to the principalities and powers in the heavenlies. This is high level, cosmic, spiritual warfare.

As we move on to Ephesians 1:20, we must see this passage in the context of verses 15–22, Paul's prayer for his Ephesian brethren. We only have space to focus on verse 19 and its relationship to verse 20.

Paul prays the church will experience the surpassing greatness of God's power" demonstrated by His raising Jesus from the dead (v. 19). The surpassing greatness of God's power in raising Jesus from the dead was for the purpose of seating Him "at His right hand in the heavenly places" (v. 20)—the place of absolute power.

Lincoln calls this "cosmic Christology." He says that "Christ's resurrection and exaltation mean that the center of gravity in God's cosmic drama of salvation has moved from the realm of earth to that of heaven." He continues saying that this event shifted the power structures of this world. Paul used Psalms 110:1 and 8:6 in 1 Corinthians 15:25–27 in speaking of Christ's rule at history's end. In Ephesians he adapts and applies them to Christ's present status as the last Adam who is already Lord over the cosmos. This means that as "head over the cosmos Christ fills it with his sovereign rule. This same note is struck later when Christ is said to have 'ascended far above all the heavens in order that he might fill the cosmos.' "[22]

Christ is "head over all things," Paul says (v. 22). While this includes His headship over the powers, it naturally and especially includes the church "which is His body" (v. 23) and His fullness (1:23; 4:13; Col. 2:9–10; John 1:16). Thus he states that Jesus is "head over all things to the church" (v. 22b; 4:15 and 5:23). He is its beginning (v. 2:20b), its life, and the goal of its growth (4:15–16).

The *church's greatest sin* is its resistance to His sole headship. While we are co-regents with Him over the powers, we are not co-heads with Him over the church.

All occurs ultimately for the benefit of God in Christ in His church. The readers of Ephesians are to see themselves as a people of destiny, part of a universal church whose head, Christ as Lord, exercises all power on its behalf. He has gifted that church with all it needs to function and to grow. In the unity of the Spirit it will grow up in all things in Christ. It will build itself up in love. It will succeed in its world mission because its head is the cosmic head of heaven and earth (Eph. 4:1–16).

In Ephesians 4:1–16 Paul says Christ has gifted His church with all it needs to function and to grow (vv. 15–16). In the unity of the Spirit (vv. 1–6) it will grow up in all things in Christ. It will build itself up in love. It will succeed in its world mission because its head is the cosmic head of heaven and earth (vv. 1–16).

As a result we have two crucial lines of truth in Ephesians, which must be stressed here. First there is the authority of the exalted cosmic Christ. Second is the authority of the exalted believers in union with their exalted Christ (Eph. 2:1–10). This is Paul's burden in Ephesians (1:18—2:10). The apostle sums it up in 2:4–6:

> But God, being rich in mercy, because of His great love with which he loved us, even when we were dead in our transgressions, made us alive together with Christ (by grace you have been saved), and raised us up with Him, and seated us with Him in the heavenly places, in Christ Jesus.

Seated with the cosmic Christ, sharing his throne, is the cosmic Christian. As the cosmic Christ, He is Lord. He is God. As the cosmic Christian in Christ, I am a man of cosmic power. It is His power which operates within me.

As the cosmic Christ, His sphere of operations is the entire universe. From the perspective of Scripture, however, He is seen operating exclusively with reference to humanity. Thus His operations in the heavenlies and on earth all relate to salvation history—His love for humanity.

As a cosmic Christian my sphere of operations is the same as His, that is, in the heavenlies and on earth. I am seated with Him in the heavenlies; I am also indwelt by Him on earth.[23]

This same apostle had already written elsewhere that "we are God's fellow workers" (1 Cor. 3:9). To work with Him, we need to share both His power and His authority. Otherwise, with nothing but natural power, we are called to do a super-natural work opposed by supernatural enemies. If that be the case, let's close shop. It cannot be done.

This is not what God has done, Paul says. He has made available to us the "surpassing greatness of His power towards us who believe" (Eph. 1:19).

God has given us a vivid demonstration of that surpassing greatness of power *(dunamis)* by the operation of the might *(kratos)* of His strength *(ischus)* which he operated *(energia)* in Christ, raising Him from the dead far above all rule *(archē)* and authority *(exousia)* and power *(dunamis)* and lordship *(kurios)* "and every name that is named, not only in this age, but also in the one to come" (vv. 19–21).[24]

I reproduce McAlpine's excellent table of all of the major power words found in the New Testament.[25] While other writers, notably Wink[26] mention power words in the New Testament, McAlpine and Arnold[27] restrict their studies to the power words which refer to high-level cosmic powers that operate above and through human power persons and power structures in society. So do I, because I believe that is Paul's approach in Ephesians and Colossians. This is also the primary approach of the other New Testament writers.

McAlpine's study of four of the nine power words used by Paul in Ephesians 1:19,21 is excellent.[28] We will focus only on those in verse 21. In Greek they are *archē*, ruler, often translated "rule" in the abstract, as here in verse 21; *exousia,* "authority;" *dunamis,* "power;" *kuriotēs,* "dominion." He misses the fifth power word, however, as do many scholars. It is *onoma,* "name."

As we look at the five power words, it is difficult to know specifically what Paul has in mind in verse 21. Each word has a variety of uses in the New Testament and are used of human as well as non-human personalities. They may even be used in an impersonal sense as reflecting a certain *Zeitgeist,* as mentioned earlier.

They are occasionally used of good cosmic beings—God and angels. Yet when we look at Paul's negative, restrictive use of these concepts in Ephesians and Colossians, we must see the principalities and powers as primarily evil. It is the believer's power-encounter warfare with evil, cosmic level principalities and powers that Paul has in view. Thus, we should probably view them as evil powers in verse 21 also.

Paul is *not* demythologizing the language of power in his use of these words here. There is no indication he wants to remove personal cosmic powers, either the elect angels or fallen angels, from our thinking, causing us to focus exclusively on human powers and social structures as some scholars affirm.

Exactly the opposite is true. In Paul's writing we see evil, personal, high-level cosmic powers manipulating men and their social institutions towards ultimate satanic evil. Human powers are not in view except as they are the visible manifestations of cosmic powers manipulating them towards evil demonic goals.

Thus in chapter 1 Paul takes the believers into the "heavenlies" (v. 3). He reveals that these heavenlies represent not only the sphere of their Christian life in Christ (vv. 13–18), and the locale in which Christ is enthroned as Lord, but also the locale of the activity of the powers (vv. 19–23).[29]

Ephesians 2

The first specific reference to the principalities and powers as evil is in 2:2. Here Paul says,

> in which you formerly walked according to the course of this world, according to the prince of the power of the air, of the spirit that is now working in the sons of disobedience.

To understand verse 2 we must begin with verse 1. There the apostle presents a shocking overview of the spiritual state of the Gentiles in particular and of all men in general who are outside of Christ (vv. 1–3).[30] After stating they were formerly "dead in trespasses and sins" in verse 1, he begins verse 2 with "in which you formerly walked."

Ephesians 2:2 is unique in the New Testament. The words *ton aiōna tou kosmou* are literally, "the age of this world." Paul says "the age of this world is evil" because it obeys "its unseen ruler (who is still operating in those who do not respond to the truth of God)" (PHILLIPS).

A literal translation of the second part of verse 2 is,

> according to the ruler of the authority of the air, of the spirit now operating in the sons of disobedience.

Arnold comments on this last phrase that not only are "non-believers pulled in to following all of the corrupt traits of this present age, but they are described as actually inspired and energized by personal evil forces." He then states that these forces "are directed by *ton archōnta tes exousias tou aēros*" (the ruler of the authority of the air).

Arnold states that "the term *archōn* is yet another expression for a personalized evil force." He concludes that the author is here, therefore, "referring to a chief or leader among the angelic powers. It may be a reference to the devil himself (cf. 4:27; 6:11) since the term is in the singular and because of the prominence ascribed to this being."

I assert that this is certainly the case. As Arnold himself points out the "Synoptics describe the devil as the *archōn ton daimonion* (Matt. 9:34; Mark 3:22; Luke 11:15) [the ruler of the demons]. John refers to the devil as the *archōn tou kosmou toutou* (John 12:31; 14:30; 16:11)" [the ruler of this world].[31]

Lincoln remarks that for Paul this age had its own god (2 Cor. 4:4). Thus there is a personal power center to the power of evil. Paul calls him "the prince of the power of the air." What does this mean? Lincoln writes that

> elsewhere in Ephesians, hostile powers inhabit the heavenly realms (cf. 3:10; 6:12). This notion has its background in Old Testament and Jewish thought where angels and spirit powers were often represented as in heaven (e.g., Job 1:6; Dan. 10:13, 21; 2 Macc 5:2; 1 Enoch 61:10; 90.21, 24); it was also developed in Philo (cf. De Spec. Leg. 1.66; De Plant. 14; De Gig. 6, 7).[32]

Lincoln then says the two terms, "the air" and "the heavenly realms," must refer to the same realm. Both are inhabited by "malevolent agencies." He says if there is any difference, perhaps "the 'air' indicates the lower reaches of that realm and therefore emphasizes the proximity of this evil power and his influence over the world."[33]

The problem some commentators have with the idea of the air above the earth, as the abode of Satan and evil spirits is again, a world view problem. How else are we to visualize the abode of these personal, but invisible beings? They are always seen as above the earth yet in close proximity to the earth.

Arnold affirms that "the air was regarded as the dwelling place of evil spirits in antiquity" and that the "air as the abode of demons is also well known to Judaism."[34]

Paul makes it clear this cosmic prince-ruler not only operates in the heavenlies or air above earth, but he is at home on earth also. Why else would Jesus himself call him "the ruler of this world" (John 12:31; 14:30; 16:11) and Paul "the god of this world" (2 Cor. 4:4)? Paul even says he is "the spirit that is now working in the sons of disobedience." What does this mean?

We can state an opinion. The preposition *in* probably means "upon" or at least, "among." Paul is *not* asserting that all the unredeemed are indwelt personally by Satan through his demons. His working in their lives is so strong, however, it is just as if he were inside of them, working from inside out. We have already seen that demons work effectively against people from without though they are usually more destructive from within.

The demonic condition of the unredeemed could not be stated more strongly. This is why I have repeatedly used this passage to refer to the *potential* demonization of the unredeemed. In the words of Arnold, the diabolical force is so entirely effective in retaining its subjects that the author can describe these victims as "sons of disobedience."

The Devil is thus seen to exercise effective and compelling power in his work of inspiring disobedience among humanity.[35]

We see then, that as Paul begins his specific interpretation of the powers, they are all evil powers. Also, while Jesus defeated them in His redemptive event, they still have liberty to work their evil among believers, men, and nations. However, the rebellious powers are not as free as before. Jesus has the power "even to subject all things to Himself" (Phil. 3:21). He will continue to "reign until He has put all his enemies under His feet" (1 Cor. 15:25). Indeed, in Ephesians they are seen as *already* under His feet (1:21; see 1 Pet. 3:22). Again we face the enigma of the "already but not yet."

Ephesians 3

Paul begins chapter 3 with a summation of the preceding verses that serves also an introduction to what is to follow. "For this reason" (v. 1a)—that the Ephesian believers be built together into a dwelling of God in the spirit (2:22)—Paul was made a minister of the gospel. He further explains the purpose of his ministry to the Gentiles was to unveil to them the mystery of Christ that the Gentiles, too, are fellow heirs and fellow members of the body, and fellow partakers of the promise in Christ Jesus through the gospel (3:1–7). Here again is the theme of unity within the Body, so central to Paul's teaching on victorious warfare.

The mystery of the Gentiles' being in the church is only part of a larger mystery, however, that embraces one dimension of the purpose of the church. The purpose is that all of creation, might see God's great plan, including the evil principalities and powers (3:10).

The NEB translation captures the concepts well:

> It was hidden for long ages in God the creator of the universe, in order that now, through the church, the wisdom of God in all its varied forms might be made known to the rulers and authorities in the realms of heaven. This is in accord with his age-long purpose, which he achieved in Christ Jesus our Lord. (Eph. 3:9–11, NEB)

Ephesians 3:10

Commentators are divided in their interpretations of verse 10. The difficulties revolve around three major questions:

1. What is "the manifold wisdom of God" about which the church testifies?
2. How does the church bear testimony to this wisdom towards "the rulers and authorities in the heavenly places"?
3. Who are these "rulers and authorities in the heavenly places"?

Let's take the last question first: Who are the rulers and authorities in the heavenly places? John Eadie discusses the various views.[36] The three major ones are: These are the elect and the fallen angels; these are the elect angels; or these are the fallen angels.

If we had only the first two views, that of both the elect and the fallen angels and that of only the elect angels, I would have to go with the former view. Yet, in light of the spiritual warfare motif of Ephesians, especially the apostle's explanation of how he is viewing the principalities and powers in this epistle (6:12), I am compelled to embrace the third view.

The principalities and powers are primarily evil spirits. While the elect angels are observing and participating in this warfare, they do not seem to be in Paul's focus in 3:10, or in any of the verses referring to principalities and powers in Ephesians' for that matter.

Second, what is the "wisdom of God" about which the church testifies to the principalities and powers?[37] We begin by examining the larger context in which Paul writes these words. That context focuses on Paul's use of "mystery" in Ephesians and Colossians.[38] God's mystery in both epistles is the Christological-redemptive mystery of God's salvation in Christ. The most common idea used by Paul in both Ephesians and Colossians for the essence of the mystery, besides the words "the mystery" themselves, is either "the mystery of Christ" or "God's mystery, that is, Christ Himself" (Eph. 3:4; Col. 2:2).

Mystery in Ephesians coordinates with Paul's view of the powers, Arnold says. "The aim of the 'mystery' is revealed in 1:9–10 to be the consummation of all things in Christ. This includes the subjugation of the hostile 'powers' to Christ." Arnold next points out that "The 'mystery' spoken of in Ephesians may very well provide a contrast to the Lydian-Phrygian 'mysteries' which were so popular. In this way the author could have employed it as a polemic against the influence of the ideas of the 'mysteries' in the churches."[39] The mystery of the mystery religions involved "receiving *ho kurios tou aeros* [the lord of the air] (cf. Eph. 2:2) as the indwelling deity."[40] The same ideas are brought forth in Colossians: Jesus has come to dethrone that spirit being.

While still on the theme of the mystery which is Christ and Christ in the believer, Arnold returns to God's election of the believer in Christ first mentioned in Ephesians 1:4f. He says that "this concept of election is closely linked with the foregoing discussion of 'the mystery.'" How is this so? Arnold says Paul's concept of election in Christ provides a "comforting and instructive counter to the fears of Christians formerly under the influence of magic, the mysteries, and astrological beliefs."[41] The same applies to Colossians.

Now we must look at the practical question: How does the church testify to the principalities and powers of the wisdom of God, that is, His redemptive plan in Christ with all of its outworkings in this world and even the next?

In his commentary on Ephesians 3:10, Wink says that

> the Church's task is articulated here as preaching to the Powers. It is engaged in a kind of spiritual warfare, but it also has a mission that carries the truth of the gospel into the very heart of power and expects some result. Are we then to envisage the conversation of the Powers? What is the Church to tell them? Where are "the heavenly places," and how is the Church to have access to powers there?[42]

Wink begins by taking the last question first, that is, how the church has access to the powers in the heavenlies. He first gives his own study of *en tois epouraniois*, in the heavenlies. He sees "the heavenlies as a dimension of reality into which believers have already, while on earth, been admitted yet in which unredeemed Powers still exercise dominion and must be fought with, preached to, and made to know the manifold wisdom of God."[43]

Wink then says that just as "God's throne is where God is effectively acting, so 'the heavenlies' are where Christ is already effectively Lord, with all Powers under his sovereignty (Eph. 1:22) even though not yet under his control (6:12)."[44]

This is an intriguing concept—what I have called the "already, but not yet" enigma of spiritual warfare. Wink comments that the

> seeming contradiction between sovereignty and control is the consequence of the struggle at the juncture between two ages. To use a modern analogy, Christ's provisional revolutionary government has already been formed in exile, and parts of the country are already effectively under its sovereignty. The old regime, however, still holds the capital and the loyalty of the army and practices brutal and indiscriminate warfare against its own people in desperate attempt to preserve its privilege and wealth. But the outcome, however long in coming, is assured.[45]

Wink then states that "the heavenlies" where

> the believer has already been established . . . [It] is thus a kind of "liberated zone," . . . although with this caveat; those who are in this "liberated zone" are not at all free from the possibility of collusion with the old Powers or even of apostasy. But they are provided a space of relative freedom from determination by the Powers.[46]

The church's "collusion" with the old powers is its most serious act of disobedience to the Lord, its Head. It is the major cause of powerlessness in the spiritual battle before us.

The church then has direct access to the evil powers because the church lives in the same realm as they do. We are a people, Wink says, of both kingdoms, the earthly and the heavenly. We are thus in continual contact with the powers but unfortunately are either only vaguely aware of it, don't know what to do, or don't care.

Now we come to the key question. What does it mean that the church is to make known "now" the manifold wisdom of God to these principalities and powers?

The simplest and most obvious answer is the best one. It means exactly what it says. The church, united with Christ in the heavenlies, the same heavenlies in which the powers exist, proclaims to them "the manifold wisdom of God." It is that simple.

I am not saying the process of doing what the apostle says the church is to do is simple. It is not. It is very complex. I am only stating that the answer to the question is simple.

Wink says it well when he states that

> it remains the Church's task not only to proclaim to *people* that they have been redeemed from the darkness that once held them in bondage (5:8–14), but also to proclaim to the *powers* that they are not supreme. That Christ is their sovereign. That those human beings under their dominion (here the concept of national angels comes immediately to mind)[47] belong to Christ.[48]

What incredible insight! This is exactly what many are discovering today in evangelism launched in a spiritual warfare context. Wink then states that the "Church does not exercise the power of the Powers, however. It has no hope of success in a frontal encounter. That is why the writer ends this paragraph celebrating the 'boldness and confidence of access through our faith in him' (Eph. 3:12)."[49]

What does this access signify? Wink says it can

> only mean access to the heavenly presence, the divine throne, the heavenly council (see 2:6, "made us sit . . . in the heavenlies"). Full admittance to that distinguished

circle awaits the future ages (2:7; see also Rev. 3:12, 21; 7:9–17; 14:1–5). But even now, through intercessory prayer, the church is confident that it has access to God's presence and power in the struggle with the Powers. It is this very confidence that causes the writer to launch immediately into prayer for his readers ("For this reason," 3:14–19).[50]

How do *intercession* and *high level cosmic spiritual warfare* work together? The church enters the heavenlies through prayer and intercession. The risen Lord is praised, worshipped, and loved through prayer. The church then intercedes for those the church has been called to redeem. Only a unified church interceding over a period of time can effectively do this. Thus again the dominant note on church unity in Ephesians (2:11—6:9).

The church declares Christ's lordship both over the powers and the unredeemed. It declares God's purpose in redeeming all men (2 Cor. 5:18–21). It then turns towards the powers. It does *not* pray against the powers. It prays only to its Lord. It proclaims the defeat of the powers. It *declares* that Christ as Lord is now displacing the power of the powers over the unredeemed peoples they have been keeping in bondage. It not only *informs* the powers of their defeat by the Lord in His church, (which is His fullness) it *enforces* their defeat by its faith and delegated authority in Christ. This is the manifold wisdom of God made known by the church to the rulers and authorities in the heavenlies to which Paul refers in Ephesians 3:10.

The question naturally follows, why is the church to proclaim the mystery of Christ to the powers? I believe the answer is obvious. If the elect angels were kept in the dark, so to speak, about the Christ event, how much more the fallen powers! Again Peter talks about the revelation of God's redemptive plan "things into which angels long to look" (1 Pet. 1:12).

Evidently even the angels only know what God wills them to know, and that, progressively. They know their part in God's plan. They know that and little more. The evil fallen angelic powers, then, know even less about God's profound plans in Christ, decreed from before the foundation of the world. This is continually born out by the ignorance of demonic powers, even Satan himself, about the true meaning of the Cross, and the fact of Christ's resurrection and the Ascension (1 Cor. 2:7–8). Of course they know more now, but only after the fact. Yet there is much they still do not know unless the church tells them. Wink remarks,[51] "To these powers, then, the church is to proclaim the divine plan made known only now in the fullness of time in Christ Jesus, that the God who is above all and through all and in all is uniting all things in Christ, things in heaven and things on earth (Eph. 4:6; 1:10)."

I believe the church's role in informing the powers is not just for information's sake. We have both an informing and an enforcing role towards the principalities and powers. We inform them to enforce against them their defeat. Perhaps that is why Paul follows with the declaration that this hidden mystery of Christ and the cosmic-earthly mission of the church are all according to God's eternal plan, carried out in Christ Jesus our Lord, who is now lord over the powers.[52]

The church can carry out its dual mission—earthly and cosmic—with boldness and confidence because we "have access through faith in Him," Paul says (v. 12). This implies worship, praise, prayer, and intercession. It also implies access through the risen Christ to the powers.

All of this is so awesome, God's plan so perfect, our resources in Christ so complete, Paul immediately breaks forth into prayer that believers may be empowered to minister the mystery. What a prayer it is! (vv. 14–21).

The church is a praying church. The church is also a warring church. It is to engage the powers in the name of the Lord. The church is to maintain that engagement offensively, not just defensively. If we do so with faith and persistence proclaiming in the Spirit the defeat of the powers over specific areas of human life, they will eventually have to yield. In the long run we will win if we will pay the price. Jesus promises that the gates of hell will not be able to prevail against His obedient, praying, warring church (Matt. 16:18).

Ephesians 4

How is all of this possible? With the singular strong man (Satan) already bound, Jesus began the process of "plundering his house" (Matt. 12:29b). Both of these statements, made prior to the Cross, the Resurrection, and the Ascension, were spoken in anticipation of the full Christ redemptive event (see John 7:37–39; Matt. 28:18–20). Then, Jesus "led captivity captive," the literal translation of Ephesians 4:8 *(Greek-English New Testament)*.

Arnold gives Ephesians 4:8–10 a good spiritual warfare perspective. "When this is viewed from the perspective of the first-century milieu and the fear of the underworld deities, one can gain a greater appreciation for the comfort the passage would bring to the readers." In other words, we begin to understand this passage when we put on our first-century, spiritual warfare eye glasses.

Arnold continues, saying that these verses

underline the cosmic supremacy of Christ in a fresh way. Christ is not only superior to the aerial spirits and the forces populating the heavens, but he is also superior to the so-called underworld deities. Christ alone holds "the keys to Hades," as another Christian writer wrote to believers in Asia Minor.[53]

On and on we could go to burn into our hearts, minds, emotions and will the fact that "we are more than conquerors through Him who loved us" (Rom. 8:37). We are on the winning side. Jesus has already won the victory. He is presently winning the battles. He will yet win the war through us, His unified, praying, warring church, climaxed by His glorious Second Coming. The powers must be made to hear the voice of our delegated authority as we attack the gates of hell in each area where God has placed us to live and minister.

I thank God that this dimension of evangelism and church planting is being rediscovered in our day.[54] I say "rediscovered" because men of God have moved in this realm in the past, usually stumbling onto this reality after much suffering and many failures.

Did the Ephesians win the war as Paul instructs them? Yes and no. Yes, because they are not recorded as falling back into spirit magic or worship. No, because the formerly pagan religious spirits changed their tactics. They became "Christian" religious spirits. Working through deceived Christian leader-teachers, as Paul had warned earlier (Acts 20:28–31), they played havoc with the Ephesian church through demonically deceived leader-teachers who, in turn, became deceivers (see 1 and 2 Tim.). Thus, I conclude with two closing words of admonition:

"Beloved, do not believe every spirit, but test the spirits to see whether they are from God; because many false prophets have gone out into the world" (1 John 4:1,2).

"But I am afraid, lest as the serpent deceived Eve by his craftiness, your minds should be led astray from the simplicity and purity of devotion to Christ" (2 Cor. 11:3).

51

Ephesians 6

Our next passage is one of the best known in all of Scripture, Ephesians 6:10–20. In this passage the apostle Paul is not writing about demonization but about warfare between the power of the Devil and power of God in the life of believers.

The conviction that Ephesians 6 is *the* manual on victorious spiritual warfare is not new to our age. All through the history of the church, believers, both theologians and lay Christians, have turned to this passage for help, especially in those hours when all the powers of hell seem to have been released against them.

The church fathers continually referred to this passage. A look at the Scripture indexes for the writing of the Ante-Nicene, Nicene and Post-Nicene fathers will reveal how often they turned to these words of Paul.[1] Ephesians 6 was also commented on continually by the great Puritan divines.[2]

First, I want to examine the passage critically. This will mean a somewhat in-depth and almost word-by-word study, where necessary and if space permits. Second, I want to be pastoral. How does Paul's teaching about the spirit world here affect our Christian life? How do we put it into practice? Third, I want to focus on evanglism. How does Paul's teaching enlighten us in the effective evangelization of those blinded by evil spirits against the truth of the Gospel?

In Ephesians 6:10–20 *Paul is bringing together all of his warfare teachings*. He has brought his readers to the point where they are now ready for his most important teaching on warfare in the entire epistle. Here is the practical application of all he has been saying in Ephesians until now. As Arnold says, Ephesians 6 is Paul's "call to acquire divine strengthening for the purpose of engaging the spirit-forces of evil (Eph. 6:10–20). It is not an irrelevant appendix to the epistle. It is a crucial part of the paraenesis to which the rest of the epistle has been pointing."[3]

Arnold next makes an important comment. He says that this

is the only place in the Pauline corpus where believers are explicitly called upon to struggle against the "principalities and powers." The "struggle" is not merely mentioned as a parenthetical aside. It is taken up by the author and elaborated on in ten verses integrally connected with the foregoing paraenesis of the epistle. (4:1—6:9)[4]

He concludes saying that in the 6:10–20 passage we discover again Paul's "significant emphasis on power." It is brought about "by the author's perception of a 'spiritual warfare' in which the readers are already engaged. This concept is present in Paul, but it is never elaborated to the degree that it is here."[5]

Arnold then asks the question why there is such a unique emphasis on cosmic level spiritual warfare in Ephesians. The answers Arnold gives all relate directly to the spirit-magic-occult lifestyle of Ephesus and the surrounding region, centered in the worship of Artemis and the saturation of the culture of Asia Minor (indeed of the Greco-Roman world) with magic, occult, spirit practices.

Ephesians 6:10–20

Paul begins his presentation with "Finally, be strong in the Lord and in the strength of His might" (v. 10).

The word "finally" here is *tou loipou* in Greek, a common expression in Paul's epistles, which literally means "for the rest."

I believe it would be accurate to paraphrase Paul's words to this point something like this:

"First, I told you about your election of God (1:3—2:27) and that the Lord Jesus already reigns as Lord at the Father's right hand, above all the cosmic forces of evil you are facing. I have also said that you are raised up with him and are seated with him in the heavenlies.

"Furthermore, you have been given the task of declaring to the principalities and powers the eternal plan of God, and to bring them into submission to the Lord by exercising your delegated authority in union with Christ.

"To do this, you have been given the Holy Spirit. Furthermore, Christ Himself dwells in you. You are one body in Christ.

"Now, let me put all of this in perspective. The Devil and the evil powers which war against you, while defeated by the Lord Jesus, are still free to continue to assault you, over and over again.

"There is no need to fear, however. Jesus alone is Lord. You have victory in Him. You are co-regents in the heavenlies in Him.

"You need to learn how to be strong in Him, however. While the Enemy will attack, God has provided all you need to be victorious Christian soldiers. Let me tell you how all of this is to be worked out in daily life."

"Finally" is followed immediately by three imperatives: be empowered (v. 10); put on (v. 11); and take up (v. 13). The last two refer directly to the armor of God.

The three imperatives, Arnold says, "are similar in meaning . . . (They) emphasize the need for divine strength in order to resist the enemy."[6]

Arnold says Paul's use of the conjunction, *oun* ("therefore," vv. 13, 14) introduces the main admonition in verse 14 by making a general reference to the need for divine power because of the supernatural, powerful, and cunning nature of the enemies," revealed in verse 12. He states that "verse 12 functions as an explication of the nature of the enemy and not as the central element in the development of 6:10–20" as some commentators suggest.

Arnold gives great importance to verse 14.[7]

> The imperative *stete* ("stand firm," v. 14) has been accurately described as the chief admonition of the passage. The admonition to acquire divine strengthening and enablement has not been given by the author as an end in itself. The strength is required for a particular purpose—that the believer might be enabled to stand against the evil "powers" and successfully resist them (vv. 11, 13, 14). "Stand firm" (v. 14) then becomes the central command of the passage.

Stand Firm

After Paul gives his main command, "Stand firm" (v. 14), he follows with four imperative participles in verses 14–16: *perizōsamenoi*, "girding about, around"; *endusamenoi*, "putting on"; *hupodēsamenoi*, literally "shoeing"; and *analabontes*, "taking up."

These four are followed by the second imperative verb in the series, *analabete*, from *analambanō*, to "take up" (v. 13). Vine says it means to "receive by deliberate and ready reception of what is offered . . . taking with the hand, taking hold, taking hold of."[8]

Arnold writes that these commands do not introduce an independent series of admonitions. They are all dependent on *stete*, "stand firm" (v. 14).[9]

> The whole of verses 14–20, then, is dependent on the main thought of verse 14—"stand!" All other thoughts are subservient to this ultimate aim. The divine armor and power are provided for the attainment of this goal. The opponents are carefully delineated so that the reader may know the nature of the enemies to be withstood. Even prayer is given with the goal of resistance in mind.

Be Strengthened

With this overview as the foundation we go back to where Paul begins in verse 10a, "Be strong." Lincoln says Paul's use of a passive command here reinforces the notion that "strength is to be drawn from an external source and corresponding to the passive in the prayer of 3:16. 'Be strengthened with power through His Spirit in the inner man.'" He continues saying that here "the external source is 'the Lord,' and the wording is again reminiscent of the Old Testament (cf. 1 Sam. 30:6; 'David strengthened himself in the Lord his God'; Zech. 10:12. 'I will make them strong in the Lord.')"[10]

Arnold comments on 6:10 on the believer's source of power in the Lord. He says this "phrase not only describes the person with whom the readers have been brought into union, but also refers to the sphere or new set of conditions in which they live, into the domain of light (5:8ff); they are no longer subjected to the tyranny of life under the control of the prince of the authority of the air (2:2) but now live under the loving headship of Christ who is Lord."[11]

He then says "Grundmann has fittingly commented, 'This place [in Christ] is to a great extend charged with the superior power which belongs to Christ.' For this reason the readers can be admonished to 'be strong.'"[12]

With this in mind, Arnold writes that the source of the strength "is more specifically defined as existing in 'the strength of the Lord's might.'" These are the "same terms the author used to describe the divine power which brought about the resurrection and exaltation of Christ (1:19–20)." Thus, he says, Paul "affirms that believers have access to this vast divine power which has already proved itself sufficient to overcome powerful diabolic opposition."[13]

Continuing with 6:10, we note the two power terms *kratos*, "might," and *ischus*, "strength." Arnold states that they "are linked in one place in Isaiah (40:26), which the author may have been thinking of as he penned 6:10."[14]

Arnold then says Paul "appears significantly indebted to Isaiah for many of his terms and metaphors, particularly with respect to the armor." Both Arnold and Lincoln continually refer to Paul's use of the Old Testament, particularly Isaiah, in all warfare imagery of Ephesians 6. Arnold states that the one Old Testament passage that stands out as having a significant correspondence to Ephesians 6:10ff is Isaiah 52.

Arnold comments that "the extended similarity of ideas throughout the wider context of Isaiah 52 with Ephesians (especially chap. 6) suggests that our author thought of the entire Isaianic passage as he wrote."[15]

The Enemy We Face

After appealing for believers to strengthen themselves with the Lord's strength and might by putting on God's armor, Paul comes forth with the rationale behind his battle cry in verses 11–12. He says that

1. They need "to stand firm against the schemes of the devil" (v. 11d).
2. They are not facing human foes (v. 12a).
3. They are facing a complex spiritual army-hierarchy of evil supernatural beings who have thoroughly infiltrated the heavens and exercises great control over the earth (v. 12b).

The "stand firm" of verse 14 is a repetition of his two prior "stand firm" statements (v. 11b and 13b). This repetition of "stand firm" three times strengthens the view that it is the central command around which all else flows. Eadie says the construction in Greek of "stand firm against" (v. 11b) is a military phrase "to stand in front of with the view of opposing." He cites secular sources revealing this use.[16] Thus it fits well the "for and against" military symbolism of Paul in these verses.

This military stance is not directed against men but against the Devil and his high level cosmic demonic powers, Paul says (vv. 11–12). His reference to the believer's principal cosmic enemy by the name "the devil" here (v. 11) and in 4:27 is unique to his writings. He only uses "the devil" here and in Hebrews 2:14. Paul's most frequently used title for the devil is "Satan." He also uses "the evil one" here (v. 16) and in 2 Thessalonians 3:3. He uses "the serpent" in 2 Corinthians 11:3 and "the god of this world" in 2 Corinthians 4:3–4. Then there is "Belial" in 2 Corinthians 6:15 and "the tempter" in 1 Thessalonians 3:5. In addition, of course, are all the power words for principalities and powers which would also include the Devil since he is the chief cosmic evil principality.

We not only face the Devil, but we must also contend with his schemes (6:11). "Schemes ("wiles" in the KJV) is the Greek word *methodia*. It is always used in a negative manner in the New Testament. Vine says it means

> craft, deceit (*meta*, after, *hodos*, away), a cunning device, a wile, and is translated "wiles (of error) in Ephesians 4:14 [A.V.] paraphrases it, "they lie in wait (to deceive)," . . . (with a view to) the craft (singular) of deceit.[17]

The idea behind *methodia* is deception. The apostle is warning us that the devil's entire system of warfare against us is based on deception. Eadie makes an excellent observation at this point. He says that the Devil has a method of warfare peculiar to himself, for it consists of "wiles." His battles are the rush of a sudden ambuscade. He fights not on a pitched field, but by sudden assault and secret and cunning onslaught.[18]

The Enemies We Face

Verse 12 is without doubt one of the most remarkable verses in the entire Bible on spiritual warfare. Paul says we struggle against high level, cosmic principalities and powers of total evil. The word for "struggle" is *palē,* a wrestling. This is the only appearance of the word in the New Testament.[19] Wuest remarks that this Greek athletic term refers to a

> contest between two in which each endeavors to throw the other . . . When we consider that the loser in a Greek wrestling contest had his eyes gorged out with resulting blindness for the rest of his days, we can form some conception of the Ephesian Greeks' reaction to Paul's illustration. The Christian wrestling against the powers of darkness is no less desperate and fateful.[20]

Paul's switch from the imagery of the soldier to that of the wrestler and then back to the soldier again should not be considered surprising. At times, in hand-to-hand combat, the soldier is also a wrestler. Paul probably used the wrestler imagery primarily to bring out that point.

Up until now the apostle has been talking in general of the evil principalities and powers. First, in 1:21 he gives a five-fold classification of the powers: rule, authority, power, dominion, and name. Next, in 4:8 he refers to "captivity" (KJV), evidently also an evil power concept. Then, in Ephesians 3:10 Paul mentions "rulers and authorities," and in 4:27 he mentions the devil for the first time. Now in Ephesians 6, Paul unites the Devil (v. 11), the Evil One (v. 16), and the rulers and the powers (v. 12) all together. For the very first time Paul clearly states what he has already implied, that our battle against the Devil is *not* with him personally or individually. It is with him only as he operates against us *through* evil, high-level, cosmic principalities and powers.

This is the third time in Ephesians the apostle uses his two primary summary words for the evil principalities and powers: *archai,* "rulers," and *exousia,* "authorities" (1:20 and 3:10).[21] I like John Eadie's observation on Ephesians 1:21, where these two words are first used in Ephesians along with *dunameos,* "might," and *kuristetos,* "lordship." He says "what the distinction of the words among themselves is, and what degrees of celestial heraldry they describe, it is impossible for us to define."[22]

That is a good statement. He recognizes that Paul is not being technical. He is simply heaping up words to describe the massive and complex hierarchy of evil supernaturalism with which the believer is at war. The same is true of 6:12. Eadie's further observations strongly support this more flexible view of these power concepts. He says the order of power in 1:21, with *archē* and *exousia* listed first as they are in 6:12 also, is reversed in Colossians 1:16. There the two are listed last. He then mentions that the last power term in 1:21, *kuriotētos,* is listed second in Colossians 1:16.

Eadie then makes an interesting comment about a possible connection between the four power terms as first used in 1:21. He says, "Whoever possesses the *archē* enjoys and displays *exousia,* and whoever is invested with the *dunamis,* wields it in his appointed *kuriotēs.*"[23]

The apostle follows rulers and powers with a phrase which is not used anywhere else in the New Testament or in the LXX: *tous kosmokratoras tou skotous toutou,* "the world rulers of this darkness" *(Greek-English New Testament).* Arnold attempts to trace the origin of this unique phrase as do other critical commentators. Many come to the same conclusion that Arnold does, that Paul did *not* create this phrase, but only borrowed it out of the world in which these believers lived. Arnold says the evidence suggests it was "current in both the magical tradition and world of astrology when the author wrote this epistle."

The term occurs a number of times in the magical papyri, "used as one of a number of descriptive titles for various gods/spirits called upon to aid the conjurer, . . . [and] as one of the many titles of the deity Helios."[24] Arnold outlines some of the results of his extensive research into the religious use of this phrase in the first century B.C.[25] He says that "the employment of *kosmokratōr* appears to be a clear example of the Ephesians' author utilizing a term from the magical/astrological tradition. It is also a likely candidate for being one of 'the names which are named' (1:21)."

Next Arnold states that "the author reinterprets the meaning of *kosmokratōr* for the Christian readers. There is not one, but many (the term is plural)." He says that the "*kosmokratōr* is not considered omnipotent, but is placed alongside the principalities and 'powers' under the leadership of the devil! Far from being beneficial or helpful deities, the *kosmokratores* are regarded as evil spirits *(pneumatika)* of 'this darkness.'"

Arnold next says that "the way the term is used in this context may serve as the author's interpretation of the Ephesian Artemis." It could also include Helios, Sarapis, or other deities claiming to possess cosmic power.

Thus, believers who formerly worshipped Artemis or adhered to magical practices now have Paul's instruction about how they are to look at the deities or spirits in which they once put their faith. Arnold says the pagan deities "are powerful and evil emissaries of the devil himself who need to be resisted with the powerful armor of God."

This reminds us of Paul's treatment of idols and their demons in 1 Corinthians 10:20–21: "The things which the Gentiles sacrifice, they sacrifice to demons [*daimonia*], and not to God; and I do not want you to become a sharer in demons." Arnold makes a clear connection between idols and the spirits in Ephesians 6. He then notes that "Paul believed that a Corinthian believer would actually be joined with demonic 'powers' if he became involved in the table fellowship of pagan deities. . . . An offering brought to them brought one under the influence of demonic 'powers.' This was because the heathen cults were the instruments of the kingdom of Satan."

Next Arnold points out that "this close association of pagan gods with 'demons' is also found in the LXX. Psalms 95:5 reads: 'For all the gods of the Gentiles are demons' (see also Deut. 32:7; Baraita 4:7; Jub. 22:16–17). The identification of the gods of the heathen with demons became even more explicit in later Judaism."

If Paul were writing these words directly to our Western religious context today, what would he say? Today we have demons of materialism, intellectualism, self-worship, the pursuit of power, position, pleasure, and possessions. In the religious realm, we have everything they had except for the physical temple of Artemis. Taking its place, however, are the many material temples plus the mystical temple of the New Age movement. The baser, grosser sides of the religious spirit world found among the magical practitioners of Paul's day is replicated in modern occultism and Satanism rapidly spreading in our world. A powerful minority is committed to unspeakable, religious, satanic evil.

In the Two-thirds World, the gods of the non-Christians are very similar to those of Ephesus, but with different names. The high level, cosmic powers of evil control these contemporary god-spirit-magical systems, however.

There is one more area of insight into the work of the powers among men which needs to be considered: the strategy of supernatural evil in manipulating human institutions and social structures to work evil among humanity. Walter Wink is the champion of this more socio-cultural institutional view of spirit evil. He says that we must see Paul including here in 6:12

> all the *archai* and *exousiai* . . . not only divine but human, not only personified but structural, not only demons and kings but the world atmosphere and power invested in institutions, laws, traditions and rituals as well, for it is the cumulative, totalizing effect of all these taken together that creates the sense of bondage of a "dominion of darkness" (see Col. 1:13) presided over by higher powers.[26]

Wink holds the *kosmokratoras* to include all who hold mastery over the world, the spirit of empire, and

> all forms of institutional idolatry, whereby religion, commerce, education, and state make their own well-being and survival the final criteria of morality, and by which

they justify the liquidation of prophets, the persecution of deviants, and the ostracism of opponents.

Wink continues saying that it is the "suprahuman dimension of power in institutions and the cosmos which must be fought, not the mere human agent." The institution will perpetuate itself no matter who the human agent "because that is what the institution requires for its survival." Finally he says that it is "this suprahuman quality which accounts for the apparent 'heavenly,' bigger than life, quasi-eternal character of the Powers."[27]

While favorably responding from the depths of my being to Wink's words, I must emphasize the strong personal supernatural dimension to this warfare motif as well as the social. In fact, the personal-spiritual dimension seems to be Paul's primary focus in Ephesians 6:10–20.

Finally Paul says we are at war with the *pneumatika tēs ponerias en tois epouranios,* "the spiritual (hosts) of evil in the heavenlies" *(Greek-English New Testament).* Arnold comments that with this phrase Paul ends his list of powers with a "comprehensive designation for all the classes of hostile spirits—*ta pneumatika tēs ponerias.*" He says that the "term should probably be viewed as an alternative expression for *pneuma* [spirit] not *pneumata* [spiritual]. Believers need to be prepared to engage all the forces of evil in battle."[28]

Eadie contributes a remarkably inspiring and insightful observation. He says that to "rouse up the Christian soldiery, the apostle brings out into bold relief the terrible foes which they are summoned to encounter." He says that as to

> their position, they are no subalterns, but foes of mighty rank, the nobility and chieftains of the fallen spirit-world; as to their office, their domain is "this darkness" in which they exercise imperial sway; as to their essence, they are not encumbered with an animal frame, but are "spirits"; and as to their character, they are "evil"— their appetite for evil only exceeds their capacity for producing it.[29]

Finally he says that their "nature is evil, their commission is evil, their work is evil. Evil and evil only are they, alike in essence and operation."

This then is the foe and his forces we face in battle.

Offensive and Defensive Weapons

Many commentators and preachers affirm that all the weapons listed in Ephesians 6:14–17, with the possible exception of the sword of the Spirit, are defensive. Is that really true? No. A warrior who never attacks the enemy but only defends himself is a trapped warrior. An army that only defends but never attacks is unfit for war. A church which does not reach out to war but only stands and defends itself is already defeated. In spiritual warfare the best defense is to go on the offense.

Walter Wink comments on this question:[30]

> It is humorous to watch the statement bob from scholar to scholar that the weapons listed here are all "defensive." . . . The Pentagon says the same about nuclear missiles. . . . The terms employed are taken straight from the legionnaire's equipment and the metaphor is of the church like the Roman wedge, the most efficient and terrifying military formation known up to that time and for some thousand years after.

Wink says Paul describes armor that is both offensive and defensive. Although the shield, helmet, breastplate, and greaves (for girding the loins) were all defensive, the other pieces of armor were offensive. The "round shield of the early [Roman] legionnaires had long since been elongated (the scutum); two-thirds covered his body and one-third covered his comrade to the left. This brilliant innovation encouraged tight ranks, since each fighter was in part dependent on his neighbor for protection." The Roman wedge was primarily for protection while the soldiers were *on the offensive*. Paul omits the legionnaire's *pilum* (javelin) and *pugio* (dagger), but the dagger was carried in the girdle and may be implied by "girding up the loins." The pilum was more for disarming than killing the enemy. "Their absence does nothing to turn the *gladius* into a 'defensive' weapon. It was the centerpiece of the Roman army's devastating military efficiency."

In referring to Paul's three-time repetition of "stand firm," Wink says this "has perhaps contributed to the idea that the Christian is not on the attack so much as trying to keep from being overwhelmed." Wink quotes Chrysostom, who was familiar with legionnaire ways, to clarify the sense of this "stand firm": "The very first feature in tactics is, to know how to stand well, and many things will depend upon that . . . Doubtless then he (Paul) does not mean merely any way of standing, but a correct way."

Wink himself refers to "stand firm" in verses 11 and 14 as having "the sense of the 'drawing up a military formation for combat.'" In verse 13 the phrase

> refers to the triumphant stance of the victor. In the latter verse it is linked with *katergasamenoi;* Bauer translates, "after proving victorious over everything, to stand ground." The writer has no notion here of Christian life as a last-ditch, rearguard, defensive operation; this is war with the powers of evil. *He depicts the church taking the fight to the enemy, and he expects the church to win.*[31] (italics mine)

Finally Wink says that "against such evil the church is well advised to stand shoulder to shoulder, shields overlapping. Hence this instruction in armaments is issued in the plural throughout the paragraph." He continues saying that

> not individuals but the whole people of God is addressed. Solitary efforts may at times be necessary, but far better when many, each individually equipped thus, can struggle (pale 6:12) together and perhaps even "prove victorious over everything . . . All this, then, figures in the Church task vis-a-vis the powers.[32]

A Look at Each Piece of the Armor

Lincoln says that Paul's presentation of the different parts of the armor of God "shows what it means to have accomplished everything necessary for battle, and explains how it is that one stands."[33]

1. *Loins girded with truth* (v. 14b). The verb in the middle voice means the Christian must gird *himself* with the truth. In Luke 12:35, 37, and 17:8, girding one's loins is a sign of readiness for service.

Lincoln feels the source of Paul's imagery was probably the Old Testament more than the Roman soldier. "The primary influence on the writer's choice of terminology at this point is LXX Isaiah 11:5, where the Messiah-King is said to have righteousness girding his loins and truth clothing his sides."[34] He next refers to E. Levine, who he says, "claims that all such references still carry allusions to the beltwrestling practices of the ancient Near East and that the wrestling belt became symbolic of soldiers ready for battle."

The question is often asked at this point, what is the "truth" that Paul has in mind? The two answers most often suggested are: The truth is the word of truth, that is, the Gospel and Jesus as the truth; the truth is the absence of all deceit. Lincoln says that "since in LXX Isaiah 11:5 truth referred to faithfulness and loyalty and what was said there of the Messiah is now applied to believers, it is likely that

that is also the force of 'truth' in this verse."[35] Others disagree. They say that truth here is the truth of the gospel (1:13) since Paul has consistently used truth in this manner in this book.

Which is it? In light of the power motif of Ephesians, I lean towards the latter. It is the gospel which is "the power of God unto salvation." Arnold says that "those who live under the influence of the powerful gospel and 'walk in the light' will live by the truth and speak truth (4:25; 5:9) and thereby resist the devil, not giving him a place (4:27)."[36] This is truth encounter.

2. *The breastplate of righteousness* (v. 14b). Again, we have the middle voice. The putting on of the breastplate of righteousness is the task of the individual believer. We also end up with two views of righteousness. The first is that "righteous" means a righteous life. The second is that it is the righteousness provided in the gospel. Wuest says, "It is not justifying righteousness but sanctifying righteousness."[37]

Lincoln, taking the same position as Wuest, again borrows a metaphor out of the Old Testament. He says that " 'the breastplate of righteousness' was part of Yahweh's armor in the depictions found in Isaiah 59:17 and Wisdom 15:18 (cf. also Isaiah 11:5, where righteousness is the Messiah's girdle)."[38] Lincoln refers to 1 Thessalonians 5:8. He says that "Paul had made the virtues of faith and love the Christian's breastplate, but he also depicted righteousness as necessary for the battle when he spoke of 'the weapons of righteousness for the right hand and the left' in 1 Corinthians 6:7."[39]

Arnold takes a different stance.[40]

> If the author of Ephesians reflects anything of Pauline tradition in his use of "righteousness," the concept of divine power is clearly present. Paul writes that the reason the Gospel can be described as the power of God has to do with the fact that it reveals the righteousness of God (Rom. 1:16). The righteousness of God is therefore construed as divine power.

While I see truth in both views, I believe Arnold is right in his power motif. The righteousness of God, in this context, is a power term. The gift of the righteousness of God to the believer totally defeats the Enemy. This righteousness of God in turn transforms the believer's life. The result of experiencing the divine righteousness is a life of righteousness.

3. *Feet shod with the preparation of the Gospel of peace* (v. 15). Again there are two primary views here. Some say the focus is on evangelism. As we march forward—thus the motif of the soldier's sandals—we will be opposed. In the midst of the war, ours is the only message of peace. Lincoln puts forward the second view. Paul here refers to readiness for spiritual warfare, Lincoln says. This is consistent with the main teaching of the entire Ephesians 6:10–20 passage. He observes that Paul here is primarily influenced by the language of an Old Testament passage "which mentions feet in connection with proclaiming the gospel of peace. The text in question is LXX Isaiah 52:7, 'as the feet of one preaching glad tidings of peace' (cf. also Nah. 1:15)."

Lincoln mentions that "Paul has used this verse in connection with the preacher of the gospel in Romans 10:15." He believes in Ephesians the "writer links the equipping of the feet not with the proclamation of the gospel of peace but with the *etoimasia* 'readiness,' of the gospel of peace." He states that "the term nowhere actually means 'firm footing,' and its more usual sense is readiness, preparedness, or preparation (cf., e.g., LXX ps. 9:17; Wis. 13:;12; Ep. Arist. 182; Josephus, Ant. 10:1.2, 9 V.L)."[41]

He concludes, saying that the "reference is, therefore, not to readiness to proclaim the gospel . . . but to the readiness or preparedness for combat and for standing in the battle that is bestowed by the gospel of peace (cf. also Meyer, 334–34; Abbot, 185; Hendriksen, 277)." While Lincoln may be correct, one view does not necessarily exclude the other.

4. *The shield of faith* (v. 16). Lincoln again goes to the Old Testament. He says "the shield was used as an image for God's protection of his people (cf., e.g., Gen. 15:1; Ps. 5:2; 18:2, 30, 35; 28:7; 33:20; 35:2; 59:11; 91:4; 115:9–11; 144:1)." He then states that Paul here uses *thureos* or *scutum,* for shield. It is the "large shield, four feet in length and two and a half feet in width, which is described by Polybius 6.23.2 as the first part of the Roman panoplia and which protected the whole body."[42]

Lincoln then looks at the place of faith in Ephesians. "Faith takes hold of God's resources in the midst of the onslaughts of evil and produces the firm resolve which douses anything the enemy throws at the believer (cf. also 1 Thess. 5:8, where faith is part of the breastplate, and 1 Peter 5:8, 9, where firm faith is necessary for resisting the devil)."

He next refers to Paul's statement that "faith will enable the believer 'to extinguish all the burning arrows of the evil one.' Burning arrows feature in the Old Testament in Psalms 7:13 and 26:18. They are the *malleoli,* arrows tipped with inflammable tar or pitch and shot off after being lit." He says that "Livy (Hist. 21.8) graphically describes how these arrows, even when not hitting the body but caught by the shield, caused panic because they blazed fiercely and tempted soldiers to throw down their burning shields and become vulnerable to the spears of their enemies."

He applies this to Ephesians 6:16. "Here the burning arrows represent every type of assault devised by the evil one, not just temptation to impure or unloving conduct but also false teaching, persecution, doubt, and despair. Faith is the power which enables believers to resist and triumph over such attacks."[43]

5. *The helmet of salvation* (v. 17). Paul introduces the next two pieces of armor with another change of verbs. The one verb "take" applies to both pieces of armor listed next, "the helmet of salvation" and "the sword of the Spirit which is the word of God." S. D. F. Salmond writing in the *Expositor's Greek New Testament* says, "The verb has its proper sense here, not merely 'take,' but 'receive,' i.e., as a gift from the Lord, a thing provided and offered by Him."[44]

The helmet is, of course, required for the defense of the head. Paul is certainly quoting from Isaiah 59:17.

> And He [God] put on righteousness like a breastplate
> And a helmet of salvation on his head.

Beautiful words indeed! The helmet of salvation protects us from the most fatal of all blows to a child of God, the doubts about his acceptance "warts and all" by God.

Lincoln says that for Paul

> what ultimately protects believers is that God has already rescued them from bondage to the prince of the realm of the air and seated them with Christ in the heavenly realms (cf. 2:1–10). By appropriating this salvation as their helmet, believers have every reason to be confident of the outcome of the battle.[45]

6. *The sword of the Spirit which is the Word of God* (v. 17). We have two technical words used here by Paul. One is the word for "sword," and the other is the

word for "the Word of God." Here for the first time in Ephesians, the Holy Spirit is seen to be the power behind the Christian warrior's use of the Word of God which is the sword God has given him for battle.

Lincoln again has a good word for us. He says that the "sharp short sword (*maxaira* opposed to *pouphaia*, the long sword) was the crucial offensive weapon in close combat." He then mentions that this "sword stands not for the Spirit but for 'the word of God.'" He then wisely states that the "Spirit is not so much the one who supplies the sword—both the helmet and the sword are to be received from God—but the one who gives it its effectiveness, its cutting edge . . . (cf. Heb. 4:12)."

Lincoln next mentions 2 Thessalonians 2:8. "The Lord Jesus will slay the lawless one with the breath of his mouth," also quoting Isaiah 11:4. Then he reminds us that in Revelation "Christ wages war with the sword of his mouth, and his word reveals people's deeds for what they are (cf. 1:16; 2:12, 16; 19:13, 15)."

Lincoln says that in

> Ephesians, however, when the Christian soldier wields the sword of the word, it is not first of all the word of judgment but the good news of salvation. *Rema* here, not *logos,* refers to the gospel (cf. also 5:26; Rom. 10:18; 1 Peter 1:25). This is "the word of truth, the gospel of your salvation" (1:13), "the gospel of peace" (6:15).[46]

Finally Lincoln states that "as the Church continues to be the reconciled and reconciling community, the gospel conquers the alienating hostile powers and brings about God's saving purposes."[47]

As we close Paul's outline of the divine armor God has provided for the Christian warrior, we discover the apostle is not finished yet (vv. 18–20). While prayer is not to be seen as an additional piece of armor, it is directly connected to all Paul has said from verses 10–17.

Prayer is not a seventh piece of spiritual armor, however. It is too grand, too foundational, too essential, too all encompassing to be listed as just another piece of spiritual armor, important as they are.

I like Arnold's way of expressing this. He says Paul's summons to prayer "completes his presentation of the spiritual weaponry." The "author appears to give prayer a more prominent place than merely the seventh among a list of spiritual weapons. He says the "author maintains a structural continuity with the foregoing delineation of the weapons by employing a participle *(proseuxomenoi)* still in dependence on the main verb 'stand' in verse 14."[48]

Arnold sees Paul as wanting "his readers to understand prayer as an essential spiritual weapon, but more than a weapon." He says "it is foundational for the deployment of all the other weapons."[49] Indeed, it is the key to effective warfare with high-level, cosmic powers of evil. In Ephesians 6 it is the *total context* in which spiritual warfare is engaged and won.

J. O. Fraser and the China Inland Mission

Just how foundational prayer is to the deployment of all the other weapons is vividly illustrated in the story of J. O. Fraser of the then China Inland Mission, now the Overseas Missionary Fellowship (OMF). Fraser, a British missionary, worked among the Lisu tribal people in southwest China from 1909 until his death in 1938. My source is his biography written by Mrs. Howard Taylor, *Behind the Ranges, Fraser of Lisuland.*[50] I quote freely from both Fraser's words and those of Mrs. Taylor with the publisher's permission.

To the Lisu, *conversion had to be deliverance from the fear of the demon spirits they worshipped,* that is, power encounter. When this did not occur, they frequently fell back into spirit homage. Fraser's early years of ministry were difficult. He soon realized that his ignorance of the spirit world was one of his major problems. This ignorance severely handicapped his converts. They suffered continual demonic attacks, many returning to their former lifestyle, pacifying the abusive spirits.[51] The result was terrible setbacks in Fraser's ministry. He had assured his converts that Jesus is mightier than the spirits, but he did not know how to teach them the way of victory. They were defeated by the demons again and again.

In one case at least, Mrs. Taylor reports that some believers were reinvaded by the spirits.[52] "Fraser was still slow to believe that demonization can be as real today as when our Lord was upon earth."[53] One of his key families went back into demonism when a family member became seriously ill. God did not heal him in spite of their prayers. A diviner told them they must return to spirit worship in order for him to be healed. They did. He died, anyway, but it was too late. They had chosen again to serve the spirits that terrified them.[54]

Then Fraser, always a man of prayer, began to build an intercessory team in England. He could not form a team in Lisuland as he had no strong believers as yet. Mrs. Taylor says this "was to become in a very real sense the power behind his work."[55] At that time Fraser himself went into a deep spiritual depression. He did not know at first what to make of it. Was it loneliness? Was it the poor food, the struggle with the language, or the deadlock in the work?

As time wore on, he realized there were influences of another kind to be reckoned with. All he had believed and rejoiced in became unreal. Even his prayers seemed to mock him. *Does God answer prayer?* The question tormented him. Thoughts of suicide persistently tempted him. Mrs. Taylor writes that "deeply were the foundations shaken in those days and nights of conflict." He soon "realized that behind it all were 'powers of darkness,' seeking to overwhelm him."

She then makes a remarkable statement. "*He dared to invade Satan's kingdom, undisputed for ages.* At first, vengeance had fallen on the Lisu inquirers, an easy prey. Now, he was himself attacked—and it was war to the death, spiritually.

"Then help came when the rainy season was at its dreariest. Someone sent him a copy of *The Overcomer,* a magazine with which Fraser was unfamiliar. It set forth the very truth needed in that strange conflict, and the truth set him free. The truth that dawned upon Fraser as he pored over the welcome pages was that *Satan is indeed a conquered foe.* All of this he had held before, as a matter of doctrine. Now, it shone out for him in letters of light that victory is ours. Deep in the Lisu mountains, he responded to the liberating power of the Cross. 'They overcame him [the great enemy] by the blood of the Lamb and the word of their testimony.' There, in that poor shack, the victory was won that was to mean life to thousands."

Fraser later told Mrs. Taylor, "I read over and over—that number of *The Overcomer.* What it showed me was that deliverance from the power of the evil one comes through definite resistance on the ground of the Cross. I had found that much of the spiritual teaching one hears does not seem to work. . . . The passive side of leaving everything to the Lord Jesus as our life, while blessedly true, was not . . . needed just then. Definite resistance on the ground of the Cross was what brought me light. For I found that *it worked.* I felt like a man perishing of thirst, to whom some beautiful, clear, cold water had begun to flow.

"People will tell you," Fraser continued, "that such and such a truth is the secret of victory. No: we need different truth at different times. 'Look to the Lord,' some will say. '*Resist the devil,*' is also Scripture (James 4:7). And I found *it worked!*"

"That cloud of depression dispersed. I found that I could have victory in the spiritual realm whenever I wanted it. The Lord Himself resisted the devil vocally: 'Get thee behind me Satan!' I, in humble dependence on Him, did the same. I talked to Satan . . . using the promises of Scripture as weapons. And they *worked*. One had to learn, gradually, how to use the new-found weapon of resistance."

Some time later, Fraser was much tried by the persistent recurrence of evil thoughts. They became obsessive. One day Fraser went out to a hidden prayer haunt and voiced his determined resistance to Satan. He combined prayer, worship, praise, and intercession. He prayed in the context of spiritual warfare and took an Ephesians 3:10 stance against the cosmic powers of evil attacking him and blinding his beloved Lisu people.

"I claimed deliverance on the ground of my Redeemer's victory on the Cross," he said. "I even shouted my resistance to Satan and all these thoughts. The obsession collapsed then and there, like a pack of cards, to return no more.

"James 4:7 is still in the Bible. Our Lord cried . . . 'with a *loud voice*' at the grave of Lazarus. He cried 'with a *loud voice*' from the Cross. In times of conflict I still find deliverance through repeating . . . out loud, appropriate Scripture, brought to my mind through the Holy Spirit. It is like crashing through opposition. 'Resist the devil and he will flee from you.' "[56]

Spiritual Warfare Lessons From Fraser

Let's look at some of the key dimensions of experience-oriented spiritual warfare based on aggressive action against Satan and high level cosmic principalities and powers rediscovered by Fraser.

1. *He had dared to "invade Satan's territory."* There is such a thing as invading Satan's territory.

   Some of His churches, Jesus said, were located in "the synagogue of Satan" (Rev. 2:9–11; 3:9), others where "Satan's throne is" (2:13). Jesus spoke of one area ruled by a "Jezebel" spirit (2:20–23), and another committed to "the deep things of Satan" (2:24).

2. *Because of this "the powers of darkness were seeking to overwhelm him."*[57]

   "God will never let this happen to an obedient, Spirit-filled child of God," we are told. "Jesus will protect him from such brutal blows." In that case Fraser must not have been an "obedient Spirit-filled, child of God" because it happened to him. Mrs. Taylor says he became so overwhelmed by Satan, he was tempted to commit suicide "and that persistently."

3. *He was himself attacked. His was a war to the death, spiritually.*

4. *His victory came when he faced the reality of what he already knew theologically,* that "Satan is indeed a conquered foe." Christ, our risen Lord has in truth bruised Satan's head upon the cross of shame. He made a show of principalities and powers, triumphing over them. (See my study on Satan as a defeated foe in chapter 52.)

5. *He learned "the already, but not yet" warfare reality.* Though already defeated, Satan was not yet completely bound. He was on a long chain and that chain reached to Lisuland. Satan and his demons had to be fought through prayer, intercession, and Ephesians 3:10 resistance.

6. *We need different truth at different times.* "Resist the devil" is also Scripture (James 4:7). Fraser found it worked! Fraser resisted the Devil vocally, using

the promises of Scripture as weapons, and they worked. He learned gradually how to use the newfound weapons of resistance.[58]

7. *Prayer is the true key to victory* in spiritual warfare, not just vocal resistance against the devil.

8. *Warfare against deeply entrenched high-level cosmic spirits needed an intercessory team,* and it meant a long period of intercession and resistance before victory would come.

9. *Victory was progressive.* It could be won, but then lost again if intercession and warfare were neglected after the initial victories.

Soon after this, the people movement began.[59] "After hours of talking it all over, the majority said they would like to become Christians," Fraser reported of family conversions. This is how a people movement begins.

Aggressive, offensive storming of hell's gates became a major part of his evangelistic and pastoral strategy. After years of battle in prayer and preaching-teaching, the harvest finally came. When it occurred more was done in a few short months of reaping after years of sowing in tears, than in all the time before.[60]

It was in that context that Fraser developed his famous concept of "the prayer of faith."[61] He knew it would take time. The strong man in a specific area is not bound by a few prayer meetings. It requires persistence in prayer. It is accomplished with time and persistent group warfare prayer. Fraser's letter on prayer and the prayer of faith contains excellent insight for today's intercessors.[62]

Mrs. Taylor wrote that

recent experience had deepened his conviction as to the vital part God had assigned in the work of His kingdom to intercessory prayer. . . . He had occasion to notice the difference between people and places that had been much prayed for and those that had not. In the former, half the work seemed to have been done already, an Unseen Ally had gone ahead to prepare the way. This made him not only persevere in prayer himself, whether he felt like it or not, but impelled him to induce and encourage Christians at home to pray.[63]

Here is a story involving most everything Paul has been teaching us about warfare with the spirit world: Territorial spirits. Warfare praying. The spirit warrior himself suffering severe demonic attacks. Battles with oppression and depression of spirit. The demonic bondage of the unconverted through occultism. Powerful, high-level, cosmic evil spirits attacking and stopping the growth of the new converts. Converts falling back to their former lifestyle. Demonization of some Christians.

We find the missionary's battles with his own unworkable theology of spiritual warfare. We find the severe sufferings involved in Christian service in places where high level territorial spirits have ruled unchallenged for centuries.

Here we discover power encounters galore, many lost, most won. The Enemy is forced to retreat, but he never gives up. His power is only measurably broken when a strong, praying, and godly *church* finally emerges in enemy's territory.

Above all, here we discover the place of prayer and intercession in kingdom ministries. It is not quick, instant prayer, but continuous, prevailing intercession. It is not one man, a spiritual lone ranger, praying alone, but groups of intercessors, thousands of miles away, who join him in persistent, systematic prayer.

The prayer of faith is his burden. When he breaks through to the rest of faith, he does not cease from battle, however. He continues to battle, but now with confidence of victory. This is Ephesians 6 in action, the Christian warrior arrayed in all his spiritual armor.

52

Hebrews, the Catholic Epistles, the Johannine Writings

The spiritual warfare dimension in Hebrews that we will briefly examine is limited to Hebrews 2:14–15. After stating his case for the superiority of the Lord Jesus Christ over both the prophets (1:1–3) and the angels (1:4–14), Paul[1] writes that we dare not drift from the eternal truth of the great salvation He provided (2:1–4). That salvation is accomplished by the temporary but real subordination of the Son, "who was made a little lower than the angels" (2:9) in the Incarnation. Since those to be redeemed are flesh and blood, Jesus partook of the same. He was truly one with us, Paul says (v. 14a).

Next Paul tells us of His mission, the purpose of the Incarnation:

> that through death He might destroy[2] him who had the power of death, that is, the devil, and release those who through fear of death were all their lifetime subject to bondage. (Heb. 2:14b–15, NKJV)

Here we see that the purpose of the divine death was twofold: to abolish (destroy, render powerless) the Devil and to remove the fearful power death holds (and thus the Devil holds) over the lives of God's children. Thus the purpose is redemptive, not primarily to redeem us from sin—though that too is implied—but to *redeem us from the power of the Devil*. The rationale behind this unique focus of Christ's redemptive act is the power over us that death gave to the Devil. His major weapon against us is death and our fear of death, Paul says. However, when Jesus suffered our death for us (2 Cor. 5:14–21), He canceled Satan's death power over us (Col. 2:14–15). In Christ's resurrection, death lost its sting (1 Cor. 15:55).

Donald Guthrie notes the paradox of Christ's use of death as a means of destroying "the maliciousness of death." The difference between His death and that of all others "lies in the fact of His sinlessness. Death for Him was caused by other men's sins."[3]

It is interesting to note that Satan actually caused the death of the Son of God (John 13:2,27). He was jubilant in having succeeded in having Jesus executed. The Resurrection and Ascension, however, completely outmaneuvered him. Demons today lament, "We thought we had Him when our master caused Him to be put to death. We thought we had won. We did not know He was to rise again. When He rose, we saw Him rise. We were helpless to interfere. He took away our power of death over his people." Thus the purpose of His death to render powerless the Enemy is more understandable, though of course, it is still filled with great mystery.

One more word must be added. The second aspect of the twofold purpose of His death in our behalf listed here is already ours. The power that death gave to the Devil is already removed. While we may fear the process of dying (the pain of dying and the separation from loved ones), we do not fear death. Death leads to His presence. Thus its enslavement of us is gone (v. 15).

The first aspect of the twofold purpose, the destruction of the Devil, is an "already, but not yet" experience for the child of God. Jesus' ministry and death already defeated the Devil. Yet, as one who is rebellious and evil, facing a yet future, final incarceration in the lake of fire, he is still active and aggressive. This fact is attested to both by Scripture and by contemporary experience. He fully realizes that Jesus has destroyed him and his works (1 John 3:8) and that the time of his execution draws near (Rev. 12:12,17). Thus while his personal destruction is "already," it is also "not yet" fully made manifest. As we have seen in our studies of Ephesians (chapters 50 and 51), we the church are called to play the important role in battle against him until the "not yet" is fully come.

SPIRITUAL WARFARE IN THE CATHOLIC (ENCYCLICAL) EPISTLES

In distinction from the Pauline epistles, which were addressed to individual churches or persons, a group of epistles was probably sent to the general Christian public: James, Peter, John, and Jude. Origen and the other church fathers in the third century began the practice of calling them the Catholic (universal) and the Encyclical Epistles.[4] We will hold our studies of James and 1 Peter until chapter 63.

2 Peter and Jude

We begin with 2 Peter and Jude because their subject matter lends itself to first consideration. Neither deals directly with the believer's warfare with principalities and powers, but both speak of the original fall of these powers. They are the only two books in the Bible which clearly do so. The rest of the Bible only mentions this fall indirectly or takes it for granted.[5] Both Peter and Jude are facing the same problem, that of false teachers and false prophets attempting to undermine the faith of the churches (2 Pet. 2:1f; Jude 3f). In the context of declaring the certainty of God's judgments upon these false teachers, both writers refer to the judgment of rebellious angels (2 Pet. 2:3–4; Jude 4–6).

Let's place the words of Peter and Jude side-by-side.

2 Peter 2:4	*Jude 6*
For if God did not spare angels when they sinned, but cast them into hell and committed them to pits of darkness, reserved for judgment;	And angels who did not keep their own domain, but abandoned their proper abode, He has kept in eternal bonds under darkness for the judgment of the great day.

The Sinning Angels

The first thing Peter and Jude tell us about angels is that some of them sinned. It is interesting to observe that angels were involved in the first sin war. They continue to be involved in ongoing war. They will yet be involved in the Revelation 12 warfare in the heavenlies, assuming the future interpretation of this passage. They will also have a major role to play in the final sin battles in the universe (Rev. 6—20).

According to Peter and Jude, angels sinned at a mysterious point in the past. According to Jesus, it was the Devil who sinned from the beginning (John 8:44). The angelic sin must then somehow be associated with Satan's sin. The question that most disturbs commentators is the occasion of this angelic fall.[6] John Calvin comments that while Peter briefly mentions here the fall of angels, he has not named the time and the manner and other circumstances of their fall. Thus, he says, "Most men are curious and make no end of inquiries on these things; . . . and indeed they who curiously inquire, do not regard edification, but seek to feed their souls with vain speculations. What is useful to us, God has made known."[7] He adds that all of the above is clear from Peter. Jude then adds the additional fact the angels who sinned, did so because they "did not keep their own domain." This is all we can be sure of.[8]

Do we need to know when and how sin was born among the angels, turning them into demons, evil spirits, unclean spirits, and Satan's angels (Matt. 25:41) to know how to deal with them? The answer to all these and similar questions is a resounding "No!" If God does not tell us all we wish to know, then that knowledge is really not necessary to our life as Christian warriors.

Sinning Angels Cast into Hell and Pits of Darkness

The sinning angels were not only cast into hell;[9] Peter says they were also committed to "pits of darkness." Peter, like Paul, makes use of Homeric imagery, Michael Green says. "Cast into hell" is only one word in Greek. It means "consigning to Tartarus." The word comes from Greek mythology. *Tartarus* "was the place of punishment for the departed spirits of the very wicked, particularly rebellious gods." The evil angels are in this place of torment now, although they must await the final judgment.[10]

Next they are confined to pits of darkness *(sirois)*, Peter says. William Barclay says *siros* meant a "pit in which a wolf or other wild animals is trapped. It means here that the wicked angels were cast into subterranean pits, and kept there in darkness and punishment. This well suits the idea of a *Tartarus* beneath the lowest depths of Hades."[11] This is not the word for pit which is used in Luke 8:31, where the demons entreated Jesus not to cast them "into the pit," the *abussos,* which Vine describes as "the abode of the demons out of which they can be let loose; Revelation 11:7; 17:8."[12]

These fallen angels are possibly now in torment of some type if Peter uses *tartarus* in the Greek traditional meaning as the place of torment of fallen gods. William Barclay says that in particular it was the place into which had been cast "the Titans and the Giants who had rebelled against Zeus, the Father of gods and men. *Tartarus,* then, was the lowest and the most terrible hell, in which those who had rebelled against divine power were kept in eternal punishment."[13]

Jude and the Fallen Angels

Certain angels chose to abandon "their own domain," Jude declares (see chap. 63). The word for "domain" here is one with which we are by now quite familiar: *archē* or "principality." Calvin writes that the fallen angels are like military deserters. They "left the station in which they had been placed." He states that "we are not to imagine a certain place in which the devils are shut up, for the apostle simply intended to teach us how miserable their condition is, since the time they apostasized and lost their dignity." Thus Calvin believes these are the same demons who are free on earth. They are not literally bound in a specific place, but, "wherever they go" he says, "they drag with them their own chains, and remain involved in darkness."[14]

Frederic Gardiner says this expression is a metaphor used of runaway slaves.[15]

Like servants seeking to escape from their master, these angels forsook the household of God in pursuit of a chimerical freedom. They exchanged that service for the dominion of the evil passions which, because they are not at unity among themselves, nor in harmony with the development of the universe, is the most galling slavery.

Gardiner, as did Calvin before him, departs from the traditional view of commentators who hold that these fallen angels are in a literal place, *tartarus* or the like. He says they are the free demons with which we war. He writes that "the Apostle further describes the apostate angels as *reserved in chains that cannot be broken*. A state of sin is not infrequently spoken of in Scripture as a prison-house, and guilt is described under the figure of bonds. See Romans 11:32; Galatians 3:22, etc.; Proverbs 5:22; Lamentations 1:14."[16]

This view rids us of the problem of some fallen angels being bound in a place of torment while others remain free. Gardiner then says, "Whatever be the precise nature of the confinement thus figuratively made known, it still leaves to Satan and his angels the power of inflicting considerable evils upon mankind, and of tempting them from the path of uprightness. Job 1:7; 2:2; Luke 4:2–13; 22:31; 1 Peter 5:8; 2 Corinthians 11:14."[17]

The rebellious angels are kept "for the judgment of the great day." This is almost identical with Peter's words in 2 Peter 2:4. If their being "kept" refers to a place of confinement awaiting future judgment, probably these fallen angels are not yet under judgment, confined in a literal *tartarus* of torment. If not they are either bound in the "pits of darkness" (2 Pet. 4) or are bound to Satan's kingdom of darkness, but are still active as principalities and powers imposing their darkness upon men and societies.

Whichever view one takes of Peter's and Jude's words we can say:

1. Angels sinned.
2. We don't know when the sin occurred.
3. Their general sin was to abandon their designated leadership role in God's creation.
4. They were expelled from God's presence. They are presently in *tartarus,* however we may interpret *tartarus* here. They are presently also in the deepest pits of darkness, under eternal bonds of darkness.

Either way, we have victory over all of them in our reigning Lord as we will soon see. Yet we must learn how to war effectively against them in both world evangelization and Christian living. We must dispel their darkness, as Jesus taught us, by letting our light shine before men. How greatly the world needs to see and hear of the true light of God reflected in Christian lives, homes, and churches, and proclamation!

SPIRITUAL WARFARE IN THE JOHANNINE WRITINGS

The range of spiritual warfare concepts in John's writings is nothing short of amazing. John's writings in his gospel and his epistles on the believer's warfare with the spirit world focus primarily on warfare with Satan. Although he does not say much about warfare with demons, he does mention the work of deceiving spirits (1 John 4:1–6).

The Gospel of John

In the gospel, John's first reference to the evil spirit world (6:70) is unique in the entire New Testament. He has Jesus saying that Judas is a devil, *diabolos,* used exclusively in the rest of the New Testament for the singular person of the devil.

I take the Lord's reference to Judas as a devil as simply a graphic manner of describing how serious his demonization was. We know from all of Scripture that there is only one Devil and he was not Judas. The next references in the gospel of John to the spirit world are a series of references that refer to the Jewish charges that Jesus was a magic-demonized power worker, to Jesus' defense of Himself against these charges, or of other's defense of him (7:20; 8:48,49,52; 10:20–21). All the rest of John's references to the spirit world in his gospel are to Satan by several of his various names (see Fig. 52.1).

1 and 2 John

In John's epistles he continues to refer primarily to "the evil one," his most frequent name for Satan. (The Book of Revelation is a totally different matter, however. John makes more reference to demons or demonized miracle workers than he does to Satan. In fact, except for the synoptic Gospels, John makes more reference to demons in Revelation than any other book in the New Testament. At the same time, he also gives a prominence to Satan unexcelled anywhere else in the New Testament.)

Figure 52.1 presents a chart of all the references to Satan and demonic principalities and powers in John's gospel and 1 and 2 John. (Third John contains no reference to the spirit world.) I have taken the references somewhat in chronological order, starting with John's gospel. Then I do the same for his epistles, uniting concepts and/or verses where the same truth is given. The concepts in John's writings bypassed are primarily the ones we already studied in Paul's writings.

John calls Satan the Devil six times, the Evil One six times, and the Liar and the Father of Lies three times. He calls him a murderer, once; a thief, once; the Wolf, once; the Deceiver, once; the Ruler of this World three times; he who is in the world once. Finally he says "the whole world lies in (the power of) the evil one."

John has an extremely negative view of the world. Like the flesh, the world is totally evil and controlled by the Devil. It is to be resisted and overcome by the believer, by faith (2:15–17; 3:1; 4:1,4–5; 5:4–5,19). There is nothing quite like this in the rest of the entire Bible. John truly had deep insight into the believer's multidimensional sin war. He also understood that behind all the evil of the flesh and of the world stands the Evil One himself.

John also has a strong negative view of those who were deceived by the Devil. They are "the children of the devil" (1 John 3:10). He was especially hard on religious leaders who resisted Jesus and accused him of being a spirit-magician. In John 8 he records Jesus as saying that:

1. The opposing religious leaders were doing "the things" which they "heard from your father [the devil]" (v. 38).
2. "You are doing the deeds of your father [the devil]" (v. 41).
3. "You are of your father the devil" (v. 44a).
4. "You want to do the desires of your father . . . he was a murderer . . . he is a liar" (v. 44).

Next are John's references to the Antichrist. Paul wrote of "The Man of Lawlessness" and "The Lawless One" (2 Thess. 2:3–12); Jesus spoke of false christs and the Abomination of Desolation (Matt. 24:4–15). It was left to John to refine and define these concepts in at least three ways: the one Antichrist "who is coming" (2:18,21); the many antichrists who were already present (2:18,22; 2 John 7); and a powerful demonic spirit which he calls "the spirit of Antichrist" (4:3). He may, however, be using this term to refer to the control of human cultures by principalities and powers of evil producing a demonic-satanic *Zeitgeist,* or spirit of the age.

John also speaks of "spirits" which deny the truth concerning the person of Christ (1 John 4:1–6). He calls them the (singular) spirit of error or falsehood. This expression is unique in the New Testament.

Figure 52.1
Evil Supernaturalism in the Writings of John
(Excluding the Book of Revelation)

A Demon or Have a Demon	Demon Possessed	The Devil	Your Father the Devil
John 7:20 John 8:48–49 John 8:52 John 10:20–21b	John 10:21a	John 8:44 1 John 3:8 (3 times) 1 John 3:10	John 8:38 John 8:41 John 8:44 (twice)

Murderer (the Devil)	Liar and Father of Lies (the Devil)	Thief (the Devil)	Wolf (the Devil)
John 8:44	John 8:44 (twice) 1 John 2:22	John 10:10a	John 10:12

The Evil One	Ruler of this World	Antichrist(s) (Spirit of Antichrist)	The Deceiver
John 17:15 1 John 2:13–14 1 John 3:12 1 John 5:18–19	John 12:31 John 14:30 John 16:11	1 John 2:18 (twice) 1 John 2:22 1 John 4:3 2 John 7	2 John 7

Of the Devil	Children of the Devil	Of the Evil One	Overcome Them, the Evil One
1 John 3:8	John 8:44 1 John 3:10	1 John 3:12	1 John 2:13–14 1 John 4:4

The Devil Sinned from the Beginning		Works of the Devil	He Who Is in the World
1 John 3:8		1 John 3:8	1 John 4:4

Spirit of Error	Idols	The Darkness	Destroy the Works of the Devil
1 John 4:6	1 John 5:21	1 John 1:5–6 1 John 2:8 1 John 2:11 (3 times)	1 John 3:8

The Spirits	Every Spirit	False Prophets	Whole World Lies in Power of Evil One
1 John 4:1	1 John 4:3	1 John 4:1	1 John 5:19

Finally there is 1 John 5:18. I will hold this passage until our last study on spiritual warfare, chapter 63.

Spiritual Warfare in the Book of Revelation

When we examine the spirit world in Revelation we face the problem of the sheer number of references to that world. It is staggering. Next to the gospel of Matthew there are more references to the work of evil supernaturalism in Revelation than anywhere else in the New Testament. The references run the entire gamut from direct satanic-demonic attack against the saints of God to the possible (but not probable) incarnation of Satan in the person of the Beast. An entire book of hundreds of pages needs to be written on these dimensions of cosmic-earthly last-times spiritual warfare from the Book of Revelation.

To summarize its contents, I have made a chart reflecting the major topics concerning evil supernaturalism in Revelation (see Fig. 52.2) and conclude this section with a few observations based on the chart.

1. *Great preeminence is given to Satan himself.* He is called by at least seven different names.

2. *John refers to what are now being called "territorial spirits."* Certain sociocultural and/or geographical areas are described as unusually strong concentrations of satanic-demonic-evil spirit activity. Some of the churches located in these areas were suffering terrible persecution, often leading to martyrdom, John reveals.

3. *References are made to places where evil is particularly strong,* such as "the Synagogue of Satan", "Babylon," called the "dwelling place of unclean spirits," "spirits of demons," and "dwelling place of every unclean spirit." Places which reveal strong satanic power in action are suffering from "the deep things of Satan." They are described as places where false prophets and prophetesses were active. Satanic-demonic warfare, sometimes successful, sometimes not so, against individual churches and Christians is described in considerable detail (Rev. 2—3; 12:17; 13:7).

4. *There is a strong focus on churches and believers needing to overcome the enemy and his attacks.* This is reminiscent of 1 John 2:13–14; 4:1–6, even Ephesians 6:10–20 and 1 Peter 5:8–9 (Rev. 2—3; 12:11).

5. *False prophets hold a dominant role.* The first group is closely related to the churches. They are evidently church leaders, both men and women (Balaam and Jezebel; Rev. 2:13–23). The second is "the false prophet." He is associated with the Beast out of the sea, evidently the one John calls the Antichrist. They both have dominant roles from Revelation 9—20.

6. *Demons are almost as prominent as Satan.* In some cases locust-like creatures emerge from the bottomless pit (Rev. 9:1f) and are identified as "demons," (Rev. 9:11,20; 16:14; 18:2). They have an evil ruler over them called "Abaddon-Apollyon" (9:1–11), i.e., Destroyer. Demons are also called "unclean spirits" and "spirits of demons." They concentrate in certain areas described as "dwelling places of demons" and "a dwelling place of every unclean spirit." Even demon worship is mentioned in a list of the most prominent sins of unrepentant mankind (Rev. 9:20–21).

7. *Sorcery, sorceries, and sorcerers are mentioned as characteristic of the unbelieving world.* Here is the religious dimension of the sins of the flesh as we have already discovered (Gal. 5:20a).

8. *The fall of Satan and the fall of angels are mentioned* (Rev. 9:1; 12:3).[18] These fallen angels are called "the angels of the dragon" (Rev. 12:7f).

9. *Various evil animal-like creatures and "beasts" are prominent.* Everything in chapters 9, 11—20 centers on their corrupting activity among the nations and their hatred of God and His people. These are evidently powerful demonic principalities and powers.

Figure 52.2

Evil Supernaturalism in the Book of Revelation

Satan
2:9,13,24
3:9
12:9
20:2,7

Devil	Dragon	Serpent (of old)	Abaddon/ Apollyon	Synagogue of Satan	Throne of Satan	Where Satan Dwells	Deep Things of Satan	Accuser of the Brethren
2:10 12:9,12 20:2,10	12:3-17 13:2,4,11 16:13 20:2	12:9,14, 15 20:2	9:11	2:9 3:9	2:13	2:13	2:24	12:10

Idols, Idolatry	Balaam, Teaching of	False Prophets		False Apostles	Overcoming (A warfare concept)
		Jezebel Prophetess	False Prophet		
2:14,20 9:20 21:8 22:15	2:14	2:20-23	13:11,14 (not named) 16:13 (named) 19:20 20:10	2:2 (see 2 Cor. 11:13)	2:7,11,17,26 3:5,12,21 12:11

Locust (Demons)	Demons	Ruler of Demons	Demon Worship	Sorcery Sorceries Sorcerers	Fall of Angels (Falling Stars)	Fall of Satan	Angels of the Dragon
9:2-12	9:11,20 16:14 18:2	9:11	9:20	9:21 18:23 21:8 22:15	9:1 12:4	12:7f	12:7-9

Beasts, Various	Babylon, Great (Mother of Harlots) (Mother of Abominations)	Unclean Spirits	Spirits of Demons	Dwelling Place of Demons	Dwelling Place of Every Unclean and Hateful Bird
9:11 with 11:7 13:1f 14:9,11 15:2 16:2,10,13 17:3f 19:19-20 20:4,10	14:8 16:19 17:1f 18:1f	16:13 17:4 18:2 21:27	16:13	18:2	18:2

10. *There is the strange role of a personified evil city* (17:1–18). It is called "Babylon the Great" who makes "all the nations of the earth drink of the wine of her immorality" (14:8; 16:19). Incredible detail is given to describe her nature, her power to corrupt, to dominate, and to rule kingdoms and nations, and to her eventual destruction (chaps. 14—18).

During this time the principalities and powers are in full manifestation until the end (19:20–21; 20:10–15). At the end, the Devil and the principalities and powers, along with death itself and hell, are cast into the lake of fire forever. The warfare of the ages is concluded, giving way to the glorious consummation of God's kingdom on earth (chaps. 21—22). Hallelujah!

SUMMARY: THE DEFEAT OF SATAN AND HIS KINGDOM

We end this exegetical section with a brief summary of the scriptural teaching on the defeat of Satan and his demonic kingdom. This will help put in balanced perspective the view of the powers given us in the New Testament.

1. *Satan's defeat began in the wilderness temptation as we have already discovered.*[19]

During a deliverance session, I once asked a demon, "When did my Master defeat your master?" I expected him to say on the cross.

"In the wilderness temptation," he answered.

I was startled. In a flash I saw the wilderness temptation as I had never seen it before. I had somehow missed the cosmic dimensions of that story until then.

"How did my Master defeat your master in the wilderness temptation?" I asked.

"Because He would not succumb. He would not succumb," he said with deep emotion, especially fear. "If we had won that battle things would be different. We would be on the winning side and you would be defeated. Now you win and we lose."

2. *Satan's defeat was carried forward by Jesus all during His sinless earthly life.*[20]

3. *The Lord Jesus continued His redemptive work and defeat of Satan by bringing deliverance to demonized men, women and children during His entire earthly ministry.*[21]

4. *The Lord maintained His redemptive work and His defeat of Satan by committing to His disciples all authority over all the power of the enemy.*[22]

5. *The Lord Jesus began the final defeat of Satan in His redemptive act on the Cross.* The focal point in all redemptive history and victory over Satan is Calvary, the substitutionary death of the Lord Jesus Christ on the cross.[23] This reality is based on at least three major truths.

   a. The wages of sin is death, or separation from God (Rom. 6:23).
   b. We are all sinners, thus merit eternal death (Rom. 3:23).
   c. The Lord Jesus Christ took our sins upon Himself and experienced in Himself the death those sins merited.

There were at least three dramatic dimensions to His death.

   a. The payment of the blood of the Lord Jesus Christ for our sins was primarily toward God.[24]
   b. The payment of the blood of the Lord Jesus Christ was for the benefit of humanity. He bore both the guilt and the penalty, as well as breaking the power, of our sins.[25]

    c. The payment of the blood of the Lord Jesus Christ for our sins was toward Satan. It canceled all claims of Satan against us, freeing us from his bondage and control.[26]

In Jesus' death on the Cross, Satan's power over obedient humanity was broken, once and for all. The Devil never understood the Cross of Christ until it was too late. He does understand it now, however.[27]

    6. *The Lord Jesus Christ carried forward the final defeat of Satan and the full redemption of humanity* in the five-fold event that includes His death, burial, resurrection, ascension and glorification.[28]

Satan did not understand that death could not hold the Lord Jesus Christ. He did not know that in His resurrection, ascension and glorification, Jesus would ascend above all principalities and powers and reign as Lord in heaven and earth. He did not know that Jesus would commit to His disciples all authority over all the power of the Enemy. He does understand and fear it now.

    7. *The Lord Jesus maintains Satan defeated and the believer redeemed through His ministry of intercession in our behalf at the right hand of God.*[29]

    8. *Finally, the Lord Jesus will complete the defeat of Satan and the redemption of humanity at His glorious second coming.*[30]

If there exists one single key to victory in spiritual warfare, this is it: God, in our behalf, has already totally defeated Satan and his demonic hosts through the Lord Jesus Christ.[31] In the name of our Lord Jesus Christ and through our union with Him, we all share in that victory over Satan and his demonic hosts.[32]

PART FIVE

Practical Considerations

On the Demonization
of Christians

53

The Reality, the Cause,
the Cure

THE REALITY

The possible demonization of true Christians is the single most controversial area of spiritual warfare today. It is also one of the most urgent areas crying for more objective studies and hands-on ministry with severely demonized believers.

Scripture, church history, and contemporary experience show that under unusual conditions of sin, either their own or the sin of others against them, some believers become demonized.

Most Christians would categorically reject the possibility of the demonization of true believers. This was my position during most of my years in Christian ministry. In fact most of us who have reversed our position on this matter were brought up with this traditional view of the non-demonization of believers.[1] We changed primarily because of accumulated experience in counseling the demonized. This has led to renewed scriptural studies and a re-examination of the position of the post-apostolic church fathers on this subject.

As we have seen, the church fathers saw that believers demonized before coming to Christ *were not automatically set free* from their indwelling demons when the Holy Spirit came into their life at conversion. They also knew full deliverance would be more process than crisis. As catechumens, new believers were built up in the truth in Christ. Then, as a final assurance of full deliverance from demons, they were dealt with by the Order of Exorcists, which the church appointed to perform this ministry. It was completed before the believers were baptized, says J. Warwick Montgomery.[2]

Finally, hundreds of Christian leaders counseling traumatized believers have discovered demonic personalities linked to the believers' lives, often dwelling inside of them and in conflict with the indwelling Holy Spirit. We must accept this reality and help them into freedom without tearing away their Christian faith by telling them that since they have demons they are not true Christians and on their way to hell. How dare anyone, to defend a theological presupposition, inflict further pain upon them!

An article reflecting the convictions of most of those who oppose deliverance ministry for believers appeared in *The Word for Today*.[3] In summary it declares that a born-again believer cannot be indwelt by a demon. The article says that to admit to demonic presence in the life of a believer is to declare that God and Satan dwell together. If the believer is seated with Christ in the heavenlies (Eph. 2:6), he is seated above these principalities and powers (Eph. 1:21–22). If the believer is in Christ and Satan has nothing in Christ (John 14:30), how can Satan have anything in the believer?

The writer of the article points out that some of the names claimed by these demons, such as lust, hatred, jealousy, and so forth, are really the works of the flesh, which the believer is to put off (Col. 3:8) or mortify (Rom. 8:13), not cast out. The notion of a demonized believer, then, is a cop-out to one's fleshly nature. Furthermore, neither Jesus, his apostles, nor the early church ever cast out demons from a believer. Those in deliverance ministry supposedly emphasize Satan and demons more than Christ and the Holy Spirit.

This is the type of controversy provoked by the subject we are dealing with. Outspoken critics of compassionate ministry take verses like the ones cited in the above article and distort their meaning. Those verses reflect the ideal for God's people. The critics choose to ignore the obvious fact that most Christians as yet do not live up to God's ideal.

All Christians know that believers can be filled with anger, rage, lust, envy, and jealousy. They can lie, steal, be unkind to others, and even abuse their children. We accept this reality and minister within this real world of Christian failure, always directing our sometimes battered and sinful brothers toward the ideal which is their birthright in Christ.

However, let demons appear in a believer's life, and, reverently speaking, God help them! They receive no sympathy from the brethren who often won't stop manhandling them until they have even gone so far as to accuse battered believers of wanting to be possessed by demons so they can continue to live a sinful life. What a strange way to minister to the suffering!

My position is that true believers can be demonized. Such demonization can range from mild to severe. I am not affirming that true believers can be demon possessed. They cannot be. Satan does not truly possess anything but his own kingdom of fallen spirits.

I am affirming that under rare and unusual conditions of sin, either the sin of the individuals in question or that of others against them, some believers become demonized. Areas of their life can—not necessarily will—come under the direct influence of Satan through demons operating from outside and inside the believer's life.[4]

Those who reject the possible demonization of Christians affirm that the Holy Spirit cannot dwell in the same body with demons.[5] This is a theological presupposition, not a biblical certainty based on scriptural exegesis. Not a single verse of Scripture states that the Holy Spirit cannot or will not dwell in a human body or any other area, where demons are present.[6] The argument is based more upon a syllogism of logic than on biblical interpretation:

The major premise: Every Christian is indwelt by the Holy Spirit.

The minor premise: The Holy Spirit cannot dwell with demons.

The conclusion: Christians cannot have demons.

In every syllogism, if either the major or the minor premise is incorrect, the conclusion is always incorrect.[7] The major premise of the above syllogism is correct (Rom. 8:9; Gal. 4:6), but where is the direct, clear, emphatic scriptural support for the minor premise? If it is lacking, then there is the possibility it is inaccurate and the conclusion false.

At least four lines of argument suggest the traditional theological presupposition concerning the impossibility of the demonization of true believers may be inaccurate.

1. The logical argument presents parallel syllogisms which suggest the possible inaccuracy of the traditional syllogism. One would be:

   The major premise: Every Christian is indwelt by the Holy Spirit.

   The minor premise: The Holy Spirit cannot dwell with sin.

   The conclusion: Christians cannot sin.

2. The negative argument is that one cannot find a single verse of Scripture which states that true believers cannot be indwelt by demons. Second Corinthians 6:14–18 and James 3:11–13 are often suggested, but when read in the context of the rest of Scripture their true meaning is clear.[8] Neither of these verses states that the Holy Spirit cannot or will not dwell in the same location with a demon. To read into these and similar verses such a view is not *exegesis,* "in which the meaning of Scripture is brought out," but *eisegesis,* "bringing a meaning into Scriptures."[9]

3. The positive argument presents case studies of severely demonized believers, and biblical principles or teaching.[10]

4. The historical argument presents past experience showing that God's people, under unusual circumstances, can become demonized.[11] As repeatedly stated, the Patristic Church recognized that true believers who had been or still were involved in idolatry, occultism, spirit homage, and magic could be demonized even after receiving Christ as their Savior.

A List of Possible Case Studies

1. First there is the case of King Saul (1 Sam. 9–31). He was a true Old Testament believer. He was filled by the Holy Spirit on more than one occasion, as we have already seen (see chapter 35). On three occasions an evil spirit entered his life, causing dramatic personality changes when the demon was in manifestation.

2. Next is the example of the rebellious nation of Israel. It is altogether possible that most of the adult Jews who had given themselves to gross spirit-idol worship were demonized when God sent them into captivity. The prophets describe in shocking detail their total surrender to the spirit world.

Israel united the cult of Baal with the worship of Jehovah (Hos. 2:13,17). The result was a deplorable syncretism which soon led Israel to reject the Law of her God. She was, in turn, rejected by God (Hos. 4:1–10). Israel became ensnared by the Devil. The people became as demonized as the Baal worshipers they had joined (Hos. 9:1,7–10,15—10:2 with 1 Cor. 19:19–22; 1 Tim. 3:6–7; 2 Tim. 2:26).

3. In the New Testament we have vivid case studies of Jews, regular synagogue attenders, who were severely demonized (Mark 1:21–28; 39).

4. The case of the demonized daughter of Abraham (Luke 13:10–17; see John 8:33–35; Gal. 3:29.) She was a true Jewish believer (v. 16). Her sickness was caused by an evil spirit (v. 11) from which Jesus set her free (v. 12).

5. The case of the demonized church family of Ananias and Sapphira (Acts 5:1–10), discussed earlier. They were believers, but Satan had filled the heart of Ananias (v. 3). "To fill is to control, the same expression used for the filling of the Holy Spirit. That is pretty strong language.

How does John's promise in 1 John 5:18 that the Evil One will not touch the believer apply in these cases? The obvious meaning of John's words here, says William Vine, is that Satan cannot "assault (the believer), in order to sever the vital union between Christ and the believer."[12] To take the word "touch" as meaning Satan cannot afflict a believer is to contradict all of Scripture. If believers give place to the Devil (Eph. 4:27), he can bring them into bondage to himself, the New Testament clearly teaches (1 Tim. 3:6–7; 5:15; 2 Tim. 2:26), or even destroy their physical life (1 Cor. 5:5; 11:30–31; 1 Tim. 1:20).

God can use Satan's touch against sinning believers to humble them. In some cases, God even allows Satan to take the life of godly, obedient, faithful believers (Rev. 2:10; 12:17; 13:7).

Warnings of the New Testament that Christians can become partly bound or controlled by Satan are very vivid. Paul cautions against the potential demonization of bishops, elders, and pastors (1 Tim. 3:6–7), Bible teachers, preachers, and prophets (2 Cor. 11:3–4,13–15; 1 Tim. 1:19–20 with 2 Tim. 2:14–26; 1 Tim. 4:1f; 1 John 4:1–4). There is the enigma of demonized "deaconesses" (1 Tim. 5:9–15) and the danger of demonized gifted Christian leaders and miracle workers (1 John 4:1–4 with Matt. 7:13–29; 2 Thess. 2:1–17; Rev. 13).

Demonized bitter, jealous, selfish, ambitious, arrogant, lying, and cursing believers are spoken of in James 3:9–15. We are also warned of the possibilities of Christians receiving another spirit (2 Cor. 11:3–4).

Finally, we have warnings about Christians giving an area of their lives over to occupancy by Satan, knowingly or unknowingly (Eph. 4:27). "Give no place to the devil," Paul says (KJV). The word "place," *topos,* is the word from which we derive the English word *topography.* Vine says it "is used of a region or locality . . . of a place which a person or thing occupies."[13] "Of the 84 times it appears in the Scripture only twice does it mean occasion . . . it usually indicates an area of occupancy."[14]

TWO EXPLANATIONS FOR THE TERRIBLE ENIGMA OF DEMONIZED CHRISTIANS

The enigma of demonized Christians may be explained two ways.

First, they were demonized before their conversion. All demons do not always automatically leave the body of demonized unbelievers when they turn to Christ. While most of us have been taught that they will, the New Testament nowhere teaches such a doctrine. To affirm otherwise is a theological presupposition, not a biblical certainty. This is especially true when the demonized are brought to Christ by the traditional Western logical-analytical approach towards evangelism. To be assured that demonized unbelievers will be set free from their demons, power-encounter evangelism may have to occur.

I have already given case studies where this happened. In some cases the individuals had difficulty coming to Christ apart from power encounter. The demons came into full manifestation while we were trying to lead them to Christ.[15] This will usually happen with severely demonized unbelievers. While the initial power encounter was decisive, it was not complete. All had to go through ongoing deliverance after their conversion. This also will almost always happen with severe demonization, at least for a period of time until the new believer can be taught self-deliverance through truth encounter. For all involved in ongoing one-on-one power evangelism, these cases are not as rare as some would have us believe. This is also true in group evangelism (Acts 8).

Second, believers become demonized after their conversion by serious sins they commit or serious sin committed against them. Satan and his evil spirits as sin personified are the believers' greatest enemies and exist to spread sin among God's people. They will attach themselves to sin areas of a believer's life and work continually to increase their control over these areas (Eph. 4:27). That control is only partial, however, never total. Thus, demonized believers are able and responsible to turn against the demons attached to their lives. One of the purposes of pre-deliverance counseling is to lead believers to confess and reject the sins in their life, and to renounce Satan and all his demonic powers.

Generally speaking, the demonic condition of demonized believers is usually mild. Most are able to maintain a normal life. They usually realize that something is wrong within them, though they seldom suspect they are suffering from demonization. Many are sincere, Spirit-filled Christians often bound by unexplainable fears, confusion, uncontrollable emotions, and other disturbing phenomena.

Often certain sins dominate their life in actual open sinful activity or in their thoughts. They are in bondage to evil imaginations and unholy fantasies. While all believers have this problem on occasion, with these believers it is often a living nightmare. They are struggling with what I call the continuum of sin. Their minds are a battleground of evil thoughts which, as godly Christians, they abhor.

Following the continuum of sin (see Fig. 17.1, p. 134), we see that evil thoughts can come from any of the three sources of sin energy, or all three at the same time. Troubled believers often fluctuate between rejecting these thoughts, practicing Philippians 4:8, and being overpowered by them. Either way, they must choose to accept or reject these sinful thoughts.

If these believers do not learn the way to victory in the warfare for their thought life, they will begin to form evil habits of imagination and fantasy. This, in turn, leads to the beginning of loss of control over their thought life. Over a period of time, loss of thought control inevitably leads to bondage to evil fantasies which soon leads to evil actions. The end can be almost total control by certain compulsive forms of sin. How many believers are in bondage to evil habits, only God knows!

Usually demonically troubled believers battle in four primary sin areas. All four areas can exist without demonization being present, but certainly demonic activity of some degree—affliction or attachment—is involved. These are the four sin areas:

1. Illicit sexual practices or fantasies out-of-control.
2. Deep-seated anger, bitterness, hatred, rage and rebellion, often leading to destructive and/or self-destructive impulses.
3. A sense of rejection, guilt, poor self-esteem, unworthiness, and shame.
4. Strange attraction to the occult and to the spirit world, often, but not always, with a desire for illicit power over circumstances and other people.

Fortunately, most demonized believers do not need dramatic, spectacular, one-on-one prolonged power encounter deliverance sessions. They usually only need to be brought through what Neil Anderson correctly calls "truth encounter." He outlines it as "Seven Steps to Freedom in Christ."[16] This can be ministered by any Spirit-filled believer. Professional deliverance ministers or counselors are not usually needed. This is part of the believer's authority which comes through our union with Christ.

Figure 53.1, "The Three Levels of Protection Around Us," illustrates how demons occasionally can gain entrance into the life of a believer after conversion through personal sin.

The schema follows the trichotomous view that the human person is made up of body, soul, and spirit. If one holds to the dichotomous view, that man is composed of only two essential dimensions of reality, his material nature, and immaterial nature, the reality is the same.

As believers, we evidently have at least three levels of protection around us: the mysterious hedge of God that the Devil complained about in Job 1—2; the wonderful angels of God who continually minister to our needs (Ps. 34:7; 91:11–13; Heb. 1:14); and the shield of faith of Ephesians 6:16. It, if used properly, will protect us from "all the flaming missiles of the evil one."

These flaming missiles—here I will limit them to direct stimulation or temptation to sin—are continually hurled against us with ever-increasing intensity. If we are emotionally and spiritually healthy believers, the arrows are deflected. At the same time, we must admit that under some severe attacks, we are almost cast down, especially if we are passing through an "evil day." By the grace of our loving Lord we are able to get back up to fight again. We wield the sword of the Spirit; we practice "all prayer"; we are restored; the Enemy retreats. He comes back again and the whole process is repeated, however.

When these temptations come against us, if we are tantalized by the sins in question, we can be in danger. Even when that happens, at first there is usually no immediate change. If we continue to compromise, however, we are soon in trouble. We begin to struggle with interpersonal relationships and are drawn towards specific sins. Yet, at first, the spirit world would usually seem to be inactive: We do not at first sense any demonic activity *in* our life, only *against* our life, and there is a world of difference.

If sin is persisted in, the wall of protection around the believer will be weakened, then breached. When this happens, Paul says, we may give the Devil a base of operation in our life (Eph. 4:27). It is not easy for demons to gain entrance into the life of a believer, but at some point, access is often gained.

The first demon inside the believer's life will work to gain entrance for other demons. From within, they have direct access to the mind, emotions, and even the believer's will. They want to injure the believer enough to marginalize him in his Christian life and ministry. They can best accomplish that task from within the believer's life.

If the believer repents and turns against the demons, many, perhaps all, will be expelled (James 4:7–8). If not, they will remain there, often in hiding, for years. They will slowly begin to affect sensitive areas of the believer's life, penetrating deeper and deeper into the very center of the believer's personality without their presence even being suspected. The believer will usually need help to get started towards freedom from their power. These are the types of believers I spend so much time with.

Figure 53.1
The Three Levels of Protection Around Us

The *hedge of God* (Job 1—2), the *angels of God* (Ps. 34:7; 91:11–13; Heb. 1:14), the *shield of faith* (Eph. 6:16) are God's three primary levels of protection, represented by the wavy line.

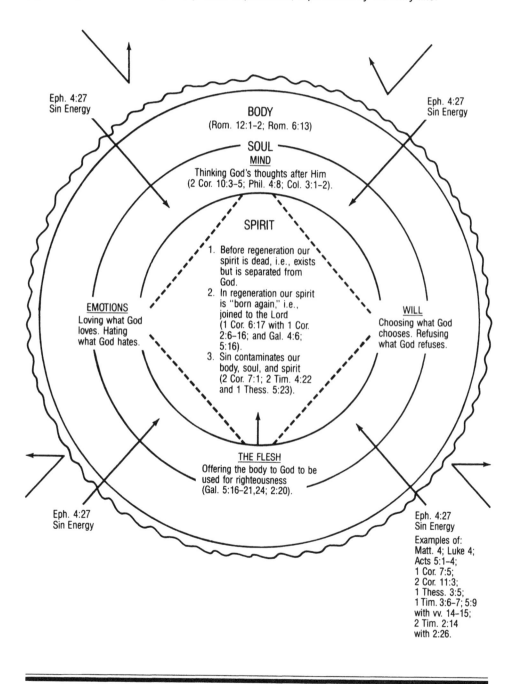

Since these matters are not dealt with in detail in Scripture, the above description comes from the accumulated experience of those who are willing to minister to demonically afflicted believers, including my own experience.

It is now time to look at the most common sin doors through which demons frequently gain entrance into human lives.

54

Six Sin Areas and the Possible Demonization of Christians

U nder unusual conditions of sin, true believers can become demonized. What are the major, identifiable sin areas which occasionally bring this about? I list six in some sense of order in which they occur, beginning even before infancy and continuing through adulthood. They are generational sin; child abuse; social sins such as anger, bitterness, rage, rejection, and rebellion; sexual sin; curses from the spirit world; and occult practices.

These sin areas do not automatically lead to demonization, and where it does occur, it can range from mild to severe. Deliverance, also, can vary from the instantaneous, in which, for example, one is totally freed at the moment of conversion, to the prolonged. In the latter case, the victim may need to practice self-deliverance (spiritual warfare focused on breaking the demonic strongholds within one's own life) over a period of time or seek the help of other believers to effect full deliverance.

GENERATIONAL SIN

Generational sin is sin judgment which moves through the family line. It is called by various other names such as tranference, inheritance, or familial sin. In some cases demons seem to become identified with a family line. This then leads to demonic transference, demonic inheritance, and potential generational demonization.

To my knowledge, direct and clearly defined biblical teaching or examples of demonic transference are not found in Scripture. What is found are divine warnings that the sins of parents can have potentially devastating consequences on their children. The context in which these warnings are given is very clear. Heads of families, usually males, have rebelled against God. God says they hate Him (Exod. 20:5). What is implied is a deliberate turning away from God. Usually, if not always, it involves serving other gods, denying God the love and obedience which His singular and absolute Lordship demands (Exod. 20:5–6; Deut. 5:9b–10; 18:9–14). Ministry with people afflicted by demons which have come down through family lines always reveals this to be the case.

In such rebellion the authority figure deliberately turns from God to serve other gods, Satan, or the spirits and to do terrible evil. They will often commit their family and future generations to the gods, the spirits, Satan, and evil.

Jewish heads of households knew whatever they did would affect their families for generations. God told them so. In times of crisis they stood before God and confessed the sins of their family, even of their nation. Outstanding biblical case studies are found in Nehemiah 1:4–9; Jeremiah 14:20, and Daniel 9:1–19.[1] The Jews understood that the sins of the fathers could affect future generations. The principle is that family sin or judgment for that sin flows through the family line, affecting later generations who had nothing to do with the sins in question.

This generational curse can be broken by family members who identify themselves with the sins of the fathers or by national leaders who identify with the sins of their nation, either before or after the fourth generation. That is what Nehemiah (Neh. 1:4–9), Jeremiah (Jer. 14:20), and Daniel did (Dan. 9:1–21).

The Jews interpreted this warning in this manner at least by the time of the divided kingdom (Jer. 31:27–30; Lam. 5:7; Ezek. 18:1–20). The negative approach of the prophets towards this "law of the inheritance of evil"[2] was not to deny its reality but correct its abuses. One abuse, according to Plumtre, was that "men found in it an explanation of their sufferings which relieved their consciences. They were suffering, they said, for the sins of their fathers, not for their own."[3]

William H. Brownlee adds further insight:[4]

> Ezekiel objects . . . to the perverse usage by which one infers that if past generations were as wicked as Ezekiel claims (2:3, chapter 16, 20, 23), then it will be of no use to repent in order to avert the doom he predicts. They say, in effect: "Of what use is repentance? Our fate is already sealed by the sins of the fathers." Against this Ezekiel directs a lengthy disputation.

Plumtre declares that the Scriptures support "the law of hereditary tendencies and punishments that fall not on the original offenders, but on their children, and the law of individual responsibility."[5]

In light of this biblical principle of the law of inheritance of evil, demonic transference or inheritance would *not* appear unlikely. The most obvious possibility would be for occult involvements of parents who rebel against God and join themselves to the no-gods of the spirit world. They usually present not only themselves to the spirits but their progeny also. Studies in non-Christian religions and occultism reveal this transference to be a fact.[6]

Finally, the experience of most, if not all, believers who are involved in deliverance ministry would reveal this dimension of demonization to be a vivid reality. Thus, it is wise to confess the sins of one's family line (Neh. 1:4–9; Jer. 14:20) and smash any potential demonic transference in the life of all new converts from non-Christian families. This would be especially true in the life of all believers from families which practiced any form of occultism, were members of non-Christian religions, or were involved in extreme forms of moral sin.

I even encourage adoptive parents, in a non-threatening manner, to take their adopted and foster children through deliverance. In several cases where severe demonization has existed since infancy, demons have declared their presence in the family line, sometimes for hundreds of years. There is no reason to doubt their claims. This gives the evil spirits a sense of ownership of the family line in question. While for Westerners this is hard to accept, it is a reality to be reckoned with. When the ownership is broken by the repentant family member, at that point the generational sin curse stops.[7]

CHILD ABUSE

The victim of child abuse becomes the victim of the sin of others, usually trusted authority figures, in childhood or youth. Because of the extent of child abuse in the United States, this dimension of evil needs special consideration.

It is one of the major evils being perpetuated through powerful evil principalities and powers in the U.S. today. It deals with that part of the human race most beloved to God, little children. The words spoken by Jesus about the relationships of the heavenly Father to children is spoken of regarding no other human social unit (Matt. 18:1–10; 19:13–15). Since Satan hates God, he especially hates what God loves most, our children. It is as simple as that.

Children are the most vulnerable and defenseless of all human beings. They cannot protect themselves from human and supernatural evil as adults can. We adults are their primary protectors. As a result, children are very susceptible to demonization (Matt. 15; Mark 9; Acts 16).

Children become adults, parents, and grandparents. Damaged, demonized adults tend to raise damaged, demonized children and grandchildren. The most strategic way to destroy humanity is to destroy man's children. The greatest good to be done to humanity is to protect and to heal its damaged children.

Abuses suffered by children today usually fall into four broad but interrelated classifications.

Four Types of Abuse	Four Common Negative Reactions
Sexual Abuse	Extreme shame and sexual problems. Fear and anger also occur.
Physical Abuse	Extreme rage and interpersonal relationship problems.
Psychological Abuse	Extreme negative self-image and a spirit of rejection. Always produces anger.
Religious Abuse	Extreme confusion about God and the Christian faith. Inability to trust God or the Son of God.

The negative reactions listed are not exhaustive. Anger, bitterness, rage, and interpersonal relationship problems will almost always accompany each of the four types of abuse.

The worst possible type of child abuse occurring today is Satanic Ritual Abuse (SRA), a combination of all four forms of abuse. It is religious abuse performed on a child to cause unspeakable pain. It is physical abuse related to sexual abuse, often rape and perversion of every imaginable and unimaginable type. It results in the most extreme form of psychological damage. The growing child is preprogrammed through this ultimate evil to malfunction as a youth and as an adult. Often the abuse splits the personality of the child, producing personality disassociation leading to Multiple Personality Disorder (MPD). Research reveals that 75 percent or more of MPDs resulted from SRA and related forms of extreme child sexual abuse.

Jay, a student at San Jose Christian College, was totally committed to Christ. He wanted to be a pastor. He was also obviously a disturbed man. Loud, boisterous, argumentative, and angry, he had the reputation among the faculty of being a troublemaker.

While I was teaching missions from the Book of Acts, Jay came alive in the class. He was excited about missions, the Lord, and people. Soon we were dealing with Satan and his attacks against God's people in Acts. We also dealt with demons. One day Jay stayed behind after class.

"Dr. Murphy, I love the Lord, but I am a difficult person to get along with. I have difficulty getting along with myself. What is wrong with me? Could I be demonized?"

Jay had been abandoned by his father and mother and rescued when he was three years old by an aunt and uncle who were drunkards and who physically fought each other. They smashed furniture and tore up the house. As a little boy, Jay had to hide to escape being beaten himself. He was not always successful escaping their rage and drunken bouts.

His aunt was the worst offender. She beat him so often he was black and blue all over his body. One day she beat him unmercifully. He had no place to hide, nowhere to go, no one to protect him.

"Dr. Murphy, I ran outside," he told me. "I was crying and screaming. I was filled with hatred for my aunt, my uncle, for everyone and especially for God. Where was God? He was supposed to be the protector of children, but He had not protected me. He gave me a bad mother and father. He gave me a bad aunt and uncle. So He was a bad God, if He even existed at all.

"I raised my fists up toward the sky and screamed my hatred against God. I then called upon the Devil, if he existed. I asked him to punish my aunt and uncle. I asked him to take my life. I was his because God had abandoned me.

"Dr. Murphy, a terrible thing happened, instantly. A dark cloud surrounded me. I could almost see and feel it. It completely covered me and it has never lifted. I have lived in that dark cloud until today. It parted some when I accepted Jesus as my Savior and Lord, but it never went away. It still envelopes me. Could it be demons?"

I had to go on the assumption that it was. I decided not to go after that "cloud" but to teach Jay to do so. Eventually he was totally delivered through self-deliverance.

ANGER, BITTERNESS, RAGE, REJECTION, AND REBELLION

These sins usually result from wrong or alleged wrong done in childhood or youth and continue on into adulthood. While reactionary sin (see Fig. 24.1, p. 172) arises because of wrong or supposed wrong done to an individual, reactionary sin itself can open the door to demons. Most demons of anger, bitterness, rage, rejection, and rebellion come in *after* the abuse as the victim gives way to anger and rage over what is happening.

Earlier I told the story of the young lady filled with bitterness against her grandparents and her parents. I presented her bitterness and sexual problems only from the perspective of the flesh. I did not mention that she was also severely demonized. She had called me because of problems with her young child, a boy about one year of age. She was certain his problems were demonic. Her child was having night terrors. Of course, night terrors are not necessarily demonic. In her child's case she was certain demons were involved because the child's toys were mysteriously thrown around the room whenever he experienced these terrors, usually more than once a week.

I always carefully probe the life of Christian parents who are having possible demonic problems with their children. A great number of the demonic problems experienced by believers are associated with their families. Demonic transference, child abuse, and dysfunctional home life are among the most frequent causes of the attachment of demons to the life of children.

In this case I did not have to do any probing. At one point in the conversation, after telling of her prolonged sexual abuse by her grandfather, she began to talk of her personal sexual fantasies.

"I love my husband very much," she said. "We have a good sexual relationship together, but Dr. Murphy, strange sexual urges often suddenly come upon me. I feel like I would like to go out on the street and just pick up some handsome, sexy man and go to a motel and have sex with him. Where does that fantasy come from? I hate it, but it comes to me over and over again."

As the session went on I began to suspect that this lovely young mother was afflicted by both sexual demons and demons related to bitterness and anger. I said nothing to her about it, however. As a rule of thumb, I never infer that a person has a demonic problem unless I make direct contact with demons in their life. It does influence the way I pray with the person, however.

As I led in prayer I prayed what is sometimes called an affirmation of faith and doctrinal prayer (see Appendix A). I continued praying in this manner with my eyes open, after asking Mary Ann to close her eyes. Suddenly she showed signs of personal discomfort. She began to rock from one side of the chair to another and to breathe abnormally. Her hands twisted and moved. Her face became distorted and ugly. I began to prepare myself for possible demonic interruption. I was not quite ready, however, for the piercing scream that came from deep within this small woman, nor for the rasping voice that cried out in protest against me.

"I-I-I-I . . . haaate . . . yoouu!"

I quickly silenced the protesting demon.

Mary Ann was startled at what had just come out of her mouth. She had no idea that she had a demonic problem. Over the course of a few counseling sessions she and her child were set free.

The pastor whom I invited to minister to her with me continued counseling her. He later discovered that her psychologist husband was also demonized. He too was set free. Today they are part of the counseling and deliverance team of his church.

Mary Ann was severely demonized by many sexual demons associated with her repeated sexual abuse as a child by her grandfather and an even larger group of social demons: anger, rage, rebellion, rejection, and bitterness were the primary ones, with bitterness leading the pack.

SEXUAL SINS

The fourth common sin door to demonic involvement in the lives of believers is the door of sexual sins and sexual malfunctions of all types. In a great majority of cases of severe demonization of adult Christians, sexual demons are present. I offer a few suggestions why:

1. Sexuality occupies an important place in human life. In a unique manner it reflects the image of God in man. God as perfect being possesses all the sublime qualities of maleness and femaleness in His one person. While God is not sexual, He has created the unique qualities of maleness and femaleness. Thus, neither man nor woman is fully complete without the other. Disturbing human sexuality disturbs the whole person. Demons recognize this fact and exploit it for evil.

2. When persons are crippled sexually, their entire being is damaged. More harm can be done to humanity by debasing sexuality than by almost any other single factor except for spirituality. Thus the most destructive form of child abuse is not physical abuse but sexual physical abuse. If a religious dimension is also added (SRA), the sexual abuse is even more destructive.

3. Sex is one of the most powerful drives in life. Men and women face some of their fiercest struggles at this point. Sex out of control leads to some of the greatest personal and social problems faced by humanity. AIDS and abortion result primarily from the abuse of sexuality, as do prostitution,

rape, incest, homosexuality, and the unimaginable range of sexual perversions humanity practices.

4. Demons of sexual abuse and perversion are floating in the air, so to speak, everywhere. They are among the most active, subtle, and vicious of all demons.

An Indian friend of mine, Brother Silas, is a successful church planter in the villages of northern India. He had planted a church in a particular Hindu village. Its young pastor invited Silas to return to visit the church. He was also anxious that Silas talk with his young wife, who had been acting strangely. She did not even want to attend church with her pastor husband.

After speaking in the church on a Sunday morning, Silas went to the pastor's small, thatched-roof mud home. The pastor's wife had not been at church that morning. When he approached the house, she was inside. Before he even came in sight, the young wife spoke out, "Brother Silas is here to see me. I must go out and meet him."

She went outside just as Silas reached the gate. As she ran towards him, she began pulling off her clothes. When she reached Silas she was totally naked. Silas knew exactly what was going on. He bound the sexual demons into submission to him. Returned to her senses, the young lady was horrified to find herself naked. She had not realized what she had just done.

In counseling her, Silas discovered that a few weeks earlier on a Sunday morning when she had stayed home from church alone, a young Hindu priest appeared at her door. He seduced her. In the act, sexual demons entered her body. Though she later repented, she was still troubled by sexual fantasies. With Brother Silas' help she was set free.

CURSES IN THE SPIRIT WORLD

Curses are a puzzle to the Western mind. We think of a curse as an expression of anger or displeasure which has no inherent power to inflict evil. Thus, the saying, "Sticks and stones may break my bones, but names will never hurt me." Is that all there is to curses?

The Bible opens and closes with curses. God pronounces the first series of curses upon Satan, mankind, and the land (Gen. 3:14–19). The last reference to the curse declares its end (Rev. 22:3). In other words, for humanity there is no escape from the power of the curse and curses until the new heavens and new earth have come and the saints are glorified with our Lord in the eternal kingdom.

Curses come from four possible sources: God, God's servants, the spirit world, and Satan's human servants. All four release spiritual energy towards the person or object cursed.

To curse is primarily an Old Testament concept. From the Old Testament world view cursing finds its meaning. Cursing is not used in the Old Testament with the Western idea of swearing or speaking dirty words. Cursing in the Old Testament is a *power concept* meant to release negative spiritual power against the object, person, or place being cursed. This is true even when God does the cursing. In fact, most curse expressions in Scripture refer to God's action or the action of His servants in accordance with His will. It is God releasing His power of judgment. That is why I call it negative spirit power even when activated by God.

So prominent is this activity of God in pronouncing curses, it can hardly be exaggerated. Of the some 202 curse contexts in Scripture, God or God through His servants is pronouncing the curse 143 times. Entire chapters are given to listing the curses sin will bring upon God's people (Deut. 27—31). One of the most prominent motifs is the curse-versus-blessing motif. Entire chapters are dedicated to it (Deut. 28—30; Num. 22—24).

So precious are the people of God in His eyes, three times He declares He will curse the one who curses His people. He also says, "Cursed is everyone who curses you" (Num. 24:9).

It is dangerous to curse another man. Only a prophet directly led of God can rightly do so. Twice God says one who curses another should be cursed himself. Thirty-one times such curses are warned against. Cindy Jacobs, in her excellent book *Possessing the Gates of the Enemy,* critiques the practice of believers who pronounce curses upon unbelievers, especially those who resist the truth. (Her section on what she calls "strike-em dead" prayers is excellent.) She wisely says, "The point that I am making, however, is that while we do rebuke Satan from controlling people, we are not to curse people. We are to call out to God and let Him decide the judgment."[8]

Satan also understands the power concept of curses. He told God twice that Job did not really love Him unselfishly. "Take Your hand off his life," Satan said. "Let me at him, and he will curse You to Your face" (Job 1:11; 2:5). It wasn't long before the command to curse God reached Job's ears. Sadly, his wife became the accusing voice of Satan to that end. "Curse God and die," she said (Job 2:9).

Under the Law given later, a person who cursed God was to be executed. The Old Testament also warns against cursing rulers. It records occasions when rulers were cursed by angry men. Shimei cursed David. David allowed it for the moment in his time of humiliation. Later he ordered him executed (1 Kings 2:8f).

T. Lewis and R. K. Harrison inform us:

> When a curse is pronounced against any person we are not to understand this as a mere wish, however violent, that disaster should overtake the person in question, any more than we are to understand that a corresponding "blessing" conveys simply a wish that prosperity should be the lot of the person on whom the blessing is involved. A curse was considered to possess an inherent power of carrying itself into effect. . . . Such curses [and blessings] possessed the power of self-realization.[9]

G. B. Funderburk says, "Indeed, the validating of pronounced blessing and the antitheses of cursing in early Bible history is amazing."[10] He cites the following:

1. Noah pronounces a curse on Canaan and a blessing on Shem and Japheth (Gen. 9:25–27).
2. Isaac blesses his twin sons and pronounces a curse upon anyone who was to curse Jacob (Gen. 27:27–28).
3. Jacob blesses his 12 sons, the most elaborate series of parental blessings in Scripture (Gen. 49:28).
4. The power released in either blessing or cursing was real. The curse was to be feared and the blessing to be coveted.

The story of Jacob and Esau is a case in point. Their seeking for the blessing of their ailing father Isaac, revolves around that blessing power concept (Gen. 27:1f). Also, Rebekah's deceptive plot for Jacob to steal the blessing of the firstborn in place of Esau is a world-view power play.

A curse uttered or written in the name of God through his authority figures was considered effective in bringing the judgment of God upon the person, place, or thing.

Moses set before Israel "the blessing and the curse" (Deut. 30:1). Jeremiah spoke of the curse upon disobedient Israel which caused the land to mourn (Jer. 23:10).

Was this world view a valid one, or was God merely accommodating himself to the superstitious world view Israel held in common with its pagan neighbors? If God accommodates to a quaint but inaccurate world view here, where does He stop? The entire Old Testament in its curse/blessing theology is built on this world view. We find it in the New Testament as well.

As Lewis and Harrison say, the curse reality

> plays an important part in Paul's interpretation of the curse. In the light of the Law all men are guilty. . . . The violator of the Law is under a curse. His doom has been pronounced. Escape is impossible. But on the cross, Jesus Christ ended the curse—"for cursed be everyone who hangs on the tree" (Gal. 3:10, 13) and a curse that has overcome its victim is a spent force.[11]

Jesus himself cursed the fig tree which bore no fruit (Mark 11:12–14) as a symbol of the doom of his fruitless people.[12] He exhorts us "bless those who curse you, pray for those who mistreat you" (Luke 6:28). Paul responds taking this even further. He says, "Bless those who persecute you; bless and curse not" (Rom. 12:14).

This is exactly what Jesus himself did from the Cross (Luke 23:34). Should we do less? Thus James' astonishment that with the same mouth, "we bless our Lord and Father; and with it we curse men, who have been made in the likeness of God; from the same mouth come both blessing and cursing. My brethren, these things ought not to be this way" (James 3:9–10).

Many believers have been victims of the curses of the Enemy pronounced by the Enemy's power workers.

Such curses are not always effective, but often they are.

Such curses do not usually involve demonization, but at times they do.

Such curses are not always allowed by God, but often they are.

Such curses do not usually have to be individually identified and defended against, but often they do.

Such curses thrive on ignorance and arrogance. They are nullified by knowledge and humility.

Such curses, to be most powerful, are "worked up" by invocations to the spirits and satanic magic. They are overcome only by the greater power of God. Sometimes God does not automatically overcome those curses on our behalf, however. We are to learn the world of spirit power curses and break them ourselves. Thus the importance of group spiritual warfare praying.

A missionary in Africa became strangely sick and lost weight at an alarming rate. The doctors were puzzled. She increased her eating, but her body would not assimilate the nutrients from the food she ate. Finally, she had to be sent home to Canada for medical treatment. The treatment did not help. She became worse and worse.

She began to attend the church where Dr. John White and Ron Blue were then leaders. In time God revealed that the source of her problem was not physical but spiritual. In a time of prayer it was discovered a curse had been placed on her. When the curse was broken, her body was then able to function normally. She was healed.[13]

THE AIRPLANE STORY

I recently read an article warning believers not to believe in or spread unfounded stories of occultism and Satanism. The writer cited the accusation that the logo used on the Proctor and Gamble products was connected with Satanism. Obviously, it is not true. Unfortunately the writer mentioned the airplane story as another untrue fable being circulated by misguided Christians.

The airplane story is true. One of my prayer partners in the San Jose area experienced it herself. She was flying out of San Jose. She sat in an aisle seat. The seat next to her was empty but the window seat was occupied by a young man. When it was time for the stewardess to serve the meal my prayer partner accepted hers. The young man refused, saying he was fasting.

"I overheard you tell the stewardess you are fasting," my friend said. "Then you must be a Christian."

"No, I am a Satanist," was the reply.

Pat was taken back by his remark. She did not know if she should look for another seat on the plane or what! She decided to stay where she was and engage the young man in conversation if he would. In fact, he was quite willing to talk of his faith and witness to the power of Satan.

In the course of the conversation, Pat asked him about the specific targets of his fasting and praying. (Such fasting and praying is a curse attempt, not humble supplication.) He said the targets were the leading churches and pastors in the San Jose area and two leading Christian missions. When Pat asked which missions were the targets, without hesitation he said they were Partners International and OC International.

This hit home. Pat's father was one of the founders of Partners International. She also is a supporter of OC International, my mission.

Within the next few years a half dozen key pastors in the San Jose area fell into immorality and were removed from their churches. Coincidence? This had never occurred before. What happened to Partners International and OC International? Ask their leadership what they experienced during the late 1980s and early 1990s.

The airplane story has now become the restaurant story. Christians in restaurants have seen groups of people gathered at tables, obviously praying. Thinking they were believers, they have approached them only to find they were Satanists "praying" to Satan and putting curses on leading pastors and Christian workers.

It has also become the supermarket story. Missionary Beverly Lewis of the World Gospel Mission reported of her experience in Argentina. A Satanist, waiting in the check-out line in a supermarket, suddenly announced to everyone that he and his group of Satanists were praying and fasting to Satan "for the destruction of the homes of the Christian leaders." Beverly then follows with the sad story of the results in her city of the curse prayer and fasting to Satan. The story is shocking and sobering.[14]

This calls us back again to the recognition that we are at war. We must learn how to mobilize believers to warfare prayer to break these demonic curses. We must not allow the biblical truth of the defeat of the demonic powers and principalities to lull us into an arrogant, indifferent complacency saying it cannot happen to us. This is biblical and historical naivete.

OCCULT PRACTICES

There are two broad types of occultism with which we are at war: non-Christian occultism and Christian occultism. A broad summary of non-Christian occultism would require pages of material. I will only mention several areas which are focal points of warfare for believers, especially in the Western world:

1. The horoscope and other astrological practices.
2. The use of ouija boards and similar methods of direct contact with and use of the power of the spirit world.
3. Fantasy role games involving the spirit world, such as "Dungeons and Dragons."
4. The acceptance and use of any psychic powers from pre-conversion days.
5. All attempts to seek psychic or spiritual healings.
6. Any practice of ESP, clairvoyance, levitation, telekinesis, astral projection, automatic handwriting, and similar practices. While some of this can be outright fraud, much induces the operation of evil spirits.
7. Any involvement in the cults, seances, belief in reincarnation, attempts to contact the dead.
8. All Eastern and mystic religions and other non-Christian religions.
9. Heavy metal rock, acid, punk, or other immoral and destructive music or groups. Many of these groups and music are demonic and occultic.[15]
10. The New Age movement. I dedicate a later chapter to this modern revival of paganism and Eastern religions.

Next is what I call "Christian" occult activity. This involves seeking for or accepting spiritual experiences within a "Christian" context without examining their true source and the motives for seeking such experiences from the perspective of Scripture (1 John 4:1).

We must first mention the minimal threefold basis for examination of spiritual experiences. First, the doctrinal content implied, especially with respect to the person of the Lord Jesus Christ, must stand up under the scrutiny of the Word (1 John 4:1–11; 1 Cor. 12:3; Rom. 10:9). Second, true experiences with the Holy Spirit produce humility, not pride. The believer is drawn closer to the Lord. Holiness of life is increased. Obedience to his Word results (Gal. 5:22–23). Love for and tolerance of all believers (1 John 2—5) also occurs. Third, the body of Christ is edified (1 Cor. 12—14). One does not seek to "draw away disciples" after himself (Acts 20:30), but seeks only to produce disciples of the Lord Jesus.

Some examples of spiritually deceived believers and deceiving spirits are helpful (2 Cor. 11:3–4; 12–15; Gal. 1:8; 1 Tim. 4:1; 2 Tim. 3:13; 1 John 4:1–6). Next, I share one case study.

An angry woman named Audrey called me. Raised in a Christian home, she was now bound to a powerful Christian cult. They won her over through power experiences in the spirit world. Her believing aunt begged her to call me, so to please her, Audrey did. She talked continually for one-half hour, not giving me time to speak. Finally I said, "Audrey, please be quiet. I have listened to you for one-half hour. Now I want you to listen to me. I am going to give you some Scripture to read. Promise you will study these Scriptures every day and pray. Ask the Holy Spirit to help you become open to the truth they contain. Then call me back and we can talk again."

She agreed. A few days later she called back. The Word of God had shaken her confidence in the source of her spiritual experience. She was trying to break with the cult but was having difficulty doing so. Internal voices threatened her. She was afraid and asked for help.

Since she lived in another city some distance away, a friend of mine and I decided it wise to counsel her in her own home. Occult objects and books filled her house. Hindu and other Eastern religion paintings lined the walls of her apartment.

They completely filled the back of my station wagon when we hauled them to the dump. A single woman in her forties, she had become trapped in New Age philosophy and was bound to a powerful and strange religious personality cult.

We first took her through the biblical plan of salvation. Already a believer, she was very cooperative. She reconfirmed her faith in the Lord Jesus as her Lord and Savior, but she was suffering greatly at the hands of the spirits. They raped her almost daily (the terrible incubi spirits already mentioned). Others disturbed her sleep, made her nervous, and filled her with fear and anxiety. Some, she was afraid, would kill her.

We began deliverance ministry with her and had good success. Yet her case was so bad and so complex we knew she would need further counseling, so we taught her self-deliverance.

With my traveling ministry I soon lost personal contact with Audrey. She did write to me from time to time. About a year later, I began to feel deep concern for her again. I was disturbed by her latest letters and cassette recordings she had sent me. Still confused in her walk with God, I feared that her mysticism was drawing lying spirits to her life again.

When OC International scheduled a missions conference in northern California, I decided to take all Audrey's recent letters and tapes with me so I could gain insight into what was occurring in her life. At the conference one evening, a lady asked to talk with me. I was amazed! What a coincidence! It was Audrey's aunt.

"I have been away so much over the past months, I have lost contact with Audrey," I explained. "She has faithfully corresponded with me, but I have not been able to answer her. I am going to reread the letters, listen again to the tapes, and answer her this week. I am convinced there are still some deceiving spirits at work in her life," I said.

"You won't have to do that," her aunt said, sadly. "Audrey is dead!"

I was shocked speechless. "What happened?" I inquired.

"She fasted till she died. You are right. She was still struggling to get totally free from the demons. She phoned me a few months ago and said that the Lord told her that she would be totally free from all her demons if she would fast for forty days.

"I told her I did not think this was of God. She finally agreed to give up the idea.

"I did not hear from her for weeks. I called, but no one answered. I called her work and found she had not gone to work for some time, so I called the police. When they broke into her apartment, they found her dead. She had left a note saying that her death was self-inflicted through fasting. She was looking forward to death so she could be with the Lord and free from her sufferings." How sad!

As I close this chapter, I must give a word of warning about involvement in any form of spirit world activity involving the use of charms, including the possession of physical objects associated with the spirit world. Because they were dedicated to the spirit world when they were made, evil spirits are often associated with them just as they are associated with places and buildings dedicated to their use. This includes paintings, "art" objects, sculptures, images, charms, fetishes, books, even some forms of extreme rock or other music associated with the spirit world.

One case study will do. It is called "Ding's Special Gift."[16]

The Blaans are traditionally animists who worship the spirits living in trees, rivers and mountains. Their belief system includes the use of charms to protect them from these spirits. Just one of these small objects, hidden in their clothing or homes, might equal the value of a carabao or a revolver.

Coming to know Christ doesn't necessarily rid new Blaan believers of their deep-rooted belief in these charms. Instead, they try to combine the two, resulting in a continuous struggle between the two spirit worlds, rather than in a victorious Christian life.

Two years ago, Ding Rogue realized this problem and began to confront believers who were still clinging to their old ways. He sometimes stops a church service to say, "There's bad spirit in here, over on this side. You have no business bringing charms into this church. You should get rid of them." Sometimes he can point out the very person. "It's like the Holy Spirit is whispering in my ear," he says, "telling me 'that's the one.'"

As a result, believers often give up their charms to be burned. This great act of sacrifice and faith opens the way for God's Spirit to work in even greater ways in the lives of the Blaan people.

The same is true in the Western world. We cannot serve two masters. Since the Lord alone is God, let's follow Him. We don't need good luck, magic, or spirit objects for protection and provision. With God as our Father, we don't need foreign gods.

Demonization and Child Abuse

55

Child Abuse

O f the six major doors through which demons attach themselves to the lives of human beings, the door of child abuse is perhaps the most common, most hideous, and the most destructive. It is universally agreed that child abuse, if terrible enough and if continued over a long enough period of time, injures the child for the rest of his life.[1] Demons exploit this injury to their evil purposes.

The spirit world knows human history as no historian will ever know it. Demons know human nature as no psychologist or psychiatrist will ever know it. They know man's propensity towards evil as no theologian will ever know it. They know the long-term affects of particular kinds of damage to human personalities on both the individual and group level as no researcher will ever know it.

With this knowledge, demonic powers have concentrated on the baser side of human nature.[2] They know humans have an insatiable inclination towards gaining power over others, especially the weak, the helpless, and the less gifted. With power comes position, possessions, and pleasure, the ultimate goal of unchecked humanity. The spirit world knows that the children of today become the adults of tomorrow. They understand that if they can exploit humanity's tendency towards the abuse of its own children, they will have done almost the ultimate in damaging the human race. Evil spirits, therefore, are *always* directly or indirectly involved in child abuse.

An Historical Perspective

The statement about humanity's tendency towards the abuse of its own children at first appearance may seem too strong. After all, if humanity did not care for its children, most of us would not be alive to read this chapter. However, recent historical and contemporary studies reveal children to be the most oppressed group of human beings in the history of humanity. Yale historian John Boswell has written a shocking book called *The Kindness of Strangers* (1985) that studies historically the abandonment of children by their parents.

Boswell never intended to write the book. The idea arose while he was researching early Christian sexual mores. In the process he came across an argument by several prominent early church theologians stating that men should not visit brothels because they faced the danger of unwittingly committing incest with a girl they may have abandoned as a child.[3]

Boswell was stunned by these writings. As he investigated, he found child abandonment a common practice throughout history. For example, in eighteenth century European cities, one third of all children who survived beyond birth were abandoned by their parents. He says the modern feeling that parents are obligated at all cost to care for every child they allow to be born—thus the conscience-calming practice of killing them through abortion before birth—is based on a middle class, economic structure.

In the ancient world and up through the modern period, that conscience was nonexistent, especially in the days before any form of birth control was possible. Society expected you would adequately rear the children you kept, but you did not necessarily keep all of them.

In our study of ancient child sacrifice in chapter 34, I used an article from *Biblical Archeology Review*. The latter part of the article also deals with infanticide and child abandonment as forms of population control down through the centuries. The authors say:[4]

> From a comparative cultural perspective, child sacrifice, or ritual infanticide, is simply a special form of infanticide. The non-institutionalized form has appeared in Graeco-Roman society and in the Christian West with more regularity than we usually are comfortable in admitting. Unwanted or abandoned children have been subjected to exposure, drowning, starvation, strangulation, smothering, and poisoning, but the most common and lethal way of disposing of unwanted children has been simply neglect.

Child abandonment continues in many parts of the developing world according to the United Nations Children's Organization.

Newsweek's cover article, "Child Labor: The Plight of the World's Youngest Workers" dated January 24, 1983, reports that "the world's youngest laborers (75 million children) sacrifice their childhood in days of endless toil."

Charisma (December, 1983) published a shocking article entitled "Throwaway Kids." The subtitle is a statement in the form of a question: "In the last two years, thousands of Americans have rejected their young. Why? The answers are elusive." The writers, Mark Kellner and Rob Kerby, call "throwaways" good kids, but unwanted by their families. They say, "It's a problem that America has known for years, but which suddenly has become worse in the last two years, say officials. It is part of the decaying structure of the once solid American home."

In light of the above representative material, I don't think my charge about "humanity's tendency towards the abuse of its own children" is far from the truth.

I Am Just a Little Girl

I was watching a film on TV which told the true story of a little girl abandoned by her abusive parents and taken to a foster home where she was further abused. The most powerful part of the film to me was the beginning, when the child was being taken by a social worker to her foster home.

Sitting on one side of the back seat of the car, almost as if she were all by herself (she was not, the social worker was with her), is a beautiful little girl, perhaps four years of age, at the most. She has her pretty hair in pigtails. She is dressed in a cute little child's dress. She also is wearing a light gray coat. Later when she got out of the car I saw her black child's shoes and small white socks on her tiny feet.

She is sitting there in a world of her own. She is emotionally alone, and her face shows it. Her eyes are expressionless, fixed, staring directly ahead. She is not looking around, taking in all the new sights as most little girls would.

When the car stops, the social worker asks for her hand so she can take her to her new "home." The beautiful, tiny hand is offered to the social worker without protest. My eyes were fixed on that tiny, lonely, little submissive hand.

As they alight from the car they begin to walk towards the foster home. Suddenly the terrible sadness of loneliness known only by an abused and abandoned little four-year-old girl breaks down my defenses and penetrates my mind and my emotions. I begin to cry.

This is not right! This is not the way it was meant to be, my soul cries out within me. My fatherly instincts are aroused. I want to reach out and rescue her, but I am not allowed to do so.

This is my little girl, my emotions suddenly shout into the depths of my being. It is true. She looks exactly like my two daughters when they were four years of age, even to her pigtails, dress, coat, shoes and socks. I can still see both of them walking like this with me, holding my hand, so long ago.

As she walks up to the home with her little hand in the hand of the social worker, she turns and faces the camera. She is facing me.

Her eyes! It is her eyes that pierce me to the core of my being. What are they saying?

"I am just a little girl," those eyes are saying to all who have eyes to see and emotions to respond. "I am meant to be loved and protected, not rejected and abused.

"I am just a little girl," her eyes continue. "I am totally unable to take care of myself. Without caring adults to feed and clothe me, I will die, but here I am, alone. No one cares about what is happening to me, especially my mommy and daddy. Why?

"I am just a little girl," her eyes tell me. "I cannot defend myself. I cannot run away to a safe place. There is no safe place for a little girl like me. I go where others take me.

"I am just a little girl." Her eyes speak their final words. She turns away from me to go where she is being taken, not where she wants to go.

She has absolutely no choice in the matter. She is not a power person. Others are. She can only submit to their power over her.

That final glance of her eyes before she turns away from me say, "I am too young, too hurt, and too alone to know what is happening to me.

"What about my future? I don't know what the word means. I have no future. I only have the now which means I must survive.

"What about my past? I don't know what that word means, either. Is the past really past or is it still part of my now? I must survive the now which is all I know, and it is a now filled with pain.

"I am too afraid to be afraid. I am too confused to think. I am too alone to talk. I am just a little girl."

With this she turns her back to the camera and on me. She is gone. She was just a little girl.

I tried to fight the tears but I could not. I cried for her. I continued to cry for the millions of little ones who are abused, rejected, and alone. They too are just little girls.

Her sad eyes still stare at me as my mind brings continual flashbacks of the little girl. Her eyes do not plead, they are too dead to plead any longer. They just stare at me, empty, emotionless, and so alone. I still have to fight back tears every time my mind decides to give me another picture of the lovely little girl with the emotionless eyes. They are the eyes of a lonely little girl.

Oh, God! If only I could have rescued her! If only I could rescue the millions of other little girls in this perverse world who are abused by those who are supposed to be their protectors. If only I could—but I can't. There are too many. Where are you, my Father, when little girls are abused and are alone?

I, too, suffer with the existence of this kind of evil in my Father's world. True, though He is the world's Creator, He is not presently the world's god. Satan is that god (2 Cor. 4:3–4). Still, He alone is really God.

One wonders about the spiritual bondage of these abused children. How many become demonized? What is the outcome of their lives as they move into adulthood?

Ministry to adult survivors of serious childhood abuse reveals that many do become demonized, while others do not.

The results are due to many unknown factors. One reason I am sure of is the sovereign intervention of God. God does r ot intervene in all evil, or there would be no evil at all. Evil has to run its course. Yet if Satan and his cohorts were allowed to do all the evil they yearn to do, human life would not be possible; it would be hell on earth.

However, millions of abused children do pick up demons, especially if SRA was the context of their abuse. When counseling survivors of premeditated, personality-altering abuse we should always be alert to the probable presence of demons. We should also always suspect the presence of evil spirits when ministering to the survivors of severe, long-term, untreated, child abuse, be they children or adults. If the abuse has been successfully treated (in a relative sense), often they are no longer there or are not in strong control as before treatment.

Effective treatment by either Christian or non-Christian counselors will often remove some of the sin handles to which demons attach themselves to a human life. While Christians widely acknowledge such success in treatment by Christian counselors, it is often denied when it comes to treatment by non-Christians.[5] This is unrealistic. All truth is eventually God's truth. If non-Christians even unconsciously build their counseling practices upon God's truth, God will honor it. In fact, that truth in itself, if acted upon, helps heal human beings.

Therefore, there is really little ground for the strong negative attitudes in many Christian circles towards all non-Christian counselors. If healing procedures are built upon God's truth, but the "healer" denies God's existence, damaged people can still be helped into less traumatic living. As Satan's strategy is always built on lies, he loses control when lies are displaced by truth. This is an important biblical principle called *truth encounter.*

Of course, the ideal is the counselor who is not only highly knowledgeable and skilled in counseling abused people, but approaches his counseling from a biblical perspective.

A CASE STUDY OF DEMONIZATION THROUGH CHILD ABUSE

This case study blends events from several cases into a composite protecting the identities of all involved. Each event reported occurred. Al was one of my delightful seminary students. Intelligent and enthusiastic, he kept a good attitude toward his studies, even when challenged theologically.

One day I received a phone call from Al. He was pastoring a small church in one of the most God-resistant cities in the U.S.[6] Al wanted the churches of his city to understand some of the spiritual warfare dimensions of evil and resistance to the gospel. He invited me to conduct a united church spiritual warfare in the city.

About six weeks after the seminar, I received an urgent phone call from Al's wife, Claire.

"Dr. Murphy, Al is demonized," she said over the phone. "He is lying on the floor in the other room and we don't know what to do. Will you help us?"

"Of course I will if I can," I replied. "Tell me what is going on."

"Ever since you left, Al has had problems. (Great encouragement for my seminars!) He began to teach our people more about spiritual warfare, giving a series on Ephesians 6. At first he did okay. Then his messages became shorter and shorter. He seemed to get confused while preaching. He couldn't follow his outline. Finally he would just end his sermon and dismiss the congregation.

"Al has always been a kind and patient husband and father, but he began to change. He became impatient with us and with people in general. He started saying and doing weird things. He became oppressed.

"Yesterday he just fell apart. He began to rant and rave. I got scared so I called Greg, our assistant pastor, and another member of our church. They came over and tried to help Al.

"As they counseled him, he suddenly went wild. He began to throw things around the room. He yelled and screamed like a madman. We could not control him. Finally we had to call emergency for help. They took him to the psychiatric ward of the hospital. He spent the night there.

"We brought him home a few hours ago. The doctor said he had suffered a severe anxiety attack of some type but felt he would be okay with the medication they gave him.

"A little while ago he began to rave again. He began to say evil things. I realized then it was not Al. He is demonized. Greg is with him now. Al is lying on the floor in a trance. Please tell us what to do."

Frankly, I did not know exactly what to do. This was another of those difficult ministry situations where you have to make immediate decisions but don't have all the information you need to make an accurate diagnosis. I had to make an immediate decision and act upon it.

Was Al truly demonized? How could I know? I could not make an accurate diagnosis just from the brief story that I had heard from an understandably distraught wife.[7] I acted on the assumption that Al was demonized. If one is careful in what he does, even if the first diagnosis is wrong, no harm will be done to the victim or those with him.

"Tell Greg to come to the phone, please," I replied.

"Greg, Dr. Murphy is on the phone. He wants to speak to you," Claire yelled to the assistant pastor.

I could hear the noise of a terrible commotion coming through the phone. I heard Al yelling and Greg trying to bring him under control.

The demons attached to Al's life heard Claire's words to Greg that I was on the phone. They knew me—they usually do—and wanted nothing to do with me—they usually don't. Suddenly the phone went dead. Claire later told me that Al pulled the phone out of the socket in the wall.

All I could do was hang up and pray. Frankly, I was scared. If Al was demonized, they had to be extremely bad demons. He could hurt himself, his wife, his children, and Greg. I prayed that God would directly intervene, that Claire would find the way to contact me again. Soon the phone rang.

"Al pulled the phone plug out of the wall," Claire said. "I'm using the phone in the kitchen. I'm scared."

"Tell Greg to command the demons to be quiet and to go down into the pit of Al's stomach and be in subjection. Tell him to keep doing this until they obey him," I instructed.

In a minute, Claire was back on the phone. "Greg did what you said and it worked. Al is conscious and the demons are gone," she said.

I doubted that they were gone but was relieved the attack had subsided.

"Tell Greg to communicate quietly that he wants to speak only to Al, not the demons. Keep it up until Al is able to respond to him. Then have him ask Al to come to the phone so I can talk with him," I said.

A few minutes of silence passed. It seemed like hours. Then Al's subdued and surprised voice came on the phone.

"Hello, Dr. Murphy. What are you doing on the phone?" He did not remember anything that had just occurred.

This began one of the longest counseling sessions I have ever had long distance. It went on for hours. Since very destructive demons seemed to be present,[8] I had to continue long enough with Al until I felt confident that he, Greg, and his wife could handle whatever would occur in the immediate future.

Al was severely demonized.[9] He did not know how long he had been in that condition, nor the causes of his demonization. Since I could not see Al, I decided to call into manifestation the ruling demon.[10] Before calling it up, however, I bound it to my authority in the Lord Jesus (Luke 10:17–19). I forbade it to go berserk again, to hurt Al or anyone else, or from pulling the phone out of the wall. It protested but obeyed.

"I am Anger," the evil spirit said, "and I am in charge here. Get away from me. Let us alone. I don't like you."

"Be quiet," I commanded. "You speak only when I ask you to speak. You will answer my questions only when I am ready for you to do so. When did you come into Al?"

"When he was two years of age," he replied.

"What was being done to him that gave you entrance into his life?" I asked.

"He was being beaten by his father," he replied.

I commanded Anger to go down into Al's stomach and to remain quiet until I told him what to do.

"Al," I asked, "did you hear who that demon was and what he said?"

"Just something about anger, but I don't know anything else that was said," Al replied.

"Al, tell me something about your home life as a child. Was it a happy home? Was it a Christian home?"

"I had always thought it was a happy home, but lately I've been wondering. It was a very strict Christian home. My dad and mom are leaders in the church. We were there every time the church doors opened," he said.

"How did you relate to your father?" I asked.

"I was afraid of him. When he became angry he would go into a rage. He often beat me so hard I was terrified. One time when I was little he punished me so bad

I messed my pants. He wouldn't let me change them. He forced me to go to school—mess and all.

"He always compared me with my older brother. He liked him more than me. He told me I was dumb, that I would never amount to anything. I always tried to please him, but with no success. I was the black sheep of the family in his eyes."

For the next hour I endeavored to get Al to tell me as much as possible about his early home life. This was pre-deliverance counseling.

Al's mother was a kind woman, but totally dominated by his father. The two did not live as husband and wife. They seldom slept in the same room together.

When Al was still a little boy, his mother would often invite him into bed with her. She soon began to fondle him sexually. He didn't know what to do. If his mother was doing it, it must be right, he reasoned. Yet, with time, he became confused and felt guilty. When he reached his teens he began to use pornography and practice autosexuality. He soon became obsessed with sex.

While his sexual relationship with his mother died out as he reached his teens, it did occur on at least one other occasion—perhaps more than once. This time it involved full sexual intercourse with her, by her initiative.[11]

This was not all of the story, however. Al was also repeatedly sexually abused by his father's brother over a period of time when Al was a small child. On one occasion he remembers that his uncle pulled him up on his lap. While sitting in the living room, talking to his father, his uncle was sexually fondling him.

"I looked across the room at my dad," Al recalled. "He had to know what was going on. I was pleading with him through my eyes to make his brother stop. He didn't do anything. He just laughed. I hated both of them."

It was at this point in my talk with Al that he confided that he had tried to commit suicide to hurt his father. "Then he would realize how badly he had hurt me and be sorry for what he had done to me. I wanted to get even with him," Al said.

I worked Al through the process of forgiving his dad, his mom, and his uncle. Though bitter against them, he was finally able to forgive them.[12] He also wanted them to face their sins against him. At the time of writing they have ignored the subject. This also is typical of this type of abuse.

Al was totally sincere in his desire to live a holy life and serve the Lord and His people. This type of Christian lifestyle destroys the grounds for demons to remain indefinitely in a life, once their presence is finally recognized and dealt with.[13]

As the demons fled, some complained, others tried to yell. I shut them down. All soon went out. I am in on-going contact with Al. He is doing great. This is post-deliverance counseling.

I gave Al's story primarily to demonstrate one of the most difficult and shocking areas of spiritual warfare, the potential demonization of children through child abuse.[14] Many believers have great difficulty accepting the demonization of innocent children. "How can a good God allow innocent children to be demonized?" Once again, we are back with the problem of evil in a universe created and upheld by an all-powerful and all-good God.

Whenever we are in a "How could God allow such and such to happen?" context, we are wrestling with this enigmatic problem. Once we understand and accept what the Scriptures teach about the awful reality of evil, arising out of the fall of Lucifer with some of the angels, followed by the fall of man, we can accept, even though we do not like it, all the evil, both natural and supernatural, which exists.

Actually, humanity is the perpetrator of almost all the evil experienced by children, however. Adults abuse, torment, torture, and kill innocent children. Adults exterminate children in wars and in concentration camps. Adults allow millions of children to go hungry, even starve to death. Adults spend their money on pleasures and vice, neglecting and injuring their own children and the children of their neighbors. Thus, adults do most of the evil suffered by children.

Much is being written about child abuse in our day. Counselors, pastors, researchers, scholars, public officials, medical practitioners, law enforcement officials, writers, and others—both secular and Christian—are alerting the public and the church to this evil in our midst. Perhaps no generation has ever been as well informed as the present one about the destructive power represented by the abuse of our children.[15]

What is needed is a fuller understanding of how this abuse, inspired as it is by demons, opens the door of the life of children to potential demonization. There are probably millions of Al's in our churches. Some, like Al, are in our pulpits. Some are in the pew. Some are out on the field as missionaries. I have taken dozens of them through deliverance from demons which entered their lives as children. They did not leave at conversion or ordination. They left only through putting into practice the deliverance procedures revealed in God's Word.

Demonized believers know they have problems. They don't know where to go to get the help they so desperately need. We will look at this issue in greater detail in the chapters which follow.

56

Christians Demonized Through Child Abuse

The almost unbelievable horrors of widespread sexual child abuse in the United States have fallen upon the public with terrible impact. Women undergoing counseling are experiencing vivid flashbacks of such abuse. Reports of child sexual abuse in day care centers are surfacing from all parts of the country. Satanic Ritual Abuse of children has exploded into the public consciousness.

Sexual abuse of children is not new. It has occurred since the fall of man. Historical literature refers to such abuse, usually indirectly. It speaks of child slavery, particularly female, child marriages, child prostitution, child sexual ritual prostitution, and more.[1]

The dominance of children and women by men in the past made such abuse easy, respectable, and expected. It also made it almost impossible for the abused to find protection or release from their bondage. The sexual abuse of children that has always existed in the Western world has rapidly increased in recent years. Major causes seem to be the breakdown of traditional Judeo-Christian ethical standards, the breakdown of the home, and the general sexual looseness which permeates our culture.

Pornography, child pornography, and the influence of explicit sexuality in the media have helped to create "sexual insanity" within the U.S.[2] The rapid growth of Satanism, witchcraft, and similar occult groups have added new dimensions of horror to child sexual abuse never before imagined.

Someone has said that children are God's greatest gifts to humanity. Jesus pronounced a special blessing upon children and childhood in Matthew 18:1–10. There He taught that:

1. Children set the example for all who wish to enter the kingdom of God. They are an example to adults, not visa versa (vv. 1–2).
2. Those who, like children, are humble are "the greatest in the kingdom of heaven" (v. 3).
3. When one receives a child in Jesus' name, he also receives Jesus (v. 4).
4. The sin of hurting a child is so terrible that Jesus says it warrants capital punishment (v. 6).
5. Stumbling blocks are inevitable, but woe to the one who becomes a stumbling block to a child (vv. 7–9)!
6. We are never to despise or look down upon one of God's little ones (v. 10a).
7. "Their angels in heaven continually behold the face of [the] Father who is in heaven" (v. 10b). This is the place of greatest familial intimacy, to be continually in the presence of God as Father.

Leaders of the Roman Catholic church are reputed to have affirmed long ago, "Give me a child until he is seven. After that anyone can have him." The first seven years are the most formative in a child's life. If the child can be formed to do God's will in those early years, few will permanently depart from following the Lord. (There are sad exceptions [1 Sam. 8:1–5]).

Also, chances are if he is malformed in the early years of his life, he will be scarred for the rest of his life. How atrocious, therefore, is any treatment of children which causes them to stumble, that is, injures them for life.

If this is true of child abuse in general, then sexual child abuse must be in a category all by itself. First, because it is child abuse and second, because it is sexual. To force any kind of sexual activity upon a child is to violate childhood. Sex has no point of contact with a child's love. Sexual exploitation of children is sex only for the benefit of the exploiter. Children are used in an unnatural manner to satisfy the perverted, selfish passions of their abusers. No wonder it is so destructive to the child.

FACTS ABOUT THE SEXUAL ABUSE OF CHILDREN

The August 25, 1985, *Los Angeles Times* reported a telephone poll of randomly chosen Americans touching on the subject of sexual child abuse.[3] The poll revealed that 27 percent[4] of the women and 16 percent of the men contacted had been sexually molested as children. Poll margin of error was 3 percent.

> According to the poll, two-thirds of the victims were girls, and 93 percent of their abusers were men about 20 years older than they. The most vulnerable age is about 10. Friends and acquaintances accounted for 41 percent of the incidents of abuse, strangers for 27 percent, and relatives for 23 percent. About half of the abusers were classified as persons in authority. . . . About 95 percent of both victims and nonvictims agreed that sexual abuse has a lasting effect on children.

The poll further revealed that only 3 percent reported the abuse to police or other authorities. Less than 50 percent who did report, reported within a year of the abuse. In 70 percent of the cases where the abuse was reported, no effective action was taken.

Physical force was used in 18 percent of the cases. In the rest, the young victims submitted for a variety of reasons. Research shows some of the reasons for such submission: helplessness ("I was afraid"); role reversal in which the victim would be responsible for the consequences, not the abuser ("I did not want to make trouble for him"); and entrapment and accommodation ("I felt there was no one I could turn to for help"). The young victims have no choice but to submit to the abuse until they can obtain power over the power of the abuser.

The latter point is important. This is a *power* issue. The damaged abusers—all are damaged persons—only find sexual satisfaction and ego support in a situation which they totally control. To totally control the situation they must find a victim who is helpless to resist their sexual perversions.

The victims, in turn, seek to find a source of power greater than the power of their abusers. This is the natural consequence of all powerlessness. It further damages the victims because they unconsciously see life as *a game of power*. They make power vows. "I will never again allow myself to be controlled by the power of others." "Wait until I am in a position of power." "I must find a way of gaining power over my abuser." When the victims become persons of power, they, in turn, are apt to exercise power over others more powerless than themselves. It becomes a never-ending circle.

Victims become angry persons. They become secretive persons whose refusal to reveal their true feelings to others is a way of exercising power over them and of protecting themselves from their power. Worst of all, victims may become abusers of their own or others' children. This abuse is the result of anger and need for power. It also can be directly demonic.

The ultimate expression of power to overcome or revenge the power of the abuser is death—either the death of the victim by suicide or the death of the abuser by murder.[5] Fortunately, most cases of overcoming the abusive power person do not lead to this drastic final contest, but many do.

CHRISTIANS AND CHILD SEXUAL ABUSE

The almost universal assumption that real Christians do not abuse children is not true. A Christian researcher friend told me a disproportionate number of believers are guilty of child abuse, even of their own children. This abuse includes psychological, physical, and sexual abuse.[6]

Al's story recorded in the last chapter is a case in point. Al's parents were believers during all the years he was physically, emotionally, and sexually abused by family members. Steve, a mission executive, told me of a stand-out case of Christian child abuse in which he had to intervene while principal of one of the largest mission schools in Africa.

A young girl had tried unsuccessfully to commit suicide. As an experienced counselor, Steve became suspicious when he investigated some of the events surrounding the attempt. He understood that the teenager had made a confused cry for help. When he felt he had gained her trust, he inquired about her home life.

Evasive at first, she finally dropped her cover-up and sobbed, "I hate myself. I don't deserve to live. I am dirty. I have to submit to my father's sexual use of me whenever he wants me."

Her father had sexually abused her since her childhood. She did not remember ever being free from his sexual use of her. The worst had occurred over the last few years, however. She had to offer herself to him so that he would not abuse her younger sisters. Her hatred for her father was surpassed only by her hatred of herself for willfully giving herself to him as if she were his mistress.

"I hate him! I hate myself! I want to die! I can't live with this emotional hell any longer," she blurted out.

Steve arranged to meet with the girl's father, an evangelical missionary. When Steve confronted him with his daughter's accusations, he strongly denied it. Steve brushed aside his denial and continued pressing the point until the father finally admitted it. What was his explanation for such sexual misconduct?

"It is my responsibility to teach my girls about sex. Rather than have them learn from others, I teach them myself. What better way is there than being loved sexually by their father?"

Steve had the unpleasant task of reporting the abuse to both the mission and the police. All three girls were removed from the missionary's home. The man and his wife were sent back to the States in shame. Not only was this man guilty of incest,[7] there is also the possibility that he is a sexual addict.[8] He seemed to want sex continually.

Such persons need the intervention of trained counselors. Their abnormal sexual appetites indicate they are damaged persons.

Child abusers and pedophiles[9] are of two broad types. There are those who know they are doing wrong and want to be free. Then there are those who justify their sexual appetites for children—even their own children. They may occasionally feel sorry if they hurt innocent people or if they get caught, but they do not want to change. The first group needs help. While the battle may be long and hard, they can and do change. The second group needs commitment in institutions which will keep them from being a threat to children in the future.

I have been involved in long-term counseling with believers who are pedophiles. Their sin involved both incest and the sexual abuse of other children. All serious pedophiles that *I have dealt with* were demonized. This is a crucial dimension of counseling usually neglected by counselors, even Christian counselors. I am not saying that all pedophiles are demonized. I don't know that they are. I am only saying that all I have dealt with were demonized. One cannot say dogmatically that all who practice any specific sins are necessarily demonized.

Rich Buhler has written an important book on child victimization called *Pain and Pretending*.[10] After giving a general overview of the sexual abuse of children which "has reached epidemic portions" in the U.S., he asks: "What about the Christian community? Tragically, the incidence of abuse does not seem to be any different. I have interviewed professionals who feel abuse may actually be higher in certain types of religious homes."

Buhler mentions the work of my friend David Peters, a professional private counselor who has also worked with secular public agencies. Peters has written an excellent book, *A Betrayal of Innocence*.[11] He reveals the results of studies on the sexual abuse of children in Christian homes. One study was done by graduate students of a Christian school of psychology. The students surveyed 150 pastors and certified Christian counselors. They report that they have dealt with almost 1,000 cases of child sexual abuse by Christians.

Buhler tells of the work of one researcher who interviewed personnel at sexual assault centers, counselors, therapists, and researchers in one part of the U.S. He says they are unanimous in their conclusion that the "rate of sexual abuse is no less in religious or Christian homes than in the general public."[12]

Could this really be true? David Peters says, "The general characteristics reported by pastors and counselors seemed basically to fit the study profile seen in secular findings. Ninety percent of the reported victims were female. Fathers and stepfathers were the most common offenders. Fathers were more often abusers than were stepfathers."

Peters states that in 64 percent of these cases, the incest began when the child was between seven and thirteen years of age. The incest reported seldom involved single incidents of molestation. Most of the cases—between 60–65 percent—were repeated incidents spanning a year or more.

In nearly half of the cases reported by Christian counselors, more than one child in the family had been molested. Sixty-two percent of the incest families were middle or upper class. Peters concludes, "Such figures make it difficult for us to follow our natural inclination to deny that child sexual abuse affects Christians in this day and age."[13]

Paula Sanford in her book *Healing Victims of Sexual Abuse*, says, "Christians desperately want to believe that the problem of sexual abuse cannot belong to them, that someone born anew could not possibly commit such an abomination." She says that her experience in counseling shows otherwise. Many of the abusers had accepted Jesus as Lord and Savior many years before they sinned in this area. Some had served as ordained ministers of the gospel. She says, "They love the Lord. Many claim to be Spirit-filled. They sit in church pews, sing in the choir, or teach in Sunday School. Some even preach from the pulpit."[14]

While conducting spiritual warfare training conferences with missionaries in Latin America, I spoke about the emotional trauma children suffer as a result of even short-term sexual abuse. One of the missionaries asked for a counseling session with me.

"Ed, I have three daughters," he said. "One of them is with us and the other two are in the U.S. in college. All three were sexually abused when they were children.

"When we lived in the U.S., we loved to have missionaries from other organizations stay with us. One week a missionary visited our church and stayed in our home. Months later one of my girls told me the missionary sexually abused her and her two sisters while he was with us.

"The abuse has had a terrible impact on all three girls. We want to know how to help them recover. Would you be willing to counsel with the daughter who is still with us?" I agreed.

She was a lovely girl. God began the process of healing the demonic trauma involved. I appeal to all those who counsel believers with sexual problems to consider possible demonic overtones. The abused often pick up demons from their abusers. Others pick them up from the air, as demons themselves confess, during the trauma of abuse and even afterwards. The more severe the trauma, the more apt the victim to come into strong demonic bondage—even demonization.

I was contacted by a Christian worker who has given his life to work with troubled teenagers. He was having sexual problems and was calling for help. He deeply loves his wife. They have children, including two girls. He told me he had sexually molested the girls in childhood and during their early teens until they were able to make him stop.

June, his wife, is a lovely woman. She loves Will. During the early years of their marriage, she did not know he was a pedophile. She did notice, however, that he was attracted to young girls. When her daughters finally told her of the sexual abuse by their father, June was overwhelmed with remorse for not having protected her girls.

June faced Will with the girls' report. He admitted it. He was deeply repentant and begged each of his daughters for their forgiveness. Both in time forgave him. Will also went to his married sons and told them what he had done to their sisters. They too, in time, forgave him.

Will and June left their ministry and withdrew from active church participation until he could be healed. They were afraid he would be discovered or would fall again because young girls were drawn to Will. He has a very appealing personality. Children love him.

These were wise moves. Will needed spiritual and psychological intervention. At last he found it in a local church that had a "12-step program" only for Christians who were pedophiles and sex addicts.[15] Will made good progress towards recovery. All was still not well, however.

That is when he came to me. After counseling him I encouraged him to purchase my spiritual warfare tape series and begin a serious study and practice of spiritual warfare. One day Will phoned me. He and June had been using the tape series, studying the accompanying spiritual warfare manual, and praying the warfare prayers. Until the day he called there had been no prior unmistakable evidence of demonization. While he often wondered if he was demonized, there was nothing to convince him that he had a demonic problem.

This day things changed, however. While Will was driving his car and praying, demons came into manifestation from inside of him, trying to take control of the car. They tried to force him to run off the road or collide with another car. He began to declare his authority in Christ over them to keep from killing himself. He was emotionally shaken—almost in tears—when he called me.

I began to pray with him over the telephone. Suddenly the demons came into manifestation. They wanted to kill Will. We both came against them in the name of Jesus. They fought back. Will fought them with his authority in Christ. I supported him. Soon he was set free while on the telephone. This was the turning point in Will's life. He continues to replay the tape series to learn better how to be victorious in his ongoing warfare with sexual spirits. He continues to meet weekly with his support group. This is an absolute necessity. Deliverance from demonization seldom by itself cures sexual addictions and perversions. It only frees the victim to be healed.[16]

All during those years in which Will sexually abused children, he was a Christian. While this is not easy to understand in light of some Scriptures, it is understandable in light of others.

57

A National Crisis of Denial

This chapter has five goals:

1. To make you aware of the problem of sexual child abuse as seen through the eyes of a national leader who has become a powerful advocate for the sexually abused child.
2. To awaken you to the sinister forces set against all efforts to advocate the cause of awareness of sexually abused children.
3. To point out the effects of evil persons within child care centers who are trying to capture as many of them as possible for general child sexual abuse and Satanic Ritual Abuse.
4. To encourage us to realize that we can help save our children if we will use the resources already at our disposal.
5. To challenge the church to teach believers about sexual child abuse, which exists even among Christians; cooperate with worthy agencies in this area; as citizens, to influence law enforcement agencies including our courts to take children's reports seriously (although not all such reports are valid) and to prosecute abusers; and minister to both the abused and the abuser who seeks help.

Second to Satan's hatred of God is his hatred for humanity made in the image of God. Every blow against the welfare of humanity is a blow against God and his kingdom. Women and children are the most vulnerable, so the evil one stimulates violence against women and abuse of children. Satan seems to hate women intensely (Gen. 3:1ff). Little wonder! Only women give birth to children, and women traditionally have given stability to our homes. By corrupting or destroying women, Satan defeats God's purposes for humanity. Yet children are even more vulnerable, and, over the long term, injuring children damages humanity more than attacking adults. If Satan can cause children unspeakable pain through the adults they unhesitatingly trust, then Satan has accomplished the ultimate evil.

In this light, child abuse becomes a spiritual warfare issue. Powerful cosmic-level demonic princes rule over the child abuse insanity now in epidemic form in the Western world. I am personally deeply grateful for the heroic Christians and non-Christians who fight for the protection of our children against the child abusers both within and outside of our homes. Their most vicious opponents, beyond the confirmed child abusers themselves, are those who gain personal or corporate profit by the continued abuse of children.

The abusers are found within our own homes. They are usually older, more powerful family members, relatives, and friends who get satisfaction or a sense of power from causing sexual, physical, emotional, and even spiritual pain to helpless children. The abusers are also found in our neighbors' homes, primarily middle class, well-educated people, often civic, educational, law enforcement, medical, and even religious leaders.

Those who profit from children's pain are primarily of two types: the child pornographers and the satanic cultists. Child pornography should be a capital offense.

Such people cause injury and death to more children than all the street gangs who have gained so much attention from the media. Some advertise special devices used in all forms of ritual sexual abuse. Others print handbooks on how to deceive and sexually seduce innocent children.

In the satanic cults, sexual, physical, psychological, and spiritual torture of little children is an essential part of the power-craze demonization characteristic of all such cults and their willing members. These people are attempting to gain control of child care centers all across this country with the express purpose of having an abundant crop of defenseless children available for their demonic delight. Outspoken and vicious opponents of the brave child advocates leading the legal warfare against child abuse in this country, they are unfortunately joined by an even larger and more dangerous group.

This larger group is represented by the apathetic, naive, and often incredulous adult public at large—Christians among them—and increased by indifferent and sometimes hostile branches of law enforcement, the judiciary, child-protection systems, social workers and so-called professionals—psychologists, psychiatrists, counselors—who will not believe the extent of this evil, nor the testimony of the abused children.

This crisis has not been alleviated since the awareness of the sexual abuse of children first fell with real force upon the consciousness of the American public in the 1970s and 1980s. This crisis has yet to reach the consciousness of the American church because, it is argued, the sexual abuse of children is not primarily a spiritual issue, but a social one. Thus it is considered to be outside the area of responsibility of Christian leaders and the Christian public at large. We are also told it is primarily a problem affecting the unconverted. Church-going Christians would not be involved in the sexual abuse of any child, let alone their own.

An outstanding national medical leader, Dr. Roland Summit is also a faithful advocate of the sexually abused child. Dr. Summit is the Head Physician of the Community Consultation Service and Assistant Clinical Professor of Psychiatry at the Harbor-UCLA Medical Center in Torrance, California. He is carrying forward an intense and often disappointing campaign to bring true understanding of this complex evil to the public in general, but more specifically to the leadership of our nation who have the power, if only they had the will, to truly help in the present crisis.

In 1983 Dr. Summit wrote a paper entitled "The Child Sexual Abuse Accommodation Syndrome."[1] In it he summarizes both the present interest in and result of increased studies in the problem of child sexual abuse which "exploded into public awareness" with the production of over 30 books on the subject and many magazine and TV features. Dr. Summit asserts that this explosion of information is saying that sexual abuse of children is "much more common and more damaging to individuals and to society than has even been acknowledged by clinical or social scientists. Support for these assertions comes from first- person accounts and from the preliminary findings of specialized sexual abuse treatment programs."

Dr. Summit next reveals the general disbelief with which the results of this research have been received by child welfare professionals. He says there exists an unreasonable skepticism among social scientists and a reluctance to accept "such unprecedented claims." A predictable counter assertion that while such sexual child abuse may be more common than first imagined, the fact that relatively few reports of abuse come in reveals "the experience for the child is not uniformly harmful." In fact, the result may be either neutral or even beneficial, some affirm.

Dr. Summit then comments that "any child trying to cope with a sexualized relationship with an adult faces an uncertain and highly variable response from whatever personal or professional resources are enlisted for help."

Next the author discloses the negative impact upon the abused child caused by the *disbelief* with which the reports of abuse have been received. This disbelief is often as damaging as the abuse itself. Interest in child abuse creates new problems for the child. It increases the likelihood that the abuse will come to light, but *fails to protect the child* from the damaging effects of general disbelief in his claims of abuse. The established intervention system does not believe the child's claim.

Dr. Summit says "the identified child victim encounters an adult world which gives grudging acknowledgment to an abstract concept of child sexual abuse, but which challenges and represses the child who presents a specific complaint of victimization." What a sad situation for the abused child to encounter!

First he says that "adult beliefs are dominated by an entrenched and self-protective mythology that passes for common sense. 'Everybody knows' that adults must protect themselves from groundless accusations of seductive or vindictive young people." An image persists of children somehow wrapped up in sexual fantasizing, acting out their fantasies, and accusing adults of being involved in sexual play with them.

Dr. Summit strongly defends the young victims by stating that most critics refuse to acknowledge that *most of the accusations have been proven to be true.* The child is not calculating or practiced, but most often fearful, tentative, and confused about the nature of the continuing sexual experience and the outcome of disclosure. "If a respectable, reasonable adult is accused of perverse, assaultive behavior by an uncertain, emotionally distraught child, most adults who hear the accusation will fault the child," he observes.

This disbelief has a terrible impact on the child victim. This disbelief on the part of adult caretakers "increases the helplessness, hopelessness, isolation and self-blame that make up the most damaging aspects of child sexual victimization." When no adult intervenes in his behalf, the child is further traumatized. This becomes a reinforcement of the child's "tendency to deal with the trauma as an intrapsychic event and to incorporate a monstrous apparition of guilt, self-blame, pain, and rage."

Acceptance and validation of the child's claims are crucial to his psychological survival. "A child molested by a father or other male in the role of parent and rejected by the mother is psychologically orphaned and almost defenseless against multiple harmful consequences," he affirms. However, a mother who becomes an advocate for her child and protects against re-abuse seems to confer on the child the power to rebuild his self-image and recover with minimum consequences.

What makes most sexual child abuse so difficult is that the abuse comes at the hand of one involved in what Dr. Summit calls "kinship trust." Thus the child is put on the defense for daring to attack a trusted authority figure. This creates a crisis of loyalty which is difficult for the child and the protecting parent. Dr. Summit states, "At a time when the child most needs love, endorsement and exculpation, the unprepared parent typically responds with horror, rejection and blame."

Dr. Summit then writes of the crucial role the mental health professional plays in this entire process. If he fails, the child is subjected to further personal harm.

Finally, Dr. Summit refers to what he calls the *accommodation syndrome.*[2]

The accommodation process intrinsic to the world of child sexual abuse inspires prejudice and rejection in any adult who chooses to remain aloof from the helplessness and pain of the child's dilemma, or who expects that a child should behave in accordance with adult concepts of self-determinism and autonomous, rational choices. Without a clear understanding of the accommodation syndrome, clinical specialists tend to reinforce the comforting belief that children are only rarely victims of unilateral sexual abuse and that among the few complaints that surface, most can be dismissed as fantasy, confusion, or a displacement of the child's own wish for power and seductive conquest.

What a powerful summary of the plight of sexually abused children! What a sad commentary on adult reaction to our children's complaints of abuse! What a heartbreaking experience for the traumatized child to be even further traumatized by an unbelieving adult world! As Christians let's believe the children.

Dr. Summit helped support the excellent work of the U.S. Attorney General's Commission on Pornography under former Attorney General Edwin Meese. He presented to the Commission a devastating indictment of the nation's leadership who are responsible to defend sexually exploited children and to prosecute or help heal their abusers. It is entitled, "Too Terrible To Hear! Barriers To Perception of Child Abuse."[3] It is a paper almost "too horrible to read." He introduces his paper with the following castigation of those people and agencies—including the church—who are responsible to protect and support our children in general, and sexually abused children in particular:[4]

I believe that as a people, as a nation, and as a collection of child caring institutions, we have maintained, like the three monkeys, a self-protective posture of see no evil, hear no evil, and speak no evil.

Sexual abuse of children, child pornography, with its companion vices of child prostitution and sexual molestation, is explained away, trivialized or simply denied wherever there is a risk of confrontation. While the greatest motivation for denial rests in each of us as adult individuals, our need to deny is bolstered by the relentless irrelevance of protective institutions and the paralyzing, calculated confusion imposed by an unknown number of influential citizens whose private lives are devoted to the sexual subjugation of children.

Protective institutions like the family, church, schools, medical and social service agencies, police, courts, government and public media are not irrelevant to most of the needs of children, but all such resources remain devoted to beliefs, policies and priorities that not only ignore but often obscure the impact of adult sexual interest in children.

If there is an enthusiastic traffic in sex with children and if little kids are consumed for the sake of its production, how could such an empire stay in hiding? I would like to reflect on seven dimensions of denial which serve as protective camouflage.

The seven dimensions of denial follow:

1. *Self-Protection.* Adults tend to band together to endorse "the unchallenged myth that child sexual abuse is practiced only by obviously degenerate strangers on somebody else's child. . . ." A continuing centuries-old tradition blames the victim and maligns the complaining parent whenever a respectable adult is accused. Any professional who speaks out for the child will be targeted also for blame.

2. *Victim Suppression.* Most sexually abused children do not report the abuse, ever. If they eventually do, it is years after the abuse began. Common sense says if one is a victim of crime, he will immediately report it. Since no report was immediately given, there has been no crime.

Here a psychology of adulthood is applied to a child. Dr. Summit later reveals that children by nature do not report abuse by adult authorities to whom they have been taught they are to submit. If those adults are family members it is even more difficult. He says, "Instead of defining the crime and forging new tools to combat it, we use our distrust of the children to avoid recognition and to resist intervention." The result is, most sex crimes involving children are never reported, and even worse, most such crimes reported are never charged.

3. *Inadequate Investigation and Evaluation.*

4. *Adversarial Inhibition.* This argument focuses on the traditional legal position that conviction of crime demands strong objective evidence. That evidence is usually not available in most child sexual abuse cases. There are no adult eye witnesses. Usually the only witness is the abused child.

The defense technique in such crimes is "aging the case" and "discrediting the victim," Summit says. If the case does go to trial, judges and juries—all of whom are adults—will side with the accused adult against his child victim.

Dr. Summit gives unique attention to the above process when it comes to SRA and other religious sexual child abuse. He speaks of child mutilation, even child sacrifice as described by dozens of children. The child's testimony is affirmed to be "too unbelievable to be believable." The result is most cases become bogged down in hopeless confusion and are terminated before going through a full trial.

5. *Kill the Messenger.* This shocking section of the paper provides an overview of the intense persecution faced by courageous individuals who have tried to expose sexual child abuse, child sex rings, and other forms of organized sexual exploitation of children. He says, "The child specialist who elicits the first disclosures of abuse will be a very unwelcome messenger."[5]

> The rapid emergence of child sexual abuse diagnostic specialists and the predictable challenge from attorneys for the defense have produced a forensic dogfight. People who were hailed a few years ago for their contributions to discovery are now being condemned as self-serving inventors and malicious witch-hunters. The tools that launched the explosive sexual abuse awareness of the last five years—anatomic dolls, figure drawing, improved physical examinations, symptom checklists and patterns of expected victim and perpetrator behavior—are denounced as instruments of abuse. The methods are attacked to invalidate the outcome, and the messengers are destroyed to challenge the message.

6. *Deliberate Deception.* The case suppression and failure of the legal system to protect the child (witness the Presidio and the McMartin child care scandals, both thrown out of court in 1990) are due to unintended denial and chronic public avoidance on one hand, and the influence of treacherous decision makers and gatekeepers on the other. He describes them as "doctors, judges, attorneys, police officers, editors, writers, school administrators, teachers and parents who are invisible pedophiles, pornophiles or cultists." He says "children describing multiple-perpetrator abuse typically implicate trusted institutions and community leaders among the peripheral players. . . . The uncertainty of sorting out enemies from friends impairs the emotional security of victims and their advocates."[6]

7. *Conceptual Chaos.* Dr. Summit's final word calls us to "hear the small voices and to overcome the enormous pain." He states:[7]

> Until a more seasoned base of knowledge develops, the speculations of the investigators will be hopelessly outclassed by the cunning of practitioners. Whatever evolution of concept the last ten years of progress have initialed, those concepts are far too immature to survive another ice age of reactive denial.

Continuing progress in defining the motivation, scope and significance of child sexual abuse in this country will require a new commitment to view a wide scope of issues relating to adult victimization of children. Every such issue is offensive to adult comfort and each will tend to fragment constructive alliances. Only an extraordinary effort and a strong sense of coalition can empower us to hear the small voices and to overcome the enormous pain.

A word needs to be said about some positive moves within the U.S. Government to help stem the tide of the sexual abuse of children in our nation. Out of the work of the former Reagan Administration,[8] directed by then Attorney General Meese, has come the most far-reaching legislation in U.S. history to help combat obscenity and sexual child abuse.

In 1984 child pornography was set apart as a distinct criminal offense. Directly resulting from the seven-point plan to combat national obscenity drawn up by the Attorney General came The Child Protection and Obscenity Enforcement Act of 1987. This in turn led to the formation of the National Obscenity Enforcement Unit of the Criminal Division of the United States Department of Justice.

Concerned Americans in general and concerned Christians in particular already have many of the necessary tools at the national level to help expose and slow down both obscenity and sexual child abuse in the U.S.A. What is now needed is effective action coupled with new understanding of the issues as Dr. Summit has brought out in his two excellent papers.

Perhaps the most heartbreaking incidents of sexual abuse have been in child care centers throughout the U.S.[9] Some of the centers are sponsored by the U.S. military, particularly the U.S. Army Presidio Day Care Center in San Francisco and West Point.[10] Most disheartening of all is that some of the child care centers where children were sexually abused were run by Christians.

The cases of the McMartin Preschool in Manhattan Beach, California, and the Presidio Day Care Center in San Francisco involved hundreds of children, 300 at McMartin and 60 at Presidio. Most disturbing is that both cases were dropped by the state prosecutors for "lack of evidence." "The charges were all too vague," it was affirmed. The abusers are today free to carry on their sexual assault on children wherever they can find them.

On March 28, 1988, Linda Goldston, staff writer of the *San Jose Mercury News*, published the findings of the Family Research Laboratory of the University of New Hampshire, which conducted the first nationwide research project of U.S. day care centers focusing on sexual child abuse. The article was entitled "Day Care Sex Abusers: 40 Percent Women." From it I have drawn the following points:[11]

1. Women are responsible for nearly 40 percent of the sexual abuse of children in the nation's day care centers and are more likely to use force and threats than men.
2. Twenty-five percent of the sexual abuse was committed by the owner or director of a center, suggesting that these perpetrators established the centers for the purpose of sexual abuse.
3. Children are still more likely to be abused at home than in day care. The estimated rate of sexual abuse is 5.5 cases per 10,000 children enrolled in day care compared to 8.9 cases per 10,000 children under age 6 at home.
4. More violent abuse occurs in the nation's 229,000 day care centers, which serve seven million children.
5. About half of the victims were more intelligent and physically attractive

than average, and were more popular and affectionate with the day care staffs. Two-thirds of the cases occurred in bathrooms, and about the same number of girls as boys were victims.

6. Women who make up the bulk of day care workers were more likely to abuse children together with other women, while men tended to act alone. Women also were "more likely than men to commit multiple sexually abusive acts and the acts involving sexual penetration."

7. A center's sterling reputation and well-trained staff have little bearing on risk of abuse. Children were "just as likely" to be abused at such prestigious centers as the McMartin Preschool in Manhattan Beach.

8. The vast majority of cases involved a single perpetrator. However, the multiple perpetrator cases are clearly the most serious ones, involving the most children, the youngest children, the most serious sexual activities, and the highest likelihood of pornography and ritualistic abuse.

9. Threats used by abusers included telling children that their parents or their pets would be killed if they told anyone about what had happened.

10. Licensing had no effect on reducing abuse. Investigators from state licensing boards tend to inspect the centers once a year and focus on such things as fire safety.

Since releasing the first edition of this book, I have talked with adults falsely accused by children of sexual abuse. Children who are disturbed, angry, seeking the approval of others, and manipulated by evil spirits do falsely accuse adults of abuse. Thus we should assume that adults are innocent until proven guilty. Each case of alleged sexual abuse must be investigated by specially trained investigators.

Furthermore, the question of repressed memories of childhood sexual abuse has suddenly emerged. Some of these memories are true. Some are false. Thus the innocent suffer with the guilty. Most false memory recall is caused by the suggestion of therapists. Their counselees are emotionally disturbed persons. The suggestions are reinforced through some combination of aggressive questioning, often accompanied by hypnosis, sexualized dream interpretation, and victimization. The longer the counseling continues, the worse the emotional state of the counselee becomes.

The phenomenon of repressed memories of childhood abuse needs careful investigation. For Christian counselors, I offer the following suggestions:

1. Never suggest childhood sexual abuse to troubled counselees.

2. If abuse is suspected, become an intercessor. Ask the Holy Spirit to bring it to the mind of the counselee. If He does not, what right do you have to do so?

3. Encourage the victim to forgive the abuser(s).[12]

4. Consider whether or not disturbed believers must remember all the causes of their emotional damage. While identifying these causes is helpful when prompted by the Holy Spirit, if a counselee does not identify them, is there then no balm in Gilead?

5. Do not encourage victims to break up their family or take their abusers to court, unless the perpetrators still represent danger to other children.

6. Take the victim through deliverance ministry as well as through emotional healing.

I believe that following these steps will help Christian counselors avoid therapist-produced "memories" of abuse, while encouraging them to fully integrate good clinical skills and spiritual resources to serve their counselees effectively.

Creative Abuse—A Calculated Evil

Writing about the relationship of pain, power, and abuse, Drs. Wilder and Friesen make several observations crucial to our spiritual warfare study.[1] Wilder says, "Abuse is the application of excessive power." For our study on child abuse in general, and sexual abuse in particular, Wilder's description of excessive power applied against a helpless child is important. The use of such power, he says, produces pain, helplessness, and finally helplessness in the abused and "ultimately in the abuser as well."

"Paradoxically, most common abuse occurs when the person in power is feeling powerless," Wilder affirms. What a profound insight! He follows with a real-life illustration of a parent, the power person, who seeks to gain greater power over his crying child by applying excessive power. He smothers the child with a pillow until he almost passes out. The crying stops. This is the application of excessive power to gain power over the child's life at that point. This is also physical child abuse, a criminal offense.

The parents stop the abuse, for the moment at least, when they see that they are now powerful enough to control the child. They will then go through a cycle of regret, recurring abuse, followed by more regret and more abuse. Wilder says that "most parents have only been partially seduced by evil and so only partially believe that they should control their children. As a result, they only partially abuse their children." This is not the case of those so fully given to evil they wish to completely control their children—their minds, bodies, wills, and spirits. This is the nature of extreme evil.

"The only way to succeed at such mind control," Wilder says, "is to apply so much power that pain, the fear of pain, and the desire for power in order to avoid pain line up with the lines of power. Here enters the calculated use of power to cause helplessness and pain in order to break the child's soul."[2]

Breaking the Soul

Wilder points out the abundance of evidence that God's purposes in creation are frequently shattered in this sinful world. In spite of this, some Christians have difficulty believing that the soul can be shattered. "Evidence, however, points to the terrible truth that we are breakable," he says (Ps. 34:18; 69:20; Prov. 15:13; 17:22).

"In the only reference to the brokenhearted in the New Testament, Christ claims that he has come to 'heal the brokenhearted.' He does not say he has come to find the piece he created and throw the rest away."[3]

Entrance of Demons Into Broken Places

Many cases of demonization are traceable to times of trauma, particularly involving assault by another person, either sexual or physical. That a person should become demonized on top of a trauma seems potently unfair, but who says we live in a fair world? Satan is the ruler of this world. Any world over which he rules will be an unfair world. "Demons are attracted to pain because 1) they 'like' the pain and suffering; 2) pain produces powerlessness which makes their offers of power attractive," Wilder notes.[4] When Jesus had fasted, he was hungry, and guess who showed up?

The attitude of Wilder and Friesen differs from the common one held by Christian counselors, psychologists, and psychiatrists who often affirm they have rarely or never discovered demons in the lives of severely abused patients. Fortunately for the victims, that attitude is beginning to change in the U.S. As I examine the many counseling sessions I have had with Christians since I was first forced by the Lord into this ministry in the mid-1970s, I have concluded that in the U.S., at least, sexual abuse after occult involvement is the number one cause of demonization in the life of Christians.

Powerless Feeling

Wilder says pain causes powerlessness. The abused wants the pain to stop. When it doesn't, the victim feels powerless. "The pain of powerless feelings can make one long desperately for power," Wilder says. "Many a person watching a loved one die has had this experience. The solution to feeling powerlessness appears to be increasing your power." This is not a solution but a trap, Wilder says. "One good definition of evil should be: Correcting powerlessness by increasing your power." Common ways to achieve power are by "plotting revenge, holding grudges, feeding bitterness, passive aggressive retaliation, attempting to control others or oneself, and explosions of rage."[5]

The First Offer of Power

God is the ultimate source of all power, demonic or otherwise, Wilder affirms. Yet God is not primarily power. Consequently "it is an insult to His nature to offer power as a solution to our troubles. The first offer of power almost always comes from demons. It doesn't matter whether this is power to heal, deliver, or get revenge. . . . Demons are power beings and they will always offer you: 1) power as a way to fix things; 2) enough power so you can give back more than you got; 3) enough power to damage you for handling it; 4) power if you give up something in return." Wilder then makes a controversial statement, yet one deserving of careful consideration: "People who seek power, even for healing, generally find it first from demons."[6]

Building on what he has written under hurting children through abuse, Wilder continues, "Now that we have some understanding of power, pain and abuse, we can consider how evil people can use abuse creatively to get the results they want." Wilder gives the illustration of a disobedient two-year-old child. His parents want to gain total power over him. He must be taught to immediately obey on command.

They throw him into the washing machine with dirty clothes, calculating how long he can remain there without dying. After a few such treatments they get the power over him they want. When he begins to disobey they remark, "Do you want a good washing?"

Mild forms of torture like this "are enough to get some control of the child's mind and body. To really control his soul, mind and spirit requires much more extensive and intense kinds of suffering for the child. Before we consider that problem let us see what mild to moderate torture does to a child's soul and mind."[7]

Alex and Betty, a handsome young couple in their thirties, had served for one term in Asia with one of the largest and oldest interdenominational, evangelical missions in the world. Alex's home was religious, but non-Christian. Betty came from a dysfunctional non-Christian family.

Betty suffered through her first term of missionary service. Busy with their young children, she was not able to enter into the ministry with Alex. The real reason for her frustration with missionary service, however, lay much deeper. She felt spiritually and emotionally dead. She had been that way all her life, before and after coming to Christ.

She knew she was a believer. Her acceptance of Christ by faith, not by feeling, while still a teenager had saved her from suicide. Her faith in God as Creator and Redeemer, in Christ as Savior and Lord, and in the indwelling Holy Spirit was more important to her than life itself. Without God, life to her was a living hell. She preferred death to a godless life.

With God, she found hope for eventual emotional healing. With God she could continue to believe, even though she could not feel His presence. She knew the Holy Spirit best. While she could not feel His presence either, she heard His voice within her[8] louder than the other voices.

Betty was convinced she had to change or she could not continue as a missionary. She had to be healed if she was to be a healer of others. She convinced Alex that she needed Christian counseling. They received permission for a medical furlough and moved to Arizona for in-depth, long-term counseling at a well-known Christian counseling center. They had been there about a year when Loretta and I met them at their request.[9]

As Betty shared what she remembered of her childhood, it became increasingly evident that she had been the victim of some type of calculated evil Satanic Ritual Abuse (SRA). Since this type of abuse always involves demonic activity (if there are exceptions, I have not heard of them), Loretta and I changed some aspects of our counseling procedures. With the limited time that was available, we wanted to do at least six things:

1. To be as sure as possible that she truly knew Christ as Savior and Lord. She did.
2. To get as full a picture as possible of her childhood and teenage life in her home.
3. To allow her the right type of counseling environment, so she would open up to Loretta and me, though we were almost strangers.

    I say almost strangers because she had obtained a copy of my tape series. She knew my voice and style of teaching. Listening to the tape series had awakened within her hope for healing and a desire to meet me. She told herself that if there were demons involved in her problems and she could be free from their influence, healing would speed up. That is exactly what happened.
4. To discover whether or not her problem had direct demonic overtones.[10]
5. To begin the deliverance process, if necessary.
6. To harmonize our ministry to her with that of her Christian psychologist. Since her psychologist had requested that we counsel with her, we were greatly encouraged at this point.

Betty's story is long and complex: I have over 100 pages of notes taken from our sessions with her and her counselor has more. As I write, she is still undergoing weekly counseling. I sum up her case as follows:

1. Hers is a story of generational demonization. It goes back at least five generations, from Betty, through her father, her grandfather, and her great-grandfather. It has passed on to one of her children.

2. Her father, a Satanist, dedicated her to Satan before she was born. The spirits told him a child would be born to him with a cleft lip and cleft palate. This would be the sign that she was especially chosen by Satan. He was to initiate her into Satanism as an infant.

3. He hated her before birth. As his father hated him, so he in turn hated her. Satanism is a hate belief system.

4. She was severely demonized before birth. The demon which called itself Hellbent came into her from her father when she was still in her mother's womb. So did Father of Hate, one of the chief demons in her life. The demons Pain, Torture, Cleft Lip, and Cleft Palate also came in at that time.[11] Destroyer came in about the time she was born.

5. She was ritually sexually abused repeatedly by her father beginning when she was about three years old. It continued until adolescence when her mother, suspecting sexual abuse was occurring, never again allowed Betty to be alone with her father.

6. Several demons came into her body when she experienced that first ritual sexual abuse at three years of age. They were Sacrifice, Spirit of Her Father, Kill, and Perversion.

7. Others came in during her on-going abuse. One called itself Lust, the other False Authority. The latter told her that what her father was doing to her was good. She had to obey him, as he was her authority.

8. Demons continued to gain entrance into her life at specific points of terrible trauma. First, a group came in when she was in the hospital for surgery on her cleft palate and cleft lip when she was three months old. The leader was Unbelief. He turned out to be the prince over all the demons, about 1,065 in total. There has been no further evidence of demonization since they were expelled.

Another leader demon under him was Stronghold of Fear. He had five demons under his command. They called themselves Terror, Dread, Panic, Anxiety, and Worry.[12] Unbelief controlled other chief demons besides Stronghold of Fear. They were called Pride, Pain, Pretending, Ignorance, Alone, Separate, and Untouchable. Next was a demon calling itself Deceive. It declared, "I came in when she was working in the inner city under Rev. Smith. Rev. Smith is the spiritual leader of the ministry. He has control spirits working through him. He is messing up all the young people working with him. He told her she is no good; she's evil to the core; that no good thing dwells in her; that she deserves to be treated like a worm; she deserves to be stomped on."

"He told her that life was supposed to be miserable. He said that if you were not miserable then you were not doing right. She has believed all these lies, but now she is turning against us."

Interesting, is it not, that the very negative things Rev. Smith told Betty were the very things the demons had been telling her since childhood. Is this part of what the apostle Paul meant when he warned that some "latter times" Christian teachers—would pay "attention to deceitful spirits" and teach "doctrines of demons"? (1 Tim. 4:1; see Matt. 16:21–23).

Finally, there was a demon named Confusion. He said, "I came in the night she got baptized." When asked how this could have occurred at baptism it said, "Because she was confused about baptism. They were telling her that if she would be baptized she would be saved, but she knew salvation was through faith in Jesus Christ. That's how I got into her life."

9. She always felt what she described as "floating pain" deep within her being. She could never get away from it. Though she tried to be a happy wife, mother and missionary, she was never happy. She always hurt deep within her.

10. Her father was told to offer her as a blood sacrifice to Satan. He tried to do so when he first ritually sexually abused her at three years of age in the basement of his home. Betty first began to be aware that she was a possible victim of SRA a few months before we met with her. She was watching a documentary on the life of the painter Goya. In some of his paintings reference was made to the occult activity mixed with the Catholicism of his day. It included child sacrifice.

While watching this documentary she had the first flashback indicating possible SRA by her father. She saw herself bound with ropes, her mouth gagged, her father engaging in bestiality and sexually abusing her. He was holding an unusual dagger and cutting her body. Blood was flowing. A relative stopped him.

Sometime after this flashback, Betty innocently attended a Renaissance Fair. (Such fairs are often controlled by occult groups.) She saw on display two elaborate daggers dedicated to occult practices. They were sacrificial knives, the same type she had seen in the flashback. Betty now knew her father had attempted to sacrifice her ritually to Satan. Finally she saw a TV show which featured adult survivors of SRA. She understood their stories as being her own, and all the pieces now began to fall into place.

11. The demons confirmed her flashbacks at every point. She was chosen by Satan through her father both to serve him and to be sacrificed by him to Satan, they said, but God intervened.

12. The principal purposes of the SRA and the demons was to break down Betty's will; to bring her under the control of her father and Satan; to cause personality splitting. Betty's conversion at 11 years of age was the turning point of her life. Now that she knew God, personally, she developed a deep hunger for Him. She began to grow as a Christian in spite of the inner pain.

13. Betty had dissociated as a child. As a result, the SRA she had suffered had been totally blanked out from her consciousness. While she could not explain the floating pain and emotional death, she knew nothing of her childhood tortures.

James G. Friesen defines dissociation in the following manner:[13]

> (It) is the act of defending against pain. It may be the most effective defense people can use, since it is 100 percent successful. When a person dissociates, he or she separates from the memory of a painful event.

> It is as simple as this: A child goes through a trauma and then pretends to be a new person, or alternate personality (alter), to whom these bad things did not happen. There is a separation from the memory. It is immediately and completely forgotten. The newly created alter "remembers" only a blank spot where the trauma happened, and there is no hint that the traumatic event could have happened. If the dissociation is complete, the amnesia is 100 percent. If you mention anything about what happened during the blank spot, there is a puzzled look on the new alter's face. "I have no idea what you are talking about."

This is what occurred in Betty's case. She had no memory of her trauma. She knew her father was evil and in bondage to pornography. The house was full of the stuff. She knew her father and mother were not a close, loving couple. She also knew her mother kept her from ever being alone with her father from adolescence on, but she did not know why, nor did she care to ask.

Finally, she knew that her love for God was an unemotional love. She could not know God as Father. That was unspeakable. She could not know Jesus as a compassionate Savior either. He was too perfect for her. She did know the Holy Spirit as her indwelling Lord. She did not feel His love, but He spoke to her and told her how to follow the Lord. In faith, she obeyed. The demons were angry with the Holy Spirit but were afraid of Him. They repeatedly told me so.

During the first counseling session Betty drew the following diagram of her relationship with God:

Figure 58.1
Betty's Relationship With God

BETTY—HER MIND

	B	B		
	A	A		
	R	R		
	R	R		
Spirit	I	I	*Soul; i.e., Emotions*
Holy Spirit	E	E	No Sense
Is	R	R	of
Here			God's Presence

This Barrier Kept
Betty's Soul from
Feeling—Knowing—God's
Presence

Every one of the demons from whom I commanded a response to my questions about their purpose in her life said their major goal was to keep her from knowing God's presence in her life. All affirmed she was a Christian and that she had become a believer in childhood.

Hellbent: "My purpose was to take her to hell. After her conversion that purpose changed. My purpose was to make her life a hell on earth."

Unbelief: "She belongs to us. She was given to us by her father in sacrifice. She doesn't remember what her father did."

Sacrifice: "He [Jesus] has redeemed her by His perfect sacrifice. He has a plan for her life and we wanted to destroy her so that plan would not be fulfilled. She finally got wise. She's been turning against us. Jesus is healing her."

Spirit of Her Father: "I came from her father. Her father told her lies and I was there working with her father, telling her these lies. She believed these lies up until recently."

Pain and Torture: "Our purpose was to torture her mind, to cut her off from the life of God. We have been hiding from her; she has not known that we were here."

Cleft Lip and Cleft Palate: "I came into her life because I didn't want her to know God. We hate her. We tormented her."

Destroyer: "My purpose was to destroy her spirit. I came into her when she was born."

False Authority: "I told her that she needed to be a loner, that she should not obey any authority. She doesn't need anybody. She should go through life by herself."

Unbelief, the Prince: "I own a place in her. I own the seat of her emotions. I get her tied up in knots. We don't want her to know God in her soul."

Separate: "I keep her from feeling the love of God."

Pride: "I keep her from knowing God as her Father. I keep her from being able to identify with Jesus."[14]

By the end of the second deliverance session with Betty, we discovered her first alter personality. I was confident she must have formed alter personalities which made it possible for her to survive the SRA and function as effectively as she did.

1. She had suffered severe and continued sexual, physical, psychological, and religious child abuse as a victim of SRA. Friesen says, "One thing we know about dissociation is that it is used only when the pain has been extreme, and it usually begins in preschool days.

"Ninety-seven percent have been subjected to serious child abuse as youngsters. Another study found that 88 percent had been abused sexually, with 83 percent having been sexually penetrated as young children. That is a horrible way to start life. Although I always hope when I meet a dissociating person that he or she will be one of those who was not sexually abused, that is not usually the case."[15]

2. That abuse was prolonged, and in the context of lack of nurture within the home. Friesen describes it this way: "The life circumstances have been dangerous, and the children continue to suffer abuse over a long period of time."[16]

3. There is the natural biological factor. Children who dissociate are very intelligent children. They have an inborn ability to transfer themselves out of the painful context into an imaginary world. They are masters at fantasizing. About 25 percent of all children seem to possess this ability, Friesen says.

4. The child who dissociates is psychologically constituted with a very vivid and creative imagination.[17] This is similar to number 3.

Betty had experienced all of these and more. She is one of the most intelligent, creative, and strongest persons I have ever met. At the end of the second counseling session with Loretta and me, Betty said, "I have felt a loss to get in touch with the Holy Spirit, and this inner child, inner compartment. . . . The last few weeks it has gone far, far away, and even the Holy Spirit, it's like He says, 'I'm here and I'm protecting this. . . .' It's like a body inside. It really sounds crazy, but . . . it's defenseless and can't fight for itself and the demons want to destroy it. As we were praying today there was a voice saying, 'You can't have the baby. You can't have the baby. You can't have the baby.' "[18] It wasn't long before we were in contact with this inner child—the baby. She could not speak, but another alter personality evidently spoke in her behalf. Thus, we were in contact with at least two alter personalities besides Betty, the host personality. During my last conversation with Betty's counselor she indicated that over 100 alter personalities have been identified, all living within Betty's body. The process of integrating these into the one host person is still in process. She will win the battle.

Betty told me some time ago, "The three things that have so damaged my life are the demonic activity, the sexual abuse (SRA), and the multiple personalities. The multiple personalities that exist within me have kept me from reaching the wholeness that I need. I understand why I have been having difficulty applying God's truth to my life. How do you apply truth to a broken personality before the pieces are put together? That personality is now being repaired. The pieces are starting to come together."

With this as a background we are ready to look at the complex question of MPD and the potential demonic dimension to this human affliction.

Demonization and Mental Health Issues

59

Multiple Personality Disorders and Demonization

T he Reverend Ernest Rockstad was one of the leading pioneers in the USA in the twentieth century among conservative evangelicals in spiritual warfare ministry and teaching. Ernie, as many of us called him, like others of us active in this ministry today was introduced into the terrible realities of the demonization of believers and their need for deliverance through demonic problems within his own family. In Ernie's case it was through demonic attachment in his own life.

For over 40 years Ernie worked with hundreds of severely demonized Christians, even bringing some of them into his home. He shared his life, his family, and all his earthly resources with bruised and battered men, women, and young people.

Ernie was an Independent Baptist. You can't be more conservative than that; yet he never allowed his theological presuppositions to blind him to the reality of human anguish. He adjusted his theology to fit the realities he was facing. As such, he was constantly in trouble, like the rest of us, with many of the brethren.

When Rockstad discovered what he called "shattered personalities" and "segmented personalities," now commonly called MPDs, "multiples," or "alter personalities,"[1] he broke open to the Christian world the whole controversial and complex reality of segmented personalities with a series of papers, audio cassettes, and lectures. In this chapter I want to quote part of a lecture by Rockstad telling how he stumbled into his amazing discovery of shattered personalities in the early 1970s. The following story taken from his audio cassette entitled "Healing the Shattered Personality" is only lightly edited.

> The Lord has seen fit for us to discover that it is possible for a person to have his personality shattered so that parts of him . . . actually fight against [other parts of] him. . . .
>   We have lived with this tragedy for years in the person of Carmen Cherry, the

daughter of a Southern Baptist evangelist, a man dedicated to soul winning. He had eleven children; Carmen is the fifth. Demons from her have declared, "We keep a book of balances. Her father talked [about Christ] too much. She's got to pay the price. We are exacting the price in her life."

The girl has suffered greatly. She became a hopeless drunkard and tried to commit suicide many times. I worked with her for over a year and couldn't contact any demons. As I counseled with her, I began to realize there was life from God there, although others had said it couldn't be possible that anybody in that condition could be a Christian.

I began to encourage her. In time she was able to read *War On the Saints*. She began to carry on the warfare. She was able to break a demon-imposed diet that she had been on for thirteen years.

At twelve years of age she quit eating and would have starved to death if she were not hospitalized and force-fed. From the time she was twelve years old she was on a very strict diet. She was told from inside what she could eat and not eat. If she transgressed in any way, she was punished terribly. The Lord helped her break this. But somehow that did not take care of the problems—the running away and the drunkenness.

Last fall we turned up in her a control being who says he owns her. I don't understand it. We have had experience with hundreds of people. We have dealt with thousands of demons. We have turned up something in Carmen that is not like anything with which we have ever dealt before.

It is not like a regular demon. We have not been able to remove it. It says it owns her. "She is mine." When I declare Jesus Christ is Lord, it replies back, "No. I am her lord. I own her. She belongs to me."

For a while it seemed she had lost her mind, completely. She begged to be recommitted to a mental hospital, but I refused to give in. We have now seen a healing take place and her mind come back to her again.

What we discovered in Carmen is a shattered, split personality. I worked with her for over a year trying to contact demons without success. One day I made my calls a little bit wider. I said, "I command you, whoever it is that is causing Carmen this trouble, in the name of the Lord Jesus Christ, you come to attention. I want to talk to you."

I repeated the command a few times. All of a sudden her head came up, a big grin on the face, shoulders back. She got up and began to strut back and forth across my counseling room floor, a completely different person, cocky, sure, confident. I looked at her in amazement and said, "Well, who are you?"

"I am Carmen. I am the real Carmen. I'm not that little mouse that you know. I'm the real one. I'm stronger than she is. I'm completely lost. She is only partly saved. Look at me. See how strong I am."

I didn't understand it. I said, "You're a demon."

"No, I'm not a demon," it said.

You know I tried to cast out that thing, to make it know it was a demon. We would have times when our people would come in to help pray and work. We worked through the months of May, June, July, August, September—and we still had it there. It was a terrible thing. We could call it up. It was a killer. We went through some awful things.

Rockstad told of physical attacks, both against himself and his wife, Ilene, and of the destruction of personal property. Finally, at Carmen's request, they put her in restraints when they worked with "The Thing," as Rockstad came to call it.

We were always calling it up—trying to get it out—with no success whatsoever. It protested being tied down.

"I'm not crazy," it said. "Don't tie me down. She is the one who is crazy. She ought to be put in the mental hospital, not me!"

Then one day I was talking to it as if it were a human being. I noticed a listening ear. I made some mention about the Bible as the Word of God. The answer came back, "Oh! No! That is not the Word of God. Men wrote that book, you know."

It was an intelligent answer. I talked some more as if I were talking to a human being. I got intelligent answers back; unbelief—but still intelligent answers. Finally I strapped her into a chair about 9:30 one morning and called this thing up. I started out with God and the Book of Genesis with Creation, through the Fall, all the way through the Bible. I taught her all day long. She sat there, interested.

"Why, I have never heard of that before. I never knew anything about that," it said.

I talked about Jesus Christ being Lord. Previously when we called this thing up, dealing with it as with a demon, it would cry out about Jesus Christ, "He's a dead man. He's a dead man. I curse His blood."

Oh, terrible things that would be said—terrible blasphemies. And to my amazement, when we had gone through the day—I had put special emphasis on the lordship of Jesus Christ—this violent thing said, "I would like to pray to Him, if I could. Would you let me pray to Him?"

She prayed. She submitted to Jesus Christ as Lord, and the violence was all gone. There was a complete change. She said, "Don't send me back down. Let me stay up."

"I can't do that," I said. "Think of all the threats you have made. You threatened to kill her; you would leave her body bloody and mangled."

"That's all changed now," she replied. "I promise you I won't do that. Besides, I would like to go to prayer meeting tonight. Would you let me go to prayer meeting?"

I didn't know what in the world to do. Finally, I unstrapped her. She went along to prayer meeting—she was a little bit strange, scared. That girl was with us from Wednesday until Saturday. On Saturday she came to me and said, "I'm getting tired of being up. I wonder if you would let me go down again now?"

I said I did not know what to do. I said, "Let's pray and lay this before the Lord!" We prayed and asked God for His will to be done, in the name of the Lord Jesus Christ. As I prayed, she changed again, and I had somebody else there, a completely different person, a lovely girl, just a lovely girl. I sat talking with her. I just mentioned something about Jesus Christ, and she said, "Who is He? I never heard of Him."

I was amazed. I couldn't believe it. We had spent the whole day instructing [the other Carmen] about Christ, and this one knew nothing about Jesus Christ, nothing about God. She was an entirely different person. As I began to tell her about Christ she said, "Oh! Tell me more. That sounds real good. I've never heard anything about that before."

I taught that girl. She drank in everything. Finally she said, "Can I pray to Him? I would like to know Him. I would like to have Him."

I could hardly believe it.

We have lost count of the number of Carmens that we have worked with. I quit counting at about one hundred seventy-five. I have prayed with retarded ones, with brilliant girls, with girls that are twelve years old, with grownups. I have prayed with segments of the personality that were utterly depraved.

With each succeeding one, they had never heard about Jesus Christ. But as we talk to them, and give them the truth about the Lord Jesus, we find that we are able to pray with them and they submit to Jesus Christ as Lord. . . .

I want to tell you that I don't understand this. I can't figure it out. Either we are being terrible deceived, or God is leading us into something which is tremendously momentous.

Rockstad then told of his concern that persons are now learning how willfully to damage another human being, primarily children, to the place where they can split their personality. This was a remarkable insight, occurring in the early 1970s before the horror of sexual child abuse and SRA were widely recognized among Christians. In SRA the abuse is carefully calculated to produce enough trauma, torture, and pain so the child will dissociate. The abuse is continued until the dissociation is well established. Demons are conjured up or down to attach themselves to these personality segments. They are preprogrammed (for lack of a better word) to gain control of the host person later in life for Satan and evil. This is exactly what Rockstad had foreseen.

Rockstad's narrative continues.

> I think this is something that is going to need to be known in our day. After we had found this out with Carmen, six weeks later Jan Smith came to us for help. They had tried to help her in casting out demons, and they had come up against a stone wall.
>
> It was the first session that Jan was there when I felt impressed to pray and then begin to command, "If there is a Jan here that does not know the Lord Jesus, I call you to attention. I call for a Jan or Janet who does not know the Lord Jesus."
>
> All of a sudden she burst out crying, and wept and wept and wept. It was a rejected Janet. She said, "Nobody loves me. Nobody cares for me."
>
> I replied, "The Lord Jesus cares for you."
>
> "Who is He?" she asked. "I never heard of Him."
>
> Now that was the Janet who was the daughter of medical missionary parents. The Jan who a number of years before had received the Lord Jesus Christ as Savior. A part of her was still in the grips of darkness.
>
> People have criticized us for this—criticized us terribly. I have had people leave my church. One man said, "This is absolutely ridiculous, that a part of me could be saved and going to heaven and a part of me lost and going to hell."
>
> Of course, I don't believe it either. That is not what this is. This is not an eternal thing. When a person is saved he is going to heaven and he is going to be there entirely. But this is a work that Satan is able to do as far as time is concerned.[2] He is able to split off parts of a person and hold that part in abeyance that the person is not wholly and completely for the Lord Jesus Christ. The person is going to have serious problems.

At the time of the segmented personality discovery (the 1970s), Rockstad had already suffered over 25 years with attacks from the brethren for his views on the demonization of some Christians and his method of expelling demons. He had been able to bear with all this, but the avalanche of criticism now coming his way for this new discovery was just too much. He resolved to quit working with segmented personalities. He would just continue his pastoral work and even cut back on his ministry to demonically afflicted believers.

Again I must remark how much evil is done against godly Christian warriors who have the courage to break new ground in counseling. Why are we so prone to seek to destroy men whose ministry challenges our theological comfort zones? We are all prouder and crueler than we are willing to admit.

The afternoon he made his decision he received a totally unsolicited phone call.

> "Hello. This is Jan. I just wanted to call and encourage you and to tell you I am getting along just fine. I wanted to tell you, too, please keep on with what you are

doing. If you don't keep on with what you are doing, what would people like me do?"

Rockstad reversed his decision:

I've been keeping on. I didn't cancel my engagements, I kept right on. We have been finding this in other people since. Let me try and identify the problem—not that we understand it.

In a traumatic experience in childhood or elsewhere along the way, *a part of the person is split off and left behind.* It is sealed off, somehow, by Satan. The personality that is split off remains at that place, at that age. Usually this segment is kept in darkness about Christ or is held in the grip of some problem.

One of the people with whom we have worked, all of her segments have been saved. They have the assurance of their salvation. They are all related to some problem in the person's life. In one case I was instructing one of the segments, a 12-year-old girl in a 28-year-old body, about the truth of her union with Christ, when she saw it and laid hold of it. She took her stand as being dead to sin in Christ and alive in Christ.[3] She merged right back, and the original person came forth, clear and strong.

These segments that are split off have an influence upon the life of the person. Sometimes you will run into a segment that absolutely hates the real person. So the person is lugging this struggle along. It is no wonder that with Carmen she discovered vodka.

In our counseling—we are dealing with Christians—we have the person declare, "I renounce Satan. I confess Jesus Christ as my Lord."

Then I make an affirmation and pray something like this:

"I declare that we refuse to have in this time anything but the work of God, the true and loving God through the Lord Jesus Christ. We choose to operate only by the Holy Spirit. We choose to operate only in the name of the Lord Jesus Christ. We refuse and repudiate all psychic and demonic workings. We want only that which comes by way of the cross of the Lord Jesus Christ. Father in heaven, block us if we do anything that is not pleasing in your sight, if we are doing anything that You don't want us to do."

Then I go on and I begin to command, "In the name of the Lord Jesus I call for the "John Doe" here who has not renounced Satan and has not accepted Jesus Christ as Lord. Is there a "John Doe" here who does not know the Lord Jesus? Will you come to attention?"

I must mention in passing, this is not hypnotism at all, because *you don't have control over the person who comes up.* Sometimes you have some terrible ones, even in Jan. We had one that came up who said, "I sure want to thank you for bringing me up. I want to have a good time. That Jan, she is so religious. She doesn't want to have any fun. Now I'm going to paint the town red tonight."

We had a real bad time with her and another one. She was a psychiatrically oriented one. Jan had been under psychiatric care for ten years. This had all been stored up in one of the segments, and when we got that segment up, all she could talk about was that she was absolutely against the Bible and prayer. She told us, "The way you take care of your emotions is to let them fly. If you get angry, go ahead and get angry. Don't hurt people, but if you have to kill an animal, just go right ahead and kill it. You've got to get these things out of you."

That was the one who called the police. The people with whom she was staying didn't know about it until they saw the lights flashing out in front. The police came to the door and said, "We've come to pick up the lady who called in to be taken to the hospital."

"There is no one here to be taken to the hospital," the family responded. Just then Jan stepped up to the police and said, "I'm the one. Can you imagine? These people are trying to get demons out of me. Isn't that ridiculous?"

It so happened that the wife in the home was a registered nurse. She said, "I'm a registered nurse. This lady is mentally ill. She is staying with us while she is counseling with our pastor."

"Oh," the police responded, "that's why she is talking about demons."

They had a time with her. She was something else. This psychiatrically oriented one was up for a number of days. She got hold of the aspirin bottle and took two dozen or more aspirin and got real, real sick. Her husband was there. Finally she got so sick she said to her husband, "Take me to Rockstad. He knows the answer to this."

They came. She wanted the plan of salvation. She wanted to hear about the Lord Jesus. Before she had absolutely rejected and refused it. But I was able to go over the Word of God with her and she prayed, and that one alter was gone and the real Jan was back again.

When you call for the segment to come, the change can be immediate or it may be gradual . . . a grin comes on the face—you can tell that somebody else is there. But sometimes it comes gradually, and I've been fooled on this.

I keep checking [when I am not certain if the segment has switched]. "Do you confess Jesus Christ as Lord?" And when it is a character which has come up it will be very perplexed. "Well, I don't know. I don't know what you are talking about."

The difference between a personality segment and a demon is that *a demon will never renounce Satan*. A demon will never, ever repudiate Satan. But when you explain to this segment about Satan, I have never yet had one but will immediately say, "Well, I sure don't want anything to do with him." And when you present the truth about Christ eventually there is a willingness to submit.

Is this true working with all such cases? I doubt it. But Rockstad says this was his experience repeatedly.

In dealing with a segment, it is very interesting that the segment will begin to talk about the real person in the third person—"She does so and so"—many times with dislike. It will be in darkness about Christ or have some problem.

When we instruct it in the truth of the Word of God and bring this segment to renounce Satan and submit to Christ, there is a merging that takes place. On confession of Jesus Christ as Lord, this thing disappears and the real person comes back again. We have never had the same one come back. It is molded into the place where it is supposed to be.

In most every case demons are associated with that particular segment. In fact, demons are able to hide in the segment of the person. That's why you need to get the demons from that particular segment. Sometimes you have to get the demons from that segment before it will submit to the Lord Jesus Christ. The segments become strongholds for the powers of darkness. This is one of the reasons that some people are retarded in getting deliverance. It takes a long time or you don't get anywhere because there are the segments that are the dwelling places of wicked spirits. They prevent the submission to Christ. The segments become hiding places to the demons.

We have known of demons counterfeiting the segments and demons that take the same name as the person. It takes some checking and discerning to recognize when this is being done.

I believe that whenever there is something that turns up and claims to be the person it should be carefully checked out by demanding what it confesses concerning Jesus Christ come in the flesh, and Jesus Christ as Lord. We are still finding this phenomenon of the shattered personality, segments of the person not saved, or somehow split off, and held by the enemy. With some people they have not been able to get help in any other way.[4]

I have quoted in detail the late Rev. Ernest Rockstad's experiences in discovering segmented, or shattered personalities in adult survivors of child abuse or trauma[5] for several reasons:

1. The condition was discovered by a nonprofessional counselor, not by a trained psychologist-counselor.

2. Rockstad revealed no prior knowledge of what is now called MPD. He discovered the condition in the context of ministering to extremely bruised people.

3. Rockstad came into his ministry with demonized segments against his own will and theology. At first he stubbornly dealt with these segments as though they were difficult demons who did not respond to proven deliverance procedures.

4. Rockstad made many errors in the early days of dealing with segmented personalities, just as he did in the early days of dealing with the demonized. This is true of all of us.

5. There is an unsophisticated simplicity, honesty, and refreshing humility in his report.

6. His account reveals the personal, historical dimension of ministry to fractured personalities in the life of a godly pastor. To see a developing ministry from a historical perspective is extremely helpful.

7. Rockstad's approach to multiplicity seems to be generally compatible with the broad, general approach of professional Christian counselors who specialize in counseling what are commonly called MPD's. Admittedly, he did not understand the complex psychological dimensions of this human phenomenon as do professionally trained counselors. While professionals will question some of his conclusions, most will not question the basic reality he discovered.

8. Rockstad's strong emphasis on the demonic dimension of personallity segmentation is greatly needed.

Every serious multiple I have dealt with has had demonic problems associated with his multiplicity. Since I am limited in on-going, hands-on experience with multiples, I am not in the position to affirm that multiplicity always involves demonization. Yet, knowing the nature of demons as I do, I would find it hard to believe that they do not try to be involved in all such cases.

In the case study on Betty given in chapter 58, the multiples would not even appear until the demons were cleared out. The demons effectively hid her segments until they were removed from her body. Either that or else the segments were afraid of the demons and would not appear—even in therapy—until the demons left.

In the case studies mentioned by Rockstad, the fragments—even the demonized ones—seem to have come up first. In the case of some of them, he said, the segments couldn't come to Christ until the demons attached to them were removed. Whatever the case may be, the interrelationship between the segments and the demons attached to them is crucial. We must learn to recognize when demons hinder the segments from renouncing Satan and receiving Jesus as Savior and Lord.[6]

9. Rockstad strongly stresses the need to consider the segments as capable of accepting Christ one by one. This is essential and, according to Rockstad, always successful when it is done in a correct, loving, and persistent manner with persons who are already believers.

10. Fusion or integration through the rebuilding of the whole personality is the goal once the segments are led to Christ. This would raise serious questions about cases where the counselors settle with segment cooperation, but separateness. Fusion is neither sought nor accomplished. Thus the personality is never made whole again, a condition that is unacceptable both the Christian and non-Christian perspectives. It may be that only those counselors who acknowledge and depend on God's creative power can help effect such integration.

11. Since most of my readers are not highly trained professional counselors, Rev. Rockstad's story is one we can all identify with. This would not be the case if this introductory chapter on multiplicity rested primarily on the writings of trained professionals.

12. Finally, Rockstad's report reveals errors in working with personality segmentation that trained Christian professionals would avoid. This is to be expected.

First, there is Ernie's apparent failure to discover (or to report) the particular abuse or trauma which led to the split personalities of Carmen and Jan. The younger and earlier segments are the first to dissociate. If there was severe physical, sexual, psychological, or religious abuse suffered at an early age—and there always is—these segments would hold the memory of that abuse. If they are led to Christ and fused without the memories they hold brought to light and faced by the traumatized person, that person will face unnecessary future difficulties in life, perhaps never being fully healed.

Second, Rockstad did not mention SRA. Perhaps he was aware of it, but he does not refer to it unless he did so toward the end of his life when the extent of SRA began to be made known. Most child abuse which produces severe dissociation is associated with sexual child abuse. The sexual child abuse that most often leads to severe dissociation is SRA.[7] Some practitioners estimate it is as high as 75 percent.

Third, he does not mention the amnesia that often exists among the segmented personalities themselves, and between the personality and the segments. The latter is probably implied in his studies, but the former is not. Nor does he mention the time gaps in the person's life, lost time that cannot be accounted for in daily life and the years of early childhood about which the victim has little or no memory.[8]

60

The Non-Demonic Reality
of Mental Illnesses

Patrick O'Brien was a well-known missionary evangelist in Mexico. I liked everything I read about him. Besides, from the viewpoint of a Murphy, an O'Brien had to be a good man.

In the late 1970s Pat's oldest son, Tom, became strangely ill while in college in the U.S. He had to be sent back to his family in Mexico. Tom's illness fit what is usually categorized as mental.[1]

The name *mental illness* is unfortunate. It gives the impression that one is crazy, emotionally weak, or too cowardly to cope with life. No truly born again believer can become mentally ill, we are often told. He has the mind of Christ so how could his mind become ill? A believer who becomes mentally ill has sin in his life. It is the believer's own fault. If he would only break with the sin patterns in his life, stop worrying and trust God, he would become well.

Thus victims of mental illness too often don't find much comfort, sympathy, or help from Christians or churches. Every organ in the believer's body can become diseased or break down, but not his brain or mind. Somehow that cannot happen to a genuine believer. However, that is exactly what happened to Tom O'Brien.

Before his illness, Tom was a delightful Christian young man, unusually compassionate and kind. After his illness, his personality changed radically. He became angry, even violent, at times. Since he was housebound—his family was forced to retire from their missionary work in Mexico and return to Los Angeles so Tom could receive medical treatment—all his violence occurred in his home. He smashed windows and furniture in his sudden fits of rage.

He was prone to nudity. He cut his hair and his clothes. His talk was confused and often profane. He seemed obsessed with sex and talked of wanting to have sex with strangers. His family was horrified. They took him to various doctors who diagnosed him as being everything from manic depressive to paranoid schizophrenic.[2] With medications, he would gradually return to semi-normal behavior. His usual cheerful, godly life style reappeared. Then, when he went off his medicine, Tom would suffer serious relapses.

Pat and his family had been home about a year when I heard about Tom's condition. Tom was under continual psychiatric care, often hospitalized for weeks on end. He would improve enough to return home. While at home his condition would worsen and he would have to be recommitted.

As I heard the reports about Tom I wondered if he might have demonic problems. I was new in deliverance counseling at the time and had the natural beginner's tendency to make snap diagnoses of demonization. I contacted Pat, asking him if he would permit me to pray with Tom. Of course he gave me permission.

I was shocked by Tom's appearance. He was skin and bones because he refused to eat. He had cut his hair almost down to his skull. It was impossible to carry on a normal conversation with him. He continually changed the subject. I asked him to read the Scriptures to me. He did so, but erratically. He could not understand most of what he was reading.

I began to pray. I began to speak out against any demons which were attached to his life. I continued to talk and pray with him for about two hours. I seemed to be making some progress. I had Tom repeat warfare prayers and doctrinal prayers with me affirming his position in Christ. Suddenly Tom stopped reading. He exploded in anger. A furious voice spoke out of his mouth, yelling "I am Satan! I am Lucifer! I hate you! I hate you! To hell with you!" While still yelling at me he struck me across the face, knocking me backwards, and then ran from the room.

I was startled. I had tried to control "the demons" but with no effect at all. This had never happened to me before. I spent the next two hours talking and praying with Pat and Judie, his wife. I tried to get information from them about the psychiatrist's diagnosis of Tom's condition. They were reluctant to tell me. Finally they admitted Tom was diagnosed as schizophrenic.[3] They categorically denied that the diagnosis could be accurate. Tom was a strong Christian, and strong Christians cannot become schizophrenic, they said.

Unfortunately I had recently read a book on counseling demonized Christians which states that schizophrenia is directly demonic. The author is a godly, experienced deliverance counselor. Most of what he writes is excellent and soundly biblical. As a result I was inclined towards the view that Tom's problem was demonic. After all, was not that a demon which spoke out against me, hit me, and claimed he was Satan and Lucifer?

When I met with Tom again there were no "manifestations" but his condition had worsened. He was catatonic.

Months passed. In the meantime Tom was ministered to by other deliverance counselors. All claimed they successfully cast hundreds of demons out of Tom's life (I couldn't even get one out), but there was no change in his condition whatsoever.

I arranged to meet with Tom once more. While disturbed by my failure to help him, I wanted to make one more attempt. Besides, I had grown in knowledge both in the demonic realm and in the area of brain-mental illness since my first long session with him. I had read everything I could on schizophrenia and related brain malfunctions. Almost every symptom described in the books and articles existed in Tom's life.

The realization that Tom's problems were primarily biological-mental came to me with disturbing clarity—not that the whole idea was new to my thinking about Tom. Long before, I had begun to believe that Tom was suffering from some kind of brain malfunction or psychosis. I could not deny the possibility of some form of demonization, either. Perhaps the two existed side by side as I had discovered in other cases.[4]

When I met with Tom this time he was in one of his occasional lucid periods. We had a great time reading Scripture, praying and talking. I tried to again minister deliverance to him. He was fully cooperative. Nothing happened. Apart from the constant interfering voices, he had no demonic reaction at all.

I occasionally visit Tom when I am in Los Angeles. He is still the same. As for his parents? They are still in denial. His has to be a demonic problem, they insist. Tom is not mentally ill. Thus they often withdraw Tom's medications, praying and believing God for his healing.

My heart goes out to Pat, Judie, and above all to Tom. Pat knows his son is not fully responsible for his actions. Yet at times he understandably becomes angry with him for the destructive effect of his bizarre behavior on the family.

The concept of reduced capacity is not popular with Christian preachers and teachers. We see the strong note of individual responsibility running all through Scripture. Thus when we are forced to face the real world of insanity or serious demonization which greatly reduces, indeed in some cases almost completely nullifies, the victim's capacity to think and act responsibly, we become both angry and impatient.[5] When our home is turned into a battlefield by a family member who acts in an anti-social manner, our frustrations and shame know no bounds. It soon leads to anger, often hidden, but there nevertheless.

Tom's experience and the sheer agony of his family's decade-long nightmare of having a beloved but seriously mentally ill son in their home compels me briefly to discuss the nature of mental-brain malfunctions. I am not a psychiatrist. Yet because I often face the dilemma of diagnosis, I have had to learn something about brain-mental-emotional malfunctions.

The greatest recent help has come from two books, one by a highly respected Christian psychiatrist, Dr. John White, *The Masks of Melancholy,* and the other by a respected professor of psychology at the Western Baptist Seminary in Portland, Oregon, Dr. Rodger K. Bufford, *Counseling the Demonic.*[6]

In the introduction to his analysis of depressive illnesses and serious brain malfunctions like schizophrenia White recognizes the failures of psychiatry. He quotes a psychiatrist colleague as saying, "Psychiatry is an orderly body of ignorance." White comments, "His view is a little extreme. I would prefer to say that psychiatry, like other human sciences, is a disorderly mass of truths, half truths, and wild ideas."[7]

White contrasts depression with depressive illness. All of us are occasionally depressed. Depressive illness and brain malfunctions like schizophrenia are much more serious. Like kidney failure or heart malfunction, they require special treatment. White observes that

> our problem arises . . . because we use the term *depression* to mean different things [such as] grief following bereavement, . . . humiliation following failure and defeat, . . . the petulant response of one whose expectations of others are never met. . . . [or] unresolved emotional problems.
>
> I am concerned more with depression (whatever its type or origin) which has assumed graver and perhaps life-threatening proportions. The distinction between the "depressions" above and what I would like to call depressive illness is not always clear, but slowly patterns are beginning to emerge and to make more sense.[8]

White writes of the struggle for acceptable definitions and classifications of the whole gamut of depressive illnesses. He says that in general, simple depressions as well as serious brain malfunctions like schizophrenia are treated by counselors of many kinds. Depressive illnesses should be treated by psychiatrists and clinical psychologists. He says that worldwide mental health physicians are beginning to cooperate with the World Mental Health Organization to adopt "a common language and more rigorous definition of terms."

Perhaps the most successful effort to date has been done in America.

> One of the most rigorous searches for clear definitions is a recent effort on the part of the American Psychiatric Association who have put out a manual known as *Diagnostic and Statistical Manual III* (DSM III). . . . Two research teams on opposite sides of the world can be reasonably sure that they understand what each other is saying if both use standard terms, such as those DSM III proposes.[9]

White shares a simplified version of some recent classifications of depressive illnesses:[10]

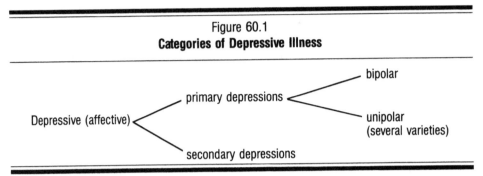

Figure 60.1
Categories of Depressive Illness

White says primary depressions arise by themselves. Secondary depressions, on the other hand, arise out of other problems including mental or physical illness. We will concentrate only on primary depressions.

Primary depressions are probably due to malfunctions in the body.[11] They are of two types. First there is bipolar depressive illness evidenced by mood swings from total despair on the one hand to manic, almost uncontrollable, excitement on the other. This has traditionally been called manic-depressive psychosis.

Unipolar depressions do not combine highs and lows. It is all gloom, despair, and darkness with never a sunny day.[12]

> To merit the description of depressive illness all of these conditions must last (a period of time). . . . All have a tendency toward spontaneous remission without any treatment after a period of time varying from several months even to a number of years. Occasionally a unipolar depression may be lifelong, or else there may be spontaneous remission only for a month or two. . . . Severe forms of bipolar illness are those in which the fluctuations from mania to melancholy are continuous.

White makes an important observation which fits Tom's story and the reaction of his parents, Pat and Judie, to his mental illness when he says, "Unfortunately Christians tend to see their depressions [and other, even more serious brain disorders] only in spiritual terms. They feel they have let God down." He follows with a case study. A Christian musician was told by her counselor if she would praise God with her music, the depression would go away. She tried, but the depression worsened. White comments, "Her symptoms were being treated while her illness was allowed to progress."

White observes that doctors often refer depressed Christians to him, but pastoral counselors seldom do so. "Perhaps they are less alert to the possibility of depressive illness," White says. "Some patients who have been receiving counseling for years have been made well in a couple of months once the real problem has been sorted out."

White continues with the problem Christians have with accepting the fact that believers can suffer depressive illnesses. He says, "Along with the depressed affect, religious patients are plagued with feelings of guilt. . . . They decide that they never were Christians or that they have committed the unpardonable sin."[13]

We dare not slip into the "all things are spiritual" mode. Some mood disorders and mental brain-psychological malfunctions among believers are not due to spiritual problems but to natural factors. Natural evil is just as real and destructive as moral evil to human beings, including believers. Thus, Christians can suffer from depressive illnesses and even more serious brain disorders like schizophrenia. Rodger Bufford tells of a Christian woman, Leila, and her battle with an obsessive compulsive disorder. She believed in deliverance. She sought to have the "demon" causing her problem cast out of her.[14]

Bufford tells us that obsessive compulsive disorders are "recurrent thoughts, ideas, images, impulses the person professes not to desire and finds repugnant, yet reports he or she is unable to resist." They are "repetitive behavioral rituals performed to produce or prevent some event or situation. The person recognizes that the activity has no relationship to the event or is clearly excessive" but cannot stop doing it.

Leila came to him for help with a compulsive pattern of washing herself. Her first appointment with Bufford was at 6:00 P.M. In order to be ready on time, Leila rose at 5:30 A.M. to shower and dress. She spent all day washing and rinsing her body, inch by inch; yet she was late for the appointment. Leila struggled with the belief that hers was a demonic problem, the result of sin. She prayed for deliverance and attended healing meetings in which others prayed for her. She experienced no change.

Bufford diagnosed Leila as obsessive-compulsive. He says there were spiritual dimensions to her problem as well. All these dimensions were addressed. Treatment also centered on practical behavior changes. Bufford says it was hard for Leila to accept the view that her problem was partly psychological, not only spiritual. So long as she viewed her problems primarily as spiritual "she believed that all she could do was pray and believe that God would heal her. This made it easy for her to justify doing nothing herself." Bufford says he "encouraged her to pray and believe, but also to work as God enabled her, to promote the healing process through her own diligent efforts. As she did so she gradually made progress."

One night I received a frantic phone call from a woman from another city. "Dr. Murphy, I am demon possessed. Please help me. I'm going to die unless you help me. I talked with Rev. _____ but he could not help me. Will you help me?" she pleaded.

My first task was to get her calmed down. I comforted her as I sought to help her out of the frenzy of emotion she was in. In time she calmed down. As I listened to her story over the space of two hours, I began to suspect her problem was not demonic. It sounded like she was suffering from some form of manic-depressive disorder.

I decided to pray with her. I always do. If there are demons present, this usually causes them to react and in some way make their presence known. Also, using what I call "Affirmation of Faith" prayers brings faith and comfort to the victim.

Many people seek help from spiritual counselors because they believe we are power people in the Holy Spirit. Thus when we calmly but authoritatively pray with them, they are immediately helped. This opens the door to more effective counseling. I am continually puzzled by Christian counselors who do not pray with and for their counselees. Those who don't pray with them, don't use Scripture with them, either. Why not?

"Elizabeth," I said, "I do not sense any demons in your life. I am not saying they are not attacking you, but you have nothing to be concerned about. They cannot hurt you! As I prayed I bound their activity against you. I will teach you how to do the same thing for yourself. You don't need to be afraid of them any longer. They are all defeated by the Holy Spirit within you."

"Oh, thank you! Thank you!" she said. "I feel better already, though I am still afraid and depressed. I'll do anything you say."

"Do you know of a Christian psychiatrist or psychologist in your area?" I asked.

"No! But I do belong to a good medical plan in a near-by hospital. They have psychiatrists there. In fact my husband already called and made an appointment for me before we were given your phone number. I don't know whether or not he is a believer. Will he try and take my faith away from me?" she asked.

"I don't think so, but you can tell him right up front you are a Christian and you do not want him to talk against your faith. Most psychiatrists will not deliberately try to undermine the religious beliefs of their patients.

"However, he may tell you that you are too religious and that your bondage to your extreme religious lifestyle is harmful to your emotional stability. Elizabeth, you *are* too religious. The type of frantic Christian activity you are involved in is an extreme. You have neglected your husband, your children, and your own physical and emotional needs. You must break off your extreme lifestyle. Are you willing to follow my suggestions?"

To make a long story short, Elizabeth went to the psychiatrist. He diagnosed her problem as a manic-depressive disorder and hospitalized her immediately. In a few weeks she came home. As long as she stays on her medication, she does well. She is a lovely, normal woman, wife, and mother. She still attends church but lives a balanced Christian life. Her non-Christian psychiatrist, a caring person, has been a great help to her.[15] What she needs now is God's healing of her manic-depressive illness, for which she and others are praying.

Finally, I am convinced that everyone, the author included, is in need of further insight into the relationship between the spirit world and mental illness. Much has been written about the spirit world, even more about mental illness. We need a book which treats both subjects and shows how each is related to the other. If God wills, I may attempt to write such a book.

61

Counseling With Wisdom

How wise we must be as counselors! We should never make diagnoses about our counselees that go beyond our range of experience and knowledge. An undiscerning counselor is a dangerous counselor, but so is an ignorant one. If knowledge is available, God expects us to search for it.

An effective Christian counselor must be an avid reader. He should read the experts, Christian and non-Christian alike. While it is advantageous to seek out gifted and well-trained Christian psychiatrists and psychologists who know how to diagnose and treat depressive illnesses, we must not ostracize non-Christian mental disease specialists.

There are non-Christians who possess great skills in the diagnosis and treatment of these illnesses. Many are compassionate and indefatigable in their drive to refine the understanding and treatment of the biological and emotional causes of depressive illnesses. These physicians have helped develop diagnostic tools which can be used by counselors to understand better what is really wrong with the people to whom we minister.[1]

Two Types of Depression

I would like to return to one area of depressive illness, that of primary depressions. They are of two broad types, bipolar and unipolar depressions.

In bipolar depression the person experiences mood swings from manic enthusiasm on one hand to depressive gloom on the other. Manic highs can give the impression of both insanity and demonization. When on a manic high, the afflicted person may appear totally out of control. He may yell, run wild, or destroy personal property; or he may simply talk, incessantly, about illusions.

One lady was certain the Lord was coming. She became so excited she took the poker from her fireplace and began to swing it wildly, shouting "Jesus is coming! Jesus is coming!" She demolished the Christmas tree and other objects before she could be brought under control. After being put on a higher dosage of medication, she became normal. In such an uncontrollable ecstasy she appeared demonized, but she was not.

In unipolar clinical depression, however, there are no manic highs. There is only gloom and despair. Such persons can become suicidal. Death is preferable to life that has become unending and ever-increasing pain.

Specialists are now convinced both bipolar and unipolar depressions are primarily biological. Dr. John White says it is now believed that both bipolar and unipolar depression illnesses are due to "the scarcity" of neurotransmitters in the brain. They are tiny electrical-chemical "dispatch riders," to use Dr. White's term, which are supposed to carry the messages contained in the nerve cells of the brain from one nerve cell to another.

> For some reason they get locked up in storage areas in the nerve cells. Treatment is aimed at either releasing them or keeping them going longer . . . we really don't take messages of the brain from one part of the brain to the other, so much as from

one nerve cell to the next. In two nerve cells in the communication network there is a tiny space filled with fluid called synapse. Area transmitters pick up messages from one side of the synapse and deliver them on to the other. Their range is rather limited.[2]

If the neurotransmitters become scarce, that is, if they are not released from nerve cell to nerve cell, the brain malfunctions. When they fail, the part of the brain which controls our moods, our powers of concentration, energy, sleep, sexual drive, appetite, and so forth are affected. We become gloomy, we lose our energy. As one psychiatrist put it, the "joy center" of the brain is sabotaged. We lose all joy for life. We lose our normal desire for love, sex, food, beauty, humor. We either want to sleep all the time or are unable to sleep at all. We either eat in wild excess, not enjoying what we eat but eating compulsively, or we cannot eat because food has lost its appeal.

It is important to realize that the behavior caused by defective brain functions often mimics similar behavioral patterns produced by demonization; thus the need for correct diagnosis. We cannot cast out non-existent demons!

My Personal Experience With Depression

It is difficult to tell the following story about myself, but I too suffered unipolar depression which many of my friends said was demonic. The agony I went through was a hell on earth. Yet it has become one of the most valuable experiences in my life.

In non-technical terms, I have been, at least up until recently, an obsessive-compulsive-compassionate-workaholic-perfectionist. None of these terms are complimentary except for compassionate. A total breakdown in 1983 climaxed my undisciplined, workaholic lifestyle. The ten years before my breakdown were completely undisciplined. While studying full-time for three years for my doctorate at the Fuller School of World Mission, I was teaching full-time at Biola University and Talbot Theological Seminary. I also served as interim pastor or pulpit minister in churches which were without pastors. One was the large Church of the Open Door in downtown Los Angeles.

Every summer I taught summer school then went overseas. I was gone as long as two months at a time, often going through many time zones from Asia to Africa and Europe. During this same period I was thrust into my spiritual warfare counseling, deliverance, and training ministry. I could not get away from the calls for spiritual warfare counseling unless I left my home. The phone rang continually.

As a compassionate person, I did what I later came to call "deliverance on demand." I became the leader of a spiritual SWAT Team, releasing the hostages by power encounter, day and night. I used to comment to Loretta, "Why are demons always so active at night when I am supposed to sleep?"

What were my motives for ministering to the suffering victims of demonization in this manner? Was it for the glory of God? Yes. The tearing down of satanic strongholds? Yes. What else? The love of work. My obsessive, compulsive, workaholic, perfectionist nature. I gained self-worth through work. This was part of my sin. *Mine was a life out of balance.*

My wife and children warned me over and over again, but I was too "spiritual" to listen. God and people needed me. I also needed them for my sense of self-worth, I was later to discover.

God had called me to be a missionary. Thus after my seven-year loan to Biola was up, I returned to OC as one of its vice presidents. As an OC vice president, I traveled overseas continually. When 1983 dawned, I was exhausted. Yet I had a schedule of continuous overseas travel with missionary conferences in the U.S. in between.

The worst experiences occurred during Christmas 1982 in Nigeria. We were ministering with an indigenous church among the Ibo tribe in northern Nigeria. Our hosts did not take very good care of us. We had to sleep in a brothel-bar-dance hall in a nearby town, the only place with rooms for rent. The madam had her room right across the hall from mine.

The Christmas season is party time in Nigeria. The people seem to party day and night. The only way to sleep was to sedate myself with strong sleeping pills. We had little food and less water. Whiskey bottles littered the filthy room. Local religious practitioners, some noticeably hostile to us, headed endless parades. They all knew we were there. The atmosphere was difficult, oppressive. We were doing evangelistic preaching at night and teaching on spiritual warfare during the day.

During one of the morning sessions, commotion broke out towards the back. A young woman suddenly jumped up, yelling and shaking her fist at me. I could not understand what she was saying, but I knew she was demonized. She began to hurl curse after curse against me. They tried vainly to restrain her. Suddenly she ran down the aisle towards me. All the time she was yelling, cursing me, and taking off her clothes. They could not restrain her until she stood partially naked right below the platform. Demonic voices were screaming out of her mouth.

Normally I can handle this type of disturbance. This time I could not. I was too exhausted and too weak to think straight! I didn't even have enough presence of mind to ask my translator what she was saying.

We struggled through the week. My partner and I were glad when it was over. When we left for the nearest airport to catch our return flight, however, we discovered that all airplane flights had been canceled because of a military coup earlier that morning. They took us back to the brothel.

After much persuasion, two businessmen agreed to drive us the 500 miles to Lagos. They promised only to drop us off at the American consulate. This began another week of terrible tension. First, we could not find a place to stay in the city; the American consulate had closed down; the Marine guard offered no help. We knew the Sudan Interior Mission had its headquarters in Lagos. They agreed to put us up. What a blessing the SIM people were to us!

To top things off, the phenomenon called *Harmattan* occurred while we were in Lagos. Harmattan refers to the rain of tons of microscopic soil particles upon large sections of Central Africa. The sand comes from the mighty Sahara Desert, thousands of miles away. It blocks out the sun like heavy, black fog. It sifts into motors and other machinery, damaging their inner workings. It is dangerous for airplanes to fly through. Thus when the siege of the nation was lifted, permitting the resumption of air travel, the Lagos International Airport remained closed due to the Harmattan. The international carrier on which we were ticketed canceled all flights into Lagos. The airplanes scheduled to land at Lagos overflew the airport. The pilots refused to land in the Harmattan.

Every day we had to go to the airport, trying to get tickets on any flight out of the country. Hundreds of people jammed the airport, entire families camping out for days. Every toilet was plugged and overflowing. Food and drink were in short supply. It all looked hopeless. We at last managed to get a seat on Alitalia, the Italian airlines, through a fluke so bizarre it would take a long story to explain. In my journal I recorded over a dozen "miracles" God performed during this two-week period.

When I arrived home I was so weak and mentally tired I could not think straight. Yet I had a month of missionary conferences and speaking engagements in different parts of the U.S. in January. All of February was booked for spiritual life—spiritual warfare conferences in Colombia, South America. All of March I was to be the principal speaker for pastors' conferences all over Argentina, South America.

I made it through February, sleeping little at night and that only with sleeping pills. I was almost in a state of panic at the loss of my ability to sleep even when I was exhausted. When I returned from Colombia, I struggled to get ready for the heavy ministry in Argentina.

The most horrible feature of my problem was my mental confusion. Though I am fluent in Spanish, I could not organize my Spanish studies. I worked on them for hours. Waves of anxiety flowed over my being. I felt terrified but did not know why. I assumed it was the Enemy, so I increased my daily times of prayer and spiritual warfare. Reflecting on the curses put on me by the Nigerian sorceress, I was convinced this was a major factor in my problem. I probably had had curses placed on me before. They were easily broken. I prayed and resisted the Devil. My condition only worsened.

Worst of all, God's presence was slowly slipping away. He was turning His back on me. He was rejecting me and I did not know why. I became withdrawn, depressed, gloomy, forbearing, and joyless. I hated the man I was becoming, but I did not know how to return to the man I was before. Everything I had leaned upon in my life was being taken away from me, even God Himself.

I lost my appetite and thirty pounds within two months. I could not sleep. While I never slept many hours at night, I had always been able to sleep anywhere. Now I could not sleep even with double doses of sleeping pills. One of the doctors said I took enough sleeping pills to put a horse to sleep, but they were ineffective for me. I remember one three-week period when I did not sleep at all, day or night.

I lost all romantic interest in my wife, Loretta. She is a very beautiful and loving woman. We had always enjoyed each other's love. I was now incapable of any form of romantic love. Worst of all was the guilt that engulfed me. I felt I must have sinned somewhere and somehow against God, and He was holding it against me. I examined and reexamined my life. I confessed every sin I could remember. I even invented sins I had never committed and confessed them, waiting for God to come back to me as He promised (Matt. 7:7–11, Luke 11:1–13). I did my part but God refused to do His. I soon became angry with God for failing to keep His promises.

The guilt increased with the realization that unless God healed me, I would be forced to cancel my Argentine trip. I finally called Argentina saying I was not going to be able to minister there due to serious illness. One of the Argentine leaders called back insisting that I come. Loretta begged me not to go. She could see the awful transformation of her husband into a totally different man.

Canceling my flight only increased my guilt. I secretly renewed the reservation without Loretta's knowing it, hoping that would ease the guilt. It didn't.

Finally I took one more step. I had a weekend missions conference in one of my supporting churches 150 miles from my home. Instead of canceling it, I decided to use it as a test of my ability to teach. If all went well, I would go to Argentina. If not, I would cancel again.

I spoke Saturday night with great liberty. I slept soundly that night for the first time in months. How weird! Yet when I awakened to go out to the nearby mountains for an early morning prayer time with my host family, I was desperate. Fear and anxiety flooded me. Waves of panic washed over me. I could hardly talk.

As I spoke in the church services, I was again confused. My mouth and tongue swelled until I had to fight to get out each word. I could hardly preach a thirty-minute message. It seemed like thirty hours. Yet as I drove home I still wanted to go to Argentina. I tried to force my voice to respond by dictating letters all the way home. When the letters were later transcribed I could not mail them. They were totally disorganized.

I canceled Argentina. I felt the guilt was going to destroy me. For the next month I went from doctor to doctor trying to get help. The doctors, all friends of mine, diagnosed my problem as fatigue and burnout. Finally one doctor, a former missionary, said, "Ed, you are suffering from severe depression. You need the intervention of a psychiatrist."

Unfortunately I had just read a book on depression written by a famous American Bible teacher. His main message was that depression is the result of sin. Of unbelief! Of worry! Of failure to trust God! No Spirit-filled, godly Christian should ever be depressed, he repeated. He was strongly critical of all antidepressant drugs. Electroconvulsive therapy—shock treatment—was anathema. It would harm the brain and blot out one's memory.

Still interpreting my illness in a spiritual context, I tried his program for beating my depression. Actually it was the same one I had been following for months. I only got worse. That teacher's book drove me to further despair. When Loretta read it, she became so indignant she threw it in the trash.

I wanted to die. Only my love for my family prevented me from seriously planning my own death. Though I could not feel love for them, I knew I loved them. My selfish death would have lead to awful sufferings for them. I often wonder how many believers suffering from severe depressive illness have committed suicide after reading that book or ones like it. How many suicides are indirectly caused by the words and writings of fundamentalist preachers and writers who are ignorant of the biological-psychological mechanics of severe depressive illness, God only knows!

Since recovery, I have had a consistent word of warning to all popular preacher-Bible teacher writers. "Don't you dare ever write beyond your expertise. You are a Bible teacher, not a psychiatrist."

I kept saying to myself, "Me, go to a psychiatrist? No Spirit-filled Christian needs a psychiatrist. We don't need psychiatrists! We have Christ!" That is what I had been taught. That is what I, in turn, had taught.

Finally one night when I felt I was going to die unless I found relief, the name of a Christian psychiatrist suddenly came into my mind. Dr. Basil Jackson, a fellow Irishman, is the director of the Jackson Psychiatric Center in Milwaukee, Wisconsin. Several years before, we had ministered together in Ghana, West Africa. Would he remember me? Could he help me?

As soon as I began to tell Basil my symptoms, in characteristic style, he cut me off and said, "Ed, I know what is wrong with you. I have treated over a thousand Christian leaders with your problem. I can help you. When can you get on a plane and come here? You are God's servant and He wants you well. I will be His instrument to help get you well."

"Basil," I said, "you know my teaching and ministry on spiritual warfare. I believe this whole thing is demonic."

"No, it is not demonic. It is a biological-brain malfunction called endogenous or clinical unipolar depression. Demons have nothing to do with it. Get your ticket. Come this week."

Within a few days Loretta and I were on our way to Wisconsin, but not before two well-known power preachers came to see me. They are both good men, my friends. They were certain my problem was demonic. They said God wanted to heal me, right now. They both laid hands on me and prayed. One of them said, "You are healed. The demonic powers are broken."

I got worse.

By the time we left for Milwaukee, I had to be partly sedated to endure the trip by plane. I do not remember anything about the flight. I only remember that when we arrived at the Jacksons' home, I was trembling so badly I could not stand up. The doctor put me under heavy sedation. For the first time in two months, I slept.

Unipolar endogenous or biological clinical depression is a malfunction of the neurotransmitters in the brain brought on by unknown factors. Stress is known to be a decisive factor, however. I had had enough of that for two lifetimes.[3]

The main treatment for this type of depression is with antidepressants, the real miracle drugs of our generation, exactly as sulfa and penicillin drugs were to the past generations.[4] In extreme cases when antidepressants alone are not able to "jump start" the brain's electrochemical factory again, electroconvulsive therapy (ECT) is occasionally needed.

ECT unfortunately has been seriously maligned by the unfair nickname "shock treatment." ECT is primarily the carefully controlled release of a low voltage electrical current into the brain to help "kick-start" the brain's own electrochemical firing mechanism to get it started again.

I had both treatments. I thank God for both of them. I had ECT because my condition was so serious my brain did not respond to the antidepressants. It worked, almost miraculously. It turned me around. Within weeks I was on my way to recovery. The antidepressants then began to work. ECT had kick-started my brain's electrochemical factory again. Contrary to the misinformation made popular by the unfortunate film, *One Flew Over the Cuckoo's Nest,* ECT is not painful at all. In fact, I was peacefully asleep during the six treatments I had. It was a most pleasant experience for me.[5]

What about memory loss? If ECT is done right and by a specialist, memory loss is reduced to a minimum. The only memory loss I suffered was memory of almost all the sufferings I went through from the time I left California and returned three months later. I have only occasional flashbacks of those days, for which I am thankful.

Basil's counseling[6] with me exposed and shattered my legalistic, work-performance oriented, burnout-for-God misbelief. First, he told me that I was an angry person. That made me angry. I had never seen myself as an angry person before. I seldom displayed anger. I had learned to internalize it as a child.

Also, my theology told me that it's a sin to be angry. It is resisting the will of God if I try to change my immediate surroundings. I thought I had to submit to everything people did to me, said about me, or requested of me in order to please God. But I finally realized I *was* angry. I was angry with people because of the demands they put on me. I was angry with God because it was my service to Him that plunged me into the agony I was now living through. Then when I needed Him, He had deserted me.

I was angry with Basil because he forbade me to read the Bible until my brain healed. I also was angry for the non-ending pain I was forced to endure. As Loretta stood by in horror, seeing me fight to endure the inner pain and still keep my sanity, Basil confessed to her, "Loretta, there is no pain like mental pain. If you have a tumor I can cut it out. If you have migraines, I can treat them. When you suffer from a chronic depressive illness, all I can do is try to find the right antidepressant, wait to see if it will work, and pray. We can sit with the victim in his pain but can do little to alleviate the pain. No cheery word will cheer the victim up. No exhortation to think positive thoughts works. It is a pain like few other pains known to man." That is why so many severely depressed people commit suicide. They see no purpose in life. All they want is a way out of their soul pain.

His counsel also focused on the real meaning of grace. "You have brought your Roman Catholic legalism and performance orientation into your Christian life," Basil told me. "You measure your personal self-esteem by how much you do to please God: how much you can serve Him, the lost, and His people. Instead of working out of restful love in His grace, you work to please Him. That is a failure to understand unconditional grace."

Finally, he said my workaholism is sin. I knew that, but was secretly proud of it. All workaholics in the kingdom have totally abused the biblical view of man, Basil said. They see themselves as if they were only spiritual beings. They miss the fact they are spiritual-physical-emotional beings. They are presently united to a body and emotional nature that must have rest, play, fun, and relaxation as well as work to survive. I felt I was too spiritual for such mundane things.

Also, he said, I was too serious. I had to lighten up and realize I had this treasure in an earthly vessel, not a glorified one. I had broken God's law of the Sabbath for over twenty-five years. Now it had caught up with me. In order to preserve my life, God stepped in and let nature itself bring my pace of life to a sudden halt.

What was the attitude of my colleagues in the ministry to my illness? While some supported my going to a psychiatrist, many others did not. One very close friend, a missionary leader, called Loretta and told her to get me out of the hospital. We were to come back to California and get on with the ministry. He said godly Christians cannot be depressed. Sin and unbelief in my life were my real problems. Another brother called. He said a word of knowledge had been given which declared that there were demons in every pill I was taking. I was to stop taking them immediately and I would be healed. (Good thing he did not know about the ECT treatment!)[7]

Sorting Out Demonic and Biological Forces in Depression

What is the relationship between biological-emotional illness and the spirit world? How do we distinguish between them? What are the symptoms revealing that demons are directly involved?

Demons are always indirectly involved and often allowed by God to afflict His people for purposes that we may never fully understand until we are with Him. That was true in my case.

I trust Tom O'Brien's experience and mine will help balance our tendencies toward over-simplification in the matter of human personality malfunctions. There are multiple forces at work against each individual life. Seldom is a person's problem unidimensional. Every person is the product of heredity, environment, experience, and choices.

Every single symptom listed as evidence of demonization can be caused by non-demonic factors. This even includes resistance to the lordship of Christ and the strange voices which usually appear in serious demonization.[8] Certain psychiatric states including brain malfunctions can and do produce similar phenomena. This is why each counseling case is unique. We must not make snap judgments. We must proceed with caution. When we are over our heads, let's not injure the counselee further. Let's refer him to others with greater expertise than ours.

Warfare Praying will not injure a non-demonized Christian if done carefully, however. Since demons are always indirectly involved, it serves them notice that they must not interfere with the counseling procedure. If hidden demons are present, it will eventually flush them out without hurting the counselee.

With experience, the deliverance counselor learns to both discern and detect the presence of evil spirits. He also learns the symptoms of non-demonic personality malfunctions. He is always ready to refer cases that don't fit the norm of demonization.

Finally, while no one is 100 percent accurate, not even the most skilled psychiatrist or the most gifted deliverance minister, our accuracy increases with time, experience, prayer, and study. We can expect nothing more of ourselves, being mortal. Yet we can expect nothing less of skilled counselors.

62

The New Age Movement

Our nation collectively faces spiritual warfare just as we do as individuals. Often that warfare is on a world view level. In our culture, the materialistic or naturalistic world view is revealed in Western humanistic rationalism. The spiritualistic world view traditionally has been represented by Christianity.

Christianity in the Western world battles competitive religious philosophies today among which are Satanism and the New Age movement. In the narrowest sense Satanism is a religious system—even though some of its practitioners affirm they do believe in the personal existence of Satan—which pays homage to an evil spirit being called Satan, the Devil, or Lucifer.

Satanism is a power religion. People worship Satan because he promises his worshippers power. With power comes position. With power and position comes possession. With power and position and possession comes pleasure. Satanists seek personal pleasure. Some of them find it in having sex with children, animals, or even with corpses. Others find it in torturing animals, children, young people, or adults. Others find it in killing animals, children, young people, or adults.

Satanism becomes to each devotee a power-towards-pleasure system. All that matters to Satanists is power towards pleasure in this life and the life to come. To "hell" with everyone else is their attitude.[1]

Satanism in the broadest sense of the word is contact with, worship of, homage to, and even use of spirit beings other than the one true God. This covers all paganism, positive and negative witchcraft, occultism, and even non-Christian religions. While it is true that Judaism and Islam are theistic systems closely related to Christianity, they reject outright Jesus as Christ, Son of God, and Lord. The New Testament teaches that apart from the personal knowledge of Christ, one does not know God (John 14:6; Acts 4:12; 1 Cor. 8:5–7; 1 John 2:22–23).

While Muslims and Jews who do not accept Jesus as Messiah claim to recognize the same God as Father as we Christians do, they do not know God the Father in a saving way. If they knew Him, they would know the Son of the Father also (1 John 2:23). The apostle Paul, himself a Jew, reveals the satanic dimension of the unbelief of all who reject Jesus as God's unique Son: "the god of this age has blinded [those] who do not believe" (2 Cor. 4:3–4).

Paul at Mars Hill (Acts 17) encountered some of the earliest humanists, the Epicureans, and the pantheists of his day, the Stoics. They were the early New Agers.

Christianity battles with all these opposing world view and religious systems. While Satanism is the most horrendous and immediately destructive, it is probably not the most dangerous to the greatest number of people worldwide, because it is too obviously evil for the general public. It has and will continue to thrive among disturbed, evil people who want a religion that champions their total selfishness, sexual perversions, sadistic nature, lack of self-discipline and disregard for others. This self-centered religion glorifies the most evil kind of sin and pain inflicted on others.

The New Age movement is so dangerous because it seems so right for modern man. It denies the objective reality of evil centered in an evil being called Satan. It inclines itself towards "good" things. It seeks to encourage the full development of human potential. It champions nature, world peace, a new world order. It seems so obviously Christian in its focus on God, Christ, good, world order, full human and earthly happiness.[2]

I would be safe to assert that the greatest threat to Christianity in the world today is the New Age movement, not Satanism, not the revival of traditional religions like Islam, not even secular humanism. The New Age movement has all the appeal of the one-world religion of the antichrist. It will not necessarily bring in the antichrist, but it is the type of all-inclusive world religion with which the antichrist will be very comfortable.

Once secular humanism was Christianity's major competition. Coming from western Europe, secular humanism swept across the U.S. from the East coast. It took over America within a few decades. It became law in this nation through major Supreme Court decisions made in the 1960s through the 1980s. Secular humanism directly contradicts the U.S. Declaration of Independence. That document declares, "We hold these truths to be self-evident, that all men are created equal. They are endowed by their creator with certain unalienable rights that among these are life, liberty and the pursuit of happiness."

The Supreme Court overturned in principle, if not in fact, this part of the Declaration of Independence. It outlawed the teaching of biblical creation in our schools; thus there is no Creator. It outlawed school-sponsored prayer. It made school-sponsored Bible reading unlawful. It said the Ten Commandments could not be taught in public schools, nor even be posted in a classroom within the public education system in the U.S.

A gigantic, national spiritual vacuum resulted. The U.S. is one of the most religious nations on earth. We cannot live without God or religion. Secular humanism left us unsatisfied. We became a nation of technicians without peace of mind. We became comfortable, middle-class consumers without real purpose in life. We became secular giants but ethical infants. We had to have a god to be truly human.

Paralleling this sweep of secular humanism in America was the birth and growth of the Age of Aquarius. It began with dissatisfied young people, but it grew in momentum till it is now one of the greatest spiritual forces at work in America. Although a syncretism of different groups, it holds basically a Far Eastern world view.

Dr. Norman Geisler, when asked to explain what the New Age movement is, points to a unique cartoon to give the answer. It is the picture of a man, "an Easterner, sitting in a Western business suit, in an Eastern Lotus position, meditating on his Macintosh."[3]

It is Shirley MacLaine, who, in her own words from her book, *Out On a Limb*, (where Shirley was when she wrote it), "When one says, 'I am god,' the sound vibrations literally align the energies of the body to a higher level. You can use, 'I am god,' or 'I am that I am' as Christ often did. Or you can extend the affirmations to fit your own needs.

The New Age movement is not new. It is the age-old hiss from the Garden when the serpent said to the woman, "You will be like God." John Denver said, "One of these days I will be so complete I won't be human. I will be a god."[4]

Geisler lists thirteen major views of reality which identify the New Age movement.

1. *It begins with pantheism.* God is all and all is god. The Bible teaches theism. Theism declares that God is "to the world what a painter is to a painting. God is to the world what a playwright is to a play."

Geisler says, "Pantheism says God is to the world what a pond is to drops. We're all little drops in an infinite point. We're all one great big drip, we're all one great big drop."

Thus God is an "It." God is not a father but a force. "May the Force be with you" is pantheism, the New Age view of God.

2. *The New Age is philosophical monism.* Monism says there is only one essence in the universe. Atheism is monism: It affirms that the one reality is matter. The New Age is monism: It says that the one reality is God.

God is nature and nature is God. God is the water, the air, the whale, the trees. "This is why New Agers show unrealistic passion for the water, the air, the whales and the trees. While we all should be concerned about the environment, the New Agers' concern is a religious concern. They are God," Geisler says.

3. *There is holism.* If nature is God and God is nature, all is God. Thus the New Age advocates holism.

4. *There is self-deification.* If God is all, pantheism; if God is all that exists, monism; if all is God, holism; then man is God, human deification. This is self-deification.

5. *This leads to imbalanced immanence.* Where do we go to find God? We do not look to the heavens above nor to the earth below. We look inside of us. There we find God.

6. *There is extreme mysticism.* This is the ultimate in mysticism. Godhood is obtainable. If you will look within, if you will center on yourself, if you will realize that you are god, if you will awaken from your amnesia, you will find god. Shirley MacLaine said the best kept secret of the twentieth century is "We are all god. But we forgot it. We have fallen into amnesia and we need to awaken from it by transcendental meditation. Godhood is obtainable by mystical experience."[5]

7. *There is reincarnation.* We gods have to learn to be God, but if we miss it in this life, we can still obtain it in the next. Or in the next! Or the next! Or the next! Geisler goes so far as to say that reincarnation is, in this sense, "the heart of the New Age movement." He says:

Life is cyclical. Christianity teaches you must be born again! The New Age Movement says you must be born again! And again! And again! And again! Christianity says you live once and you die once. The New Age Movement says you live over and over again. You live and die! You live and die! And live and die!

Hindus have been the great champions of reincarnation. Their basic social system, the infamous caste system, rises or falls with their belief in reincarnation and karma, or destiny. While the New Age form of reincarnation does not advocate a caste system, it still possesses this semi-fatalistic view of human life. Thus, the need to be reborn over and over until one finally gets it right.

This also helps explain the positive view of New Agers toward abortion. If 4,300 women per day abort an unborn baby in the U.S., that is acceptable. According to many New Agers, it is because these babies sinned in a previous life. They are "punished" by abortion. Yet they will have a chance for another birth yet to come.

Reincarnation leads to other extremes, also. For example, Geisler says, "You know what homosexual New Agers say? Why am I homosexual? Because I have a female soul from a previous life trapped in a male body and I can't help it."

8. *There is illusion.* This means good and evil are one and the same thing. This is a hard concept to grasp until we go back to pantheism, monism, holism, and self-deification. If God is all, and all is God, then whatever exists is God. Thus, what we call good and what we call evil are only different sides of the same coin which we call God. Thus, since all is God, both good and bad are really illusions. God is both good and evil. Geisler remarks that Isaiah 6 says God is so holy that the angels sing, "Holy, holy, holy." If the New Agers are right there should be "an antiphonal choir in heaven. One side would be singing 'holy' and the other side would be singing 'unholy.' One side would be singing 'Thou art good.' And the other side would be singing 'Thou art evil.'"

9. *There is animism.* The universe is alive. It is all spirit. Geisler points out that

many of our young people are being taught the Gaia principle, that there is a living force behind everything . . . . This is animism. This is paganism. This is why we sent missionaries to . . . the world because they believed in this pagan idea that everything is living. And now it is being taught in the name of science in our universities and our schools in America today.

10. *There is evolutionism.* The world, that is human society, is evolving. Geisler remarks that New Agers don't believe in Darwinian evolution—they are concerned about spiritual evolution. They are not concerned about the theory that man came from animals. They are concerned about the fact that man can evolve into God.

This is pantheistic evolution. "If it sounds contradictory, it is," Geisler says. "How can god evolve into God? . . . *New Ageism is a complex system of self-contradictory ideas.*"

11. *There is optimism.* "New Agers are incurable optimists, not pessimists," Geisler says. This appeals irresistibly to our pessimistic world. New Agers believe that the world is getting better and better. This is the dawning of the age of Aquarius. The millennium is coming and the New Agers are going to bring it in. They believe that one day the entire world will be won and all world leaders will work together. There is a New Age coming.

Presently they see the United Nations as their international headquarters, so to speak. The U.N. does not know this. The New Agers do, and that is all that matters. They have already taken steps to guide and shape the U.N. to accomplish their missionary task: a New Age meditation center already exists in the U.N.; and a catch word both in the U.N. and in New Age is "new world order."

Not that everyone who uses this phrase is a New Ager, however. President George Bush is an example. He is reputed to be a true "born again" believer, not a New Ager. Yet he often uses this catch word, probably unwittingly.

The "new world order" is the order of the day in the U.N. Since the New Age is not considered a religion as such, but as more a movement among people of all religions or non-religious faith, many U.N. leaders see in New Age teaching a desirable world philosophy.[6] In fact, some prominent men in the U.N. are New Agers. Finally, the U.N. concept of the world as a "global village" in need of one eclectic world view which will draw all people together perfectly sets the stage for the entrance of the New Age movement.

We must remember that the New Age movement is primarily Eastern theology married to Western technology. It does not have the high visibility of other religious movements with their world headquarters: no Vatican City, no World Council of Churches headquarters, no Mormon Temple, no Southern Baptist headquarters. It has no international center at all but is a broad coalition of various and divergent organizations, headed by different persons towards the same goal and all sharing a broad, unified world view.

Their strategy is to gradually develop their goal of a new world order through a new world consciousness. This conversion process will be accomplished by a new world spiritual energy field, the god force within each human being. They use every person, organization, concept, or whatever, which can be harnessed toward the emergence of the new world order.

This broad, unorganized movement—some call it "the Aquarius Conspiracy"—takes in all and every group whose goal is a new world order. Some of the groups are not even religious. This does not matter. When the end goal is finally accomplished, all will become religious, for all will recognize they are god. All have this one thing in common. They seek a new world order, a world human brotherhood of peace.

Geisler calls this "cosmic humanism," "mystical humanism," and "human potential."

12. *There is globalism.* Globalism naturally arises out of social evolutionism and almost deterministic optimism. The entire human race will become one. This is the world as one global village.

13. *There is syncretism.* We have dealt with the scourge of syncretism several times in our study. Webster defines syncretism as "the combination of different forms of belief or practices." That is a good definition reflecting what the New Age must do to bring about the new world order. All religious and philosophies must be combined. They must be blended into one soup, not a casserole with each maintaining its own distinctives while united with the rest. All religions will be combined into one eclectic world religion.

Geisler speaks of the "world meditation of the New Age Movement." It begins well with Genesis 1:1 and 3,

> In the beginning God created the heavens and the earth. Then God said, "Let there be light"; and there was light.

It is the second verse of the New Age Genesis where we forever part company with New Age theology:[7]

> Now is the time for the new beginning. I am co-creator with God. And it is a new heaven that comes. The good will of God is expressed on earth through me. The kingdom of light and love and peace and understanding come through me. I am doing my part to reveal its realities.

> I begin with me. I am a living soul and the Spirit of God dwells in me, as me. I and the Father are one. All the Father has is mine. I'm truth. I am the Christ of God.

This syncretism of the New Age totally rejects the exclusiveness of Jesus Christ. It is a demonic, counterfeit, religious system which is now the fastest growing religious movement in America. Geisler says that in spite of a report in your paper recently where only 25,000 people alleged to identify themselves as New Agers, roughly two-thirds of America is heavily influenced by the New Age Movement. What is the basis for this statement?

First, as indicated by the Gallop Poll of 1982, one-third of all Americans believe in reincarnation. Second, according to the same poll two-thirds of Americans read astrology reports. Half of those who do, believe them. Also, two-thirds of Americans claim to have extra sensory perceptions. Four out of ten have had contact with the dead. These are all central beliefs of the New Age.

It is not that these people are all New Agers. Most are not. It is simply that several of the major teachings of New Age theology are already believed by almost two-thirds of Americans.

Perhaps most dangerous of all, for two generations the U.S. public has been conditioned for the acceptance of the New Age world view by the media. That media conditioning is at an all-time high point today. We begin with TV and the movies. *2001: A Space Odyssey* was a block-buster movie. The climax of the movie focused on human life in embryo form. This was seen as the central life force of the universe. This is New Age theology.

Then came the TV programs which voiced New Age theology. The two key ones which began to soften the ground for the acceptance of the occult were "I Dream of Jeannie" and "Bewitched." Now we have "Kung Fu" and cartoons like "He Man," "Masters of the Universe," "Captain Planet," and "The Planeteers." These are all New Age cartoons.

Next came films and more TV programs all advocating New Age philosophy: *E.T.*, "Smurfs," *Poltergeist*, "Fragglerocks," *Side Kick, Beetle Juice, Teenage Mutant Ninja Turtles,* "Meditation Scene," and *The Dark Crystal,* a pantheistic allegory.

"Powerful films like *The Exorcist,* the Indiana Jones series, *The Mystical Force,* and the *Star Wars* series, make New Age teaching acceptable," Geisler says. "But the winners were *Star Wars, The Empire Strikes Back, Return of the Jedi,* and *Willow.* Willow is a sorcerer. Then came *Solar Babies, Close Encounters,* and *Ghost Busters."*

All of them have one thing is common: a spiritual energy field, a life force field that permeates all things. It is a cosmic, mystical force. George Lucas named it "The Force."

Norman Geisler tells the following story about George Lucas. For years Lucas attended a liberal Methodist church. He was turned off by it. He had a mystical experience when he was six and another later as a teenager. He was an avid reader of the novels of Carlos Casteneda. Lucas turned the life force into the Force which Obewan Canobe, Yoda, and Luke Sky Walker, the hero, learned to tap into. Three times in the first movie Lucas calls this life force "the religion of the Jedi."

A George Lucas biography, *Skywalking,* was written by Dale Pollock. The writer, here quoted by Geisler, identifies the source of the force.

"The force embraces passive oriental philosophies and the Judeo-Christian ethic of responsibility and self-sacrifice. Joda," that's the little green slimy guy in the pond [Geisler's comment], "Joda's philosophy is Buddhist. He tells Luke that the force requires him to be calm, at peace, and passive. It should be used for knowledge and defense, not greed and aggression." He [Pollock] admits that it has a Buddhist source: "Lucas' concept of the force was heavily influenced by Carlos Casteneda's tales of power, an account of a Mexican Indian sorcerer." In fact [Geisler continues], in *Willow,* Willow is a sorcerer, Don Juan, who uses the phrase, "life force," whom

Lucas turned into Ben Canobe, the familiar wise man who aids the hero in his difficult mission."[7]

Perhaps even more successful from the perspective of New Age strategy is the success of the movement in infiltrating American education. The New Age has correctly perceived the public school system to be their mission field. Where could you find a more captive audience? Where could you find a more strategic audience to affect world control for the next century? Geisler says that

> it all started in 1954 with the publication of Alice Baily's book *Education in the New Age.* She is a disciple of Helen Petrovalbolvatsky, a Russian mystic, co-founder of the Theosophy Society. It is published by Lucas Publishing Company, originally called Lucifer Publishing Company. Others have followed her philosophy, many not even realizing the New Age world view behind her suggestions.

Textbooks published by tax dollars containing both subtle and even more overt occultic New Age philosophy are increasingly being used in classrooms throughout the U.S. Some are replete with New Age buzz words like "new consciousness," "energy fields," "centering," "holistic," "transcendental," "interdependent," "global village," "planetary vision," "meditation," "higher consciousness," "humanism," "full inner potential," "transcendent power," "tapping into the force," "new birth," "the untapped energy of the universe," and so forth. All of these words in themselves are neutral. Skillfully used, they condition children and young people, already on their way through TV and the movies, towards a New Age world view.

Norman Geisler quotes from a textbook used in the public schools in Arkansas. He says that one chapter, subtitled "Future Energy," "explores the energy of life. Then they quote from one of the world's great experts on energy, Yoda:'My ally is the force and a powerful ally it is. Life creates it, makes it grow, its energy surrounds us and binds us, luminous beings are we. You must feel the force around you, hear the tree, the rock, everywhere.'"

Geisler then comments, "I thought you couldn't teach religion in the public schools. Well, you can't teach the Christian religion, but you can teach New Age religion." Geisler continues saying the same textbook has a section on photography showing "spirit photos," as they call them, teaching young people that there is a spiritual force here that we haven't tapped into.

He tells of a series of a fifteen-book curriculum for kindergarten through sixth grade called *Impressions.* They contain both horror and occultic stories. The teaching manual for the third grade suggests "write and chant a magic spell to make objects in the room float."

Geisler next tells of educational programs with neutral titles that are primarily New Age. One is called New Age Accelerated Learning. It uses New Age books. It is followed in some parts of San Diego, California. He says the authors draw their techniques from mental yoga, music, sleep walking, physiology, hypnosis, autogenics, parapsychology, and drama.

Next he mentions a page out of an ROTC book in high school. Albert Einstein, who was a pantheist, is quoted. When asked if he believed in God he said, "Yes, I believe in the god of Spinoza." Spinoza was a pantheist. Albert Einstein said, "Imagination is more important than knowledge. *By our imaginations we have the power to do or to be anything we desire.*"

Some schools are stressing confluent education. Dr. Beverly Galean, former project director for three federally funded programs in Los Angeles, said, "Once we see that we are all god then I think the whole purpose of human life is to re-own the God likeness within us."

In some learning centers for school teachers, yoga is openly taught and paid for with tax dollars. Mind control is advocated. Chanting is practiced. Meditation and relaxation techniques assuming the famous Hindu lotus position is taught. Astral projection is encouraged. Occult role games like Dungeons and Dragons are played. Children are told that there are two mysterious regions that need further exploration, outer space and inner space. You explore outer space through the telescope and space travel. You explore inner space by assuming the lotus position and meditating on the force within you.

Geisler talks about another educational program called QR, Quieting Reflex, used in our public schools. One book used is entitled *Meditating With Children: the Art of Concentration and Centering* by Debra Rosemond. It's called a workbook on New Age educational methods. The New Age journal says the book successfully integrates yoga, concentration, meditation, creative fantasy, psychology, and most assuredly love in a way that clearly shows interesting adults a path to fulfilling their child's spiritual need.

He then tells of John Danfey's book *A Religion for the New Age*. The author says that

> I am convinced that the battle for humankind's future must be waged and won in the public school classroom by teachers who correctly perceive their role as the proselytizers of the new faith, a religion of humanity that recognizes and respects the spark of what theologians call divinity in every human being.

> These teachers must embody the same selfless dedication as the most rabid fundamentalist preachers for they will be ministers of another sort, utilizing a classroom instead of a pulpit to convey humanist values in whatever subject they teach regardless of the education level, preschool, day care or large state university.

The New Age has captivated many business organizations. Some of their training programs for their employees involve New Age philosophy. Then there is the captivity of some branches of the health industry and of the music industry. Very different from rock music, New Age music for meditation and relaxation helps one "converse with nature, to be one with the universe."

Finally, there is the influence of New Age theology on the church. Subtle pantheistic views are being taught. Counterfeit theology becomes a substitute for biblical theology. Dominion theology and prosperity theology are really New Age concepts. Many sincere Christian leaders do not recognize this. Extremes in signs-and-wonders theology, name-it-and-claim-it, visualization, and mystical meditation come close to the claims and practices of Science of Mind. Whatever you can visualize you can claim. That you can have and you can be anything your imagination can create is not biblical. It is demonic.

Often as I listen to certain TV evangelists and preachers, I am shocked at their lack of biblical exposition. They are little more than performances and personality cults, full of emotionalism and tend towards dangerous mysticism. They show little true biblical teaching or skilful use of reason and objective truth. I am afraid their power over people and power to raise money is demonic, even though they may be sincere Christians.

In closing I have extracted from Dr. Geisler's material the major contrasts between Christianity and the New Age movement concerning God and man (see Fig. 62.1).

Geisler concludes, "There are only two religions, one is spelled DO and you will be accepted. And the other is spelled DONE, it is finished. 'I have finished the work which thou gavest me to do.' It's done. That's Christianity. It's a free gift."

The New Age movement is a satanic movement of self-deification diametrically opposed to Christianity. The terrible danger arises from its deceptive packaging. It even has infiltrated the Christian church, and we need to remind ourselves of those words of 1 John 4:1, "Beloved, do not believe every spirit, but test the spirits to see whether they are from God; because many false prophets have gone out into the world."

Figure 62.1
Biblical Christianity vs. New Age Thought

Bible	*New Age Movement*
God is . . .	
Father	Force
Personal	Impersonal
Only good	Good and evil
Created all things	All things
Jesus is . . .	
Second person of Godhead	Man who took on Christ office
God and man	God in man
Died and rose from dead	Died and was reincarnated
Man is . . .	
Made like God	God
Evil in present state	Basically good
Spirit and body	Basically spirit
After death, body will be resurrected	After death, body reincarnated
Saved by God's grace	Saved by human works

63

The Road to Personal Victory in Spiritual Warfare
James 4:1–8

The warfare issues in the believer's life may be demonic attachment *(demonization)* or demonic affliction. God permits all of us to suffer demonic affliction. Though it hurts, it is good for us. As the apostle Peter says in a different context,

> Therefore, since Christ has suffered in the flesh, arm yourselves also with the same purpose, because he who has suffered in the flesh has ceased from sin, so as to live the rest of the time in the flesh no longer for the lusts of men, but for the will of God. (1 Peter 4:1–2)

My primary focus in this chapter will slant James' general warfare teaching towards helping demonized believers into freedom in Christ.[1] I believe this will be helpful in light of the strong focus on the possible demonization of Christians through sin we have been dealing with throughout our study.

I am *not* affirming that James had this in mind when he penned these words. He probably did not. He is laying down principles which cover spiritual warfare in general. Yet, as a teacher, I can legitimately slant James' words toward the more serious form of demonic attack against believers, what I have called demonic attachment or demonization. The principles I present will cover all forms of Satanic attack, however.

JAMES 4:1–8

Our study is based on one of the most complete how to passages on spiritual warfare in Scripture, James 4:1–8a. While there are several outstanding warfare passages in Scripture, the James 4 passage has become the key passage in my own counseling ministry.

It is the only passage that deals with all three dimensions of the believer's multidimensional sin problem, the flesh, the world, and evil supernaturalism. It is the only passage that takes us in sequential order through the steps necessary towards full victory. While its primary focus is the spiritual warfare faced by Christians, with slight adaptation it can be used with non-Christians as well. Finally, it can be used with all believers, not just demonized Christians. It contains foundational counseling principles to use with all Christians who are struggling in their spiritual life.

The 45–10–45 Deliverance Approach

We will begin by looking at James 4:1–8a from the perspective of what I call a 45–10–45 deliverance counseling procedure. For effective deliverance we need to spend about 45 percent of our time in pre-deliverance counseling with troubled believers. Another 45 percent of the time is spent in post-deliverance counseling.

Only about 10 percent of the time is spent in actual deliverance. This broad procedure has proved correct and effective in most cases of deliverance counseling.

Using the James 4 passage, the first 45 percent, or pre-deliverance counseling, is found in verses 1–6. The 10 percent, the actual deliverance process is found in verse 7. Finally, the second 45 percent, or post-deliverance counseling, is found in verse 8.

Post-deliverance counseling, in one sense, is the most important step of the deliverance counseling procedure. It will often involve continued on-going deliverance for the following reasons.

1. In the initial, decisive deliverance, on occasions, some demons are able to remain buried within the personality of the victim.
2. Other evil spirits may enter the still partially open doors of the victim's life or exploit the weaknesses in the personality not yet strengthened.
3. The newly delivered believer is just learning how to walk in victory and obedience to the Holy Spirit.
4. The spiritual healing of the damaged soul, spirit, and memories is a process.[2]
5. The individual will be assaulted aggressively by the Enemy, who will attempt to regain partial control of the life he has just lost to the Holy Spirit.
6. The believer may have to return to live in a hostile environment in which demonic forces are greatly active.

All of the above is normal for those freed from demonization. There is nothing to fear. The sincerely committed believer who seeks a holy life in the Spirit's power will eventually emerge triumphant (1 John 4:4). The attacks only serve to strengthen, not weaken the weary spiritual warrior.

Facing the Sins of the Flesh (vv. 1–3)

James' words here will serve as a good review of all we have studied to date on the believer's multidimensional spiritual warfare, not just warfare with the spirit world. James begins where sin usually begins, with the flesh. He twice refers to the "pleasures that wage war in your members" (vv. 1b,3b). We and the counselee must examine our life and seek to identify the activities of the flesh in all three areas. We are to confess and reject them. We claim the cleansing of the blood of Christ. We commit ourselves to the lordship of Christ and to His indwelling presence for a life of holiness.

The specific flesh focus in James 4 is on the social sins, however. These refer to fractured interpersonal relationships (vv. 1–3). The background context to that of the two kinds of wisdom mentioned in James 3:13–18, evil "wisdom" in contrast with "the wisdom from above." This evil wisdom reveals itself in the area of destructive interpersonal relationships (vv. 14–16). James first mentions bitterness (v. 14). This would be bitterness against others, circumstances, ourselves, and God (Heb. 12:15).

Next he twice mentions jealousy (vv. 14, 16), followed by selfishness (v. 14), then self-centered ambition (vv. 14, 16), arrogance (v. 14), and self-deception, or lying against the truth (v. 14). Perhaps the major door of defeat for believers struggling with interpersonal conflicts is lack of forgiveness. It leads to the bitterness, jealousy, selfishness, ambition, arrogance, and self-deception James speaks of here. When we are angry with others and refuse to forgive them, we open the door to all kinds of interpersonal conflicts and sin.

Thus, when counseling believers, I walk them through the reactionary sin diagram we have already studied (see p. 172). This is a key counseling tool in my ministry. If they do not choose to respond at this point, they will not come into full victory.

The two-fold fruit of these bitter, prideful, negative emotions is revealed in 3:16. First, there is "disorder." God's order is violated. There is confusion and lack of peace within, tension, broken relationships, and hurt feelings with others. Second is what James calls "every evil thing." These prideful, negative attitudes are the open door to all kinds of potential evil (Heb. 12:15). Sin energy, like a mighty negative spiritual magnet, draws Satan and his demons. Where deep interpersonal conflicts exist among believers, the Evil One is there. Such conflict with others cannot be accepted in our homes, churches, or even in our communities. Better to suffer harm ourselves than to harm others, especially those who are part of the body of Christ.

One of the single most prominent New Testament teachings concerning believers is God's appeal that we strive "to preserve the unity of the Spirit in the bond of peace" (Eph. 4:3). If I am aware of broken relationships between myself and other members of the body of Christ, I must not rest until I have done all I can to restore these relationships (Matt. 5:21–25; 6:12–15; 18:21–35; Mark 11:22–26).

Where broken relationships exist, the Evil One is there. If we don't want him in our midst, we must walk in peace with all who believe (Col. 3:8–17) and even with unbelievers, wherever this is possible. The apostle exhorts us, "If possible, so far as it depends upon you, be at peace with all men. Never take your own revenge, beloved, but leave room for the wrath of God, for it is written, 'Vengeance is Mine, I will repay,' says the Lord" (Rom. 12:18–19).

The apostle Paul also reminds us, "For the kingdom of God is not eating and drinking—pleasing myself at the expense of the feelings of others; see context vv. 1–16—but righteousness and peace and joy in the Holy Spirit. So then let us pursue the things which make for peace and the building up of one another" (Rom. 14:17,19).

Evil wisdom has its origin in the total spectrum of sin, James affirms in chapter 3. It comes from all three of the multidimensional sources of sin (v. 15). Most vivid is the fact it is energized by demons. James is not saying those who reveal this negative wisdom in their life are necessarily demonized. He is saying that all, without exception, have allowed demonic powers to operate against their life at this point. What is coming out of their mouth comes from a heart which has given the Devil a foothold (Acts 5:3; Eph. 4:27). The spirit behind such bitter jealousy, selfish ambition, quarrels, conflicts, envy, anger, bitterness, and rage is a demonic spirit.

This will not usually involve deliverance. It will always involve obedience, however. I, as a man of God, must judge myself at this point. I must cease from the rationalizations I have been pursuing as a cover-up for my sins. I must face the fact that these wrong attitudes are sin. They come from the offended flesh. They come from the world which tells me, when I am hurt, I must defend myself. I must hurt the one who hurts me.

Above all, they come from the Devil. By nursing my grudges, by allowing a bitter root to remain in my life, I have given Satan a sin handle in my life. He holds on to it, fiercely. He will try to penetrate deeper into my being to disturb even further my walk with God and my brethren. I must remove the sin handle of lack of forgiveness by repentance and confession so I can again walk with an ungrieved Holy Spirit.

In some cases, however, more often than we care to admit, demons have been able to walk into a Christian life through the open door of on-going unforgiveness and anger. Demons of anger, rage, bitterness, hate, and other interpersonal relationship demons are among the most common found in the lives of demonized Christians. Whatever be the case, if we obey the apostolic teaching here, we will be freed from that influence.

To add impact upon impact, James follows through on his theme of interpersonal conflicts in 4:1–2. He says these conflicts are the sure evidence of a life lived in the flesh. The flesh manifests itself in quarrels (vv. 1–2), conflicts (v. 1), hatreds, "you commit murder" (v. 2 with Matt. 5:21–24; Heb. 12:15), and envy (v. 2).

He then picks up a new evidence of the flesh life. It is the area of an ineffective personal prayer life (vv. 2b–3). The biblical ideal of a consistent prayer life is that of an earnest, but restful, personal prayer life arising out of a restful life of fellowship with the Lord, submission to His lordship, and acceptance of both joy and suffering as essential elements of a normal Christian life and ministry. Also it arises out of a restful life of fellowship with the brethren, and wherever possible, as much as it lies within us, with all men. The interpersonal conflict activity of the flesh hinders this kind of prayer life and produces personal prayer confusion (vv. 2b–3a).

James next uses two more summary words for "flesh." First are "pleasures that wage war in your members" (vv. 1b,3b); and "wrong motives" (v. 3). Why do we want what we pray for? What are our motives: personal pleasure or the glory of God?

Facing the Ungodly Values of the World (vv. 4–5)

James next says we are to break with the ungodly values set by the world which have gained some control, often strong control, in our life (vv. 4–5). As we have seen, the world represents the collective socialization of the activities of the flesh all under the over-arching subtle control of evil supernaturalism (Eph. 2:2; John 12:31; 14:30; 16:11; 2 Cor. 4:3–4; 1 John 5:19; Eph. 6:10–12).

James sums up the world's value system which subtly tries to draw us into its orbit by two graphic evils. First is pride, or selfish ambition (3:14–16; 4:1–2a). Next is lust (4:2a; 1 John 2:15–17.) He affirms that following the world's lustful and prideful values brings hostility between us and God (v. 4). Finally, James affirms that God's love for us, as is true of all true "marital" love, is a jealous love (v. 5). To love the world and God at the same time is spiritual adultery (v. 4). It grieves the Holy Spirit within us (v. 5).

God's Great Affirmation of Grace (v. 6a)

Grace is a crucial area of warfare counseling. Many believers are so battered by bruised emotions, personal failures, and demons, they have lost hope. By the time they find a deliverance counselor, they often have had long-term and ineffective counseling. While they may have been helped, their primary problem still remains. Undiscovered and undealt with sin and, often, evil spirits, are tormenting their lives. They believe God doesn't care about them any longer. Will deliverance counseling really help them on the way to recovery? Many have given up hope that they can truly change.

James knows this. Thus he interrupts the normal flow of his teaching with this carte blanche promise, God "gives a greater grace." "Grace that is greater than all our sin," as the hymn writer put it. Whatever our problem, God's grace is greater, James is saying. He is promising us that God's grace is available to every warring believer. His grace will eventually bring every warring believer into victory.

What is grace? Vine gives two pages of explanation,[3] but in this case, I prefer

Webster's definition. He says grace comes "from Latin *gratia*, favor, from *gratus*, pleasant; from a root seen in Greek, *chairō*, to rejoice . . . love . . . favor, good will, or kindness, disposition to oblige another; the love and favor of God; divine influence renewing the heart and restoring from sin; a state of reconciliation to God . . . mercy; pardon; favor conferred."

God not only gives this kind of grace, but he gives it so abundantly that James is at a loss for words as to how to describe it. So he says, "He gives a greater grace." God's grace is greater than all our sin. His grace is greater than all the bruising we suffered as children and youths. His grace is greater than all the demons. His grace is greater than all the Devil's power to do us harm. He will bestow this grace upon us now, and begin our full and complete deliverance, now. This is what James is saying in verse 6a.

One of our main problems is our negative reaction to all the sufferings spiritual warfare entails. We often complain, "Lord, why me? I merit better than what I am getting." If we got what we merited, we would be in deep trouble. In fact, we would be on our way to hell. It is not personal merit that we focus on. It is His grace that meets our needs in spite of our personal lack of merit.

This truth only hits home when we are alone with God. During times like this the greatness of His grace towards us in Christ begins to overwhelm us. Filled with gratitude for His grace, we begin to understand that from the beginning to its consummation in the kingdom of God our entire Christian life owes its existence solely to the amazing grace of God (Eph. 1:3–7; 2:4–10).

God's One Essential Qualification (v. 6b)

"God is opposed to the proud" (James 4:6b). This quote from the LXX version of Proverbs 3:34 is so crucial in counseling warrior-believers that Peter also refers to it in his great teaching on spiritual warfare (1 Pet. 5:5). The writer of Proverbs has much to say about pride. For example: "Everyone who is proud in heart is an abomination to the LORD" (Prov. 16:5). "Pride goes before destruction, And a haughty spirit before stumbling" (Prov. 16:18).

"God is opposed to the proud, but gives grace to the humble," James says (v. 6b). He continues applying this truth in verse 10. "Humble yourselves in the presence of the Lord, and He will exalt you." Pride was at the heart of Satan's original sin and that of the fallen angels. Pride was the basis of man's misbelief of God's plan and his Word. Pride is still the snare by which Satan traps believers (1 Tim. 3:6; 5:9 with vv. 14–15; 2 Tim. 2:14 with 26; 1 Peter 5:5–11). Pride is one of the first things which will stop deliverance.

I was ministering to a demonized believer. She had made progress. Many demons had been identified and expelled from her life. All was not well with her, however. She was a proud woman. She felt she was uniquely gifted by God in wisdom, speaking gifts, and some of the more exotic, spectacular gifts. I knew we had yet to deal with the principal demon still attached to her life. I suspected, but was not sure what it would call itself.

Finally, during one session a spirit came up from within the woman. She began to brag about her powers in the Holy Spirit, her gifts of speech and persuasion.

I looked her right in the eyes and asked, "Who are you?"

"I am Pride," the haughty spirit said.

This was the stronghold in her life. I shut Pride down and spoke to the lady about her pride problems. She was offended. She knew the demon of pride was there. She wanted it out, but she did not want to humble herself.

We got stuck at that point. Deliverance totally stopped. She walked away from that session with her head up in the air like a strutting peacock. She never came back.

I met her twice after that. The chance meetings were at least a year apart. In each case I saw her at a distance. As she approached me I looked directly and deeply into her eyes. In each case Pride came up—without going into demonic manifestation—to meet me. She was something to see and talk to!

She never again sought counsel. So far as I know she still lives a prideful Christian life, exercising her controlling spiritual "gifts" among the people of God. Probably few believers suspect the spiritual mixture that exists in her life.

James 4:6b also tells us how to experience all the genuine grace from God that we need: He "gives grace to the humble." We find grace by humbling ourselves. Again, it seems only pride will hinder that flow of grace. This is where I spend a great deal of time in pre-deliverance counseling. I want to help the believer discover the grounds of sin in his life which allow afflicting spirits to hinder his Christian life. If pride and selfishness lead him to hide from me willful sin areas (he cannot hide them from God, Ps. 139:1f), victory in his warfare is made very difficult.

Our task is to help the believer know who he is in Christ, to help him take his position as an heir of God and joint heir with Christ. It is also to help him identify any grounds of sin yet remaining in his life: to confess them, to break with them, to repent, and to receive God's cleansing and forgiveness. Finally, our task is to help the believer break the hold of any demons still hanging on in his life. This is more truth encounter than power encounter.

Sometimes the believer is not aware of all the evil done to him in his past. He is not even fully aware of certain dimensions of his personal life which provide sin handles, or soul-bruising handles, to which demons often attach themselves. When this state exists we ask the Holy Spirit to reveal anything which gives the oppressing spirits grounds to continue afflicting the believer's life. Amazing things occur in this prayer process.

One time the Reverend Tom White and I were ministering to a godly young man from a severely dysfunctional family. He, with his brothers and sisters, had been abandoned by their father as young children. Their mother could not care for them. She placed them in different foster homes leaving them there for years. When she remarried, she brought her children back into the home again. After a few years the stepfather, too, abandoned them. Back went the children to different foster homes.

They are all troubled young adults now. Jerry, the man we were ministering to, found the Lord in his early twenties. He then led two of his brothers and one of his sisters to Christ. A strong Christian, Jerry was nevertheless deeply insecure and driven by uncontrollable emotional ups and downs. He was also demonized, not severely, but enough to hurt his life and threaten his ability to hold down a job.

I had taken him through one successful deliverance session. Since Tom was visiting in my home he agreed to be with me for my next counseling session with Jerry. Most of Jerry's early childhood memories were removed from his consciousness. I knew there had to be an event or series of unbearable events in his past life which partly held the secret to his troubled present. Those events had seriously damaged his ego as a man. We knew it would be helpful if they were surfaced and healed so Jerry could get on with his life.

As Tom led us in prayer he asked the Holy Spirit to take Jerry back in his memory to any crisis events which held his life in bondage until today. After praying for a time, Jerry began to see events as they had occurred in the past. One critical moment suddenly appeared. His mother was taking him back to the foster home. He was being abandoned for the second time, not by his father and stepfather, but by his mother.

He began to cry. His body shook with fear. Suddenly he pleaded in a child's voice, "Oh, Mother! Don't leave me! Don't leave me again!" He wept uncontrollably. When he recovered, he began to pray. He forgave his mother. He forgave his father and stepfather. He forgave God, whom he felt had abandoned him also. As a result, the healing process accelerated forward from that day to the present. He now enjoys emotional health and freedom from all demonization.

The final section of James' spiritual warfare teaching focuses on God's final commands and promises.

Command One: "Submit Therefore to God" (v. 7a)

This command could not be more terse. At the same time, it could not be more comprehensive. It represents an appeal to apply the teachings just received. The "therefore" of verse 7 refers, as a minimum, to all he has been saying from verses 1–7. Verses 1–3 are a repetition of his impassioned exhortations about the two wisdoms in 3:13–18. Thus, his "therefore" has to do with the flesh-world-demonic (3:15) sin problems with which believers are at war.

The believer's sin problem must be identified and dealt with. James is immediately going to move into his command involving total submission to God. Confession of sin is part of the process of that submission. According to Scripture, our sins, both generational and personal, need to be confessed to God (1 John 1:6–20; 2:1–2; Ps. 139:23–24).

To truly submit to God, these sin questions must be faced. If the believer is truly ready to come into victory in his life, he will be ready to humble himself before God and in the presence of the counselor. He will honestly deal with the sin areas and sin handles in his life. While this does not imply crippling subjectivism on the believer's part nor morbid probing on the part of the counselor, if sin is hidden, victory will not come (Ps. 32:1–7; 51:1–17; 66:16–20; 139:1–24).

James 5:13–16 strongly emphasizes confession, revealing the need to confess our sins to a prayer-share-healing partner. The counselor becomes one of these partners during the counseling process. The believer will need other additional prayer-share-healing partners besides the counselor, however.

If I sense that the counselee is attempting to cover over sin in his life, I stop the counseling session. I will try to jar the believer's conscience by using verses like 1 John 1:7,9; 2:1–2; James 1:13–22; Psalms 66:16–20; 139:23–24. If demonization is involved, demonic interference will often occur at this point. The believer may become confused. He may just stare, not able to understand what is being said.

There may be a torrent of voices in his mind reacting, denouncing, ridiculing, and contradicting. There may be internal expressions of fear, anger, rebellion, blasphemy, and so forth. If this occurs it can usually be controlled through quiet rebuke or through prayer releasing the believer's mind to respond to the indwelling Holy Spirit. Demons occasionally break into vocal manifestation. This also can be controlled. The demons should be shut down, not allowed to speak or to interfere with the counseling process.

"Submit therefore to God" implies a surrender to the lordship of Christ. It is a total commitment of the whole person and each individual area of the life to the lordship of God. *Without doubt, this surrender to God is the principle key to victory in spiritual warfare.* Ultimately, Christ's lordship is the central focus of God's redemptive plan (Eph. 1:9–10,20–23; 2:4–7; 3:4,9–11; Phil. 2:9–11; 3:20–21; Col. 1:16–19,25–27; 2:2–3,9–10; 3:1; 1 Cor. 15:24–25; Heb. 1:8,10,12; 12:2; 1 Pet. 3:22). It is also the pathway to breaking all demonic bondage.

None of us lives 100 percent of the time perfectly obedient to the lordship of Christ over every area of our life. This is due to the deceitfulness of our flesh. Yet, all of us, by faith, should reach the place of total surrender to the Lord as *our* Lord. This is what Romans 6:1f,12:1–2, 1 Corinthians 6:19–20 and related passages are all about. If the troubled believer wilfully holds back an area of his life for himself, he will find it difficult to resist the Devil successfully and see him flee as James promises in verse 8.

At this point, I usually begin by explaining who Jesus is as Lord. I stress his exaltation to absolute lordship in the universe by God the Father. Then I raise the question, using Scripture, of the lordship of Christ in the counselee's life. I eventually turn to 1 Corinthians 6:19–20, then to Romans 6:11–13 and 12:1–3. In 1 Corinthians 6:19–20 the apostle Paul says, "Or do you not know that your body is a temple of the Holy Spirit who is in you, whom you have from God, and that you are not your own? For you have been bought with a price: therefore glorify God in your body."

Here I often give my own personal testimony of how God used these verses to totally change the course of my life. During a period of deep spiritual crisis, the Holy Spirit gripped my heart with the truth of these verses and led me, by faith, into a total commitment to God. It was like signing a blank page (see Fig. 63.1). I hadn't the faintest notion what God wanted to do with my life, but I was ready to accept by faith whatever God willed for my life.

Figure 63.1
The Blank Page Commitment

God's Plan
for
My Life

Sign here _____

Date _____

That was in 1949. In one sense I have not had to go back and re-sign that blank page since I signed it once and for all by faith that day. Yet, in another sense, I have to sign it again at every crisis point of my life.

Next I take the counselee to Romans 12:1–2 and 6:11–13. In Romans 12:1–2 the apostle Paul says

> I urge you therefore, brethren, by the mercies of God, to present your bodies a living and holy sacrifice, acceptable to God, which is your spiritual service of worship. And do not be conformed to this world, but be transformed by the renewing of your mind, that you may prove what the will of God is, that which is good and acceptable and perfect.

I explain that when I present my body as a living sacrifice, that is presenting all of me. All of me lives in my body. If God has my body, He has all of me. Paul's prior description of the presenting of the body in Romans 6:13b is extremely vivid and to the point. He writes, "Present yourselves to God as those alive from the dead, and your members as instruments of righteousness to God."

I then proceed to pray with the counselee. I first lead him to present himself completely unto God. Next, I lead him to present the members of his body, one by one to God, as instruments of righteousness. (See the Group Deliverance Prayer, Appendix C.)

This is usually a very moving prayer and commitment time. The counselee knows he is entering into a deeper experiential union with Christ as Lord and as the Light of his life than he has ever experienced before. The demons know this also. In the case of severely demonized believers if there has not been demonic protest or interference until now, it will usually occur at this point. If not, it may appear in the next command given by James.

Command Two: "Resist the Devil" (v. 7b)

"How do we resist the Devil?" many believers ask. The best answer is, "The same way the Lord Jesus Christ resisted him. By verbal confrontation based on the truth of God's Word" (Matt. 4:1–11 with Luke 4:1–13). Jesus handled these power encounters with the Devil through *truth encounter.*

With truth encounter in mind, I take the counselee through Ephesians 6. In Ephesians 6:18–20 the apostle Paul reveals four key dimensions of the believer's defeat of the Devil: the shield of faith (v. 16); the helmet of full salvation (v. 17a; Acts 10:38; 1 John 3:8; Col. 2:15; Heb. 2:14–15); the *rhēma* of the Word of God (v. 17b); and prayer in the Holy Spirit (v. 18).

With truth encounter in mind, I next take the counselee to 1 Peter 5:8–11. This passage, like the Ephesians 6 passage, can be used at any point in the counseling process. I usually bring it in here, however, because Peter also gives us a "resist the devil" command similar to James's "resist the devil."

The apostle Peter here confirms all we have seen in this book. He begins with a dual command. "Be of sober spirit, be on the alert." "Sober" is the verb *nēphō.* J. Ramsey Michaels says the best translation would be, "Pay attention!"[4] Peter uses the same word in reference to prayer in 4:7, "Be of . . . sober spirit for the purpose of prayer." "Pay attention to your prayer life," he is saying. That is a good word for all of us.

He then follows with, "Be on the alert." The Greek word is *grēgoreō.* Vine says it means "to keep awake, be watchful."[5] Michaels says it means "wake up!" He writes, "These strong imperatives are simply a call to the readers to prepare themselves in mind and spirit for decisive battle with their one great enemy, the devil."[6] He mentions that these two commands not only appear in reference to prayer in 1 Peter 4:7, but in reference to the totality of their Christian life in 1 Peter 1:13.

Peter next gives the three-fold rationale behind the commands. They have an adversary, the Devil. That adversary, the Devil, prowls about like a roaring lion (see Ps. 22:12–13; Ezek. 22:25). The apostle Paul uses a similar phrase in 2 Timothy 4:17 also. He says, "I was delivered out of the lion's mouth." All are references to the enemies of God's people. In 1 Peter 5 we have the principal enemy who manipulates all our human enemies in order to devour us. Here he is clearly identified as our one adversary, the Devil.

Peter says our roaring adversary is "seeking someone to devour." This is a strong word. Can the Devil devour careless Christians, even severely bruised Christians? Peter seems to think so. Then why, whenever I find myself trying to stress the terrible evil power that Satan brings against God's children, do many believers quickly revert to 1 John 5:18, "the evil one does not touch him"?

The word translated "touch" in 1 John 5:18 is the Greek word *haptō*. It has many varied meanings. In the context stated by John here, Vine says touch means "to assault, in order to sever the vital union between Christ and the believer."[7] Satan cannot do that to any true believer.

If no believer could even be touched by Satan were literally true, then Peter is wrong. He should have written, "The Devil is only a paper tiger. While he prowls about, he can only roar. He cannot bite. He is not allowed to hurt a believer. Therefore, don't pay any attention to him. He is all roar and no devour." Also Paul should have written, "Don't bother to take up the full armor of God. You have all been born of God. The Devil cannot touch you."

Peter follows with another command. "Resist him firm in your faith." "Resist" here is the same word James uses in James 4:7b. I paraphrase Peter: "Here is our adversary. He is presently prowling about your life twenty-four hours a day, seven days a week, and fifty-two weeks a year. He wants to devour you. How do we handle such a vicious enemy? By being sober! By being watchful! By resisting him, firm in our faith! By knowing all our brethren worldwide in every age face the same kind of warfare. Finally, by realizing God is involved in this entire process! He allows it. Indeed, He even commands it in order to perfect, strengthen, and establish us" (vv. 8–10).

This resistance of the Devil is a daily, on-going resistance, both offensive and defensive (Matt. 16:18). This is the usual stress in Scripture. For example, we put on the full armor of God, daily. We live in the fullness of Christ, daily. We pray in the Spirit, daily. It can also refer to crisis points of resistance. Paul and Jesus both mention unique evil days or hours (Eph. 6:13; Luke 22:53). These demand the believer's offensive and defensive use of the armor.

Actually, all parts of the armor are all to be used all of the time in both types of spiritual combat. As Dr. Ray Stedman often says, the Christian soldier is "completely fearless, continually cheerful, and constantly in trouble." How true this is!

In our resistance of the Devil, we are to be forcible. Martin Luther, who, of all the reformers, gave the greatest attention to spiritual warfare, understood the power of aggressive vocal resistance against the Devil. According to C. S. Lewis, Luther wrote, "The best way to drive out the devil, if he will not yield to texts of Scripture, is to jeer and flout him, for he cannot bear scorn."[8] C. S. Lewis then has Sir Thomas Moore saying, "The devil . . . the prowde spirite cannot endure to be mocked."[9]

Demons are evil, and I tell them so. They are liars, deceivers, and killers, and I tell them so. They are doomed to burn in hell for eternity and I tell them so, with all scorn and disdain. This approach creates problems for some believers, who declare that we should not rebuke the Devil or his foul spirits. They use Jude 8–9 to support their timid position:

> Yet in the same manner these men also by dreaming defile the flesh, and reject authority, and revile angelic majesties. But Michael the archangel, when he disputed with the devil and argued about the body of Moses did not dare pronounce against him railing judgment, but said, "The Lord rebuke you."

First, we must look at the context. Jude is writing about false teachers, not spiritual warfare counselors (vv. 4–23). These men follow "their own ungodly lusts." They are "worldly minded, devoid of the Spirit" (vv. 18–19). The NIV probably captures the meaning: they "reject authority and slander celestial beings." In other words, they neither respect the authorities in the heavens nor those on earth. This is not true of spiritual warfare resistance or counseling.

Second, Jude is telling this unique story not to teach us what is lawful and unlawful in warfare against Satan and his demons. He is using the story to illustrate what he affirms in verse 10a: "But these men revile the things they do not understand."

Third, when we resist the Devil, we are resisting *fallen angelic majesties*. They are the principalities and powers mentioned by Paul in Ephesians 6:10–12. The powerful ruling principalities and powers are not usually handled by individual believers, alone, separated from the body. This should only be done by a body of believers, over a period of time, and at great cost in prayer, fasting, and confrontational Warfare Praying, as we saw in our study of Ephesians.

While we despise these principalities and powers, we have a healthy respect for their power. It is dangerous for believers to singlehandedly take on spiritual principalities and powers beyond their knowledge, their faith, and their experience. Believers who do so can get in serious spiritual trouble. In most occasions, however, the principalities and powers simply ignore them.

When it comes to handling the demons which afflict individuals, these can be handled by godly, mature, and experienced believers who are taught forceful, aggressive spiritual warfare. While we, like Luther, challenge their authority and declare them to be worthless scum, the garbage pit of the universe, as I like to tell them, this is not reviling angelic majesties. This is resistance against fallen majesties who are now the garbage of the universe.

They have lost whatever majesty they once had. As I also delight to tell them, they are fit only to provide fuel for the lake of fire. They are worthless, despicable scum destined to be tormented forever in hell. When I tell them this, they usually react in anger and in fear. They admit my words are true, however. They can be made to confess they are all that I call them, and more.

Finally, let's remember that the verbal confrontation between Michael and the Devil to which Jude refers took place before the Christ event. Christ dethroned these principalities and powers from their place of majesty. They are not majesties any more, none of them. They, with their master, Satan, are now in disgrace. We hold them in holy contempt. They are all under our collective authority as the church. We handle them with the delegated authority given us by the Son of God himself. Jesus told us to cast demons out in his name and that is what we do.

Next, Peter commands, resist him "firm in your faith." Faith here is undoubtedly the whole gospel with special focus on the defeat of Satan (Heb. 2:14–15; 1 John 3:8). It is the gospel which gives us our position in Christ.

Christ is our life. Christ is our Lord. We are in Him and He is in us. We are seated with Him in the heavenlies. We have the *rhēma* of the Lord God, the sword of the Spirit. We are clothed with the full armor of God, including the shield of faith which extinguishes all the flaming missiles of the Evil One. What, then, have we to fear?

Finally, Peter concludes with a four-fold rationale behind his teaching.

1. The afflictions we face in warfare with the adversary are those born by all believers of all places and all times. As they overcome, so can we (v. 9c).

2. These warfare sufferings are necessary. They are good for us. Though they cause pain, there is a divine purpose to them (v. 10).

3. The one who allows these afflictions and sufferings is "the God of all grace" (v. 10b).

4. The God of all grace is also the God of all glory, and he will share that glory with us in Christ, after we have suffered (v. 10c).

With this study from Peter, we return again to James 4.

Promise One: "He will Flee From You" (v. 7b)

He must flee from you. The choice is not his. It is God's and God's alone. Often his flight is instantaneous. More often, however, it is a gradual process begun by a crisis. Thus again the importance of the 45–10–45 deliverance counseling procedure. The second 45 percent is the one that counts. This is always the key to on-going victory in spiritual warfare.

The only exception to the promise the Devil will flee is if God speaks to us directly—as He did to Paul—saying He chooses to allow the demonic affliction to continue, maybe indefinitely. Using messengers of Satan, God is accomplishing deeper sanctification purposes in our life which He can do in no other way. There has been and will continue to be more than one 2 Corinthians 12:7–10 believer. This is not the norm, of course. That is why I stress God must give to us a word of confirmation that this continued demonic affliction is His will and for our spiritual benefit.

The enemy eventually must flee from us, James promises. While demons will complain, bluff, and argue, they will always eventually leave. This is God's promise.

Command Three: "Draw Near to God" (v. 8a)

Worship him, praise him, love him, glorify him, James is saying. Dr. Bill Bright, Founder and Director of Campus Crusade for Christ speaks of how the power of worship and praise spoken to the Lord breaks demonic strongholds in the lives of believers. Dr. Bright begins by referring to the angelic chorus in Revelation 4 and 5 who are occupied in constant praise of our God.[10]

> Surely that which occupies the total time and energies of that great heavenly host must be a fitting pattern for us to follow here on earth.
>
> So often we underestimate the importance of praise. Many have the idea that praise is a beautiful esthetic exercise but has little practical value. But if praise is the highest occupation of that great heavenly angelic host there must be some valid reason for it. And there is.
>
> Praise is our most powerful weapon in spiritual conflict. Satan is allergic to praise. So where there is massive triumphant praise, Satan is paralyzed, bound, and banished.
>
> When the Lord inhabits the praises of His people, the influence of the enemy is driven away. If our battle is not against flesh and blood, but against the evil rulers of the unseen world, then we need to use powerful spiritual weapons, and triumphant overcoming praise is the most effective weapon at our disposal.

Praise which results in constant victory is continuous praise, praise that is a vocation, a way of life. Let us make it our regular practice to arm ourselves for spiritual conflict with a lifestyle of continuous praise.

Promise Two: "He Will Draw Near to You" (v. 8b)

The believer will begin to know the Lord's presence as never before. With some it occurs instantaneously, as soon as the bondage of the last abusive demon is broken. With others there is some immediate change and freedom in the Lord, but it will take time before they reach an acceptable level of the conscious felt presence of God.

One morally pure woman had been sexually abused over a period of years by her husband. She had been forced to watch graphic pornographic videos with him while "making love." She felt dirty, even though she knew God's forgiveness. In a deep prayer time during a deliverance counseling session she suddenly saw herself with the Lord. She was dressed in a new, white wedding gown. She was as pure as a virgin bride. She wept with the joy of His presence.

In another case, a man too, saw a vision. He had been terribly abused both physically and sexually as a child. The Lord picked him up—he saw himself in child form—and held him in His arms on His lap (Mark 10:13–16). The man wept like a little child. The Lord had drawn near to him as James promises.

This is the way to victory in spiritual warfare. It is the only way to live until we are in His personal presence where we shall see Him, face to face.

Amen. Hallelujah! The Devil is defeated!

64

Dangers and Pitfalls of Spiritual Warfare

All of human history and all human-divine encounters have taken place in the context of spiritual warfare. The entire biblical account, from Genesis 3, where spiritual warfare began for humanity, to Revelation 20, where it ends even for Satan and his evil kingdom, expresses ongoing conflict between good and evil.

Spiritual warfare defined throughout this book refers both to the believer's multi-dimensional war against personal sin and to warfare with Satan and his fallen angels. All Christians and churches are to learn spiritual warfare (2 Cor. 2:11; 10:3–5; 11:3). Dangers and pitfalls lurk, however, in this area of life and ministry. In this chapter, we will examine ten of these.

Pitfall One: Not Dealing Adequately With Sin

We have already examined in depth the sin problem. We discovered that sin is *personal* in that we war against our own flesh; that it is *social* in that we battle worldly influences around us; that it is *supernatural* in that it is fostered by Satan's invisible, cosmic kingdom of evil made up of Satan himself and all the demonic hierarchy under his command (Eph. 6:10–20). I have called this third area "evil supernaturalism."

One of the greatest pitfalls in spiritual warfare teaching and counseling is the tendency to consider only one of these three forces to be the major cause of human sin, while neglecting the other two. Since the Fall, all three work together in promoting human evil. In any particular case, one force may be the primary cause. That area would require special attention, but *all three areas* should be carefully dealt with in spiritual warfare counseling and deliverance ministry.

The televangelist scandals that rocked the charismatic world in the late 1980s were certainly due as much to the sin of these highly visible Christian leaders loving "the world" and "the things in the world" (1 John 2:15 NASB) as to the lusts of the flesh. To be adequately counseled and restored, such persons would have to be taught to crucify the flesh and the lusts that come from within. They would need to learn to deal with the world's fourfold temptations to lust: the temptations to lust for power, for position, for pleasure, and for possessions (1 John 2:15–17).

But did only the lusts of the flesh and the lusts of the world lead to their downfall, or did the devil and his demons have any part? Of course they did! That is why the first pitfall warns against failing to recognize the interaction between the personal, social, and supernatural aspects of sin.

Our spiritual warfare ministry and counseling are too often ineffective because of our limited understanding of the complexity of human evil. Regardless of where the sin originates—from the flesh, the world, or evil supernaturalism—it must be dealt with on all three levels because all three are *always* involved.

Pitfall Two: Inadequate Pre-Deliverance Counseling

Failure to counsel adequately before attempting deliverance (if deliverance is needed) is the second pitfall. The purpose of pre-deliverance counseling is to discover what is truly occurring in the counselee's life. If there is demonic activity, the purpose is to help the individual understand the "sin handles" to which demons have possibly attached themselves. Demonic powers gain entrance only through sin areas in a person's life. Sin areas give demons something to hold on to, hence the term "sin handles." The apostle Paul refers to them as "grounds" or "footholds" (PHILLIPS) in the believer's life (Eph. 4:27).

In chapter 54 we examined generational or familial sin, discovering that such sin comes as a judgment from God. It often involves strong demonic influence, even demonization, which seems to pass down through a family's line from one generation to the next.

The enemy may have gained entrance into the family by one of several ways: through dedication of oneself or the family to an occult organization, a non-Christian religion, a god (which Paul calls a "no god" in Gal. 4:7), or evil spirits; or through curses put on a family or its members (including self-curses). Demons may have come through the commitment of a family head to sinful businesses such as crime, prostitution, or pornography, palmistry, New Age practices, conducting seances, reading tarot cards, venerating ancestors, or producing and selling occult literature. In addition, demons may enter through acts of violence and bloodshed, abuse, deceit, or various kinds of similar sinful acts.

Generational demonization will usually continue until someone in that family line finally takes responsibility for the ancestral sins, repents, and claims the cleansing blood of Christ to break the demonic power. After this occurs, all curses can be broken and the demons cast out. Such acceptance of responsibility for generational sin, repentance, and cleansing needs to precede deliverance. If the person falls back into the family sin, then repents, generational sin may have to be broken again.

Finally, we must never forget that people often come into bondage to sin because they have been the victim of the sins of others. Even if the person is too young to sin personally or to remember the abuse itself, reactions against it can erupt into sins such as anger, rage, hatred (including self-hate), shame, rejection (including self-rejection), rebellion, and even attempts at suicide. Victims may also develop a myriad of sexual problems, such as excessive masturbation, promiscuity, sexual addictions, and frigidity. Victimized people are often drawn into these types of sinful behavior without knowing why.

Only as such sin areas are recognized by the person and dealt with through confession, repentance, and forgiveness through the cleansing power of Christ can total freedom from demonic attachment truly occur. That freedom usually occurs over a period of time, but it can occur instantly.

Unfortunately, many who practice spiritual warfare ministry and deliverance counseling often fall short at this point. Too often the counselor or deliverance minister goes directly after the demons, battling them sometimes for hours until the demons' suffering becomes so extreme that they leave or are "cast out" of the victim—but for how long?

If effective pre-deliverance counseling is short-circuited, the deliverance will usually only be temporary. If the sin handles still remain, the original demons can easily return—with reinforcements (Matt. 12:42–45)! If the original demons are forbidden to return, millions of other "free-floating" demons like them are ready to latch onto the still existing sin handles in the believer's life. Truly, "the last state of that man becomes worse than the first" (Matt. 12:45 NASB).

Pitfall Three: Inadequate Post-Deliverance Counseling

The third pitfall in spiritual warfare ministry is the failure to adequately counsel those who have experienced deliverance. Why is such counseling so important? Consider these ten reasons:

1. Post-deliverance counseling over a course of time may be required to discover all of the sin handles.
2. Newly delivered believers are only beginning to walk in full victory. Like the rest of us, they are still susceptible to demonic deceptions.
3. Newly delivered believers will be assaulted by the enemy, who will attempt to regain control and even extend his previous influence. We must teach our counselees how to discern and overcome these counterattacks.
4. Newly delivered believers may have to return to live or work in a hostile environment or to a place where demonic forces are active.
5. Such believers may not be fully aware of the extent to which evil forces have attached themselves to their lives. A partial deliverance is a deliverance in process, a deliverance that needs to be continued. The Holy Spirit often reveals such situations over a period of time and usually through ongoing counseling.
6. These believers may need deep and painful humbling to break a prideful and rebellious spirit. Often only after a person has been freed from demonization is God able to deal fully with such character flaws (John 4:1–10).
7. Frequently, all the demons attached to the life of the victim are not exposed and expelled in the initial deliverance session, even when the gifting of the deliverance ministers is spectacular and the freeing power of the Holy Spirit very obvious.
8. Scripture's way of overcoming the adversary demands time to be learned and practiced in one's daily life. (See 2 Cor. 10:3–5; Eph. 6:10–20, James 4:1–8; 1 Peter 5:8–11; and Rev. 12:11.)
9. Where extreme sexual abuse, physical harm, religious deception, or emotional damage have occurred, victims will usually need ongoing spiritual and professional counseling and healing. Where necessary we must be willing to refer such counselees to professionals better skilled than ourselves in such delicate areas of counseling for emotional and mental health.
10. Finally, deliverance is often more a process than a single crisis event or even a series of such events. Newly delivered persons, like new believers, must be encouraged to join a support group of persons whom I have identified elsewhere in our study as "James 5:16 prayer-share-healing partners." As they do so, ongoing deliverance will usually occur over a period of time. This serves to build their faith in the power of God operating in their *own* lives and in the lives of their James 5:16 partners.

When I do ongoing deliverance counseling, I follow what I have called a "45-10-45" spiritual warfare counseling ministry. Forty-five percent of my time is given to pre-deliverance counseling, 45 percent to post-deliverance counseling, and only about 10 percent of the time is needed for actual deliverance.

Pitfall Four: Incorrect Diagnosis

The fourth pitfall in spiritual warfare ministry is the problem of incorrect diagnosis. The most important question the counselor must ask God, himself, and his ministry team is, "What is truly occurring within the counselee's life? How do we know what aspects of the person's problem are biological, physiological, psychological, or the results of human tendencies or the world around us?" At times the problem is a combination of physiological malfunctions (such as hormone imbalances and/or brain malfunctions), emotional bruising, and the complications of mild to severe demonization.

The importance of correct diagnosis cannot be overestimated. Generally speaking, there are two extremes. The first extreme is trying to handle all serious human personality malfunctions exclusively through medication and/or counseling. If demonization exists, the demons, of course, delight in this approach because their presence remains undiscovered. Though the counselee may receive a certain amount of help with the emotional or physiological aspects of his problem, the demons remain, and total freedom eludes the client.

The second extreme is trying to cast out nonexistent demons. This is the unfortunate practice of many sincere deliverance ministers who do not accept the value of psychological counseling, even by Christians psychologists or psychiatrists.

When asked to speak to a group of students studying to be psychologists at a major Christian university, I told them, in essence, the following:

> You are responsible before God and man to learn spiritual warfare counseling, including deliverance. If you do not do so, you are violating the Scriptures and the commission of God. You are sent out to set the captives free.

> Even ethically, you are obligated to learn spiritual warfare and deliverance. You will be paid to help people into freedom in their lives. If you ignore the possibilities that they may be demonized or under demonic harassment, you betray them.

> You have the best of both worlds. You can help them through the specialized counseling training you are receiving. And you can set them free from bondage to the enemy. You need that training.

The primary problem of much training for professional counselors in psychology or psychiatry is that of an inadequate world view. These Christian professionals are often trained in programs that deny or minimize the importance of key dimensions of a fully biblical world view. Their counseling procedures may be generally compatible with biblical truth, even while their view of reality as counselors is nearly blind to the operation of evil supernaturalism. Or if such counselors acknowledge the reality of personal evil, their training has not helped them integrate such knowledge into their practice.

In wanting all counselors to integrate the revealed knowledge of the Bible with the empirical knowledge of behavioral science, we must remember that the Bible does not use modern technical language. It does not speak of emotional depression by name, nor does it name or deal directly with major depressive illnesses such as manic depressive disorder, schizophrenia, or major clinical depression. Neither do the Scriptures refer directly to the terrible phenomenon of multiple personality disorder (see chapters 59 and 60).

The Bible is not a textbook on modern psychology. It does not touch on every conceivable evil to which the human personality is subject. It does, however, present us with broad principles for healing which must be applied appropriately in every individual and cultural context.

How do we learn to minister to people with these illnesses? Only by experience. Those who affirm that the Bible provides us with all we need to know about the condition of fallen humanity (including medical conditions) and reject extra-biblical experience as a legitimate teacher are wrong. Nothing is truly learned apart from experience. Even learning from Scripture involves learning from experience. And genuine experiential, empirical learning always proceeds from and remains accountable to revealed knowledge.

We help those with biological disorders by recognizing that these are not caused *directly* by demons. The same is often true of emotional and even spiritual depression. If we treat them all *primarily* as a result of demonization, we will be attempting to cast out nonexistent demons. We must also recognize, however, that demons can mimic psychological disorders. Furthermore, in some cases of serious personality malfunction, it is not a case of either biological causes or demonic causes but of both biological and demonic causes. In such cases, the counselee's problems result from a combination of physiological and psychological damage which is best dealt with through effective medical treatment, counseling, and deliverance.

In such cases, how do demons occasionally enter the lives of their victims? No one knows for sure. We do know that demons deliberately take advantage of debilitating human weaknesses, especially those that affect the brain. When people, even believers, do not have full control of their mental and emotional faculties, demons are sometimes able to secretly attach themselves to these wounded areas of the victim's life.

This method of demonic entry happened to an Alzheimer's patient who was a nationally known Christian leader and is now deceased. The demons actually spoke through their victim, cursing and saying all manner of evil. The man's wife knew this could not be her husband and stopped the demonic evil through warfare praying and direct rebuke.

In one serious case I was handling, the individual's problems were both *physiological* and demonic, but I did not know it. I cast demons out of the victim's life, but he showed no improvement when the demons were eliminated. If his problems had been *psychological* and demonic, he would have shown marked improvement.

This individual suffered, however, from one of the three main depressive disorders. When he received psychiatric intervention, he showed great improvement. If he went off his medications, however, he reverted back to his prior state. Though demons went out of his life when he was ministered to, other demons evidently returned when he went off his medications.

How is this possible? While one cannot always be certain, they evidently came in due to his inability to resist their entrance when his symptoms reappeared in the absence of his medications. As long as he is on his medications, he has control of his faculties and is able to live a normal Christian life. Since he is a strong Christian and understands spiritual warfare, he now has no problem in resisting the entrance of demons into his life.

Pitfall Five: Overestimating Satan's Power

The fifth major pitfall in spiritual warfare counseling is that of overestimating the power and authority of Satan and his kingdom. What follows is a summary of the biblical teaching on the absolute defeat of evil supernaturalism by the Lord Jesus (see also pp. 424–425):

1. The Lord Jesus has already bound the strong man (Matt. 12:22–29).
2. The Lord Jesus has already proclaimed release to the captives and recovery of sight to the blind and has set free the oppressed (Luke 4:16–19; Acts 10:38; Eph. 4:8; 2 Cor. 4:3–6).
3. God has already taken all of us as His children out of the kingdom of darkness and placed us in the kingdom of His Son (Col. 1:12–14).
4. The Lord Jesus has rendered the devil powerless against His elect and has delivered all of His children from slavery to him (Heb. 2:14–18).
5. The Lord Jesus has already totally destroyed the works of the devil in the lives of all the children of God (1 John 3:1–10a).
6. All this was accomplished in His redemptive event by the Lord Jesus on our behalf as the Representative Man, the Last Adam, and the Second Man (Phil. 2:5–11; 1 Cor. 15:45–47; Heb. 2:9–18).
7. God's Word declares Jesus' lordship over Satan and his kingdom (Matt. 28:18; Mark 16:19; Eph. 1:19–23; Phil. 2:9–11; 1 Pet. 3:22).
8. Jesus totally defeated the entire kingdom of evil supernaturalism on our behalf (Col. 2:13–15).
9. God promises all obedient believers victory in spiritual warfare over Satan and his entire kingdom of evil (Rom. 16:20; 2 Cor. 2:11; 10:3–5; Eph. 2:6; 3:10; 6:10–20; Col. 2:8–15; James 4:7–8; 1 Pet. 5:8–11; 1 John 2:12–14; 5:18–19; Rev. 12:11).

Pitfall Six: Underestimating Satan's Power

This pitfall is perhaps more common than the former. Many more believers underestimate Satan's power rather than overestimate it.

Those of us who deal with the demonic realm are continually accused of granting too much power to Satan and his demons. That is not true. We believe that Satan is a defeated foe and that Jesus has already bound him. Only on the basis of our Lord's victory do we command the demonic to leave. Instead, we believe that those who criticize us most strongly do not themselves grant to Satan the terrible power that, according to Scripture, he possesses and will continue to possess until he is put into the lake of fire (Rev. 20:10).

If space would permit we could look at the some 328 references to evil supernaturalism found in the New Testament (see pp. 288–293; see also graphs and references to the Johannine writings alone, pp. 419–424). From them we could draw up a startling list revealing that our foe's defeat is as multifaceted and progressive as is our salvation and as is the manifestation of God's reign on the earth. The Lord Jesus has already defeated Satan, yet he still resists. For example:

- Satan has yet to be crushed under our feet (Rom. 16:20).
- He can still take advantage of us if we are ignorant of his schemes, and most believers are. Even those of us in continual contact with him feel we are only just beginning to understand the vast complexity of his schemes against us (2 Cor. 11:2–4).
- He can deceive our minds *as he did Eve* and lead us astray (2 Cor. 11:3).
- His schemes are so horrendous it takes all of *God's* armor (our frail Christian-human armor is useless) to be able to "resist in the evil day" and "stand firm" against him (Eph. 6:10; 3:20).
- We can "fall into the condemnation incurred by the devil" and even "fall . . . into the snare (the control) of the devil" (1 Tim. 3:6–7).

Does the apostle Paul really mean this, or is he using hyperbole or writing mythology? Can a true believer actually fall into the same condemnation incurred by the devil? That's strong language for believers whose protection by the power of God from Satan's power is allegedly absolute and unconditional, as some teach.

One of the most intriguing situations we who minister deliverance to believers often confront is this: Too many of those needing our help—including pastors and their spouses—belong to the very churches and denominations where it is dogmatically affirmed Christians cannot have demons. I wonder why? What would happen if demons came into manifestation in public in such churches? They occasionally do.

Canadian psychiatrist, teacher, and deliverance minister John White tells the story of this occurring in a Texas church where he was asked to preach. He told them beforehand that if he accepted the invitation, he would speak on spiritual warfare and invite afflicted people to come forward for prayer.

One of those who came forward for prayer was the pastor's wife. As Dr. White began to pray for her, demons came openly into manifestation. The pastor's wife started to hiss like a serpent. She fell to the ground, making grotesque bodily movements like those of a serpent.

How embarrassing! Her husband, the pastor, was one who categorically states that Christians cannot be demonized.

One final word about Satan's power against believers. Paul says that some of the deaconesses in the churches in Asia in his day had "already turned aside to follow Satan" (1 Tim. 5:15). Paul evidently assumed his readers would know they were true believers, as it was common knowledge believers could sin and still be Christians. Furthermore, the sins they were guilty of were not only common in their day but in our day also: they went back on a pledge made to the church (v. 12); they became idle (v. 13); they became gossips and busybodies (v. 13).

Can a true Christian turn aside and follow Satan in an area of his life instead of following the Lord? Yes! We all do on occasion. We all are aware of the case of the believer at Corinth who was guilty of incest. He was a true believer, the apostle Paul tells us (1 Cor. 5:1–5). He had turned aside to follow Satan in one area of his life but he still belonged to the Lord.

What is the essence of what I am saying? Our enemies, while defeated, are very much alive. If you don't believe me, look at your own life. Have you had any bouts with the enemy lately? If not, you are the only believer alive who hasn't.

"Defeated yet resisting. It *sounds* like a contradiction," many complain. That's because they have not thought through the implications of the "already-but-not-yet" principle (see p. 417).

Pitfall Seven: Evil People in Our Midst

This pitfall and the three that follow all focus on potential deception and/or counterfeit manifestations of the Spirit's presence among the people of God. All need to be dealt with in greater depth in future studies. The need is crucial for God's people. We must have insightful but balanced teaching on what is occurring in our midst in the area of deception.

Evil people in our midst (2 Thess. 3:1–2) may be satanic plants, occultists or New Agers. I have had contact with one husband and wife "team" who go from conference to conference, attempting to put curses on believers, especially high-visibility Christian leaders including myself.

Recently I had a letter and several telephone calls from one church which knows it has satanic plants in its midst and is under a curse or curses. The church purchased an abortion clinic and turned it into church offices. One of the church leaders wrote that soon afterward "unborn babies began to die in the womb (from the first trimester to a full term) immediately after the closing of the clinic and to date the number is 27, far [above] the normal." He states that "the only people that have not been affected are staff and their wives and unwed mothers, to which our church has a ministry."

During our last phone call (Dec. 19, 1995), the leader informed me the cycle of the deaths of unborn children seems to have been broken. Their prayer team has been putting into practice basic principles I (and probably others) shared with them. They have had confrontations with some of the "planted" Satanists within their assembly. In one case of deliverance involving power encounter, the demons were forced to reveal part of Satan's strategy against the church. At the time of writing, the battle continues but the momentum has swung in the church's direction. God is honoring their faith and warfare praying.

"We have learned more about the strategy of Satan and how to block his tactics against our people and the church than in all the long years of our church's existence," the leader told me.

The perseverance of this church in spiritual warfare is crucial, since it is one of the largest and most effective in reaching its community for Christ in its area.

Pitfall Eight: The Pitfall of Blended Gifts

Some in our midst have received false gifts from the spirit world operating alongside of their genuine gifts. In my deliverance ministry I have run into this phenomenon. The most common occurrences of this phenomenon that I have run into is in the case of the gift of tongues. The person will have a genuine gift of tongues and a false gift of tongues at the same time. In one case, I contacted three tongues operating in an individual; two of them were false tongues, and one was genuine.

In the case of the false tongues, the individual said that the tongues took over and controlled him; he did not really have control over the tongues. I would suggest that this phenomenon is evidence of false tongues in general. When an individual is controlled by the tongue, that is pretty good evidence that the tongue is false. As in all of the gifts, the individual has control of the gifts; he is not controlled by them. I have not worked out a typology or a good system for identifying false gifts operating alongside true gifts, but the basic test mentioned in the book concerning spiritual gifts would apply (pp. 41–42; 371–373).

Too often, the presence of these false gifts becomes apparent only when the individual seeks deliverance counseling or when other dimensions of his life lead discerning Christians to the opinion that the individual needs counseling.

Pitfall Nine: The Pitfall of Unbalanced Emphasis
on Specific Manifestations of the Holy Spirit

In the twentieth century, Christianity has emphasized the Holy Spirit perhaps more than it has at any time since the apostolic period. This emphasis has resulted in incredible blessings as the Spirit has been released among God's people to function freely in our midst. A movement of God's Spirit among the people of God is reaching a new zenith. Some relate its beginnings to the Holiness movement of the closing years of the last century. It continued growing through the birth of the Pentecostal churches during the first quarter of the twentieth century.

Pentecostals characteristically emphasize a life-transforming *experience* of the

Holy Spirit. Baptism with, or by, the Holy Spirit is for Pentecostals an experience, not primarily a doctrine of the faith simply to be believed. Pentecostals typically believe that this baptism of the Holy Spirit is distinct and subsequent to conversion, that it is evidenced initially by speaking in tongues, and that its chief purpose is that of empowering believers for supernatural ministry. In terms of Holy-Spirit renewal in this century, Pentecostalism is the first wave.

Then came the charismatic movement in the 50's, the second wave. Like their Pentecostal siblings, charismatics also emphasize the baptism of the Holy Spirit as a post-conversion experience of empowerment, but they are less insistent on tongues as the necessary evidence of the baptism. Also, unlike Pentecostals, many charismatics have chosen to remain in their traditional churches, while others have formed the many independent charismatic churches that now cover North America.

The third-wave movement emerged in the late 70's and early 80's. It, even more than the charismatic movement, has spread renewal among conservative evangelicals who have been traditionally opposed to some of the phenomena especially associated with the Pentecostal and the charismatic movements. Third wavers (of whom I am one) do not consider themselves Pentecostals or charismatics and prefer to describe their fresh encounter with the Holy Spirit as a "filling with the Holy Spirit," not their "baptism with/by the Spirit." Third wavers believe they were baptized with, or by, the Spirit when they were born again by the Spirit. Yet third wavers agree in many ways with their Pentecostal and charismatic siblings on the reality of the Holy Spirit's gifts for and empowerment of believers today.

While these three waves of the Holy Spirit do not exhaust His renewal in the churches, these streams of renewal constitute the cutting edge in renewal and world evangelism in our day. The first two waves alone are "outstripping most other Christian bodies in their rate of growth" worldwide.[1] Through these three waves and in other ways, it is clear that the Holy Spirit is renewing millions of Christians and awakening many unchurched and non-Christian peoples to life in Christ.

Revival Worldwide

We are probably on the threshold of the greatest movement of worldwide, apostolic-like renewal and evangelism in the history of the church. Africa, the scene of revival for years, is now experiencing village-wide conversions to Christ through demonstrations of the Spirit's power, especially among Muslims. The churches of several Asian nations are experiencing renewal, and even historically resistant countries such as Japan and parts of China are responding to the gospel in ways that encourage missions observers to expect broad renewal and accelerated evangelism soon.

For many years, the church in Latin America has led the world in rapid growth. Today it is estimated that some 400 people come to Christ each hour! During the last decade, the number of Latin American Protestants (evangelicals) increased from 18.6 million to 59.4 million—a 220% increase, nine times the population growth rate. Mega-churches of several thousands of members are springing up, and many churches are actively planting daughter churches. Latin American churches are now organizing to further world evangelism and are sending missionaries to the ends of the earth.

In the English-speaking countries, Australia and New Zealand are evidencing signs of renewal, while churches in Canada are developing a hunger for God, renewal, and evangelism. Europe is now the new "dark continent." Indifference to the gospel, the rise of cults, and the growth of non-Christian religions such as Hinduism and Islam are everywhere. But there are encouraging changes in many churches, especially those in the British Isles. Even indifferent countries like Switzerland and Austria are beginning to show new response to the gospel. And the renewal extends to the formerly communist countries of Europe and Asia, where social and political upheaval has created a new openness to the gospel.

Threats to Renewal

What an hour to be alive! We are witnessing a passion unique in church history to see churches renewed, believers filled with a new love for Christ, and the lost reached, especially in resistant countries. Yet I believe that this marvelous revival is threatened. Because a central goal of all authentic renewal is world evangelism, genuine renewal threatens Satan's kingdom in the greatest possible way. Satan, therefore, attacks renewal severely; he wages spiritual warfare against the renewing, evangelizing church.

Threats to ongoing renewal and evangelism assume many forms, but here I will focus on two threats that come from emphasizing specific manifestations of the Holy Spirit in an unbalanced way. I discuss these threats not as an outsider to renewal, but as an enthusiastic part of it. Renewal of believers and equipping them for world evangelism has been the goal of my ministry since I went into missions in 1957. While I identify myself as a third waver, I am also pro-Pentecostal and pro-charismatic. With that sincere identification, I appeal to my charismatic and Pentecostal brothers and sisters not to be offended by my discussion of the first of these two threats.

Equating Church Culture with Renewal Itself

This first threat is that of mistakenly identifying one church culture with the movement or renewal of the Holy Spirit itself. I am concerned that the current renewal is in danger of becoming only a Pentecostal and charismatic movement, instead of fulfilling its larger purpose of being a movement of God among all who yearn for revival.

My concern is not what God is doing or wants to do in our midst, but a style of public meetings in which pre-programmed noise and emotions energized by the flesh, not by the Spirit, are imposed on the audience. The sound and emotions do not arise because the Holy Spirit is directly touching the emotions of His people, but because those leading the meeting are doing so themselves. We all know that only the Spirit of God can come upon His people and lift them outside of their self-consciousness and bring them directly into His presence. Too often, leaders feel that if they make enough noise and stir up the emotions of God's people, then God will visit His people. But, emotion and sound, even religious emotion and sound, simply must not automatically be equated with the work of the Holy Spirit. They may come more directly from the flesh than from the Spirit's intervention as John Arnot, the leader of the Toronto Revival, is quick to point out.

We all recognize that people have to live normal lives in revival times. The demands of family, work, and school are always there. People cannot live in church. That does not mean they have left the revival atmosphere behind them. They carry it with them into their daily relationships.

My next statement asking if God wants us to be quiet, speechless in the presence of His majesty was out of place. While we meet as a group, times of quietness may occur, but at the same time people are caught up in the emotions as the Holy Spirit works in their midst. Such experiences are visual and occur during the revival when we are one in His presence but mixed spirits may also become involved, i.e., the Holy Spirit, counterfeit spirits, and the human spirit. I have witnessed these myself. This concern is not original with me. Even John Arnot, the main human instrument of the Toronto Movement, expresses this concern in his superb book, *The Father's Blessing*.

Finally, as the movement subsides into a more steady state in the post renewal period, which always occurs, the individual church cultures, which have been used by God to stabilize His church for centuries, will be introduced again. The danger of trying in ourselves to reproduce those unique days of renewal when the time has passed is obvious to all students of church history.

My remarks about the dangers of resisting the historic legitimate wide diversity with the body of Christ are still valid. The benefits one part of Christ's diverse Body receives from other equal but different parts of the Body are wonderful. (1 Cor. 12:4–27, Eph. 4:1–16) The creative Holy Spirit must not be grieved, all in the name of promoting a spiritual renewal/revival.

Seeking Specific Manifestations as Essential to Renewal

Another aspect of this threat to renewal deserves mention. This aspect is the view that certain specific manifestations of the Spirit are essential to renewal and revival. Yet nowhere in Scripture are we taught to seek specific manifestations of the Holy Spirit. We are taught to seek the Spirit Himself; His sanctifying ministry; His gifts; His filling; and we are taught not to quench or grieve Him. But no specific manifestations of these dimensions of His ministry are essential to each renewal and revival. Only the freedom of the Holy Spirit to do what He wants to do and what He alone can do is essential. John Arnot also advocates this position.

As John White points out, what the Holy Spirit does can be disturbing enough without our culturally conditioned manifestations being imposed also. The Holy Spirit will often come with fire. Our demand that His fire manifest itself in our preconceived ways will lead only to wild fire! Yet, as White shows in his study *When the Spirit Comes with Power,* strange spiritual phenomena have almost always accompanied revival movements.[2]

Non-Pentecostals will discover that all real revivals are accompanied by spiritual phenomena that many find strange. Stephen Strang observes that "Calvinists today are usually a dignified lot. So I was surprised to read this description of their meetings in France in the late 16th and 17th centuries . . . : 'Such persons would suddenly *fall backwards,* and while extended at full length on the ground, undergo *strange* and apparently *involuntary contortions;* their chests would seem to heave, their stomachs be inflated'" (emphasis mine).[3]

I don't know if this is really a spiritual warfare issue. During revival movements, some believers might engage in such action in the excitement of the moment, however, I am sure some Pentecostals will also be surprised to discover that what occurs in some of their revival services has occurred in the past in non-Pentecostal revivals. Some of the same phenomena occurring today were common, especially during the Great Awakening of the 18th century under Wesley, Whitefield, and Jonathan Edwards. I would like to make several observations however.

First, in the words of John White, "We must be cautious in evaluating new religious movements. Many new movements are mediocre and a few, extremely dangerous. False fire burns fiercely, and the angel of light still spreads his wings, and the elect continue to be deceived." Second, in true visitations of the Spirit, the phenomena which have occurred were *not sought.* People experiencing them were often embarrassed, especially when they occurred in public. Third, spiritual manifestations "unduly emphasized" open the door to the flesh, the world, and evil supernaturalism.

White warns against seeking specific spiritual phenomena as essential to revival: "It is a mistake to encourage such behavior (weeping, shaking violently, crying out, losing consciousness, falling down, becoming uncontrollably agitated). One reason is that encouragement inspires insecure people to imitate it. But the behavior can occur spontaneously and regularly."[4] "We should be scared of emotionalism, the artificial manipulation of emotion," but not of true emotions caused by a vivid experience with God.[5]

Renewal through the "Toronto Blessing"

With these principles in mind, I consider the renewal known as the "Toronto Blessing" and offer an evaluation with both affirmation and caution. The Toronto Blessing originated in January, 1994, at the Toronto Vineyard Christian Fellowship (now named the Toronto Airport Christian Fellowship). The Blessing itself consisted of an overwhelming experience of divine joy, expressed through what became dubbed as "holy laughter." Many who have experienced this blessing testify to an enduring dimension of joy in the Lord they had not experienced previously and to new dimensions of freedom, vitality, anointing, and effectiveness in their ministries. Services at this location have been held six nights a week now for more than two years.

The movement has had a worldwide impact. As of May, 1995, over 250,000 believers from over fifty nations had come to Toronto. These included hundreds of experienced pastors, missionaries, teachers, evangelists, and ministry leaders. Those receiving the blessing in Toronto carried its effects to some 7,000 churches in North America and some 4,000 churches in England.[6] Locally, *Toronto Life* magazine called the Toronto Blessing the number-one tourist attraction of 1995.

Why do people come for the Toronto Blessing? Without doubt, it is because they have a hunger for God. While it is not necessary for people to go to Toronto to receive a new anointing from God's Spirit, one cannot ignore the fact that in this church in that city, many are finding God in a new way. Whether we believe all the manifestations are of God or not does not nullify the reality of this spiritual hunger. To my knowledge, we have never witnessed the hunger for God we are witnessing today (evidenced in America not only by the Toronto Blessing, but also by the burgeoning men's renewal movement, Promise Keepers, which has been remarkably controversy-free within evangelical circles). This was true in 1996, but may or may not be occurring today.

Evaluations of the "Toronto Blessing"

While I have not witnessed services at this Toronto Fellowship firsthand, I have consulted a number of sources carefully. The February 1996 issue of the Toronto Fellowship's own magazine *Spread the Fire* carries testimonials from those whose lives were deeply touched by the Blessing, along with a study by the sociologist Dr. Margaret Poloma documenting "incredible life changes" this renewal has produced.

Families and marriages have been healed, and some 90% surveyed said their time in Toronto resulted in their being "more in love with Jesus than ever before."[7]

Two European leaders, who are very experienced in spiritual warfare, visited me in 1996. They had recently attended the meetings at the Toronto Fellowship. They came away from the meetings quite concerned. They detected the presence of what I call, "blended spirits," i.e., counterfeit religious spirits working at the same time that the Holy Spirit was in operation. The counterfeit spirits will do just that, counterfeit the work of the Holy Spirit.

In all honesty, I must confess that the men attended the Toronto meeting with a suspicious attitude to begin with. Therefore, their report must be filtered through that reality. They told me that they began to resist counterfeit spirits during the meeting. The result was a considerable subduing of the Toronto phenomena, much to the consternation of those leading the service. Many others, both first-hand witnesses and those evaluating the movement using first-hand reports, evaluate parts of the movement negatively. Concern over the way the renewal was being pastored at the time (and not renewal itself) led ultimately to the Fellowship's being asked in 1996 by the Association of Vineyard Churches to leave the Association, which it did.

As already mentioned, I have read with great interest *The Father's Blessing* by the Fellowship's senior pastor, John Arnot. I agree with another reviewer who wrote:

> John is unassuming and unpretentious, and he radiates gentleness, kindness and humility. He writes as he lives—nondefensively and nonagressively in relation to people, and passionately in relation to God. To read the book is to read the man.... Few, if any, will agree with everything they read, but all who read should examine the context, remember the man, and ask for divine light before sounding a negative.[8]

Now to the most crucial question of all, is this Toronto Blessing movement a genuine renewal by the Holy Spirit? At least three views are commonly given:

1. The movement is a work of the Holy Spirit.
2. The movement is demonic.
3. The movement is a mixture of good and bad, true and false, with an uncertain future.

I submit a fourth view: The movement has all the evidences of being a revival movement, but it must be worked out in the context of spiritual warfare.

Sustaining Renewal through Spiritual Warfare

If the leaders of the Toronto renewal view it from a spiritual-warfare perspective and proceed accordingly, then the renewal has a good and certain future. Such a way of going forward means bringing to bear all that this book has explained about sin and spiritual warfare being multidimensional. Warfare against the flesh keeps us from wrongly emphasizing or demanding certain spiritual manifestations as proofs of the Spirit's presence, work, or power. Warfare against the world keeps us from being snared in the power, position, possessions, and pleasure syndrome by the attention of the media (see chapters 25 and 26). Warfare against evil supernaturalism keeps us vigilant regarding the onslaught of spirits that counterfeit manifestations of the Holy Spirit and that otherwise attack the leaders and people of any revival movement.

From this spiritual-warfare perspective, I recommend three courses of action that I believe will help the Toronto renewal fulfill God's intentions for it. *First, guard the Spirit's freedom, and keep the renewal focused on spreading the gospel.* Make sure we are not trying to spread Toronto manifestations but renewal in the Holy Spirit who chooses to manifest Himself in various ways. Our desire to see specific manifestations repeated and spread as assurance that the Spirit is truly at work is a pitfall that denies the Spirit's freedom and opens us to spiritual deception and the manipulation of the flesh to create such (counterfeit) manifestations. But one result of true spiritual renewal that we should seek is the transformation of believers into the image of Christ. As this occurs, believers grow in their compassion for others and follow Jesus in His ministry of loving the poor, the sick, and those in the most desperate conditions. Our flesh, conforming to the mold of the world, may be repulsed by these who often feel alienated from our middle-class church cultures, but God's Spirit draws us to them in the name of Jesus. As we grow in compassion for others and in passion for our Lord, we also pursue worldwide evangelism more intensely. Increased commitment to evangelism results naturally from true spiritual renewal. Renewal without an increased impetus to evangelism is false or seriously flawed.

In response to both animal sounds and other phenomena, I suggest that the most godly prophetic interceptors at Toronto fast and pray for 24 hours or until God says, "Yes" or "No." If He says no, then I am wrong, and I am willing to be wrong.

In the 1996 revision, I suggested that the leadership at Toronto ask God to remove the animal sounds and actions. John Arnot did exactly that and God responded "no." (see *The Father's Blessing,* pages 164–183) If that was good enough for John, it's good enough for me.

Implement a strategy for combatting the demonic activity all renewal stimulates. Take the offensive both in small-group and public intercessory prayer. All the people at a meeting should be informed that demonic powers are present. Then they should be briefly instructed in the three commands and the two promises of James 4:1–8a (see chapter 63). The leader then leads the congregation in taking their spiritual authority against all demons assigned against the meeting (Rev. 12:11; Eph. 3:10). The demons have entered the church's territory and are under the church's delegated authority. They are to be bound to silence and commanded to release the people and to leave their minds and emotions alone.

Also, all free-floating unattached demons are to exit the building. God is then petitioned to fill the building with His warring angels, forcing all the free spirits outside. The meeting will then continue without their interference. Spiritual warfare intercessors can be stationed at the entrances to the building. As people enter, prayer can be directed to God against any spirits they bring with them.

This procedure should be repeated every evening. We never win the battle once and for all until the war is finally over. I believe that this kind of united warfare in group prayer in all our public services is a missing dimension in effective spiritual warfare (along with group deliverance; see Appendix C). I have followed this procedure and experienced its good results countless times.

This is my appraisal of the Toronto movement. May God purify His people and make them wise as serpents and harmless as doves as they guide this movement. May this be the beginning of the worldwide revival we all yearn for. May we let God be God and do only and all that He wants to do among us!

Pitfall Ten: Ministry Outside the Area of Our Faith and Experience

What do I mean by "ministering outside the area of our faith and experience"? The concept comes from Paul's teaching in Romans 12:3.

> For through the grace given to me I say to every man among you not to think more highly of himself than he ought to think; but to think so as to have sound judgement, as God has allotted to each a measure of faith. (NASB)

The context is twofold: first, the faith which enables us to obey God's commands as found in verses 1–3a; second, the measure of ministry faith that God has allotted to each one of us. Each, of course, has its source only in the grace of God (v. 3 with 1 Cor. 15:10; Eph. 4:7).

The truth of this verse rests on this principle: As we begin our ministry in spiritual warfare, God will increase our anointing (if that is the right word) progressively, to enable us to move into increasingly more difficult dimensions of warfare.

Most of us begin with spiritual warfare ministry focused on our own life. We learn how to submit to God, resist the devil, draw near to God, and experience His drawing near to us (James 4:1–8a; see also chapter 63). If we find demonic activity in our own lives, we can learn self-deliverance even if it takes the ministry of others to us in order to get us started.

Some of us rapidly move beyond self-deliverance. We may find demonic activity within our family members and quite naturally attempt ministry of deliverance to them. Others are too frightened to work with their family members, and they insist that someone else help set their loved ones free. As these believers observe the way others minister to their family member, they often learn how to continue the ministry, if needed, themselves. Still others do not want or are not able to move into any dimension of spiritual warfare ministry. Some feel they are involved in enough spiritual warfare with only their own life.

Ministry to oneself I call the *personal level* of spiritual warfare. When we help other members of our family, we move into the elementary steps of what I call the *pastoral level* of spiritual warfare. The next step in the pastoral level of spiritual warfare involves being part of an occasional spiritual warfare and even deliverance ministry to others. Some go so far as to form a local-church deliverance team. Finally, there are the more advanced levels of spiritual warfare ministry. I call them the *cosmic* and the *evangelistic levels.*

In one sense these last two are the same. The cosmic level has to do with the demonic princes who rule territorially and socially; that is, they partly control different areas of society such as the commercial, political, educational, religious, legal, and military. These cosmic princes may rule on a local, regional, or even a national level. There perhaps are others who rule on an international level. Their purpose is to keep mankind in bondage to the flesh, the world, and the devil, and to stop people from coming to Christ as Savior and Lord. Thus, the cosmic and evangelistic levels go together.

I distinguish between these two levels only to emphasize evangelism. Satan's main goal, always, is to keep people from coming to Christ. The church's mission is to bring people to Christ. Thus the kingdom of Satan and the kingdom of God clash fiercely, especially in the area of world evangelism. The cosmic and evangelistic levels of spiritual warfare also go together because they are usually part of a strategy to break demonic strongholds that control specific people groups and even geographic locations. We encounter these strongholds as we seek to evangelize these people groups.

The question of territorial spirits, that is, the identity of powerful high-level demonic personages who rule geographical or socio-cultural people groups has become a major concern to many of us who are involved in world evangelism. Our search for effective strategies to break the power of these spiritual beings, however, has caused controversy. The main reason is that we do not know how the early church dealt with territorial spirits.

The main approach being taken today is often called "spirit mapping." The term came from one of the outstanding researchers in spiritual warfare, George Otis, Jr. He defines spiritual mapping in a simple, logical manner. It is an attempt to see a particular town or area "as it really is, not as it appears to be."[9] How the area to be evangelized really is depends on what spiritual powers control the minds of the people in the area to be evangelized.

What is the belief system of the people? Who are the spiritual powers they fear, worship, and serve? How did the people come into bondage to them?

With this and similar information, we can now pray effectively for the people in question. We can identify the spirits that control their lives. We can ask God to subdue the activity of these spirits who blind the people to the truth of the gospel (2 Cor. 4:3–4). We can ask God to free them so they can make their own decision for or against Christ without the deceptive influence of these cosmic spirits. This and this alone is the aim of spiritual mapping.[10]

Closing Comments

Many today are emphasizing cosmic level spiritual warfare in order to speed up world evangelism. Cosmic level warfare is essential to world evangelism, and the desire to wage warfare at that level for this result is commendable.[11] But I must caution against people seeking to do spiritual warfare at this level without sufficient understanding or experience.

Believers who have not been through spiritual warfare boot camp are certainly not ready to "dethrone" cosmic level spiritual powers. Not only do such believers bring disrepute on the whole area of strategic level spiritual warfare, but they also can open themselves to spiritual attack from such powers. Even highly experienced spiritual warriors have made mistakes in attacking demonic princes by themselves. One believer told me that he had been praying for some time that God would reveal to him the center of the major demonic activity which covered his entire city As he was praying, God gave him a vision of city hall and grotesque spiritual beings hovering over the city hall and nearby buildings.

He was driving his car at the time. He became so upset he began to engage these demonic principalities in warfare. When he did so, a tremendous power overwhelmed him, forcing him to pull the car off the road in order not to suffer a severe accident. When he had recovered sufficiently to pray, he cried out, "Lord, why did that happen to me?"

The Lord replied, "You asked me to show you where the center of the demonic control operating in the city is located. I did that. But I did not tell you to come alone in warfare against them."

"I learned a lesson I'll never forget," the brother told me. "If I do engage in such a ministry, I will only do it in the company with a good number of other believers who have gifts and experience sufficient to wage this type of high-level cosmic warfare."

What is even more alarming to me is to see some high-visibility spiritual "warriors" giving the impression to untaught believers that, under their guidance, they can dethrone these principalities and powers in one or two days of emotionally charged deliverance sessions. Some go so far as to affirm that when this occurs the demonic princes will be removed from the city once and for all. Yet the history of the expansion of Christianity reveals that this type of battle is not won in a few short conferences led by power persons (see chapter 51). What happens when the power people leave the community? While they may have, in the words of one insightful sister, "beat up a bit" on the demonic stronghold, they have by no means dethroned the demons, and they certainly have not broken their complex, deceptive hold over the community in question.

I see the need for at least four steps in this process:

1. To neutralize and defeat this type of evil force, we need to start with long-range, united intercessory ministries, accompanied by widespread repentance on the part of believers and the practice of a godly kingdom lifestyle by the believers in churches of the area. Often it takes years of crying to God day and night to bring this about.
2. The believers need spiritual boot camp training; that is, learning to put on and use the spiritual weapons that God has given to us. This preparation for intense spiritual warfare includes cleansing our own lives of any possible demonic powers and ministering to our family members as well.
3. We should join with other more experienced believers and learn what I call limited warfare counseling and limited warfare praying as already mentioned.
4. We must all be in subjection to and in fellowship with mature believers. Immature believers are a danger to themselves more than they are to the kingdom of evil. When the more mature and experienced warriors believe we are ready, we can then move on to greater spiritual encounters in warfare praying.

We are at war. The Captain of our salvation has delegated to us authority over "all the powers of the evil one" (Luke 10:17–19). Yet Satan and his demons, though defeated by the Lord on our behalf, are not dead. Their defeat, like our salvation in the kingdom of God, is being enacted in time and is thus both already begun and assured. Evil supernatural beings remain active, deceiving the nations and the children of God whenever and wherever they can. Thus Paul commands us not to be "ignorant of Satan's schemes" (2 Cor. 2:11 NASB).

Spiritual warfare is the very context in which we live and minister as God's sons and daughters—His soldiers. We would do well to master the Christian soldier's instruction manual given us in the word of God. We would do well to know the schemes of the enemy so that he will not be able to take advantage of us (2 Cor. 2:11).

We would do well to judge and evaluate all our spiritual warfare teaching and practice by the word of God *and* the proven history and experience of the church. We must avoid nonbiblical and questionable methodology, critiquing all "prophetic pronouncements" about spiritual warfare strategy and testing the spirits

(1 John 4:1). We should be accountable to mature and godly men and women (James 5:16) for all aspects of our spiritual warfare counseling and ministry. The goal of every ministry must be the glory of God through the edification of His Church and the evangelization of "every creature."

Endnotes

Abbreviations
ISBE   *The International Standard Bible Encyclopedia,* Revised
NICNT   New International Commentary on the New Testament
TDNT   *Theological Dictionary of the New Testament*
TNTC   Tyndale New Testament Commentary
TOTC   Tyndale Old Testament Commentary
WBC   The Word Biblical Commentary
ZPEB   *The Zondervan Pictorial Encyclopedia of the Bible*

Preface to the Second Revised Edition
1. Clinton E. Arnold, *Three Crucial Questions About Spiritual Warfare,* Baker Books, 1992, 140.

Introduction
1. See Merrill F Unger, *What Demons Can Do to Saints* (Chicago: Moody, 1977) and C. Fred Dickason, *Demon Possession and the Christian* (Westchester, Ill.: Crossway, 1989).
2. This type of willful defiance of the spirit world in the power and name of the Lord Jesus Christ by one who once served it is called a "power encounter."
3. As is often the case with believers who have been "demonized," set free, and gone on to a close walk with the Lord, Carolyn became quite sensitive to the spirit world. She is acutely aware of the presence of evil spirits in people and places, even in homes and stores. She has also been wonderfully used to help free other demonically afflicted believers.
4. "World view" refers to one's most fundamental view of reality. See chapter 1. What I experienced here is also called a "paradigm shift."
5. 1 will define *spiritual warfare* in more detail in later chapters.
6. For a look at the contrasting notions of *demon possession* and *demonization* see chapter 8.
7. It is amazing to realize that these words are warnings to church pastors (elders). Can pastors be demonized? We will see later in our study.
8. Satanology is the doctrine of Satan; demonology, that of demons; hamartology, the doctrine of sin; soteriology, the doctrine of salvation.
9. *Spiritual warfare* is war with sin and sinful personalities. While all human beings are victims of spiritual warfare, its primary combatants are God and His angels and children, who are opposed by Satan and his demons. It is warfare between the kingdom of God and the kingdom of the Devil.

Chapter 1: World View Clash
1. See Bryant Myers, "The Excluded Middle," *MARC Newsletter,* June, 1991.
2. World view has to do with one's personal or a group's collective view of reality. There are really then two realities. There is reality as God has made it and sees it. Then there is reality as we finite and imperfect human beings perceive it. My friend Charles Kraft writes that "we see the world (both physical and all other aspects of it) as we have been taught to see it. It is part of our world view to assume that our way of seeing the world is right . . . . We from Western nations bordering the North Atlantic have been taught or allowed to assume that our perception of reality is the same as the absolute REALITY itself . . . . This is the problem of world view." *Christianity With Power: Your World View and Your Experience With the Supernatural* (Ann Arbor, Mich.: Vine Books, 1989), 23–24.
3. *Contextualization* is the process of adapting to a lifestyle or point of view different from our own to such a degree that our behavior becomes normal for the new context in which we find ourselves. It is an essential part of cross-cultural living and ministry.
4. James W. Sire, *The Universe Next Door* (Downers Grove, Ill.: Intervarsity, 1976), 17.
5. Paul Hiebert, *Cultural Anthropology* (Philadelphia: J. B. Lippincott Company, 1976), 371.
6. For an excellent and scholarly presentation and critique of this process by a reputable Christian scientist, see A. E. Wilder Smith, *Man's Origin, Man's Destiny* (Wheaton, Ill.: Harold Shaw, 1974).
7. For a critique of this view see Arthur C. Custance, *The Mysterious Matters of Mind* (Grand Rapids, Mich.: Zondervan, 1980).
8. For an excellent discussion of the inescapable tension between one's limited personal or group world view, Western world views, and key elements of a biblical world view, see Charles Kraft, *Christianity With Power.*
9. Sire, 66.
10. Vergilius Ferm, ed., *An Encyclopedia of Religion* (New York: The Philosophical Library, 1945), 518.

11. Sire, 66.
12. Paul Hiebert, "The Flaw of the Excluded Middle," *Missiology* 10 (January, 1982), 35–47.
13. Myers, 3.
14. Myers, 3.
15. Myers, 4.
16. Myers, 4.
17. Traditional world view is often described as not believing in germs or science of any form but only in spirit forces operating directly, every moment of the day, in "nature" until nature has become almost totally unpredictable. Bronislaw Malinowski in his classic *Magic, Science and Religion* (Garden City, N.Y.: Doubleday Anchor, 1954), 17–36, denies that the traditionalist holds to a totally mystical world view. "On the contrary," he says, "traditional people understand the difference between religion, magic, and science." By observation they have created a true science by which they also live their lives. While admitting malevolent spirits can interfere in the course of nature, they do not attribute all negative experience as necessarily coming directly from evil spirits or angry ancestral ghosts.
18. J. Warwick Montgomery, "Exorcism: Is It For Real?", *Christianity Today* (July 26, 1974). Jeffrey Burton Russell of the University of California in Santa Barbara, California, traces the development of satanology and demonology up through the 5th century A.D. In his book *Satan: The Early Christian Tradition* (Ithaca, N.Y.: Cornell University Press, 1987), he begins with the apostolic fathers—Clement of Rome, Ignatius, Polycarp, Papias, and others—and continues through the age of Augustine. He graphically describes the activity within the post- first century Church of the Order of Exorcists.
19. Michael Green, *I Believe in Satan's Downfall* (Grand Rapids, Mich.: Eerdmans, 1981), 112.
20. *Power encounter*, mentioned earlier in the Introduction, is a crisis point of encounter in the on-going spiritual warfare between supernatural personages in which Christians are directly involved. Its goal is the glory of God, the defeat of the "no-gods" (Gal. 4:8–9), and the obedience of men to the one true God and His only begotten Son, the Lord Jesus Christ (John 1:14,16; 3:16; 1 John 4:9–10). Much is being written today about power encounter. See the bibliography for several outstanding books and articles dealing with this area of spiritual warfare.
21. The question of territorial spirits seems to be causing considerable controversy and opposition among Christians today. Some of it is justified by the careless, unscriptural, and shallow way these spirits are dealt with by some Christian leaders. However, the Bible does speak of spirits who exercise control over peoples and geographical areas.

Chapter 2: The Spiritual Warfare Dimension of a Biblical World View

1. H. B. Kuhn, "God, Names Of," in Merrill C. Tenney, ed., *ZPEB* (Grand Rapids, Mich.: Zondervan, 1977) 2:760–766.
2. See Gordon J. Wenham, *Genesis 1—15,* WBC (Waco, Texas: Word, 1987), 316–322.
3. Kuhn, 761–762.
4. God was, however, probably known as Yahweh by His people before the Exodus (Gen. 2:4f; 3:1f; 4:1f; 4:26; 12:1f; 14:22 etc.).
5. Kuhn, 762.
6. James W. Sire, *The Universe Next Door* (Downers Grove, Ill.: InterVarsity, 1978), 21–27.
7. Edward T. Ramsdwell in Vergilius Ferm, ed., *An Encyclopedia of Religion* (New York: The Philosophical Library, 1945), 714.
8. Ferm, 557; see also Sire, 129–148.
9. Shirley MacLaine, interview. *Time* (December 7, 1987), 64.
10. *Time,* 66.
11. Howard F. Vos, *Religions in a Changing World* (Chicago: Moody, 1959), 83–84.
12. This is the theology of the New Age movement. It is the theology made popular by the *Star Wars* series of films. The "Force," i.e., God, is both good and bad. (See chapter 62 for a study on the New Age.)
13. For excellent popular presentations of this dimension of reality see my friend Frank Peretti's excellent books, *This Present Darkness* (Westchester, Ill.: Crossway, 1986) and *Piercing the Darkness* (Westchester, Ill.: Crossway, 1989).

Chapter 3: Cosmic Rebellion: The Problem of Evil

1. William Dyrness, *Christian Apologetics in a World Community* (Downers Grove, Ill.: InterVarsity, 1983), 153.
2. C. S. Lewis, *The Problem of Pain* (London: Fontana, 1962), 1f.

3. "... that is, never made at the beginnings of a religion," Lewis writes in a footnote. "After belief in God has been accepted, theodicies explaining, or explaining away, the miseries of life, will naturally appear often enough," Lewis, 4.
4. E. S. Brightman in *An Encyclopedia of Religion*, Vergilius Ferm, ed. (New York: The Philosophical Library, 1943), 264.
5. Jeffrey Burton Russell, *Satan: The Early Christian Tradition* (Ithaca, N.Y.: Cornell University Press, 1987b), 51ff.
6. Russell, 53.
7. For the reader who wants to pursue the problem of evil and theodicy in greater detail, I would recommend the following: William Dyrness, *Christian Apologetics in a World Community;* S. Paul Schilling, *God and Human Anguish* (Nashville: Abingdon, 1977); M. Scott Peck, *The People of the Lie: The Hope for Healing Human Evil* (New York: Simon and Schuster, 1983); and Edward J. Carnell, *An Introduction to Christian Apologetics* (Grand Rapids, Mich.: Eerdmans, 1948).
8. As we will later see, the Bible was written to a world thoroughly knowledgeable of the spirit world, of a devil, fallen angels, and other evil cosmic-spiritual beings. Since their existence was universally accepted, it was not necessary to prove or explain their origin, existence, or involvement in human affairs. The biblical revelation about evil supernaturalism simply builds upon, corrects, and expands upon what was already known. See Merrill F. Unger, *Biblical Demonology* (Chicago: Scripture Press, 1955) and Jeffrey Burton Russell, *The Devil: Perceptions of Evil from Antiquity to Primitive Christianity* (Ithaca, N.Y.: Cornell University Press, 1987).
9. For further study see Russell, *Devil*, 174–220. This book provides valuable background to the understanding of evil supernaturalism prevalent in both the Old and New Testaments.
10. W. E. Vine, *An Expository Dictionary of New Testament Words* (London: Oliphants, 1953), 278–279.
11. I do not use the term "exorcism" to refer to the Christian's ministry of evicting demons from human lives. I use "deliverance" and similar terms. Exorcism carries the idea of magic, incantations, and similar non-biblical practices.
12. Merrill F. Unger, *Demons in the World Today* (Wheaton, Ill.: Tyndale, 1971), 10. Unger's three books (see bibliography) are important to an understanding of the spirit world within biblical cultures.
13. See H. L. Ellison, "Leviathan," in *ZPEB*, Merrill C. Tenney, ed. (Grand Rapids, Mich.: Zondervan, 1977) 3:912.
14. John D. W. Watts, *Isaiah 1—33*, WBC (Waco, Texas: Word, 1985), 251.
15. The sudden emergence of strong opposition among some evangelicals to the contemporary attempt to understand the activity of such evil spirits and to guide the people of God into warfare against them puzzles me. Fortunately for Daniel, such opposition either was not forthcoming or was ignored by him.
16. The use of "pit," "bottomless pit," "abyss," and "deep" to describe the underworld and the abode of some demons is very confusing in the New Testament. Both the KJV and NAS translate the same Greek word *abussos* in different manners. The NEB is more consistent using "abyss" for *abussos*. Vine says *abussos* is an adjective "used as a noun denoting the abyss. It is a compound of *a*, intensive and *bussos*, a depth." He says "it describes an immeasurable depth, the underworld, the lower regions, the abyss of Sheol." Its reference in Luke 8:31 and Revelation (it is used seven times in Revelation) "is to the lower regions as the abode of demons (I would qualify this with 'some demons'), out of which they can be let loose, Revelation 9:1,2,11; 11:7; 17:8; 20:1,3." (Vine 1:142; see also W. L. Liefeld, "Abyss," in *ZPEB* 1:30–31.
17. Vine 2:213. See H. Buis, "Hell," in *ZPEB* 3:114–117.
18. Not every one would agree with this last statement. In fact, I am not sure myself that this is the correct interpretation of 2 Peter 2:4 and Jude 6. See chapter 52 for my attempt to wrestle with these difficult passages.
19. This would be the premillenial eschatological view of these verses. For those holding other views of eschatology, there is still the understanding of a future outpouring of evil supernaturalism before the second coming of Christ.

Chapter 4: Rebellion in the Heavenlies and on Earth
1. Bernard Ramm wrestles with these days of creation in his superb book, *The Christian View of Science and Scripture* (Grand Rapids, Mich.: Eerdmans, 1954), 173–228. So does Gordon J. Wenham, *Genesis 1—15*, WBC (Waco, Texas: Word, 1987), 1–40.

2. For an outline of other suggested partial answers, see Paul S. Schilling, *God and Human Anguish* (Nashville: Abingdon, 1977).
3. For a discussion about angels created in God's image, see C. Fred Dickason, *Angels, Elect and Evil* (Chicago: Moody, 1975), 32.
4. Schilling, 206, 209.
5. M. Scott Peck, *People of the Lie* (New York: Simon and Schuster, 1983), 204.
6. I say "possibly" because there is no scriptural proof that Isaiah is referring to the fall of an angelic creature called Lucifer, i.e., "Day Star" (NEB says "Star of Dawn") who later became Satan. See N. Green, "Day Star," in *ISBE*, Geoffrey W. Bromiley, ed., (Grand Rapids, Mich.: Eerdmans, 1989) 1:879. The belief that this is a reference to the fall of the one who later became Satan or the Devil is based on tradition, not on biblical exegesis.
7. See Dickason, 30–32, 39–42; also Hebrews 2:9–18.
8. Merrill F. Unger, *Biblical Demonology* (Chicago: Scripture Press, 1955), 62–76.
9. See Robert H. Mounce, *The Book of Revelation*, NICNT (Grand Rapids, Mich.: Eerdmans, 1977), 191–193, for the view that the stars are angelic personages.
10. Edward J. Carnell, *An Introduction to Christian Apologetics* (Grand Rapids, Mich.: Eerdmans, 1948), 280.
11. Carnell, 280–281.
12. Carnell, 281–282.
13. Carnell, 282.
14. Ramm, 188–189, 195–210.
15. See H. Buis, "Hell" in *ZPEB*, Merrill C. Tenney, ed. (Grand Rapids, Mich.: Zondervan, 1977) 3:114–117.
16. For a popular examination of hell see "The Rekindling of Hell," *U.S. News and World Report* (March 28, 1991), 56f.
17. Besides the study of Genesis 3 done here, chaps. 6, 7, 27–29 are important too. The entire biblical revelation concerning the activity of evil supernaturalism in the believer's sin war rests upon the truths taught in Genesis 3.
18. While not accepting all his conclusions, I believe Gordon J. Wenham's study entitled *Genesis 1—15* is outstanding in its reverent, yet scholarly review of the divergent views of Genesis in general and Genesis 3 in particular (WBC (Waco, Texas: Word, 1987)).
19. Wenham, 72–81.

Chapter 5: The Source of All Rebellion

1. Dialogue from my tape recording of session.
2. Again I must state that I do not usually allow dialogue with demons using the vocal cords of their victims. The exact procedure depends on each deliverance case, of course. Usually demons can be dealt with by allowing them to speak only to the mind of their victim. At times, however, there may be value in allowing the vocal approach as I did in this case.
3. Not all fear is demonic; usually it is not. Demons do, however, seem to specialize in causing specific problems in the lives of their victims. This is biblical. First Samuel 16:14f describes a demon of terror. If allowed to speak he might call himself Terror. In 18:10 and 19:9, Saul is again demonized. These demons might call themselves Madness, Insanity, Rage, Anger, Murder, Kill, etc. In 1 Kings 22:22 we have "a lying spirit." He might call himself Deception, Liar, or Spirit of Deception or Spirit of Lying. In Mark 9:25 Jesus addresses the demon as a "deaf and dumb" spirit. He could have called himself Deaf-Mute. In Matthew 12:27 a ruling demon was called Beelzebul, Master of the Dwelling, or Beelzebub, Master of Spirits (see D. E. Aune, "Beelzebul" in *ISBE* (Grand Rapids, Mich., Eerdmans, 1989) 1:447–448). Demons are called "unclean spirits" in the New Testament. Some may have called themselves Unclean or Uncleanness. These are only suggestions based on experience with demons. Church history also supports these views.
4. Leon Morris, *The Gospel According to John*, NICNT (Grand Rapids, Mich.: Eerdmans, 1977), 73.
5. Morris, 463–464.
6. Edith Schaeffer, *Affliction* (London: Hodder and Stoughton, 1984).

Chapter 6: Cosmic-Earthly Warfare Begins: Genesis 3

1. See A. E. Cundall "Adam" and H. C. Leopold "Eve," in *ZPEB*, Merrill C. Tenney, ed., (Grand Rapids, Mich.: Zondervan, 1977) 1:53–56; 2:419.
2. See Gordon J. Wenham, *Genesis 1—15*, WBC (Waco, Texas: Word, 1987), xxvi, xlv–liii, 5–91.
3. John Calvin, *Genesis* (Grand Rapids, Mich.: Baker, 1989) 1:139.

4. I will assume, but not argue for, the Mosaic authorship of Genesis; see H. C. Leopold "Genesis," in *ZPEB* 2:678–695.
5. Wenham, 49–81. For an overview of the allegorical school of biblical interpretation see Bernard Ramm, *Protestant Biblical Interpretation* (Grand Rapids, Mich.: Baker, 1977), 23–45, 121, 125.
6. R. Payne Smith "Genesis," in *A Bible Commentary for English Readers,* Charles John Ellicott, ed. (New York: Cassell and Company, 1954) 1:23.
7. For an in-depth discussion of Moses' teaching style adopted in the early chapters of Genesis and especially Genesis 3, see Calvin 1:139–142.

   Probably the average citizen at that time, if he could read at all, was not a skilled reader. Even if he could read, written records were not readily available to the masses. The main channels of education were oral tradition and the practice of scribes and teachers who read aloud from the written texts to their students or to the masses.

   Illiterates, semi-literates or literates who lack their own written records tend to develop amazing capacities for memorization, however. Thus to help them in their memorization of large amounts of information in biblical times, vivid symbolism was used commonly in both historical accounts and teaching materials. In Genesis 3 Moses adopted a teaching style suitable to people who think in word pictures and through symbols.

   Our Lord's use of parables and symbolism to teach the masses the profoundest truths is a case in point. In His itinerant teaching He could not "carry his Bible" with Him. Nor could His listeners follow His teaching with "their Bibles"! All had to be communicated verbally. To enhance the learning process, Jesus did what Moses did in Genesis 3. He resorted to symbolism and illustrations from the everyday life of His audience to teach the mysteries of God.
8. Calvin 1:145.
9. This is probably because the point of the narrative has nothing to do with Balaam's surprise or lack of surprise when his donkey spoke to him. God usually goes right to the point of His stories, paying no attention to such peripheral issues which cause more critical modern readers almost panic. Woe unto us! We are great at asking peripheral questions, poor at asking the key questions.
10. See my study on Luke 10:17–19 in chapter 40.
11. John Peter Lange, "Genesis," in *Commentary on the Holy Scriptures* (Grand Rapids, Mich.: Zondervan, 1969) 1:228.
12. Calvin, 149–150.

Chapter 7: Warfare in the Garden

1. Not all believers will agree with this statement. We should not let our differences about how God inspired the biblical writers nor the extent of that inspiration to keep us apart as believers. Someday we will fully understand this and similar controversial questions.
2. D. M. Lake, "Mind," in *ZPEB*, Merrill C. Tenney, ed., (Grand Rapids, Mich.: Zondervan, 1977) 4:228.
3. J. M. Lower, "Heart," in *ZPEB* 3:58–60.
4. Lake, 229.
5. W. E. Vine, *An Expository Dictionary of New Testament Words* (London: Oliphants, 1953) 3:69.
6. See chapter 62 in this book for my overview of the movement.
7. I once was stopped right in the middle of a conference for Christian leaders while teaching on the gift of prophecy in today's church. The individual said, "Our prophecies are just as valid and infallible as biblical prophecy." After a series of serious problems arising out of this erroneous view, the leaders of the movement had to reassess their views of prophecy. To their credit they rejected the notion that modern prophecy is as binding upon believers as are the prophetic Scriptures.
8. Another area of great controversy in today's church centers around "signs and wonders." See John Wimber and Kevin Springer, *Power Evangelism*, 1986, and *Power Healing*, 1987 (San Francisco: Harper and Row). Whether or not one agrees with Wimber, the two books brilliantly set forth the biblical, theological, historical, and contemporary foundation for today's emphasis on miracles, signs, and wonders. See also John White, *When the Spirit Comes With Power* (Downers Grove, Ill.: InterVarsity, 1988).
9. John Calvin, *Calvin's Commentaries* (Grand Rapids, Mich.: Baker, 1989) 1:150–151.
10. Ray C. Stedman, *Spiritual Warfare* (Portland, Ore.: Multnomah, 1975), 48.
11. See C. S. Lewis, *The Screwtape Letters* (London: Fontana, 1963) for insight into how Satan,

through his cosmic level powers and "worker" demons ("Wormwood") plant evil ideas in the mind of human beings.

12. John Peter Lange, *Commentary on the Holy Scriptures* (Grand Rapids, Mich.: Zondervan, 1969) 1:229.
13. See Wenham's insightful discussion of the serpent's words and Eve's reaction to them: (Gordon J. Wenham, *Genesis 1—15* [Waco, Texas: Word, 1987]) 72–76, 85, 88–91.
14. Wenham, 61–65, 67–72.
15. Lange 1:230.
16. Calvin, 151.
17. Newport J. D. White, *The Expositor's Greek New Testament*, W. Robertson Nicoll, ed., (Grand Rapids, Mich.: Eerdmans) 4:109.
18. Calvin, 152.
19. Donald Guthrie, *The Pastoral Epistles* (Grand Rapids, Mich.: Eerdmans, 1983a), 77.
20. Calvin, 154–157.

Chapter 8: The Potential Demonization of the Unredeemed

1. John Murray, "Fall, The" in Merrill C. Tenney, ed., *ZPEB* (Grand Rapids, Mich.: Zondervan, 1977) 2:492–494.
2. Murray, 493.
3. Adam Clark, *The Holy Bible: Commentary and Critical Notes* (Cincinnati, Ohio: Applegate and Company, 1828) 2:420.
4. John Calvin, *Calvin's Commentaries* (Grand Rapids, Mich.: Baker, 1989) 21:220–221.
5. The "if" clause here does not imply doubt, but a statement of fact. See Calvin 20:191–192; Clark, 315.
6. Some commentators struggle with applying *o theos* (god) to Satan. Adam Clark is one of them. He argues "the god of this world who blinds the unbelievers to the light of the Gospel is God Himself." He quotes St. Augustine as saying it was the opinion of all the ancients "including Irenaeus, Tertullian, Chrysostom, Theodorot, Photitus, Theophylact and, of course, Augustine" (Clark 2:315–326). As we study the great church fathers, however, we are often bewildered at some of their interpretations of Scripture. Usually historical reasons will be found for their occasional strange views. Commenting on the strange interpretations of some of the Fathers, Calvin wrote, "we see what the heat of controversy does in carrying on disputes. Had all these men calmly read Paul's words in 2 Corinthians 4:3–4, it would never have occurred to any of them to twist them in this way into a forced meaning; but as they were harassed by their opponents, they were more concerned to refute them, than to investigate Paul's meaning" (Calvin 20:193). I agree with Calvin, as do most modern critical commentators.
7. Calvin 20:192.
8. Calvin 20:193–194.
9. Lewis Sperry Chafer, *Systematic Theology* (Dallas, Texas: Dallas Seminary Press, 1947) 2:51.
10. Michael Green, *I Believe in Satan's Downfall* (Grand Rapids: Mich.: Eerdmans, 1981), 54.
11. Neil Anderson, *The Bondage Breaker* (Eugene, Ore.: Harvest House, 1990a).
12. Tom White, *The Believer's Guide to Spiritual Warfare* (Ann Arbor, Mich.: Servant Publications, 1990), 22. I see four levels: cosmic, personal, pastoral, and evangelistic.
13. Merrill F. Unger, *What Demons Can Do to Saints* (Chicago: Moody, 1977), 90.
14. That is not the name I would choose for myself, but it is the name others give me and my colleagues of all theological persuasions who constantly minister deliverance to the suffering, the demonically afflicted, and usually mentally-emotionally "agonized" fellow human beings. When criticized for my ministry, I often repeat D. L. Moody's famous words, "I like my way of doing it better than your way of not doing it."
15. I say thrice removed because none of the biblical writers describe their own experiences with demons, but only that of others. This means that the modern biblical translator and commentator is almost 2,000 years removed from the stories presented by the biblical writers. Also, he is living in a world view context quite different from that of the biblical writers.
16. J. Warwick Montgomery, ed., *Demon Possession* (Minneapolis, Minn.: Bethany Fellowship, 1976).
17. We will deal with the extremely controversial issue of the possible demonization of some true Christians later in our study.
18. Timothy M. Warner, *Spiritual Warfare* (Wheaton, Ill.: Crossway, 1991), 79–80. For other excellent critiques of the words *demon possessed, demon possession* and related words, and the preference for *demonization*, see Fred C. Dickason, *Demon Possession and the*

Christian (Westchester, Ill.: Crossway, 1989) 37–40; Murphy in Peter C. Wagner and Douglas F. Pennoyer, *Wrestling With Dark Angels* (Ventura, Calif.: Regal, 1990), 20–22; Mark Bubeck, *The Adversary* (Chicago: Moody, 1975), 83–92; *The Satanic Revival* (San Bernardino, Calif.: Here's Life Publishers, Inc., 1991), 45f; Anderson, *The Bondage Breaker;* White, 44–46; Unger, 86f; Green, 126. Unfortunately other outstanding books like R. Bufford's *Counseling and the Demonic* (Dallas, Texas: Word, 1988), consistently use "demon possession"; see page 102f.

19. Unger, 86f.
20. William Vine, *An Expository Dictionary of New Testament Words* (London, Oliphants, 1953) 1:291–292.
21. Unger, 86–87.
22. Unger, 86–87.
23. Dickason, 37–38.
24. The only persons who may be truly "demon possessed" are those who, like spiritist mediums, actually and consciously invite evil spirits to possess them. This voluntary possession is unlike the involuntary demonization recorded in Scripture. Perhaps the Antichrist and the Beasts (if these are persons) of Revelation will be examples of persons truly possessed by Satan or other powerful evil spirits.
25. Rodger K. Bufford, *Counseling and the Demonic* (Dallas, Texas: Word, 1988), 110–111.
26. I do not usually allow or hold demons in manifestation but try to keep them quiet and speak only to the mind of the victim. On other occasions, as Jesus and Paul did, when they come up into manifestation I may hold them there for purposes I will mention later. If done right, it both frightens and weakens them.
27. The question of demons of fear and others that take on functional as well as other names will be dealt with later. I am only recounting here what occurred. I recorded the session so the demon's voice and those of several others are recorded and can easily be distinguished from the voice of the young lady.
28. I say "usually" because they will not reveal all that is going on in the life of their victim. They will usually only reveal partial truth. They will hide all that they are able to hide. Also what they do reveal may not be 100% true in all its details. The main thrust of what they are forced to reveal will usually be true if one knows how to compel them to tell the truth.
29. Some "deliverance ministers" have such a negative view of counseling they refuse to do pre-deliverance or post-deliverance counseling. They say Jesus did not and they do not. They follow what a pastor friend calls the "yank and jerk" method. They "yank out" the easier demons and get the tough ones out in a series of "jerks" and send the person on their way with perhaps a few written helps and declare their mission completed. I wonder what becomes of these poor people a few days or weeks later? Since I have not done accurate scientific research to discover the answer, I cannot say. I do have enough personal experience with this procedure, however, to know that the latter state of many of these people becomes worse than the first (Matt. 12:43–45).
30. John R. W. Stott, *The Epistles of John*, TNTC (Grand Rapids, Mich.: Eerdmans, 1983), 193.
31. Francis Foulkes, *Ephesians*, TNTC (Grand Rapids, Mich.: Eerdmans, 1982), 69–70.
32. John Calvin, *Commentary on the Gospel of Luke* (Grand Rapids, Mich.: Baker, 1989) 16:24.
33. Calvin, 24.
34. See my in-depth study of Luke 10:17–21 in chapter 40.

Chapter 9: Abundant and Conquering: John 10, Romans 6–7

1. William Vine, *An Expository Dictionary of New Testament Words* (London: Oliphants, 1953) 2:317.
2. Leon Morris, *The Gospel According to John*, NICNT (Grand Rapids, Mich.: Eerdmans, 1977), 82.
3. See also John 5:24,26,29,40; 6:33,35,48,53; 8:12; 11:25; 14:6; 20:21; 1 John 1:1–3; 3:14–15; 5:11–13,20; Revelation.
4. George Eldon Ladd, *A Theology of the New Testament* (Grand Rapids, Mich.: Eerdmans, 1983), 254.
5. Ladd, 257.
6. Ladd, 257.
7. We will deal later with the biblical basis for such "demons" and contrast them with emotional states.
8. Dr. Mark Bubeck is a pioneer in combining spiritual warfare revival and prayer ministry in the United States. His three books are musts for balanced, biblical and relevant teaching

in these three areas. For examples of Doctrinal Praying, some mixed with Warfare Praying, see Bubeck's three important books, *The Adversary* (Chicago: Moody, 1975), 93f; *Overcoming the Adversary* (Chicago: Moody, 1984), 26–27, 42–43, 63, 71–72, 81, 90–91, 101–102, 110–111, 120, 136–137; *The Satanic Revival* (San Bernardino, Calif.: Here's Life Publishers, Inc., 1991), 110–113, 130–133, 145–147, 160–163, 181–184, 205–207, 220–223.

9. Dr. V. Raymond Edman, *They Found the Secret* (Grand Rapids, Mich.: Zondervan, n.d.). See also his *The Disciplines of Life* (Minneapolis, Minn.: World Wide Publications, 1948).

10. J. B. Lightfoot, *Saint Paul's Epistle to the Galatians* (New York: MacMillan, 1902), 180.

11. John Calvin, *Romans* (Grand Rapids, Mich.: Baker, 1989), Vol. xix, xxxiii.

12. David C. Needham, *Birthright* (Portland, Ore.: Multnomah, 1982) 69–86, 239–258. See his discussion with an anonymous second person about the believer's so-called two natures. It not only makes for interesting reading, but it is a powerful discourse on who we are in Christ. We are not two persons; nor are we a split personality. We are one, new person in Christ.

13. For in-depth study of the words referring to the dark side of man's immaterial nature, see Needham. Also see his superb discussion of our union with Christ and the Holy Spirit's presence in our life, 119–206. His parable of the lustful television program is especially interesting, 77–80.

14. Mark Bubeck, *Overcoming the Adversary,* 25–26.

15. In 6:19 he speaks of "the weakness of your flesh." This would refer to their humanity. Their very humanness made it difficult to understand deep spiritual truth. I believe this is similar to his use of the flesh in 2 Corinthians 10:3–4. He uses it not precisely in a moral sense (though that may also be implied), but as an expression of human weakness itself.

Chapter 10: Its Ecstasy: Romans 8

1. John Calvin, *Romans* (Grand Rapids, Mich.: Baker, 1989), devotes 57 pages to Romans 8. For scholarly, profound relevant studies of Romans 8:1–17, see John Murray, *The Epistle to the Romans* (Grand Rapids, Mich.: Eerdmans, 1977) and John Calvin, *Calvin's Commentaries* (Grand Rapids, Mich.: Baker, 1989). E. H. Gifford's *Romans* (Minneapolis, Minn.: The James Family, 2500 James Avenue North, 1977), H. P. Liddon's *Romans* (Minneapolis, Minn.: James and Klock Christian Publishing Co., 1977) and William Barclay's *The Epistle to the Romans* (Philadelphia: Westminster, 1958–1960) are also excellent.

2. The second clause found in the KJV "who walk not after the flesh but after the Spirit" does not have support in the oldest and largest number of manuscripts. It belongs where it is repeated at the end of verse 4. Calvin's editor admits this but says, "It being placed here does not, however, interfere with the meaning" (Calvin, 275).

3. For excellent studies on these truths in the context of spiritual warfare see Mark Bubeck, *Overcoming the Adversary* (Chicago: Moody, 1984), 36–63; Neil Anderson, *Victory Over Darkness* (Ventura, Calif.: Regal, 1990b), 37–67; and *The Bondage Breaker* (Eugene, Ore.: Harvest House, 1990a), 75–91; Tim Warner, *Spiritual Warfare* (Wheaton, Ill.: Crossway, 1991), 60–67. While George E. Ladd's study in his *A Theology of the New Testament* (Grand Rapids, Mich.: Eerdmans, 1983) is not necessarily from a spiritual warfare perspective, his presentation of the Christian life is superb (479–494, 511–530).

4. Dr. Neil Anderson's treatment of the subject of who the believer is in union with the Christ who indwells us by His Spirit and how to appropriate the victory this brings to our Christian life is outstanding (Anderson, 1990b, 9–67). George Ladd's treatment of this subject is very profound, though theological and somewhat awesome. He sees "in Christ" and "in the Spirit" in relationship to this age and our present experience of the age to come. It is thorough, exciting, even if to some, controversial reading (479–494).

5. Murray, 275.

6. Murray, 276.

7. James D. G. Dunn, *Romans 1—8*, WBC (Waco, Texas: Word, 1988a), 435.

8. Murray, 276. See also Romans 8:6,10,11; John 6:63; 1 Corinthians 15:45; especially 2 Corinthians 3:6,17,18; Galatians 6:8.

9. Murray, 277.

10. Murray, 278.

11. Calvin, 282.

12. Calvin's editor, 282.

13. Verse 9 represents one of the key verses about the indwelling of the Spirit of God in all of Scripture. He indwells every true believer, regardless of his immaturity in the faith. Existence in the Spirit is life. Without the Spirit is death. Jude's graphic outline of the condition of professing Christians who are not regenerate concludes with these words, "These are the ones

who cause divisions, worldly minded, devoid of the Spirit" (Jude 19). Romans 8:9 equates "the Spirit," "the Spirit of God," and "the Spirit of Christ"; thus my affirmation that Christ is now exalted at the right hand of God as head over all things pertaining to His church (Eph. 1:20–23). He indwells every believer and his body, however, only in the person of the Holy Spirit (John 14:16–18 with Gal. 4:6; Acts 16:6–7 with Rom. 8:9). This verse, as well as others like it, form some of the strongest arguments for the Holy Trinity in all of Scripture.

14. Thus any doctrine of physical healing which is based on the teaching that our bodies have already been redeemed, as is true of our souls or spirits, is contrary to Scripture. One can practice and teach an effective biblical healing ministry, without building it upon an obvious distortion of Scripture.

15. See Murray's excellent exposition of these verses (292–299). Also Calvin (293–302); Dunn (446–464); Gifford (151–154); Denny in W. Robertson Nicoll is excellent (*The Expositor's Greek New Testament* [Grand Rapids, Mich.: Eerdmans] 2:647–6648). So with F. F. Bruce in the TNTC (*Romans* [Grand Rapids, Mich.: Eerdmans, 1983], 164–168).

16. Calvin, 294.

17. Dunn says, "The usage may reflect the current way of expressing opposition between God and evil in terms of good and evil spirits, such as we find in the DSS . . . 'spirit of truth' and 'spirit of falsehood'—especially 1Q53, 18ff; spirit of fornication, jealousy, envy, error, etc. . . . Here Paul speaks of Israel's condition under the law as equivalent to that of the Gentiles under the elemental spirits . . . Galatians 4:9 and 5:1" (449–450). This is an important quote in light of the presence of evil spirits of fornication, jealousy, error, etc., discovered in people's lives in our day.

18. Available for $40.00 plus $4.00 postage and handling from OC International, P.O. Box 36900, Colorado Springs, CO 80936–6900.

Chapter 11: Its Agony: Romans 8

1. John Murray, *The Epistle to the Romans*, NICNT (Grand Rapids, Mich.: Eerdmans, 1977), 300–301.

2. See 1 Peter 1:3–9,13; 4:12–13,19.

3. Again I must point out the error of much modern application of a "healing in the atonement" theology. Healing is in the Atonement exactly as the new heavens and the new earth are in the Atonement. But we have not experienced those dimensions of the Atonement as yet. The latter (the "healing" of the physical creation) and the former (the total healing of our bodies) will occur in the future and at the same time.

4. One does not need to resort to this kind of misuse of the Scriptures to defend his practice of speaking or praying in tongues. If the practice is biblical, it can easily be defended from other passages of Scripture.

5. John Calvin, *Calvin's Commentaries* (Grand Rapids, Mich.: Baker, 1989), 311.

6. Calvin, 311–312.

7. John Murray's article "Foreknow, Foreknowledge" in Merrill C. Tenney, ed., *ZPEB* (Grand Rapids, Mich.: Zondervan, 1977) 2:590–593, is without doubt one of the best summaries of these two divergent views in print today.

8. Calvin, 320.

9. Calvin, 325.

10. James D. G. Dunn, *Romans 1—8*, WBC (Waco, Texas: Word, 1988a), 510–511.

11. Calvin, 327.

12. Ruth Tucker, *From Jerusalem to Irian Jaya* (Grand Rapids, Mich.: Zondervan, 1983), 34–35.

13. Murray, 332.

14. William Barclay, *Romans,* The Daily Bible Study Series (Philadelphia: Westminster, 1958–60), 123, in 20 Vol. Series.

15. Barclay, 123.

16. Dunn, 513.

17. Similarly, Murray, 333.

18. E. H. Gifford, *Romans* (Minneapolis, Minn.: The James Family, 2500 James Avenue North, 1977), 163.

19. Gifford, 163.

20. Gifford, 163.

21. Barclay, 124.

22. It is to Dunn's credit that he admits the possibility of such a "force" against believers. Barclay's description of Paul's choice of words in the context of the astrological views of his day

is excellent (124). He does not, however, apply Paul's words to the spiritual reality behind astrology as does Dunn.

23. Dunn, 513.
24. Murray, 334.
25. Dunn, 513.
26. Barclay, 124–125.
27. Dunn, 513.
28. Godet in Gifford, 164.
29. See Argentina-born Rev. Ed Silvoso's exciting chapter on the present move of the Holy Spirit in formerly resistant Argentina (where I spent my first years as a new missionary, 1958–1962) in C. Peter Wagner, ed., *Territorial Spirits* (Chichester, England: Sovereign World Limited, 1991b), 109–115.

Chapter 12: The Reality of Below Normal Performance

1. Phillips translation.
2. See Delling in Gerhard Kittel, *TDNT* (Grand Rapids, Mich.: Eerdmans, 1977–1978) 8:73–74. Delling's discussion of *teleios*, translated "perfect" as used in Matthew 5:48, is worth studying. He says the context in which *teleios* is used for our being "perfect" or "complete" as the Father is "perfect, complete, undivided" in Matthew 5:48 refers to the believer's relationships to his fellow man, while in Matthew 19:21a the focus is on our "undivided" relationship to God. The NEB translation of Matthew 5:48 captures well this idea.
3. Hell is a reality. The New Testament is filled with references to it, many from the lips of Jesus Himself. This was not His main message, however. His main message was the kingdom of God and eternal life.
4. No one in my circle of contacts talked about demons in those days. If they did, I didn't hear them. None of my professors or fellow students did. Satan was believed to be alive, but he primarily lived in biblical times, on the "mission field," and in theology textbooks. We were not taught how demons attempt to resist and deceive believers. We were told we were to resist the Devil, but we had no real "handles" on this to know what it meant.
5. From author's notes taken while participating in the Bible study.
6. See Neil T. Anderson, *Victory Over the Darkness* (Ventura, Calif.: Regal, 1990b), 51f for an excellent study of who we are in Christ, also in a spiritual warfare context.
7. Peter E. Gilquist, "Spiritual Warfare: Bearing the Bruises of Battle," *Christianity Today,* August 8, 1980.
8. God is sovereign. I do not doubt that He was using this painful incident to help me to fail so that I might learn lessons I could not learn in any other way.
9. See also Acts 13:48; Romans 8:28–30; 9:6–24; 11:1–36; 1 Peter 1:1–9.
10. See also 1 Corinthians 10:16; 11:25; Ephesians 1:7; 2:13; Colossians 1:12–14; 2:9–13; Hebrews 9:13–28; 10:10–14,19–22; 1 Peter 1:2,18–21; 1 John 1:7; 2:1–2; Revelation 1:5.
11. See also Galatians 4:6; Ephesians 2:18,22; 3:16–21; Titus 3:4–7.
12. See chap. 59 of our study where I attempt to deal more in depth with the relationship of demons to personality malfunctions. This is one of the most troublesome areas of counseling and spiritual warfare ministry.
13. I am not questioning the validity of experiences with the Holy Spirit nor even that of the particular experience she sought for and received. I am questioning the teaching that such experiences in themselves, will cure wounded people. Learning how to walk in the Spirit, appropriate the promises of God, resist the Devil, and receive on-going "healing" by the Spirit all takes time. Thorough, on-going counseling by a trained and spiritually gifted counselor will be necessary in the case of severely emotionally, physically, and spiritually damaged people. This is especially true if personality splitting has occurred. (See chapter 59.)
14. Again, while salvation can be seen as the total picture of God's dealing with us which would also include sanctification, I am not using salvation in its broadest aspect. I am using salvation as the initial work of God by which He forgives all our sins in Christ and takes us out of the kingdom of darkness and into the kingdom of His dear Son (Col. 1:13). Sanctification is the process of living as a son of the kingdom.

Chapter 13: What Is Happening to Me? A Multidimensional Sin War

1. Donald Grey Barnhouse, *The Invisible War* (Grand Rapids, Mich.: Zondervan, 1965), 172.
2. C. Fred Dickason, *Demon Possession and the Christian* (Westchester, Ill.: Crossway, 1989), 63–64.

3. D. Martyn Lloyd-Jones, *Exposition of Ephesians* (Grand Rapids, Mich.: Baker, 1987–88) 1:418–419.

4. Lloyd-Jones, 417–420.

5. Ray Stedman, *Spiritual Warfare* (Portland, Ore.: Multnomah, 1975), 13–14.

6. Stedman, 47.

7. Neil T. Anderson, *Victory Over the Darkness* (Ventura, Calif.: Regal, 1990b), 81–82.

Chapter 14: The Flesh, the Believer, and the Demonic

1. Rodger K. Bufford, *Counseling and the Demonic* (Dallas, Texas: Word, 1988), 143.

2. Bufford, 143.

3. R. K. Harrison, "Flesh (in the O.T.)" in Merrill C. Tenney, *ZPEB* (Grand Rapids, Mich.: Zondervan, 1977) 2:548.

4. W. A. Elwell, "The Flesh in the New Testament" in *ZPEB* 2:548–549.

5. Vine, *An Expository Dictionary of New Testament Words* (London: Oliphants, 1953) 2:107–108.

6. Eduard Schweizer in Kittel's *TDNT* (Grand Rapids, Mich.: Eerdmans, 1977) 7:98–151. Schweizer surveys the use of *sarx* in the Greek world, in the Old Testament, in Judaism, which includes its use in the Dead Sea Scrolls, the Targums, the Talmud and Midrash, the Apocrypha and Pseudepigrapha, Philo and Josephus. In the New Testament he explores the use of *sarx* in the "Synoptic Gospels and Acts"; in "Paul"; in "Colossians, Ephesians and the Pastoral Epistles"; in "John"; in "Hebrews"; in "The Catholic Epistles" and a study of the adjectives *sarkinos* and *sarkikos*. He continues with a nine-page summary of the use of *sarx* in the "Post-New Testament Period," the "Apocryphal Acts," the "Apologists," and finally in "Gnosticism."

7. Elwell, 549.

8. Stedman, *Spiritual Warfare* (Portland, Ore.: Multnomah, 1975), 48.

9. Neil T. Anderson, *The Bondage Breaker* (Eugene, Ore.: Harvest House, 1990a) 69–85; David C. Needham, *Birthright* (Portland, Ore.: Multnomah, 1982), 39–86, 239–272.

10. See Romans 6—8; 2 Corinthians 2—5; Ephesians 2:1–22; Colossians 2—3.

Chapter 15: Walking in the Spirit: Galatians 5

1. For those who object saying that the flesh is not a person like a spirit, what difference does that make? It is a question of a totally evil part of the believer's being cohabiting with the Holy Spirit that is the issue. The human flesh, which is so bad it is totally unredeemable, is no better than a demon which is also totally unredeemable. Jesus said the worst evils come out of the heart of men (Matt. 15:19). Yet the Holy Spirit lives in that potentially evil heart which is only progressively being sanctified. Deliverance counseling reveals, in full harmony with Scripture, that the Holy Spirit wars against indwelling demons just as He does with the indwelling flesh.

2. D. Martyn Lloyd-Jones, *Exposition of Ephesians* (Grand Rapids, Mich.: Baker, 1987) 1:74.

3. Neil T. Anderson, *The Bondage Breaker* (Eugene, Ore.: Harvest House, 1990a), 79–80.

4. See Dick Hillis, *Not Made For Quitting* (Minneapolis, Minn.: Dimension Books, Bethany Fellowship, 1973).

5. See W. A. Elwell in Merrill C. Tenney, ed., *ZPEB* (Grand Rapids, Mich.: Zondervan, 1977), 2:548–549. He says Paul uses *sarx* four times "where no negative moral judgment is implied and the word bears no connotation of evil at all" (Gal. 1:16; 2:16; 3:13–14); eight times where a negative moral judgment is made; *sarx* becomes descriptive of man's baser nature or is defined as being simply "evil" (Gal. 5:13,16,17 [twice]; 19, 24; 6:8 [twice]; five times "where *sarx* is not sinful per se, but tends in that direction" (Gal. 3:3; 4:23,29; 6:12–13).

6. Norman B. Harrison, *His Side Versus Our Side* (Minneapolis, Minn.: The Harrison Service, 3112 Hennepin Avenue, 1940), 83–84.

7. Richard N. Longenecker, *Galatians,* WBC (Dallas, Texas: Word, 1990), 239.

8. Longenecker, 239.

9. Longenecker, 239–241.

10. Anthropological dualism, according to Longenecker, views the physical body as evil per se. It must be mortified in some manner in order to achieve a true Christian experience. This was the view Martin Luther so strongly resisted in his day. (See William Barclay's [*Galatians* (Philadelphia: Westminster, 1958), 23–24] account of Luther's experiences at this point.)

11. Longenecker, 239–241.

12. Longenecker, 241.

13. W. Barclay, *Flesh and Spirit* (Philadelphia: Westminster, 1978), 22.

14. Longenecker, 244–245.
15. See John White, *When the Spirit Comes in Power* (Downers Grove, Ill.: InterVarsity, 1988).
16. Longenecker, 245.
17. With the personification of the flesh dwelling and warring within the believer, Paul's personification of the unholy, unredeemable flesh cohabiting the believer's body with the Holy Spirit is just as difficult to comprehend as an unredeemable unholy spirit dwelling with the Holy Spirit within the same body, as already mentioned. The Holy Spirit is not afraid of the demon, is He? He is certainly not contaminated by dwelling spatially with a demon, is He? Here again we face a world view problem, spatiality. God exists in His own universe which is saturated with demons. He allows Satan to come before His holy throne evidently "daily" (if daily fits when talking about God) and lie and accuse us. That doesn't bother God at all. I am certain it bothers Satan more than it bothers God. Demons dwelling within believers are much more uncomfortable with the presence of the Holy Spirit than He is with them. In deliverance ministries with believers the demons continually complain of His presence and warfare against them. Why does He not immediately expel them when He enters a human body where they are present? For the same reason He does not expel them from the same universe in which He and they are present. We don't know because God has not told us (Deut. 29:29; Ps. 139:6; Rom. 11:32–36).
18. Longenecker, 245.
19. Barclay, 50.
20. Matthew Henry, *Matthew Henry's Commentary on the Whole Bible* (New York: Revell, 1935) 6:676.

Chapter 16: Moral Sins: Galatians 5

1. Thomas Ice and Robert Dean, Jr., *A Holy Rebellion* (Eugene, Ore.: Harvest House, 1990), 81–84.
2. This is the opinion of many critical commentators. This addition is not at all necessary as *porneia* is often used in Scripture for all kinds of illicit sexual relations. In Matthew 5:32 and 19:9 and similar passages it would include adultery, not just fornication (see William E. Vine, *An Expository Dictionary of New Testament Words* [London: Oliphants, 1953] 2:125). Fredrich Hauck and Siegfried Schulz who write on the use of *porneia* and related words in Kittel agree (see Hauck/Schulz in Gerhard Kittel, *TDNT* [Grand Rapids, Mich.: Eerdmans, 1977] 6:579–595; see especially the New Testament usage on pp. 590–595).
3. Ronald Y. K. Fung, *The Epistle to the Galatians*, NICNT (Grand Rapids, Mich.: Eerdmans, 1989), Figure 17.1, 254.
4. Richard N. Longenecker, *Galatians*, WBC (Dallas, Texas: Word, 1990), 252.
5. Longenecker, 254.
6. William Barclay, *Galatians* (Philadelphia: Westminster, 1958–60), 51.
7. Herman Ridderbos, *The Epistle of Paul to the Church of Galatia* (Grand Rapids, Mich.: Eerdmans, 1976), 205.
8. John A. Broadus, *Matthew* (Valley Forge, Penn.: Judson Press, 1886), 109.
9. Harriet Koskoff, "In Love With Porn," *West Magazine*, San Jose Mercury News, January, 1989, 11–18.
10. John Hubner, "In Love With Porn," *West Magazine*, San Jose Mercury News, January, 1989, 11–18.
11. Dr. James Dobson, *Combating the Darkness: the Pornography Commission's Final Report* (Colorado Springs, Co.: Focus on the Family, August, 1986), 1–4.
12. Rev. Bill Hybels, "The Sin That So Easily Entangles," *Moody Monthly* (April, 1989).
13. Quoted by Hubner, 14.
14. He writes that this freedom came as he used my audio cassette and study manual series called *Spiritual Warfare*, 16 cassettes and a 112-page self-help study manual. For information, write OC International, Inc., P.O. Box 36900, Colorado Springs, CO 80936-6900.

Chapter 17: The Age of Eros

1. It is outside the scope of this book to deal with the controversial issue of whether or not "fallen" pastors should be allowed back in the pastoral ministry. Feelings are strong on both sides of the issue.
2. A. W. Tozer in Randy C. Alcorn, *Christians in the Wake of the Sexual Revolution* (Portland, Ore.: Multnomah, 1985), 23.
3. Alcorn, 24–25.

4. I speak primarily to men because men are usually more susceptible to visual sexual stimulation than women. Increasingly, however, some women are facing similar problems.
5. Maureen Grant, "I Was Not Immune: Temptation Did Come," *Decision* (January, 1988).
6. Bondage to illicit sexual practices or being driven by sexual desires until they almost totally control one's life can become an addiction as strong as nicotine, drugs, etc. (see Patrick Carnes, *Out of the Shadows: Understanding Sexual Addiction* [Minneapolis, Minn.: CompCare Publishers, 1983]). In such cases direct demonic attachment to the life of the "addict" is also very common.

Chapter 18: Homosexuality in Biblical Perspective

1. Ronald Y. K. Fung, *The Epistle to the Galatians,* NICNT (Grand Rapids, Mich.: Eerdmans, 1989), 255.
2. William E. Vine, *An Expository Dictionary of New Testament Words* (London: Oliphants, 1953) 4:166–167.
3. John White, *Eros Defiled: The Christian and Sexual Sin* (Downers Grove, Ill.: InterVarsity, 1977).
4. Walter C. Kaiser, *Toward Old Testament Ethics* (Grand Rapids, Mich.: Zondervan, 1983), 118.
5. White, 105.
6. We are now witnessing attempts to approve of homosexuality by declaring it is primarily due to brain functions. Thus it is biologically based, not learned behavior. That *some* life-long homosexuals may *occasionally* reveal unusual brain patterns does not prove homosexuality is a biologically determined sexual pattern. It is just as possible that the brain patterns (if they truly exist) are the result of intense continual, long-term homosexual abuse.
7. *Time* (October 31, 1969). While this is an older article than I would prefer to quote, its analysis of homosexuality in the U.S. is unsurpassed. Its conclusions are still held by many secular counselors working with homosexuals. Since it is written by non-Christians we would not agree with all of its ethical conclusions since they are not based on Christian ethics but situation ethics.
8. White, 103–139.
9. E. M. Yamauchi, "Fertility Cults" in *ZPEB* 2:531–532.
10. Kaiser, 195–199; see R. L. Alden, "Sodom" in *ZPEB* 5:466–468.
11. Rev. John McClintock and James Strong, *Encyclopedia of Biblical, Theological and Ecclesiastical Literature* (New York: Harper and Brother Publishers, 1891) 9:857–858.
12. Charles John Ellicott, *A Bible Commentary for English Readers* (New York: Cassell and Company, 1954) 7:304.
13. Vine 2:19.
14. G. G. Findlay in W. Robertson Nicoll, *The Expositor's Greek New Testament* (Grand Rapids, Mich.: Eerdmans) 2:817.
15. F. W. Grosheide, *The First Epistle to the Corinthians,* NICNT (Grand Rapids, Mich.: Eerdmans, 1976), 140.
16. White, 112–113.
17. Gordon D. Fee, *The First Epistle to the Corinthians,* NICNT (Grand Rapids, Mich.: Eerdmans, 1989), 242–244.
18. William Barclay, *First Corinthians* (Philadelphia: Westminster, 1958–60), 58.
19. Barclay, 60.
20. Findlay, 817.
21. Ellicott, 304.
22. Matthew Henry, *Matthew Henry's Commentary on the Whole Bible* (New York: Revell, 1935) 6:533.
23. Leon Morris, *I Corinthians* (Grand Rapids, Mich.: Eerdmans, 1983b), 97–98.
24. Henry 6:533.
25. W. C. Kaiser, Jr., "Name" in *ZPEB* 4:360–366.
26. Morris, 98.
27. Henry, 533–534.
28. Barclay, 60–62. This is a good reminder in our day when a new focus on God's miraculous power has arisen among evangelicals. While extremes do exist, some of the evangelical opposition to this power emphasis is totally unfounded both from the perspective of Scripture and contemporary Christian experience (see Murphy, *Spiritual Gifts and the Great Commission,* 1975, 100–129; Wm. Carey).
29. *Addiction* is a carefully chosen word. Webster defines *addiction* as "the state of being devoted or surrendered to something habitually or obsessively." A former homosexual

says, "Addictions (and homosexuality is an addiction) are degenerative, a moral cancer. The addiction produces pain so the intensity of the addicted must be increased in order to continue numbing the pain. . . . Addictions bring frustration and loneliness. . . . Such is the addiction of homosexuality . . . pain . . . frustration and loneliness. (Bob Gentles, "Road Back Home from Homosexuality," *The Forum* [October 1990]).

30. Gentles, 5.

Chapter 19: Homosexuality and Contemporary Ministry

1. Ronald Y. K. Fung, *The Epistle to the Galatians* (Grand Rapids, Mich.: Eerdmans, 1989), 255.
2. Christian psychiatrist Dr. M. Scott Peck in his remarkable book *People of the Lie* admits that "Evil people are easy to hate." He then reminds us of Saint Augustine's caution that we "hate the sin but love the sinner" (M. Scott Peck, *People of the Lie* [New York: Simon and Schuster, 1983], 9).
3. *Pastoral Renewal* (April, 1981).
4. Don Baker, *Beyond Rejection: The Church, Homosexuality and Hope* (Portland, Ore.: Multnomah, 1985), 3.
5. For someone struggling with homosexuality or interested in knowing where to find help for friends who are, I list some of the outstanding Christian organizations in the U.S. who specialize in helping homosexuals. While there are probably many more groups, these are the ones I am most familiar with.

   Love In Action
   P.O. Box 2655
   San Rafael, CA 94912

   Mentanoia Ministries
   P.O. Box 33039
   Seattle, WA 98133

   LIFE Ministry
   P.O. Box 353
   New York, NY 10185

   Homosexuals Anonymous
   c/o Guest Learning Center
   P.O. Box 7881
   Reading, PA 19603

6. *Eternity* (October 1962), 22.
7. Practicing homosexuals seem more prone to demonization than others who are wrestling with sexual sin. Perhaps it is because homosexuality is so totally contrary to human sexuality as created by God. Also it is marked out by the apostle Paul as a unique expression of human rebellion against God as Creator and Father alongside of idolatry (Rom. 1:18–28).

   Strong demonic powers often attach themselves to homosexual bondage, making that bondage even more intense. I will give a case study of a Christian leader indwelt by homosexual demons later in our study. I have dealt with many cases of believers demonized by homosexual demons.

Chapter 20: Autosexuality

1. In my spiritual warfare teaching and counseling I often have to defend giving such prominence to this illicit (in my opinion) sexual practice. I give importance to this aspect of warfare with the flesh because autosexual stimulation is so common among Christians, even Christian leaders. It is part of the general sexual looseness gaining such control in the church today. While wishing to avoid the unhealthy "guilt" trip produced by rigid, legalistic, and uncompassionate traditional views of masturbation, I fear encouraging the slide in the opposite direction to be just as dangerous. I believe the biblical commands toward purity of mind are undermined by our laissez faire attitude towards autosexuality.
2. Norman L. Geisler, *Ethics: Alternatives and Issues* (Grand Rapids, Mich.: Zondervan, 1975), 200.
3. Earl D. Wilson, *Sexual Sanity* (Downers Grove, Ill.: InterVarsity, 1984), 63.
4. Psychologist Randy C. Alcorn, in his excellent book already referred to, gives a similar

definition of masturbation. He says, "Masturbation is the stimulation of one's own sex organs to find sexual pleasure or release" (Randy C. Alcorn, *Christians in the Wake of the Sexual Revolution* [Portland, Ore.: Multnomah, 1985], 213).

5. Wilson, 61.
6. For a Protestant overview of the Roman Catholic view of this passage and sexual practices which do not lead to procreation, see John White, *Eros Defiled: The Christian and Sexual Sin* (Downers Grove, Ill.: InverVarsity, 1977), 36–37. Roman Catholic books on sexuality would be primary sources of the Catholic position.
7. Alcorn, 214.
8. Geisler, 199.
9. Geisler, 200.
10. Geisler, 200–201.
11. Wilson, 63–64.
12. Wilson, 65; White, 36.
13. Alcorn, 216–217.

Chapter 21: Indecency
1. W. E. Vine, *An Expository Dictionary of New Testament Words* (London: Oliphants, 1953) 2:310.
2. Ronald Y. K. Fung, *The Epistle to the Galatians* (Grand Rapids, Mich.: Eerdmans, 1989), 255.
3. Fung, 255–256.
4. I am not commenting on whether or not the sexually fallen or deceptive Christian leader should ever be allowed a place of public and strategic leadership in the church. Personally, I could not do it. I would feel that I had disqualified myself from any high visibility leadership role in light of 1 Timothy 3:1–7 and Titus 1:5–11. This is an opinion, not a certainty I would apply to all cases.
5. There were very direct demonic dimensions to the husband's sexual bondage. Not until the sexual and other demons were recognized and expelled from his life over a period of time did he become free so as to respond to non-confrontive Christian counseling. His spiritual warfare was more than warfare with the flesh (his distorted and perverse sexual lusts), warfare with the world (the world of media which produced the wild sexual films he watched and the world of business which makes such morally filthy videos available in video shops which are open to the public), but very strong warfare with evil supernaturalism. He was demonized from childhood due to severe sexual abuse he had been subjected to as a child.
6. Anonymous, "Video Seduction," *Moody Monthly* (May, 1987), 28–30.
7. A group of cable television companies in 1991, by their own choice, removed MTV from their TV programming because of the open sexuality of Madonna and Cher. We salute their sensitivity to this sexual assault upon America's youth. Oh, that others would follow their example!

Chapter 22: Religious Sins
1. W. E. Vine, *An Expository Dictionary of New Testament Words* (London: Oliphants, 1953) 2:244.
2. Ronald Y. K. Fung, *The Epistle to the Galatians* (Grand Rapids, Mich.: Eerdmans, 1989), 256.
3. Vine, like Fung, brings this out in his treatment of idolatry, 2:244–245.
4. See Mrs. Howard Taylor, *Behind the Ranges: Fraser of Lisuland* (Overseas Missionary Fellowship, 1956).
5. P. H. Garber, "Idol" in G. W. Bromiley, ed. *ISBE* (Grand Rapids, Mich.: Eerdmans, 1989–91), 2:794–800.
6. F. B. Huey, Jr., "Idolatry" in Merrill C. Tenney, ed., *ZPEB* (Grand Rapids, Mich.: Zondervan, 1977) 3:242–249.
7. Garber, 798–799.
8. Huey, 247–248.
9. Garber, 798.
10. Huey, 246.
11. Huey, 248.
12. Garber, 799.
13. Huey, 248.
14. Fung, 256.
15. Vine 3:51–52.
16. Fung, 256–257.

17. For more in-depth studies see the articles on divination, witchcraft, and sorcery in the *ISBE* and *ZPEB*.
18. For two helpful books on this topic, see *War on the Saints* by Jessie Penn- Lewis and Evan Roberts (New York: Thomas E. Lowe, Ltd., 1987) and *The Beautiful Side of Evil* by Johanna Michaelsen (Eugene, Ore.: Harvest House, 1982).

Chapter 23: Social Sins
1. Ronald Y. K. Fung, *The Epistle to the Galatians* (Grand Rapids, Mich.: Eerdmans, 1989), 257.
2. Fung, 258.
3. For a history of Pentecostalism by a Pentecostal scholar see John Thomas Nichol, *Pentecostalism* (New York: Harper & Row, 1966). For one which includes a history of the Charismatic movement by a non- Pentecostal and non-Charismatic, see C. Peter Wagner's excellent book, *How To Have a Healing Ministry Without Making Your Church Sick* (Ventura, Calif.: Regal, 1988b).
4. For the best information on both the Charismatic and Pentecostal movements, see Stanley M. Burgess and Gary B. McGee, *Dictionary of Pentecostal and Charismatic Movements* (Grand Rapids, Mich.: Zondervan, 1989).
5. The first wave of widespread renewal of the century was the Pentecostal movement, according to researchers. The second was the Charismatic movement. A third renewal movement is being called The Third Wave. The name probably originated from the creative mind of church growth expert C. Peter Wagner of the School of World Missions of Fuller Theological Seminary. See, *The Third Wave of the Holy Spirit* (Ann Arbor, Mich.: Vine Books, Servant Publications, 1988a) and *How To Have a Healing Ministry.*

Chapter 24: Bitterness and Intemperance
1. Reactionary sin is the sin reaction of abused persons against their abusers, against innocent third parties, and even against God. The diagram on page 172 shows how such sin operates. Follow the arrows from (1) Activator to (2) Victim. The victim then becomes an activator of sin (3) against the abuser (4); or, if in an inferior power position, the victim turns his anger against other, innocent people (5). This produces a chain reaction spreading sin often for generations. It must be stopped by the choice of the victims to forgive their abusers as Christ has forgiven them, even if the abusers do not seek forgiveness. This is the example set by Jesus as recorded in 1 Peter 2:21–25; 3:8–18.
2. See the following beneficial books by David A. Seamands, Professor of Pastoral Studies at Asbury Theological Seminary: *Healing for Damaged Emotions* (Wheaton, Ill.: Victor, 1985a) and *Healing Grace* (Wheaton, Ill.: Victor, 1988).
3. Seamands says low self-esteem is Satan's number one tactic of deception with Christians *(Healing for Damaged Emotions, 48–96).*
4. William Backus' two books, *Telling Yourself the Truth* (Minneapolis, Minn.: Bethany House, 1980) and *Telling the Truth to Troubled People* (Minneapolis, Minn.: Bethany House, 1985) are outstanding.
5. Ronald Y. K. Fung, *The Epistle to the Galatians,* NICNT (Grand Rapids, Mich.: Eerdmans, 1989), 258.
6. Fung, 259.
7. Fung, 259. Not everyone will agree with Fung's more liberal attitude towards wine. Let each be persuaded in his own mind.
8. W. E. Vine, *An Expository Dictionary of New Testament Words* (London: Oliphants, 1953) 2:57.
9. Fung, 260.
10. Vine 2:295.
11. Fung, 260.
12. While I understand what Fung is trying to say, I must state that the "sins committed in the sphere of the body" can also be committed by disembodied spirits operating through human beings and even animals. Furthermore, as in the case of incubi and succubi, gross sexual sins can be committed by evil spirits by direct sexual contact with the body of their victim. I have dealt with several such cases. They are grotesque. The victims suffer greatly, because what they experience is abusive rape.
13. Fung, 261.
14. Fung, 262.
15. George Eldon Ladd, *A Theology of the New Testament* (Grand Rapids, Mich.: Eerdmans, 1983), 571.

16. I. H. Marshall in Merrill C. Tenney, ed., *ZPEB* (Grand Rapids, Mich.: Zondervan, 1977) 3:801–809.

Chapter 25: The Gospel and Culture

1. William E. Vine, *An Expository Dictionary of New Testament Words* (London: Oliphants, 1953) 4:233.
2. Dick Hillis, *Is There Only One Way?* (Santa Ana, Calif.: Vision House Publications, 1974); Alan R. Tippett, *Verdict Theology* (Lincoln, Ill.: Lincoln Christian College Press, 1969), 3–94.
3. Don Richardson, *Peace Child* (Ventura, Calif.: Regal. 1982) and *Eternity in Their Hearts* (Ventura, Calif.: Regal, 1982b).
4. Don M. McCurry, ed., *The Gospel and Islam* (Monrovia, Calif.: MARC/World Vision, 1979). George Otis, Jr., *The Last of the Giants* (Tarrytown, N.Y.: Revell, 1991).
5. Almost every people or cultural group will be composed of subgroups which see themselves as different than the people of the host culture, i.e., the "us versus them" mentality. Seldom does a major cultural or people group come to Christ but often subgroups within the larger people group do become Christians. For lack of a better word I use *subculture* to refer to these groups.
6. The concept of functional substitutes was a major theme in the teaching and writing of my teacher and mentor, the late Dr. Alan Tippett, former Professor of Anthropology at the Fuller School of World Mission. See Alan R. Tippett in bibliography; 1967; 1970, 28f; 1971; 1973, 167–168; 1975; 1987, 144–221.
7. I define a *missionary* as "any Christian who takes the gospel to a culture different than his own." This includes Two-thirds World missionaries as well as Western missionaries.
8. For the finality of Jesus Christ see Robert E. Speer, *The Finality of Jesus Christ* (London: Fleming H. Revell, 1933); W. A. Visser't Hooft, *No Other Name* (Philadelphia: Westminster, 1963); Lesslie Newbigin, *The Finality of Christ* (Richmond, Va.: John Knox, 1969); and Hendrick Kraemer, *The Christian Message in a Non-Christian World* (Grand Rapids, Mich.: Kregel Publications, 1961).
9. Webster defines syncretism as "the combination of different forms of belief or practice."
10. "Traditional Mayan Life Challenged: Evangelical Church, Catholics Compete," *San Jose Mercury News* (March 20, 1991).
11. Charles Colson, *The Body* (Dallas: Word, 1992), 165–171. To those unfamiliar with American television, "Donahuism" refers to the social views frequently expressed on *The Phil Donahue Show,* a TV talk show that once attracted the largest viewing audience. Lately, however, Donahue's ratings crashed, and the show has been cancelled.
12. For my prior discussion of Nihilism, see chapters 1 and 17.
13. Colson, 176.
14. Colson, 180.

Chapter 26: The World's Power, Its Character, Our Victory

1. William E. Vine, *An Expository Dictionary of New Testament Words* (London: Oliphants, Ltd., 1953) 4:233–234.
2. Leon Morris, *The Gospel According to John,* NICNT (Grand Rapids, Mich.: Eerdmans, 1977), 126.
3. Morris, 127.
4. Morris, 127.
5. Morris, 128.
6. Kenneth S. Wuest, *Exegesis of I John* (Grand Rapids, Mich.: Eerdmans, 1983) 2:125.
7. Wuest, 126–127.
8. John R. W. Stott, *The Epistles of John,* TNTC (Grand Rapids, Mich.: Eerdmans, 1983), 99.
9. Wuest, 127.
10. David C. Needham, *Birthright* (Portland, Ore.: Multnomah, 1982), appendix, 265–266.
11. C. H. Dodd in Stott, *The Epistles of John,* 100.
12. William Barclay, *The Letters of John,* The Daily Study Bible (Philadelphia: Westminster, 1960), 68.
13. Wuest, 127.
14. Wuest, 128.
15. Stott, 100.
16. Cal Thomas, "A Moral Alarm Clock," *San Jose Mercury News,* (January 28, 1988).
17. Vine, 4:233.

18. Trench, *Galatians,* in Kenneth S. Wuest, *Wuest's Word Studies* (Grand Rapids, Mich.: Eerdmans, 1983) 1:33.
19. Wuest, 33.
20. Wuest, 34.
21. John Eadie, *Commentary on the Epistle to the Galatians* (Minneapolis, Minn.: James and Klock Christian Publishing Company, 1977a), 467–468.
22. Michael Novak, "Awakening from Nihilism," *First Things* (August/September, 1994): 18–22.

Chapter 27: Warfare in Paradise

1. Gordon J. Wenham, *Genesis 1—15* (Waco, Texas: Word, 1987), xxi.
2. Wenham, xlv–xlvi, 39–40.
3. Wenham, xxxvii–xlv, 58–59.
4. For the differences see Wenham, xlv–L, 8–10, 21–23, 36–38, 52–57.
5. Wenham, xlix, 33.
6. Wenham, xlix, L.
7. G. Ernest Wright, *The Old Testament Against Its Environment* (Oberlin, Ohio: Graduate School of Theology, 1949), 9–41.
8. For further study of the image of God, see the critical commentaries on Genesis in bibliography and major books on systematic theology and any major Bible dictionary or encyclopedia for an overview of the most commonly-held opinions. *ISBE* and *ZPEB* have excellent overviews.
9. Dr. Fred Dickason (as well as other Bible scholars) is of the opinion that possibly angels too "were created in the image and likeness of God just as was man" (Dickason, *Angels Elect and Evil* [Chicago: Moody, 1975], 32). This may be true, but the Bible says nothing about the matter. That does not mean that Dickason is wrong.

    The focus of the Bible is on the God-man relationship, not on the God-angel relationship. While the latter is occasionally spoken of, the Bible's purpose is not to develop an involved theology of angels in relationship to God their Creator, but more a theology of man in relationship with God. Angelic activity is primarily revealed in Scripture in the God-man relationship.
10. Wenham, 38.
11. Derek Kidner, *Genesis,* TNTC (Downers Grove, Ill.: InterVarsity, 1967), 52.
12. Kidner, 53.
13. *Serpent* literally meant "snake," according to Wenham, 45, 72.
14. This is the view of Adam Clark. See Adam Clark, *The Holy Bible: Commentary and Critical Notes* (Cincinnati, Ohio: Applegate and Co., 1828), 39–41.
15. For an interesting treatment of this question, see Francis Schaeffer, *Genesis in Space and Time* (Downers Grove, Ill.: InterVarsity, 1976), 75–77.
16. Wenham, 72.
17. Wenham, 73.
18. Wenham, 73.
19. Jeffrey Burton Russell, *The Devil: Perceptions of Evil from Antiquity to Primitive Christianity* (Ithaca, N.Y.: Cornell University Press, 1987a), 182.
20. A. R. Fausset gives an outstanding brief overview of this position in *Fausset's Bible Dictionary* (Grand Rapids, Mich.: Zondervan, 1969), 637.
21. W. H. Griffith Thomas quoting James Orr's *Image of God in Man,* in Thomas, *Genesis: A Devotional Commentary* (Grand Rapids, Mich.: Eerdmans, 1953), 47.
22. John Calvin, *Genesis* (Grand Rapids, Mich.: Baker, 1989), 140.
23. Wenham, 72.
24. C. F. Keil and F. Delitzsch, *Commentary on the Old Testament* (Peabody, Mass.: Hendrickson Publishers, 1989) 1:92.
25. Keil and Delitzsch, 93.
26. Keil and Delitzsch, 93–94.
27. Gordon J. Wenham, *Genesis 1—15,* WBC (Waco, Texas: Word, 1987), 75–76.
28. Francis Schaeffer, *Genesis in Space and Time* (Downers Grove, Ill.: InterVarsity, 1976), 85.
29. Schaeffer, 86.
30. Matthew Henry, *Commentary on the Whole Bible* (New York: Fleming H. Revell, 1935) 1:25–26.
31. Derek Kidner, *Genesis,* TNTC (Downers Grove, Ill.: InterVarsity, 1967), 69.
32. Kidner, 69.
33. H. C. Leupold, *Exposition of Genesis* (Grand Rapids, Mich.: Baker, 1987) 1:180.

34. Leupold, 155–157.
35. Leupold, 157–158.
36. Leupold, 159.
37. It is outside of the purpose of our study to deal with the separate judgments first upon the woman (v. 16) and then upon the man (v. 17–19). The outstanding commentaries I have been quoting all have excellent material on these two subjects. Schaeffer's insights are outstanding, 69f.
38. Keil and Delitzsch, 107.
39. Leupold, 180.
40. Keil and Delitzsch, 107.
41. Leupold, 183–184.
42. Leupold, 183.

Chapter 28: Enmity Between the Seeds: Genesis 3:15

1. John Calvin, *Genesis* (Grand Rapids, Mich.: Baker, 1989), 165. Calvin's discourse on this matter is worth reading, 165–167.
2. See Merrill F. Unger, *Biblical Demonology* (Chicago, Ill.: Scripture Press, 1955; Jeffrey Burton Russell, *The Devil: Perceptions of Evil from Antiquity to Primitive Christianity* (Ithaca, N.Y.: Cornell University Press, 1987a); see the articles on the Religions of the Biblical World in G. W. Bromiley, ed., *ISBE* Grand Rapids, Mich.: Zondervan, 1985) 3:79–128.
3. Russell, 174f; Unger, 1955, 9f; and G. Ernest Wright's two books, *The Old Testament Against Its Environment* (Oberlin, Ohio: Oberlin Graduate School of Theology, 1949); *The God Who Acts* (London: SCM Press, Ltd., 1969).
4. Gordon J. Wenham, *Genesis 1–15,* WBC (Waco, Texas: Word, 1987), 72–73.
5. R. Payne Smith in Charles John Ellicott, *A Bible Commentary for English Readers* (New York: Cassell and Company, 1954) 1:25.
6. The expression "cursed are you" is very strong. It usually means to invoke God's judgment on someone. For an excellent discussion, see Wenham, 78.
7. H. C. Leupold, *Exposition of Genesis* (Grand Rapids, Mich.: Baker, 1987), 161.
8. Leupold's refutation of that view is outstanding, 232; see also Victor P. Hamilton, *The Book of Genesis: Chapters 1–17* (Grand Rapids, Mich.: Eerdmans, 1990), 196–197; and Smith in Ellicott, 25.
9. Smith, 25.
10. As to why the helpless animal should be cursed along with Satan, see Calvin, 165–168.
11. Leupold, 163.
12. Leupold, 162; see Calvin, 165–167.
13. Wenham does have a thorough overview of the entire serpent episode.
14. Adam Clarke thinks it was an ape or similar creature; *The Holy Bible: Commentary and Critical Notes* (Cincinnati, Ohio: Applegate and Co., 1828), 40f.
15. Jeffrey Burton Russell has written an outstanding series of books on Satan and personal evil, starting from antiquity through modern times. In his first book, *The Devil: Perceptions of Evil from Antiquity to Primitive Christianity,* he ascribes evil to God. (This is a New Age concept, whether or not Russell is aware of it.) Adopting an evolutionary view of the development of Hebrew theism, he affirms that God was both good and bad. When the Jews realized this was unacceptable to their view of God, they split God in two, "the good aspect of the God" became "the Lord." The "bad aspect" became "the Devil." He says the Jews thus unconsciously moved to absolute dualism (also a New Age concept.)
    I find this a totally unacceptable view of Hebrew theism.
    For a refutation of this and similar evolutionary views of the Hebrew faith see the superb books already mentioned by G. Ernest Wright, Professor of Old Testament History and Theology at Harvard University, entitled *The Old Testament Against Its Environment* and *The God Who Acts.*
16. Calvin, 168–169.
17. Matthew Henry, *Commentary on the Whole Bible* (London: Fleming H. Revell, 1935) 1:29.
18. Henry, 29–30.
19. Henry, 30.
20. Henry, 30.
21. Henry, 30.
22. Henry, 30–31.

Chapter 29: The Messianic Promise: Genesis 3:15

1. H. C. Leupold, *Exposition of Genesis* (Grand Rapids, Mich.: Baker, 1987), 163.
2. See Victor P. Hamilton, *The Book of Genesis: Chapters 1—17* (Grand Rapids, Mich.: Eerdmans, 1990), 197 for an outline of negative views.
3. Gordon J. Wenham, *Genesis 1—15*, WBC (Waco, Texas: Word, 1987), 80.
4. Wenham, 80.
5. Wenham, 80.
6. Wenham, 80–81.
7. The other authors I have referred to with great frequency hold to similar views, i.e., John Calvin, R. Payne Smith, Griffith Thomas, Adam Clarke, C. F. Keil and F. Delitzsch, John Peter Lange, Francis A. Schaeffer, Gordon Wenham, Victor Hamilton, H. C. Leupold, and Derek Kidner. Leupold says this not only in his commentary, but in his masterful overview of Genesis in *ZPEB* 2:678–695.
8. R. Payne Smith in Charles John Ellicott, *Bible Commentary for English Readers* (New York: Cassell and Company, 1954) 1:25.
9. Smith, 25.
10. Francis Schaeffer, *Genesis in Space and Time* (Downers Grove, Ill.: InterVarsity, 1976), 103.
11. Schaeffer, 103–104.
12. Schaeffer, 104.
13. Schaeffer, 104–105.
14. Schaeffer, 104–105.
15. Leupold, 164–165. Leupold says the Hebrew word for enmity here can only be used between persons or morally responsible agents, never of animals.
16. William E. Vine, *An Expository Dictionary of New Testament Words* (London, Oliphants, 1953) 1:147.

Chapter 30: The Beginning of Warfare Between the Two Seeds: Genesis 4:1–8

1. H. C. Leupold, *Exposition of Genesis* (Grand Rapids, Mich.: Baker, 1987), 189.
2. Leupold, 189–190, notation mine.
3. For the significance of Abel's name see Gordon J. Wenham, *Genesis 1—15*, WBC (Waco, Texas: Word, 1987), 102–103.
4. Wenham, 104.
5. Victor P. Hamilton, *The Book of Genesis: Chapters 1—17* (Grand Rapids, Mich.: Eerdmans, 1990); 222–223 Wenham, 104.
6. Wenham outlines the five major explanations given by most commentators, 104; Hamilton also gives various opinions, 223–224.
7. Wenham, 104.
8. See John Calvin, *Genesis* (Grand Rapids, Mich.: Baker, 1989), 194–196.
9. Hamilton, 224–225.
10. Wenham, 104.
11. Calvin, 197.
12. Hamilton tells why, 225–228, as does Wenham, 104–106.
13. Wenham, 105, and most other major commentators.
14. C. F. Keil and F. Delitzsch, *Exposition of Genesis* (Grand Rapids, Mich.: Baker, 1987) 1:112.
15. Hamilton, 227.
16. Wenham, 105. See his detailed discussion, 104–106.
17. Wenham, 106.
18. Hamilton, 227.
19. Keil and Delitzsch, 112.
20. Leupold, 202.
21. Leupold, 202.
22. Leupold, 202.
23. Wenham, 106.
24. For excellent commentary see Wenham, 106; Hamilton, 228–230; Calvin, 204–205; Leupold, 203–204; R. Payne Smith in Charles John Ellicott, *A Bible Commentary for English Readers* (New York: Cassell and Company) 1:29; Matthew Henry, *Commentary on the Whole Bible* (New York: Fleming H. Revell, 1935) 390–400; Adam Clark, *The Holy Bible: Commentary and Critical Notes* (Cincinnati, Ohio: Applegate and Company, 1857), 47; W. H. Griffith Thomas, *Genesis: A Devotional Commentary* (Grand Rapids, Mich.: Eerdmans, 1953), 57; W. P. Patterson in James Hasting's, *A Dictionary of the Bible* (Edinburg: T. and T.

Clark, 1910) 1:338–339; Rev. John McClintock and James Strong, *Encyclopedia of Biblical, Theological, and Ecclesiastical Literature* (New York: Harper and Brother Publishers, 1891) 2:12–14.
25. Hamilton, 230.
26. Leupold, 204.
27. Wenham, 106.
28. Keil and Delitzsch, 113.

Chapter 31: The "Watchers" of Genesis 6 and the Call of Noah
1. Walter Kaiser, *Toward Old Testament Ethics* (Grand Rapids, Mich.: Zondervan, 1983), 249.
2. Gordon J. Wenham, *Genesis 1—15*, WBC (Waco, Texas: Word, 1987), 136.
3. See Wenham for details.
4. G. H. Livingston in Merrill C. Tenney, ed., *ZPEB* (Grand Rapids, Mich.: Zondervan, 1977) 5:493–494.
5. Livingston, 493.
6. Livingston, 493–494.
7. See Victor P. Hamilton, *The Book of Genesis: Chapters 1—17* (Grand Rapids, Mich.: Eerdmans, 1990), 262–265; Wenham, 139–141; John Calvin, *Genesis* (Grand Rapids, Mich.: Baker, 1989), 237–239; C. F. Keil and F. Delitzsch, *Exposition of Genesis* (Grand Rapids, Mich.: Baker, 1987), 127–134.
8. Hamilton, 263–264.
9. Keil and Delitzsch, 128. For a thorough and fair presentation of this view, see Wenham, 139–140.
10. Wenham, 140. Many well-known scholars hold this position. A few examples are Merrill Unger, *Biblical Demonology* (Chicago, Ill.: Scripture Press, 1955), 45–52; J. Warwick Montgomery, *Principalities and Powers* (Minneapolis, Minn.: Bethany Fellowship, 1975), 50; Arno C. Gaebelein, *The Conflict of the Ages* (New York, N.Y.: Publication Office "Our Hope," 1933); Donald G. Barnhouse, *The Invisible War* (Grand Rapids, Mich.: Zondervan, 1965), 104–105.
11. C. Fred Dickason, *Angels, Elect and Evil* (Chicago, Ill.: Moody, 1975), 59.
12. See in the bibliography, Wagner, 1991a, 1991b, 1992; Jacobs, 1991; McAlpine, 1991.
13. See John E. Goldingay, *Daniel* (Waco, Texas: Word, 1989), 92–94, 96, 213–215, 290f; Joyce E. Baldwin, *Daniel* (Downers Grove, Ill.: InterVarsity, 1978), 112–113, 158f, 167, 178f; F. F. Bruce, *Hebrews*, in NICNT (Grand Rapids, Mich.: 1977), 33.
14. Jeffrey Burton Russell, *The Devil: Perceptions of Evil from Antiquity to Primitive Christianity* (Ithaca, N.Y.: Cornell University Press, 1987a), 170, 188 (see note 17, also), 191–197, 206, 208, 241, 246, 256. For a good, concise outline of the concept of watcher angels, see A. E. Hill's article in G. W. Bromiley, ed., *ISBE* (Grand Rapids, Mich.: Eerdmans, 1991) 4:1023–1024.
15. Wenham says that "the 'angel' interpretation is at once the oldest view and that of most modern commentators. It is assumed in the earliest Jewish exegesis (e.g., the books of 1 Enoch 6:2ff; Jubilees 5:1), LXX, Philo (De Gigant 2:358), Josephus (Ant. 1:31) and the Dead Sea Scrolls (1QapGen 2:1; CD 2:17–19). The New Testament (2 Peter 2:4, Jude 6,7) and the earliest Christian writers (e.g., Justin, Irenaeus, Clement of Alexandria, Tertullian, Origen) also take this line," 139.
16. Wenham, 139.
17. Wenham, 141.
18. Wenham, 141.
19. Wenham, 140.
20. The Sethite view is also the view of most of the highly acclaimed commentaries, both old and new, which I have been using in these studies in Genesis. A few outstanding examples are Calvin, Matthew Henry, Lange, Keil and Delitzsch, R. Payne Smith, Clark, and others.
21. Those in this category are Victor P. Hamilton; Derek Kidner, *Genesis* (Downers Grove, Ill.: InterVarsity,1967); Francis Schaeffer, *Genesis in Space and Time* (Downers Grove, Ill.: InterVarsity, 1976).
22. Kidner, 83.
23. Kidner, 84. For an excellent discussion of the Sethite versus the angelic view, see Keil and Delitzsch's extensive notes and footnotes (132–137). For a good summary of both views, and one of the most outstanding treatments of satanology and demonology in a systematic theology, see Lewis Sperry Chafer, *Systematic Theology* (Dallas, Texas: Dallas Seminary Press, 1947) 23. Whether or not one agrees with Chafer's dispensational view of the

Bible, few who write on systematic theology surpass Chafer's treatment of satanology and demonology. See also Lewis Sperry Chafer, *Satan—His Motive and Methods* (Grand Rapids, Mich.: Zondervan, 1969).

24. Kidner, 84.
25. Jeffrey Burton Russell, *Lucifer: The Devil in the Middle Ages* (Ithaca, N.Y.: Cornell University Press, 1986a), 206; see also 77, 181–183, 297; and Russell, 1987a, 73, 92–93, 194. In his book *Witchcraft in the Middle Ages* (Ithaca, N.Y.: Cornell University Press, 1985), his material on incubi and succubai is too extensive to even list. See his index (386, 392). Kurt Koch, *Christian Counseling and Occultism* (Grand Rapids, Mich.: Kregel Publications, 1978b), 162–164. Also see Keil and Delitzsch, 132–137; Chafer, 1957, 3:26.
26. Kidner, 83–84.
27. Wenham, 141–142; Hamilton, 266–269. Both discuss the difficulties with finding the best translation of this verse.
28. Hamilton, 266.
29. Keil and Delitzsch, 134.
30. Calvin, 240–241.
31. Wenham, 142.
32. Hamilton, 268–269.
33. W. B. Wallis writing on "Nephilim" in *ZPEB* 4:409 provides superb support for the position I take here. Writing about these men he says, "There is nothing demonic or mythological in the story." These men were born of normal human marriages.
34. Hamilton, 270.
35. H. C. Leupold, *Exposition of Genesis* (Grand Rapids, Mich.: Baker, 1987), 258.
36. Leupold, 258–259.
37. Leupold, 259.
38. Wallis, 409.

Chapter 32: Spiritual Warfare From the Flood to the Call of Abraham

1. I am assuming that the sons of God were not fallen watcher angels, but mortal men. As already mentioned, the main problem with the fallen angel view is the problem of incubi producing sperm, thus potentially creating angelic/human life and impregnating women, out of which union emerges a hybrid demon-man creature which is more manlike in his lifestyle than fallen angels. This is a major stumbling block to the acceptance of that ancient view. In almost twenty years of research and experience of expelling sexual demons from their human victims, even though some, both male and female, were, before their deliverance, regularly raped, or, in the case of consent, had regular sexual intercourse with incubi or succubi, demonic impregnation never occurred. While some sensationalistic books and movies have been built around this theme, I see no sound biblical, historical, or contemporary evidence for such phenomena.
2. John Calvin, Genesis (Grand Rapids, Mich.: Baker, 1987), 245.
3. Calvin, 324. Calvin criticizes some Jewish views which held to upwards 340 years.
4. Leupold says that "Noah lived 58 years after the birth of Abraham. Shem did not die until Jacob was 48 years old . . . Shem even outlived Abraham." H. C. Leupold, *Exposition of Genesis* (Grand Rapids, Mich.: Baker, 1987), 395–396.
5. See William LaSor in G. W. Bromiley ed., *ISBE* (Grand Rapids, Mich.: Eerdmans, 1991) 4:481.
6. See Gordon J. Wenham, *Genesis 1—15,* WBC (Waco, Texas: Word, 1987), 222–223, and Victor P. Hamilton, *The Book of Genesis: Chapters 1—17* (Grand Rapids, Mich.: Eerdmans, 1990), 337–339. Hamilton has a more positive view of Nimrod as a historic king than does Wenham. Calvin follows the more negative view of Nimrod as do most commentators including Leupold.
7. See the major prophets, especially Isaiah 14:1–23; also the last book of the Bible, Revelation, chapters 17–18.
8. Calvin, 316–320, and Leupold, 365–368, provide important commentary on this.
9. Leupold, 367.
10. Calvin, 316–320; also Wenham, 222.
11. Wenham, 245.
12. Wenham, 245.
13. Wenham, 242.

14. See further E. A. Speiser, "Word Plays on the Creation Epic's Version of the Founding of Babylon," in J. J. Finkelstein and M. Greenberg, ed., *Oriental and Biblical Studies*, (Philadelphia: University of Pennsylvania, 1967), 53–61; Hamilton, 352.
15. Calvin, 323–324.
16. Hamilton, 352.
17. M. J. A. Horsnell, writing on the religions of Assyria in Babylonia in the *ISBE* says, "Typical of a major temple complex was the ziggurat, a great man-made multi-staged mountain of earth and brick up to 90 m. (300 ft.) square and 45 m. (150 ft.) high (cf. Gen. 11:1–11, the tower of Babel). On its top, approached by long stairways (cf. the ladder in Jacob's dream in Gen. 28:12), was the 'high temple.' At the bottom was the 'low temple.' The significance of the ziggurat is unclear but it may have been perceived as a giant altar that provided a link between earth and heaven (cf. Ezek. 43:13–17, which describes an altar like a miniature stepped ziggurat). Others have seen it as the throne of the deity (cf. Isa. 14:13)" 4:85–95. See D. J. Wiseman in *ZPEB* 5:846–849.
18. Hamilton, 353.
19. Hamilton, 363.
20. A. A. MacRae in Merrill C. Tenney, ed., *ZPEB* (Grand Rapids, Mich.: Zondervan, 1977) 2:439.
21. F. W. Bush, "Plagues of Egypt" in *ISBE* 3:878–880.
22. The question of God hardening Pharaoh's heart has provoked controversy for centuries. All the commentaries and reference works cited in our study deal in depth with this troublesome issue. For my part, God is God. He does what He does and what He does is always just (Rom. 3:5–6) because He is God. He judges sin in His manner. Egypt is to be judged for its centuries of rebellion and idolatry. God will use the natural hardness of Pharaoh's heart to accomplish His righteous judgments upon this wicked nation. So He has done throughout history and will continue to do until the end.
23. Petros Octavianus, 1980, author's personal notes.
24. See G. Ernest Wright's view of *The God Who Acts* (London: SCM Press, Ltd., 1969). Most critical commentaries and reference works have excellent studies on the plagues and the religious encounter dimensions of the Exodus. We have already referred to the *ISBE* article by F. W. Bush on the Plagues of Egypt (3:878–880). See the *ISBE* articles on "The Book of Exodus," "Date of Exodus," "Route of Exodus," and the "Exodus" (2:222–241). See the *ZPEB* on "Exodus," "Book of Exodus," and "Plagues of Egypt" (4:805–807). Most helpful is Professor John I. Durham's commentary *Exodus*, WBC (Waco, Texas: Word, 1987) and Alan Cole, *TOTC* (Downers Grove, Ill.: InterVarsity, 1973).
25. See Wenham, 221; Leupold, 364f.
26. See Wenham, 220–227; Hamilton, 330–348.
27. See Wenham, 221–222.
28. Hamilton, 336. Wenham agrees, 221.
29. For a discussion of Canaan's boundaries see Numbers 33:2–12 and Aharoni, *The Land of the Bible* (London: Burns and Oates, 1966), 61–70, 221. See also Hamilton, 336.

Chapter 33: Warfare With the Gods

1. M. J. A. Horsnell, "Religions of the Biblical World: Assyria and Babylonia" in G. W. Bromiley, ed., *ISBE* (Grand Rapids, Mich.: Eerdmans, 1989) 4:85–89. His article is superb.
2. Horsnell, 86.
3. See H. A. Hoffner, Jr., "Dagon" and H. G. Stigers, "Dagon, Temples of" in Merrill C. Tenney, ed., *ZPEB* (Grand Rapids, Mich.: Zondervan, 1977) 2:2–6. Most of the article is on the role of Dagon within Philistine culture. It does, however, cover the origin of the cult in the Euphrates Valley.
4. Horsnell, 87.
5. Horsnell, 87.
6. Horsnell, 87–91.
7. Horsnell, 92.
8. Some commentators try to escape the problem of Abraham's pagan background by pointing out that while the Scriptures speak of the idolatry of Abraham's ancestors and family they never specifically speak of Abraham as being an idolater and polytheist. I don't believe this argument fits the general thrust of Genesis 11—12 and Joshua 24.
   First, Joshua does not separate Abraham from the sins of the "fathers." By implication he includes Abraham as participating in the general lifestyle of his pagan family (Josh. 24:2–3,14).

Second, this is the whole point behind this and other dramatic accounts of God's election. God calls whom He will, which means He always calls undeserving sinners, usually the least expected.

9. W. S. LaSor, "Religions of the Biblical World: Egypt" in *ISBE* 4:101–107.
10. Gordon J. Wenham, *Genesis 1—15*, WBC (Waco, Texas: Word, 1987), 225.
11. Victor J. Hamilton, *The Book of Genesis: Chapters 1—17* (Grand Rapids, Mich.: Eerdmans, 1990), 341.
12. Wenham, 226.
13. A. E. Cundall, "Baal" in *ZPEB* 1:431–433.
14. Cundall, 432.
15. Cundall, 432.
16. Ashtoreth was her most popular name. She was also known as Ashtoroth (the plural), Ishtar, Aphrodite, Athah, Naaman, Asthart, Astarte, Venus, Astarter, Atargatis, and Asheroth (see A. E. Cundall, W. White, Jr., "Ashtoreth" in *ZPEB* 1:359–361, and A. H. Sayce and K. G. Jung, "Ashtoreth" in *ISBE* 1:319–320.
17. W. White, Jr., in *ZPEB* 1:359–361. See also A. H. Sayce and K. G. Jung in *ISBE* 1:319–320.
18. White. 359.
19. The writer found parts of two Asthoreth figurines while searching through piles of pottery and other debris discarded by archaeologists near the ancient site of Bet Shean in Galilee (with the archaeologists' permission). Both had grossly exaggerated breasts, which White refers to in his article, 1:359–361.
20. White, 360. See White's interesting discussion of the myths of Inanna and Isthar, 360.
21. The reader will find a reasonably good but brief overview in E. M. Yamauchi's article "Fertility Cults" in *ZPEB* 2:531–532.
22. White, 360.
23. White, 361.
24. Hamilton, 436.
25. Derek Kidner, *Genesis*, TOTC (Downers Grove, Ill.: InterVarsity, 1967), 125.

Chapter 34: The Low Point in Spiritual Warfare: Human Sacrifice

1. See Leviticus 17:7, Deuteronomy 32:16–18.
2. Simon J. DeVries in his commentary on 1 Kings in the Word series reveals his world view problems with this passage. He says the lying spirit is "the spirit (. . . evidently the spirit of prophetic inspiration, personified) who does the deceiving." He does not identify it as a lying, demonic spirit (*I Kings*, WBC [Waco, Texas: Word, 1985], 268).
3. See Matthew Henry's further insights, *Commentary on the Whole Bible* (New York: Fleming H. Revell, 1935) 2:702–704.
4. E. E. Carpenter, "Human Sacrifice" in G. W. Bromiley, ed., *ISBE* (Grand Rapids, Mich.: Eerdmans, 1989) 4:258–260.
5. Carpenter, 259.
6. Lawrence E. Stager and Samuel R. Wolff, "Child Sacrifice at Carthage—and in the Bible" *Biblical Archaelogy Review* (January—February, 1984) 30–51. The following scripture quotations are these authors' translations.
7. Stager and Wolff, 32.
8. The animals were seen as substitutes for the sacrifice of children. Strange as it may seem, as Phoenician culture advanced, child sacrifice increased in relationship to substitute animal sacrifices. See the *BAR* article for a thorough insight into this hideous practice of parents sacrificing their own children to the gods, particularly to Baal and his consort "Tanit Ashtart." *BAR* calls it "the bloody cult," 48.
9. Carpenter, 259.
10. Stager and Wolff, 32ff.
11. Yet syncretism was the number one problem which God had to deal with in the life of His fickle people from before the time of Abraham until the Exile. If he had dealt with them on New Testament standards few would have been saved. He accepted men where He found them and worked across centuries through His power, His prophets, and His Word to gradually bring them to Himself, free from the demonic deceptions of counterfeit religions and religious experiences and the immorality of the flesh and the lusts and vain glory of the world. How else can we explain Abraham's pagan religious early life (assumed), occasional lying, adultery with Hagar (Was it right in God's eyes for His man to have a wife and a concubine or practice polygamy? See Walter C. Kaiser, *Toward Old Testament Ethics* (Grand Rapids, Mich.: Zondervan, 1983), 181f). Would Jacob's lifestyle be accepted

today? He was, for years, a deceiver, a liar, a polygamist. His son Judah visited a temple prostitute and was guilty of incest (Gen. 38:12) and kept concubines. What about "the foreign gods" found among his family members, including his beloved Rachel (Gen. 31,34)? God said nothing about these moral and religious failures in the beginning. He has plenty to say about them today, however (see Don Richardson, *Eternity in Their Hearts* [Ventura, Calif.: Regal, 1982b].

12. Carpenter, 259–260.

Chapter 35: Of Kings and Prophets

1. Personal notes by the author written while listening to Dr. Mouw at Biola University in the early 1950s.
2. I say "the world" because Saul was acting exactly like the world of his day said a monarch should act. In fact, Saul at his worst was a saint in comparison to the kings of his day. Thus, Saul was facing and losing a multidimensional sin war, i.e., warfare with the flesh, the world, and as we will soon discover, with evil supernaturalism.
3. Again we discover the spirit world as seen throughout the grid of the Old Testament world view. Demonic spirits, even Satan himself (Job 1—2) cannot severely harass or demonize a sinning believer unless given direct permission by God. Thus the Old Testament writers describe the evil spirit as "an evil spirit from the Lord" (16:14; 18:10; 19:9) (See our discussion of this issue in the last chapter).
4. Ralph W. Klein, *I Samuel,* WBC (Waco, Texas: Word, 1983), 165. His insightful words on pages 165–167 are excellent, distinguishing between David and Saul at this point.
5. See Klein's discussion of the cultural context of this musical "exorcism" of evil spirits, 165–166.
6. I am indebted to my former professor of anthropology, the late Dr. Allan Tippett, for ideas for my study of 1 Kings 18 and Isaiah 57. I heard him give a lecture on both chapters many years ago.
7. See Lawrence E. Stager and Samuel R. Wolff, "Child Sacrifice at Carthage—and in the Bible" *Biblical Archaeology Review* (January—February, 1984) 39–43.
8. Mention should be made of the popular use of indirect references to the fall of Satan in Isa. 14 and Ezek. 28. This practice is unwise. Both passages were written in a given cultural context to convey a specific understandable message to the readers who felt intimidated by the presence of powerful, but wicked rulers, the king of Babylon (Isaiah 14:4) and the king of Tyre (Ezek. 28:2f).

   John D. Watts in his excellent treatment of Isaiah 14 (*Isaiah 1—33,* WBC [Waco, Texas: Word, 1985], 205–212) says this is a mythological poem, probably of Canaanite origin, used here to refer to the yet future fall of the king of Babylon and his co-tyrants. He says its use by some of the church fathers and modern commentators to refer to the fall of Lucifer has no support from the text itself. He states. "When the poem has been used in apocryphal and Christian circles to picture the fall of an angelic Satan, the reference must be to the shadowy mythical background of the poem rather than to the poem itself. It is significant that the account of the fall of Satan (Rev. 12) makes no reference to Isaiah 14" (212).

   This is an acceptable view. As a "shadowy mythological" poem it can be used to illustrate how Satan, as a tyrant ruler aspiring to be like God, was cast out of heaven. However, why not use Revelation 12:3f for the fall of Satan? It does not matter how we view this passage, either as history or prophecy yet to be fulfilled, the story is the same. (See also Luke 10:18.)

   What we have said about Isaiah 14 also applies to Ezekiel 28. This is the account of the fall of the ambitious arrogant king/ruler of Tyre. He, too, sees himself as God or a god. "I am a god," he says, "I sit in the seat of gods" (or "God," NAS marginal note).

   It was a common practice for powerful rulers to see themselves as a god in those days. Some took on the name of a god. They even tried to have their divinity accepted among their subjects. We are all familiar with this practice in both Egyptian and Roman history. This same arrogant pretense to be a god was characteristic of rulers like the king's of Babylon and Tyre. Isaiah had spoken about the Egyptians, perhaps referring to their god-kings in this manner; "now the Egyptians are men and not God" (Isa. 31:3).

   Leslie C. Allen in his commentary on Ezekiel (Leslie C. Allen, *Ezekiel 20—48,* WBC [Waco, Texas: Word, 1990], 93–95) says Ezekiel 28 clearly is dealing with the king of Tyre. He says, "The target of Ezekiel's judgment oracle [there are two separate oracles, vv. 1–11,12–29] is the ruler of Tyre, Ethball II. His claim centers in the impregnability of his island city and the survival of his power. These claims were doubtless echoed by or attributed to him by Tyrian exiles known to Ezekiel and his Jewish compatriots in Babylon."

Allen then comments, "for Ezekiel they constituted a challenge to God and His ongoing purposes. . . . The self-confidence of the king . . . was an attitude of proud defiance against Yahweh, as well as against Nebuchadnezzar. . . . Whether an ancient, Near Eastern concept of divine kinship has contributed to the imagery . . . is by no means certain" (93).

Allen ends his study by referring to the application of 28:11–15 to Satan by the third and fourth century church fathers, Tertullian, Origen, John Cassian, Cyril of Jerusalem, and Jerome. He says this is an erroneous view. "It is a case of exegeting an element of Christian belief by means of Scripture and endeavoring to provide it with extrabiblical warrant and to fit the passage into the framework of the Christian faith. However, it is guilty of detaching the passage from its literary setting."

Chapter 36: The Temptation

1. Most of the major books on spiritual warfare have good studies on the person, character, and activity of the Devil. Most outstanding are *Angels, Elect and Evil* by C. Fred Dickason; "Satanology" and "Demonology" in Lewis Sperry Chafer's *Systematic Theology* and Chafer's *Satan—His Motives and Methods; The Invisible War* by Donald Barnhouse; *Satan, His Personality, Power and Overthrow* by E. M. Bounds; *I Believe in Satan's Downfall* by Michael Green; *Satan Cast Out* by Leahy; *The Devil: Perceptions of Evil from Antiquity to Primitive Christianity* by Jeffrey Burton Russell; *Satan: The Early Church Tradition* by Jeffrey Burton Russell; *Unmasking the Powers* by Walter Wink. Daniel P. Fuller's overview of "Satan" in G. W. Bromiley, ed., *ISBE* (Grand Rapids, Mich.: Eerdmans, 1989) 4:340–344 and D. E. Hiebert's overview in Merrill C. Tenney, ed., *ZPEB* (Grand Rapids, Mich.: Zondervan, 1977) 5:282–286 are excellent. Both contain excellent bibliographies.
2. Jeffrey Burton Russell, *The Devil: Perceptions of Evil from Antiquity to Primitive Christianity* (Ithaca, N.Y.: Cornell University Press, 1987a), 174. For an exhaustive historical study of the person of the Devil there is nothing to compare with the five-volume set by Jeffrey Burton Russell. *Lucifer: The Devil in the Middle Ages* (1986a); *Mephistopheles: The Devil In the Modern World* (1986b); *The Devil: Perceptions of Evil from Antiquity to Primitive Christianity* (1987a); *Satan: The Early Christian Tradition* (1987b); *The Prince of Darkness: Radical Evil and the Power of Good in History* (1988). All are published by Cornell University Press in Ithaca, New York.

   Russell does not hold a high view of Scripture. As a result he takes great liberty as he handles the Old Testament text and in his evolutionary syncretistic views of Satan and demons in both the Old and New Testament. His books are for scholars and historians. In spite of the faults mentioned above they are in a class by themselves, surpassing anything else in print today.
3. See Gordon Wenham, *Genesis 1—15*, WBC (Waco, Texas: Word, 1987), 41–91.
4. Jeffrey Burton Russell in interview by Michael G. Maudlin, "The Life and Times of the Prince of Darkness," *Christianity Today* (August 20, 1990) 21.
5. Russell, 1987a, 174.
6. Russell, 1987a, 227.
7. Russell, 1987a, 221–222 in a footnote.
8. Clinton E. Arnold, "Giving the Devil His Due," *Christianity Today* (August 20, 1990). It is in the same edition of *Christianity Today* as the interview with Jeffrey Burton Russell entitled "The Life and Times of the Prince of Darkness." For both a brief historical overview of the concept of the Devil and a brief overview of the Devil's place in Scripture the two articles are superb. Clinton Arnold has also written an excellent book called *Ephesians: Power and Magic* (Cambridge: Cambridge University Press, 1989), 17. I use it in later studies in this book.
9. Kenneth S. Wuest, *Wuest's Word Studies* (Grand Rapids, Mich.: Eerdmans, 1983) 1:26.
10. John A. Broadus, *Matthew* (Valley Forge, Penn.: Judson Press, 1886), 279.
11. Wuest, 1:25–26.
12. C. L. Blomberg, "Temptation of Jesus," in *ISBE* 4:784–786.
13. Most critical commentators have excellent material on the temptation accounts. G. W. Bromiley in *ISBE* 4:784–786, and Merrill C. Tenney in *ZPEB* 5:671–672 give outstanding overviews. For detailed and reverent studies of the temptation story, nothing surpasses Rev. Alfred Edersheim's commentary found in his classic *The Life and Times of Jesus the Messiah,* (New York: Longmans, Green and Company, 1899, Book 3, 1:291–307), and

G. Campbell Morgan's *The Crises of the Christ* (New York: Fleming H. Revell, 1936), 149–210.

14. Broadus handles this issue well, 63, as does Morgan.
15. Wuest, 25.
16. A. B. Bruce in W. Robertson Nicoll, *The Expositor's Greek New Testament* (Grand Rapids, Mich.: Eerdmans) 1:343.
17. Bruce, 343–344.
18. For a fascinating article on Satan's pseudo-logic revealed in the temptation story, see C. G. Kehn, "Discerning the Devil's Deductions," *Christianity Today* (November 10, 1972) 10–12.
19. Broadus, 64–65.
20. Norval Geldenhuys, *Commentary on the Gospel of Luke*, NICNT (Grand Rapids, Mich.: Eerdmans, 1977), 162–163; also William Barclay, *Matthew*, The Daily Study Bible (Philadelphia: Westminster, 1958) 1:62.
21. Bruce, 90.
22. P. D. Johnson, "Temptation of Christ" in *ZPEB* 5:671–672; Broadus, 65; Barclay, 62–63.
23. See Barclay for his fascinating ideas, 62–63.
24. John Calvin, *Calvin's Commentaries* (Grand Rapids, Mich.: Baker, 1989) 13:217–218.
25. Broadus, 67.
26. Bruce, 487.
27. Broadus, 68.
28. James Morrison, *A Practical Commentary on the Gospel According to Matthew* (London: Hodder and Stoughton, 1985), 50.
29. Bruce, 488.
30. Geldenhuys, 163.
31. Geldenhuys, 163.

Chapter 37: In the Synagogue: Mark 1

1. George E. Ladd, *A Theology of the New Testament* (Grand Rapids, Mich., 1983), 66–67.
2. See Robert A. Guelich, *Mark 1—8:26*, WBC (Dallas, Texas: Word, 1989), 55–56.
3. R. Alan Cole, *Mark*, TNTC (Grand Rapids, Mich.: Eerdmans, 1983), 61.
4. One of the great advantages to the believer in receiving "user friendly" teaching about spiritual warfare is that he can, alone, or with a James 5:16 prayer-share-healing partner, begin to learn self-deliverance. Many have experienced this with my spiritual warfare cassette tape series and have contacted me to share their testimony.

    Just as I was writing this chapter I received a long letter from a Christian counselor. He writes with great joy, that the tape series helped him identify the doors through which terribly abusive demons had entered his life as a child and teenager. Through self-deliverance he is now free. What a difference this should make not only in his own life but in the life of those he counsels. Praise the Lord!

    Some have even been set free while driving in their car. Demons do not seem to be allowed by God to disturb their driving so as to injure or kill them. In these cases the exodus of the demons will usually begin without serious bodily disturbances, allowing the person to get to a safer place to continue the process. Since deliverance is usually a process, not a once-and-for-all instant event, the process may continue for a short period of time.
5. Cole, 61.
6. *Greek-English New Testament* (Washington, D.C.: Christianity Today Publishers, 1976), 71–74.
7. William L. Lane, *Commentary on the Gospel of Mark*, NICNT (Grand Rapids, Mich.: Eerdmans, 1975), 73.
8. Guelich, 56.
9. Kenneth S. Wuest, *Wuest's Word Studies* (Grand Rapids, Mich.: Eerdmans, 1983), 33.
10. Lane, 73.
11. William E. Vine, *An Expository Dictionary of New Testament Words* (London: Oliphants, 1953) 1:302.
12. Vine 1:302, and 4:144.
13. Wuest, 33.
14. Wuest, 33–34.
15. Wuest, 34.

16. Lane, 76.
17. Wuest, 35.

Chapter 38: Among the Tombs: Mark 5

1. Joachim Jeremias, *The Proclamation of Jesus* (New York: Charles Scribners and Sons, 1971), 85–96.
2. Jeremias, 93.
3. Jeremias, 93–94.
4. Merrill F. Unger, *What Demons Can Do to Saints* (Chicago: Moody, 1977), 129.
5. Alfred Edersheim, *The Life and Times of Jesus the Messiah* (New York: Longmans, Green, and Company, 1889) 1:607.
6. Whenever Jesus had personal contact with non-Jews, the Gospel writers are careful to tell us (Mark 7:24–30; Matt. 8:5–13; John 12:20–21). Also at this stage in His ministry our Lord's mission was primarily a Jewish mission (Matt. 15:24).
7. There are primarily two broad methods of establishing truth (theology) from Scripture. There is the inductive method. One starts with the particular and moves towards forming conclusions, i.e., generalizations. This is the so-called scientific method. We examine enough facts to be able to form general conclusions. The conclusions are always to be open to the critique of new factual discoveries, however. This is the only way to formulate biblical theology. Then there is deduction. We start with a presupposition or a previously proved statement (the latter is the ideal; the former is the problem) and examine each particular in light of the general. This is the method used in syllogistic thinking, as we will see in later studies. It has serious built-in weaknesses, however. It must be used very carefully or we will arrive at erroneous conclusions.
8. One reason I mention this is because this story is continually used by writers to draw up a list of the symptoms of demonization. This is an inaccurate approach to the story. At the most it can be used only to draw up a suggested list of some of the symptoms of some of the most severe forms of demonization in a religious adult male or perhaps, more accurately, of a first-century Jewish religious adult male. While I may be going too far in saying this because there are supracultural elements here, yet I am disturbed at an inductive approach which ignores the uniqueness of this account.
9. William Barclay, *The Gospel of Mark,* The Daily Study Bible (Philadelphia: Westminster, 1958), 116–117.
10. Mark 1:23,26–27,34,39; 3:11,15,22,30; 5:2,8; 6:7,13; 7:25–26,29–30; 9:17–25,38; 16:5,17.
11. Edersheim, 607–609.
12. Robert A. Guelich, *Mark 1—8:26* (Waco, Texas: Word, 1989), 278.
13. Edersheim, 479.
14. Kenneth S. Wuest, *Wuest's Word Studies* (Grand Rapids, Mich.: Eerdmans, 1983), 101.
15. William E. Vine, *An Expository Dictionary of New Testament Words* (London: Oliphants, 1953) 1:263–264.
16. Wuest, 101.
17. See Larry W. Hurtado, *Mark* (Peabody, Mass.: Hendrickson, 1989), 71–87, for his ideas why Jesus forbid demons to reveal who He was.
18. See Wuest, 102–103; Guelich, 279; John Calvin, *Calvin's Commentaries* (Grand Rapids, Mich.: Baker, 1989), 430f.
19. R. Alan Cole, *Mark* (Peabody, Mass.: Hendrickson, 1989), 27–28.
20. Cole, 97–98.
21. Wuest, 103.
22. Guelich, 279.
23. Guelich, 279.
24. Guelich, 280–281; Cole, 98.
25. Barclay, 118.
26. Barclay, 118.
27. Guelich, 281.
28. Hurtado, 71.
29. Barclay, 118.
30. Hurtado, 71.
31. William L. Lane, *Commentary on the Gospel of Mark* (Grand Rapids, Mich.: Eerdmans, 1975), 185.
32. A. A. Bruce, *The Synoptic Gospels* (Grand Rapids, Mich.: Eerdmans), 372.

33. In a footnote, Lane mentions H. Ridderbos' book *The Coming Kingdom* (Philadelphia, 1962, 113–115), which gives a survey of seven principal interpretations of the swine incident, 186.
34. Guelich, 282.
35. Hurtado, 84.
36. Wuest, 103.
37. Vine 2:156.
38. Bruce, 37.
39. Vine 2:327.
40. Cole, 98–99.
41. Barclay, 119.
42. John A. Broadus, *Matthew* (Valley Forge, Penn.: Judson Press, 1886), 192.
43. Wuest, 106.
44. Bruce, 373.
45. John Hunter, *Impact* (Fort Washington, Penn.: Christian Literature Crusade, 1966), 114–115.

Chapter 39: Foundations and Lessons From a Failure: Mark 9

1. Robert A. Guelich, *Mark 1—8:26*, WBC (Waco, Texas: Word, 1989), 321.
2. Larry W. Hurtado, *Mark* (Peabody, Mass.: Hendrickson, 1989), 61–62.
3. William E. Vine, *An Expository Dictionary of New Testament Words* (London, Oliphants, Ltd., 1953) 2:37.
4. Vine 1:188.
5. Several books on spiritual warfare give accounts of ministry to demonized children. A few good books on spiritual warfare in reference to children are now in print. John Bibee's *Spirit Flyer Series for Children* (InterVarsity Press, 6 vols.) contain spiritual warfare teachings for children. Dr. James Wilder's book *A Redemptive Response to Satanism* (see bibliography) is written to help parents guide their children safely through the present revival of Satanism and witchcraft cults which is occurring in our day. Another excellent book on ministering to children by my friend Neil Anderson is *The Seduction of Our Children* (Eugene, Ore.: Harvest House, 1991c).
6. Vine 2:291.
7. James Morrison, *A Practical Commentary on the Gospel According to Matthew* (London: Hodder and Stoughton, 1895), 303, 306.
8. Morrison, 307.
9. Morrison, 307.

Chapter 40: The Success of the Seventy: Luke 10

1. Norval Geldenhuys, *Commentary on the Gospel of Mark*, NICNT (Grand Rapids, Mich.: Eerdmans, 1977), 306.
2. Geldenhuys, 307.
3. Leon Morris, *Luke* (Grand Rapids, Mich.: Eerdmans, 1983), 185.
4. Geldenhuys, 302.
5. Geldenhuys, 302.
6. Geldenhuys, 302–305.
7. William E. Vine, *An Expository Dictionary of New Testament Words* (London, Oliphants, 1953) 3:196–197.
8. I have made an extensive list of the Psalms whose major focus is on spiritual warfare, a deeply instructive and comforting study. David's enemies can be seen as flesh and blood alone or as flesh and blood as the agents of the principalities and powers operating through them.
9. Rev. E. H. Plumtree in Charles John Ellicott, *A Bible Commentary for English Readers* (New York: Cassell and Company) 6:292.
10. Matthew Henry, *Commentary on the Whole Bible* (New York: Fleming H. Revell, 1935), 683. Many spiritual warfare books focus on the offensive as well as the defensive spiritual warfare ministry of the spiritual warrior (see Jacobs, 1991; Christenson, 1990, 93–192; Wagner's books; Bubeck's books; Tom White, 1990; Warner, 1991, 77f; Kraft, 1989, 133f; to mention a few outstanding ones).

Chapter 41: Beginnings in Acts: Acts 2, 4

1. Dr. Arthur Glasser, "Satan's Attacks in Acts" from personal notes taken by author, 1976.
2. For excellent discussion of what is commonly called the "Johannine question" see Leon Morris' overview on the gospel of John in *ISBE* 2:1098–1107 and also I. H. Marshall's superb overview of Johannine theology, also in *ISBE* 2:1081–1091. Morris also does a study on John the apostle in the same volume, 1107–1108. Morris has written one of the greatest commentaries in print today on the gospel of John in NICNT. There is nothing quite like it in both scholarship and fidelity to John's gospel as the Word of God. Donald Guthrie's article, "Johannine Theology" in *ZPEB* 3:623–636 is also excellent. R. E. Hayden does a masterful study on "John, Gospel of" in the same volume, 657–674, and G. A. Turner on "John, The Apostle," 637–641. All are outstanding.
3. For example we have Paul's synagogue ministry given in detail in Acts 13. After that, little detail is ever mentioned about his ongoing synagogue ministry. Acts 14:1,17 are examples. In the latter Luke writes, "According to Paul's custom." The same applies to his preaching to all Gentile crowds. The major example is Athens (Acts 17:22f). A condensed version is given in Acts 14:14–18. After that mention is made that he preached to Gentiles but no further outline of his message is given.
4. John Wimber with Kevin Springer, *Power Evangelism* (San Francisco: Harper & Row, 1986).
5. John Wimber with Kevin Springer, *Power Healing* (San Francisco: Harper & Row, 1987).
6. F. F. Bruce, *The Book of Acts,* NICNT (Grand Rapids, Mich.: Eerdmans, 1977), 96.
7. R. J. Knowling in W. Robertson Nicoll, *Expositor's Greek New Testament—The Acts of the Apostles* (Grand Rapids, Mich.: Eerdmans, no date), 125.
8. Walter Wink, *Naming the Powers* (Philadelphia: Fortress, 1984), 161.
9. See G. F. Hawthorne, "Name," *ISBE* 3:481–483 and Walter C. Kaiser, Jr.'s, equally excellent study in *ZPEB* 4:360–366.
10. Hawthorne, 481.
11. Hawthorne, 482–483.
12. Hawthorne, 482–483.
13. Wink, 1984, 20–21.
14. Wink, 21–22.
15. John Bright, *The Kingdom of God* (New York: Abington, 1952), 218.
16. William B. Barclay, *Acts of the Apostles,* The Daily Study Bible (Philadelphia: Westminster, 1958–1960), 122.

Chapter 42: Ananias and Sapphira: Acts 5

1. During the first 14 years of the history of the Jerusalem church recorded in Acts the church evidently experienced four major persecutions: Acts 3—4; Acts 5:17–42; Acts 6:8—8:3a and 9:1–2; Acts 12:1–24. These four cover a time period from A.D. 30 to A.D. 44. (See F. F. Bruce, *ISBE* 1:42–43 for further insight.)
2. The word *Satan,* as we have seen, is a translation of the Greek word meaning "adversary." As we have repeatedly observed, he is revealed in the Scripture as the adversary of God (Matt. 4:1–11; 12:26–29; Luke 22:3–4; Acts 10:38), and humanity (Luke 13:10–16; Acts 26:18; 2 Thess. 2:9–10; 1 John 2:7–8; 5:18–19; Rev. 20:1–10). He is especially the adversary of God's people, however (Luke 22:31; Rom. 16:20; 1 Cor. 5:5; 7:5; 2 Cor. 2:11; 11:3,13–15; 12:7; 1 Thess. 2:18; 1 Tim. 1:19–20; Rev. 12:9–13).
3. William E. Vine, *An Expository Dictionary of New Testament Words* (London: Oliphants, 1953) 2:96.
4. William Barclay, *The Acts of the Apostles,* The Daily Study Bible (Philadelphia: Westminster, 1955), 42–43.
5. While working on this chapter I received a fascinating letter from Rev. Kent Yinger, OC Director for Europe dated December 13, 1991. He lives in Germany. He writes, "I recently ran across an interesting news item in a German evangelical publication (*idea-Spektrum* from the German Evangelical Alliance, Issue #49, 1991, p. 8), which I thought would interest you. It says: 'The three exorcists of the Catholic Church in Italy don't know what to do any longer with the great flood of telephone calls: about 600 people per day call up, because they believe they are possessed by the devil. The head exorcist, Father Gabriel Amorth, who gave this information added, "One could truly speak of a 'satanic emergency situation'"."

This is further proof that we are living in a day of renewed demonic activity, world wide. Whether or not these 600 persons a day are truly demonized is to beg the point.

They are all troubled people. They are aware that demons can invade the bodies of human beings, even church members. We must minister to them the liberating power of Christ's victory of the powers.

6. I give more detail about SRA in chapter 58. The readers will find excellent accurate material in James G. Friesen's *Uncovering The Mystery of MPD* (Friesen, 1991). Note his chapter entitled "Satanic Ritual Abuse," 69–104. It thoroughly analyzes Satanism, occultism in general, and satanic cults. Also very important is Dr. James Wilder's *A Redemptive Response to Satanism* (1992). The *Passport Magazine* special edition called "America's Best Kept Secret" is the best expose in shortened form (1986). All contain bibliographies and sources for further examination of this ultimate evil.

7. In the case of MPD there is evidence one alter can do evil, even committing serious crimes such as murder, without the host personality even being aware of it. If so, this will cause a revolution in our judicial system in the future. In this sense, some alter personalities may be even more dangerous than demons. Such wicked alters are probably all demonized. If so, the demons are ultimately the source of the evil practiced by the alter. All of this represents an area of research desperately crying for attention. Neil Anderson, in his superb book *Released From Bondage* (1991b) raises some crucial questions about ministry to multiples.

Chapter 43: Philip's Ministry at Samaria and Peter's Encounter with Simon Magus: Acts 8

1. For an excellent study of Samaria see the detailed studies in Merrill C. Tenney, ed., *ZPEB* (Grand Rapids, Mich.: Zondervan, 1977) "Samaria, City of," 232–240; "Samaria, Territory of," 240–242; "Samaritans," 244–247; and "The Samaritan Penteteuch" by A. A. MacRae 5:242–244. Also in G. W. Bromiley, ed., *ISBE* (Grand Rapids, Mich.: Eerdmans, 1989) see "Samaria" by A. Van Selms, 295–298; "Samaria, Country of" by W. S. LaSor, 298–303; and "Samaritans" by R. T. Anderson 4:303–308.

2. See F. F. Bruce, *The Book of Acts* (Grand Rapids, Mich.: Eerdmans, 1977), 178–180; D. E. Aune, "Simon Magus," in *ISBE* 4:516–518; B. F. Harris, "Simon Magus," in *ZPEB* 5:442–444; I. Howard Marshall, *Acts* (Grand Rapids, Mich.: Eerdmans, 1983), 155–160, all for excellent studies on the life of Simon Magus and his impact on church history.

3. Harris, 443. See also B. F. Harris, "Magic and Sorcery" in *ZPEB* 4:35–37; and J. K. Kelso, "Magician" in *ZPEB* 4:37–38.

4. D. E. Aune, "Magic: Magician" in *ISBE* 3:213–219.

5. Aune 3:218.

6. Aune 3:218–219.

7. Aune 3:219.

8. Aune 3:219. Aune notes that the charge that Jesus was a magician has also been preserved outside the New Testament in both pagan and Jewish traditions. Jewish sources: T. B. Sanhedrin 43a; cf. Klausner, 18–47; pagan traditions: Origen Contra Clesum i.6, 38; Koran 5:113.

9. Aune 3:219.

10. Aune 3:219. See his excellent outline of the Old Testament polemic against magic, 214–216.

11. Harris, 443.

12. Argentina, South America is a country where evangelism through power encounter is flourishing today. It has not always been that way. I served as a missionary in Argentina from 1958–1962 when it was one of the most resistant nations to the gospel in the world. All that began to change in the 1980s (see in bibliography Silvoso, 1987, 1989; and Wagner 1991, 1991a, 1991b, 1992).

   Argentina is now in the midst of a dramatic spiritual awakening. All is being led by Argentine Christian leaders, not by missionaries. Among the men God has raised up are Carlos Annacondia and Rev. Omar Cabrera. Both engage in mass evangelism crusades where they encounter the spirits continually.

13. Harris, 443.

14. Harris, 442.

15. Alexander Whyte, *Bible Characters* (London: Oliphants, Ltd.) 6:197–198.

16. Acts 8:10 according to Walter Wink, *Naming the Powers* (Philadelphia: Fortress, 1984), 161.

17. Aune, 4:517–518; also Harris, 442–444.

18. Whyte, 201–202.

Chapter 44: Paul's Encounter With Elymas and the Spirit
Medium of Philippi: Acts 13, 16

1. For an excellent study of Paul's encounter with Elymas the magician, see John Calvin, *Acts* (Grand Rapids, Mich.: Baker, 1989) 18:505–512.
2. F. F. Bruce, *The Book of Acts*, NICNT (Grand Rapids, Mich.: Eerdmans, 1977), 264.
3. William M. Ramsay, *St. Paul, The Traveler and Roman Citizen* (Grand Rapids, Mich.: Baker, 1962), 76.
4. For the distinction between these three areas of reality, see Bronislaw Malinowski's classic *Magic, Science and Religion* (Garden City, N.Y.: Doubleday Anchor Books, 1954).
5. Ramsay, 78–79.
6. Bruce, 140.
7. Thomas Walker, *The Acts of the Apostles* (Chicago: Moody, 1965), 285.
8. I. Howard Marshall, *Acts*, TNTC (Grand Rapids, Mich.: Eerdmans, 1983), 219–220.
9. Ramsay, 79.
10. Ramsay, 81.
11. William E. Vine, *An Expository Dictionary of New Testament Words* (London: Oliphants, 1953) 2:275.
12. Vine 4:187–188.
13. Vine 3:333.
14. Chrysostom in Bruce, 265.
15. Vine 3:77.
16. Walker, 287.
17. The *ISBE* has one of the most outstanding summaries of the religions of the biblical world in print today (G. W. Bromiley, ed. [Grand Rapids, Mich.: Eerdmans, 1989], 4:79–129). Of special importance for this study is the article on the religions of Asia Minor, 79–84, and of the Greco-Roman world, 107–117.
18. Bruce, 333.
19. Bruce, 332.
20. R. J. Knowling, *The Acts of the Apostles*, in W. Robertson Nicoll, *Expositor's Greek New Testament* (Grand Rapids, Mich.: Eerdmans) 2:347.
21. Vine 1:266.
22. Knowling, 348.
23. Richard B. Rackham, *The Acts of the Apostles* (London: Methuen and Company, Ltd., 1953), 283.
24. Vine 1:328.
25. Ramsay, 215.
26. Knowling, 347.
27. Bruce, 329–330. An excellent overview of the city continues through p. 339.
28. See Bruce, 330–335 for further comment on this story. Also see his superb study of Paul entitled *Paul: Apostle of the Heart Set Free* (Grand Rapids, Mich.: Eerdmans, 1981), 218–222.

Chapter 45: Idolatry at Athens and Corinth: Acts 17, 1 Corinthians 8—10

1. For excellent studies on Athens, see A. Rupprecht in Merrill C. Tenney, ed., *ZPEB* (Grand Rapids, Mich.: Zondervan, 1977) 1:403–407; D. H. Madvig in G. W. Bromiley, ed., *ISBE* (Grand Rapids, Mich.: Eerdmans, 1989) 1:351–352; and Kenneth F. W. Prior, *The Gospel in a Pagan Society* (InterVarsity, 1975); F. F. Bruce, *Paul: Apostle of the Heart Set Free* (Grand Rapids, Mich.: Eerdmans, 1981); F. F. Bruce, *The Book of the Acts* (Grand Rapids, Mich.: Eerdmans, 1977a).
2. Thomas Walker, *The Acts of the Apostles* (Chicago: Moody, 1965), 371.
3. F. F. Bruce, 1771a, 350–351; R. W. Vunderink, "Epicureans" in *ISBE* 2:12—122.
4. Everett F. Harrison, *Acts: The Expanding Church* (Chicago: Moody, 1975), 269.
5. William M. Ramsay, *St. Paul, The Traveler and Roman Citizen* (Grand Rapids, Mich: Baker, 1962), 246–247.
6. Harrison, 269.
7. Harrison, 269.
8. Harrison, 273; see also I. Howard Marshall, *Acts* (Grand Rapids, Mich.: Eerdmans, 1983), 291.

9. Prior, 1975.
10. Prior, 22.
11. Michael Green, *Evangelism in the Early Church* (Grand Rapids, Mich.: Eerdmans, 1970), 127.
12. E. M. Blaicklock, *The Acts of the Apostles* (Grand Rapids, Mich.: Eerdmans, 1959), 31.
13. Gordon D. Fee, *The First Epistle to the Corinthians* (Grand Rapids, Mich.: Eerdmans, 1989), 3.
14. Fee, 2. Gordon E. Fee's introduction on 1 Corinthians 8—10 is most outstanding. He sees Paul's teaching in all of chapters 8—11:1 as focusing on this question of idols, idolatry, meat sacrificed to idols, demons, and participating in temple feasts. It is very sobering reading. See pages 357–490.
15. F. F. Bruce, 1977a, 366–367.
16. Fee, 1989, 370.
17. Leon Morris, *The First Epistle of Paul to the Corinthians* (Grand Rapids, Mich.: Eerdmans, 1983b), 125–126.
18. Morris, 127.
19. See Romans 14 where Paul deals again in depth with the same subject.
20. Morris, 131.
21. Fee, 454–455.
22. Fee, 455.
23. Fee, 455.
24. Fee, 463.
25. Fee, 464–465.
26. See Fee's excellent detailed study on this fact, 465–477; also Morris, 144–148.
27. Fee, 471–472.
28. Fee, 472.
29. Fee, 472–473.
30. Fee, 474.
31. Fee, 475.

Chapter 46: The Nature of Power Encounters

1. William E. Vine, *Expository Dictionary of New Testament Words* (London: Oliphants, 1953) 1:319.
2. Vine 1:263.
3. F. F. Bruce, *The Book of the Acts* (Grand Rapids, Mich.: Eerdmans, 1977a), 388–389.
4. Timothy M. Warner in "Power Encounter with the Demonic" in Dr. Robert E. Coleman, *Evangelism on the Cutting Edge* (Old Tappan, N.J.: Revell, 1986), 90.
5. Warner, 90.
6. Warner seems to imply this in his excellent article "Teaching Power Encounter," 1986. He avoids that error, however, in his outstanding book, *Spiritual Warfare: Victory Over the Powers of the Dark World* (1991).
7. Tim Stafford, "Testing the Wine from John Wimber's Vineyard," *Christianity Today* (August 8, 1986) 18–19.
8. Frank Peretti, *This Present Darkness* (Westchester, Ill.: Crossway, 1986), and *Piercing the Darkness* (Westchester, Ill.: Crossway, 1989).
9. I was allowing the demons to come into controlled manifestation as I was working with his pastor and elders. I felt they had to hear and see demonic activity instead of just believing the victim that it was truly demons speaking in his mind. I still do this on many occasions.

Chapter 47: Power Encounters at Ephesus (Acts 19)

1. Clinton E. Arnold, *Ephesians, Power and Magic* (Cambridge: Cambridge University Press, 1989), 14–20.
2. Andre Kole and Al Janssen, *From Illusion to Reality* (San Bernardino, Calif.: Here's Life Publishers, 1984).
3. See D. E. Aune, "Magic, Magician" in G. W. Bromiley, ed., *ISBE* (Grand Rapids, Mich.: Eerdmans, 1990) 3:213–219; B. F. Harris, "Magic and Sorcery" in Merrill C. Tenney, ed., *ZPEB* (Grand Rapids, Mich.: Zondervan, 1977) 4:35–37; and J. L. Kelso, "Magician" in *ZPEB* 4:37–38.

4. Arnold, 14–20.
5. Arnold, 16.
6. F. F. Bruce, *Paul: Apostle of the Heart Set Free* (Grand Rapids, Mich.: Eerdmans, 1981), 291–292.
7. Arnold, 19–20.
8. Arnold, 39.
9. William E. Vine, *Expository Dictionary of New Testament Words* (London: Oliphants, 1953) 1:72, 192; F. F. Bruce, *The Acts of the Apostles*, NICNT (Grand Rapids, Mich.: Eerdmans, 1977), 389.
10. R. J. Knowling, *The Acts of the Apostles* in W. Robertson Nicoll, *Expositors Greek New Testament* (Grand Rapids, Mich.: Eerdmans) 2:405–406.
11. See Knowling; and I. Howard Marshall, *Acts*, TNTC (Grand Rapids, Mich.: Eerdmans, 1983) for further comments on Acts 19:11–12.
12. Knowling, 406.
13. Arnold, 31. See his list of texts and subjects which have been discovered revealing how widespread Jewish magic was in the biblical world in Paul's day.
14. F. F. Bruce, *The Book of Acts*, NICNT (Grand Rapids, Mich.: Eerdmans, 1977), 389–390.
15. Bruce, 1977, 389–390.
16. See James Morrison, *A Practical Commentary on the Gospel According to Matthew* (London: Hodder and Stoughton, 1895) for excellent historical background to Jewish exorcism in the days of Jesus and later years, 206–208. See also John A. Broadus, *Matthew* (Valley Forge, Penn.: Judson Press, 1886), 269.
17. Morrison, 206–208. See also D. E. Aune, 245.
18. For the view of a secular anthropologist see Ari Kiev, *Magic, Faith and Healing* (New York, N.Y.: The Free Press, 1964).
19. Marshall, 311–312.
20. F. F. Bruce, *The Book of Acts* (Grand Rapids, Mich.: Eerdmans, 1977), 391–392.
21. Marshall, 317.
22. Marshall, 317–318.
23. Arnold, 20–28. His study is worth the price of the book.
24. Arnold, 27.

Chapter 48: Galatians, 1 and 2 Thessalonians

1. Richard H. Longenecker, *Galatians*, WBC (Dallas, Texas: Word, 1990), lxi. Only after this book was complete did Clinton Arnold's excellent new book *Powers of Darkness: Principalities and Powers in Paul's Letter* (Downer's Grove, Ill.: InterVarsity, 1992) come to my attention. It confirms and enlarges upon much of what I have written in this section. I wish I had had this book while doing my work and recommend it heartily.
2. The Judaizers were believing Jews who insisted that the law of Moses, including the ceremonial laws, must be kept by all, even Gentiles, to be truly Christians. Paul's major theological battles were with these people, also called "those from James" (Gal. 2:12) and those "of the sect of the Pharisees" (Acts 15:5).
3. See Longenecker's discussion of Paul's opponents in Galatia, lxxxix–c.
4. Frederic Rendall, *The Epistle to the Galatians*, in W. Robertson Nicoll, *The Expositor's Greek New Testament* (Grand Rapids, Mich.: Eerdmans) 3:152.
5. R. Alan Cole, *Galatians* (Grand Rapids, Mich.: Eerdmans, 1983), 42.
6. F. F. Bruce, *1 and 2 Thessalonians*, WBC (Waco, Texas: Word, 1982), xxxv.
7. Bruce, xxxiv.
8. George Eldon Ladd, *A Theology of the New Testament* (Grand Rapids, Mich.: Eerdmans, 1983), 65.
9. Bruce, 55.
10. Leon Morris, *1 and 2 Thessalonians*, NICNT (Grand Rapids, Mich.: Eerdmans, 1983), 64.
11. Bruce, 63.
12. Bruce, 63. See also 1 Cor. 15:58; Phil. 2:16; Gal. 2:2; 4:11; 2 Cor. 6:1. Cp. Isa. 65:23 with 49:4.
13. Matthew Henry, *Commentary on the Whole Bible* (New York: Fleming H. Revell, 1935) 6:779.
14. Bruce, 162.
15. William E. Vine, *An Expository Dictionary of New Testament Words* (London: Oliphants, 1953) 1:65–55, 208–209.

16. Leon Morris, *The First and Second Epistles to the Thessalonians,* NICNT (Grand Rapids, Mich.: Eerdmans, 1977), 213.
17. Morris, 1977, 213.
18. Morris, 1977, 213.
19. Morris, 1977, 218.
20. Morris, 1977, 219–220.
21. Morris, 1977, 220–222.
22. Morris, 1977, 222.
23. Morris, 1977, 222–224.
24. Morris, 1977, 227. Morris gives a brief outline of the various interpretations of who the restrainer is and the fact of his removal before the lawless one is allowed to appear (Morris, 1977, 224–227). Yet he does not mention one widely held view that the restrainer is the Holy Spirit within the church. The Holy Spirit abides in this evil world in the temple of God, His church. This is the most commonly held view of those who see the Rapture, i.e., the "catching up" of the church, before the seven years' tribulation period spoken of by Daniel and Jesus. Thus one's eschatology partly determines one's view of this yet-future event.

   Morris does briefly refer to this view with a negative comment in a reference to the mystery of lawlessness in verse 7. He says,

   > The animated style we noted in verse 3 continues. Once again Paul rushes on without completing his sentence. His point is that although the lawless principle is at work already it cannot reach its climax at present because of the restrainer. That climax will be reached only when the restrainer is "taken out of the way." This is not explained. Even so it seems definite enough to exclude some suggestions as to the identity of the restrainer, e.g., that which thinks of the Holy Spirit (e.g., the *Scofield Reference Bible*). While it would be easy to think of the Spirit as restraining the forces of evil it is impossible to envisage Him as being "taken out of the way." Such an idea does not appear in Scripture. (Morris, 1977, 228–229)

   Not everyone would agree with Morris' position at this point.
25. Morris, 1977, 227.
26. Morris, 1977, 229.
27. Morris, 1977, 231.
28. Morris, 1977, 231.
29. Morris, 1977, 231.
30. Morris, 1977, 232.
31. Morris, 1977, 233.
32. Morris, 1977, 234.
33. Morris, 1977, 234.
34. Morris, 1977, 236.

Chapter 49: 1 and 2 Corinthians, Romans, and the Pastoral Epistles

1. While not holding to this view, Gordon Fee admits that "there has been a growing consensus over many years that the 'rulers' are demonic powers, or at least that by these words Paul wants the Corinthians to see demonic powers as lying behind the activity of the earthly rulers." (This is my personal position.) Gordon D. Fee, *The First Epistle to the Corinthians,* NICNT (Grand Rapids, Mich.: Eerdmans, 1989), 103.
2. Fee, 196.
3. See Fee's discussion of this issue, 203–204, 206.
4. Fee, 208–214.
5. See Leon Morris, *I Corinthians* (Grand Rapids, Mich.: Eerdmans, 1983), 88–89; also Rodger K. Bufford, *Counseling and the Demonic* (Dallas, Texas: Word, 1988), 47.
6. Morris, 167.
7. Fee, 577–578.
8. Merrill F. Unger, *New Testament Teaching on Tongues* (Grand Rapids, Mich.: Kregel, 1972), 1–3.
9. This does not mean all tongues are demonic or false. If I accept all the gifts in operation, I must also accept tongues as a present-day gift of the Spirit.
10. If we followed Paul's teachings here, a lot of the opposition to tongues, in time, would probably melt away by itself.

11. See Philip E. Hughes, *The Second Epistle to the Corinthians,* NICNT (Grand Rapids, Mich.: Eerdmans, 1977), 59f, for an excellent discussion of the various views on the identify of the person in question in this passage.

12. See John White, *The Masks of Melancholy: A Christian Physician Looks at Depression and Suicide* (Downers Grove, Ill.: InterVarsity, 1982).

13. See comments on chapters 10—13 in, e.g., Ralph P. Martin, *2 Corinthians,* WBC (Waco, Texas: Word, 1986), 40; and Victor P. Furnish, *2 Corinthians,* Anchor Bible (Garden City, N.Y.: Doubleday, 1984), 32A.

14. Much is being written today about satanic strongholds in the mind: some of it good, some questionable. The word translated "stronghold" is *ochuroma.* Literally, Vine says, it means "a fortress," but in this verse, its use is metaphorical, referring to "those things in which mere human confidence is imposed," *An Expository Dictionary of New Testament Words* (London: Oliphants, Ltd., 1953) 1:156.

15. Martin, 388–424; R. G. V. Tasker, *II Corinthians* (Grand Rapids, Mich.: Eerdmans, 1983), 169–179.

16. While some may debate it, I cannot see how it can be denied that pride was the sin of Satan and his angels. It was also the sin of our first parents (Gen. 3:1ff).

17. Vine 1:156.

18. For our study of Romans 6—8, see chapter 10.

19. James Denney, *St. Paul's Epistle to the Romans* in W. Robertson Nicoll, *The Expositor's Greek New Testament* (Grand Rapids, Mich.: Eerdmans) 2:722.

20. John Murray, *The Epistle to the Romans* (Grand Rapids, Mich.: Eerdmans, 1977) 2:237.

21. Murray, 236–237. Murray's entire discussion of verses 17–20 exactly, but in greater detail, parallels what I am saying here.

22. Paul uses "God of peace" frequently. See Rom. 15:33; 1 Cor. 14:33; 2 Cor. 13:11; Phil. 4:5; 1 Thess. 5:23; Heb. 13:20.

23. John Calvin, *Romans* (Grand Rapids, Mich.: Baker, 1989) xix:551.

24. The Pastorals are truly letters, more than any other of Paul's writings, except for Philemon. Guthrie has a good discussion of their free-flowing, letter-like style (Donald Guthrie, *The Pastoral Epistles* [Grand Rapids, Mich.: Eerdmans, 1983], 11–12). Guthrie has written identical overviews on the Pastoral Epistles both in *ISBE* (Grand Rapids, Mich.: Eerdmans, 1990) 3:679–687, and *ZPEB* (Grand Rapids, Mich.: Zondervan, 1977) 4:611–619.

25. Kenneth S. Wuest, *The Pastoral Epistles* (Grand Rapids, Mich.: Eerdmans, 1973) 2:5.

26. First and Second Timothy were written to Timothy, the apostolic leader of the church at Ephesus (1 Tim. 1:3f). For a better understanding, they should be studied after Ephesians. They reveal how false teachers were decimating that great church as well as others in Asia.

27. Guthrie, 67.

28. Guthrie, 67.

29. Guthrie, 67.

30. See Cindy Jacobs, *Possessing the Gates of the Enemy* (Tarrytown, N.Y.: Chosen Books, Fleming H. Revell, 1991), 21f.

31. Guthrie, 69.

32. Vine, 3:119.

33. Wuest, 58.

34. Newport J. D. White, *First Timothy* in Nicoll 4:114.

35. White, 114.

36. See James Robison's personal story in *Winning the Real War* (Lake Mary, Fla.: Creation House, 1991).

37. See Wuest, 66–68; Guthrie, 91–93.

38. See 2 Cor. 11:3–4,13–15; 2 Tim. 1:15—2:14; 3:1–17; 4:3–4.

39. Guthrie, 92. See my comments on Gnosticism on pages 000.

40. Guthrie's discussion of these verses is excellent, 100–101.

41. Vine 1:35.

42. Guthrie believes it is immorality, 104.

43. Guthrie, 149.

44. Guthrie, 149.

45. Guthrie, 154–155.

46. Guthrie, 155.
47. Guthrie, 155.

Chapter 50: Colossians and Ephesians

1. In Bob and Gretchen Passantino, "The Kingdom Strikes Back," *Christianity Today* (November 11, 1991), 62.
2. For excellent studies on the Colossian Heresy see Peter T. O'Brien, *Colossians, Philemon,* WBC (Waco, Texas: Word, 1982), xxx–xli; H. M. Carson, *Colossians and Philemon* (Grand Rapids, Mich.: Eerdmans, 1983); John Eadie, *Colossians* (Minneapolis, Minn.: James and Klock Publishing Co., 1977a), ix–xxxix; Ralph Martin, "Colossians," Merrill C. Tenney, ed., *ZPEB* 1:914–918; F. F. Bruce, "Colossians," in G. W. Bromiley, ed., *ISBE* 1:733–735.
3. F. F. Bruce and E. K. Simpson, *The Epistles to the Ephesians and the Colossians,* NICNT (Grand Rapids, Mich.: Eerdmans, 1977), 165–166.
4. Bruce, 167. We have referred to Gnosticism before. For a good overview see A. M. Renwick, "Gnosticism," in *ISBE* 2:484–490, and A. F. Walls, "Gnosticism," in *ZPEB* 2:736–739. All the commentaries used in this chapter also contain excellent material on Gnosticism.
5. Carson, 17–18.
6. O'Brien, 29.
7. For a word study on thrones, dominions, rulers, and authorities, see note 25.
8. O'Brien, 46–47.
9. O'Brien, 110.
10. O'Brien has a detailed and outstanding discussion of the phrase as used by Paul in Colossians, 129–132. So does Ronald Fung in *The Epistle to the Galatians* (Grand Rapids, Mich: Eerdmans, 1988), 181, 188–192.
11. William E. Vine, *An Expository Dictionary of New Testament Words* (London: Oliphants, Ltd.) 3:306.
12. O'Brien, 131.
13. O'Brien, 127–128.
14. Ray C. Stedman, "Off Witchcraft" (Palo Alto, Calif.: Discovery Publishing), Dec. 6, 1970.
15. Clinton E. Arnold, *Ephesians: Power and Magic* (Cambridge: Cambridge University Press, 1989), 47.
16. Arnold, 47. The word *Pseudepigrapha* literally means "false writing," or writings attributed to a person who did not write them. In the case of the Old Testament, the writers wrote to honor the name of their biblical heroes. The term is applied to a group of Jewish writings written in the first century before Christ. They, with the Apocrypha, are the writings of the intertestamental period. For a good overview see George E. Ladd's article in *ISBE* 3:1040–1043.
17. Arnold, 47.
18. Arnold, 47.
19. Thomas H. McAlpine, *Facing the Powers* (Monrovia, Calif.: MARC, 1991).
20. First, the church is blessed by God in the heavenlies (1:3). Second, Christ is Lord of the heavenlies (1:21–23). Third, the church is co-regent with Christ in the heavenlies (2:6). Fourth, the church witnesses to the principalities and powers in the heavenlies (3:10). Finally, the church wars with the evil powers in the heavenlies (6:10–20).
21. Andrew T. Lincoln, *Ephesians,* WBC (Waco, Texas: Word, 1990), 21. (See his full discussion about "in Christ," 21–22).
22. Lincoln, xc.
23. See Frank Peretti's two fictionalized accounts of this reality, *This Present Darkness* (Westchester, Ill.: Crossway, 1986) and *Piercing the Darkness* (Westchester, Ill.: Crossway, 1989).
24. A free-flowing translation of parts of verses 19–21 revealing the amazing series of power words used by Paul, all heaped up together.
25. From McAlpine, 87–88; used by permission. The New Testament Word Field for "Powers": What words are used for the powers? The following list of words and texts represents an initial cut. The list of words follows Louw and Nida, whose recent lexicon lists words by semantic domain or field (like a thesaurus).
    The English word following is the word generally used in the NRSV. The list of occurrences is cross-checked against both Bauer-Arndt-Gingrich (BAG) and Kittel (TDNT) lexicons. In most cases the words have other meanings as well, so not all the texts in which the words occur are cited. This list should be compared with the rather fuller listings in Morton Kelsey's, *Discernment: A Study in Ecstasy and Evil* (New York: Paulist, 1978), 51–85.

Words	Occurrences
aiōn "age"	Eph. 2:2, 3:9; Col. 1:26. So BAG (27 #4, with bibliography). Sasse regards Eph. 2:2 as possible; rejects Eph. 2:7; 3:9; Col. 1:26 (TDNT 1:197–209).
archē "ruler"	Luke 12:11*; 20:20*; Rom. 8:38; 1 Cor. 15:24; Eph. 1:21; 3:10; 6:12; Col. 1:16; 2:10, 15; Titus 3:1*; Jude 6** (* = human referent; ** = "rule"). So BAG (111–12 #3,4). Delling notes regular collocation with *exousia*, with exception of Jude 6 (TDNT 1:478–89). Appears 56x in NT (MG 110–111).
archōn "ruler"	Matt. 9:34; 12:24; Mark 3:22; Luke 11:15; John 12:31; 14:30; 16:11 (refers to devil); 1 Cor. 2:6–8; Eph. 2:2. So BAG (113 #3), Delling (TDNT 1:478–89).
dunamis "power"	Matt. 24:29//Mark 13:25//Luke 21:26; Rom. 8:38; 1 Cor. 15:24; Eph. 1:21; 1 Peter 3:22. So BAG (206–207 #6, citing also Acts 8:10; omitting Matt. 24:29 par), Grundmann (TDNT 2:284–317).
exousia "authority"	Luke 12:11*; Rom. 13:1[bis]*, 2*, 3*; 1 Cor. 15:24; Eph. 1:21; 3:10; 6:12; Col. 1:16; 2:10, 15; Titus 3:1*; 1 Peter 3:22 (* = human referent). So BAG (277–28, #4, with bibliography, and including Eph. 2:2, "domain of the air"). See Foerster for general discussion and bibliography (TDNT 2:560–575). Appears 102x in NT (MG 347–48).
thronos "throne"	Col. 1:16. So BAG (364–65 #2b), Schmitz (TDNT 3:160–167).
kosmokratōr "cosmic power"	Eph. 6:12. So BAG (446), Michaelis (TDNT 3:905–15).
kuriotēs "dominion"	Eph. 1:21; Col. 1:16. So BAG (461–62 #3), Foerster (TDNT 3:1096–97). Appears 4x in NT.
pneumatikon "spiritual force"	Eph. 6:12. So BAG (685 #3).

BAG   Bauer, Walter, William F. Arndt, and F. Wilbur Gingrich, *A Greek-English Lexicon of the New Testament and other early Christian literature* (Chicago: Univ. of Chicago Press; Cambridge: Cambridge Univ. Press, 1957).

LN   Louw, Johannes P. and Eugene A. Nida, eds., *Greek-English Lexicon of the New Testament based on semantic domains* (New York: United Bible Societies, 1988) 2 vols.

MG   Mouton and Gedden, *A Greek Concordance to the New Testament.*

TDNT   Kittel, Gerhard, ed. *Theological Dictionary of the New Testament* (Grand Rapids, Mich.: Eerdmans, 1964–76) 10 vols.

26. Walter Wink, *Naming the Powers* (Philadelphia: Fortress, 1984), 6–12. See also his *Unmasking the Powers* (1986).
27. Arnold, 59–69.
28. McAlpine, 87–89.
29. See in bibliography especially Green (1981), Wagner (1991a; 1991b), Arnold (1989), McAlpine (1991), Wink (1984; 1986). Tom White's *The Believer's Guide to Spiritual Warfare* (1990) contains excellent help in this area (31f, 129f). The same is true of Cindy Jacob's *Possessing the Gates of the Enemy.* There is no book in print like Cindy's book, as Wagner says in his foreword (11–14).
30. For good commentary on v. 1, see Lincoln, 91–93. On v. 2., see Arnold, 39.
31. Arnold, 60.
32. Lincoln, 95–96.
33. Lincoln, 96.
34. Arnold, 60.
35. Arnold, 61.
36. John Eadie, *Ephesians* (Minneapolis, Minn.: James and Klock Christian Publishing Co., 1977), 230–235. Eadie eloquently presents the elect angel view. D. Martyn Lloyd-Jones embraces the elect-and-fallen- angels view, as do most of the commentators. See D. Martyn Lloyd-Jones, *Exposition of Ephesians* (Grand Rapids, Mich.: Baker, 1988) 3:80.

37. Lincoln, Arnold, Calvin, Eadie, *Expositor's Greek New Testament,* and all the other good expositions of this passage give the various views.
38. The apostle refers to "mystery" six times in Ephesians (1:9; 3:3, 4, 9; 5:32; 6:19), and four times in Colossians (1:26, 27; 2:2; 4:3). His use of mystery in both epistles is basically the same.
39. Arnold, 127.
40. Arnold, 127.
41. See Arnold's full discussion, 126–128.
42. Wink, 1984, 89.
43. Wink, 1984, 89.
44. Wink, 1984, 92.
45. Wink, 1984, 92.
46. Wink, 1984, 92–93.
47. Wink, 1984, also believes in what we have called the watcher angels. He calls them "the angels of the ethne." Paul is speaking of the conversion of *panta ta ethne,* all the nations (3:8). Wink says this demands that the church preach to the national angels of the nations, 93–94.
48. Wink, 1984, 94.
49. Wink, 1984, 94.
50. Wink, 1984, 94–95.
51. Wink, 1984, 95.
52. Revelation gives us two helpful pictures. See chapter 52.
53. Arnold, 58.
54. There are several excellent books just off the press totally dedicated to this cosmic level spiritual warfare and power encounter dimension of evangelism.

    Besides the books of Arnold and Wink which deal with these realities in a general overview, some key books are: John Dawson's *Taking Our Cities for God* (1989) and Jacobs (1991) and McAlpine *Powers* (1991) mentioned above; Peter Wagner's *Territorial Spirits* (1991a), *Engaging the Enemy* (1991b), *Warfare Prayer* (1992).

    The man of God who in many ways is setting the pace for this dimension of evangelism is Rev. Edgar Silvoso of Argentina. We worked together for many years in OC, where Edgar was part of the Luis Palau team when Palau was part of OC.

    I had the privilege of serving as the first president of Ed's mission, Harvest Evangelism, a spin-off of OC, to help him get started in his amazing ministry. I still serve on his board. It is also my privilege to serve as one of Ed's closest advisors. What a privilege to work with such a man of God!

    I believe that Edgar is one of God's gifts to His church today, especially in the area of urban evangelism in the Two-thirds World. He has pioneered urban evangelism in a spiritual warfare—Ephesians 3:10 context with great success. For insights into how he leads Harvest Evangelism to help churches penetrate the spirit realm, claiming cities for God see in the bibliography Silvoso (no date; 1987; 1989) and Silvoso in Wagner (1991a, 109f; 1991b, 109f; 1992, 6f); in McAlpine (1991, 91–93) and Jacobs (1991, 121f).

Chapter 51: Ephesians 6
1. The *Ante-Nicene Fathers* were edited by Alexander Roberts and James Donaldson, 1981. *The Nicene Fathers* and *Post-Nicene Fathers* were edited by Philip Schaff and Henry Wace, 1979 and 1982. The complete set of 38 volumes is published by Eerdmans.
2. Perhaps the most exhaustive study ever done is one done by William Gurnall, *The Christian in Complete Armor* (Edinburgh: The Banner of Truth Trust, 1987).
3. Clinton E. Arnold, *Ephesians: Power and Magic* (Cambridge: Cambridge University Press, 1989), 103.
4. Arnold, 103.
5. Arnold, 104.
6. Arnold, 105.
7. Arnold, 105.
8. William E. Vine, *An Expository Dictionary of New Testament Words* (London: Oliphants, 1953) 3:255.
9. Arnold, 105–106.
10. Andrew T. Lincoln, *Ephesians,* WBC (Dallas, Texas: Word, 1990), 441.
11. Arnold, 108.
12. Arnold, 109.

13. Arnold, 108.
14. Arnold, 108.
15. Arnold, 109.
16. John Eadie, *Ephesians* (Minneapolis, Minn.: James and Klock Publishing Co., 1977), 457.
17. Vine 4:216.
18. Eadie, 458.
19. Vine 4:293.
20. Kenneth Wuest, *Ephesians in the Greek New Testament* (Grand Rapids, Mich.: Eerdmans, 1983) 1:141.
21. For a study of these words, see Arnold, Lincoln, Wink and Eadie.
22. Eadie, 101.
23. Eadie, 101.
24. Arnold, 65.
25. Arnold, 67–68.
26. Walter Wink, *Naming the Powers,* (Philadelphia: Fortress, 1984), 85.
27. Wink, 86.
28. Arnold, 68.
29. Eadie, 461.
30. Wink, 86.
31. Wink, 87.
32. Wink, 88–89.
33. Lincoln, 447.
34. Lincoln, 447. See also Ps. 65:6; 18:32,39; 1 Pet. 1:13.
35. Lincoln, 448.
36. Arnold, 110.
37. Wuest 1:143.
38. Lincoln. 448.
39. Lincoln, 448.
40. Arnold, 110–111.
41. Lincoln, 448.
42. Lincoln, 449.
43. Lincoln, 449–450.
44. S. D. F. Salmond, in W. R. Nicoll, *The Expositor's Greek New Testament* (Grand Rapids, Mich.: Eerdmans) 3:388.
45. Lincoln, 451.
46. Lincoln, 451.
47. Lincoln, 451.
48. Arnold, 112.
49. Arnold, 112.
50. Mrs. Howard Taylor, *Behind the Ranges, Fraser of Lisuland* (London: Overseas Missionary Fellowship, 1956).
51. Taylor, 42, 67, 70.
52. Taylor, 68. Again, church history reveals that under unusual conditions of sin, true believers can be reinvaded by evil spirits without losing their salvation.
53. Taylor, 71–72.
54. Taylor, 73.
55. Taylor, 73–75.
56. Taylor, 5, 47, 55–57, 74, 85f.
57. Taylor, 89–92.
58. Taylor, 91.
59. Taylor, 94f.
60. Taylor, 146f.
61. Taylor, 98f, 105f.
62. Taylor, 107–117.
63. Taylor, 188.

Chapter 52: Hebrews, the Catholic Epistles, the Johannine Writings

1. There is no end to the debate over the authorship of Hebrews. For excellent summaries of the arguments, see F. F. Bruce, "Hebrews, Epistle to the," in Merrill C. Tenney, ed., *ZPEB* (Grand Rapids, Mich.: Zondervan, 1977) 3:87–93; Donald Guthrie, "Hebrews, Epistle to the," in G. W. Bromiley, ed., *ISBE* (Grand Rapids, Mich.: Eerdmans, 1989) 2:663–670. Since

I am writing with other concerns in mind, however, I will assume the Pauline authorship of Hebrews. This is the historical view of the church.

2. For excellent insight into the meaning of the word *katargeo*, here translated "destroy," see William E. Vine, *An Expository Dictionary of New Testament Words* (London: Oliphants, 1953) 1:13–14; and Gerhard Delling in Gerhard Kittel, *TDNT* (Grand Rapids, Mich.: Eerdmans, 1977) 1:452–454. Delling's full discussion well fits my "already but not yet" view of the destruction of Satan. See also F. F. Bruce, *The Epistle to the Hebrews* (Grand Rapids, Mich.: Eerdmans, 1977), 48–51, for an excellent commentary.

3. Donald Guthrie, *Hebrews* (Grand Rapids, Mich.: Eerdmans, 1983), 92.

4. D. M. Pratt, "Catholic Epistles," in *ISBE* 1:622–623.

5. For a thorough overview of the many difficult and critical issues presented by 2 Peter and Jude, see Richard J. Bauckham, *Jude, 2 Peter*, WBC (Waco, Texas: Word, 1983). Unfortunately he accepts a second-century date for both books. One of the best thorough studies of the critical issues from a more conservative stance is Michael Green's excellent commentary, *2 Peter and Jude* (Grand Rapids, Mich.: Eerdmans, 1983), 13–53. Green honestly faces the critical problems in holding to the traditional views of the authority of both epistles but concludes affirming the traditional Petrine authority of Peter and the authorship of Jude by St. Jude, the half-brother of Jesus, 41–46.

6. Tom White, *The Believer's Guide to Spiritual Warfare* (Ann Arbor, Mich.: Servant, 1990), 31–34, outlines the common views of both the origin of demons and the fall of angels.

7. John Calvin, *II Peter and Jude* (Grand Rapids, Mich.: Baker, 1989), 396–397.

8. Calvin, 397.

9. H. Buis in *ZPEB* 1:114–117. For excellent studies on this issue see Buis, *ISBE* 1:277–279. Also see Green, 98–9, Vine: 142; 2:212–213. See the *ZPEB* and *ISBE* for their studies on "Pit" and "Abyss."

10. Green, 98.

11. William Barclay, *Letters of James and Peter* (Philadelphia: Westminster, 1960),379–384, gives an excellent overview of the development within Judaism of divergent views on the fall of angels. His overview directly relates to 2 Peter and Jude.

12. Vine, 1:142.

13. Barclay, 379.

14. Calvin, 435–436.

15. Frederic Gardiner, *The Last of the Epistles: Commentary on the Epistle of St. Jude* (Boston: John P. Jewell, 1856), 23.

16. Gardiner, 77.

17. Gardiner, 78.

18. See Robert H. Mounce's important discussion of stars as symbols of angels in biblical and Jewish writings, *The Book of Revelation* (Grand Rapids, Mich.: Eerdmans, 1977), 192–193.

19. See Matthew 4:1–11; Mark 1:12–13; Luke 4:1–13.

20. See Luke 4:13 with Matthew 16:21–23; John 8:29,46; 14:30; 16:11; 17:1–4; 2 Corinthians 5:21; Philippians 2:15–18; Hebrews 2:18; 4:14–16; 5:7–11a.

21. See Mark 1:21–28; Matthew 12:22–29; Acts 10:38.

22. See Luke 9:1–2 with Mark 6:7–13; Luke 10:1,17–19.

23. See John 3:14–16; 10:11,14–18; [Isa. 53]; thus 1 Corinthians 1:17–18,21–23a; 2:1–2; Galatians 5:11; 6:14; Colossians 1:20; Hebrews 12:2,24; 13:20.

24. See Matthew 20:28; Romans 3:23–26; 5:9–11; Ephesians 5:2; Colossians 1:19–20; Hebrews 2:17; 9:11–14; 1 Peter 1:18–19; 1 John 1:7; 2:1–2; 4:10.

25. See Isaiah 53:4–6; Matthew 26:28; Luke 19:10; Acts 20:28; Romans 5:8–11; 2 Corinthians 5:21; Galatians 3:13; Ephesians 1:7; 2:13; Titus 2:14; Hebrews 2:9; 10:10; 13:12; 1 Peter 1:2; 3:18; Revelation 1:5; 5:9; 7:14.

26. See Colossians 2:13–15 with Ephesians 6:12; Hebrews 2:14–15; 1 John 3:8; Revelation 12:11.

27. See John 13:1–2,27; 1 Corinthians 2:1–2,6–8; Hebrews 2:14–15; Colossians 2:13–15; Revelation 12:11 with Ephesians 3:10.

28. See John 2:18–21; 10:17–18; 1 Corinthians 15:1–4; Acts 1:9; Hebrews 1:3–13; Ephesians 1:19–23.

29. Romans 8:33–34 with Revelation 12:10–11; 1 John 2:2; Hebrews 7:25; Matthew 28:18; 1 Peter 3:22; Ephesians 1:20–22; 2:6; 3:10.

30. See 1 Thessalonians 4:13–18; 2 Thessalonians 1:6–10; 2:1–4,8; Revelation 20:10 with Matthew 25:41.

31. See Matthew 28:18–20; Ephesians 1:20–22; Colossians 2:15 and Hebrews 2:14; 1 John 3:8.
32. See Luke 10:17–19; Ephesians 2:6; 3:10; 6:10–20; James 4:7–8; 1 Peter 5:8–11; 1 John 4:1–4; 5:18–19.

Chapter 53: The Reality, the Cause, the Cure

1. A great number of major sources on spiritual warfare I use in this book come from men and women who have experienced this change of view.
2. J. Warwick Montgomery, "Exorcism: Is it for Real?", *Christianity Today* (July 26, 1974).
3. "Can Christians Be Demon Possessed?", *The Word for Today* 6, 5–6.
4. Charles R. Swindoll, *Demonism: How to Win Against the Devil* (Portland, Ore.: Multnomah, 1981). This is Swindoll's position also, 10–11, 15–19.
5. See C. Fred Dickason, *Demon Possession and the Christian* (Westchester, Ill.: Crossway, 1989), 33–45, 73–348.
6. Dickason, 81–127.
7. See Dickason's similar syllogisms, 131–133.
8. Dickason, 81–100.
9. Bernard Ramm, *Protestant Biblical Interpretation* (Grand Rapids, Mich.: Baker, 1977), 110–111.
10. Dickason, 101–127.
11. See Dickason, 149–213; Montgomery; Jeffrey Burton Russell, *Satan: The Early Christian Tradition* (Ithaca, N.Y.: Cornell University Press, 1987b), 30f; Swindoll, 13–22; Merrill F. Unger, *Demons in the World Today* (Wheaton, Ill.: Tyndale, 1971), 116–117, and *What Demons Can Do to Saints* (Chicago: Moody, 1977), 28f; James G. Friesen, *Uncovering the Mystery of MPD* (San Bernardino, Calif.: Here's Life Publishers, 1991); Timothy M. Warner, *Spiritual Warfare* (Wheaton, Ill.: Crossway, 1991); Thomas White, *The Believer's Guide to Spiritual Warfare* (Ann Arbor, Mich.: Servant, 1990). See all of C. Peter Wagner's books, Neil Anderson, Kurt Koch, Michael Green, Charles Kraft.
12. William E. Vine, *Expository Dictionary of New Testament Words* (London: Oliphants, 1953) 3:145.
13. Vine 3:185–186.
14. Conrad Murrell, *Practical Demonology: Tactics for Demon Warfare* (Bentley, Penn. 71407: Saber Publications, 1974), 63.
15. While this type of power encounter will often occur with severely demonized unbelievers, it can usually be stopped. This is the procedure I now follow. The demons are shut down. They are forbidden to manifest themselves and even to hinder the thinking process of the unsaved person. It is our authority in Christ which brings them under control. With some, admittedly, this may not work or works with great difficulty. The immediate goal is always the same, both with unbelievers and believers, however. It is, wherever possible, to have the counselee fully lucid and in control of his mind while we minister to him. (See Neil Anderson's excellent outline of this procedure in *Released from Bondage* [San Bernardino, Calif.: Here's Life Publishers, 1991b], 183–247). Thus the power encounter becomes a "truth encounter," a term I learned from Neil Anderson. Even power encounters are really truth encounters as it is the truth of God's power working through our life (and, in the case of the demonized believers, through their life also) that we rely upon to bring demonic powers into submission.
16. Anderson, 229f. For those wanting separate copies of the "Steps to Freedom in Christ," write Dr. Neil Anderson, Freedom in Christ Ministries, 491 E. Lambert Road, La Habra, CA 90631.

Chapter 54: Six Sin Areas and the Possible Demonization of Christians

1. We are witnessing a renewed understanding in our day of national sin which needs to be confessed, repented of, and forgiveness sought. See John Dawson's *Taking Our Cities for God* (Lake Mary, Fla.: Creation House, 1989); and Cindy Jacobs, *Possessing the Gates of the Enemy* (Tarrytown, N.Y.: Chosen Books, Fleming H. Revell, 1991).
2. Rev. E. H. Plumtre, *Jeremiah*, in Charles John Ellicott, *A Bible Commentary for English Readers* (New York: Cassell and Company) 5:107–108.
3. Plumtre, 107–108.
4. William H. Brownlee, *Ezekiel 1—19*, WBC (Waco, Texas: Word, 1986), 282–283.
5. Plumtre, 107–108.

6. See Merrill F. Unger, *Demons in the World Today* (Wheaton, Ill.: Tyndale, 1971), 82–83, 177–178, 192; Merrill F. Unger, *What Demons Can Do to Saints* (Chicago: Moody, 1977), 135–139, 142–144, 155, 165, 178–179.
7. See Appendix C for Group Prayer for generational sins (plus other sin handles).
8. Jacobs, 131–133.
9. See T. Lewis and R. K. Harrison, "Curse" in G. W. Bromiley, ed.. *ISBE* (Grand Rapids, Mich.: Eerdmans, 1989–91) 1:837–838.
10. G. B. Funderburk, "Curse" in Merrill C. Tenney, ed., *ZPEB* (Grand Rapids, Mich.: Zondervan, 1977) 1:1045–1046.
11. Lewis and Harrison, 838.
12. Lewis and Harrison, 839.
13. John White and Ron Blue, series of cassette recordings on spiritual warfare. Exact title and dates not available.
14. Beverly Lewis, "Missionary Prayer Report," *World Gospel Magazine,* (November, 1985).
15. See Bob Larson, *Rock* (Wheaton, Ill.: Tyndale, 1980); Bob MacKenzie, *Bands, Boppers and Believers* (Cape Town, South Africa Printpak Books, 1986).
16. "Ding's Special Gift," *In Other Words* (December, 1987).

Chapter 55: Child Abuse

1. One single instance of child abuse can be enough. If it is a terrible enough violation of the child's sense of relationship to others, especially to adult authority-protective figures, and if it is painful almost beyond endurance, it can scar a child for life. Usually child abuse continues over a period of time, however. This has the most destructive effects on a child's development as a human being. They will need healing from God to become whole persons.
2. I am not affirming that Satan does not concentrate on the nicer side of human nature, i.e., man's intellectual, creative, aesthetic, artistic, compassionate, religious, and other noble and God-given abilities. In the long run supernatural evil more effectively seduces men from a life of obedience to God through these avenues than through man's capacity for more gross forms of evil.
3. John Boswell, "The Unwanted Children of Times Past," *U.S. News & World Report* (May 1, 1989), 62.
4. Lawrence E. Stager and Samuel R. Wolff, "Child Sacrifice at Carthage—Religious Rite or Population Control?" *Biblical Archaeology Review* (January-February, 1984), 51.
5. I am not affirming treatment by non-Christian counselors is as effective in breaking demonic attachment as is treatment by skilled Christian counselors who know the reality of the spirit world. It is not. How many Christian counselors are there, however, who know the spirit world? The ideal would be a well-trained counselor who is both a devout, godly Christian and also knows the world of supernatural evil. This is what I look for when I refer abused children and the adult survivors of child abuse. Unfortunately, such Christian counselors are hard to find.
6. In missiology we often work with what we call a resistance-receptivity scale or axis. The axis runs from −10 to +10. On the resistance side of the axis, we place peoples, communities, cities, even nations which show resistance to the gospel. They may run from highly resistant (−10 to −7), to moderately resistant (−6 to −4), to mildly resistant (−3 to −1). On the plus side of the axis are those mildly receptive (+1 to +3), moderately receptive (+4 to +6), and highly receptive (+7 to +10). The axis is simply a pragmatic working tool to help visualize a people's present attitude towards the gospel. Al's city was highly resistant, perhaps a −8 on the scale or axis. Resistant communities are controlled by high level cosmic spirits of great power. (See bibliography Silvoso, 1987, 1989, no date; Wagner, 1991a, 1991b, 1991c, 1992.)
7. The brazen actions of Al could have their source in any number of physiological-psychological problems. I have had similar cases in which demons were not directly involved. The problems were rooted in other areas requiring the intervention of medical doctors and psychiatrists. Thus, the importance of correct diagnosis. (See Rodger K. Bufford, *Counseling and the Demonic* [Dallas, Texas: Word, 1988], 48–50.)
8. I say "seemed," for at this point it had not been proven to my satisfaction that Al's problem was demonic. Not being present prohibited me from observing any "body language" which often gives clues to possible demonic presence.
9. Not all will agree with my diagnosis because Al was a Christian and a pastor. That is their privilege. I don't feel obligated to debate about theories of reality and unreality. I am too interested in "real" reality and the hurting people living with their "unreal" reality of pain

and suffering. When I confront demons attached to the life of a true Christian (either internal or external), I accept their presence and work to get the person free. Also, I do not debate with the suffering victim my selfish theological presuppositions. At this point I refuse to give any ground. What exists really exists, whether or not it fits our theological presuppositions. What demons do, they do.

10. Some do not believe it is ever wise to bring or allow demons to come into manifestation or speak through the vocal cords of their victims. Again, this is an opinion area. Jesus and Paul clearly dealt with demons in manifestation (Mark 1; Acts 16:16–18) and probably when not in manifestation. I do also. I usually do *not* bring them into manifestation, however. At times I do when this seems to be the wisest procedure. Since there is biblical support for both approaches, let each do as God leads and trains him.

11. Later, when I dealt with some of the other demons in Al, one leader called itself "Sex." He came in during the incest with his mother. This is consistent with many similar cases. It does not always occur in incestuous relationships with children, but it often does. I believe it should always be suspected. Children and adult survivors of such abuse should be taught spiritual warfare as a matter of course in a nonalarming, nonthreatening manner. (See Neil Anderson, *Released from Bondage* [San Bernardino, Calif.: Here's Life Publishers, 1991b], 229f.)

12. For many this is often the most difficult point. They have lived secretly hating their abusive family members for all of their lives. In the case of SRA and abuse amounting to sheer torture, often leading to personality dissociation, forgiveness becomes almost impossible at the beginning of counseling. It usually comes with time, however.

13. Probably most demons leave the believer's life without his even knowing they were there. This usually occurs in times of deep seeking after God. Demons then become so miserable in the believer's life they begin to leave. They are really being expelled by the indwelling Spirit of God. Some do manage to remain for years, as in Al's case—the "mystery of iniquity" at work.

14. In our last chapter we saw the demonization of children through generational sin. Often they go together, but not always. The generational demonization of children can occur in the best of Christian homes where no abuse of the child was experienced.

15. For an excellent list of organizations, mental health practitioners, and law enforcement departments in the U.S., write Personal Safety for Children and Youth, 8366 East San Sebastian Drive, Scottsdale, Arizona 85258 (phone 602-948-2101). Perhaps the best source of information available on all forms of child abuse in the U.S. is Reuben E. Epstein's newsletters. He calls his organization "Uniquity." The address is 215 Fourth Street, P.O. Box 6, Galt, California 95632 (phone 209-745-2111; outside of California, 800-521-7771). His catalog number 17, 1987, is an almost exhaustive (for that date) listing of books, audiovisuals, "show me" dolls for teaching about child abuse, audiocassettes, play therapy books and objects as well as substance abuse, wife abuse, and personality disorder, 31 pages.

For a thorough summary publication by a Christian organization about the current epidemic in the U.S. of the sexual abuse of children, including incest and SRA, see "America's Best Kept Secret," Special Report, *Passport Magazine,* 1986, Calvary Chapel of West Covina, 1432 West Puente, West Covina, California. All the books used in the following chapters also have excellent bibliographies on child abuse.

The largest national non-profit, charity combating child abuse in the U.S.A. is Child Help, USA. They have established the National Child Abuse Hotline (phone 800-4-A-CHILD; i.e., 800-433-4453). The address of the national headquarters is 6463 Independence Area, Woodland Hills, California 91367. They have a strong spiritual focus. Outstanding personalities, including Christians, are involved. Some of the Christians are Dr. Billy Graham, Dr. Lloyd Ogilvie, Mr. and Mrs. Roy Rogers, Mr. Efrem Zimbalist, Jr., and Roman Catholic leaders.

Chapter 56: Christians Demonized Through Child Abuse

1. For a fictionalized account of sexual child abuse in biblical times involved with Baal worship, see Mary Ellen Keith and Deborah Elder Champagne's, *The Scarlet Cord: The Dramatic Life of Rahab* (Nashville: Nelson, 1985). The novel is based on accurate historical research.

2. See Dr. Earl D. Wilson's important book, *Sexual Sanity* (Downers Grove, Ill.: InterVarsity, 1984); Randy Alcorn's *Christians in the Wake of the Sexual Revolution* (Portland, Ore.:

Multnomah, 1985); Dr. John White's *Eros Defiled: The Christian and Sexual Sin* (Downers Grove, Ill.: InterVarsity, 1977).

3. The Los Angeles *Times* poll defined sexual abuse as "sexual intercourse, oral copulation, sodomy, fondling, taking nude photographs, and exhibitionism." Evidently the questions of SRA and longevity of abuse were not raised.

4. Some figures run as high as one-third of girls presently 18 years of age or under. When one considers the personal shame often connected to admitting abuse and the dissociation factor (James G. Friesen, *Uncovering the Mystery of MPD* [San Bernardino, Calif.: Here's Life Publishers, 1991], 41f), this estimate would not seem to be far from reality.

5. On April 29, 1989, the *San Jose Mercury News* published an article entitled "Kids Who Kill Leave Behind a Dearth of Answers" and subtitled, "In 1988, 44 Parents in State Were Killed by Their Kids"; Pamela Kramer was the writer. The article says, "Kids are not supposed to be killers . . . especially . . . of their parents." Dr. Luis J. West, Professor and Chairman of the Department of Psychiatry of the University of California, Los Angeles, says, "Children who kill their parents almost always fall into at least one of three basic categories. . . . The first is mental illness. . . . The second is children reacting to severe abuse or neglect by parents. . . . Experts say the child may see no other options to end a horrible situation than to kill the abusive parent. The third category is composed of children who have become delinquent or criminal, sometimes behaviorally disturbed. The first type of killer generally commits the crime alone. The second . . . involves a friend or friends. The third type may or may not involve friends."

6. For those who find this difficult to accept, see Paula Sanford, *Healing Victims of Sexual Abuse* (Tulsa, Okla.: Victory House, Inc., 1988); John L. Sanford, *Why Some Christians Commit Adultery* (Tulsa, Okla.: Victory House, Inc., 1989); Charles Mylander, *Running the Red Lights: Putting the Brakes on Sexual Temptation* (Ventura, Calif.: Regal, 1986); John White, *Eros Defiled*.

7. Incest is another of "America's Best Kept Secrets," *Passport Magazine* (1986). One of the key books that helped shock the public and the psychological world to face the fact of widespread incest in the U.S. is Dr. Susan Forward and Craig Buck's *Betrayal of Innocence: Incest and Its Devastation* (New York, N.Y.: Penguin Books, 1978). Dr. Forward is one of the world's leading authorities on incest and sexual abuse.

8. Sexual addiction is a relatively new word for most people. Its premise is that those whose lives are controlled by sex are sexual addicts, just like those whose lives are controlled by alcohol or drugs are called alcoholics and drug addicts. Dr. Patrick Carnes' book *Out of the Shadows: Understanding Sexual Addiction* (Minneapolis, Minn.: CompCare Publishers, 1983) is an excellent introduction to this complex subject.

9. A pedophile is an adult who is sexually attracted to children. Some are attracted only to girls, others to boys, others to both. While they are capable of normal sexual relations with adults, they prefer children.

10. Rich Buhler, *Pain and Pretending* (Nashville: Nelson, 1988), 32–33.

11. David Peters, *A Betrayal of Innocence* (Waco, Texas: Word, 1986).

12. Buhler, 34.

13. Peters, 19–20.

14. Paula Sanford, *Healing Victims of Sexual Abuse* (Tulsa, Okla.: Victory House, Inc., 1988), iv, viii.

15. The "Twelve-Step Program" came out of Alcoholics Anonymous. It has been proven effective for all kinds of addictions. Many churches are organizing Christian support groups based on a more Christianized 12-step program. The "higher power" is recognized to be God or Jesus, not a god of one's imagination. The Christian program is primarily for believers. If unbelievers seek to attend, they are first led to personal faith in Christ. The ministry thus becomes both evangelistic and building up in the faith of believers.

16. For further discussion see my tape series listed in the bibliography, *Spiritual Warfare*.

Chapter 57: A National Crisis of Denial

1. Dr. Summit's address is the Harbor-UCLA Medical Center, 1000 West Carson Street, Torrance, California, 90509. He is also a founding member of Parents Anonymous.

2. Dr. Roland Summit, "The Child Sexual Abuse Accommodation Syndrome," *Child Abuse and Neglect* (1983), 180.

3. Presented to the Attorney General's Commission on Pornography, Miami, Florida, November 20, 1985. Also available by writing Dr. Summit's office in Torrance, California.

4. Summit, 1985, 1.

5. Summit, 1985, 5.
6. Summit, 1985, 8.
7. Summit, 1985, 9.
8. This is not a statement of particular endorsement of the Reagan presidency, but only giving honor where honor is due. The former president's policies, both as governor of California and as president, towards the mentally ill were as destructive to hurting people as his stance on child pornography was beneficial to child victims.
9. For a remarkably gripping and thoroughly documented case study of one child care center whose directors were convicted of terrible sexual child abuse, the Country Walk Baby Sitting Service, see Jan Hollinsworth, *Unspeakable Acts* (New York: Congdon and Weed, 1986).
10. Linda Goldston, "Day Care Sex Abusers: 40% Women," *San Jose Mercury News* (March 22, 1988); "Army of the Night: Child Abuse at the Presidio," *West Magazine* of *San Jose Mercury News* (July 24, 1988), 14–23; Joanna Michaels, " 'The Teacher Hurt Me, Mommy': The Sex-Abuse Scandal at West Point," *Redbook,* (January, 1986), 106–108, 142.
11. Goldston.
12. Charles H. Kraft, *Deep Wounds, Deep Healing* (Ann Arbor, Mich.: Vine Books, 1993), 152–153. The whole book is valuable.

Chapter 58: Creative Abuse—A Calculated Evil

1. James Wilder and James Friesen, "Restoration of Those Exposed To Extreme Evil As Children" (Van Nuys, Calif.: The Shepherd's House, 1989). Friesen's landmark book on MPD, *Uncovering the Mystery of MPD* (1991), is the first scholarly, well-documented in-depth book on MPD written by a trained and experienced Christian psychologist. Dr. Wilder has also written a book on the ultimate evil of Satanism, *A Redemptive Response to Satanism* (Downers Grove, Ill.: InterVarsity, 1992).
2. Wilder, 2–3.
3. Wilder, 3.
4. Wilder, 3–4.
5. Wilder, 4.
6. Wilder, 4.
7. Wilder, 4–5.
8. There is a disturbing and unbiblical trend in some conservative evangelical circles *towards* a subtle form of Bibliolatry and *against* Christian mysticism and Christian revivalism. God, it would seem, no longer speaks directly to His people—only indirectly through the Bible—and that primarily from the pulpit. When we read the Bible, that is God speaking to us, we are told. When we pray we speak to God.

   While this is true, is it the whole truth? Is God limited in His speech to direct quotes from the Bible? Does He no longer (as He has in the past) fellowship with His people, direct their lives, meet their needs, and answer their personal questions as they wait upon Him? While all He says will be in harmony with His infallible revelation in the Bible, He also likes to give personal words directly to His children.

   Terry Muck writes under "God and Oral" (written at the time of the Oral Roberts question about raising $4.5 million in contributions): "It would be a sad day, indeed, if we thought God was finished talking. So in our skepticism over Roberts' understanding of this particular message, let us not deny the fact that God speaks clearly and frequently to us. In fact, the evidence of God's desire to communicate with us is so overwhelming, it seems obvious the only thing that could silence his voice would be our unwillingness to listen."

   Muck admits that "it can be difficult to pick out God's voice from all the rest. Satan has been known to disguise his ingratiating pap so the casual listener could mistake it for a signal from God. We can even be the victims of our own earnest desires to minister as faithfully and fully as possible. We trust the latter was the case with Roberts."

   Yet the facts are clear. "Throughout history God has talked to countless human beings," Muck says. "Even by today's loquacious standards, God has been a veritable blabbermouth." He follows with a condensed historical overview of God's talking individually to human beings. "This has been the position of the Church for 2,000 years and the Old Testament position for hundreds of years before Christ." (Terry Muck, "God and Oral," *Christianity Today* [March 20, 1987]; see also John White, *When the Spirit Comes with Power* [Downers Grove, Ill.: InterVarsity, 1988]).
9. Generally speaking, experienced missionaries are among my strongest backers in the type of spiritual warfare teaching being presented in this book, even if their mission in general

and their mission executives in particular are resistant to the more controversial aspects of this teaching. This support exists for many reasons. First, missionaries often run into evangelistic and discipleship problems with nationals which seem to imply direct demonic activity. Second, missionaries, generally speaking, are among the most courageous and honest people on earth. If it were not so, they would never make it on the mission field. Third, they are usually "people" people. Whatever truly helps people and is consistent with general biblical principles (everything which truly helps people is always consistent with biblical principles), they will accept. They are looking for such help. It was missionaries, I assume many of them graduates of Dallas Theological Seminary, who corrected the late Dr. Merrill Unger's view about the potential demonization of some Christians (see Unger, *Demons in the World Today* (Wheaton, Ill.: Tyndale, 1971, 116–117.)

10. By "direct demonic overtones" I mean *demonization*. All human problems always have indirect demonic overtones given the nature of personal evil in the universe.

11. This is not to affirm that cleft palate and cleft lip are necessarily demonic. Usually, like all physical afflictions which have resulted from the Fall, they are not directly demonic. In this case, they were. I do not know if the presence of the demons Cleft-Palate and Cleft-Lip in the unborn child produced the physical malfunction, came in after the physical problem began to form in the womb, or if it was just coincidental. All three are possibilities.

12. Of course such psychological states are not necessarily directly demonic. Most of the time they are not. Demons who "specialize" (if that is the best word) either permanently or for a time in helping produce or reinforce these negative states usually take on functional names like these. While some people are very uncomfortable admitting the possibility, I can only answer, "What is, is. I like my way of finding them better than other people's way of not finding them."

13. Friesen, 62–63.

14. Notes and tape recording of demons in manifestation before being expelled from Betty's life.

15. Friesen, 64.

16. Friesen, 42.

17. Friesen, 42.

18. Taken directly from the cassette recording of the counseling session.

Chapter 59: Multiple Personality Disorders and Demonization

1. Ernie's use of shattered or segmented personality to refer to extreme cases of dissociation is more accurate than the more commonly used terms, multiple (or alter) personality. Multiple Personality Disorder (MPD) implies that the traumatized individual is composed of more than one personality. God created each human being with one unique personality. That one personality, however, can be shattered, segmented, broken, and smashed into pieces, that is, split into different parts, each fragment dissociated from the others and from the original whole personality. Each part is *not* a different personality, however, but *only a part* of the one original personality created by God. The healing process, too involved to describe here, has as its goal helping each segment to "grow up" by its own choice and the power of God, progressively, starting with the youngest fragment, into the whole personality as it was originally created by God, until all are one at the biological age of the traumatized person. In the process, as Ernie's story reveals, many (all in the case of SRA and related abuse) will need to be delivered from the demons attached to them. Each segment will also need to be led to Christ which results *not* in the blending of many different personalities into one but in the restoring and healing of the one original personality. Again, I choose to use Ernie's description over against that of many Christian counselors because his reveals *most* of these elements. Finally, Ernie did occasionally call the segmented personalities, multiple personalities. In the interest of consistency I have substituted segment or fragment (his favorite words) in the text.

2. Some take the opposite view. They believe MPD is a gift of God which enables horribly abused children to endure pain which would otherwise drive them to insanity or kill them. Satan takes advantage of multiples and seeks to demonize them just as he does non-MPDs.

3. Rockstad was an outstanding teacher/preacher on the believer's union with Christ. He practiced long and in-depth pre- and post-deliverance counseling. He was one of the first deliverance counselors to focus on the victory that comes to the believer as he learns to take his position in Christ as dead to sin, alive to and in Christ, reigning with Christ.

4. Rockstad, "Healing the Shattered Personality," audio cassette recording (Andover, Kansas: Faith and Life Publications, 1970).

5. I have not stated what type of abuse Carmen Cherry (and the others) were subjected to because Rockstad does not reveal this in his writings or audio cassette tape.

6. See James G. Friesen, *Uncovering the Mystery of MPD* (San Bernardino, Calif.: Here's Life Publishers, 1991).

7. See Friesen, 69f, and Neil T. Anderson, *Released from Bondage* (San Bernardino, Calif.: Here's Life Publishers, 1991b), 207–228.

8. For further help in this complex area, see Friesen, and Rodger K. Bufford, *Counseling and the Demonic* (Dallas, Texas: Word, 1988).

Chapter 60: The Non-Demonic Reality of Mental Illness

1. This is a composite story, based on experiences with people with similar problems.

2. See Ed Clendaniel, "Crying Out for Help: The Horror of Schizophrenia", *San Jose Mercury News* (March 18, 1990); and "Brain Changes Found in Schizophrenics", *San Jose Mercury News* (March 22, 1990).

   The noted Christian psychiatrist, Dr. John White, says, "We are finding that schizophrenias are a complex of different physical entities, some of which have already been separated off and understood, others remaining obscure. Knowing that in schizophrenia the biochemistry of the brain is disturbed, we hope that the key to healing all schizophrenics will be found some day." "Demonization and Mental Health," three-tape audio cassette series, tape #2a.

3. To my knowledge, the best practical book on schizophrenia in print today is *Surviving Schizophrenia: A Family Manual* (New York: Harper) by Dr. E. Fuller Torrey, a clinical and research psychiatrist who specializes in working with schizophrenia. Every counselor should buy and read this book. Every family with a disturbed family member who has been diagnosed schizophrenic should have this book.

   Quoting Torrey, I give these more common symptoms of schizophrenia:

   a.) Two of the following
      i. delusions
      ii. prominent auditory hallucinations
      iii. incoherence or marked loosening of associations
      iv. catatonic behavior
      v. flat or grossly inappropriate affect
   b.) Bizarre delusions . . .
   c.) Prominent auditory hallucinations consisting of voices keeping up a running commentary on the person's behavior, or two or more voices conversing with each other.

   Dr. Torrey comments that though DSM III has been helpful, serious problems still exist in accurate diagnosis (74–75).

   The most important symptoms, says Dr. Torrey are "auditory hallucinations of any kind." Thus the problem the counselor faces in ascertaining if these auditory hallucinations are truly hallucinations (schizophrenia) or demons or even alter personalities. All three can produce voices from within or from outside of the victim's head. In some mental states the voices may be more external than internal but both can occur.

   Dr. Torrey says that research has established "emphatically the biological bases for schizophrenia and manic-depressive psychosis as brain disease; they are nothing more, and nothing less, than diseases like multiple sclerosis, Alzheimer's disease, and Parkinson's disease" (p. xiii). Is there shame connected with Parkinson's disease? Of course not. The same should be true of schizophrenia.

4. See Rodger K. Bufford, *Counseling and the Demonic* (Dallas, Texas: Word, 1988), 116f; Marion H. Nelson, *Why Christians Crack Up* (Chicago: Moody, 1976), 135–148; John White, *The Masks of Melancholy* (Downers Grove, Ill.: InterVarsity, 1982), 27–39.

5. Bufford, 73–77, 110–111.

6. White; Bufford.

7. White, 60.

8. White, 60–61.

9. White, 63.

10. White, 63.

11. See Bufford, 68–72, 78f, 199.

12. White, 63–64.

13. White, 77–78; see Bufford, 51f.

14. Bufford, 88–89.
15. I am not comfortable with the words *psychiatrist* or *psychologist*, especially for Christian counselors. Both words are built on the Greek word *psyche,* soul. Psychology is thus the science of human souls. Psychiatrists and psychologists usually see themselves as doctors or healers of the human soul. But only God can truly heal broken, sick souls. Psychology and psychiatry do use truths based on careful human observation and reflection, but they also incorporate teachings and practices based on fundamental spiritual error and even deception. This mixture of truth and error occurs especially in psychotherapy, some of which is not biblically based. As God is the healer of human souls, His Word is the source of truth that heals. Thus, trained Christian counselors (a better word than psychiatrist or psychologist) who know how to apply God's truth to hurting people, who know the spirit world, who are not afraid to engage in deliverance ministry where necessary, and who are experienced in working with all forms of personality dissociation make the ideal persons to minister to troubled persons, both Christians and non-Christians.

Chapter 61: Counseling With Wisdom

1. See endnote 15, chapter 60, especially my strong caution about psychotherapy. Had time permitted, I would have rewritten portions of this chapter to cohere better with the concerns raised in that note.
2. Dr. John White, personal letter to author.
3. John White, *The Masks of Melancholy* (Downers Grove, Ill.: InterVarsity, 1982), 127–135. White's discussion on how these neurotransmitters work in relationship to what he describes as the whole "electro-chemical-facory-cum-microcomputer-cum- communicator system" within the brain cells is fascinating and very understandable, but too long to record here.
4. Antidepressant drugs help restore the activity of the retired or malfunctioning neurotransmitters.
5. White does a thorough analysis of the pros and cons of ECT. It is must reading for those counseling the clinically depressed, 210–221.
6. Dr. Jackson did not use psychotherapy, but counseled me from the Scriptures as this chapter reveals. While he denied that demons were my primary problem, he did *not* mean they were completely uninvolved; my primary problem was physical. Demons involved indirectly would leave once their point of contact in my weakened spiritual-emotional life was dealt with. His remarks and my comments must be interpreted in that light.
7. Many believers have anti-science bias especially an anti-social science bias. We need to recognize both the value and the limitations of science.
   "Christians need have no fear of science provided we remember three things," says John White. "First, scientists are merely investigating the laws of our Creator. They sometimes make serious mistakes in their investigations and arrive at wrong conclusions. But if they pursue matters far enough, they can only find truth, for truth is all there is to find. But because scientists make mistakes, all scientific conclusions must be tentative. Sooner or later the most unshakable and the most firmly founded ideas crumble and fall.
   "Consequently, it matters little whether science supports Scripture or not. If today's science opposes, we need not fear for today's theory will be replaced by another tomorrow. By the same token it is unwise to rejoice in science's support of Scripture. Who are scientists that they presume to 'confirm' the Word of the living God?
   "Finally, science is only one of the many ways of discovering truth and has serious limitations. It becomes dangerous only when we worship it, that is, when we assume it is the high road to all understanding. It can offer us no help with life's deepest questions. (Why do I exist? Why is there a universe? Does life have any meaning? How can we determine what is important in life?)" (60).
8. Rodger K. Bufford, *Counseling and the Demonic* (Dallas, Texas: Word, 1988), is good on this area.

Chapter 62: The New Age Movement

1. For excellent insight into Satanism and satanic cults see James Wilder, *A Redemptive Response to Satanism* (Downers Grove, Ill.: InterVarsity, 1992); Bob Larson, *Satanism: The Seduction of America's Youth* (Nashville: Nelson, 1989); Mark Bubeck, *The Satanic Revival* (San Bernardino, Calif.: Here's Life Publishers, Inc., 1991); Phil Phillips, *Halloween and Satanism* (Lancaster, Penn.: Starburst Publishers, 1987); Jerry Johnson, *The Edge of Evil*

(Dallas, Texas: Word, 1989); James G. Friesen, *Uncovering the Mystery of MPD* (San Bernardino, Calif.: Here's Life Publishers, 1991).

2. Dr. Norman L. Geisler and Yutaka J. Amano, *The Reincarnation Sensation* (Wheaton, Ill.: Tyndale, 1986); Neil T. Anderson, *Walking Through the Darkness* (San Bernardino, Calif.: Here's Life Publishers, 1991a); Douglas Groothuis, *Unmasking the New Age* (Downers Grove, Ill.: InterVarsity, 1986), *Confronting the New Age* (Downers Grove, Ill.: InterVarsity, 1988), *Revealing the New Age Jesus* (Downers Grove, Ill.: InterVarsity, 1990).

3. All quotes from Dr. Norman Geisler are from a series of lectures Dr. Geisler gave at the Los Gatos Christian Church, Los Gatos, California in 1990. The tapes of these lectures from which I draw all my materials are available. Write Los Gatos Christian Church, 16845 Hicks Road, Los Gatos, California 95030. Phone 408-268-1411. Ask for the Tapes Ministry Department. After completing this chapter I discovered *The Reincarnation Sensation* by Norman L. Geisler and Yutaka J. Amano (Wheaton, Ill.: Tyndale, 1986). Many items in Dr. Geisler's three lectures appear in his book.

4. "The Wiz of Show Biz," *Newsweek* (December 20, 1976), 68.

5. According to Geisler, 1990 cassette recordings.

6. Robert Muller, *New Genesis: Shaping a Global Spirituality* (New York: Doubleday, 1982).

7. Dale Pollock, *Skywalking: The Life and Films of George Lucas* (New York: Harmony Books, 1983), 140.

Chapter 63: The Road to Personal Victory in Spiritual Warfare: James 4:1–8

1. See Neil Anderson, 1990a, 1990b, 1991b in bibliography.

2. See David Seamand's *Healing For Damaged Emotions* (Wheaton, Ill.: Victor, 1985a); *Healing of Memories* (Wheaton, Ill.: Victor, 1985b); and *Healing Grace* (Wheaton, Ill.: Victor, 1988).

3. William E. Vine, *An Expository Dictionary of New Testament Words* (London: Oliphants, 1953) 2:169–170.

4. J. Ramsey Michaels, *1 Peter,* WBC (Waco, Texas: Word, 1988).

5. Vine 4:201.

6. Michaels, 297.

7. Vine 2:145.

8. C. S. Lewis, *The Screwtape Letters* (London: Fontana Books, 1963), 7.

9. Lewis, 7.

10. Bill Bright, *Praise and Worship,* Audio cassette series (San Bernardino, Calif.: Campus Crusade for Christ, 1987).

Chapter 64: The Dangers and Pitfalls of Spiritual Warfare

1. Stanley Burgess, Gary McGee, and Patrick Alexander, *Dictionary of Pentecostal and Charismatic Movements* (Grand Rapids: Zondervan, 1989), 3.

2. John White, *When the Spirit Comes with Power* (Downers Grove, IL: InterVarsity Press, 1988).

3. Stephen Strang, "Floored in Toronto," *Charisma* (February, 1996): 106.

4. White, 45.

5. White, 51.

6. Stephen Strang, "More, Lord," *Charisma* (May, 1995): 102.

7. Margaret Poloma, "By Their Fruits," *Spread the Fire,* Toronto Airport Christian Fellowship (February, 1996): 8.

8. John Arnott, *The Father's Blessing* (Altamonte Springs, FL: Creation House, 1995).

9. C. Peter Wagner, *Breaking Strongholds in Your City* (Ventura, CA: Regal, 1993): 14.

10. Wagner, 17–19.

11. Two major groups stress strategic-level spiritual warfare today. This first operates in fellowship with the A.D. 2000 United Prayer Track Networking Structure. Within this group, I am a member of The Spiritual Warfare Network, which is directed internationally by C. Peter Wagner. The Network draws together many of the most balanced and experienced leaders in spiritual warfare worldwide. Its members have written most of the outstanding books on spiritual warfare available. These are serious men and women with the most years of experience both in research and practice of strategic, cosmic-level spiritual warfare.

The second group is difficult to define because it is not organized in a large structure. In this group are many pastors, conference speakers, and other intercessors. These are zealous for God and His kingdom, but they are not accountable to a larger, more experienced group. Inexperienced, untaught people within this second group are those about whom I am most concerned regarding their involvement in cosmic-level spiritual warfare.

Appendices & Select Bibliography

The Daily Affirmation of Faith

Today I deliberately choose to submit myself fully to God as He has made Himself known to me through the Holy Scripture, which I honestly accept as the only inspired, infallible, authoritative standard for all life and practice. In this day I will not judge God, His work, myself, or others on the basis of feelings or circumstances.

1. I recognize by faith that the triune God is worthy of all honor, praise, and worship as the Creator, sustainer, and end of all things. I confess that God, as my creator, made me for Himself. In this day I therefore choose to live for Him (Rev. 5:9–10; Isa. 43:1,7,21; Rev. 4:11).
2. I recognize by faith that God loved me and chose me in Jesus Christ before time began (Eph. 1:1–7).
3. I recognize by faith that God has proven His love to me in sending His Son to die in my place, in whom every provision has already been made for my past, present, and future needs through His representative work, and that I have been quickened, raised, seated with Jesus Christ in the heavenlies, and anointed with the Holy Spirit (Rom. 5:6–11; 8:28–39; Phil. 1:6; 4:6–7,13,19; Eph. 1:3; 2:5–6; Acts 2:1–4,33).
4. I recognize by faith that God has accepted me since I have received Jesus Christ as my Lord and Savior (John 1:12; Eph. 1:6); that He has forgiven me (Eph. 1:7); adopted me into His family, assuming every responsibility for me (John 17:11, 17; Eph. 1:5; Phil. 1:6); given me eternal life (John 3:16; 1 John 5:9–13); applied the perfect righteousness of Christ to me so that I am now justified (Rom. 5:1; 8:3–4; 10:4); made me complete in Christ (Col. 2:10); and offers Himself to me as my daily sufficiency through prayer and the decisions of faith (1 Cor. 1:30; Col. 1:27; Gal. 2:20; John 14:13–14; Matt. 21:22; Rom. 6:1–19; Heb. 4:1–3,11).
5. I recognize by faith that the Holy Spirit has baptized me into the body of Christ (1 Cor. 12:13); sealed me (Eph. 1:13–14); anointed me for life and service (Acts 1:8; John 7:37–39); seeks to lead me into a deeper walk with Jesus Christ (John 14:16–18; 15:26–27; 16:13–15; Rom. 8:11–16); and to fill my life with Himself (Eph. 5:18).
6. I recognize by faith that only God can deal with sin and only God can produce holiness of life. I confess that in my salvation my part was only to receive Him and that He dealt with my sin and saved me. Now I confess that in order to live a holy life, I can only surrender to His will and receive Him as my sanctification; trusting Him to do whatever may be necessary in my life, without and within, so I may be enabled to live today in purity, freedom, rest, and power for His glory (John 1:12; 1 Cor. 1:30; 2 Cor. 9:8; Gal. 2:20; Heb. 4:9; 1 John 5:4; Jude 24).

Having confessed that God is worthy of all praise, that the Scriptures are the only authoritative standard, that only God can deal with sin and produce holiness of life, I again recognize my total dependence upon Him and submission to Him. I accept the truth that praying in faith is absolutely necessary for the realization of the will and grace of God in my daily life (1 John 5:14–15; James 2:6; 4:2–3; 5:16–18; Phil. 4:6–7; Heb. 4:1–13; 11:6, 24–28).

Recognizing that faith is a total response to God by which the daily provisions the Lord has furnished in Himself are appropriated, I therefore make the following decisions of faith:

1. For this day (Heb. 3:6,13,15; 4:7) I make the decision of faith to surrender wholly to the authority of God as He has revealed Himself in the Scripture—to obey Him.

    I confess my sin, face the sinful reality of my old nature, and deliberately choose to walk in the light, in step with Christ, throughout the hours of this day (Rom. 6:16–20; Phil. 2:12–13; 1 John 1:7,9).

2. For this day I make the decision of faith to surrender wholly to the authority of God as revealed in the Scripture—to believe Him. I accept only his Word as final authority. I now believe that since I have confessed my sin He has forgiven and cleansed me (1 John 1:9). I accept at full value His Word of promise to be my sufficiency and rest, and will conduct myself accordingly (Exod. 33:1; 1 Cor. 1:30; 2 Cor. 9:8; Phil. 4:19).

3. For this day I make the decision of faith to recognize that God has made every provision so that I may fulfill His will and calling. Therefore, I will not make any excuse for my sin and failure (1 Thess. 5:24).

4. For this day I make the decision of faith deliberately to receive from God that provision which He has made for me. I renounce all self-effort to live the Christian life and to perform God's service; renounce all sinful praying which asks God to change circumstances and people so that I may be more spiritual; renounce all drawing back from the work of the Holy Spirit within and the call of God without; and renounce all nonbiblical motives, goals, and activities which serve my sinful pride.

   a. I now sincerely receive Jesus Christ as my sanctification, particularly as my cleansing from the old nature, and ask the Holy Spirit to apply to me the work of Christ accomplished for me in the Crucifixion. In cooperation with and dependence upon Him, I obey the command to "put off the old man" (Rom. 6:1–14; 1 Cor. 1:30; Gal. 6:14; Eph. 4:22).

   b. I now sincerely receive Jesus Christ as my sanctification, particularly as my enablement moment by moment to live above sin, and ask the Holy Spirit to apply to me the work of the Resurrection so that I may walk in newness of life. I confess that only God can deal with my sin and only God can produce holiness and the fruit of the Spirit in my life. In cooperation with and dependence upon Him, I obey the command to "put on the new man" (Rom. 6:1–4; Eph. 4:24).

   c. I now sincerely receive Jesus Christ as my deliverance from Satan and take my position with Him in the heavenlies, asking the Holy Spirit to apply to me the work of the Ascension. In His name I submit myself to God and stand against all of Satan's influence and subtlety. In cooperation with and dependence upon God, I obey the command to "resist the devil" (Eph. 1:2–23; 2:5; 5:27; 6:10–18; Col. 1:13; Heb. 2:14–15; James 4:7; 1 Pet. 3:22; 5:8–9).

   d. I now sincerely receive the Holy Spirit as my anointing for every aspect of life and service for today. I fully open my life to Him to fill me afresh in obedience to the command to "be filled with the Holy Spirit" (Eph. 5:18; John 7:37–39; 14:16–17; 15:26–27; 16:7–15; Acts 1:8).

    Having made this confession and these decisions of faith, I now receive God's promised rest for this day (Heb. 4:1–13). Therefore, I relax in the trust of faith, knowing that in the moment of temptation, trial, or need, the Lord Himself will be there as my strength and sufficiency (1 Cor. 10:13).

(This affirmation was composed by Dr. Victor Matthews, Professor Emeritus of Systematic Theology, Grand Rapids Baptist Bible College and Seminary [as quoted in Mark Bubeck, *The Adversary* (Chicago: Moody Press, 1975) 136–140]. Used by permission.)

Warfare Prayer

Heavenly Father, I bow in worship and praise before you. I cover myself with the blood of the Lord Jesus Christ as my protection during this time of prayer. I surrender myself completely and unreservedly in every area of my life to yourself. I do take a stand against all the workings of Satan that would hinder me in this time of prayer, and I address myself only to the true and living God and refuse any involvement of Satan in my prayer.

Satan, I command you, in the name of the Lord Jesus Christ, to leave my presence with all your demons, and I bring the blood of the Lord Jesus Christ between us.

Heavenly Father, I worship you, and I give you praise. I recognize that you are worthy to receive all glory and honor and praise. I renew my allegiance to you and pray that the blessed Holy Spirit would enable me in this time of prayer. I am thankful, heavenly Father, that you have loved me from past eternity, that you sent the Lord Jesus Christ into the world to die as my substitute that I would be redeemed. I am thankful that the Lord Jesus Christ came as my representative, and that through Him you have completely forgiven me; you have given me eternal life; you have given me the perfect righteousness of the Lord Jesus Christ so I am now justified. I am thankful that in Him you have made me complete, and that you have offered yourself to me to be my strength.

Heavenly Father, come and open my eyes that I might see how great you are and how complete your provision is for this new day. I do, in the name of the Lord Jesus Christ, take my place with Christ in the heavenlies with all principalities and powers (powers of darkness and wicked spirits) under my feet. I am thankful that the victory the Lord Jesus Christ won for me on the Cross and in His resurrection has been given to me and that I am seated with the Lord Jesus Christ in the heavenlies; therefore, I declare that all principalities and powers and all wicked spirits are subject to me in the name of the Lord Jesus Christ.

I am thankful for the armor you have provided, and I put on the girdle of truth, the breastplate of righteousness, the sandals of peace, the helmet of salvation. I lift up the shield of faith against all the fiery darts of the Enemy, and take in my hand the sword of the Spirit, the Word of God, and use your Word against all the forces of evil in my life; and I put on this armor and live and pray in complete dependence upon you, blessed Holy Spirit.

I am grateful, heavenly Father, that the Lord Jesus Christ spoiled all principalities and powers and made a show of them openly and triumphed over them in Himself. I claim all that victory for my life today. I reject out of my life all the insinuations, the accusations, and the temptations of Satan. I affirm that the Word of God is true, and I choose to live today in the light of God's Word. I choose, heavenly Father, to live in obedience to you and in fellowship with yourself.

Open my eyes and show me the areas of my life that would not please you. Work in my life that there be no ground to give Satan a foothold against me. Show me any area of weakness. Show me any area of my life that I must deal with so that I would please you. I do in every way today stand for you and the ministry of the Holy Spirit in my life.

By faith and in dependence upon you, I put off the old man and stand into all the victory of the Crucifixion where the Lord Jesus Christ provided cleansing from the old nature. I put on the new man and stand into all the victory of the Resurrection and the provision He has made for me there to live above sin. Therefore, in this day, I put off the old nature with its selfishness, and I put on the new nature with its love. I put off the old nature with its fear and I put on the new nature with its courage. I put off the old nature with its weakness and with all its deceitful lusts and I put on the new nature with all its righteousness and purity.

I do in every way stand into the victory of the Ascension and the glorification of the Son of God where all principalities and powers were made subject to Him, and I claim my place in Christ victorious with Him over all the enemies of my soul. Blessed Holy Spirit, I pray that you would fill me. Come into my life, break down every idol, and cast out every foe.

I am thankful, heavenly Father, for the expression of your will for my daily life as you have shown me in your Word. I therefore claim all the will of God for today. I am thankful that you have blessed me with all spiritual blessings in heavenly places in Christ Jesus. I am thankful that you have begotten me unto a living hope by the resurrection of Jesus Christ from the dead. I am thankful that you have made a provision so that today I can live filled with the Spirit of God with love and joy and self-control in my life. And I recognize that this is your will for me, and I therefore reject and resist all the endeavors of Satan and of these demons to rob me of the will of God. I hold up the shield of faith against all the accusations and against all the insinuations that Satan would put in my mind.

I do, in the name of the Lord Jesus Christ, completely surrender myself to you, heavenly Father, as a living sacrifice. I choose not to be conformed to this world. I choose to be transformed by the renewing of my mind, and I pray that you would show me your will and enable me to walk in all the fullness of the will of God today.

I am thankful, heavenly Father, that the weapons of our warfare are not of the flesh, but mighty through God to the pulling down of strongholds, to the casting down of imaginations and every lofty thing raised up against the knowledge of God, and to bring every thought into obedience to the Lord Jesus Christ. Therefore in my own life today I tear down the strongholds of Satan, and I smash the plans of Satan that have been formed against me. I tear down the strongholds of Satan against my mind, and I choose to think my thoughts after you, blessed Holy Spirit. I affirm, heavenly Father, that you have not given us the spirit of fear, but of power and of love and of a sound mind. I break and smash the strongholds of Satan formed against my emotions today, and I give my will to you, and choose to make the right decisions of faith. I smash the strongholds of Satan formed against my body today, and I give my body to you, recognizing that I am your temple; and I rejoice in your mercy and your goodness.

Heavenly Father, I pray that now through this day you would quicken me; show me the way that Satan is hindering and tempting and lying and counterfeiting and distorting the truth in my life. Enable me to be the kind of person that would please you. Enable me to be aggressive in prayer. Enable me to be aggressive mentally and to think your thoughts after you, and to give you your rightful place in my life.

Again, I now cover myself with the blood of the Lord Jesus Christ and pray that you, blessed Holy Spirit, would bring all the work of the Crucifixion, all the work of the Resurrection, all the work of the glorification, and all the work of Pentecost into my life today. I yield my life to you. I refuse to be discouraged. You are the God of all hope. You have proven your power by resurrecting Jesus Christ from the dead, and I claim in every way your victory over all satanic forces active in my life, and I reject these forces; and I pray in the name of the Lord Jesus Christ with thanksgiving. Amen.

This prayer is taken from Mark Bubeck's book *The Adversary* (Chicago: Moody Press, 1975) and was written by Dr. Victor Matthews and lightly edited by Dr. Neil T. Anderson. Used by permission.

Group Deliverance Prayer

Dear heavenly Father, in the name of the Lord Jesus, as your servant, I come before you right now in behalf of these your people. Father, these are your people. You have taken them out of the kingdom of darkness. You have placed them in the kingdom of your dear Son.

We are your people. You are not angry with us. You were in Christ reconciling us unto yourself. Jesus' blood was the propitiation for our sins. It covered our sins. It satisfied all the demands of your justice and your holiness. You say in your Word, "There is therefore now no condemnation to those who are in Christ Jesus." We are all in Christ Jesus. You do not condemn us.

Father, you are not the accuser. You convict us of sins so we will confess our sins to you and reject their influence in our life. You never haunt us with accusations saying we are evil; no good, worthless, unacceptable to you; so bad we are not true Christians. We know that such accusations only come from the Enemy.

You don't condemn your children. You don't accuse your children. You love us. Oh, God, oh, Lord Jesus, you said in your Word, "If you then being evil (and we are) know how to give good things to your children, how much more shall your heavenly Father give good things to those who ask Him?"

Oh, Father, thank you that you are my father, that you are our father. Thank you that your Spirit in us cries, "Abba Father," "my own dear father." Your Spirit within all of my brothers and sisters here in your presence right now is crying to you in their behalf, "Abba Father." The Spirit Himself within us is making intercession for us right now with groanings that we cannot even utter. We bless you, our Father and our God, that you know the mind of the Spirit. Thus, you answer His cries because He prays according to your will through us and we bless you for that.

Lord Jesus, we thank you right now that by faith, with the eyes of our spirit, we see you enthroned at the right hand of God interceding for all of us. We also see all demons, all evil principalities and powers placed in subjection to you. You alone are Lord. Lord Jesus you say to us in your Word that all authority has been given to you in heaven and on earth. You alone are Lord! You are our Lord! With our mouth we confess, Jesus, you are my Lord! You are our Lord! Your Father has established you as head over all things pertaining to your church and we belong to your church, Lord Jesus. We honor you right now and we bless you as the Lord of our life.

Lord Jesus, you have bound Satan. You dethroned the Enemy. You took upon yourself human flesh that "through death you might render powerless him who had power over death, that is the devil, in order that you might free us who were in bondage to him." We thank you that you have already freed us from that bondage. We thank you that you have already rendered Satan powerless against us.

Thank you, Father, that when you placed our sins upon your Son, you nailed the death debt decree which was against us to the Cross. Thus you disarmed the evil rulers and authorities that had enslaved us. You triumphed over the demonic principalities and powers. The whole kingdom of evil supernaturalism has been humiliated and defeated by you. Lord Jesus, you made a public display of our defeated enemies. Your angels and all of creation joyfully witnessed the defeat of these fallen angelic beings who had rebelled against your Father. You dethroned them and you defeated them. You tell us in your Word that since we are born of God the Evil One cannot touch us. You have given us authority over "scorpions and serpents and over all the work of the enemy." You have said to us "Nothing shall by any means hurt" us. You have given to us authority over the kingdom of Satan and we thank you for it.

In the name of Jesus Christ, I speak to the evil spirit world in behalf of my brothers and sisters who are here before God. Every demonic power which has been assigned against us to disturb this meeting, get out of here! You have no place here.

We, right now, break every demonic curse placed upon us as individuals and as a group. Jesus has born all curses for us. We send you cursing evil spirits out of this room, away from our lives, back to the one who sent you here. Get out now. God's angels are now removing you from our presence. Every demonic power, every enemy of Jesus Christ attached to the lives of any of God's people gathered here, I command you in the name of Jesus, be silent! Any evil spirits hiding within the lives of my brothers and sisters, in the name of Jesus, I command you go into the pit of their stomach. You are bound there and you cannot whisper to their minds. You cannot touch their bodies. You cannot disturb their emotions nor influence their will. You cannot do anything. You are bound and you are to shut up and when we tell you to go, you will go and not return. You cannot call upon Satan or any other demonic powers to assist you.

We seal off this entire building by the authority we have in Jesus Christ the Lord. We command every external spirit that has nothing to do with the lives of these, God's people, get out of this room right now! Get out and you cannot come back!

Father, you said you send your angels as ministering spirits to minister to us, your heirs of salvation. You say that the angel of the Lord "camps round about those who fear Him and delivers them." We ask you right now that your angels will camp right around this room and seal us off from all activity of any external evil spirits. They have nothing to do with what's going on here. Father, may your angels expel every demonic power that has been sent against us by evil persons. We bless you for that. You are doing so right now. They are being sent back in anger and defeat to those who sent them against us.

Now Father, we want to come together before you as the representatives of our family line. We want to confess the ancestral, generational sins we are guilty of as families. Those sins which we share in as part of a rebellious lineage.

We also want to deal with the sins that have resulted from the abuse we experienced as children. We want to forgive those who have hurt us. We want to ask you to forgive and to bless those who have sinned against us. You told us we are to forgive as we have been forgiven.

Finally, we are going to confess to you in a general way the sinful choices we have made, the sinful activities that have opened the door to demonic attachment to our life. Thank you that you are going to hear our confession, Father, because you said that you forgive us and cleanse us when we confess our sins. We thank you that you are going to forgive us right now.

Brothers and sisters, don't be afraid of what we are going to do now. I want you to speak out loud after me the words which I speak in your behalf before God. Even if some of the sins I confess in behalf of all of us here you are not personally guilty of, confess them anyway, out loud after me. Thus, we minister in behalf of others in this room who have experienced the curse of those sins.

Dear heavenly Father, I am your child. *(Repeat.)* You have redeemed me. *(Continue repeating out loud each phrase.)* You have taken me out of the kingdom of darkness. You have placed me in the kingdom of your Son. As far as the east is from the west you have removed my iniquities from me. You promise me in your Word that my sins and my iniquities, you remember no more. How I bless you for that.

Dear Father, I want to come before you as the representative of my ancestral line, of my family line. Hear my confession as I confess to you the sins of my fathers as the Scriptures teach.

Father, we are a rebellious family. We have rebelled against your Word. We have grieved your Spirit. We have served other gods. We are guilty of sexual sins. We have abused other people. We have been filled with anger and rage and self-pity, with rejection and bitterness. We have hurt other people. We have gossiped. We have stolen, lied, and committed iniquity. We are a sinful people. I ask you right now to forgive me, my parents, my grandparents, my family line for the sins we have committed. I ask you right now to cancel out the sinful transference that you have pronounced in your Word when you said that the sins of my fathers and my father's fathers would come down through the family line unto the third and fourth generation.

Father, I represent a new generation. I want to serve you. I want my children to serve you. Right now I ask you to forgive my family members. I pray with Jesus when he said, "Father, forgive them for they know not what they are doing." In behalf of those who are still alive, Father, forgive them. Bring them to repentance. Don't lay their sin to their charge. Father, for me, as the representative of my family, forgive me for my involvement in the sins of my family line. I thank you that the generational curse is broken in your eyes right now. Jesus bore that curse for me and my family.

Then, dear Father, you know I was abused as a child. You know I came from a dysfunctional family. My parents didn't raise me as I should have been raised. Since my early childhood there were problems in my life, there were sexual problems, there were problems of anger, bitterness, shame, a sense of unworthiness, and rejection. Oh, Father, forgive me for these negative dimensions of my life. Father, you know the people whose very name brings a negative reaction within me. They hurt me. They abused me sexually. They abused me physically. They abused me religiously. They sinned against me. Right now, I confess to you my reactionary sin against them, my bitterness, anger, even hatred and rage against these people.

Let's take a moment and let God bring some of those names to our minds. Silently choose to forgive those people one by one. Don't hold back. Remember what Jesus said, "If you do not forgive the transgressions committed against you, your heavenly Father will not forgive you." He said when you are standing, praying, "Forgive, if you have anything against anyone that your heavenly Father may forgive you." That's a principle of the kingdom of God.

If the name of someone comes to your mind, someone who did something so awful against you that you have battled for years with anger and unforgiveness, you might not emotionally feel you can forgive as God commands. That is understandable. That results from the serious emotional bruising that you have suffered at the hands of other people. The healing of your emotions will come in time, but you are able now to begin obeying the command of God by choosing to forgive them.

It will help you if you can accept the fact that the persons who did you harm were in all probability themselves the victims of somebody else's abuse. That's why they acted the way they did against you. That doesn't absolve them of their accountability, but very often those who have victimized you were themselves first victimized by others. The cycle of sin must be broken and you must make that break right now. The indwelling Holy Spirit will help you right now. Say,

Father, forgive them. *(Mention all the names that come to your mind.)* They did not know what they were doing. Father, by faith, I choose to forgive them right now.

Perhaps you too have been guilty of the same type of sin against other people. You have been so angry with your parents, brothers or sisters, grandparents or relatives, or a babysitter or friend, people of different race, ethnic group, social class, or whoever it might be, that you, in turn, have poured out your anger on other people. Perhaps you too have victimized your loved ones, your husband or wife or your children or your parents or others and you want to right now ask God to forgive you. Do it, quietly. We will all pray silently for a few moments. Ask the Holy Spirit to bring to your mind those who need your forgiveness.

The Lord, by His Spirit, will bring other names to your mind later today, tomorrow, and the days ahead. You can continue to choose to forgive.

Now, repeat after me as I pray.

Dear Father, I choose to forgive all of these people whose names you have brought to my mind. I choose to forgive everyone whose name you will yet bring to my mind in the days ahead. I have been angry with them. I have hated them. I have been bitter towards them. I have fantasized harm happening to them because they hurt me so much. Father, forgive them. They didn't know what they were doing. They, themselves, were victims of sins committed against them in their childhood, through their family line or by other sinful people. Father, right now, by faith, I choose to forgive all those who have sinned against me. I forgive all of them without exception, especially that one person who did me so much harm. I have battled for years with my inability and/or unwillingness to forgive him, her, and the others. I do it now, by faith, by the power of your Spirit.

Lord, more than that, by faith I choose to love them with your love. In myself I don't find that love. In your love for me I can extend my love and your love to them.

I want them to be redeemed. I don't want them to go to hell. May your grace work in their life if they are still alive and bring them to repentance for the evil that they have done just, Father, as you have done with me. I want them to love you the way I love you. Now, dear Father, I right now claim your promise that if I confess my sins (and I have done that) you are faithful and just to forgive me my sins and to cleanse me from all unrighteousness. Thank you, Father, that you have forgiven me and that I am now free to forgive them.

Dear Father, I have more confession to make to you. I have wilfully sinned against you from my childhood until now. You know those sins that I have committed, wilfully. I am ashamed. Lord, I know that you want to forgive me and set me free.

Lord, I now confess all my sins to you. I confess and renounce all my sexual sins, both in actual sexual activity as well as those of the mind and imagination. Cleanse me, Father. I confess and reject my sins of anger, pride, stubbornness, bitterness, rejection, shame, wanting my own way, contention, division, worldly ambitions—all of this evil, oh, God, I am ashamed of it all. I have sinned against you and ask you to forgive me.

Now Lord, I take all of my sins in one group and lay them before you. I renounce them. I confess them. I reject them. I want nothing to do with them. I want to be pure. I want to be a person of God. You have said in your Word, "Be ye holy because I am holy." I want to be holy. I claim your promise that if I confess these sins as I have now done, that you are faithful and just and you are forgiving me right now. The blood of Jesus Christ, your Son, is being applied to my heart right now. I am being washed clean. I am no longer guilty. I am free. Thank you, Father. I bless your wonderful name.

Now, brothers and sisters, we are going to break all demonic activity which these sins have drawn to our life. Just relax. Don't fight anything that takes place inside of you. You are not going to be embarrassed. Nothing is going to hurt you. I am going to speak out as your representative. Don't try to analyze what is going on. Just listen and let the Spirit of God do what He does.

Jesus said, "I cast out demons by the Spirit of God . . . ." Jesus by His Holy Spirit dwells inside of you. He is going to evict those squatters. He is going to break their attachment to any area of your life. He is going to send them where He wants them to go because there is no longer any grounds for them to be attached to your life. They can only be attached to you because of sin grounds. We have removed those sin grounds.

Just listen and relax. Don't be afraid. Just let the Spirit of God do what He does. If you feel something strange occurring inside of you don't worry about it. Nothing is going to hurt you. Anything that doesn't belong inside of you is going to begin to go out. However, don't depend on any feelings. Just relax in the presence of God. Let the Spirit of God apply to your life what I am now going to do as your spokesman, what we are going to do together:

In the name of Jesus Christ, I stand as the representative of these, my brothers and sisters. I now take my position with these my brethren as reigning with Jesus Christ. I speak and we speak to every enemy of Jesus Christ, every demonic power that has been assigned and attached to the lives of my brothers and sisters here.

All of you evil spirits who have come down through the family line, your right to afflict their life has been broken. They have confessed the sins of their fathers. Any of you who have come in as a curse placed upon them as children, that curse has been broken. Any of you demonic powers who have become attached to the lives of my brothers and sisters through the abuse they suffered as children, you no longer have any place in their life. They have forgiven those who have done harm against them. Every demonic power who in any way is attached to the lives of my brothers and sisters because of sins which they themselves have committed, you must now go. You no longer have any grounds in their life.

As a servant of God, I come into the spirit world and right now in the name of Jesus Christ, I draw you away from and out of the life of these my brothers and sisters. I break your attachment to their lives. In the name of Jesus Christ, I command you to go, right now, quietly the same way you came in, and do not return. Go to where Jesus sends you and you cannot come back. My brothers and sisters are being set free.

I would like all of you to pray out loud with me: Thank you, dear Father. *(Repeat each phrase.)* I bless you that you have forgiven my sins. Spirit of God, I bless you, praise you and thank you today that you have set me free. Anything that was internal in my life has quietly gone the same way it came in. Anything external to my life has been broken away. The bondage that I have been facing is now diminishing and will continue to diminish in the days ahead. Thank you, Lord Jesus, that you promised in your Word, "If the Son shall set you free, you shall be free indeed." Lord, I thank you that you have set me free right now. I just want to worship you. I want to draw near to you. I ask you to draw near to me now.

Just praise Him, dear brothers and sisters. Thank Him in your own heart. If your practice is to pray out loud quietly, then do so. Just worship Him right now. Thank Him for what He has done for you and for the life of all of God's people here. Just in your own way, pray. If you want to stand up and bless Him, do it. If you want to just sit where you are that is perfectly acceptable. Just praise Him. Don't shout and disturb others, but praise Him out loud. Pray with joy and faith. Pray and praise.

Now, I would like you to follow me in this last united prayer, out loud.

Dear heavenly Father. (Repeat.) I lift my heart to you right now. I worship you. Oh, I love you. You are my Father. You don't judge me. You don't condemn me. I belong to you. You called me to be your child. You separated me from this world. You took me out of the kingdom of darkness and placed me into the kingdom of your Son. I worship you right now. Thank you, Father, that I am free. I bless you, I am free from the bondage that was mine in these areas of my life that I have brought before you. I thank you that within my being I sense as never before the flow of your Spirit, the freedom to go out into the world and face those former sources of temptation and not be drawn to them because I am free. Your Spirit has made me free. Bless your wonderful name. Draw near to my life, now. Make me to be the child you want me to be. I pray all of this in the name of your beloved Son, the Lord Jesus and for your glory. Amen.

(An actual [edited] group spiritual warfare prayer led by Dr. Ed Murphy in churches in the U.S.A. and around the world.)

Requirements for Deliverance and Staying Free from Further Demonization

REQUIREMENTS FOR DELIVERANCE

1. Be assured of salvation through personal faith in the Lord Jesus Christ.
2. Humble yourself before God. Be totally open and honest with Him.
3. Confess and renounce the sin of your family line.
4. Confess and renounce your own sins.
5. Choose to forgive everyone who has hurt, rejected, or offended you, especially those who have injured you the most deeply (an act of faith and obedience; your emotions have nothing to do with the matter).
6. Ask God to forgive, redeem, and cleanse those who have hurt you. Desire (by faith) their salvation and spiritual well-being.
7. Commit the totality of your life to the absolute lordship of the Lord Jesus Christ.
8. Speak out against Satan and his demons declaring they no longer have any place in your life. Their sin grounds have been removed. They must now leave your life and not return.

REQUIREMENTS TO STAY FREE FROM FURTHER DEMONIZATION

1. Practice "The Daily Affirmation of Faith." This is the "word of your testimony" (Rev. 12:11; Eph. 3:10). (See Appendix A.)
2. Repeat the "Warfare Prayer" found in Appendix B. When you feel internal resistance to this prayer, it is demonic. Practice James 4:7–8a until the demons leave. Tell them to leave quietly and with no harm to you.
3. Study Ephesians 6:1–20 daily. By faith put on the whole armor of God. That armor is yours in Christ, i.e., he is the armor (Rom. 13:12–14; 2 Cor. 6:7; 10:4; Gal. 3:27). Pray according to Ephesians 6:18–20.
4. Stay away from all sinful practices. Avoid any environment which will lead you into temptation. Avoid the companionship of persons who could lead you back into sin.
5. Begin daily Bible study. Don't be concerned if you don't understand everything in the Bible. Keep reading.
6. Join a Bible-believing, Christ-honoring local church. Attend faithfully. Attend Sunday School with your age group.
7. Try and get into a small Bible study-prayer group, a James 5:16 prayer-share-healing group.
8. Pray daily. Start a prayer list of things and persons you want to pray for. God will answer your prayers.

APPENDIX E

How I Learned to Pray
for the Lost

Here is a remarkable testimony which should be a real help to many. Since the nature of the testimony is personal, the writer requested that her name be withheld.

"This is the result of my search for the right way of praying for the unsaved. I have found it to produce amazing results in a very short time. After more than 20 years of fruitless praying, it seemed that there was no possible chance for my loved ones ever to return to the faith. But after only a few weeks of the type of praying that I have outlined here, I have seen them studying the Bible by the hour and attending every church service possible. Their whole attitude toward Chrisianity has changed, and all resistance seems to be gone. I have taken my place of authority in Christ and am using it against the Enemy. I have not looked at myself to see if I am fit or not; I have just taken my place and have prayed that the Holy Spirit may do His convicting work. If each and every member of the body of Christ would do this, what a change would be made in this world."

Believers everywhere are burdened for unsaved or backsliding loved ones. However, many are praying in the spirit of fear and worry instead of in faith.

This has caused me to seek for definite light on how to pray, feeling the need of praying the right prayer, and also the need for a definite promise or word from God on which to base my faith when praying for the unsaved. Praise God—He never fails to give such needed help.

Perhaps because the salvation of some seemed to me to be an impossibility, the first verse of Scripture that was given to me was Mark 10:27, "With God all things are possible."

The next Scripture verse had occupied my attention for some time, but it took on a new meaning. "For the weapons of our warfare are not carnal, but mighty through God to the pulling down of strongholds; casting down imaginations (speculations) and every high thing that exalteth itself against the knowledge of God and bring into captivity every thought to the obedience of Christ" (2 Cor. 10:4,5). This shows the mighty power of our spiritual weapons. We must pray that all of this will be accomplished in the ones for whom we are concerned; that is, that the works of the Enemy will be torn down.

Finally, I was given the solid foundation for my prayers—the basis of redemption. In reality, Christ's redemption purchased all mankind, so that we may say that each one is actually God's purchased possession, although he is still held by the Enemy. We must, through the prayer of faith, claim and take for God in the name of the Lord Jesus that which is rightfully His. This can be done only on the basis of redemption. This is not meant to imply that, because all persons have been purchased by God through redemption, they are automatically saved. They must believe and accept the gospel for themselves; our intercession enables them to do this.

To pray in the name of the Lord Jesus is to ask for, or to claim, the things which the blood of Christ has secured. Therefore, each individual for whom prayer is made should be claimed by name as God's purchased possession, in the name of the Lord Jesus and on the basis of His shed blood.

We should claim the tearing down of all the works of Satan, such as false doctrine, unbelief, atheistic teaching and hatred, which the Enemy may have built up in their thinking. We must pray that their very thoughts will be brought into captivity to the obedience of Christ.

With the authority of the name of the Lord Jesus, we must claim their deliverance from the power and persuasion of the Evil One and from the love of the world and the lust of the flesh. We should also pray that their conscience may be convicted, that God may bring them to the point of repentance and that they may listen and believe as they hear or read the Word of God. Our prayer must be that God's will and purposes may be accomplished in and through them.

Intercession must be persistent—not to persuade God, for redemption is by God, but because of the Enemy. Our prayer and resistance are against the Enemy—the awful owner and ruler of darkness. It is our duty before God to fight for the souls for whom Christ died. Just as some must preach to them the good news of redemption, others must fight the powers of darkness on their behalf through prayer.

Satan yields only what and when he must, and he renews his attacks in subtle ways. Therefore, prayer must be definite and persistent, even long after definite results are seen. We must pray for the new Christian even after he begins to be established in the faith.

We will find that as we pray, the Holy Spirit will give new directions. At one time I was interceding for a soul and began to feel that my prayers were largely ineffective, when the Holy Spirit inspired me to begin presenting that person to God in the name of the Lord Jesus. As I obeyed this leading, praying, "I present so-and-so to God in the name of the Lord Jesus," I felt that my prayers were gradually becoming more effective. It seemed that I was drawing that person from deep within the very camp of the Enemy. Then I was able to proceed as usual claiming every detail of that life for God, using the power of the blood against the Enemy. This is true warfare in the spiritual realm. Thank God that our spiritual weapons are mighty and that our authority in Christ is far above all the authority of the rulers, powers and forces of darkness, so that the Enemy must yield. It takes faith and patience and persistence.

Reprint from "Back to the Bible" broadcast. Used by permission.

SELECT BIBLIOGRAPHY

Here are listed mainly titles for which full bibliographical information is not given elsewhere. The many other sources cited in the main text are documented fully in the Endnotes.

Anderson, Neil T. 1990a, *The Bondage Breaker.* Eugene, Ore.: Harvest House.

———. 1990b, *Victory Over the Darkness.* Ventura, Calif.: Regal.

———. 1991a, *Walking Through the Darkness.* San Bernardino, Calif.: Here's Life.

———. 1991b, *Released from Bondage.* San Bernardino, Calif: Here's Life.

———. 1991c, *The Seduction of Our Children.* Eugene, Ore.: Harvest House.

Bibee, John. 1989, *Spirit Flyer Series for Children.* Downers Grove, Ill.: InterVarsity.

Boswell, John. 1989, *The Kindness of Strangers: The Abandonment of Children in Western Europe from Late Antiquity to the Renaissance.* New York: Pantheon.

Bubeck, Mark. 1975, *The Adversary.* Chicago: Moody Press.

———. 1984, *Overcoming the Adversary.* Chicago: Moody Press.

———. 1991, *The Satanic Revival.* San Bernardino, Calif.: Here's Life.

Christenson, Evelyn. 1990, *Battling the Prince of Darkness.* Wheaton, Ill.: Victor Books.

Custance, Arthur. 1980, *The Mysterious Matter of Mind.* Grand Rapids, Mich.: Zondervan.

Dawson, John. 1989, *Taking Our Cities for God.* Lake Mary, Fla.: Creation House.

Green, Michael. 1981, *I Believe in Satan's Downfall.* Grand Rapids, Mich.: Eerdmans.

———. 1991, *Exposing the Prince of Darkness.* Ann Arbor, Mich.: Servant.

Horrobin, Peter. 1991, *Healing Through Deliverance.* Chichester, England: Sovereign World Limited.

Jacobs, Cindy. 1991, *Possessing the Gates of the Enemy.* Tarrytown, N.Y.: Chosen Books.

Koch, Kurt. 1971, *Between Christ and Satan.* Grand Rapids, Mich.: Kregel.

———. 1972, *Occult Bondage and Deliverance.* Grand Rapids: Kregel.

———. 1973, *Demonology Past and Present.* Grand Rapids: Kregel.

———. 1978a, *Occult ABC.* Grand Rapids: Kregel.

———. 1978b, *Christian Counseling and Occultism.* Grand Rapids: Kregel.

———. 1978c, *Satan's Devices.* Grand Rapids: Kregel.

Kraft, Charles. 1991, "What Kind of Encounters Do We Need in Our Christian Witness?" *Evangelical Missions Quarterly.* 27 (7/July): 258.

———. 1989, *Christianity With Power.* Ann Arbor, Mich.: Servant.

McAlpine, Thomas H. 1991, *Facing the Powers: What Are the Options?* Monrovia, Calif.: MARC World Vision.

Montgomery, John Warwick. 1974, "Exorcism: Is It for Real?" *Christianity Today,* July 26.

———. 1975, *Principalities and Powers: A New Look at the World of the Occult.* Minneapolis, Minnesota: Bethany Fellowship.

Murphy, Edward. 1975, *Spiritual Gifts and the Great Commission.* Pasadena, Calif.: William Carey Library.

———. 1990a, *Spiritual Warfare.* (audio cassette series and manual) Colorado Springs, Col. 80936–6900: OC International, Inc., P.O. Box 36900.

Silvoso, Edgardo. 1987, "Prayer Power: The Turnaround in Argentina." *Global Church Growth Bulletin.* 24 (Jul.—Sept.): 4–5.

———. 1989, "Spiritual Warfare in Argentina and the Plan Resistencia." *Spiritual Warfare Track Workshop,* Lausanne II, Congress on World Evangelism, Manila, Philippines, July 11–20.

———. 1991, "Prayer Power in Argentina." In *Territorial Spirits,* C. Peter Wagner, editor. Chichester, England: Sovereign World Limited.

Smith, A. E. Wilder. 1974, *Man's Origin, Man's Destiny.* Wheaton, Ill.: Harold Shaw.

Tippett, Alan. 1967, *Solomon Islands Christianity.* New York: Friendship Press.

———. 1970, *Church Growth and the Word of God.* Grand Rapids, Mich.: Eerdmans.

———. 1971, *People Movements in Southern Polynesia.* Chicago: Moody Press.

———. 1973, *God, Man and Church Growth.* Grand Rapids, Mich.: Eerdmans.

———. 1975, "Evangelization Among Animists." In *Let the Earth Hear His Voice.* Minneapolis, Minn.: Worldwide Publications.

———. 1987, *Introduction to Missiology.* Pasadena, Calif.: William Carey Library.

Unger, Merrill F. 1955, *Biblical Demonology.* Chicago: Scripture Press.

———. 1971, *Demons in the World Today.* Wheaton, Ill.: Tyndale House.

———. 1977, *What Demons Can Do To Saints.* Chicago: Moody Press.

Wagner, C. Peter. 1991a, "Spiritual Power in Urban Evangelism: Dynamic Lessons in Argentina." *Evangelical Missions Quarterly.* 27 (4/April): 130–137.

———. 1991b, editor, *Territorial Spirits.* Chichester, England: Sovereign World Limited.

———. 1991c, editor, *Engaging the Enemy.* Ventura, Calif.: Regal Books.

———. 1992 *Warfare Prayer.* Ventura, Calif.: Regal Books.

Warner, Timothy. 1991, *Spiritual Warfare.* Wheaton, Ill.: Crossway Books.

White, Tom. 1990, *The Believer's Guide to Spiritual Warfare.* Ann Arbor, Mich.: Servant.

Wilder, James. 1992, *A Redemptive Response to Satanism.* Downers Grove, Ill.: InterVarsity.

Wycliffe Bible Translators. 1987, "Ding's Special Gift." *In Other Words.* Huntington Beach, Calif.: Wycliffe Bible Translators, December.

Scripture Index

Subject Index

the people of earth, 9–10; Of Israel, 9f; only God is God, 24f, 91; only non-creature, 24f; perfection of, 24; predetermination, 99; self-revelation of, 9f; transcendence of, 9–11; Trinity, 11–12, 71; true God, 9f, 11

Gods (See Belief Systems, Idols, Idolatry, Religions), are demons, 51; astral pieties, 162; fertility gods, goddesses, 161–62, 239f; Greco-Roman, 159, 162–65; high gods, 6, 162; Israel, battle with, 158–62, 232–33, 237–57; Mesopotamian pantheon, 238–40; No-gods nonentities, 10, 346–52

Gods, names of in Bible: Aphrodite, 158; Artemis, 351–52; Asherim, 161; Apollo, 324–28; Asthtart and related names, 241f, 562; Baal (See Baal, Baalism), 239f; Baal-Ashtoreth combination, 249f; Bel, 162; Bagon, 162, 239; Dionysus, 175; Milcom, 162; Sarapis, 82; Sin, moon god, 159; Tanit, 247–48; Various, 239–50; Zeus, 162, 319

Gnosticism, 320, 556

Groaning, church, Holy Spirit, universe, 77

Guatemala, 181

Handwriting, demonic, 286–87

Healing(s), demonic, 306f; divine, xiii, 5–6, 305, 309, 346f, 547; in atonement, critical view, 547

Heavenlies, the, 393–94, 397–01

Hell, 10, 22, 27, 89, 90, 97f, 274

Holy Spirit, abiding, 64; agent of divine power; 140–41; anointing, 160; baptized with, 114, 167–69, 529; cohabitation with flesh and demons, 110–17; crisis experiences with, 65, 113f; empowers believers, 70f, 168; filling of, 168, 529; gift of, 111f, 528–29; gifts of (See Spiritual Gifts), 70, 114f, 167–69, 371–73; groanings of, 77; indwelling, 70f, 95; indwelling of Christ in/with, 70–73; intercessor ministry of, 77, 95; power of, 140–41, 528–35; received by faith, 11f; regeneration by, 95; 140–41; unbalances, emphasis on manifestations of, 528–35; walking by/in, 72f, 92f, 98, 108f, 110–17; warfare by, 110–17

Homosexual(s), Homosexuality, 136–147; abuse, 145–47, 373–74, 551; active/passive roles, 139; biblical view, 136–42; bondage to, 136–42, 551–52; Christian

homosexuals, 145–47; deliverance from, 139–42; demonic dimension, 142–43, 145, 147; forgivable sin, 136–142; gay rights day, movement, parades, etc., 143–47; infiltrating churches, 144–45; spiritual warfare issues, 43f; support group necessity of, 138, 141–42; victory over, 137, 139–42, 146–47

"I am just a little girl," 450–58

Idols, Idolatry (See Belief Systems), 10–11, 119, 158–64, 328–38, 358; Christian involvements, 158; demonic dimensions, 329–38; immorality, cultic, 329–38; sin of Gentiles, 158

Incest, among humans, 122, 173, 369–70, 455, 459–62, 582; among the gods, 239–40

Incantations, 164

Incubi/Succubai, 225, 554

Israel (See Judaism, Jews), 159f, 195–96, 202f

Jacob, 561

Jeroboam, 161

Jesus Christ, the Lord, Blood of, 95, 98, 140–41; cosmic christology, 389–90, 393–01; defeat of Satan, 206, 240, 277, 288f, 293, 298–99, 424–25; power of, 92, 390–402; Second Coming of, 361–67; union with, 390–402

Johannine Writings, 419–25

Job, 434–35

Joshua, 237–44

Josiah, King, 162

Judaism, Jews, Hebrews (See Israel), 11–12, 135, 195f, 202f, 208f, 222f, 266

Judaizers, 113, 117, 357, 572

Judas, 415–20

Justification/Justified, 73, 79, 140–41, 176

Kingdom, conflict between kingdoms of God/Satan, x, xiii, 12–13, 17f, 28f, 100f, 288f; of God, 12–13, 17f, 28f, 63, 100f, 176, 273, 289, 293, 298–99, 308–09, 353; of Satan, 12–13, 17f, 21–23, 28f, 100f, 277, 289f, 295, 299, 308

Law, freedom from the law; Mosaic/Old Testament, 67f; of love, 119; of the spirit of life, 71f; of sin and death, 68–69, 71f; works of, 66f, 111f

Leaders, 154f, 158–59, 189, 303; deceived, 19–20, 128f, 284–86; double standard,

Person Index